William Beckford

Leading business men of Lewiston, Augusta and vicinity, embracing, also,

Auburn, Gardiner, Waterville, Oakland, Dexter, Fairfield, Skowhegan, Hallowell, Richmond, Bath, Brunswick, Freeport, Canton, Buckfield, Mechanic Falls, South Paris, Norway, Farm

William Beckford

Leading business men of Lewiston, Augusta and vicinity, embracing, also,
Auburn, Gardiner, Waterville, Oakland, Dexter, Fairfield, Skowhegan, Hallowell, Richmond, Bath, Brunswick, Freeport, Canton, Buckfield, Mechanic Falls, South Paris, Norway, Farm

ISBN/EAN: 9783337727857

Printed in Europe, USA, Canada, Australia, Japan

Cover: Foto ©ninafisch / pixelio.de

More available books at **www.hansebooks.com**

COMMONWEALTH
Loan and Trust Co.

CAPITAL, - - $100,000.00.

Paid into the Treasury in Cash.

Eastern Office, 131 Devonshire St., Boston, Mass.

Western Office, KANSAS CITY.

Offers to Savings Banks, Insurance Companies, Investors of Trust Funds and Private Investors.

7 PER CENT. GUARANTEED FIRST MORTGAGE

WESTERN FARM AND CITY LOANS.

And their

6 per cent. Debenture Bonds.

These Bonds are **SECURED** by **FIRST MORTGAGE** loans to the amount of 105 per cent. of all Bonds issued, deposited with the

Boston Safe Deposit and Trust Company, Trustee.

And each bond bears the Certification of the Trust Co., to that effect. The **PRINCIPAL** and **INTEREST** of all securities sold by us are paid at our **BOSTON OFFICE**. We **GUARANTEE** every loan that we sell, and offer nothing but strictly **FIRST-CLASS SECURITIES**.

SEND FOR OUR BOOK TO INVESTORS.

C. A. PARKS,   **W. W. MASON,**

President and Western Manager.   Treasurer and Eastern Manager.

[ESTABLISHED 1839.]

B. THURSTON & CO.,
PRINTERS AND PUBLISHERS,

97 1-2 Exchange and 108 Market Streets,

PORTLAND, MAINE.

BROWN THURSTON.   GEORGE H. WATKINS.

WE PUBLISH

HISTORY OF NORWAY, MAINE, royal octavo, 676 pp., Ill., (sheep, $5 00), cloth,	$4.00
HISTORY OF THE 16TH MAINE REGIMENT, by Maj. A. R. Small, 300 pp., Ill.,	1.50
HISTORY OF PARSONSFIELD, 516 pp., 100 Ill., cloth,	3.50
WILLEY'S ANTI-SLAVERY HISTORY, 12mo, 514 pp., Ill.,	2.00
PORTLAND CITY DIRECTORY, Annual,	2.50
CRAWFORD'S WHITE MOUNTAINS, 228 pp., Ill.,	1.50
THURSTON GENEALOGIES, 600 pp., by mail,	5.25
GREENE'S QUESTIONS IN SURGERY,	1.00
YORK DEEDS, 6 vols., over 600 pp. each, per vol.,	5.00
YORK WILLS, 1 vol., 965 pp.,	5.00
THE STANLEY FAMILY, 352 pp., Ill.,	3.00
THE MARSTON GENEALOGY, 604 pp., Ill , cloth,	4.00
A TALE OF HOME AND WAR, 200 pp.,	1.25

Agents Wanted for "Baptist Hymn Writers and their Hymns."

Large *commission* to good agents.

We also have an extensive

JOB PRINTING OFFICE,

Where All kinds of Printing is done quickly, cheaply and well.

MILLIONS INVESTED WITHOUT LOSS.

Kansas Investment Company
—OF—
TOPEKA, KANSAS.

Cash Capital and Surplus, $ 600,000
Guarantee,   1,100,000

7 PER CENT. Kansas Mortgages. Principal and Interest Guaranteed and Payable in Gold.

6 PER CENT. Gold Debenture Bonds. Interest Payable Quarterly.

These Bonds are Secured by First Mortgages, and are

Absolutely Safe.

BOSTON SAFE DEPOSIT AND TRUST CO., TRUSTEES.

Before investing elsewhere, investigate these Securities and see a large list of Banks, Trustees and Individual Trustees. Send for our new pamphlet, just out.

Boston Office, 101 Devonshire St., Corner of Water.

H. E. BALL, Pres.   } *Topeka,*   GEO. C. MORRELL, Vice-Pres. } *Boston*
B. R. WHEELER, Sec. } *Kan.*   P. T. BARTLETT, Asst. Sec.   } *Mass.*

Agent in Gardiner, Maine :

ISAAC J. CARR,
President of the
GARDINER NATIONAL BANK.
Office :— Gardiner National Bank.

LEADING

BUSINESS MEN

OF

LEWISTON, AUGUSTA

AND VICINITY,

EMBRACING, ALSO,

AUBURN, GARDINER, WATERVILLE, OAKLAND, DEXTER, FAIRFIELD, SKOWHEGAN, HALLOWELL, RICHMOND, BATH, BRUNSWICK, FREEPORT, CANTON, BUCKFIELD, MECHANIC FALLS, SOUTH PARIS, NORWAY, FARMINGTON AND WINTHROP,

WITH AN

HISTORICAL SKETCH OF EACH PLACE,

ILLUSTRATED.

BOSTON.
MERCANTILE PUBLISHING COMPANY,
258 Purchase Street.
1889.

PREFACE.

"I am wonderfully delighted to see a body of men thriving in their own fortunes, and at the same time promoting the public stock, or, in other words, raising estates for their own families, by bringing into the country whatever is wanting, and carrying out of it whatever is superfluous. Nature seems to have taken particular care to disseminate her blessings among the different regions of the world, with an eye to their mutual intercourse and traffic among mankind, that the nations of the several parts of the globe might have a kind of dependence upon one another, and be united together by their common interests."—*Addison.*

In offering this book to the public the aim of the publishers has been to present in a concise manner the principal events in the history of this section of the State, and a brief review of its leading business interests.

In the following pages will be found descriptions of the immense manufacturing establishments, to whose influence Maine owes much of its fame as a manufacturing centre. We doubt if there is a section of New England, with the same population, whose manufactures are so celebrated the world over, as are those of Maine. The financial institutions and wholesale and retail houses described in this volume are also leaders in their particular lines, and their push and enterprise is rapidly extending the influence of this section of the State as a great trade center.

In conclusion, we beg to extend our hearty thanks for the liberal patronage this work has received. Our advance orders have necessitated the printing of *twelve thousand* copies to supply the demand.

MERCANTILE PUBLISHING CO.

COPYRIGHT,
MERCANTILE PUBLISHING CO.
1888.

Introduction to Business Notices.

In the following pages will be found brief notices of the principal Business firms of the section under review. While the majority are old, established houses and leader in every sense of the word, we have mentioned others who, though recntly established, are, through their enterprise and ability, deserving of notice. Abundant evidences of energy and talent have been met with in every department of commercial, professional and social life. We commend these firms as a whole, to the favorable attention of all into whose hands this volume may fall, believing that they well represent the business interests of this section of Maine.

THE PUBLISHERS.

LEADING BUSINESS MEN.

INDEX TO NOTICES.

AGRICULTURAL IMPLEMENTS.

	PAGE
Emerson, Charles S.	96
Holt, Hiram Co., The	246
Hobbs, M. C. & Co	256
Royal, W. B. & Co	282

ATTORNEYS.

Belcher, S. Clifford	247
Bearce & Stearns	287
Bisbee, George D	320
Chandler, David H	202
Greenleaf, E. O.	250
Stilphen, A. C.	147
Stevens, Greenlief T	224

BOOKSELLERS AND STATIONERS.

Bixby & Buck	184
Cushing, George	190
Chandler & Estes	60
Douglass & Cook	36
Denuison, B. L.	334
Ellis, W. W.	35
Estes, Nelson D.	43
Fernald, J. M.	52
Mitchell, W. A.	315
Stacy, E. M.	225
Stevens, Byron	332
Townsend, A. W.	336

BANKS AND BANKERS.

Auburn Savings	81
Augusta "	129
Bath "	349
Brunswick Savings Institution	328
First National, The (Augusta)	131
First " (Bath)	343
Franklin County Savings (Farmington)	244
Granite National (Augusta)	137
Gardiner "	162
Gardiner Savings Institution	158
Hallowell National	173
Lincoln " (Bath)	346
Manufacturers National (Lewiston)	65
Merchants " (Gardiner)	167
Marine " (Bath)	348
May, Samuel E. & Co	58
National Shoe & Leather (Auburn)	93
Northern National (Hallowell)	174
Oakland " (Gardiner)	169
People's Savings (Lewiston)	72
People's Trust Co. (Farmington)	243
People's Twenty-Five Cent Savings (Bath)	351
Pejepscott National (Brunswick)	329
Sagadahoc " (Bath)	350
Winthrop "	298

BOOK BINDERS.

Neal, Mrs.	46
Smith & Reid	117

INDEX

BAKERS AND CONFECTIONERS.

Cummings, S. A.	136
Dickson, John	55
Johnson & Percival	121
Norris, F. B.	46
Otten, A.	216
Snow, F. D.	330

BOOT AND SHOE MANUFACTURERS.

Bailey, L. M.	315
Caldwell & Libby	306
Cobb, John F. & Co.	80
Cummings, C. B. & Sons	288
Cushman, Ara Co.	97
Davis, H. E. & Co.	318
Dennison, H. P.	314
Dingley, Foss & Co.	85
Jordan, M. V. B.	317
Morgan, W. F. & Co.	303
Smith, Pray & Co.	92
Wise & Cooper	94

BOOTS AND SHOES—Retail.

Atwood, J. F.	82
Attwood, George B.	83
Atkins, Edwin H.	176
Clair, J. B.	222
Day, F. I.	47
Hersey, F. L.	124
Hatch Brothers	261
Hatch, Davis, Jr.	346
Kenney & Swett	293
Kenney & Plummer	281
Loud, Percy	207
Lemont, M. M.	350
Morrell, C. O.	52
Stone, W. R.	126
Stephenson, A. L.	151
Soule, S. & Son	163
Swain, A.	227
Smith, C. R.	279
Shaw, A. S. & Co.	310

CARRIAGES MANUF'S AND DEALERS.

Benson, H. A. & Co.	225
Bicknell, S. & Son	311
Clark, Hiram	122
Flinn James T.	222
Gilson, P. H.	160
Litchfield, C. J. & Co.	83
Libby, J. B.	150
Nevens, C. T.	81
Packard, C. F. & Co.	252
Smith & Gardiner	168
Wade & Dunton	60
Wilshire, George H. & Co.	215
Warren, F. A. & Son	32

CROCKERY, CHINA AND GLASS.

Ballard, George S.	124
Darrah, J. G.	213
Lander, J. C.	146
Pierce, A. J.	130
Wood Daniel	62

CLOTHING MANUFACTURERS.

Bucknam, J. A. & Co.	268
Dunning, M. S.	352
Dillaway, S.	354
McGrillis, N. L.	197

CIGAR MANUFACTURERS.

Kane & Stuber	161
Lowell, D. W.	55
Lowell & Putnam	211

COAL & WOOD, HAY & STRAW.

Ayer & Greeley	226
Briggs, C. H.	84
Currier, S.	174
Chaney, J. F.	332
Dorman, H. P. & Co.	68
Dow & Green	217
Davis, S. G.	300
Flood, G. S. & Co.	213
Hayden, J. F.	353
Hagar, W. S.	305
Olys, William B.	342
Potter, A. H.	160
Robbins, L. C.	44
Smith, H. R. & Son	84
Stone, E.	124
Spear & Whitmore	331
Wood, J. N.	71

DENTISTS.

Bailey, Emery	58
Bryant, Charles	135
Bates, H. A.	345
Bigelow, F. B.	87
Damon, M. L.	223
Davis, J. W.	231
Hardy, B. M.	200
Leavitt, H. & Son	183
Merrill, E. C.	261
Roberts, E. J.	132
Titcomb, A. C.	138
Woodbury, N. & Son	61

DOOR, SASH AND BLIND MANUFACTURING.

Bangs Brothers	131
Hathaway, C. L.	295
Johnson, James A.	35
Maxim, S. P. & Son	279
Stevens, D. B.	38

DRESSMAKERS.

Randall, William Mrs.	262
Wilder, K. F. Miss	256
Welch, M. N. Miss	265

INDEX.

DRUGGISTS.

Anderson Samuel	341
Allen, C. W.	329
Abbott, Charles A.	40
Allen, G. M.	59
Auburn Drug and Chemical Co.	85
Alden, Burt L. & Co.	94
Barbour, H. W.	54
Bixby & Buck	184
Bridgham, Levi	108
Clark, R. W.	48
Cushing, Horatio W.	189
Cushing, George	190
Cotton, F. M.	287
Dorr, George W.	206
Fuller, W. H.	185
Field, J. M.	224
Gilman, F. H.	226
Goulding, George W.	227
Gerry, A. M.	280
Harden, C. H.	152
Houlehan, John C.	154
Hawes, J. Q. A.	177
Heath, Alden A.	178
Jackson, J. A.	150
Johnson, E. W.	330
Kimball, O. W. & Co.	41
Low, Ira H.	217
Mixer, J. M.	128
Marr, C. E.	263
Noyes, A. O. Mrs.	288
Norway Medicine Co.	289
Olfene, E. A.	41
Partridge, Charles K.	119
Partridge, Frank R.	121
Patten, R. T.	186
Robinson, William A.	84
Reynolds, Nathan	311
Rawson, J. A.	322
Springall & Co	196
Shurtleff, F. A.	278
Tarbox, S. O.	261
Thomas, M. B.	312
Towne, J. S.	334
Wakefield Brothers	43
Warren, G. E.	153
Walker, J. C.	271
Wilson, F. H.	332

DRY AND FANCY GOODS.

Atwood, C. B. & Sons	322
Atkins, O. A.	82
Bartlett, F. & Son	89
Bussell & Weston	139
Brown, George W.	156
Bucknam, J. A. & Co	268

Bolster, N. Dayton	277
Bowker, C. W. & Co.	283
Boardman, S. J.	330
Childs & Staples	311
Chickering, J. F.	317
Darrah, W. C.	59
Ehrenfried, George	47
Files, Everett F.	239
Gallert, D.	206
Gore & Davis	315
Hill Brothers	89
Hamlen, C. N.	117
Heselton Bros. & Co.	187
Hines, J. W.	251
Howe & Ridlon	288
Ireland, S. S.	195
Kelly E. O.	290
Little, Z. F.	146
Lowell, E. H.	254
Mooney, F. P. Mrs.	51
Norton, A. C.	255
Paul, E. S. & Co.	35
Philbrook & Leighton	124
Preble, Sidney T.	177
Presby, L. A. & Co.	205
Pelletier, O. J.	218
Piper, G. T. & Co.	236
Purington, John L.	354
Prince, S. B. & Z. S.	293
Percy, D. T. & Son.	360
Ramsdell, H.	243
Rice, H. H.	263
Soper, L. H.	209
Smith, Harmon	307
Stetson, G. C.	333
Tuttle & Frazier	238
Tuttle George A.	343
Tubbs, C. N. & Co.	291
White & Wildes	184
Webb, F. C. & Co.	335

FRUIT, CONFECTIONERY AND CIGARS.

Bangs, F. A.	254
Eaton, Charles A.	44
Foye, D. W.	236
Field, William R.	335
Goss, A. D. & E. F.	86
Hatch, John C.	43
Harlow, A. E.	53
Learned, Amos	238
Morton, L. J.	272
Pollister, S. A.	95
Porter, W. A.	283
Royal, M. N. & Co.	274
Stackpole, George	216
Spinney & Hayes	353

FLOUR, GRAIN AND FEED.

Bartlett & Dennis	156
Brewster, W. E.	107
Beaumont Edward	337
Cony, Daniel A. & Co.	115
Currier, S.	174
Dill, Benj. U.	102
Day & Co.	177
Gardner, Benjamin	131
Ham, J. B. & Co.	38
Holway, Oscar & Co.	98
Hooker, C. A.	356
Jackson & Curtis	304
McGrillis, C. P.	105
McLure & Danforth	222
Mitchell, G. J.	340
Mallet E. B., Jr.	314
Parrott, B. F. & Co.	123
Partridge & Danforth	294
Ranger & Butler	265
Savage, Frank J.	235
Tibbetts, J. E. & Co.	86
Tufts, M. P.	200
Willis Henry & Co.	95
Woodbury, Morrill & Gage	189
Wait, Charles S.	256
Waterville Grist Mill, The	208

FURNITURE AND CARPETS.

Allen, Daniel & Co.	40
Allen, George A.	94
Adams, T. H.	264
Bradford, Conant & Co.	33
Blake, L. L. & Co.	48
Cummings, Charles S.	288
Emerson, O. E.	207
Fairbrother, E. F. & Co.	183
Groves, Oscar H.	126
Perry, D. B.	270
Preble & Keene	152
Record, S.	49
Sturgis, Charles M.	116
Snell, George	354
Titcomb & Cole	253
Vaughan, Thomas	39
Wells, A. L. & Co.	118
Wheeler, W. H.	228

FURNITURE MANUFACTURERS.

Batchelder, J. & Son	224
Cilley, J. A. & Co.	233
Fairfield Furniture Co.	232
Flagg, Charles & Son	304
Moore, W. H.	155
Trask, T. O.	247
Wadsworth Brothers	151

FRUIT AND PRODUCE—Wholesale.

Bolster, H. N.	279
Crowell, C. S. & Co	55
Downing, G. P.	287
Soule, R. W.	121
Wing, F. A. & Co.	207

FISH AND OYSTERS.

Atwood, Abram	36
Jenkins, Charles	138
Moulton, M. S. & Co.	127
Sabourin Elie	45

GROCERIES AND PROVISIONS.

Atwood, Abram	36
Atwood, C. B. & Sons	322
Atwood & Lowell	92
Arnold, George D.	190
Blake, Spear & Co.	66
Bicknell Henry W.	123
Baker, Thomas M.	126
Boynton & Farr	130
Braun Brothers & Co.	154
Bartlett & Dennis	156
Brewster, W. E.	107
Bolster, N. Dayton	277
Briggs, F. C.	278
Bennett, J. C. & Co.	295
Barron, F. W.	331
Chase & Bean	92
Crafts, A. B.	99
Cony, Daniel A. & Co.	115
Caswell, H. C.	132
Childs & Staples	311
Chickering, J. F.	317
Chase, H. L. & W. E.	357
Douglas, E. C.	38
Dingley, John & Co.	83
Dill, Benjamin U.	102
Day & Co.	177
Dyer, A. C.	280
Fuller, T. & Son	124
Fuller, James E.	129
Fuller, A. & Son	164
Fogg, F. J.	196
Garner, John	69
Gordon, A. K. P.	96
Gardiner Beef Co.	170
Gerry, E.	264
Gould, D. C. & Co.	346
Gilbert & Foss.	294
Gore & Davis.	315
Hutchins, E. H.	40
Howard Brothers	45
Haskell, I. N. & Co.	91
Hill, Lucius.	121
Haskell, George D.	136
Harrington, A. C.	176

INDEX.

Hillman, R. S.	188	Webber, F. L.	138
Hines, J. W.	251	Wakefield, C. E. & Son	149
Howe & Ridlon	288	Woodbury, Morrill & Gage	189
Harris, R. C.	344	Wiggin & Nye	236
Hamlin, J. H.	310	Waugh, James H	255
Harris, F. N. (Wholesale)	252	Wait, Charles S.	256
Jones, Levi & Co	208	Witham, L. E. & Co.	263
Jordan, B. R. & Co	329	Williams, A. F.	353
Lord, J. C. & Son	60	Webber, W. G. & Co	304
Libby, George C.	122	Webb, F. C. & Co.	335
Lowell & Simmons	174	**HOTELS.**	
Leighton & Haines	196	Andrews House	279
Lincoln, W. M.	206	Cony House	139
Leonard, A. W.	221	Commercial House	345
Lowell, E. H.	254	Cushing Hotel	317
Mitchell, Isaiah	89	De Witt, The	70
McGrillis, C. P.	195	Exchange Hotel (Lewiston)	69
Marshall, Paul	215	Elm House (Auburn)	97
Morse & Cannon	216	Elm House (Farmington)	253
McLure & Danforth	222	Elm House (Norway)	286
McDonald, F. H. Co	274	Evans Hotel	166
Morin, E. D.	332	Elmwood Hotel	210
Nealey & Miller	33	Exchange Hotel (Farmington)	254
Nichols, T. L.	355	Elms, The (Mechanic Falls)	271
Peabody, J. L. & Co.	58	Franklin House	140
Penley, Arthur M.	87	Fairfield House	235
Peables & Garcelon	89	Heselton Hotel	188
Parsons, J.	55	Harlow House	316
Penley, Albert M.	94	Lincoln House	68
Pulsifer, W.	95	Park House	98
Pinkham, H. D.	178	Rockingham Hotel	73
Pierce, A. A.	184	Revere House	95
Patterson, H. D. & Co.	186	Stoddard House	260
Prescott, E. S.	190	Tebbetts, C. C.	294
Pooler, Fred.	214	Tontine Hotel	331
Preston, L. G.	254	Willows "	245
Peterson, W. O.	337	Winthrop House	209
Partridge & Danforth	294	**HOUSE AND SIGN PAINTERS.**	
Roche & Curran	42	Bubier & Mason	67
Ring, William H.	169	Beale, C. & Co.	140
Rogers, L. W.	216	Berry, John W.	165
Ranger & Butler	265	Davies, George F.	208
Russell, Walter S.	342	Dunham, A. H.	280
Stevens & Goss	82	Manchester, J. R.	128
Stevens, Edwin T.	86	Redmond, James B.	227
Symmes, J. C	88	Sherman, J. M	65
Savage, C. B.	129	Storah, F. H. & Co	93
Smith, Tobey & Co	161	Spaulding & Kennison	214
Spaulding, A. C. & Bro.	306	Shepard, J. H.	354
Smith, Harmon	307	Walker, E. L.	189
Snow, L. D.	335	**HATS AND GENT'S FURNISHINGS.**	
Thompson & Howes	185	Davis, E. E. & Co.	114
Towne, Edwin	207	Hamlin, J. H.	310
Tufts, M. P.	260	Kane & Stuber	161
Tarbox, S. O.	261	Murphy, T. J	34
Tubbs, C. N. & Co.	291	Mathews, F. W.	116
Umberhine, I. F.	306		
Voter, Warren S.	307		

INDEX.

HARNESS, TRUNKS, ETC.

Callahan, T. F. & Co.	66
Chase, L. W.	191
Carsley, J. W.	255
Covel, N. & W. C.	345
Dickinson, S. A.	209
Fish, S. D. & Son	194
Farrar, Byron	250
Graves, E. A.	336
Hamlen, H. H.	125
Longley, J. P.	40
Littlefield, Fred & Co.	164
Michaud, George B.	45
Philbrook, G. C.	237
Robbins, F. A.	212
Sager, R. A.	150
Scott, James B.	344
Tucker, C. S.	291
Wood & Walker	90
Williams, J. D.	283
Warren, F. A. & Son	321

LAUNDRIES AND DYE HOUSES.

Barbier, Emile	130
Dirigo Laundry (D. B. Morse)	272
Hatch, H. E.	340
Le Blanc, Joseph	53
Low Brothers (Star laundry)	211
Norway, August	293
Quimby, A. K. P.	52
Wing, L. B.	153

LIME, HAY, CEMENT, ETC.

Flood, G. S. & Co.	213
Nichols, Read	355
Sawtelle, J. R.	156

LIVERY, BOARDING AND SALE STABLES.

Alexander & Hubbard	334
Bradbury, R. S	87
Bryant, G. A.	140
Cony, G. A. & H.	133
Chase, L. W.	191
Cummings, O. M.	293
Dunning, Charles W.	348
Emerson, S. L.	90
Golder, I. S.	48
Hanson, F. M.	213
Hill, C. A.	214
Jowell, William	151
Legard, George E.	316
Mills Brothers	223
Mitchell, W. A.	315
Perkins, Hiram	272
Savage, Parker N.	138
Shorey, C. & Co.	208
Trask, C. F.	152
Tasker, E. D. & Co.	159
Wilshire, George H. & Co.	215
Waterman & Jordan	271

LUMBER MFGS. AND PLANING MILLS.

Allen, M. J.	190
Brown, S. T. & E. M.	330
Bradstreet, J. S. & F. T.	159
Clark & Milliken	305
Canton Steam Mill Co.	309
Duren, A. H. & C. E.	233
Davis, S. G.	300
Flanders, E. A.	200
Gray, Joshua & Son	163
Gould, C. A.	265
Haley, James E.	352
Hathaway, C. L.	295
Irish, C. M. & H. A.	322
Jordan, Frost & Co.	37
Jewett, H. W. & Co.	162
Kennebec Framing & Lumber Co.	231
Lawrence Brothers	105
Maxcy S. N. Mfg. Co.	157
Nye, Stephen A.	233
Oakland Mfg. Co.	148
Pingree, R. C. & Co.	35
Prescott, J. F.	244
Ranger, George W.	264
Totman, N. & Sons	233
Totman, E. & Co.	236
Trafton, N. A.	294
Varney, J.	349
Weston & Brainard	183

MISCELLANEOUS.

Auburn, Historical Sketch of	74
Augusta, " " "	100
Bearce & Clifford Construction Co., The	38
Bath, Historical Sketch of	338
Buckfield, " " "	318
Brunswick, " " "	323
Brown, Levi G. (horseshoeing)	251
Conant, S. F. (compound vapor bath)	182
Canton, Historical Sketch of	308
Chase, Homer N. & Co. (nurserymen)	320
Dickey, H. H. & Son (leather belting)	34
Dexter, Historical Sketch of	191
Drake, G. (baskets)	265
Dunbar, M. C. (human hair)	41
Equitable Mortgage Co.	300
Field, D. P. & Co. (ice)	67
Fairfield, Historical Sketch of	229
Farmington, " " "	230
Farmington Mfg. Co. The, (car protectors)	257
Freeport, Historical Sketch of	313
Gardiner, " " "	141
Gower, John (book publications)	290
Horton & Pierce (rubber goods)	37
Heath & Tainter (sewing machines)	51
Hallowell, Historical Sketch of	170
Hooper C. T. & Sons (wall papers, curtains)	359
Kennebec Light & Heat Co.	113
Lewis, E. E. (architect)	169

INDEX.

Moses, Charles T. (corn packer).......... 198
Mechanic Falls, Historical Sketch of....... 266
Mason, W. W. (trucking)................ 347
Newman, Lara & Co. (ice)................ 65
Norway, Historical Sketch of.............. 284
Norway Tanning Co...................... 286
Oakland, Historical Sketch of............. 218
Oxford County Dairying Asso............. 322
Roak, George M. (florist).................. 88
Riggs, G. L. & A. S. (tanners)............. 256
Richmond, Historical Sketch of........... 301
Singer Mufg. Co........................... 49
Stone, H. L. (bicycles)..................... 126
Skowhegan, Historical Sketch of 179
South Paris, Historical Sketch of......... 275
Trafton, N. A. (cattle and sheep).......... 204
Varney, E. V. (horse-shoeing)............. 262
Waterville, Historical Sketch of........... 200
Winthrop, Historical Sketch of............ 296
Young, Freeland (billiards)................ 290

MANUFACTURERS.

Bailey's C. M. Sons & Co. (oil cloths)...... 290
Dunn Edge Tool Co....................... 220
Eureka Hosiery Co......................... 90
Emerson & Stevens Mufg. Co.(scythes, axes) 224
Fuller & Co. (whiting and putty).......... 175
Hutchins, H. Wesley (boxes)............. 82
Hubbard & Blake (edge tools)............ 223
Holt Hiram Co., The (hay knives)........ 246
Irish, F. L. & Co. (brush blocks).......... 324
Irish, C. M. & H. A (brush blocks)........ 322
Jackson, J. S. & Son (block mfrs.)......... 357
Lewiston Machine Co..................... 37
Lewiston Bleachery & Dye Works 54
Lucas, C. H. (screw drivers).............. 310
Morse, Mark (paper boxes)............... 96
Marshall, C. (shovel handles)............. 225
Pulsifer, J. Roak (leather counters)........ 90
Paris Mufg. Co. (children's carts, etc.).... 277
Skinner, H. B. & Co. (bobbins, spools, etc.) 72
Wheeler, Charles E. (fishing rods)......... 262
Withington, C. & Sons (brushes).......... 321

MARBLE AND GRANITE.

Auburn Marble and Monumental Works... 91
Augusta Marble Works................... 127
Augusta and Waterville Marble Works.... 130
Blaisdell, Stephen......................... 223
Boston, E. C.............................. 305
Faught, Henry M.......................... 128
Gardiner Marble Works................... 101
Morse & Bridges.......................... 107
O'Connell, J. J........................... 47
O'Connor & Owen......................... 202
Verrill A. J. & Co......................... 86

MACHINISTS AND FOUNDERS.

Carman & Thompson...................... 54
Dexter Machine Co........................ 195
Dustin & Hubbard Mfg. Co................ 221
Eagle Iron Works.......................... 177
Field, Edwin F 48
Fay & Scott............................... 199
Gay & Parsons............................ 120
Greenwood, Chester....................... 257
Holmes Gear Works, The.................. 167
Hallowell Iron Foundry.................... 175
Jones, A. C............................... 278
Jumper, Charles H 39
King, A. B. & Co.......................... 46
Perry, Joseph............................. 156
Penney, J. W. & Sons..................... 273
Purinton, F. H............................. 328
Robbins & Sons........................... 163
Watson, S. J.............................. 350

MASONS AND CARPENTERS.

Chauey, H. W............................. 187
Colby, C. H............................... 333
Gilpatrick, F.............................. 215
Hayden & Robinson....................... 217
Jordan, C. A 90
Libby, W. A............................... 68

MILLINERY AND FANCY GOODS.

Atwood, L. Mrs............................ 58
Bigelow, H. H. Mrs........................ 189
Chase, F. E. Mrs.......................... 287
Chase, E. A. Miss......................... 336
Dean, N. E. Miss.......................... 282
Dillingham, A. Miss....................... 315
Emery, A. L. Miss......................... 300
Flagg, B. R. Mrs.......................... 185
Frizzell, B. F. Mr. & Mrs.................. 222
Farnham, Julia A. Mrs.................... 228
Hacker, A. Miss........................... 337
Jordan, L. M. Miss........................ 134
Lemont, J. T. Mrs......................... 66
Page, George R........................... 68
Packard, G. M............................. 292
Rouse, E. A. W. Mrs...................... 342
Stewart. G. C............................. 247
Smith, M. A. Mrs.......................... 336
Wilson, C. R. Mrs......................... 304

PLUMBERS AND GAS FITTERS.

Green, John............................... 237
Goodwin, W. R............................ 64
Johnson, D. H............................. 176
Learned & Brown.......................... 208
Smith, John B, & Co...................... 61
Taber, Henry A........................... 212
Ward, A. D................................ 123

PICTURE FRAMES AND ENGRAVINGS.

Excelsior Picture Frame Co	280
Knowlton, D. P.	125
Piper, J. C.	345
Wardwell, H. B.	66

PIANOS, ORGANS, MUSICAL INSTRUMENTS AND MUSIC.

Allen, C. A.	250
Bucknam, J. A. & Co.	268
Ballard, L. W.	39
Barker, M. B. Mrs.	56
Bean & Hamlin.	139
Chadwick, W. E.	212
Carpenter, Gilbert H.	216
Glover, George H	62
Hunt, Charles C.	136
Hughes, J. D.	164
Heath & Tainter.	51
Lothrop, W. L.	62
Laughton, N. J.	63
Taylor, N. S.	47
Towle, George F.	311
Wheeler, W. J.	281
Washburn, J. G.	351

PUBLISHERS, PRINTERS, ETC.

Callahan, George A.	67
Calvert & Waldron.	73
Dexter Gazette.	197
Farmington Chronicle.	253
Goodwin, H. L.	264
Howard H. W. Printing Co., The.	341
Knowlton, D. H. & Co.	246
Knowlton, McLeary & Co.	246
Morse, W. S.	93
Thompson, J. W.	309
Weeks, W. H.	45
White, Charles R	158

PHOTOGRAPHERS.

Ayer, George O.	127
Call, B. L.	195
Carleton, C. G.	209
Hendee, J. S.	138
Hawkes, N. S.	186
Higgins, J. C. & Son.	355
Hatch, A.	354
Kimball, A. W	305
McIntosh, George.	109
Reed, A. O.	334
Stanley, F. E.	50
Sturtevant, E. E.	185
Starbird, E. R.	255
Vose, S. S. & Son.	213
Worthley, W. E. G	63

PAPER MFRS. AND DEALERS.

Bowdoin Paper Mfg. Co.	337
Hollinsworth & Whitney Paper Co.	158
Poland Paper Co.	274
Richards Paper Co.	167
Wood, Robinson & Co.	92
Warren, S. D. & Co.	102

RESTAURANTS.

Bennett, I.	123
Bridge, W. C.	274
Cressey, D. B.	42
Fairgrieve's Restaurant.	191
Hibbert, Samuel.	41
Harrison, George W.	344
Potter, A. G.	56

REAL ESTATE INSURANCE & INVESTMENT SECURITIES.

Bailey, A.	152
Berry, Arthur L.	161
Conant, F. A. & Co.	50
Davis, Farr & Co.	125
Davis, A. E.	217
Davenport George P.	358
Franklin Company, The.	34
Garcelon & Hunton.	96
Howe, Freeland.	292
Hall, W. T.	306
Kendall, J. C.	316
Lydston, William.	56
Maine Benefit Association.	98
Macomber, George E.	133
Maxcy, Josiah & Sons.	154
Neal, W. B.	165
Pennell, William M.	331
Small, J. T. & Co.	60
Stoddard, J L.	164
Voter, F. E.	261

SHIP BROKERS AND COMMISSION MERCHANTS.

Drake, James B.	343
Davenport, George P.	358
Olys, William B.	342

SHIP CHANDLERY, CORDAGE, ETC.

Donnell, J. T. & Co	353
Johnson Brothers.	355
Lord, H. S.	346

SCHOOLS AND COLLEGES.

Abbott Family School.	248
Colby University.	210
Dirigo Business College.	125
Farmington State Normal.	258
Lewiston Commercial, The.	70

INDEX.

STEAMSHIP LINES.

Eastern Steamship Co.	358
Kennebec Steamboat Co.	166
Kennebec Steam Towing Co.	159

STOVES, HARDWARE, ETC.

Allen, D. W. & Co.	208
Brooks, George B.	91
Brooks, S. S. & Co.	130
Blackwell, S. H.	235
Day, Joseph H.	46
Doran Furnace Co.	187
Emerson, O. E.	207
Folsom, C. W.	220
Farrar, S. L.	352
Greenwood, Charles	44
Goss, A. L. & E. F.	62
Hardy, J. D.	247
Johnson, D. H.	176
Lander, J. C.	146
Leavitt, W. C.	294
Pratt, T. L. & Co.	51
Richardson & Libby	282
Swanton, Jameson & Co.	347
Umberhine, I. F.	300
Watson & Co.	351
Winslow, J. A. & Son	342
Williamson, O.	136
Ward, A. D.	123

SPORTING GOODS, ETC.

Catland, T. R.	42
Cross, George W.	163
Fairbanks, J. A.	137
Houghton, C. R.	312
Littlefield, John F.	71
Sabourin Elie.	45

TEXTILE MANUFACTURERS.

Androscoggin Mills.	57
Avon Mill.	71
Abbott, Amos & Co.	194
Bates Manufacturing Co.	57
Barker Mills.	97
Continental Mills.	72
Edwards Manufacturing Co.	137

TAILORS AND CLOTHIERS.

Andrews, L. H.	356
Blaisdell, H. S.	117
Bicknell & Neal.	155
B. B. C. C. (B. L. Filene).	350
Carter, E. B.	186
Davis, E. E. & Co.	114
Dolloff & Dunham.	217
Dwinal, O. B. & C. H.	271
Douglas, J. L.	347

Estes & Ward.	184
Elliott, F. Q.	291
Hall, A. J.	120
Hawthorne, W.	357
Isaacson, S. A. & I. B.	64
Johnson, A. A.	225
Kenney & Plummer.	281
Lincoln, G. W.	198
Ledyard, William	348
Martin, P. E. & Co.	52
Maher, J. J. & Co.	134
Nason, Charles H.	129
Pinkham & Sherburne.	128
Partridge, B. W.	153
Richards & Merrill.	40
Sykes, R. M. & Co.	53
Small, E. N.	206
Salley, U. G.	237
Snow, A. J.	356
Soule, Fred S.	317
Snow, Jordan	335
Twombly, J. H. & Co.	85

UNDERTAKERS.

Allen, Daniel & Co.	40
Adams, T. H.	264
Crane, F. E. & Co.	43
Clark, John M.	347
Dillingham, C. W.	300
Dorman, R. S.	321
Flagg, Charles & Son	304
Knowlton, D. & Son	122
Perry, D. B.	270
Sturgis, Charles M.	116
Vaughan, Thomas	39
Wells, A. L. & Co.	118
Wheeler, W. H.	228

WATCHES AND JEWELRY.

Anthoine, A. W. & W. B.	50
Blethen, H. A.	198
Blake, E. G.	245
Clifford, C. W.	352
Davis, A. A.	329
Field, J. M.	224
Goodridge, F. J.	211
Hayden, Charles F.	359
Lord & Lowell.	115
Lambard, J. S.	159
Lovejoy, F. A.	215
Presson, George McL.	244
Rogers, G. S. & G. L.	150
Richards, S.	278
Springall, John W.	196
Smith, O. W.	317
Wright, A. S.	70
Wood, J. H	209
Woodward, C. A.	157

VARIETY STORES.

Bolster, H. N	279
Crossman, C. P.	63
Frizzle, B. F. Mr. and Mrs	222
Hillman, R. S.	188
Owen, F. H	134
Smith, L. A	251

WATER COMPANIES.

Augusta Water Works	111
Gardiner Water Co	160
Richmond Water Co	303
Waterville Water Co	214

HISTORICAL REVIEW

—— OF THE ——

CITY OF LEWISTON.

INTRODUCTION.

THE genesis and evolution of a New England city is an event of large historical signification and broad interest. From the solitude of a wilderness to the bustling prosperity of a great and enterprising city, there is a range of progress wide enough to cover almost every form of human activity, and every transition of human life. First, a few settlers' camps clustering around the river; then a frontier village with all its privations and haunting fears; then a town just opening up to the conceptions of national life and commercial possibilities; finally, the railroads and mills rapidly develop the long nourished germs into the intenser and more highly-organized action of municipal life. To understand the history of any city or country, one must know the character of the people, and the peculiar conditions of the environment which have affected their progress. To one interested in the welfare and destiny of the human race as suggested in its history, no less than to one on whom the charms and beauties of his native place have a strong, affectionate hold, the study of the growth of so representative a city as Lewiston reveals much of interest and value, and amply repays careful and continued study.

IN THE DAY OF SMALL THINGS.

Nature is not impartial, as we are sometimes asked to believe. She has her special favorites, on whom she lavishes her choicest treasures, and whose successful development is inevitable. When she gives vast motor power situated in a community and an age pre-eminent for manufacturing, it is not without a meaning, as a century or two plainly declares. As we grope among the misty traditions and mistier records that throw their feeble light on the early life of the now great industrial center of Lewiston, we find that its charms and superiority were early recognized. Upon the aboriginal mind, the glimmer of a thought of what the place was fitted for and destined to became, could never have dawned, yet in their own crude way they seem to have been not incapable of appreciating it. Lured, not unlikely, by the music of the falls, in harmony with their own impetuous natures, they seem to have frequented this locality, even to have made it the favorite meeting-place and center of the tribe in this part of the State, which went by the euphonius title of Anasagunticooks. With their peculiar predeliction for high-sounding epithets, they dubbed the Lewiston Falls "Amitgonpontook," which we doubt if they themselves thoroughly understood, and certainly no one since has mastered its meaning to any marked extent. What sort of jubilations the Anasagunticooks used to enjoy themselves here withal, is not at the present time definitely known, but it doubtless was not much advanced on the usual manner of people of their range of intelligence. They seem to have had a modified form of the ancient eastern religion of ancestor worship, and the fact that this was a great burial place of the tribe, undoubtedly made it a center for their religious life and ceremonies. They seem to have been quite numerous, though far from strong and active. Numerous skeletons have been discovered in various parts of Lewiston, and these silent memorials will perhaps still occasionally recall dim visions of a forgotten past, when the names and memories of its early inhabitants shall be known by the place no more.

Any one who follows the Androscoggin river up its broad, rushing course can see that the great falls that constitute its chief superiority, make it much more difficult, indeed impracticable for navigation, compared with the Kennebec or the Penobscot; consequently, though the region at its mouth was settled about 1630, one of the earliest places so favored in the State, yet the portions of valuable land farther up the stream were settled later than many spots on the two other great rivers of Maine. It is unnecessary to go into a consideration of all the fluctuations and transitions of ownership through which the Androscoggin region, known as the Pejepscot Purchase, passed during the middle of the seventeenth century. Prominent among the Indian chieftains who were active in these land treaties, was a certain Warumbee, a man of unusual discernment and ability, supposed to have had his headquarters in this vicinity. The endless disputes between proprietors, settlers and original owners, doubtless helped to retard the settlement of Lewiston, which was not practically effected until the year 1770.

The original movers for the founding of Lewiston were two Boston merchants, Jonathan Bagley and Moses Little, also prominent members of the Pejepscot Company, who in 1767 obtained a grant for the country about Lewiston Falls, and immediately set about the colonizing and developing of the region, whose advantages they were not slow to perceive. They decided to call the prospective town Lewiston, but for what reason does not appear. The ground surveyed was about five miles square, along the north side of the river, around the falls. The first actual settler was Paul Hildreth, who arrived with his wife and infant child in the summer of 1770, from New Gloucester, N. H., and had soon erected his log cabin on the river bank, near the present situation of the Continental mills. The family returned to New Gloucester, where they spent the following winter, but came back and spent with two other families, several lonely seasons here before the gloom and loneliness were lighted up by the arrival of other strong spirits like their own. The families of David Pettingill and Mr. Varnan of Dracut, Massachusetts, were also settled here in

LEWISTON FROM DAVID'S MOUNTAIN, 1888.

the years 1770–71, and the former, particularly, became very influential in building up the new settlement. Lawrence J. Harris accomplished more, perhaps, than any other one man in laying the foundations of Lewiston. He came in the autumn of 1770, with a company of eight workmen, and erected the frame of a mill at the falls, which he completed in the following spring, when he made a permanent settlement here. In consideration of his services he received large grants of land from the proprietors, Capt. Little and Col. Bagley, in addition to one hundred acres for each of his five sons to be selected in any part of the plantation, so that his family was very influential in building up the little town. The small size of the place was one great protection against Indian hostilities, which were never suffered here, except by rumor and anticipation, the surrounding Indians always remaining friendly.

The town was surveyed and laid out into fifty lots of one hundred acres each, by Amos Davis, in 1773, who himself settled here in 1774. The same year witnessed considerable accessions to their numbers, among others, Israel Herrick, Jesse Wright, Jacob Barker, Thomas and James Coburn with their families, helped to increase the now steadily-growing village. The Revolutionary War caused many families to settle back from the coast, beyond the reach of the English marauders, and the excessive taxation. Among others who were valuable accessions in 1775, were James Garcelon, Josiah Mitchell, Joel Thompson, Stephen Coffin, Mark Pettingill, and Joel Wright. Daniel Reed, Jonathan Hodgkins, Ebenezer Ham, and Stephen Cummings, also came during the next few years, and added weight to the business and affairs of the place. Amos Davis was a leader in town affairs during its early history. He was the most prominent in advancing the interests of the Friends' Society in this vicinity, and among other gifts to advance the town, bequeathed the land on Sabattis Street, for the old burying ground. He also built a small wooden building which served for a number of years as the meeting and schoolhouse.

Israel Herrick founded one of the ablest and strongest of Maine families. His son John founded the first tavern in this vicinity, and served the town for many years and in various capacities. He was long chairman of the selectmen, and was a member for many years of the Massachusetts Legislature, also taking part in the making of the State Constitution in 1820. He was widely noted for his unfailing generosity. Of his sons, Oliver won distinction as a captain in the war of 1812, and Ebenezer was elected to Congress, where he was a great honor to his native State, ranking among Maine's greatest legislators.

James Garcelon was one of the leading members of the first board of Selectmen, and among his descendants has been a Governor of the State.

Among the descendants of Ebenezer Ham, founder of the Ham family of Lewiston, have been some of our most distinguished military and municipal officers.

Daniel Reed was one of the youngest settlers in the new town, and gaining great respect and honor as the first school teacher, became one of the most influential of the town's citizens. He served in the town government for twenty-six years, being chairman twelve; was town clerk fifteen years; served one term in the Massachusetts Legislature, and four in the Maine Legislature; he was appointed by President Washington to be the first postmaster of Lewiston, in 1795, and held the position for about forty years.

A census of the town, taken in 1788, showed that there were seventy-six families settled here, and this number kept constantly increasing. Among other leading men who came about this time, were Messrs. Pettingill, Cole, Smith, Hinckley, Merrill Carvill, Ames, Hatch, Banks, Mitchell, Field, Lake, and Thorn. Lewiston, though very small at the time, had three representatives in the Revolutionary War, David Pettingill, who died in the service, his son Benjamin, and Joel Thompson. The town by rapid growth had increased to three hundred and thirty families in 1793. The records of the early meetings, held for the formation of a local government, together with other town documents have been lost, but in 1795, in response to a petition presented the year before, a town charter was granted to the citizens of Lewiston, and a town government soon organized. The first selectmen were John Herrick, James Garcelon, Joel Thompson, Winslow Ames, and Daniel Davis. The first town clerk was Noah Litchfield, who held the office for eight years; among his successors have been Daniel Read, for fifteen years; Winslow Ames, one year; Joel Thompson, six years;

Nathaniel Reynolds, one year; Wm. Garcelon, seven years; Stephen H. Read, four years; John M. Frye, one year; S. G. Phillips, three years; E. P. Tobie, twenty-three years; John Smith, one year.

At the time of incorporation, the Gore settlement was added to the Lewiston settlement in establishing the town. Among other traditions as to the name of Lewis-

LISBON STREET IN 1888.

ton, is one ascribing it to an Indian of the region, named Lewis, who is said to have entered a canoe above the falls, while in a state of intoxication, and drifting away in the current, was carried over the falls and drowned. Just before going over he shouted (?) out to the observing spectators that they should name the falls "Lewis Falls." This rather apochryphal story contains in itself all refutation necessary, and it would require a great deal of credulity, as well as ignorance of the Indian mind, to deem it true for a minute. Like some of the myths which grew up in prehistoric days as an explanation of existing facts, it was undoubtedly an after-growth, devised by some ingenious mind anxious to solve the inexplicable problem of the origin of the town's name.

The closing years of the last century found the town already well established, growing steadily, with premonitions of its future prosperity just dawning in the most observing minds of its citizens. The center of the town was at what is now Lowell's Corner, and about this quite a country trading business had been built up by David Davis, James Lowell and Nathan Reynolds. The only manufacturing, thus far, was that of the saw and grist mills, but the magnificent water power of the falls had not escaped observation, and plans of improvement were lying dormant, which were destined to spring up in great enterprises early in the following century. The only means of communication with Portland and other towns was by means of the stage and team routes, and Lewiston was then considered quite remote in the backwoods, but here by itself in the woods were being laid the foundations of one of the most magnificent industrial developments New England has known.

THE PROGRESS OF THE NINETEENTH CENTURY.

The first few years of the century witnessed no remarkable events or growth, but by the end of the first decade it was already recognized as a town of great promise. The greatest industrial achievement up to that time, was the erection by Col. Little, in 1809, of a large saw, grist, fulling and carding mill combined, at a favorable place near the falls. Unfortunately this was burned in 1814. In the year 1811-12, the erection of the first meeting-house in the southern part of the town was a marked sign of progress. The town took a decided interest in the war of 1812, though the war brought only trouble and loss to itself. A company was raised here in 1812, under the command of Capt. Oliver Herrick, and it suffered severe loss in the engagement on Lake Champlain, July 2, 1813. A considerable number of volunteers from this town were slain. In Sept. 1814, Col. Walter R. Blaisdell of Lewiston, raised a regiment in this vicinity, two companies being from this city, which performed valuable services in the field. After the war a wave of greater progress set in, and business men from this and other states began to discover and discuss the great advantage of Lewiston as a mill site.

In 1818, the Baptist church edifice was erected at a cost of $2,260, and in 1820 the Freewill Baptists also erected a church building. During this time the school interests were advancing, chiefly owing to the untiring efforts of "Master Bond," a man of much force of character and mind, who was in charge of Lewiston's schools from 1809 to 1839.

The growth and extent of the milling interests of Lewiston, are eminently worthy of exceptional and careful mention. Not later than 1819, a decided start in this direction had been taken in the erection of a woolen mill, which was burned in 1820. But a larger and better mill was erected in 1830, and its success was the breeze which kindled the growing plans for utilization of the vast water power here into a blaze. In 1834, as the result of long work and thorough planning on the part of Lewiston and other capitalists, the first great stock company, the Lewiston Falls Manufacturing Co., with a capital of $100,000, was incorporated and started operations in the manufacturing of satinet. Thomas B. Harding was the first man to manufacture cotton, Lewiston's great specialty, setting up two looms here in 1844. The Great Androscoggin

Falls, Dams, Locks and Canal Company, incorporated in 1836, with $100,000 capital, was the first to adequately develope the magnificent water power of the falls. The name was changed in 1845 to the Lewiston Water Power Company, and the massive granite locks at the falls, and the great canal, sixty-two feet wide, three-quarters of a mile long, supplying all the mills, were the results of their valuable work. The stocks

VIEW ON THE CANAL.

and works of this company passed into the hands of the Franklin Company, by purchase, in 1857. The great dam of adamantine strength, completed at an outlay of $100,000 in 1863-64, was the work of this latter company. The Lincoln Mill was one of the earliest large mills to start cotton manufacturing, dating its work since 1846. It has a capacity of 21,744 spindles, producing 3,500,000 yards of sheeting per annum, but has not been run steadily the last few years.

The first mill erected on the canal was the Bates, No. 1, which was incorporated in 1850, and commenced manufacturing cotton goods in 1852. Bates No. 2 was completed and started in 1854; No. 3 in 1863; and No. 4 in 1881. The whole number of spindles in this great series of mills, is 63,672; annual consumption of cotton, 5,184,000 pounds; annual production of goods, 10,400,000 yards of quilts, ginghams, chevoits, towels, dress goods, shirtings, colored duck, cottonades, and seersuckers. Over 1,600 hands, male and female, are employed, and the monthly pay roll is around $55,000.

Next, in the order of time, is the Hill Company, incorporated in 1850, and operations began in 1854. Two large mill buildings are kept constantly humming to the tune of 51,630 spindles, and 8,600,000 yards of cotton goods, chiefly shirtings, sheetings and twills are run out every year. A thousand hands are employed, and about $26,000 paid out every month in wages.

The Androscoggin Mills were incorporated in 1860, and commenced manufacturing in 1861. These large mills, containing about 60,000 spindles, and producing annually 9,227,000 yards of cotton goods, together with numerous outlying buildings, comprise the extensive plant of this company. They employ a thousand hands, and the monthly pay roll is estimated at about $45,000.

The Continental Mills, incorporated 1865, began operations 1866, contain 70,000 spindles, have an annual production of 17,500,000 yards, sheetings and drillings, an employeé force of 1,200 hands, and a pay roll of $40,000 per month.

A WALK IN THE PARK.

Besides these great cotton mills are: the Lewiston Bleachery, with three hundred and sixteen employeés, and a monthly pay roll of $25,000; the D. Cowan & Company Mill, producing 300,000 yards woolen goods annually, with a hundred and eighty-five employeés and a monthly pay roll of $3,700; the Cumberland Mill, producing $300,000 worth of woolen goods per annum, with fifty employeés and monthly pay roll of $2,000; the Avon Mill, manufacturing quantities of quilts and towels. Not counting in the machine shops we thus find that, estimating roughly, in the great cotton industry alone, 245,000 spindles are kept constantly at work, 45,727,000 yards of various kinds of cotton goods, produced every year, 4,800 persons employed, and $166,900 every month or $1,992,000 annually paid in wages. When we remember that this great industrial development has raised the population from two thousand to over twenty thousand, and all the material wealth it has brought to the people, we can better appreciate how much Lewiston owes to its magnificent situation and its inexhaustible water supply. The development of its manufacturing industries has largely increased the extent of all its other commercial interests, and made it the center and leading city of all this part of the State.

While this great industrial advance was being made, Lewiston was forging steadily forward in other and all lines. Her religious growth was fostered by the establishment and maintenance of numerous church societies. Her educational affairs were advanced by the opening of the High School in 1850, and of the Maine State Seminary in 1855. The Lewiston Journal was established May 21, 1847 by Wm. H. Waldron & Co.; the first editor was Dr. F. Lane, succeeded by Wm. H. Waldron and Nelson Dingley, Jr. The issue of the Daily Journal was commenced in 1861, contemporaneously with the incorporation of the city. The charter for the city government of Lewiston was granted, but the government was not organized until the following year, and the first mayor, Jacob B. Ham, inaugurated in 1863.

The patriotic interest in the civil war was very deep and enthusiastic in Lewiston, as is shown by the fact that the first regiment in the State was largely organized here. Capt. N. J. Jackson of Lewiston, was chosen Colonel of the First Maine Infantry and performed gallant services at the front, for which he was promoted to be a Brigadier-General. Capt. Silas B. Osgood, Col. Wm. R. Ham (slain at Cold Harbor), Major Knowlton (slain in the Shenandoah Valley), and Lieut.-Col. Edwin Illsley, were among the gallant officers who upheld the honor of Lewiston, and of whose glory she was nobly proud, even amid the suffering and loss of battle days.

The large number of eleven hundred and fifty soldiers were enlisted here, only sixteen of these being drafted. Lewiston generously furnished her full quota of men without delay, being represented in almost every regiment which left the State. The contributions of money from Lewiston were constant and large. Among other amounts furnished were, $31,970.00 for the support of soldier's families, and $100,275 for bounties. A Ladies' Aid Society was actively and devotedly employed throughout the struggle, and the valuable assistance rendered in all lines, is far beyond the possibility of computation. One hundred and twelve officers and privates fell during the war, and their death brought irremedial grief to many Lewiston homes. As a fitting token of gratitude and honor, the names of all who fell are inscribed on the beautiful Soldiers' Monument, designed and executed by Mr. Franklin Simmons, artist, of Lewiston. The occasion of the unveiling of the monument, February 28, 1868, was appropriately celebrated, the address being made by the Hon. Wm. P. Frye. The monument is located near the northeast corner of the City Park.

An important event in the history of Lewiston, was its incorporation as a city in 1862. Owing to the unsettled state of affairs, produced by the war, the city government was not immediately organized, the first mayor, Hon. Jacob B. Ham, being elected and inaugurated in the next year. The list of chief city officials has been as follows: Mayors, Jacob B. Ham, 1863-64; Wm. P. Frye, 1865-66; Geo. H. Pilsbury, 1867; Isaac N. Parker, 1868-69; Wm. H. Stevens, 1870; Alonzo Garcelon, 1871; David Cowan, 1872; N. W. Farwell, 1873; H. H. Dickey, 1864; Edmund Russell, 1875-77; Jesse S. Lyford, 1878; Joseph H. Day, 1879-80; Mandeville T. Ludden, 1881; David Farrar, 1882; Alonzo M. Garcelon, 1883; Nelson Howard, 1884; Charles Walker, 1885; David Cowan, 1886; D. J. McGillicuddy, 1887; Horace C. Little, 1888. Of these honorable gentlemen, the following are deceased :

Jacob B. Ham, Isaac N. Parker, David Cowan, N. W. Farwell, H. H. Dickey, Edmund Russell, M. T. Ludden, Wm. H. Stevens. The Hon. Wm. P. Frye is well-known throughout the country as the able representative of Maine in the United States Senate. Lewiston has been represented in the gubernatorial chair of Maine by such talented men as Ex-Governors Dingley and Garcelon. The City Clerks of Lewiston, since its incorporation, have been as follows: E. P. Tobie, 1863-75; E. A. Nash, 1876-77; F. D. Lyford, 1878; C. F. Goff, 1879; E. A. Nash, 1880-82; W. J.

A LEWISTON RESIDENCE.

Rodick, 1683-85; John Sabin, 1886-87; John F. Putnam, 1888. In this connection, special honor should be given to the veteran clerk, Mr. E. P. Tobie, who served the town and city up to the time of his death, 1875, for nearly forty years. The work of compilation, by Mr. John F. Putnam, is of great value to all interested in the statistics and history of Lewiston.

The financial history since the war has coincided in Lewiston with the general experience of the country. There has been real and solid advance, though the undue inflation and sudden depressions which have occurred since the war, have not been entirely escaped here. The magnificent power of Lewiston's almost unlimited water supply has served as a rock foundation for her business interests, and renders them certain of great development and expansion in coming years.

The population of Lewiston has advanced as follows: — 1830, 1,549; 1840, 1,801; 1850, 7,584; 1860, 7,428; 1863, 8,761; 1870, 13,602; 1880, 19,083. At the present time it is estimated at a little over 20,000, which is now steadily advancing. A study of these statistics bears corroborative evidence to what has been already said of the immense impetus given to the growth of the city by the introduction of the milling in 1836, and its subsequent development. This is also demonstrated by the increased valuation of the city. Since 1856, the yearly valuations has been estimated as follows: —

1856,	$2,214,068	1872,	$10,443,165
1857,	2,451,091	1873,	11,591,054
1858,	1,983,593	1874,	12,794,376
1859,	2,429,529	1875,	12,645,206
1860,	2,509,104	1876,	11,873,130
1861,	2,974,414	1877,	11,740,602
1862,	3,338,698	1878,	10,003,845
1863,	3,864,616	1879,	9,152,121
1864,	4,024,202	1880,	9,743,979
1865,	4,322,041	1881,	9,957,257
1866,	4,957,699	1882,	10,338,160
1867,	4,435,990	1883,	10,655.217
1868,	5,615,568	1884,	11,107,166
1869,	6,048,000	1885,	11,314,331
1870,	6,271,719	1886,	11,301,356
1871,	9,866,354	1887,	10,813,088

One of the greatest undertakings ever made by the city was that resulting in the erection of the City Hall, in 1866. This fine building, one of the largest and most beautiful of its kind in the State and New England, is a striking testimony to the enterprise and liberality of Lewiston's citizens. It is built of brick, with fine granite trimmings, and both externally and internally is handsomely and elaborately furnished and adorned. The cost of the building was $200,000. It contains a large and admirably selected and arranged public library, bearing ample evidence to the intelligence and strength of intellectual things in Lewiston. There is also a finely arranged and decorated hall, admitted to be "one of the finest in New England," capable of seating about 2,500 people. Here numerous dramatic, operatic, orchestral, and other first-class entertainments are furnished, to the delight and instruction of the citizens. (see page 30.)

Among other members of the present city government, outside of those already mentioned are the following, Aldermen — A. D. Barker, W. H. White, M. A. Coyne, Fred L. Farr, P. X. Angers, M. A. Murphy, F. L. Hoyt; City Treasurer — David Farrar; Auditor — E. L. R. Hunt; Solicitor — W. H. Judkins; Chief Engineer — I. B. Merrill; Marshal — S. A. Cummings; Collector — E. G. Woodside.

The advance and power of business interests in Lewiston have been largely due to the untiring efforts and coöperating plans of its leading commercial men. The present Board of Trade has the following officers: President — C. I. Barker; First Vice-president — T. E. Eustis; Second Vice-president — S. D. Wakefield; Secretary — Horace C. Little; Treasurer — B. Peck. Other members of Board of Management: F. W. Dana, R. C. Reynolds, I. N. Wood, A. B. Nealy, C. H. Osgood, E. P. Ham. The membership of this important organization contains the leading business men of the city, and is contributing an inestimable amount to the progress and development of the city's interests.

Bates College, one of the leading institutions of education in the State, is situated at Lewiston. It was incorporated in 1856, with an endowment of $15,000. The collegiate course was first established in 1863, when its name was changed from "Maine State Seminary," to Bates College, in honor of the munificence of its chief benefactor, Benj. E. Bates, of Boston, who has given over $200,000 to the institution. The Rev. Oren B. Cheney, D.D., formerly of Augusta, the first president, being elected in 1856, has continued to exercise the duties of this office with ability and satisfaction up to the present time. The faculty is composed of ten able scholars and

BATES COLLEGE.

instructors, and the standard of work is maintained at the highest rank. There are about one hundred and fifty students at the present time in all departments. Among the principal buildings are Hathorn, Nichols and Parker Halls, and the Gymnasium. The Nichols Latin School is the preparatory department to the college. The Theological School, established in 1870, is one of the important departments of the college, and is admirably conducted and supported. Faculty of the College: Rev. Orin B. Cheney, D.D., President; J. Y. Stanton, A.M., Prof. of Latin and Greek; R. C. Stanly, A.M., Prof. of Chemistry and Geology; Thomas L. Agnell, A.M., Prof. of Modern Languages; Geo. C. Chase, Prof. of Rhetoric and English Literature; B. F. Hayes, Prof. Mental and Moral Philosophy; J. M. Rand, Prof. Mathematics. Faculty of the Theological School: Rev. Orin B. Cheney, D.D., President; Rev. John Fullonton, D.D., Prof. of Ecclesiastical History and Pastoral Theology; Rev. B. F. Hayes, D.D., Prof. of the Evidences of Christianity, and Moral Science; Prof. J. A. Howe, D.D., Prof. of Homiletics; T. H. Rich, A.M., Prof. of Hebrew.

The region around Lewiston is one of the most beautiful in this delightful State. The drives over fine roads in every direction reveal innumerable prospects of beauty, and Maranocook and many other beautiful resorts are brought almost next door by the railroad. Being furnished with admirable rail connections, both with Portland, Bath, Waterville, Bangor, etc., has been an inestimable boon to the growth of the city, both socially and commercially. Among the leading churches which represent the religious life of the city are the Pine Street Congregational and Free Baptist churches; the Maine Street Free Baptist; the Bates Street Baptist; the Park Street Methodist; the Hammond Street Methodist; the Trinity Episcopal; the St. Joseph's Roman Catholic, and Bates Street Universalist.

HISTORICAL SKETCH OF LEWISTON.

The water supply of the city is deserving of especial mention. In 1874, the first movement was made which resulted in the present admirable and efficient system. In 1876, the city, by a popular vote, authorized the purchase of the old saw mill site for $200,000, together with the right to take from the Androscoggin river such supplies of water as the city should need for domestic or mechanical uses. The pumping station was erected at this point, and this was completed in 1878, at a cost of $455,-509, commencing operations in December of that year. The city reservoir was built on Mitchell's Hill, about two miles from the city, at a cost of about $40,000. It is capacious, and thoroughly fitted with the best facilities for storing and purifying

LEWISTON WATER WORKS.

the water supply. The city is constantly making improvements, and has succeeded in obtaining for the growing population one of the most satisfactory water systems in the state. Of recent years more careful and extended attention has been given to the question of sewerage, and measures have been taken and are now being meditated for placing this department in the best position to meet the wants and demands of a constantly increasing population. Sanitary measures in general are essentially and thoroughly considered here, and executed with great rapidity and good results. The City Physician is Dr. R. R. Ricker, and all work in this department receives prompt and effective care. One department of the City Government especially worthy of mention is that of Police, which is conducted with great fidelity and the most careful attention to the interests of the citizens. This department is under the superintendence of City Marshal S. A. Cummings. To Lewiston belongs the honor of being one of the first cities in the United States to establish a long-needed reform, by adding a police-matron to its officials. Mrs. Eliza E. Knowlton has performed the large and important duties of this office with the most satisfactory results, and has demonstrated effectively the need and value of this great work. This is but one evidence of the liberal and progressive spirit exhibited by the citizens of Lewiston in advancing their municipal life to the highest possible standard. The Fire Department of Lewiston is almost celebrated for the perfection of its technique and efficiency of its services. Lewiston has had some several fires, but has never suffered from a widespread conflagration, and this is largely due to the magnificent work and thorough reliability of this department. The Chief Engineer is I. B. Merrill, who with four assistants, renders the efficiency of the department a matter of perfect confidence. Over $12,000 is annually spent upon this department by the city, and the security of its manufacturing, commercial, public and domestic property most reliably obtained. This fact adds not a little to its superiority as an industrial site.

LEWISTON CITY BUILDING.

The corner-stone was laid July 4, 1871. The building was dedicated Dec. 5, 1872. The interior of large hall, 80x165, and 37 feet and 2 inches high. The floor will seat 1,600 people; the galleries will seat 672. The building is 165 feet on Park street, 180 feet on Pine street, 40 feet on Lisbon street. The height from the sidewalk to cornice, 100 feet. The height of spire is 206 feet. The vane is 9 feet long.

THE BAND STAND.

VIEW IN THE PARK.

The religious and philanthropic work of the city is also maintained by numerous benevolent institutions and societies. The social life of the city is of that refined and elevated type which is often seen in an atmosphere charged with high educational ideals. The presence of the college adds a tone of culture and progress which is most perceptible and valuable. It also affords exceptionable privileges to the young men of Lewiston to obtain a liberal education at home and with greatest facility. The social amenities are fostered by many large and active societies which receive especial attention here from the generous tendencies of the citizens. The public-school system is naturally and thoroughly elevated in its type and management. It has been modeled according to the highest standards, and placed under the control of broadly-educated and able officers. The people are also generous in its support, realizing its surpassing importance. During the past year the appropriation of the city to the public schools was $24,000; total receipts being $35,430, and total expenditures $37,502. $1,500 was also appropriated by the city for an evening school, for the advantage of those who, working in the day, could not improve the usual opportunities. For the coming year $28,000 for day schools only, and $1,500 for evening schools were appropriated by the city. Under the able management of the Superintendent of Schools, Mr. A. M. Edwards, with a talented corps of assistants and teachers, the work is conducted thoroughly and satisfactorily, and the finest advantages afforded the children of Lewiston. The Free High School is strong and progressive in all departments, affording a broad education in the fundamental principles of higher learning, and fitting those who take the classical directly for college. The advances made in this department have been correlative with the city's growth, and based on the discoveries and laws of modern learning.

Lewiston has built its prosperity upon a broad and substantial basis of great natural advantages, but it also shown the highest energy and skill in making the superstructure solid and durable. To the sacrificing and far-reaching efforts of its citizens is chiefly due the great success which has worthily rewarded them, and the merit of that prosperity is shown both in its substantial nature and promise of endurance, and in the moderate and wise manner in which they have made use of it to obtain a higher culture and more liberal development as men and citizens. With such a history of achievements, and so powerful and highly developed an internal life at present, though of course much work is yet to be done in the future, the city of Lewiston may face it with confidence and hope. The growth of the past has been harmonious along all lines, and at the present time the city presents one of the most satisfactory and brilliant pictures of the prosperity and enterprise of New England's sturdy race. As the successes and rewards of the past have come as the well-earned result of hard, steady efforts and wise planning, so, beyond question, the future contains yet more happy and prosperous fruits of this progressive spirit on which the second greatest city of the Garden State has been firmly and grandly built up.

LEADING BUSINESS MEN

OF

LEWISTON.

Nealey & Miller, Wholesale and Retail Dealers in Groceries, Flour, and Provisions, Corner Bates and Main Streets, Lewiston. Among the many houses engaged in the handling of Groceries and Provisions in this vicinity, that of Nealey & Miller is clearly entitled to be given a leading position, and this fact is so generally known that we hardly consider it necessary to detail at length our reasons for ascribing such prominence to it. Carrying on business both wholesale and retail, this concern as a matter of course must distribute an immense quantity of goods in the course of a year, and although we have no idea what the total value of the firm's annual business is, still we feel confident that it is unsurpassed in this locality. This representative enterprise was inaugurated 1860 as H. Day & Co., and later Day & Nealey, and the existing co-partnership was not consummated until 1882. Mr. A. B. Nealey is known to many by reason of his connection with the State Legislature, and his associate in business, Mr. C. H. Miller, has served the public as a member of the City Council. Both of these gentlemen have shown that it is possible to utilize in the direction of public affairs the same qualities which yield success in the prosecution of private business enterprises and it would be well for tax payers in general if more of our successful men of business could be elected to protect their interests. Messrs. Nealey & Miller carry on an establishment occupying three floors, measuring 25x100 feet and located at the corner of Bates and Main Sts. Groceries, Flour, Meats, and Provisions are handled very extensively, and employment is afforded to twelve assistants. It is not the practice here, as it is in some stores where both kinds of business are done to neglect retail for wholesale customers, and a prime cause of this concern's general popularity is found in the courteous and prompt attention given to the smallest buyer.

Bradford, Conant & Co., Wholesale and Retail Dealers in Furniture, Carpets and Draperies, 199 and 201 Lisbon Street, Lewiston. It is not hard to guess the reason for the acknowledged superiority of the goods handled by the house of Bradford, Conant & Co., after inspecting the stock carried at the spacious warerooms on Lisbon Street, for the more thoroughly the examiner is acquainted with such goods, the more clearly he will be able to appreciate the thoroughness with which they are made, and the beauty and originality of their designs. This business enterprise is one of which every public-spirited citizen of Lewiston has reason to be proud, for it has been conducted for over half a century, (having been inaugurated in 1835) and has always been under the control of men remarkable alike for strict integrity and far-seeing enterprise. The founders were Messrs. Pinkham & Bradford, who were succeeded by the firm of Bradford & Conant, the present style being Bradford, Conant & Co., adopted in 1863. As now constituted, the firm is made up of Messrs. J. C. Bradford, and Granville Blake, and Mrs. Lucy W. Conant. The factory is located at East Auburn, and contains three floors, of the dimensions of 100x75 feet. The Furniture here produced has found its way into many a home, and it presents a refreshing contrast to the "ginger-bread work," so generally supplied to the public. It is made to *wear* as well as to sell, and hence is the cheapest, as well as the handsomest, in many respects of any in the market. The stock of Carpets carried is also worthy of mention, for it includes Staple and Standard Goods of all grades, and will be found complete in all departments, from the cheapest Woolen to the most expensive Brussels or Wilton Velvet. Customers are at all times assured prompt and courteous attention, and not the least inducement is the perfect confidence which may be placed in all representations made.

3

The Franklin Company, Mill and Real Estate Owners. Office under DeWitt House, Park Street, Lewiston. We have little need to remind our readers, or at least such of them as are residents of Lewiston or vicinity, of the important services that the "Franklin Company" has rendered in developing and more fully extending the business interests of that city for these have been so pronounced and so well-applied as to have been in the highest degree productive and successful. The Company to which we have reference was incorporated in the year 1854, with a capital of $1,000,000 and its stockholders and controlling spirits have been from its inception, made up of our most prominent and most truly representative citizens. Among the important and valuable pieces of property owned by this organization may be mentioned the Lincoln Mills, one half the Lewiston Bleachery, the DeWitt House and many other buildings, as well as several hundred acres of land most eligibly and centrally located in the city of Lewiston. No intelligent person need be told that the estimation in which the ownership of property in any given locality is held, depends very largely upon the course of conduct pursued by the heavier owners of real estate in that vicinity and, this being accepted as a fact, no argument is required to show that the gentlemen associated together under the name of the Franklin Company have exerted a powerful influence in maintaining values, as they are all evidently strong personal believers in Lewiston and her future, and indeed a perusal of the names of the Company's officers and directors will show that they are those of men who have shown their public spirit in many other ways beside those connected with their association in the Company. Treasurer, Wm. B. Wood; Clerk and Acting Agent, Wm. D. Pennell; Directors, Wm. B. Wood, Lyman Nichols, Nathan Cushing, F. L. Richardson, Edward L. Wood. William P. Frye, Jacob Edwards. Those desiring to put money into real estate for business or investment purposes would best conserve their own interests by ascertaining what the Franklin Company has to offer, as it is prepared to dispose of extremely desirable property at low figures to the right parties.

T. J. Murphy, "The Hatter," Sign of Gold Hat, Lewiston. It is said that the waiters in the fashionable hotel dining-rooms in Boston and New York, have a habit of looking at the name in the hats of strangers whom they are called upon to serve, and if it is that of a fashionable and high-priced hatter, they will show the guest every attention with the expectation of getting a fat fee, while if it is some name unknown to them, they will allow the unfortunate owner of the "tile" to nearly starve rather than bother with waiting upon him. The advantage of procuring a Hat from "Murphy, the Hatter," of this city is, that it is not necessary to look inside of it to learn its superior quality, for this is plainly manifest to all who know a good article of the kind when they see it. The business carried on by Mr. Murphy was founded in 1868, by Messrs. P. P. & A. L. Getchell, who were succeeded by the present owner in 1873. His celebrity is by no means confined to Lewiston, as both a wholesale and a retail business are done throughout this portion of the State. The "Sign of the Gold Hat" indicates where Mr. Murphy's establishment is located, and callers will find themselves well repaid as the stock carried is so heavy and varied, and the prices so low, as to offer exceptional inducements to buyers. Gents' Furnishing and Fine Fur Goods are handled, as well as Hats, and four competent assistants employed. Mr. Murphy is well-known in this city, and was formerly connected with the Common Council. He has done much to advance our local business interests, and fully deserves the personal popularity he enjoys.

H. H. Dickey & Son, Top Roll Coverers; Manufacturers of Leather Belting. Loom Straps and Pickers, and Dealers in Rubber Belting, Roller, Clearer and Slasher Cloths, Lacings, Rivets, etc., Main Street, near the Canal, Lewiston. This, of course, is not the proper place in which to present an essay on the economical transmission of power, but, nevertheless, the importance of the subject is so great that one might well be pardoned for discussing it at almost any time. Although the various industrial journals throughout the country have had much to say on this question, still it may be truly stated that the majority of our manufacturers do not properly appreciate the great gain which may be often made by proper attention to this single detail of their establishments. Where power is transmitted by means of belts, their material, construction and adjustment have much to do with their efficiency, and in the single matter of adjustment alone, it is obvious that whether a belt be so loose as to slip excessively, or so tight as to induce unnecessary wear upon the bearings as well as upon itself, there must be a waste of power, and consequently a sacrifice of efficiency. We need not go into a consideration of the influence of material, etc., upon the comparative economy of belting, but will simply state that care exercised in the selection of either Leather or Rubber Belting, will be amply repaid. One of the best known houses in this State, in connection with the manufacture and sale of Belts, is that of H. H. Dickey & Son, and an evidence of the esteem in which the goods they handle are held, is seen in their already large and steadily increasing business. Operations were begun in 1854, by Mr. H. H. Dickey, and just twenty-two years later the firm-name became as at present. Mr. William Dickey has now sole charge of the extensive business, and that he proposes to fully maintain the prestige of the establishment is seen by the care exercised in the manufacture and selection of the goods offered for sale. He is a native of Nashua, N. H., and a member of the Masons and Odd Fellows. Three floors are occupied, measuring 60x40 feet, and ten assistants employed, orders being promptly filled and shipped all through the States. Leather Belting is extensively manufactured, and Rubber Belting, Roller, Clearer, and Slasher Cloths, Lacings, Rivets, etc., are dealt in largely. Blacksmiths' Aprons, Loom Straps, Pickers, etc., are also in stock, and all goods are supplied at the lowest market rates.

LEADING BUSINESS MEN OF LEWISTON.

R. C. Pingree & Co., manufacturers of Long and Short Lumber, office 136 Main Street, Lewiston. The Lumber interests of this section would be but very imperfectly represented in these pages, were not mention made of the house of R. C. Pingree & Co., and this would still be the case, if every other house engaged in this line of trade were treated of to the exclusion of the one mentioned, for this concern, since its establishment in 1855, has taken a position among the leaders in the leading industry of Maine. Business was commenced by Messrs. S. R. Bearce & Co., just about a third of a century ago, and it has been continued under the present style since 1875. Mr. R. C. Pingree is a native of New Hampshire, while Mr. S. R. B. Pingree was born in this State and in this city. Mr. Pingree, senior, is a Justice of the Peace, and stands very high in the Masonic Fraternity. It is impossible, considering the limited space at our disposal to give any adequate description of the extensive manufacturing plant which this house is obliged to maintain, in order to keep pace with the orders received, but some faint conception of its magnitude may perhaps be gained from the statement that the annual out-put amounts to about 22,000,000 feet, equally divided between Long and Short Lumber. Employment is afforded to one hundred and seventy-five hands and both a wholesale and retail business is done. A three hundred horse-power engine is required in combination with extensive water-power, to run the necessary machinery, and the facilities at hand are so large and so admirably arranged as to permit the prompt and accurate filling of orders at all times. An extensive Planing-Mill is maintained, run by water-power, in which every kind of Moulding and House Trimming is manufactured. We need not say that this concern is a credit to the city, for that is self-evident, but we must take this opportunity to express our appreciation of the sterling integrity which characterizes its management.

W. W. Ellis, Fine Paper, Envelopes and Miscellaneous Stationery, Engraved Wedding and Visiting Cards, a Specialty. No. 2 Frye Block, Lisbon Street, Lewiston. What must without doubt be considered as one of the leading houses of the kind in this State, is that conducted by Mr. W. W. Ellis at No. 2 Frye Block, Lisbon Street. This enterprise has been in operation since 1880, and from the first has been characterized by liberal yet discriminating management, and by the honorable method employed in every department. Mr. Ellis was born in Boston, Mass., and is very generally known throughout Lewiston and vicinity. The premises utilized by him comprise two floors of the dimensions of 75x25 feet, and an immense stock is carried, consisting of Fine Paper, Envelopes and Miscellaneous Stationery, Blank-books, Art Goods, Albums, etc., together with Pictures, Picture Frames, and similar articles of utility and ornament. Special attention is given to Mercantile Printing, and those who contemplate having anything done in this line would do well to examine the advantages offered by Mr. Ellis, as he is prepared to furnish thoroughly artistic work, and no merchant can afford to have his printing done in a cheap and inferior manner. Orders are filled at short notice, and no fancy prices are quoted. Engraved Wedding and Visiting Cards are another specialty, and this concern is an authority as regards correct style in the getting up of these useful little messengers. The assortment of Art Goods, Pictures, etc., shown is much too extensive to allow of our describing it, but it is well worth visiting and ranks favorably with that offered at a much more pretentious establishment. Picture Frames are made to order at prices as low as the lowest, and can be supplied at very short notice.

E. S. Paul & Co., Wholesale and Retail Dealers in Dry and Fancy Goods, 174 Lisbon Street, Lewiston. There is more than one house in this city engaged in the handling of Dry and Fancy Goods, of which no public-spirited citizen of Lewiston has any reason to be ashamed, but among them all we question if one could be found more worthy of the highest praise and appreciation than that conducted by Messrs. E. S. Paul & Co., at No. 174 Lisbon St. We feel no doubt but that we will be supported in this assertion by a large majority of those acquainted with the facts in the case, as the record of this house has been such as to merit its receiving the highest confidence and most liberal support of residents of this vicinity. Business was begun in 1867, under the style of Goddard & Paul, and was so continued up to 1876, when the present firm-name was adopted. As now constituted, the firm is made up of Mr. E. S. Paul, a native of Buxton, Mr. A. W. Fowles, who was born in Whitefield, and Mr. W. A. Paul, who claims Auburn as his birthplace. We need not allude to these gentlemen further personally, other than to remark that the senior partner has been a member of the Auburn Board of Aldermen, and was connected with the School Committee of that city. The firm occupy four floors of the dimensions of 100x50 feet, to carry on their extensive operations, and give employment to thirty assistants. Dry and Fancy Goods of every variety are constantly in stock, and a wholesale, retail and manufacturing business is done, Cloaks and Dresses being made very extensively. A special feature of the business is the manufacture and sale of ladies' outside garments, of which a full assortment of all sizes and prices is carried. These are warranted first-class in every respect. Low prices prevail in every department, and only reliable goods are handled.

Jas. A. Johnson, Manufacturer of Doors, Sash and Blinds, Glazed Windows, Door and Window Frames. Factory, Cross Canal, Lewiston. There is going to be an active demand for Doors, Blinds, etc., as long as houses are built and occupied and as this is the case, it follows that no line of business is more staple and firmly established than that of the Door and Blind Manufacturer. Mr. James A. Johnson of this city is very prominently identified with the industry in question, for he has carried on his present establishment since 1885 (at which date he succeeded Mr. J. Miller, who began operations in 1872), and has built up a heavy and increasing patronage. Mr. Johnson was born in Parsonfield, Me., and is well known in Lewiston and vicinity. His facilities for furnishing Doors, Sash, Blinds, etc., are of the best, and he is entirely competent to meet all reasonable demands as regards the character of his productions and the celerity with which orders are filled. Employment is given to five assistants, and the latest improved machinery is utilized in the handling of stock. Building operations have been greatly simplified by the establishment and the successful results attained by such enterprises as this, and the cost of building has also been materially lessened.

Douglass & Cook, Books, Stationery, Paper Hangings, Window Shades, Pictures and Frames. Frames Made to Order. 188 Lisbon Street, Lewiston. "A beautiful store and an elegant stock" is perhaps as short and yet as correct a description as can be given of the establishment carried on under the firm name of Douglass & Cook at No. 188 Lisbon Street, and if business relations are entered into with this house, it will be found that the favorable impression first made will only be deepened and added to. This enterprise was inaugurated about a score of years ago by Mr. Oscar G. Douglass, who was born in this State, and has been City Marshal of Lewiston. In 1872, the firm of Douglass & Cook was formed, and, although Mr. Cook retired about 12 years later, the business has been continued by the senior partner since without change of style. The premises in use are of the dimensions of 95 x 35 feet, and comprise one floor and a basement. Employment is afforded to three efficient assistants, and a really remarkable assortment of goods is carried, including Books, Stationery, Window Shades, Pictures, Frames and Paper Hangings. These latter, although we have placed them last upon the list, are well worthy of careful examination, for Mr. Douglass does a very large business in the sale of Wall Paper, and at all times is prepared to supply the latest novelties and the most approved designs at the lowest market rates. He handles the productions of the best manufacturers in the country, and his goods are sure to give satisfaction. Pictures are also dealt in very extensively, and Paintings, Engravings, Etchings, Photographs, etc., are shown in great variety. A specialty is made of the manufacture of Picture Frames to Order, and some decided bargains may be had in this line, while a full supply of the leading Papers and Periodicals is always on hand.

Abram Atwood, Wholesale and Retail Dealer in Meat, Fruit, Vegetables and Fish. Oysters a specialty in their season. 159 Lisbon Street, Lewiston. Those who have done business with Mr. Abram Atwood long enough to have become familiar with his methods and the excellence of his service, need not be advised to patronize his establishment in the future, but as there are doubtless many among our readers who have not had this experience we think it will be both pleasant and well-advised for us to call attention to some of the many advantages he has to offer. To begin with his store is a fine and commodious one (60x25 feet in size and including one floor and a basement) and it is very completely fitted up for the carrying on of the business in the best possible manner. Dealing as he does in such perishable commodities as Meat, Fish, Oysters, Fruit, Vegetables, etc., Mr. Atwood has spared no expense to provide the most approved means of preserving the same when the weather is warm or otherwise unfavorable, and he has found his reward in the character of his patronage, for no one likes to purchase articles of food which have been improperly cared for. He was born in Wellfleet, Mass., and is widely and favorably known in Lewiston and also in Auburn where he has been in this business for 20 years. A large and varied stock is at all times carried of the goods we have mentioned, and during their season a specialty is made of the sale of Oysters. All the most popular varieties of these delicious bivalves being handled. Three assistants are employed and all orders promptly and satisfactorily filled.

S. A. Cummings, Manufacturer of Confectionery, 223 Main Street, Lewiston. The progress made in every department of manufacture of late years has not failed to include that of Confectionery, and such of our readers as like sweets can now congratulate themselves that never before was it possible to secure Confections of such excellent quality at the present low prices. Although the immoderate consumption of Candy is doubtless hurtful, (as is also that of Beef or any other article of food), still it is now generally conceded by physicians that Confectionery is entirely harmless when used as it should be, and common sense corroborates this view of the subject, as evidences are afforded on every side that its habitual use is not at all incompatible with the most exhuberant health. It is to be taken for granted of course, that pure goods only shall be used, and such are by no means hard to obtain here in Lewiston, as Mr. S. A. Cummings, of No. 223 Main Street, is prepared to furnish them in any desired quantity, either at wholesale or retail. He is a manufacturer as well as a dealer, and hence is able to put his prices down to the lowest notch at which first-class materials can be furnished. The premises utilized are 75x30 feet in dimensions, and three capable and efficient assistants are employed. Not only Confectionery, but also Fruits, Tobacco, Cigars, etc., are handled, and those capable of appreciating a fine glass of Soda Water will find Mr. Cummings ready to supply the purest and most delicious Fruit Syrups in combination with Fresh and Sparkling Soda. This gentleman is a native of Belgrade, Me., and has been a member of our City Council, was Clerk of Board of Overseers of Poor for five years, Deputy Sheriff of Androscoggin County, and is now City Marshal. He began operations here in 1884, and has made hosts of friends by integrity and close attention to business.

LEADING BUSINESS MEN OF LEWISTON.

Jordan, Frost & Co., Eastern, Western and Southern Lumber, Mouldings, Gutters and Brackets, Steam Planing Mill and Lumber Yard Foot of Cross Canal, Lewiston. It has long been known to builders and others interested, that the house of Jordan, Frost & Co., offered special advantages to those desiring lumber of any description and the result has been that the firm in question has done a very large and prosperous business. Although we have spoken in the past tense it is to be understood that the same desirable condition of affairs exists at the present time, as indeed no one could doubt who is familiar with the honorable business methods employed and the low rates at which goods are supplied. This representative enterprise was inaugurated some twenty years ago under the present firm name, the gentlemen carrying it on being Messrs. A. E. Frost and F. M. Jordan. These gentlemen are now the sole proprietors, and Mr. Wm. Jordan's interest having been purchased by the other partners in 1880, are extremely well-known in this community. Mr. Frost is a native of Tewksbury, Mass., while his associate in business was born in Auburn, Me. Eastern, Western and Southern Lumber is very extensively handled, and Mouldings, Gutters and Brackets are manufactured in considerable quantities, a steam planing mill being run at the foot of Cross Canal. A specialty is made of kiln-dried hard wood flooring and sheathing. Employment is given to twenty men and great pains are taken to insure the prompt and accurate filling of all orders.

Lewiston Machine Co., opposite Upper Maine Central Depot, Lewiston. The manufacture of textile machinery is one of the great industries of the country, and it is one that cannot be carried on successfully unless conservatism be combined with enterprise, and economy with liberal business methods. This may seem a contradiction of terms, but it is only apparently so, and every manufacturer will apprehend our real meaning, which is economy as to every detail of manufacture, but enlightened liberality as regards the acquisition of desirable patents and the employment of the best available skill. Many changes have been made in American textile machinery within the last quarter-century, and as a rule it is run over one third faster than was formerly the case. English mill-owners and operatives visiting this country always remark this, and it is generally understood that man for man, the production of a cotton or woolen mill here is considerably greater than in the Old Country. Higher speed involves the necessity of more perfect design and construction, and it is owing to the perfection which its products in the shape of Textile Machinery have attained, that the Lewiston Machine Company is in so prosperous a condition. It was organized in 1864, with a capital of $100,000, and has for its present officers and directors the following widely-known gentlemen: President, C. I. Barker; Treasurer, F. Kelley; Agent, R. C. Reynolds; Directors, N. Dingley, jr., John W. Farwell. C. I. Barker, E. S. Davis, James Dempsey, E. T. Gile, and L. L. Shaw. An extremely elaborate and costly plant is maintained, including one of the best foundries in the State, and employment is given to two hundred hands.

The furnishing of strictly reliable and first-class Machinery at the lowest market rates is the aim of those having this enterprise in charge, and the large and increasing sales show that this design is fully and satisfactorily carried out. The works are located opposite the Upper Maine Central Depot, and cover a considerable area of ground.

Horton & Peirce, Dealers in Rubber Goods, 87 Lisbon Street, Lewiston. So general and important are the applications which have been made of Rubber Goods, that they have become one of the great necessities of civilization in this climate at all events, and by their judicious use, enough can be saved in doctor's bills in the course of a year to more than square the account. To begin with, everybody ought to have a pair of Rubber Boots. When we say everybody, we mean everybody,—young or old, rich or poor, and these indispensable articles are now supplied at such low rates that they are within the means of all. It is always the truest economy, however, to get a good quality of Rubber Goods, and this may be done by patronizing the establishment conducted by Messrs. Horton & Peirce, at No. 87 Lisbon Street, for these gentlemen carry one of the most complete stocks in the State of Maine, comprising all grades and kinds of Rubber Goods, and will fully guarantee every article sold to prove precisely as represented. They do a wholesale and retail business, and occupy one floor of the dimensions of 35x40 feet, together with a basement of the same size. Among the articles in stock, the following may be enumerated: Ladies' and Gents' Mackintosh Garments; Gents' and Boys' Rubber Coats, in all weights and sizes; Ladies', Misses' and Children's Rubber Circulars, in various colors. Special attention given to Ladies' Cloth Surface Garments, in all latest close-fitting styles. Cotton and Rubber Hose, all weights and sizes; Elastic Stockings. Anklets, Leggins, Armlets, etc., made to order on short notice. Elastic Bands in great variety. White Hospital Sheeting, Bandage Gum and Sheet Horse Covers and Hoods. Wagon Boots, Blankets, Nursing Bottles, with Fittings, Nipples, Tubes and Brushes. Lycoming & Goodyear Glove Rubber Boots, and Foot-Wear in all styles. Rubber Hats, Gloves, Mittens, Tubing, Mats, Leggins, Aprons, Crib Sheets, Dress Shields, Capes, Bibs, Sponge Bags, etc. Foot-Balls, Dolls, Rattles, Combs, Chair Tips, Corks, Face Bags, Cots, Ice Bags, Pants, Matting, Stair Treads, Window Cleaners, etc. Physicians' Supplies and Druggists' Sundries, Air and Water Beds, Pillows, Cushions, Rings, Syringes, Atomizers, Tubing, Hot Water Bottles, and the list might be almost indefinitely extended. But enough has been said to give an idea of the resources of the establishment, and no one wishing anything made of Rubber can afford to let this store remain unvisited. A full stock of Gents' Furnishing Goods has recently been added, which are sold at low prices. Mr. W. R. Horton is a native of Reading, Mass., while Mr. A. F. Peirce was born in Waltham, in the same State, and these gentlemen possess advantages in the handling of the articles mentioned, which would be hard to parallel elsewhere.

D. B. Stevens, Manufacturer of Doors, Blinds, Sash, etc., 34 Main Street, Lewiston. An establishment which has come to be known by builders and others as the headquarters for Carpenters' Supplies and similar articles, is that carried on by Mr. D. B. Stevens at No. 34 Main Street. Business was begun by Mr. Stevens in 1871, and he has steadily increased the scope of his operations until now customers throughout this section are supplied. He is a native of Woodstock, Me., and is very widely known in Lewiston and vicinity, and a member of the Free Masons and Grand Army. The premises occupied for the storage and sale of goods comprise two floors of the dimensions of 75 x 30 feet, and an extensive stock is constantly carried of Doors, Sash, Blinds, Door and Window Frames, Glazed Windows, Mouldings, Brackets, etc., as well as a complete assortment of Carpenters' Supplies, including Butts, Knobs, Locks, Weights, Cord, etc. Many of these goods are manufactured by Mr. Stevens at his Planing Mill on Cross Canal, which occupies two floors, measuring 40 x 60 feet, and requires about 10-horse power to run the machinery used. Employment is given to ten assistants, and we must not forget to mention that an important department of the business is the painting of blinds to order, this work being done in the very best manner and at short notice. Low prices prevail at Mr. Stevens' establishment, and orders are promptly and accurately filled.

J. B. Ham & Co., Millers. Flour, Grain and Feed. Mill and Office in Grand Trunk Yard, Lewiston. It is impossible to make a review of the leading industries of Lewiston and vicinity without the attention soon being called to the trade in Flour, Grain, Feed, etc., for this is of so much importance that it occupies a very high comparative position when the totals for each branch of trade are footed up, and engages the best efforts of some of the most prominent of our citizens. There, for instance, is the firm of J. B. Ham & Co. This house begun operations in 1872, and has now built up a business which easily entitles it to a position in the very front rank of those concerns conducting similar establishments. Since the decease of Mr. J. B. Ham, which occurred in September, 1888, the business has been conducted by his son, E. J. Ham, under the same firm-name. Mr. Ham is a native of Lewiston. The senior partner was the first Mayor of this city, and held the office for two terms; also had been Representative to the Legislature. A large and admirably equipped Grist Mill is maintained, located in Grand Trunk Yard, and Flour, Grain, Feed, etc., are handled very extensively—Grinding in car lots being done, many wholesale houses being supplied. Employment is given to six assistants, and every order is assured early and careful attention. No lower rates are fixed anywhere, and that the advantages offered are fully appreciated is evidenced by the steadily increasing business done.

The Bearce & Clifford Construction Company. Teams for Heavy Trucking furnished at Lowest Cash Prices. No. 242 Haymarket Square, Lewiston. It is becoming more and more the custom—in fact, it may be said to be a well-nigh universal practice at the present day—to do work of any magnitude on the "contract system," and, although some objections have doubtless been raised to this method of doing business, they have been aimed more directly at the employment of irresponsible parties than at the system itself. As prominent and widely-known a firm of contractors as can be found in this State, is that of The Bearce & Clifford Construction Company, whose office is at No. 242 Haymarket Square, and the reputation of this concern for probity and entire reliability is as high as the operations of the firm are extensive. One of the latest examples of their work is that afforded by the dam built for the Little Androscoggin Water Power Company, at Auburn, in the construction of which a force of ninety men was employed night and day. Mr. S R. Bearce is a native of this State, while Mr. J. D. Clifford was born in Columbus, Ohio, both gentlemen being connected with the Board of Trade, and Mr. Bearce with the Odd Fellows. Contracts will be entered into for the Building of Masonry of any description, and the experience and facilities of this concern are such that it has but little to fear from competition when good work is demanded. A very large Trucking business is also done, in which employment is given to twenty-five men, sixty horses and twenty two trucks. Teams are furnished at the lowest cash prices, and first-class service in every respect is guaranteed. The shortest notice only is required to assure the supplying of transportation facilities in any desired amount, and very low rates are made on large orders.

E. C. Douglas, Dealer in Groceries, and Provisions, Meats and Fish, also Fruits and Confectionery. No. 259 Lisbon Street, Lewiston. The establishment carried on by Mr. E. C. Douglas at No. 259 Lisbon Street has been known to the public for a number of years, but has never borne a higher reputation than it has since the present proprietor assumed control in 1884. Mr. Douglas is well known about town being a prominent business man and was a member of the City Council for 1886-87, and his trade is rapidly and steadily increasing, under the influence of the close attention he gives to the wants of the public. The store utilized measures 65x30 feet and the stock on hand is remarkable alike for extent and variety. It comprises Choice Family Groceries, Provisions, Meats and Fish, together with full lines of Fruit and Confectionery. It will thus be seen that a full assortment of household supplies is to be had at this one store and not a few people recognize the advantages of doing all their marketing at one establishment and place their orders with Mr. Douglas. He employs two competent and polite assistants, and as long as he adheres to his present practice of giving a full equivalent for every cent he receives, he may confidently rely on the continued favor of the public. Goods are promptly delivered and are sure to prove as represented.

L. W. Ballard, sole agent for the celebrated Knabe Pianos, also Organs and Sheet Music, Lewiston. A piano or an organ costs a good deal of money, even when supplied at the lowest possible rates and very few people can afford to invest such a sum without being assured that they are getting value for value. It is owing to the comparatively high price which must be put on a first-class instrument that some unscrupulous dealers offer pianos and organs intrinsically worthless, at much lower rates than can be made on any article of merit. If you wish a piano, buy it of a responsible house, for such can sell good instruments as cheap as anybody and a poor one is dear at any price. If any information is desired relative to musical instruments or merchandise, call on Mr. L. W. Ballard, under Music Hall, and he will be found willing and able to lend all necessary aid. He began the sale of Pianos, etc., here in 1867, and now conducts one of the finest establishments of the kind in the State, acting as sole agent for the celebrated Knabe Pianos, as well as those produced by Behr Brothers of New York, and the Emerson Piano Co , of Boston, while he also represents the Estey Organ Co., which in our opinion makes the finest cabinet organ in the world. Sheet Music, Instruction Books,—in fact everything in the musical line, may be obtained through Mr. Ballard at the lowest market rates. His goods are fully guaranteed and his representations may be implicitly relied upon.

Chas. H. Jumper, Brass Founder; Manufacturer of all kinds of Brass and Composition Castings, and Zincs for Batteries. Shop, corner of Canal and Ash Streets, Lewiston. As it is often of great importance to know where Brass or Composition Castings may be made of fine finish and accurate proportions, we take this opportunity of calling the attention of those interested, to the establishment of Mr. Charles H. Jumper, at the corner of Canal and Ash Streets, for facilities are there at hand for the casting of such materials in a thoroughly first-class manner, and the work which has been turned out in the past is an assurance of what may confidently be expected in the future. The enterprise was inaugurated in 1867, by Mr. John F. Loomis, and passed under the control of its present proprietor some twelve years later. Mr. Jumper was born in New Gloucester, Me., and is connected with the Free Masons. He is a thorough mechanic himself, and only employs such to assist him, and as a consequence his establishment has attained a reputation for fine and accurate work, which is as high as it is deserved. One floor is occupied of the dimensions of 25x40 feet, and Brass and Composition Castings, Zincs for Batteries, etc., are manufactured to order. Also, Weights for trotting horses are manufactured to order. Especial attention is given to the making of Models, and those realizing the importance of having such made in the very best manner, would do well to patronize Mr. Jumper, when they have occasion for skillful work of this kind. Repairing is also done at short notice, and all prices are fair and reasonable.

Thomas Vaughan, Dealer in Furniture, Carpeting, Coffins, Caskets, and Robes. No. 231 and 233 Lisbon Street, Lewiston. Although it is unquestionably true that the furniture dealers of Lewiston and vicinity are many and enterprising, still there are some houses in this

line of business that are particularly worthy of patronage, and we have no hesitation in saying that one of the foremost of these is that of which Mr. Thomas Vaughan is the proprietor, located in his new building at 231 and 233 Lisbon Street. Mr. Vaughan ought to understand his business by this time at any rate, for he has carried it on for nearly a quarter of a century, having founded it in 1865. He occupies premises comprising five floors of the dimensions of 75x25 feet, and carries a stock of Furniture, Carpets, etc., such as only a dealer of ability and experience could get together. It embraces goods of all grades and prices and, coming from the most reputable manufacturers, is guaranteed to prove as represented in every instance. Whether you want to spend $100 or one-tenth that sum on furniture, call on Mr. Vaughan and you will get polite attention, prompt service and satisfactory goods *at bottom prices*. Undertaking is made a special branch of the business, and a complete stock of Coffins, Caskets, Robes, and Funeral Goods of all descriptions, is always on hand. Everything necessary will be furnished if desired, including Hearses, Hacks, etc., and the charges are made as low as the nature of the accommodations supplied will permit. Mr. Vaughan is a well-known citizen and is very generally and highly esteemed in the community.

Richards & Merrill, Merchant Tailors, and dealers in Ready-Made Clothing and Gents' Furnishing Goods, Lyceum Hall Block, Lisbon Street, Lewiston. Important as the Clothing trade is in this city and numerous and influential as are the houses engaged in it, there is no difficulty experienced in choosing the representative and leading concern in this line of business, for no one acquainted with the facts in the case would think of disputing the claims of Messrs. Richards & Merrill to that honor. This firm began operations in 1853, so that the first quarter-century of its existence has now been reached, and one might search very long amongst the history of the business enterprises of this State before coming across a record which would parallel in all respects that held by the house alluded to. One of its most prominent characteristics is keeping faith with its customers. Messrs. Richards & Merrill never intentionally allow an article to leave their store which will not prove in each and every respect fully equal to the representations made concerning it, and as a consequence those who know the firm best place the most implicit confidence in its promises and statements. Mr. D. O. Richards is a native of Durham, while Mr. J. L. Merrill was born in Yarmouth, and both these gentlemen are members of the Royal Arcanum, and are likewise connected with the Board of Trade. Two floors are utilized of the dimensions of 85x30 feet, and the stock of Ready-Made Clothing and Gents' Furnishing Goods carried is one of the largest in the entire State, and certainly the most extensive in this portion of it. Suits are on hand of all sizes and styles, and those wishing garments which can be depended upon should visit this establishment where they will find courteous attention and low prices. All grades of Ready-Made Clothing are handled, and for those who prefer custom work special provision is made, a department of the store being exclusively assigned to this branch and the most skillful and experienced tailors employed. Satisfaction is guaranteed and no exorbitant rates are charged.

E. H. Hutchins, Grocer, 25 Main Street Lewiston. If there were no other reason for making mention of the establishment conducted by Mr. E. H. Hutchins at No. 25 Main Street, than that of its long standing, it would still be worthy of a place in our columns, for this is the oldest grocery store in the city, having been opened about a half-century ago. But Mr. Hutchins is not dependent upon this fact for the celebrity his enterprise has attained, but rather is it due to the methods which have governed its management since he assumed possession in 1875. He is a native of Rumford, Me., of which town he was formerly postmaster. Mr. Hutchins has largely increased the trade of the establishment of which he is now proprietor, and has done so by a very simple process—making it desirable to do business there. He has proved to the satisfaction of the public that he handles reliable goods, that he guarantees them to prove as represented, that he extends courteous treatment toward all and that his prices are as low as the lowest. Under these circumstances his success is not to be wondered at. A very large and varied stock is carried and three active and polite assistants are at hand to give all orders prompt and careful attention.

Charles A. Abbott, Apothecary, corner Lisbon and Main Streets, Lewiston. One of the oldest established enterprises of the kind in Lewiston, is that conducted by Mr. Charles A. Abbott, at the corner of Lisbon and Main Streets. This undertaking was founded over thirty years ago, and passed through several hands before coming into the possession of its present proprietor, in 1884. Mr. Abbott was born in Dover, New Hampshire, and is a member of the Masons and Knights of Honor. The premises utilized by him are of the dimensions of 35x25 feet, and are very completely fitted up for the carrying on of a first class retail Apothecary business. The stock, which includes Drugs, Medicines, Toilet Articles, etc., is both large and well-selected, and has been chosen with a special view to the carrying on of an extensive Prescription trade. It comprises Standard Drugs, etc., from the most reputable producers and wholesalers in the country, and is thoroughly desirable in every respect. Mr. Abbott is also well provided with all the necessary apparatus for the handling, mixing, etc., of the articles which he deals in, and not the least popular feature of his establishment is the maintainance of the lowest possible prices in every department. Pains are taken to give all callers prompt and polite attention, and Prescriptions are filled without undue delay, at all times.

Daniel Allen & Co., Manufacturers of and Dealers in Furniture, Coffins, Caskets, Robes, etc. Also, Carpetings of all kinds. No. 225 Lisbon Street, opposite Post Office, Lewiston. It is but right that among the most prominent business enterprises of this city, mention should be made of that conducted by Messrs. Daniel Allen & Co., at No. 225 Lisbon Street, opposite the Post-office, for this establishment is one of the largest in this portion of the State, and it has attained its present size by hard work and intelligent management on the part of those carrying it on. The inauguration of the enterprise in question, was in the year 1870, by Messrs. Carter, Allen & Maxwell, and the present firm-name was adopted some fourteen years later. Mr. Allen is a native of Bowdoin, Me., and formerly connected with the School Committee in that place and in Webster, afterward being a member of the Common Council of this city. Mr. Allen, whose death occurred in March, 1888, since which date the business has been in charge of Mr. William Allen, who was with him for three years previous, was very well and favorably known in Lewiston and vicinity, and the house bearing his name was the first to announce that it was prepared to undertake the entire charge of funerals, its services in this capacity, being of a very high order of merit and in great demand. Embalming, etc., will be done in accordance with the most approved modern methods, and Coffins, Caskets, Robes, etc., are supplied at the very lowest rates. The premises occupied comprise five floors of the dimensions of 100x25 feet, and a magnificent assortment of Carpets and Furniture is shown, including goods of all patterns and grades, and the productions of some of the best manufacturers in the country. Employment is afforded to eight assistants, and we need hardly say that every article sold is guaranteed to prove just as represented.

O. W. Kimball & Co., Druggists and Apothecaries, Jobbers and Retailers of extra quality of Spruce Gum, 260 Lisbon Street, Lewiston. The amount of Spruce Gum which is annually marketed in this State would surprise many of our readers, and indeed it is hard to realize what becomes of the immense quantity produced. That Spruce Gum is the only gum fit to use, is becoming more clearly understood every day, and provided it be of first-class quality there can be but little doubt that it is not only non-injurious, but in some cases positively beneficial. The house of O. W. Kimball & Co., of this city, has gained an extended reputation for fair dealing and strictly honorable business methods, but we question if it has established a higher name in any special department than it has in that devoted to the handling of Spruce Gum, which it is prepared to supply, either at wholesale or retail, at the lowest market rates. One floor is occupied of the dimensions of 55 x 25 feet, and an extremely varied stock is on hand, comprising Drugs, Medicines, Chemicals, Cutlery, and Druggists' Sundries of about every description. Business was begun in 1874, under the present firm name, and since that date a trade has been built up which need not shrink from comparison with that of any similar establishment in this city. Mr. Kimball is a native of Augusta, and a member of the Odd Fellows. Employment is afforded to three courteous and thoroughly competent assistants, and either wholesale or retail orders will receive early and careful attention. The assortment of Medicines, Drugs, etc., is most complete, and it is therefore possible for this house to guarantee satisfaction in the filling of prescriptions, etc., as the utmost care is exercised and reasonable charges made.

Samuel Hibbert's Eating House. Meals served at all hours. 105 Lisbon Street, Lewiston. "There's no place like home," says the old song that has found its way to the hearts of millions of people, and that there is "more truth than poetry" in that assertion, we are sure our readers will agree. But one cannot always be at home, and therefore the only course to pursue is to patronize establishments that are as homelike as possible. In this connection, we really take pleasure in calling our readers' attention to the enterprise carried on by Mr. Samuel Hibbert, at 105 Lisbon Street, for at this place one can feel as much at home as liberal business methods, prompt and willing service, and choice and well-cooked food can make him. Mr. Hibbert is a native of England, and has been identified with his present undertaking since 1886. He is a member of the Free Masons, and has a very large circle of friends in Lewiston and vicinity, for he is a gentleman of social disposition, and his business is one particularly favorable to the making of acquaintances. The premises occupied comprise two floors of the dimensions of 55x30 feet, employment being afforded to five efficient assistants. Meals are served at all hours, and every effort is made to avoid those tedious waits so annoying to anybody whose time is of value. Mr. Hibbert supplies his table with the best that the market affords, and his prices are very low for such superior accommodations.

M. C. Dunbar, Hair Goods and Embroideries, 131 Lisbon Street, Lewiston. 'Dunbar's' has become a very familiar term to the ladies of this city for the establishment carried on under that name is one of the most popular enterprises of the kind to be found anywhere, and has been conducted ever since 1876. It was started at the date mentioned by Mrs. M. C. Dunbar. The premises utilized are located at No. 131 Lisbon Street, and measure 40x22 feet. Hair Goods, Embroideries, etc., are very extensively handled, and the latest fashionable novelties in these lines are to be had here as soon as they appear in the market. Especial attention is given to supplying fine human hair of any desired shade, and an extensive and valuable stock of such goods is always on hand. Custom Hair Work is also an important branch of the business, orders being filled without delay and at most reasonable rates. Employment is given to two experienced and efficient assistants, and prompt and courteous attention is assured to every caller. Embroidery Work to order and Stamping is another popular feature of the enterprise, and many ladies avail themselves of the opportunity to have their embroidering done at low prices.

E. A. Olfene, Registered Druggist, No. 123 Lisbon Street, Lewiston. Other things being equal, it is undoubtedly the wisest plan to purchase your Drugs and Medicines of the concern doing the largest business. Drugs depend on their freshness for much of their virtue, and an establishment that receives but a small amount of patronage, must inevitably carry some goods in stock for months and even years. This is unavoidable, and therefore we say, patronize a concern that does a big business, that is constantly renewing its stock, and that can supply you with fresh, pure, and in short, *reliable* goods at the lowest market rates. An enterprise of just this character is that carried on by E. A. Olfene, at No. 123 Lisbon Street. Business was begun by this concern in 1887, succeeded by the present style in 1888, and the public were quick to note the advantages offered, and to support an undertaking so liberally and intelligently managed. Mr. Olfene is a native of Gray, Me., and is a skillful and experienced Pharmacist, familiar with every detail of his business. The store measures about 65x40 feet, and is elegantly and conveniently fitted up. The stock carried is of course large, but it is constantly being renewed, and is made up exclusively of fresh and desirable goods. Prescriptions are compounded without delay at most reasonable rates, and Toilet Articles, Fancy Goods, etc., can also be purchased of this concern to excellent advantage.

LEADING BUSINESS MEN OF LEWISTON.

Cressey's New City Restaurant, Ice Cream and Oyster Rooms, 107 Lisbon Street, Lewiston. Food and health are so intimately connected that it is hard to determine who exercises the most influence over the health of a community — a successful physician or a widely patronized saloon-keeper, but one thing is sure — if people would have more regard for what they eat there would be a great falling off in the demand for drugs. It takes an old campaigner, however, to fully appreciate the importance of good food and plenty of it, for such a man has often known what it was to be deprived of even the poorest sustenance and has learned that no one who wants to retain health and strength can afford to neglect his stomach. Mr. D. B. Cressey, who carries on the "New City Restaurant" at No. 107 Lisbon Street, has more than once been in a position to realize what it means to "fight on an empty stomach," for he has a war record of which any man might well feel proud, and is now a prominent member of the Grand Army. He has evidently determined to afford everybody in his vicinity an opportunity to obtain a "square meal" at a reasonable price for since he inaugurated the enterprise we have mentioned, in 1886, he has spared no efforts to accommodate the public in the most liberal manner at the lowest possible rates. He is a native of Milford, Me., and, it goes without saying, is one of the most popular men in this community as his honorable business methods are universally appreciated, and the merits of his establishment conceded by all. Two floors are occupied, measuring 85x40 feet, and six assistants are employed. This is the largest and best equipped restaurant in the entire State. It has accommodations for seating 225 people at one time, and on some occasions dines 2000 at a meal. The Ice Cream apparatus is run by water power and cost $1000, being one of the most complete in New England. There is also a commodious dining-room for the use of military and fire companies, etc., where the "boys" can have a good time as well as prompt service, meals being cooked to order at all hours. Table board by the day or week is furnished and the rates for regular boarders are very low indeed. Ice Cream and Confectionery are largely handled and Oysters in every style made a specialty in their season.

Roche & Curran, dealers in Meat, Fish, Groceries, Provisions and Flour, 249 Main Street, Lewiston. Of course in so extensive a community as that to be found in Lewiston and vicinity, there must be many establishments devoted to the sale of Family Stores, etc., and so in fact there is, but few among them handle so great a variety of these goods as that conducted by Messrs. Roche & Curran at No. 249 Main Street. This enterprise was inaugurated in 1886, and has already reached a much greater development than that of many similar undertakings of double its age. Messrs. Edward Roche and James Curran are both natives of Lewiston and are well and favorably known about the city. They have worked hard to gain success, and no one familiar with their business methods will begrudge them the heavy trade they have built up, for it has been attained by entirely legitimate means, and is being steadily added to in the same way. One floor and a basement are occupied and a very heavy and varied stock is carried, comprising Meat, Fish, Groceries Provisions, Flour, Fruit, Confectionery, etc., together with a choice assortment of Tobacco and Cigars. Employment is afforded two efficient and polite assistants and customers are attended to with promptness and courtesy. Messrs. Roche & Curran sell at the lowest market rates but do *not* offer low prices on account of handling inferior stock. All goods sold by them are warranted to prove as represented, and orders are delivered accurately and promptly.

T. R. Catland, Machinist and Locksmith, dealer in Cutlery and Sporting Goods of all kinds. Stencil Cutting Key Fitting and Repairing of all kinds of Light Machinist's work, No. 120 Lisbon St., Lewiston, Me. It is a source of much amusement to those who are not members of the fraternity themselves, to see the tenderness with which the true sportsman regards his gun, fishing-rod, etc., and they cannot understand why he should consider them as anything more than pieces of iron or wood of a certain value. But to those who "know how it is themselves" no explanation is needed and they would as soon think of laughing at a man for showing affection for his wife and family as they would on account of his fondness for the companions of his sports. We feel sure that we number many lovers of field-sports among our readers, and hence take special pleasure in directing attention to the establishment of Mr. T. R. Catland at No. 120 Lisbon Street, for this gentleman is excellently prepared to serve them and we can recommend the goods he handles as being strictly reliable and sure to prove as represented. Mr. Catland was born in Damariscotta, Me., and became connected with the establishment he now conducts in 1887, succeeding Mr. H. A. Whitney. The premises utilized comprise one floor of the dimensions of 50x30 feet, and both a wholesale and retail business is done, sporting goods of all descriptions being extensively handled. Fine lines of cutlery, locksmith's goods, etc., are carried, and among the first-named articles are many specially adapted to sportsmen's use. Gun and locksmithing is done in the very best manner and the repairing of umbrellas, cutting of stencil plates, etc., are very important branches of the business. Mr. Catland's work is both neat and durable and his prices are equitable and fair. Mr. Catland is also agent for the celebrated Springfield Roadster.

LEADING BUSINESS MEN OF LEWISTON.

F. E. Crane & Co., Undertakers, dealers in Coffins, Caskets and Floral Designs. Embalming a specialty. No. 57 Main Street, Lewiston. Residence, 21 Spring St., cor. Hampshire St., Auburn. It is quite unnecessary to argue as to the advisability of employing an Undertaker possessed of a thorough knowledge of every detail of his business where the services of such a practitioner are required, for the reasons for so doing are so obvious that space would only be wasted in setting them down in detail. Therefore, when we declare that Messrs. F. E. Crane & Co. have given abundant evidence that they are well prepared to satisfactorily attend to all the multifarious details of a city undertaking business, we think that the reason of the liberal patronage they receive is already sufficiently plain. This firm commenced operations here in 1886, and soon gained the confidence and respect of the community by the liberal and dignified way in which all commissions were executed. The warerooms are located at No. 57 Main Street, and as some one is in attendance at all hours of the day or night, orders can be given at any time, and will be acted upon with promptness and skill. Mr. Crane's residence is at 21 Spring Street, Auburn, and instructions may be left at that address if preferred. He is a native of Fayette, Maine, and is connected with the Knights of Pythias, Odd Fellows, Ancient Order of United Workmen and the Red Men. This house makes a specialty of Embalming, and is prepared to undertake the same in accordance with the most approved scientific methods, on reasonable terms. Coffins, Caskets and Floral Designs are dealt in, and a sufficient variety is kept in stock to suit all tastes and conditions.

Wakefield Brothers, Apothecaries, 114 Lisbon Street, Lewiston. It is just a score of years since the enterprise conducted by Wakefield Brothers was inaugurated, and during that extended period of time, a record has been made, of which the firm alluded to may well be proud. Their establishment is located at No. 114 Lisbon Street, one spacious floor being occupied, and a heavy and valuable stock carried, consisting of Drugs, Medicines and Chemicals in great variety, a full line of Patent Medicines and Toilet Articles, Fancy Goods, etc. The firm is constituted of Messrs. S. D. and E. Wakefield, both of these gentlemen being natives of Lewiston, and extremely well-known here. Although conducting a general Drug business, this concern gives especial attention to the Compounding of Physicians' Prescriptions, and we feel assured that no Pharmacy in Maine is better prepared to give entire satisfaction to customers in this most important department. Carrying a full assortment of costly as well as of ordinary Drugs, etc., and making it a point to see that no ingredients are used that are injuriously affected by age or other causes, this firm offers advantages in the filling of Prescriptions that are well worthy of being taken into consideration, and that they are appreciated is proved by the heavy patronage enjoyed. Reasonable rates are maintained, and two efficient assistants are at hand to give prompt attention to customers.

John C. Hatch, Successor to Johnston & Hatch, Manufacturer of Cigars, No. 64 Lisbon Street, Lewiston. The story of the non-smoker who informed the habitual smoker that during the past 20 years he had wasted money enough on tobacco to buy him a house, but who was forced to confess, in response to a question, that he owned no house, himself although his income was as large as that of the man he sought to instruct, is enough to provoke a smile to be sure, but it is something more inasmuch as it contains the gist of the oft-mooted question regarding the extravagance of tobacco using. Tobacco costs money undoubtedly, so does beef and rump steak cost more than shin-bone, but for all that is it advisable to always sacrifice everything to so-called economy and deny oneself every enjoyment because, forsooth, they are not to be had for nothing? No, we do not think so, and in very few ways will money expended, return so high an interest in enjoyment as in the purchase of tobacco. If you are a smoker call on Mr. John C. Hatch at No. 64 Lisbon Street, the sign of the "Big Indian," and sample some of his cigars. He makes 'em and therefore knows just what he is selling and saving all middlemen's profit is able to furnish a very superior article at a low price. Cigars, Tobacco, Smokers' Articles, etc., are handled very extensively, a wholesale and retail business being done, and employment afforded to six assistants. This enterprise was originated in 1879 by Messrs. Johnston & Hatch and came into the sole possession of Mr. Hatch in 1885. He is a native of Jackson, Me., and a member of the Odd Fellows, having a large circle of friends in this vicinity. His goods are always reliable and his prices so low as to make his establishment a favorite with veteran smokers.

Nelson D. Estes, dealer in Stationery, Periodicals, Blank Books, Albums, Novelties, &c, Room Paper and Window Shades. Wholesale dealer in Paper, Twine and Paper Bags, 258 Lisbon Street, Lewiston. It is no wonder that the establishment of which Mr. Nelson D. Estes is the proprietor is one of the most popular in the entire city, for Mr. Estes gives close attention to the wishes of his customers, and has built up his present extensive trade by dint of hard work and unstinting liberality in catering to the demands of the public. Mr. B. W. Parker founded the undertaking some thirteen years ago, but Mr. Estes assumed control in 1884, and has since been sole manager. The premises occupied are 55x30 feet in size and are well filled by a stock of Books, Stationery, Blank Books, Albums, Wallets, Games, Wall Papers, Window Shades and Cutlery, together with Periodicals and a well-chosen Circulating Library of 800 volumes. This latter feature is one of the most popular departments of the business, for many people take advantage of the opportunity thus presented to obtain the best of reading at a nominal cost. Mr. Estes is a native of Lewiston and is very well known throughout this vicinity. He takes orders for Job Printing and delivers the same at short notice, guaranteeing the work to be first class in every respect, while the prices are entirely satisfactory. Customers receive prompt and polite attention, and may depend upon getting reliable goods at bottom rates.

LEADING BUSINESS MEN OF LEWISTON.

Charles Greenwood, dealer in Hardware and Factory Supplies, Stoves, Ranges and Furnaces. Plumbing, Steam Heating and Ventilating a Specialty. 191 Lisbon Street, Lewiston. An establishment which merits special mention as being one of the most completely equipped of its kind in the entire State is that conducted by Mr. Charles Greenwood at No. 191 Lisbon Street, and an idea of the magnitude of the business done and the size of the stock carried may be gained from the fact that the premises occupied comprise three floors of the dimensions of 100x25 feet. Mr. Greenwood is a native of Farmington, Maine, a member of the Odd Fellows, and began operations here in 1879. It is hardly necessary to say anything about his qualifications as a business man when reviewing the great establishment of which he is proprietor, as no better evidence could be wanted on this point than that afforded by the many signs of prosperity noticeable on every side. An immense stock is carried, made up of Hardware, Factory Supplies, Stoves, Ranges, Furnaces, etc., as well as an extensive and complete assortment of Tin and Wooden Ware, Pocket and Table Cutlery, Kitchen Furnishing Goods and other articles too numerous to mention. Employment is given to 14 assistants, and a specialty is made of the prompt and skillful filling of all orders for Plumbing, Steam Heating and Ventilating. The importance of securing the best possible methods of heating and ventilation, is too well known to all intelligent people to require dwelling upon here, and we will simply state that Mr. Greenwood guarantees satisfaction, both as regards the design and the execution of his work. Jobbing of every description in Tin, Sheet Iron, Zinc and Copper, is done at the shortest notice, and owing to the employment of skilled and careful workmen and the use of the best materials, a strict guarantee is given that all commissions of this kind will be filled in the most thorough and substantial manner. Low rates prevail and the business shows a steady and decided increase.

Chas. A. Eaton, dealer in Fine Confectionery and Fruit, Cigars and Tobacco, 72 Lisbon Street, opposite Music Hall entrance, Lewiston. The establishment conducted by Mr. Chas. A. Eaton at No. 72 Lisbon Street, has certainly peculiar advantages of location, for it is opposite the entrance to Music Hall and is prominently as well as centrally situated, but as favorable as its position is, it would never have attained its present popularity, were it not for the fact that the goods and the prices are satisfactory, and the management is enterprising and liberal. Mr. Eaton has not been identified with this enterprise for many years, but he is thoroughly acquainted with the business in every detail, and gives close personal attention to the carrying on of affairs. One floor, of the dimensions of 45x18 feet is occupied, and a heavy and varied stock is carried, comprising fine Confectionery and Fruit, together with Cigars, Tobacco, etc. Mr. Eaton takes pains to offer none but fresh and finely-flavored confections, and has attained an enviable reputation in this respect. His prices are as low as can be quoted on grades of similar excellence, and the Fruit he handles is also sold at low rates, an extensive assortment being generally on hand. Choice Cigars and Tobacco attract the users of the "weed,"; and the most fastidious can here find a Cigar to suit him.

L. C. Robbins, Successor to A. W. Patten, dealer in Coal, Wood and Pressed Hay, Office and Yard, Opposite Catholic Church, Main Street. Agent for Pratt's Poultry and Cattle Food. The last two years have been by no means favorable to the development of the Coal trade, for the many disturbances at the mines and elsewhere have so seriously interfered with the supply of Coal as to cripple and embarrass even the old established houses, so that the outlook for the formation of new ones has not been at all promising. Still such enterprises have been inaugurated, and some of them have met with success. Among these latter being that of which Mr. L. C. Robbins is now the proprietor, located at 270 Main Street, opposite the Catholic Church. Mr. Robbins is a native of Leeds and is connected with the Odd Fellows. The undertaking with which he is identified was founded in 1886 by Messrs. Small & Patten, later, A. W. Patten. Mr. L. C. Robbins taking sole possession in 1888. Hard Wood, Soft Wood, Birch Slabs, Birch Edgings, Spruce Edgings, Spruce Slabs, also a few cords of Choice Rock Maple, fitted or unfitted. Good Coal of all kinds. I shall endeavor to furnish at the market prices Pressed Hay and Straw. Agents for Pratt's Food for Poultry, Horses and cattle. Office and Yard at No. 270 Main Street, Opposite Catholic Church. L. C. Robbins, Lewiston. He is prepared to fill every order at short notice in a perfectly satisfactory manner. Wood will be sawed and split to suit customers, and the lowest market rates are charged for every commodity dealt in. Those who have done business with Mr. Robbins speak in the highest terms of the careful attention he gives to orders, and we can heartily commend this enterprise to our readers.

LEADING BUSINESS MEN OF LEWISTON.

W. H. Weeks, Book and Job Printer, 232 Lisbon Street, Lewiston. The question of who invented printing with movable type, is not settled yet, and the advocates of Gutenberg are hard-pressed by their opponents, who present the names of more than one old-time worthy to this honor, but it seems to us that after all it is of more practical importance to know who is best prepared to do printing at the present day, and in this connection take opportunity to mention the Job Printing establishment of Mr. William H. Weeks, as we believe that it would be hard to find one better prepared to fill all orders that may be intrusted to it in a thoroughly satisfactory manner. Mr. Weeks was born in this city, and founded the business with which he is now connected in 1874. He is constantly adding to the resources of his office, and makes it a point to obtain the most tasteful and fashionable type for use where ornament is considered, and by so doing, as well as by the taste he has shown in its arrangement, he has gained a reputation in the line of Artistic Typography which is as gratifying as it is deserved. One floor, of the dimensions of 65x20 feet, is occupied at No. 232 Lisbon Street, equipped with three large presses, requiring 3½ horse-power to run them, and employment is afforded to seven assistants. The "Labor Advocate" is printed by Mr. Weeks, and therefore the many comments which have been made upon its neat appearance are direct compliments to his capacity in this line. Orders, either large or small, are promptly filled, and the lowest market rates prevail.

Geo. B. Michaud, Dealer in Harnesses, Whips, Blankets, Robes, Horse Collars, Brushes, etc. Repairing neatly and promptly attended to. No. 289 Lisbon Street, Lewiston. A Harness which does not combine good material and good workmanship is a dangerous article to use, and those who think they are saving money by purchasing an inferior harness at a price slightly below the market price for standard goods, are making a big mistake, and one that may cost them many times the small sum they apparently save. By patronizing the right dealer, it is possible to get a strictly first-class Harness at a moderate figure, and if you doubt this assertion, just call on Mr. Geo. B. Michaud, at No. 289 Lisbon Street, and inspect his goods and prices. This gentleman does not handle inferior stock, and if you buy an article of him, you may safely depend on its proving as represented. Yet his prices are very reasonable, and anything in the line of Harnesses, Whips, Blankets, Robes, Horse Collars, Brushes, etc., can be bought of him to excellent advantage. Mr. Michaud is a native of Canada, and became proprietor of his present establishment in 1887, succeeding Mr. A. Dodge, who opened it in 1884. A large and growing business has been built up by Mr. Michaud, who gives special attention to Repairing and fills orders with neatness and dispatch, his charges being moderate and fair.

Howard Bros., Dealers in Groceries, Provisions, and all kinds of Country Produce, 40 Ash Street, Lewiston. When Messrs. Howard Bros. began operations here, in 1884, they had by no means a clear field to work in, and there were not a few who prophesied utter and early failure, giving as a reason the belief that there was too much competition. Well, four years have passed and the enterprise has not failed as yet, and what is more, was never farther from failure than at the present time, judging from the heavy business now done. This success is all the more worthy of appreciative mention from the fact that it has been won by honorable and legitimate means, and so is richly deserved. The firm is constituted of Messrs. Charles N., James C., and Emery N. Howard, all of whom are natives of Readfield, Me. Mr. E. N. Howard has held various important offices in Presque Isle, among them that of Superintendent of the School Committee, and each of the gentlemen mentioned is well known in this vicinity. The premises utilized measure 60x20 feet, and Groceries, Provisions, Tobacco, Confectionery, etc., are very extensively dealt in, as are also all kinds of Country Produce. The store is located at No. 40 Ash Street, and callers are always assured of receiving prompt and courteous attention. Having already alluded to the large trade that has been built up, it is not necessary to say that excellent inducements are offered to customers, or that reliable goods are exclusively handled. These things speak for themselves, so we will simply add — "give Messrs. Howard Bros. a call."

Elie Sabourin, Dealer in all Kinds of Fish at Wholesale and Retail. Fresh Water Fish a Specialty. Guns, Fishing Tackle, and all Kinds of Sporting Goods, 318 Lisbon Street, Lewiston.  Fish is one of the most popular articles of food we have, and it is well that it is so, for it is both cheap and healthful. The only disadvantage connected with the use of it, is that it must be perfectly fresh in order to be palatable and nutritious, and there is no difficulty in obtaining perfectly fresh fish if you only know where to look for it. For instance make a call on Mr. Elie Sabourin, doing business at No. 326 Lisbon Street, and you will find that his stock of Fish, Oysters, Clams, etc., is full and complete and that every article sold by him is guaranteed to be satisfactory and to prove as represented. Mr. Sabourin is a native of Vermont and inaugurated the enterprise to which we have reference in 1880. He has built up a very large and growing business, and is now better prepared than ever before to supply anything in his line at the lowest market rates, and to give prompt and careful attention to orders. Employment is given to two assistants, and customers are assured courteous and satisfactory attention. Orders will be delivered when promised, and if patrons so desire they will be waited upon at their residences and their orders carefully noted.

Mrs. Neal's Book Bindery, Journal Block, Lewiston. The establishment known as Mrs. Neal's Book Bindery, located in Journal Block, has a most enviable reputation for the turning out of excellent and durable work, and during the score of years that it has been in operation, it has built up a large and growing patronage, not only by reason of the nature of the results attained, but also on account of the low prices at which every description of Bookbinding, etc., is done. There is scarcely a house but what contains a tile of old magazines, an assortment of sheet-music, or something else that would be made a hundred times more convenient and useful by being properly bound, and we wish to call the attention of our readers to the fact that at the establishment under mention particular care is taken in the doing of work of this kind. Ruling and Blank Book work of every description is also done to order in a superior manner at short notice, and very low rates are maintained in every department, as low in fact as the use of the best stock and the employment of skilled labor will permit. Lettering on books, traveling or shopping bags, pocketbooks, etc., is done promptly and at short notice. Such an establishment is a public benefit, and richly deserves most cordial support.

A. B. King & Co., Machinists, Manufacturers of Elevators, Dowel Machines, Saw Arbors, etc., etc., also General Job Work and Repairing, 48 Main Street, Lewiston. As the majority of manufacturers and others who have occasion to purchase a steam engine are not practical mechanics it is impossible for them to personally judge of the merits or demerits of any special style of machine until they have given it a practical trial in their own business, and therefore they must be largely if not entirely dependent upon the representations of the house supplying them in the selection of an engine suited to their needs. On this account it is obvious that only a reputable concern should be patronized, and in this connection we take pleasure in calling the favorable attention of our readers to the advantages offered by the house known as King & Loring, although Mr. King is now sole proprietor, owing to the death of his associate in 1887. This firm began operations in 1883 and from the beginning proceeded on the assumption that the interests of its customers were identical with their own. They have therefore sought to handle only such goods, as in their opinion as experienced mechanics, would do all that was claimed for them and as a result have had little reason to complain that their efforts to serve the public were unappreciated. Three floors are occupied of the dimensions of 25x45 feet and ten assistants are employed. All kinds of job work and repairing are done with neatness and despatch and a heavy stock is carried of Steam Engines, Boilers, Wood-working Machinery, Shafting, Pulleys, Hangers, Steam and Water Pipes, Fittings, etc. The store is at No. 48 Main Street, and those wishing anything in the lines mentioned should make it a point to call and inspect the advantages offered. Mr. King is a native of Monmouth, Me., and is extremely well-known to the trade in this State.

Joseph H. Day, Dealer in Builders' Hardware, Manufacturers' Supplies, Carpenters' Tools, Fine Cutlery, etc., 235 Main Street, near Bates Street, Lewiston. There is no question as to the status of Mr. Joseph H. Day, in the commercial community, and we therefore feel that our action in including his name among those of other prominent business men of this vicinity, needs no justification. His establishment is located at No. 235 Main Street, and the business there carried on was founded in 1875, by J. H. Day & Co., but since 1883, the present proprietor has conducted it alone. He is a native of St. Albans, Me., and the wide-spread esteem in which he is held here in Lewiston may be judged from his having been chosen as Mayor of the city in '79-'80. As a member of the Water Commission, he has fully maintained his reputation as a far-seeing man of affairs, and from first to last has earned the gratitude of every believer in an honest and economical municipal government. The premises occupied by Mr. Day in the prosecution of his business are 75x40 feet in dimensions, and employment is given to five competent and active assistants in attending to the many orders received, as both a wholesale and retail business is done, and no expense is spared in the prompt and accurate filling of every order. Builders' Hardware, Manufacturers' Supplies, Iron, Steel, Bolts, Glass, Paints, Oils, Sewer Pipe, Powder—in fact almost an endless variety of goods in these lines is carried, together with a fine assortment of Carpenters' Tools, Cutlery, Cordage, Bird Cages, Clothes Wringers, etc. Mr. Day endeavors to handle no goods but those he has reason to believe will give satisfaction, and he strictly guarantees that every article leaving his store will prove just as represented.

F. B. Norris, Manufacturer of Fine Confectionery, 61 Main Street, Lewiston. That the public in general is becoming more critical, year by year, is a fact too evident and too well-known to require argument, and in scarcely any branch of manufacture is this more clearly shown than in that of the Confectioner. Every dealer in Candy, who has had any amount of experience can testify, that goods that were once sought for are now no longer salable, and it must have been noticed by many who are not habitual users of Confectionery, that the tendency for some years has been in the direction of more delicate flavors and a generally higher grade of goods. Mr. F. B. Norris, of No. 61 Main Street, owes much of his success to his recognizing this advance in the public taste, and catering to it by producing uniformly satisfactory Confections, for his goods are very popular in this vicinity, and to say a piece of Candy came from "Norris's" is enough to guarantee its purity and wholesomeness. Mr. Norris was born in Maine, and succeeded to this business in 1887. One floor is occupied, measuring 50x30 feet, and a large trade is carried on in Fruits, as well as Confectionery, while a well-equipped lunch-room is a very popular feature of the establishment. Employment is afforded to seven assistants, and the large patronage enjoyed is promptly handled and steadily added to.

F. I. Day, Dealer in Boots and Shoes, 5 Journal Block, Lisbon Street. Mr. F. I. Day, who carries on the well-known Boot and Shoe store in this city, will observe the 25th anniversary of the founding of his business during the current year, and it may well be supposed that if he is not able to suit the taste of the public in foot-wear, it is not from lack of experience. But in point of fact we never heard any one charge Mr. Day with not being able to suit the public taste, and indeed if such a charge were made, it would not require refutation other than that provided by the liberal patronage bestowed upon the enterprise of which the gentleman alluded to is the proprietor. People are not in the habit of trading at a store where goods are not kept to suit them; and a call at Mr. Day's establishment at almost any time would show a liveliness of trade which can only be explained in one way — the furnishing of satisfactory articles at bottom prices. The premises occupied comprise one floor and a basement of the dimensions of 65x30 feet, and the stock on hand is certainly extensive and varied enough to suit all tastes, being made up of goods adapted to the wear of adults and children of both sexes, and including the latest fashionable novelties in every department. Four assistants are employed, and prompt and polite attention is assured to all. Mr. Day was born in Brunswick. Me., and has been a member of our Municipal Government, having served on the Board of Aldermen. He is a representative citizen and very widely known.

J. J. O'Connell, Marble Works. All Shades of American and Italian Marble in Monuments, Headstones and Tablets, 137 Main Street, Lewiston. Although it is very true that skilled labor commands a high price, it by no means follows that it is contrary to the dictates of economy to employ such, for it not infrequently happens that this very skill is capable of turning out work so much faster than unskilled labor can do, that the difference in price is really against the latter. In stone-cutting for instance, some houses charge exhorbitant rates on the strength of their reputation, when, actually, equally good, if not better work, is to be had elsewhere, at from one-half to two-thirds their prices. Call on Mr. J. J. O'Connell, at No. 137 Main Street, this city, and see what he has to offer in the way of fine stone-cutting, and more especially in Cemetery Work. We have no hesitation in saying that some of the most artistic and beautiful Marble-Cutting ever done in this State, has been done at this establishment, and that at rates which would scarcely buy far inferior work at certain more pretentious houses. Mr. O'Connell was born in this city, and the inception of his present business dates back to 1877. The premises occupied are 40x20 feet in dimensions, and employment is given to eight assistants, who, taken as a whole, will bear the severest comparison, both as regards skill and care. with the employes of any Marble Works in this section. All Shades of American and Italian Marble are made into Monuments, Tablets, Headstones, etc., and orders are guaranteed prompt and satisfactory fulfillment at the very lowest possible prices.

Geo. Ehrenfried's Fancy Dry Goods Store, 96 Lisbon Street, Lewiston. An establishment which has been carried on for twenty-three years, and which has been a leader in its line for the greater part of that time, is certainly worthy of particular mention in any review of Lewiston's business enterprises, and hence we need make no apologies for calling the attention of our readers to the undertaking carried on by Mr. Geo. Ehrenfried, at No. 96 Lisbon St. This gentleman is a native of Germany, and has a very large circle of friends in this vicinity, being a member of the Odd Fellows and Knights of Pythias, besides being known as one of the most liberal and enterprising business men in town. One floor and a basement, of the dimensions of 85x35 feet, are utilized, for Mr. Ehrenfried carries one of the largest and most complete stocks of Fancy Dry Goods and Small Wares to be found in this section, and it requires no small amount of room to accommodate that, as well as the many customers who throng his store, brought there by the well-earned reputation it enjoys for offering reliable goods at the lowest market rates. Mr. Ehrenfried is a careful and yet an enterprising buyer, and his long experience enables him to provide his customers with just what they want, and what the prevailing fashion demands. Employment is given to five efficient and courteous assistants, and callers will receive prompt and polite attention, the goods being guaranteed to prove as represented in every instance.

N. S. Taylor, Violin Maker and Repairer, 149 Lisbon St., Lewiston. Special Attention to Old Instruments. Bows Carefully repaired. Choice Old Violin Wood for Sale. Italian Strings Always on Hand. The violin is conceded by musicians to be the most perfect musical instrument yet constructed, and no better evidence of its superiority could be asked than the fact that a violin in the hands of a master is capable of approximating very closely to the tones of the human voice itself. But no other instrument is so dependent on the material used in its construction for excellence, and even where suitable material is used the result will be very unsatisfactory unless skill is manifested by the maker. When we say that Mr. N. S. Taylor, of No. 149 Lisbon Street, has met with great success since he began his present business in 1887, we speak the simple truth, for the public (or rather the musical portion of it) have been quick to recognize the advantages derivable from patronizing Mr. Taylor, and have therefore given him most cordial support. He is a maker of Violins, and neglects nothing that will tend to improve the instruments he produces. Repairing is given particular attention, a specialty being made of the handling of old instruments, and the most pronounced lover of music may safely leave his violin with Mr. Taylor, for this gentleman thinks as much of a good violin as anybody can, and may be depended upon to handle it with care and discretion. Bows are also repaired in a first-class manner at short notice, and Italian Strings are constantly carried in stock, as is also Choice Old Violin Wood. Mr. Taylor is reasonable in his charges and is deserving of every success.

Edwin F. Field, Machinist, Manufacturer of Shafting, Pulleys, Steam Engines, Saw Arbors, Matches &c., New and Second-hand Engines, Boilers, Machinery, etc. Agent for "Tanite" Solid Emery Wheels and Emery Grinders, Canal Street, rear Music Hall, Lewiston. An establishment which has gained an enviable reputation among the business men of Lewiston and vicinity, for turning out the best of work at comparatively short notice, is that conducted by Edwin F. Field at No. 36 Canal Street, rear of Music Hall, and anyone wishing anything in the line of Shafting, Pulley, Saw Arbors, Matches or Steam Engines would best serve their own interests by giving this concern a call, as not only are the goods handled by it first-class, but the prices charged are such as to add to the advantages extended. This enterprise was inaugurated in 1872 by Mr. Edwin F. Field, who was born in this city and is very widely known in mechanical and engineering circles. Two floors are utilized, 65x40 feet in dimensions and employment is given to eleven assistants. Machine work in great variety is done, repairing being given special attention and where circumstances are such that a job must be "rushed" through, the entire resources of the establishment may be concentrated upon it, thus avoiding in many cases very expensive delay. A heavy stock of New and Second hand Goods is carried, including Engines, Boilers, Machinery, etc., and Boiler Repairing, and Tube Setting are neatly and thoroughly done. Cotton and Woolen Machinery is given special and prompt attention and all needed repairs are made with that celerity and durability only attainable with the best facilities and the most experienced workmen.

R. W. Clark, Druggist, dealer in Drugs, Medicines and Chemicals, Fancy and Toilet Articles, corner Main and Bates Streets, Lewiston. Fifteen years may be considered either a long or a short space of time, according to the point of view from which it is regarded, but when a business enterprise has been conducted uninterruptedly for that period, it may certainly be looked upon as firmly established. Mr. R. W. Clark has been identified with the establishment located at the corner of Main and Bates Streets, ever since 1873, and we feel that we are justified in saying that he enjoys the confidence of the public to a pronounced degree. And it is right that he should, for he has always striven to render faithful and acceptable service to customers, and has neglected no means to increase the value of the enterprise he conducts to the community in general. Mr. Clark was born in China, Maine, and is a member of the Odd Fellows (Canton). He is an experienced, skilled, and careful druggist and carries a large stock of Drugs, Medicines and Chemicals, giving particular and personal attention to the compounding of prescriptions, and charging the lowest possible rates for all orders of this kind. The premises occupied are 38x27 feet in dimensions, and contain a beautiful selection of Fancy and Toilet Articles which are quoted at reasonable prices, and which comprise the latest and most successful novelties. Patrons are given prompt and polite attention and their wishes are carefully regarded.

L. L. Blake & Co., Manufacterers of and Dealers in Furniture, Carpets and Draperies, 155 Lisbon Street, Lewiston. Undertaking a Specialty. No better advice can be given to those contemplating the purchase of Furniture or Carpets than to pay regard to *future* as well as to present wants. By so doing, much annoyance may oftentimes be avoided and the truest economy subserved, insomuch as it is better to pay more outright and secure a durable, as well as fashionable article than it is to put up with inferior articles whose only merit is their low, first cost, and which soon become shabby and unsatisfactory. This counsel is not the outcome of our individual experience alone, but is what anyone having an adequate knowledge of the subject will offer. To procure reliable goods, visit a reliable house, and to find a reliable house, proceed to No. 155 Lisbon Street, and enter the establishment of Messrs. L. L Blake & Co. There you will find a truly magnificent assortment of Furniture, Carpets and Draperies of every description, and it is our opinion that, quality considered, no greater bargains in the goods mentioned are obtainable in Lewiston. Certainly, Mr. Blake ought to know how to buy and sell to advantage, for he inaugurated this enterprise in 1856, under the firm-name of A. K. P. & L. L. Blake, and for a quarter-century past has carried it on alone under the present style. He is a native of Gray, in which town he has been a Selectman and member of the School Committee for many years, and he has also been a member of our City Council. The premises utilized are of the dimensions of 100x25 feet, and comprise five floors, and an immense business is done in the manufacture and sale of the articles handled, employment being given to eight assistants. A specialty is made of Undertaking, and every possible modern facility is at hand to enable this department of the business to be carried on in a thoroughly satisfactory manner, low rates being maintained.

I. S. Golder, Livery Stable, 18 Franklin Street, Lewiston. No one at all acquainted with the beautiful drives in the vicinity of Lewiston and Auburn can wonder that there is a steady and increasing demand for desirable turnouts, and this demand is growing all the time. A firm who are particularly well fitted to satisfy the most fastidious in the matter of fine accommodations and good turnouts is I. S. Golder, for his long experience enables him to select a good horse and one that will suit his customers. The premises are located at 18 Franklin Street, and afford accommodations for a large number of horses and carriages, employment being given to a number of careful and experienced assistants. A Hack, Livery and Boarding Stable is carried on, and carriages will be furnished for any occasion at short notice and careful and experienced drivers are furnished if desired. Mr. Golder does a large Livery business for he keeps everything connected with this branch of the business in first-class condition. The horses furnished to patrons are not the wrecks too often furnished at stables, but are all good-looking animals, fine roadsters, and a drive behind one is a rare enjoyment. He is well-known in both business and social circles in Lewiston, and his stable is one of the best patronized in the city.

S. Record, Dealer in New and Second-hand Furniture, 57 Main Street, and 59 Lower Main Street, Lewiston. There may be, and undoubtedly in one sense of the word is, a market price for everything, below which no article can be obtained excepting under a peculiar combination of circumstances, but nevertheless it would be hard to convince an old and careful buyer of furniture that this commodity has a fixed and certain value for he has long since discovered by experience that what is generally considered as the market price is really the lowest figure at which the article can be sold, plus the extra amount called for by the individual or the concern selling the same. Thus it follows that at some establishments much greater bargains may be had than at others, and not a few of our Lewiston citizens are firmly convinced that Mr. S. Record of No. 57 Main Street, is prepared to supply furniture, either new or second-hand, at more liberal rates than any other dealer in this vicinity. Mr. Record was born in this State and inaugurated his present enterprise in 1879. The large business he now does shows that he has attained a high reputation in his special line and we believe that there is no question but what one would have to search carefully and far before meeting with such an array of inducements in the Furniture and House Furnishing goods line as are offered by Mr. Record. Second-hand household goods of all kinds. Great bargains in Second-hand Carpets, Straw Matting, Floor Oil Cloths. Parties coming to Lewiston should not fail to visit this big establishment and see his large collection of second-hand articles. He occupies eight floors 26 feet wide and 60 feet long. Mr. Record is at all times ready to show goods and render such information as it is within his power to give. All grades of furniture are dealt in and the variety shown will suit all tastes and purses.

The Singer Manufacturing Company, Branch 217 Lisbon Street, Lewiston, S. D. LaRoe, Agent. What is there to be said new of the Singer Sewing Machine? It has been before the public for years, it has met and overcome competition of all kinds, it has gone into such general use that no other make can compare with it for an instant in this respect and it stands to-day at the head of the list as regards celebrity and general usefulness. Imitations of it without number have been made, business honor and integrity — even common decency — have been cast to the winds by some of its rivals; money has been spent like water to counteract its overwhelming popularity with the people, but to no avail, so far as superseding it, or even seriously interfering with its sale is concerned. A machine must have real and positive merits to withstand such assaults and it must be carefully constructed of the best materials to establish the record for fine work and durability which has so long been held by the productions of the Singer Manufacturing Company. Their Lewiston branch was opened in 1879, and in 1887 Mr. S. D. LaRoe assumed entire charge of it. He has proved himself to be the right man in the right place for he has "boomed" the Singer in a manner in which it was never "boomed" before in this vicinity, and has caused his rivals to gloomily ponder on their probable future. Mr. LaRoe was born in New York State and is one of the most popular "Sewing Machine men" in the State. He believes in the Singer, talks Singer and acts Singer and if he don't cause the sales of that "old reliable" to mount up to heights never reached before in this corner of the Union it won't be any fault of his for he means business and relaxes no effort to attain that desirable result.

J. P. Longley, Manufacturer and Dealer in Fine Harnesses of all descriptions, Trunks and Traveling Bags, No. 179 Main Street, Lewiston. There is no doubt, whatever, but that the undertaking conducted by Mr. J. P. Longley at No. 179 Main Street, is a truly representa-

tive one in every sense of the word, for not only has it been carried on in this city for over forty years, but for the greater part of that time it has held its present leading position. Mr. Longley is a native of Greene, Me., and began operations alone in 1847. Business was afterward continued under the style of Longley & Jordan, but in 1861 Mr. Longley assumed sole control again and has since retained it. The premises occupied, comprise three floors, and the manufacture and sale of Fine Harnesses of all descriptions, Trunks and Traveling Bags, Horse Clothing, Blankets, Robes, etc., are very extensively carried on, employment being given to seven experienced and efficient assistants. A specialty is made of the Celebrated California and Cynthaana Trotting and Racing Boots, a complete line being carried of these valuable articles. Every order is assured prompt attention and can be filled without delay, as a full selection of sizes is constantly maintained. These famous Boots need no words of praise from us. They have received the warmest endorsements from prominent horsemen, and are, without doubt, practically unequalled in their special line. The Harnesses made and sold by Mr. Longley are also standard articles. They have stood the test of years of service under all conditions, and have a reputation of their own for durability and perfection of workmanship. Made of selected materials by picked workmen, it would be strange if they were not far superior to the common article in the market, and experience has, as we have said, well established their merits. Low prices are quoted on all the goods sold here, and during the proper season special inducements are offered in Seal Skins and other Fur Garments.

F. A. Conant & Co., Insurance and Real Estate Agents, Room 2 Savings Bank Block, Lewiston. A concern which has gained the reputation of being one of the most reliable as well as one of the most enterprising in this section of the State is that one whose card is printed above, and its operations are rapidly extending as our residents become more generally conversant with the advantages it has to offer. Business was inaugurated by Mr. F. A. Conant in 1883, and was continued by him alone up to 1887, when Mr. J. Edward Lawrence became associated with him under the present firm name. Mr. Conant was born in Topsham, Maine, and is extremely well known in this city as a prominent Odd Fellow. Mr. Lawrence is a native of Richmond, Maine, and his association with Mr. Conant has doubtless been mutually profitable, for both gentlemen are thoroughly acquainted with the Insurance and Real Estate business and spare no efforts to serve their customers in so superior a manner that relations are made permanent which would otherwise be quickly dissolved. In the Insurance branch of this firm's business companies are represented having total assets of over $100,000,000, their names being as follows: Continental Insurance Co., of New York; Buffalo German Ins. Co., of New York; American Fire Ins. Co., of Philadelphia; Insurance Co., of North America, Philadelphia; Orient Ins. Co., of Hartford, Connecticut; Merchants Ins. Co., of Newark, New Jersey; Meriden Ins. Co., of Meriden, Connecticut; Traders Ins. Co., of Chicago, Illinois; Holyoke Mutual of Salem; Girard Mutual of Philadelphia; Anglo Nevada of San Francisco, also the New England Mutual Life Insurance of Boston. These organizations are among the most celebrated and popular in the country, and taken in connection with the Lancashire, the Sun, the London and Lancashire, and the Northern Insurance Companies of England, form a list which is hardly susceptible of improvement. F. A. Conant & Co., are prepared to make as favorable rates as any agency can in the insurance line, and their rapidly increasing business shows that this fact is being taken advantage of. They are also in a position to lend valuable assistance in the buying, selling, renting or mortgaging of real estate, taking charge of same, collecting rents, etc., and being satisfied with reasonable commissions are able to guarantee satisfaction to their customers.

F. E. Stanley, Artist Photographer, Sands Building, Lisbon Street, Lewiston. It is not too much to say that the so-called "Dry-Plate Process" has practically revolutionized photography, and the vast improvement in photographic work observable during the past few years, is largely due to the employment of the new system. Mr. F. E. Stanley of this city is without doubt one of the best-known photographers in the United States, and portraits bearing his name are accepted as the standard in all parts of the country, yet notwithstanding his exceptional reputation, there are comparatively few people aware that he was one of the first to manufacture and use the now universally used process to which we have already alluded. Mr. Stanley was among the first to make practical use of this valuable discovery, and he now carries on a factory for the manufacture of Dry Plates, his productions being highly esteemed in the market for their uniformity and general reliability. But it is as an Artist Photographer that Mr. Stanley excels, and after a visit to his magnificent Studio and Reception Rooms, it is difficult to avoid too much enthusiasm when making mention of what is to be seen there. The entire upper floor is occupied in the Sands Building on Lisbon Street, (also a dry-plate factory of three stories). An elegantly furnished apartment, forty feet square, is utilized for the display of some characteristic samples of Mr. Stanley's work, and no competent and disinterested judge can visit this room without becoming convinced that the fame of the establishment with which it is connected, has been honestly won. Taken as a whole, this is the largest Photographic Studio in New England, with the exception of that occupied by a single Boston concern, and as regards elaborateness and beauty of appointment, it is second to none. Lewiston people may well feel proud of the existence in their midst of an undertaking that is conducted on a more extensive scale even than those in New England's metropolis, but they are not asked to support the enterprise on the ground of local pride by any means. *The work produced here is unsurpassed.* Few establishments in the United States can equal it, and the branch studio maintained at Bridgton, Me., also turns out photographs of the highest order of excellence. Photographing of every description is done, and finishing in Crayon, Pastel, Water Colors and India Ink, will be attended to in the most artistic manner. Mr. Stanley is a native of Kingfield, Maine, and is one of the best known of our Lewiston business men. He has done much to advance the interests of the city, both directly and indirectly, and takes a genuine and an excusable pride in maintaining the reputation his establishment now holds. And now in closing, let us say a few words about prices. Mr. Stanley makes his charges as low as is consistent with the attainment of the best results. He is able to do so, having every facility, and having had long and varied experience. It is possible to obtain photographs cheaper than he will make them, and some may think they cannot afford to patronize him. You cannot afford to do otherwise. A poor photograph is one of the most expensive things imaginable at any price, for it is absolutely useless, and is certainly not ornamental. Better not spend a cent on a portrait, if you cannot afford to get a good one, but the prices quoted by Mr. Stanley are so reasonable, that no good excuse can be given by anybody for not taking advantage of them.

T. L. Pratt & Co., 183 Lisbon Street, Lewiston.
The variety of Stoves and Ranges open to the inspection of buyers is so great that choice often becomes a difficult matter, but guided by the advice of a responsible dealer who handles nothing but goods of best makes choice is no longer difficult; so if you want a Stove or a Range or Kitchen Furnishing Goods of any kind just give Mr. T. L. Pratt a call at his store 183 Lisbon Street, and he can supply you if anybody can, for his stock is large and so is his experience, and his goods are as trustworthy as his prices are low. Perhaps you think this rather too high praise. Well, go and see for yourself, and if you don't find it to be fully justified by facts you are under no obligation to act upon it. Mr. Pratt's business was established in 1872 by Messrs. Buckley and Pratt in Auburn, who were succeeded in 1874 by Messrs. Pratt and Jones, removing to Lewiston, who carried it on up to 1877, since which date Mr. Pratt has continued it by himself. He is one of the best known of our business men, and owes his success to having made the interests of his patrons his own. Two floors 75x25 feet are utilized, together with a basement, and the large stock carried includes Stoves, Ranges, Hardware, Paints, Varnishes and Brushes, Tinware, Iron-ware, Wooden-ware, Farming Tools, Plated Ware and Cutlery, Tin, Copper, and Sheet-iron work done with a thoroughness and skill worthy of the highest praise.

Mrs. F. P. Mooney, Ladies and Gents' Furnishings, 245 Lisbon Street, Lewiston We doubt if there is another establishment precisely similar to that carried on by Mrs. F. P. Mooney, at No. 245 Lisbon Street, in the city of Lewiston, and indeed the liberal support which this enterprise receives, would seem to indicate that it had the field practically to itself. Mrs. Mooney handles Ladies' and Gents' Furnishings, and Dressmaking Goods in general, and makes a specialty of the doing of Sewing Work of all descriptions at short notice, and in the best possible manner. Her stock will be found to be skillfully and carefully selected, and as for her prices, they speak for themselves, the quality of the goods being guaranteed. As a Dressmaker, we feel that we can heartily and unreservedly recommend Mrs. Mooney, for she is not only experienced and expert in such work, but also has admirable taste in the adapting of costumes to the individualities of their wearers. Every detail of the work is carefully and thoroughly done, and the result is found to prove satisfactory. Mrs. Mooney is in a position to fill orders at short notice, and her charges are very reasonable.

Heath & Tainter, Sole Agents for the Household, New Home, and Domestic Sewing Machines, Mason & Hamlin, Worcester and Dyer & Hughes Organs, also a full line of Domestic Paper Patterns, 171 Lisbon Street, Lewiston. Every family should have a sewing machine of course, and every family should have one of first-class make, for an inferior sewing machine is not to be tolerated in these days of progress. There is certainly no reason why residents of Lewiston and vicinity should not have the best that the market affords in this line, for a single concern here (that of Heath & Tainter, doing business at No. 171 Lisbon Street) handles the Domestic, the New Home, and the Household Machines, and if these are not first-class articles, then there are none to be found in the market. The firm is constituted of Messrs. E. M. Heath and F. E. Tainter, the former a native of Princeton and the latter of Dixfield. Both are members of the Odd Fellows (Canton) and Mr. Heath is also connected with the Masons and the Knights of Pythias. One floor and a basement, measuring 85x30 feet are occupied and employment given to three assistants. All kinds of machines are repaired at short notice, and machines are rented at reasonable charges. Go to the sign of the Gold Machine at No. 171 Lisbon Street, and you will receive prompt attention and honorable dealing. A full line of Domestic Paper Patterns is carried, also Mason & Hamlin, Worcester, and Dyer & Hughes Organs, are very extensively handled. These instruments sell on their merits, for they are of superior design and construction and are offered at prices that speak for themselves.

J. M. Fernald, Bookseller, Stationer and Newsdealer, No. 71 Lisbon Street, under Music Hall, Lewiston. It is easy enough to say to young people making a start in life—"Be diligent, industrious and honest, and you will succeed;" it is a very simple thing to do to advise every ambitious youth on the threshold of mercantile life, to learn his business thoroughly in every detail so that he cannot fail, but the young people of the present age are practically inclined, and so are very apt to ask—"What assurance have I that in these times of strict competition, superior excellence will be appreciated and rewarded?" Then it is that the history of such an establishment as that conducted by Mr. J. M. Fernald can be pointed out with profit, for no better example could be wished of the results of a high combination of ability and industry. In the year 1877, the gentleman in question began operations in a little store having a frontage of 4½ feet, and correspondingly humble in all its appointments. Scarcely a decade has elapsed, but his business now requires the occupancy of a store measuring 85x35 feet, the employment of six assistants and the carrying of one of the largest assortment of books in the entire State; in fact, we believe, positively, the largest assortment, if Portland be excluded. Now this wonderful growth is not the result of "luck," it is not the result of an immense amount of capital skillfully handled, but it is the result of faith, of patience, of courage, and above all, of industry, and therefore should prove the highest incentive to every wide-awake and determined beginner in life who has brains enough to fully realize the truth of the axiom—"like causes, produce like results." Mr. Fernald was born in Houlton, Me., and is a leading member of the Odd Fellows. He is a very popular member of the community, and few men could have attained his present position and excited less envy in the minds of competitors. He supplies New and Second-hand Books on every subject, as well as Blank Books, Newspapers, Magazines, Albums, Games, etc. Second-hand School Books are made a specialty, and parents may often make a decided saving by calling at No. 71 Lisbon Street.

Troy Laundry, 12 Ash Street, Lewiston, A. K. P. Quimby, Proprietor. Hot and Cold Baths. It would be difficult to find a more genuinely useful enterprise than that conducted by Mr. A. K. P. Quimby, at No. 12 Ash Street. Public Laundries have long since "come to stay," in spite of the determined opposition that greeted their advent, and the establishment to which we have reference, is one of the best equipped public laundries in the State. It is not only well-equipped, but well-managed also, and we can assure our readers that the utmost care is used in handling the fabrics submitted for cleansing, and lowest prices are charged; 10 cents only for Shirts, and Collars and Cuffs for 2 cents each. Plain Family Washing for 35 cents a dozen. As to the nature of the results attained, we have only to call attention to the announcement made by Mr. Quimby, at the head of all of his laundry lists—"All work guaranteed to give satisfaction, or no charge will be made." It will be seen that Mr. Quimby feels confident of his ability to suit the most fastidious, and indeed there is no reason why he should not, for since his connection with this enterprise in 1887, complaints have been extremely "few and far between," and whenever made, have been promptly and cheerfully attended to. Mr. Quimby was born in Farmington, and is thoroughly acquainted with his chosen business in every detail. He employs three competent and careful assistants, and delivers all work at short notice. Spacious premises are occupied, and Hot and Cold Baths may be had at low prices, (25 cents each, 5 tickets for $1.00,) the best of facilities being provided, and any desired heat obtained.

C. O. Morrell, Dealer in Boots, Shoes and Rubbers of all kinds, corner of Main and Lisbon Streets, sign of Big Black Boot, Lewiston. The store carried on by Mr. C. O. Morrell, at the corner of Main and Lisbon Streets, is gaining in popularity daily, and present indications are that it will soon become one of the largest patronized establishments of the kind is Lewiston. This gratifying state of affairs is not the result of "bull luck," by any means, but is the legitimate outcome of the earnest and intelligent efforts Mr. Morrell has made to build up a trade since he assumed control in 1883. At this date he succeeded Mr. C. S. Newell, who founded the undertaking in 1872. The store is 50x25 feet in dimensions, and no space is thrown away, for the stock carried is large enough to utilize all available room, and it is as varied as it is extensive, comprising Boots, Shoes and Rubbers of every description, adapted to the use of Ladies, Gentlemen, Boys, Misses and Children. Mr. Morrell has an idea that a stock, to be attractive, must be constantly being renewed, and he puts his prices at figures that make his goods more lively, thus enabling him to be continually offering fresh articles. Carrying a complete stock of each line of goods, he is able to fit the most difficult feet, and whether you want a Dress, Business or Working Shoe, he can supply it at bottom figures, every time. An important department of the business is the repairing of Boots, Shoes and Rubbers, and every preparation has been made to insure satisfaction in the filling of such orders. Sufficient assistance is at hand to enable customers to be served without delay, and the "Sign of the Big Black Boot" will be found a very desirable place to trade.

P. E. Martin & Co., Merchant Tailor, 80 Lisbon Street. We often hear of people being frightened before they are hurt, and in one sense of the word this is true concerning many who never think of having their garments made to order on account of the absurdly erroneous ideas they have concerning the cost of custom work. Visions of sixty dollar Suits and fifty dollar Overcoats flit through their brains, and they shudder to think of the awful extravagance of those wearing such apparel. Well, they are right. That is to say, a man who gives any such prices for his clothing, is either extravagant or else he has an income so far beyond that of ordinary work-a-day mortals that he is to be envied perhaps, but certainly not imitated. Custom-made Clothing of excellent

LEADING BUSINESS MEN OF LEWISTON.

and durable quality may be had for about half such sums as those mentioned, and a visit to the establishment of P. E. Martin & Co., at 80 Lisbon Street, will prove this to anybody's satisfaction. Mr. Martin inaugurated his present enterprise in 1877, and not a few have discovered the unusual advantages he offers to customers as his large and growing business indicates. One floor is occupied, measuring 50x25 feet, and employment is given to twelve skilled assistants. We have not Mr. Martin's price-list at hand, but we are sufficiently familiar with the average of his charges to assure our readers that they are as low as the lowest for honest and desirable work. A fine assortment of Suitings, etc., is at hand to select from, and orders will be filled at very short notice.

A. E. Harlow, Dealer in Fruit and Confectionery, 58 Lisbon Street, Lewiston. Residents of Lewiston take a well-founded pride in their city and its "institutions," and one of the most popular establishments among them, is that conducted by Mr. A. E. Harlow at No. 58 Lisbon Street. There is ample excuse for the favorable manner in which this enterprise is regarded, for there is not a similar undertaking in Maine that is more liberally or progressively conducted, and the elegant store and extensive stock are certainly worthy of the highest encomiums. Mr. Harlow was born in Winthrop and is a member of the Knights of Pythias. The premises utilized by him, comprise two floors of the dimensions of 50x30 feet, and the business done, includes manufacturing. Wholesale and retail Confectionery of about every description is made and sold, and the delicious flavoring, etc., of Mr. Harlow's productions, is so well known that we only need give it passing mention. Great care is exercised in the selection of material and in its after handling, and we can confidently recommend the Confectionery made here, as being not only palatable but healthful as well. Mr. Harlow is in a position to quote bottom prices on his goods, and the very heavy trade he carries on is proof that the inducements he offers are generally understood. Fruit and Soda Water are sold as well as Confections, and as four competent and polite assistants are employed, prompt attention may be given to every caller.

Joseph LeBlanc, Proprietor of the Lewiston Steam Dye House, Clothing of all Descriptions Cleansed, Dyed, and Neatly Repaired. Ladies' Dresses Cleansed, Dyed and Finished Without Ripping, No. 141 Main Street, Lewiston. Perhaps some of our readers on seeing the heading of this article will exclaim, "Oh those dye houses are frauds! I have had the last thing dyed I ever will have for I never yet got the worth of my money!" But hold on a minute. Have you ever tried the Lewiston Steam Dye House, of which Mr. Joseph LeBlanc is the proprietor? No? Ah! We thought not! You should remember that there are dye houses and dye houses, and that because you have chanced so far to have dealings only with incompetent dyers it by no means follows that all dyeing establishments are worthy of condemnation. Mr. LeBlanc is a native of Canada and inaugurated his present enterprise in this city in 1886. He began operations with no flourish of trumpets whatever, confident that the merits of his work had only to become known to insure him a large patronage, and the progress of time has proved his confidence to be well-founded. Premises are occupied at No. 141 Main Street, of the dimensions of 35x25 feet and an 8-horse steam boiler supplies the necessary steam, etc. Employment is given to five assistants, and a specialty is made of the handling of Clothing of all descriptions, the same being Cleansed, Dyed, and Neatly Repaired at the shortest possible notice. Ladies' Dresses are Cleansed, Dyed, and Finished without Ripping, and a feature of the business which will be of particular interest to all housekeepers is the thorough Steam Cleansing of Feather Beds, Pillows, Bolsters, Curled Hair, etc. House furnishing goods are dyed in the most fashionable colors and finished in the most skillful manner, and Ostrich Plumes are given the utmost attention, and are Curled, Cleansed, and Dyed any desired shade.

R. M. Sykes & Co., Dealer in Clothing, No. 54 Lisbon Street, Opposite Lyceum Hall. The general introduction of machinery may have worked hardship in some cases and doubtless there are many instances in which it has done so, temporarily at least, but on the whole the benefits accruing from its use must far exceed its effects in other directions, and in no special line have these benefits been more manifest or more widely disseminated than in that relating to the manufacture of Clothing. That a man can dress better to-day on a salary of $10.00 a week than he could a score of years ago on $15.00 is a fact too evident and widely-known to call for proof, and when we consider that from the time the wool leaves the sheep's back to when the goods, into which it has been made, are cut and sewed into shape, it has been handled almost entirely by machinery, we will see the potent influence exerted by this agency. A gentleman who is exceptionally well-acquainted with the history and progress of Clothing manufacture having been engaged in it for over a quarter of a century, is Mr. R. M. Sykes of the firm of R. M. Sykes & Co., doing business at No. 54 Lisbon Street, opposite Lyceum Hall. This concern began operations in 1858, and has for many years been considered as one of the "institutions" of Lewiston. Mr. Sykes was born in Gorham, and is connected with the Free Masons and the Grand Army, having hosts of friends throughout this vicinity. Two floors are occupied of the dimensions of 95x35 and 40x35 feet respectively, and a magnificent assortment is constantly carried of Mens', Boys' and Childrens' Clothing and Gents' Furnishings. There are three courteous and well-informed assistants employed and callers will meet with every attention, and need feel under no obligation to buy as it is considered no trouble to show goods by this concern, which has a reputation for fair-dealing and low prices of which it may well feel proud. Satisfaction is guaranteed as all goods are strictly warranted to be as represented.

Lewiston Bleachery and Dye Works.

Bleaching, Coloring and Finishing of all kinds of Fabrics. Capital Stock, $300,000. Incorporated January, 1872. Directors, Jacob Edwards, Lyman Nichols, George Dexter, Thomas Wigzlesworth, Theophilus W. Walker; James Dempsey, Treasurer, Lewiston. An enterprise of vast importance as regards its influence upon the interests of Lewiston, is that carried on in this city under the name of the "Lewiston Bleachery and Dye Works," and were it given an amount of space in this book commensurate with its comparative merits, it would cover several of our pages, and this amount of information could be readily compiled if necessary, for an undertaking of the nature of that alluded to involves the carrying on of so large a number of delicate and intricate operations, that a full description of them would be both voluminous and interesting. The Bleaching, Coloring and Finishing of Cotton Goods are done at these works for all this portion of New England, and as this part of the country produces a much larger quantity of the articles mentioned than is required for its own consumption, some idea of the magnitude of the task may be attained, especially when we add that some five hundred horse-power is utilized in the running of the machinery used in performing the same. The plant covers about ten acres of ground, and about one-half of this space is covered with buildings, of which ten are used altogether, employment being afforded to three hundred and seventy hands. It would be idle for us to mention the quality of the work done, for it speaks for itself, and need fear no rivalry.

Carman & Thompson,

Steam Heating Engineers, Practical Pipers and Machinists, Manufacturers and dealers in Radiators, Valves, Steam and Gas Pipe and Fittings, Boilers, Engines, Pumps, Shafting, Pulleys, Hangers, and Engineers' Supplies, 48 Main Street, Lewiston. Heating by steam has long since passed the experimental stage, and practically all well-informed men now agree that this is the cheapest, the safest, the most convenient, and, on the whole, the most healthful manner of supplying artificial heat. The arguments which have been urged against steam heating, had their rise in an imperfect knowledge of the subject, and have no foundation in fact, when directed against a properly-designed and constructed steam-heating plant. But we would most earnestly caution such of our readers as may contemplate the adoption of this system, to be sure and place their orders in competent hands, as otherwise, serious risk will be run, and much unnecessary expense incurred. The firm of Carman and Thompson are well and favorably known as Steam Heating Engineers. William W. Carman and George F. Thompson are men who have made this branch of engineering a special study, and their practical experience has been such as to greatly aid them in obtaining a comprehensive idea of the difficulties to be overcome in their profession. They are Practical Pipers and Machinists, and are extensive manufacturers of and dealers in Radiators, Valves, Steam and Gas Pipe and Fittings, Boilers, Engines, Pumps, Shafting, Pulleys, Hangers, and Engineers' Supplies in general. Employment is afforded to forty competent assistants. The firm will furnish Estimates and Plans for the heating of Residences, Public Buildings, Greenhouses, etc., at short notice, and their facilities are such as to easily enable them to meet all honorable competition, both as regards the thoroughness of the work done, and the prices fixed upon the same. It is always well to deal with responsible parties, and particularly so when purchasing anything in Messrs. Carman & Thompson's line.

H. W. Barbour,

Druggist, 268 Lisbon Street, Lewiston. While the question of adulteration of food is of the highest importance, and is deserving of all the attention which has been given it, still it is well to bear in mind that other substances than those adapted to food are susceptible of adulteration, and that equally grave consequences may follow such treatment. That a physician's prescription may be rendered entirely useless by being compounded with impure material, requires no demonstration, common sense teaches every person that such might easily be the case. The importance, therefore, of having recipes filled at a perfectly reliable establishment, can hardly be over-estimated, and the people of Lewiston and vicinity are fortunate in having so skillfully and carefully managed a pharmacy in their midst as that carried on by Mr. H. W. Barbour, at No. 268 Lisbon Street. The reputation of this establishment is of course well known to most of our readers, the proprietor having been in business here for over thirty years, so this is one of the best-known drug stores in this part of the State, and is as popular as it is well known. Mr. Barbour carries a full stock of Pure Drugs, Medicines, and Chemicals at all times, and devotes his best energies to the task of so conducting his prescription department as to give unqualified satisfaction to all who may patronize him. Precision and promptness are assured. Very moderate prices are quoted, and no pains are spared to maintain and increase the popularity of this branch of the business. All the new and popular proprietary medicines, together with a carefully selected assortment of Toilet Articles, Perfumery, Fancy Goods, etc., are to be found here. He is also sole proprietor of the celebrated Cosmetic, Floral Cream, one of the most popular articles for the complexion that has ever been introduced. Its large and increasing sale and the unsolicited testimony of many ladies and leading physicians in this city, prove it to be almost the perfection of art, so that no lady's toilet is now deemed complete without it. It is not a paint, contains no injurious ingredients, and does not merely cover, but most effectually removes Moth, Tan, Freckles, and Sunburn from the face, causing it to look Fresh, Transparent and Smooth, however wrinkled or injured by the application of rancid preparations or irritating washes. All this the proprietor warrants it to do, and will refund the money to any lady who purchases it at his store, No. 268 Lisbon Street, if it fails to accomplish what it is recommended to do. This seems fair, and he will do as he says. If it does accomplish what he says, it is invaluable, if not, it costs you nothing, your money is returned. Ladies, give it a trial.

LEADING BUSINESS MEN OF LEWISTON.

C. S. Crowell & Co., Commission Merchants, Wholesale Dealers in Foreign and Domestic Fruit, Country Produce, etc., 161 Main Street, near Lisbon, Lewiston. As long as so large and important a share of our business operations is carried on through Commission Merchants it is obvious that the standing of any community in the mercantile world will be largely dependent upon the character and ability of those giving their attention to this branch of trade, and we therefore feel that no review of Lewiston's business interests would be complete were not mention made of such Commission Houses as might truthfully be called "representative." Prominent among these, is that conducted by Messrs. C. S. Crowell & Co., at No. 161 Main Street, near Lisbon, for during the 14 years that this enterprise has been in operation (it was started in 1874) it has increased and developed, until now it is well worthy to be chosen as a leader among similar undertakings prosecuted in this vicinity. Mr. C. S. Crowell is a native of Vassalboro, Me., and was formerly connected with our City Council. He is well known here, in business circles particularly, and is as generally esteemed as he is well known. A strictly wholesale business is done. Foreign and Domestic Fruit, Country Produce, etc., being extensively handled throughout the State, and the attention of those interested is called to the advantages derivable from dealing with this popular house. Returns are promptly made, and although it is not pretended that impossibilities can be accomplished and articles sold way above the market rates, still those consigning goods to Messrs. C. S. Crowell & Co., may safely depend upon having their interests looked out for as carefully as could be wished.

J. Parsons, Wholesale Dealer in Flour, Teas, Coffees, Spices, Tobaccos and Cigars, Haymarket Square, Lewiston. Among the most important wholesale houses of this city, mention should be made of that conducted by Mr. J. Parsons in Haymarket Square, for this is one of the most largely patronized in this section of the State, and the constant increase of its business proves that its future is to be a very bright one. The enterprise alluded to was inaugurated by Messrs. W. F. Trufant & Co., in 1879, and came into the possession of its present proprietor in 1887. Mr. Parsons had previously had an extended experience, however, in this same branch of trade, having carried it on since 1868, and so was admirably prepared to advance the interests of his new undertaking. That he has done so, no one familiar with the present extent of his trade can for a moment doubt, and this has been done by hard work and intelligent effort to meet every reasonable demand of his patrons. He is a native of Auburn, and is a member of the Free Masons, having a large circle of friends in this vicinity. The premises in use include one floor and a basement, and the stock carried is a very large and desirable one, comprising Flour, Teas, Coffees, Spices, Tobaccos and Cigars. A Grist Mill is run at West Minot, and grain can be furnished at bottom rates. Employment is afforded to four assistants, and all orders are attended to with the utmost celerity and accuracy. Mr. Parsons is prepared to offer his customers genuine inducements, and dealers handling goods in his line should give him a call.

D. W. Lowell, Manufacturer of fine Havana and Domestic Cigars, 182 Lisbon Street, Lewiston. Some physicians consider the use of tobacco injurious, others consider it harmless, and not a few advise and advocate its use on the ground that it is positively beneficial. This is a true statement in a nutshell of the prevailing condition of scientific belief on the subject and it indicates as all can see that the authorities themselves are greatly at variance. But there is one thing they *do* agree on and that is if you use tobacco use that which is good, pure, and free from noxious adulteration. To obtain tobacco of this kind a reputable and well-known house should be patronized that caters to the best class of custom and does so large a business that it can afford to exercise the greatest care in the selection of the stock it handles and thus be in a position to positively assure its patrons that the goods supplied are sure to prove as represented. It is just such an enterprise that is conducted by Mr. D. W. Lowell at No. 182 Lisbon Street, and smokers grow enthusiastic when describing the variety of cigars and tobacco he has to offer, for they assert that for evenness and delicacy of flavor some of his special brands are without a rival at the price at which they are sold. The premises utilized measure 100x15 feet and there is employment given to ten assistants in filling the many orders received for Mr. Lowell's popular productions. He is the sole manufacturer of the famous "Weston" brand and in this alone a very large business is done. Both wholesale and retail orders are filled at the lowest market rates and courteous attention is given all callers.

John Dickson, Lewiston Bakery. Wedding and Fancy Cakes a Specialty. No. 217 Main Street, Lewiston. If "health is wealth," as we are told it is, then good Bread must be considered as the road to "wealth," for certainly it is hard to keep one's health while eating poor bread. A public Bakery that produces an excellent article in this line, and that can be depended upon to furnish a uniformly superior grade of Cake, Pastry, etc., is that conducted by Mr. John Dickson, at No. 217 Main Street. Mr. Dickson was born in Scotland, and began operations here in 1884. He is connected with the Free Masons, and also with the Knights of Pythias, having a large circle of friends in this city. The premises utilized by him are of the dimensions of 55x35 feet, and employment is given to four efficient assistants. Although, as we have said, dealing extensively in Bread of fine quality, Mr. Dickson gives particular attention to the production of Wedding and Fancy Cakes, and he is known as one of the foremost makers of these goods in Lewiston. Some beautiful and original designs are controlled by him in the moulding and shaping of Wedding Cakes, and his prices are remarkably low, when the nature of the materials used and results attained are considered. Such orders are delivered promptly when promised, and entire satisfaction is guaranteed.

Wm. Lydston, Real Estate Agent, No. 247 Lisbon Street, Lewiston. Also Agent for the White Bronze Monuments and Head Markers. Prominent among those who have striven earnestly and successfully to advance the best interests of Lewiston, stands Mr. William Lydston

ENDORSED BY SCIENTISTS AS PRACTICALLY Indestructible

BETTER AND CHEAPER THAN ANY STONE.

Over 500 Beautiful Designs.

Send for Price List & Circulars.

MANUFACTURED BY
MONUMENTAL BRONZE COMPANY,
BRIDGEPORT, CONN.

the popular Real Estate Agent, and those at all familiar with this gentleman's past record, will join us in ascribing to him a large share of the credit fairly due to the public-spirited citizens who have labored early and late to give this municipality the position to which its extent and importance entitle it. Mr. Lydston is a native of Bowdoin, and since coming to this city has been closely identified with municipal affairs. He has served in both branches of the City Council and held the position of Street Commissioner for seven years. He became interested in the handling of Real Estate in 1874 and has since become an authority in relation to such property as his opportunities for becoming intimately acquainted with it have been of the best, and he has improved them to their full extent. He is prepared to Buy, Sell, or Exchange Real Estate, and to negotiate Loans and Collect Rents. The advantages of being represented by a man of Mr. Lydston's experience and position are obvious and many property owners avail themselves of his services. His office is located at No. 247 Lisbon Street, and callers may see samples of the famous White Bronze Monuments and Head Markers for which Mr. Lydston is agent. These Monuments, etc., are much preferable to those made of stone, as they are practically indestructible and will not corrode or moss over, even if put under shade trees. They are supplied at reasonable rates and a variety of tasteful designs are offered.

Mrs. M. B. Barker, (formery Mrs. M. B. Sprague,) Dealer in Pianos, Organs and Musical Merchandise. Pianos and Organs to Let. No. 42 Lisbon Street, Lewiston. We believe that the public generally appreciate the fact that the cheapest Piano or Organ to buy is an instrument that is strictly first-class in every respect, and hence we will not waste space in arguing as to the truth of this proposition. Those who think that the lowest-priced instrument is invariably the cheapest are very decidedly mistaken, but as such people only learn (if they learn at all) from experience, we will not address them in this brief article. It is no harder to obtain one's money's worth in the purchase of a Piano or an Organ, than in the buying of any other standard article of trade, but it is necessary to bear in mind the fact, that to secure honorable treatment, you must deal with an honorable establishment. This store, conducted by Mrs. M. B. Barker, (formerly Mrs. Sprague), has gained so wide-spread a reputation for entire reliability, that few, if any, of the residents of Lewiston or vicinity can be ignorant of it. Mrs. Barker deals in Pianos, Organs and Musical Merchandise in general, and occupies one floor of the dimensions of 80x35 feet, at No. 42 Lisbon Street. She represents the "Behning," and other first-class Pianos, and is prepared to furnish either a Piano or an Organ at the manufacturers' price. Instruments may be hired here at reasonable rates, and will be delivered promptly when agreed upon. Frames, Pictures, Christmas, Easter and Birthday Cards are also dealt in largely, and very reasonable rates quoted on the same.

A. G. Potter, Proprietor of Central Dining Room, 5½ Central Block, 171 Main Street, Lewiston. A good-natured hungry man is a phenomenon very rarely seen, for when anyone is really hungry, he is apt to forget politeness and everything else except his desire to be well fed as soon as possible. Good nature is a highly desirable thing for every man to have, and as the satisfying of hunger will go so far toward assuring it, we take pleasure in calling the attention of our readers to the Central Dining Room, located at No. 5½ Central Block, No. 171 Main Street, for every man eating at that popular resort is sure to leave it in a happy frame of mind, that is, if a hearty and nutritious meal at a fair price can bring about that result. The proprietor of this establishment is Mr. A. G. Potter, who is a native of this State and who founded the undertaking in question in 1877. The entire premises utilized comprise three floors of the dimensions of 55x40 feet, there being 14 desirable rooms available for the accommodation of lodgers. Temporary or permanent sojourners in Lewiston will find that it would be difficult to hit upon a more satisfactory and economical plan of living than to lodge and board at this establishment, for it combines the advantages of a hotel with those of a boarding house, and has few if any of the drawbacks of either. Mr. Potter supplies his tables with plenty of healthful, nutritious and seasonable food, stinting neither in quality or quantity. Employment is afforded to five competent assistants, the service is prompt and the cooking good, and in fact the person who can't be satisfied here must be very hard to suit.

ANDROSCOGGIN MILLS.

Androscoggin Mills, Cotton Goods of all kinds, Canal Street, Lewiston, Me. Lewiston is known to be the principal seat of the manufacture of cotton goods in this State, and as the Androscoggin Mills easily take the precedence in this city in the industry mentioned, they may reasonably be accepted as making up the representative enterprise of the State of Maine as regards the manufacture of Sheetings, Shirtings, Seersuckers, Grain Bags, Etc. This great enterprise was inaugurated in 1860, and requires a capital of $1,000,000 for its prosecution, there being 1,000 operatives employed, and 62,000 spindles and 1,358 looms run. About 210,000 yards of Cotton Goods, and 60,000 Bags are produced weekly, and a better idea of what a great quantity this is may be gained from the fact that 210,000 yards are more than 119 miles, or in other words, the weekly output of cloth from these mills would more than reach from Portland to Boston. To properly handle the immense amount of "raw material" utilized in the carrying-on of an enterprise of such magnitude requires a very extensive and superior equipment, and an inspection of the Androscoggin Mills will show that all necessary facilities are at hand to enable goods to be made combining a maximum of excellence with a minimum of cost. Three large buildings are occupied, two of them three and the other five stories in height, and a spacious store-house one hundred feet square is also utilized. Both water and steam-power are required to drive the necessary machinery, and a boiler house, measuring 75x38 feet, together with an engine house of about the same size, are maintained. The Treasurer is Mr. George F. Fabyan, Boston, and the Resident Agent, Mr. George W. Bean, the Selling Agents being Messrs. Bliss, Fabyan & Co., of No. 100 Summer Street, Boston, Mass. To satisfactorily dispose of so heavy an amount of goods as this corporation produces is of itself a task of no mean magnitude, but its performance is greatly facilitated by their high reputation for durability and general excellence, and a brisk demand exists for them among consumers.

Bates Manufacturing Co., Manufacturers of Ginghams, Seersuckers, Table Cloths, Quilts, Damasks, Etc., Canal Street, foot of Pine, Lewiston, Me. The residents of Lewiston and vicinity are so accustomed to the sight of the great mills located in that city that they are very apt to forget what truly stupendous enterprises they are, and how much the prosperity of the municipality is bound up in them. Taking only one—that conducted by the Bates Manufacturing Company—as an example, we find that this enterprise was inaugurated in 1852; that it requires the occupancy of four immense five-story buildings of the dimensions of 275x75 feet, and that it affords employment to over 1,800 operatives. Now, without taking into consideration the amount which this corporation pays out in taxation, without even considering the increased value given to real estate by the attracting to this community of the large number of people directly and indirectly connected with the mills, think of the grocers, the butchers, the tradesmen of all kinds who owe the bulk of their business to the employees of this company, and it will be seen that its influence in the development of Lewiston's business has been, and is, potent and far-reaching. Ginghams, Seersuckers, Shirtings, Quilts, Damasks, Tablecloths, and all kinds of Colored Cotton Goods are made, and 68,032 spindles and 1,550 looms are kept in operation to supply the market. The company has a capital of $1,000,000, and a board of officers made up of the following gentlemen: President, J. W. Clark; Treasurer, Jacob Edwards; Agent, H. L. Pratt, of Lewiston; Directors, Jacob Edwards, Dexter N. Richards, Jas. W. Clark, J. W. Brown, Jos. H. Gray, O. H. Alford, Moses Kimball. The Paymaster and Clerk is Mr. Ralph W. Potter, of Lewiston, and the Selling Agents, Bliss, Fabyan & Co., of Boston.

Samuel E. May & Co., Bankers and Brokers, and Dealers in Government Securities, No. 17 Lisbon Street, Lewiston. In directing the particular attention of our readers to the banking house of Messrs. Samuel E. May & Co., doing business at No. 17 Lisbon Street, this city, we feel that however strongly tempted we may be to eulogize the honorable business methods of this old, established concern, it will perhaps be as well for us to remain silent, as otherwise our praise may be considered as presumptuous, and the expression of our honest appreciation as offensive patronage. Nevertheless we are inclined to take the risk of being put in a false position as we are endeavoring to make this history of the commercial development of Lewiston as complete as possible, and the concern to which we have reference has played an important part in the bringing about of that development. Messrs. Samuel E. May & Co., began operation in 1863, and continued without change until the death of the senior partner in 1886, since which time the business has been carried on under the same firm-name, so well and so favorably known to our merchants and to investors in general. The office is conveniently located at No. 17 Lisbon Street, in the Board of Trade Rooms, and seekers after information will find Mr. Wheelock at all times ready to lend such counsel and assistance as may be suggested by his long and varied experience. The favorable relations established by this house during its extended and honorable career, give it peculiar advantages in negotiating loans, etc., and enable it to fully protect the interests of its customers. Government Securities, and all first-class Investment Securities are dealt in very extensively, principally New England, City, County, and R. R. Bonds, also Letters of Credit and Foreign Drafts, and those seeking a safe investment for surplus funds would do well to ascertain what Messrs. S. E. May & Co., can do for them in this line.

Mrs. L. Atwood, Fine Millinery, No. 9 Lisbon Street, Lewiston. The ladies of this city are to be congratulated on having so first-class an establishment so easy of access as that conducted by Mrs. L. Atwood at No. 9 Lisbon Street, and that they appreciate the advantages which this lady offers in the course of her business operations is proved by the liberal and constantly increasing patronage accorded her. Mrs. Atwood's enterprise was inaugurated in 1876, being the pioneer in its line in this city, and its celebrity is by no means confined to Lewiston, but extends for a considerable distance throughout the vicinity of the city. Fine Millinery of all descriptions is handled and the stock exhibited is well worth careful inspection, for it comprises all the most fashionable and popular novelties in the goods mentioned, and the utmost taste has been shown in its selection and arrangement. The store is 65x35 feet in dimensions and employment is afforded to six skilled assistants, a specialty being made of custom work, and no pains spared to keep up the very high reputation long since won by this establishment in this department of its business. Ribbons, Laces, and all kinds of Trimmings may be had here at the lowest market rates, and their quality is at all times guaranteed to prove as represented. It is in the Embroidery Department, however that Mrs. Atwood's enterprise is most widely and favorably known, and the specimens shown of this industry are beyond description and must be seen to be appreciated. Embroidery is done to order at low prices and very elegant effects are obtained.

Dr. Emery Bailey, Dentist, Journal Block, 20 Lisbon Street, Lewiston. It is a thing to be regretted, that so many people invariably associate the idea of Dental operations with more or less severe pain to the one operated upon, for such a state of feeling results in the teeth being neglected and allowed to go to ruin, when, if they were attended to in time, they might have done good service for years to come. It may be stated with perfect truth, that by the use of the improved appliances, etc., furnished to Dentists of the present day, it is possible for a skilled operator to entirely avoid the infliction of pain in the majority of cases, and if those whose teeth require attention would only submit them to a competent dentist in season, they would save themselves much inconvenience, expense and anxiety. Care should of course be taken to select a practitioner who is fully informed regarding the latest accepted theories, etc., of his profession, and in this connection we beg leave to call attention to the admirable facilities at the command of Dr. Emery Bailey, at his spacious and finely equipped rooms in Journal Block, No. 20 Lisbon Street. This gentleman has served the Lewiston public in his present capacity since 1876, and there is not a Dentist in the city (or for that matter, in the State either) that holds a higher or more deserved reputation for giving careful attention to the best interests of his patrons. Dr. Bailey was born in Woolwich, Me., and is connected with the Free Masons and K. of P., of which he holds the office of Grand Prelate of Grand Lodge, with the Royal Arcanum and Red Men, of which he is Sachem. He carries on Dentistry in all its branches, and is very popular, owing to the gentleness and care he uses, as well as to the thoroughness and skill with which he carries out every operation entered upon. His charges are always moderate, and we can cordially advise our readers to make use of his services.

J. L. Peabody & Co., Central Market, Dealers in Meats, Groceries and Provisions, Oysters and Fish. A Full Line of Choice Cigars and Confectionery. No. 169 Main Street, Central Block, Lewiston. There are many reasons why the Central Market should be the favorite, which it undoubtedly is with the general public, and these reasons are so sound and conclusive that there is no danger of the establishment in question losing its popularity, under its present management at least. The enterprise was inaugurated in 1874, under the firm name of Daily & Peabody, and ten years later the present style was adopted — J. L. Peabody & Co. Mr. Peabody is a native of New Portland and is connected with the Odd Fellows. He is very well known about town, for during his extended business career in this city he has made many friends and has gained a well deserved reputation for enterprise and liberal methods. The premises utilized by Mr. Peabody are located at No. 169 Main Street, (Central Block) and are of the dimensions of 65x30 feet. One reason for the great popularity enjoyed by the undertaking is to be found in the variety and extent of the stock on hand, for it includes not only Meats, Groceries and Provisions of all kinds, but also Fish and Oysters and a full line of Choice Cigars and Selected Confectionery. The prices are as low as the lowest, for goods of equal quality, and the employment of two assistants makes it possible to assure prompt and courteous attention to all.

A. W. & W. B. Anthoine, First-Class Watchmakers and Jewelers, 75 Lisbon Street, Lewiston. No better evidence of the wealth and general prosperity of a community need be asked for, than that afforded by the successful carrying on in its midst, of such an enterprise as that conducted by Messrs. A. W. & W. B. Anthoine, at No. 75 Lisbon Street. This undertaking was founded in 1889, by Mr. A. W. Anthoine, who is a native of Windham, and it was carried on by him alone up to 1887, when Mr. W. B. Anthoine became associated with him, this gentleman being a native of Biddeford. The premises occupied are of the dimensions of 45x18 feet, and afford accommodation for an extremely large and varied stock of Watches, Jewelry, Silver Ware, Precious Stones, etc. These goods are offered at the very lowest market rates, and we know of no establishment in the State where the retail buyer enjoys more advantages, for every article sold is fully warranted to prove as represented, while lower prices are quoted than many irresponsible dealers are able to offer, for this firm enjoys the most favorable relations with manufacturers and wholesalers, and gives its customers the full benefit of this state of affairs. All the leading makes of Watches are handled, and a reliable timekeeper may be purchased for a reasonable sum, while French Clocks are also largely dealt in as well as those of American manufacture. The assortment of Solid and Plated Silver Ware, is complete in every department, and embraces all the latest and most fashionable designs, and the Solid Gold Goods offered are also remarkable for beauty and for novelty. Particular attention is given to the Repairing of Fine Watches, and many of our readers will doubtless be glad to learn where they may have work of this kind done with the assurance of a satisfactory result. Employment is given to three competent and polite assistants, and orders for Custom Work, Repairing, etc., are filled at short notice. Both members of the firm are very well-known about town, and the senior partner is connected with the Knights of Pythias, while Mr. W. B. Anthoine belongs to the Odd Fellows.

Darrah's Kid Glove Store, No. 117 Lisbon Street, Lewiston. Every person that desires to appear well-dressed should remember that it is in the minor details of the toilet that the most care should be exercised, for it is apt to be just here that the difference between perfect and imperfect dress is most observable. The matter of gloves is a very important one in this connection and no one can afford to be careless in the selection of these articles for if the gloves be ill-fitting or of bad style they will spoil the effect of the most elaborate costume. As there is such a great difference in the hands of people — one having a long and slender hand, while another's is just the reverse — the only way to assure getting a good fit is to visit an establishment which makes a specialty of Gloves, and carries so large a stock as to be able to guarantee that satisfaction will be given in this respect. A Lewiston enterprise which for many years has held a leading position among similar houses in this portion of the State is that located at No. 117 Lisbon Street, and known as "Darrah's Kid Glove Store," and all our readers who may be in need of Gloves should certainly give this establishment a call, as they will find as large and select a stock and as low prices as are obtainable anywhere. Mr. W. C. Darrah founded the business he now conducts over 20 years ago and has steadily added to his trade until now it has reached immense proportions. Ladies' and Gentlemen's Gloves of all descriptions are offered, made and finished in first-class style and guaranteed as to fit and durability. Employment is afforded to two assistants and no delay is experienced in being waited upon, excepting at rare intervals. A specialty is made of the sale of Infant's Wear, and many beautiful goods are shown in this department.

G. M. Allen, (Successor to Teague & Hale), Registered Druggist, 28 Lisbon Street, Lewiston, Me. It is safe to say that there are few, if any, establishments in this city that are better known to the public at large than is that conducted by G. M. Allen, (Successor to Teague & Hale,) at Nos. 28 and 30 Lisbon Street. Operations were begun by Mr. W. A. Teague, in 1884, and in 1885, Mr. S. A. Hale was admitted to partnership under the existing firm-name. Mr. Allen succeeded to the business March 1, 1888. This gentleman is a native of Waldoboro, and had an experience of thirteen years before coming here. He is a member of the Knights of Pythias, Odd Fellows and Red Men. Originally, Mr. Teague confined his efforts to the carrying on of a first-class drug store, but on becoming associated with Mr. Hale, another store was obtained, adjoining the old one, and the business of Cigar Manufacturing was engaged in. Great success has been won in this new field of effort, but the drug department is by no means neglected, and no pains are spared to carry on a Family Pharmacy that shall be satisfactory in every respect. Employment is given to a competent assistant, and every customer receives prompt and careful attention. Prescriptions are filled with the utmost accuracy and at extremely low rates, the assortment of Drugs, Medicines, and Chemicals in stock, being very extensive and made up of fresh and pure goods. A full line of attractive Holiday Goods is offered which is not excelled in the city for beauty and variety. Mr. Allen pays particular attention to the sale of the "Nordeck" Cigar, and if you want an enjoyable and fragrant smoke at a small expense, just try one of these popular Cigars.

Chandler & Estes, Dealers in School and Miscellaneous Books, Blank Books, Stationery, Paper Hangings, Window Shades, Pictures and Frames, Artists' Materials and Fancy Goods, 100 Lisbon Street, Lewiston. If Mr. J. C. Batcheller, when he founded the business now carried on by Messrs. Chandler & Estes, could have forseen the way in which it was destined to develop, he would doubtless have been proud of his work, but forty years is a long time and nearly that period has elapsed since he inaugurated the enterprise alluded to in 1849. Ten years later he was succeeded by Dresser & Varney, who in 1865 gave place to Mr. T. M. Varney, and he in turn to French Brothers in 1870. In 1877 Mr. Benjamin Chandler assumed control and in 1880 this gentleman entered into partnership with Mr. I. H. Estes under the present firm name. Mr. Chandler was born in Unity, Me., and Mr. Estes in this city, the former being connected with the Free Masons and the latter with the Odd Fellows and the Knights of Honor. The relative position of the enterprise carried on by this house is soon stated. It stands at the head. Occupying a store of the dimensions of 85x40 feet, every inch of available space is utilized for the accommodation of a stock as varied as it is extensive, and as desirable as it is varied. School and Miscellaneous Books are largely dealt in and a fine assortment of Blank Books is shown, containing shapes and sizes suitable for about all the many purposes to which these articles are put. An elegant selection of fashionable Stationery is also offered and in the line of Paper-hangings it would be difficult indeed to excel the variety exhibited. Window Shades in the most popular patterns are at hand and the prices quoted on them are so low as to merit special attention, while the collection of pictures exhibited must be seen to be appreciated. Artists' Materials of choice quality are sold at bottom prices, and the firm act as agents for the Boston Papers, and carry a complete assortment of the leading periodicals and news publications.

J. T. Small & Co., Real Estate Brokers and Auctioneers, City and Country Property Bought, Sold and Exchanged, Rents Collected, Mortgages Negotiated, No. 3 Lyceum Block, Lisbon Street. Any person — stranger or old resident — who may wish to obtain information regarding Lewiston Real Estate, would do well to call upon Messrs. J. T. Small & Co., at Room 3, Lyceum Hall Block, Lisbon Street, and make known his wishes to them. This firm makes a specialty of the handling of this class of property, and are regarded as authorities concerning it. They do a large business, but find time to give all customers prompt and painstaking attention, cheerfully affording any information in their power to give. Complete lists are kept of the desirable Real Estate on the market, either for hire or sale, and many weary steps and not a few disappointments may be avoided by "house-hunters" who will make use of the facilities here provided. City, Farm, and Country Property handled. The negotiation of Mortgages and Loans is a prominent feature of the business and no firm in Lewiston is better fitted to assure satisfaction to all parties concerned in the carrying on of such operations, Mr. Small having been engaged extensively in Real Estate for the past twenty years, not only in New England, but in the South and West. He buys, sells and exchanges. Those wishing to raise money either on Real Estate or personal property at a low rate of interest, or any business transacted in the auction line, will find that their interests would be best served by leaving their orders here. The business has been conducted in such a manner as to inspire the fullest confidence, and all customers find that promptness and reliability which alone insure success. This firm deals in all kinds of investments, but makes a specialty of Western and Southern Loans. The facilities for effecting safe investments are thus unsurpassed. This firm also transacts a general insurance business and are agents for the Dwelling House Insurance Co., of Boston, Mass.

J. C. Lord & Son, Dealers in Groceries, Flour, Meats and Provisions. No. 30 Ash Street. No one can visit the store of J. C. Lord & Son, located at No. 30 Ash Street, without at once becoming aware that a more than usually large business is done there and the more completely investigations are carried out, the more plainly evident it will become that this is one of the leading establishments of the kind in this city, and yet it is not of very long standing either, comparatively speaking. Business was begun in 1861 by J. C. Lord, who succeeded to the business of L. P. Huntoon in 1888. He is a native of Albany, N. Y.; and his son, E. J., of Lewiston. Both are members of the Odd Fellows. Mr. E. J. Lord belongs to the Red Men. Their knowledge of the Grocery and Provision trade is best vouched for by the brilliant success that has attended their efforts to increase the scope of their operations. The premises occupied include one floor and a basement and measure 65x20 feet. An immense stock is carried, particularly in the line of Flour. Messrs. Lord & Son make a specialty of this valuable product, and offer an unsurpassed assortment of standard and popular brands at bottom prices. Staple and Fancy Groceries, Meats, and Provisions are also handled very extensively, and attention might well be given to the excellence of the various grades of Tea and Coffee offered, and the remarkably reasonable prices quoted in this department. Messrs. Lord & Son employ three competent and polite assistants and guarantee the prompt delivery of orders.

Wade & Dunton, Manufacturers of and Dealers in Carriages and Sleighs, Park Street, Lewiston. The average man does not buy a Carriage or Sleigh every day in the week, by any means, and when he does purchase one,  it is but natural that he should be anxious to get a vehicle on which he can depend, for, monetary considerations aside, one does not like to trust his family, or even himself, in a carriage which there is any reason to believe is not strongly and dura-

LEADING BUSINESS MEN OF LEWISTON.

bly made. It is principally for this reason that we should advise such of our readers as contemplate the purchase of a vehicle of this description to visit the establishment of Messrs. Wade & Dunton, on Park Street, for there they will find a large and varied assortment of the productions of all the best makers (for this firm does not confine itself to the handling of its own productions,) and each and every carriage sold is fully guaranteed to prove as represented in every respect. This business was founded in 1857, by Messrs. Potter, Thompson & Co., who were succeeded by the existing firm in 1887. Mr. T. W. Wade was born in N. Y., and Mr. E. L. Dunton in Gardiner. Three buildings are occupied, measuring 45x60, 50x75 and 38x40 feet in dimensions, respectively, and employment is afforded to eighteen assistants; Order Work and Repairing being done at short notice, in the best possible manner. No house is in a position to extend more positive and genuine advantages to its customers, as regards both quality of work and lowness of price, and that this fact is appreciated the constantly increasing business shows.

Drs. N. Woodbury & Son, Dentists, Pilsbury Block. Lewiston. "If 'twere done at all, 'twere best 'twere done quickly," is a Shakespearian quotation which may be studied with profit by all requiring the services of a dentist, for in their case the old saying "delays are dangerous," applies ten-fold. If people would more generally make a rule of visiting a competent dental operator at the first symptoms of decay in a tooth, they would save themselves much pain and more money. But it is well to assure one's self as to the competency of the dentist before submitting to his guidance and perhaps the best way of doing this is to ascertain the popular sentiment of the community concerning him. Applying this test, we believe the preference in Lewiston would surely be given to Drs. N. Woodbury & Son, for these gentlemen have practiced dentistry here since 1871 and long prior to that date followed the same profession elsewhere, Dr. N. Woodbury having had an experience extending over a score of years in Auburn and Skowhegan. Both are natives of Auburn and are widely known in that city as well as in Lewiston Two rooms are occupied in Pilsbury Block, and every improved facility is at hand for the carrying on of Dentistry in all its branches. Engagements may be made in advance and annoying delays thus avoided, and all that care and gentleness can do to make things as agreeable as possible for patients will be done, while operations are carried on with great thoroughness and at reasonable rates.

John B. Smith & Co., Practical Pipers and Plumbers, Wholesale and Retail Dealers in Boiler Tubes, Wrought Iron Pipe, Fittings, Valves, etc., Lead Pipe, and Plumbing Material, 40 Lower Main Street, Lewiston. It seems to be impossible for some people to appreciate the importance of having such work as Steam and Gas Fitting done only by those who combine experience and skill, and yet it would seem as if the frequent instances occurring on every side of waste or damage caused by defective pipe laying would be of themselves enough to convince the most careless that not everybody is competent to undertake work of this description. Take it in Steam heating alone and it will be found that much of the undisputed economy of that method over the system of heating by Stoves, Furnaces, etc., may be lost by the improper arrangement or unworkmanlike fitting of Pipes and hence consideration of economy, not less than of safety demand that only skilled men should be entrusted with the carrying out of the necessary operations. Messrs. John B. Smith & Co., of No. 40 Lower Main Street, this city, make a specialty of Piping and Plumbing, and have every facility to fill orders at the very shortest notice and at the least possible expense. Carrying as they do what is regarded by competent critics as the largest and most complete stock of Pipe, Tubing, and such goods in the State, they are prepared to furnish anything in these lines without delay and at the lowest market rates. The business was begun in 1873 by Messrs. Smith & McClure and came under the control of the present firm in 1880. Mr. Smith was born in Lowell, Mass., and is one of the most widely and favorably known of our citizens, having been connected with the Board of Aldermen for two years. The premises occupied are 45x35 feet in size and employment is afforded to twenty assistants. This firm are agents for the Gurney Hot

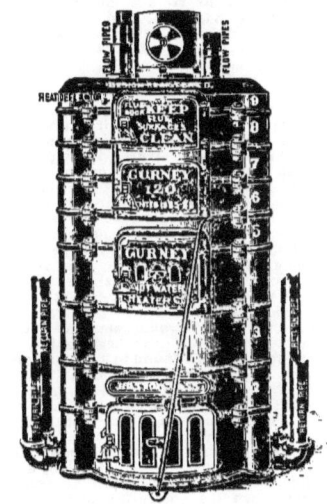

Water Heater, and make a specialty of hot water heating, both a wholesale and retail business being done and Boiler Tubes, Wrought Iron Pipe, Fittings, Valves, Lead Pipe and Plumbing Material very extensively dealt in.

W. L. Lothrop, agent for Ivers & Pond Pianos, 186 Lisbon street, Lewiston. If there was but one kind of piano manufactured, the task of choosing an instrument would be entirely done away with, and the imaginative and descriptive powers of many a hard-working salesman would not be so heavily drawn upon, as they are under present conditions. But there are many styles of piano on the market — some excellent, more good, still more fair, and even more yet positively bad. Those who buy as cheap an instrument as possible will choose the latter, and afterward repent having done so. Others will pay a fair price and get a fair or good piano, and a few will order the highest-priced instrument to be found; having plenty of money, and believing the most expensive to be necessarily the best. This belief is entirely erroneous. It is not only possible, but easy, to obtain as fine a piano as is manufactured, without paying an exorbitant price, and the way to do it is to visit Mr. W. L. Lothrop, at No. 186 Lisbon Street, and order an "Ivers & Pond." "How do we know this?" you ask. By experience. The Ivers & Pond piano is a high-grade, modern-built instrument, of sweet and powerful tone, responsive action, great durability, and beautiful finish, and it is sold at a fair and reasonable price. *These pianos always give satisfaction,* and you will never regret having chosen one. Mr. Lothrop is a native of Leeds, Maine, and is connected with both the Masons and the Odd Fellows. He has been the county agent for the Ivers & Pond Pianos since 1886, has made many sales, and has shown the instrument he handles to be the equal of all, and the superior of two-thirds of the pianos on the market today.

Daniel Wood, Dealer in Crockery, China, and Glass Ware, Kerosene Goods, Cutlery, and Rogers' Silver Plated Ware, Lisbon Street, Lewiston. If there be any among our readers who are disposed to believe that there is not an active demand in this community for goods of the finest quality and most beautiful design we would certainly advise an inspection of the stock of Mr. Daniel Wood, for this gentleman has been engaged in his present business here for 21 years, but has been in business in Lewiston for 40 years, and would not be apt to offer goods which he did not have good reason to believe would be in strong demand. As elegant an assortment of Crockery, China, and Glass Ware as is to be found in this portion of the State, may be seen at his establishment, No. 151 Lisbon Street, and no further proof can be needed of the general culture of the community than the immense quantity of the finest goods annually sold by Mr. Wood. He is a native of Acton, Me., and began operations here in 1848. In 1849 as Wood & Weeks. Seven years later he became sole proprietor, and has since continued the enterprise alone. He is one of the most universally respected of our citizens, and it is to be regretted that his dislike for public office has prevented his experience and integrity being employed in the direction of our municipal government, with the exception of a single term which he served as Councilman. But nevertheless Mr. Wood has earned the gratitude of the public by supplying reliable and desirable goods at fair rates and we can do no better than to heartily advise all wishing anything in the line of Crockery, Glass Ware, Kerosene Goods, Cutlery, Rogers' Silver Plated Ware to procure the same at this store. It is of the dimensions of 25x100 feet, and two courteous and well-informed attendants will give customers prompt attention. Wedgewood, Majolica and Japanese Wares are made specialties and many beautiful novelties are shown.

A. L. & E. F. Goss, Stoves, Agricultural Implements, etc., 41, 43 & 45 Main St., Lewiston. The enterprise conducted by Messrs. A. L. & E. F. Goss has been in operation for over a quarter of a century, this firm succeeding Mr. John Goss in 1865. To state that this concern ranks with the leading houses in the State engaged in handling Stoves, Furnaces, Agricultural and Dairy Implements, etc., is but to call attention to a well-known fact, for it is generally understood among the purchasing public that both as regards the variety and quality of the stock carried and the prices quoted on the same, Messrs. A. L. & E. F. Goss have no reason to fear comparison with any of their competitors. Both members of the firm are natives of Danville and both are well known. Mr. A. L. Goss having been a member of the Lewiston and Auburn City Council while Mr. E. F. Goss has represented the same community in the Legislature. The premises occupied are very spacious consisting of four floors and basement of the dimensions of 65x90 together with a large store house for agricultural implements 1 Main St.— From these figures some idea may be gained of the size of the stock carried, and as the firm confines itself to no special make of goods but seeks to supply its customers with all such as experience has proved to be of real value under the conditions of practical use, it is obvious that no better place can be found at which to purchase anything in its line. Among the more popular of their specialties may be mentioned the "Royal Clarion" and the "Royal Grand" Ranges, and the "Dining Room Companion," this latter stove being manufactured and patented by the firm. It is made in ten different styles and finishes and is without doubt one of the very best Parlor Cook Stoves on the market, being elegant in design, economical of fuel and requiring but little attention. Refrigerators and Dairy Goods are also very extensively handled at wholesale and retail, and in the line of Agricultural Implements no other house in the State can make such a showing, for not only is the assortment unequalled, but every provision is made for carrying a full line of repairs in stock for all the different class of goods they handle. This of itself gives them a large trade to supply the wear and tear of their extensive sales for the last twenty-three years, which accommodation their patrons greatly appreciate.

George H. Glover, Musical Instruments, 149 Lisbon Street, Lewiston. The motto "get the best" is an excellent one to follow when making purchases of any kind, as a general thing, but it is particularly worthy of observance when choosing a musical instrument, as an inferior article of this kind is dear at any price. Such of our Lewiston readers as are musically inclined, will be glad to learn of an establishment where Pianos, Organs and other musical instruments may be obtained at the lowest market rates, and of guaranteed quality, and we therefore take pleasure in calling their attention to the enterprise conducted by Mr. George H. Glover at No. 149 Lisbon Street. One floor of the dimensions of 75x50 is occupied, and an extensive stock carried, comprising not only musical instruments but also musical merchandise in General. Mr. Glover began operations in 1877, then being located in Auburn. Ten years later he removed to his present quarters and is now better prepared than ever before to assure satisfaction to his customers. Representing the Chickering, Prescott and Hallett & Davis he is certainly well able to supply the best that is to be had in the piano line, while as special agent for the Prescott Organs he can offer equal inducements in that direction. Brass Instruments, Music, Musical Merchandise etc., are furnished at prices that cannot fail to be satisfactory, and the goods are in all cases reliable and first-class. Mr. Glover is a teacher of the Cornet and also gives instruction regarding the use of other instruments. Pianos and Organs are tuned at short notice in a first-class manner, and especial attention is given to the general repairing of musical instruments.

W. E. G. Worthley, Photographer, Pillsbury Block, Lewiston. That homely old proverb which declares that "The proof of the pudding is in the eating" goes straight to the root of the matter, as indeed all those homely old proverbs are wont to do, and no better instance of it can be found in modern life than that afforded by the work of the photographer. One may talk of "light and shade" of "attention to details" of "artistic handling of a subject," for hours and it will not give half the real insight into a photographer's skill that could be obtained by a few minutes' examination of his work. So we will not take up space in describing the many excellencies of the productions of Mr. W. E. G. Worthley of this city, but will simply invite our readers to visit his studio in Pillsbury Block, over the Young Men's Christian Association, and see for themselves. This gentleman was born in Phillips, Me., and is a member of the Odd Fellows. He inaugurated his present enterprise in 1870 and has built up a very large and steadily increasing patronage by his prompt attention to orders and by always striving to do his best. Photographs of any desired size will be made and those who are not familiar with such work are the most outspoken in their praise of the system of finish and generally satisfactory character of Mr. Worthley's productions. India Ink and Crayon Portraits are also made in the very best manner and at low prices and a fine line of colored photographs is at hand for the inspection of those interested, and orders for coloring are executed in a superior manner and at low prices. The premises are 50x45 feet in dimensions, and employment is afforded to two assistants.

C. P. Crossman, Proprietor of the Boston 5 Cent Store, 5 and 10 Cent Counter Supplies at Wholesale and Retail, No. 88 Lisbon Street, Opposite Music Hall, Lewiston. Lewiston's "Boston 5 Cent Store" is one that fully deserves its name, for after a thorough inspection of its stock and prices and a comparison of them with those of Bailey (who conducts what is by far the most extensive establishment of the kind in Boston or New England) we are prepared to assert that the comparison is by no means entirely in favor of the Metropolitan enterprise. Of course it would be absurd to intimate that our Lewiston store contained so heavy a stock, but it is a fact that in those lines that are carried by it, it offers fully as great inducements to buyers as Mr. Bailey ever did. The "Boston 5 Cent Store" was founded in 1881 by Messrs. Crossman & Davis and a year later Mr. C. P. Crossman assumed sole control, which he has since continued. He is a native of Smithfield, Rhode Island, and possessed of that liberal enterprise and readiness to take advantage of any peculiarity of the market without which, great success in such a business as he is engaged in is impossible. The premises occupied are of the dimensions of 65x40 feet and a really tremendous stock of Glass, China, Crockery, Baskets, Tin Ware, in short all that endless array of articles carried in a store of this kind, is on hand and sold at wholesale and retail. Employment is afforded to four active and polite assistants and any article in stock will be promptly and cheerfully shown.

N. J. Laughton, Pianos and Organs, 84 Lisbon Street, Lewiston, and 17 Court Street, Auburn. There is no more satisfying or gratifying evidence of the general prosperity of the people of this country, than that afforded by the immense number of Pianos and Organs sold annually, for although of course some of these instruments find their way into the homes of the rich, the great majority of them are purchased by working people. By this expression we mean, of course, all those who support themselves by the labor of their hands or brains as distinguished from those who are in receipt of an adequate income without necessity for personal exertion. The charms of music in the home, have been too often and too eloquently described to need mention here, and the demand existing for musical instruments shows that these charms are generally appreciated. We have no set advice to offer regarding the selection of a Piano or an Organ, other than "get the best." Don't buy an unreliable instrument at any price, and to get a reliable one, patronize a reliable dealer. Mr. N. J. Laughton of No. 84 Lisbon Street, Lewiston, and 17 Court Street, Auburn, acts as agent for some of the best manufacturers in this country, and no mistake will be made by those leaving an order with him. He is a native of Auburn, a member of the Odd Fellows, and represents such houses as Decker Brothers, Wilcox & White, Kranch & Bach, etc. One floor, measuring 45x25 feet is occupied, and employment given to two efficient assistants. A branch store at Auburn was opened in March 1888, with a full line of Pianos, Organs, and Musical Merchandise. No one wanting a Piano or an Organ should neglect paying Mr. Laughton a visit.

The Blue Store, S. A. & I. B. Isaacson Proprietors, One Price Clothing Establishment, Corner Lisbon and Ash Street, Lewiston. Since the "Blue Store" came under the control of its present proprietors it has become one of the "institutions" of Lewiston and the advantages it has to offer in the way of Clothing, etc., are so pronounced and unusual that it may be considered as having no competitor in its own special line of business. One reason why it is in a position to offer inducements so greatly superior to those of rival houses is to be found in the fact that it is a branch of a large Boston concern. The Blue Store was originally opened in 1881, but it was not until 1886 that Messrs. S. A. & I. B. Isaacson took it in charge. They have built up a business such as under ordinary circumstances would have been the work of a full decade in less than two years, and have done it too by strictly legitimate and honorable methods. Some few dealers may complain because of the sudden cessation of the enormous profits they used to make, but what is their loss is the people's gain and the people show that they appreciate it by liberally patronizing the house that sounded the death-knell of exhorbitant figures. Two floors are in use of the dimensions of 85x35 feet, and a stock of Clothing is carried which it would be very difficult to equal in this city. Hats, Furnishing Goods, etc., are also exhibited in profusion and employment is afforded to ten assistants. Mr. S. A. Isaacson is a native of Russia and Mr. I. B. Isaacson of Boston, Mass., both gentlemen being connected with the Knights of Pythias and the first-named with the Odd Fellows as well. Not only is the concern a leading one in business circles, but the gentlemen constituting it are also very prominent socially and have hosts of friends throughout this section.

W. R. Goodwin, Steam and Gas Fitter, and dealer in Steam and Gas Fitters' Tools and Supplies. Hot Water Heating a Specialty. No. 30 Main Street, Lewiston. Although Steam and Hot Water Heating are becoming more and more popular and widely used, as their advantages become better known, still there have been instances in which they utterly failed to give satisfaction, for with these systems of heating, much more than when stoves or furnaces are used, a great deal depends upon the manner in which the necessary apparatus is adjusted. The moral is plain. Be sure that those who undertake to put in operation such arrangements for heating, are competent and responsible parties, and no mistake can possibly be made on this score if Mr. W. R. Goodwin be employed, for he has attained a reputation for skillful and thorough work in this line that could only have been won by sheer force of merit. Business was begun by Mr. David Bickford, and in 1886 this gentleman became associated with Mr. W. R. Goodwin, succeeded by Mr. Goodwin in 1887. One floor is occupied measuring 40 x 25 feet, and Wrought Iron Pipe, Fittings, etc., are extensively dealt in. There are six competent and careful assistants employed, and those favoring this house with an order for either new work or repairing, may feel positively assured that the same will be filled in the most conscientious manner and at the lowest market rates. This is a representative house and one worthy of unreserved commendation.

Manufacturers' National Bank, Lewiston. Although our National Banking system is no doubt imperfect in certain respects still it approaches as closely to perfection as most schemes of human origin, and on the whole has made a record since the war of which its sponsers need not be ashamed. It is not for us to act as a champion of the system for if any defence of it may be needed there are far abler pens than ours ready to enlist in such a cause, but we cannot refrain from suggesting that the most severe critics of our National Banks have not as a rule met with such brilliant success in the conduct of their private business affairs as to indicate that they were born financiers or far-seeing managers. Even the most prejudiced person however would scarcely have the audacity to deny that the Manufacturers' National Bank of this city had been of great service to our local business men since its establishment in 1875, for such a denial would be of no avail even if made, so generally convinced is the community of the value of the aid extended by the institution mentioned. It has a capital of $200,000 and a surplus of $33,000, and its management has shown on more than one occasion that they have an abiding faith in this city and its business men, and are therefore prepared to show their faith by their works in every legitimate way. The officers: Messrs. J. M. Robbins, President; C. I. Barker, Vice-president; and Addison Small, Cashier, are all well-known and highly esteemed citizens both in public and private life, and the present condition of the bank is the strongest possible endorsement of their faithfulness and zeal. The Board of Directors consists of Messrs. J. M. Robbins, C. I. Barker, E. S. Davis, James Munroe, T. E. Eustis, Oliver Newman and L. L. Blake, and there is no reason to doubt that the high record of the past will be fully maintained if not improved upon with the progress of time.

J. M. Sherman, Painter, Grainer, Glazier, Paper Hanger and Fancy Decorator, No. 96 Chestnut Street. "In the elder days of art" all decoration and beautiful artistic work was confined to the religious and public buildings and the palaces of the favored rich. Now, through the advancing influences of civilization, the achievements and effects of artistic coloring are brought within the reach of almost every one who can appreciate their value, and the higher tone and happiness which have thus been brought into our life is of the greatest influence and value. The refined taste exhibited everywhere in this branch of business causes one to stop and wonder if this industry has not reached the height of perfection. Among the well-known business firms of Lewiston is the familiar name of J. M. Sherman, whose business is located at No. 96 Chestnut Street. As a painter he has no superior in this section of the State, and as the business was established here in 1872 by Mr. Sherman, it is recognized as one of the leading ones in Lewiston, Mr. Sherman being favored by the finest class of custom in the city, as he does very fine work in House Painting, Decorating, Paper Hanging and Fancy Ceiling Work, Etc., six experienced hands being employed. The shop occupied consists of one and one-half stories, containing two floors 18x30 feet in dimensions. This enterprising house is ready within short notice to execute any order which may be entrusted to them, and perfect satisfaction guaranteed. Mr. Sherman was born in Belfast, Me., and is a well-known citizen, being a member of the City Government; also a member of the Odd Fellows, Knights of Pythias, G. A. R. and Order of the Red Men.

Newman, Lara & Co., Dealers in Ice, Lewiston. Americans traveling abroad, and more particularly in England, find much to admire and much to condemn, but they are unanimous in declaring that their native country is beyond comparison with any other in one respect at least, and that is the general use of ice in warm weather. For instance, they say that in England such a thing as "ice water" as we understand it is practically unknown, excepting in such hotels and other public resorts as specially cater to American tastes, what the English call "ice water" being merely water that has been somewhat cooled by being kept in a refrigerator for a while. The use of ice over here is increasing rapidly, and, as our readers well know, Maine is the most important field of supply for this indispensable article. The enterprise of our citizens engaged in the ice business has greatly developed our resources in this direction, and the State is so far north that it is very exceptional to have what is known as a "short crop." Messrs. Newman, Lara & Co., of this city, are extremely well-known in connection with the handling of ice, and their many customers will be pleased to know that they are better than ever prepared to supply their rapidly increasing list of patrons at the present time. This concern began operations in 1872, and have since gained an enviable reputation for the uniform superiority of their service and the lowness of their rates. Mr. Oliver Newman was born in Carthage, Me., and has been a member of the Board of Aldermen of this city, while Mr. Lara is a native of Turner, Me., and has served in various important public positions, such as County Treasurer, Councilman and Alderman of the city of Auburn. Mr. E. L. Philoon, who has been in the employ of this firm for many years, was in 1887 admitted to partnership. He is a native of Livermore, where for years he held positions as Chairman of Selectmen and Superintendent of School Committee. He has also served his adopted city of Auburn on school boards. He is thoroughly acquainted with ice business in all its departments and is determined that his firm shall continue to merit the confidence of its patrons. Orders for ice left with Messrs. Peables & Garcelon, or Mr. A. K. P. Jordan, popular grocers of Auburn, receive prompt attention. The firm maintain an extensive ice-plant, including two storage houses of the dimensions of 100x160 and 30x60 feet respectively, having a capacity of about 4,500 tons. Employment is afforded to fifty men in winter and ten in summer, and as prompt attention is given to all complaints of poor service, etc. customers are assured a regular and abundant supply of ice.

Blake, Spear & Co., Dealers in Groceries and Provisions, Main Street, Lewiston. Among the many establishments located in Lewiston and devoted to the sale of Groceries and Provisions, we do not know of any that offer more genuine advantages to its customers than that carried on by Messrs. Blake, Spear & Co., of Main Street. This enterprise was inaugurated by the above-named gentlemen, and its development has been in accordance with its merits, the business now done being sufficiently large to call for the employment of competent and experienced assistants. The members of the firm are very well known in this vicinity. The premises occupied are commodious, and contain an extensive assortment of Groceries, Provisions, etc., that give ample evidence of having been carefully selected by competent hands. Appealing especially to Family Trade, Messrs. Blake, Spear & Co. pay particular attention to handling goods of such a character as to be especially adapted to household use, and sell nothing that they believe to be unworthy of trial. While placing their prices at the lowest possible figures, they do not lose sight of the fact that the best class of patrons prefer quality to quantity, and so take pains to furnish only reliable articles. Prompt and polite attention to customers is insisted upon at this store, and orders are quickly and accurately delivered.

Mrs. J. T. Lemont, Fine Millinery, Corsets, Etc., 117 Lisbon Street, Lewiston. As there is no portion of the costume more conspicuous, so there is none that exerts a greater influence over the entire appearance than does the hat or bonnet which may be worn, and every lady should use care in selecting this part of her apparel, for in no other is a proper individuality more pleasing and effective. In order to learn what is best suited to one's personal needs there is no other way equal to visiting an establishment where a complete variety of the latest fashionable productions in the millinery line are kept in stock, and there inspecting the different shapes and combinations. It is important of course to know that the styles on exhibition are such as are worn in the best society, and the only way to make "assurance doubly sure" on this point is to patronize a house of leading reputation, and there is no similar establishment of which this may be more truly said than that conducted by Mrs. J. T. Lemont, at No. 117 Lisbon Street. This enterprise had its inception in 1867, and has long been held in the highest estimation by the ladies of Lewiston and vicinity, for they have found that the goods supplied are always reliable and first-class, while the prices are uniformly reasonable. One floor, measuring 55x25 feet, is occupied, and Fine Millinery of all descriptions is kept constantly on hand. Both Trimmed and Untrimmed Hats and Bonnets are handled, and Custom Work is done at short notice in the most tasteful and artistic manner. A very full line of Corsets, Bustles, etc., is carried, including Warner's, Ferris's and Geo. Frost's goods, and no greater inducements are attainable elsewhere than are offered here in this special department.

T. F. Callahan & Co., Manufacturers of and dealer in Trunks and Traveling Bags, 286 Lisbon Street, Lewiston. None but experienced travelers appreciate the importance of having a trunk that can be depended upon to preserve its contents intact, for none but such people have had an opportunity to realize how little protection the ordinary cheap trunk affords. The best, surest and most economical way to purchase a good article of this kind is to buy of the manufacturer direct, and if you want the neatest, strongest, most durable and most convenient trunk that is to be had, you can do no better than to place your order with Messrs. T. F. Callahan & Co., doing business at No. 286 Lisbon Street. This firm is made up of Messrs. T. F. and E. A. Callahan, both of whom are natives of this city and prominent citizens, Mr. T. F. Callahan having served in both branches of the City Council, and now occupying the position of Water Commissioner. The premises utilized are of the dimensions of 75x30 feet, and Trunks, Traveling Bags, Shawl Straps, Trunk Straps, Etc., are manufactured and sold both at Wholesale and Retail. Trunks of all kinds will be made to order or repaired at short notice, and at prices that cannot fail to please. An extensive stock of Hats, Caps, Umbrellas, and Gentlemen's Furnishing Goods in general, is also carried, and all the fashionable novelties in Head-wear, Collars, Neckties, Scarfs, Etc., are obtained at the earliest possible moment and offered for sale at bottom prices. This is a representative establishment, and well deserves the pronounced success it has won.

H. B. Wardwell, Dealer in Fine Art Goods, Picture Frames, Engravings, Oil Paintings, Artists' Supplies, Stationery, etc., 29 Lisbon Street, Lewiston. An establishment which no art-lover can afford to remain in ignorance of is that conducted by Mr. H. B. Wardwell at No. 29 Lisbon Street, and we can promise such as have not already visited it a rare treat, for a most magnificent display of Fine Art Goods is there made, and it is so tastefully and artistically arranged as to greatly add to the effect of the articles exhibited. Mr. Wardwell, who conducted a similar enterprise at Auburn for some years opened his present store in 1887, and has rapidly built up a large patronage as the inducements he has to offer are many and decided, and so large and varied a stock is carried that all tastes may be suited. The premises utilized are of the dimensions of 70x40 feet, and employment is afforded to four competent assistants. Oil Paintings, Engravings, Etchings, Statuary, Artists' Materials, Stationery, etc., are supplied at surprisingly low prices, and it is clearly evident that Mr. Wardwell must have a most intimate acquaintance with every detail of his business to enable him to conduct operations on so liberal a basis. Picture Framing is made a specialty, and all kinds of frames will be made to order from the plainest to the most elaborate. Mr. Wardwell is a member of the Odd Fellows, and has gained many friends in and about Lewiston. He is courteous and obliging and fully deserves his growing popularity.

Bubier & Mason, House and Carriage Painters and Paper Hangers, 82 Bates Street, Lewiston. Other things being equal, it is always more economical to have a thing done skillfully than unskillfully, and if this simple truth were more generally borne in mind, much vexation and not a little money would be saved. It is a popular belief that anybody can paint a house, and so they can — after a fashion. But to paint a house properly requires skill and experience, and although the first cost of having the work done in the best manner may be greater, the superior durability of it will more than make up for the difference, to say nothing of the gain made in appearance. Messrs. Bubier & Mason have won a high reputation for the excellence of their work since beginning operations in 1886, and we have no hesitation in heartily commending them to such of our readers as may wish anything done in the way of House or Carriage Painting. The firm is made up of Messrs. E. Mason and J. D. Bubier, both of whom are natives of Maine and thoroughly acquainted with every detail of their business. One floor, of the dimensions of 30x45 feet, is occupied at No. 82 Bates Street, and employment is given to four competent assistants. Orders will be given immediate attention, and satisfaction is confidently guaranteed.

Geo. A. Callahan, Steam Job Printer, 21 Lisbon Street, Lewiston. This may be called the "age of printer's ink" for the virtues of this magic fluid (which by the way isn't a fluid at all, but more properly a paste) are now universally recognized, and the man who wishes to buy at low rates makes equally free use of it with the man who wishes to sell at a profit. One of the chief principles of success in business is — "Procure a good article and then let the public know of it", for the world is too wide to allow every man to know his neighbors' business, and therefore it is not to be expected that a large trade can be built up unless measures are taken to see that the community at large are informed as to the inducements offered. Modern job printing has become an art, and the day when any amateur with a handpress and an unlimited supply of self-confidence could successfully compete for work of this kind has gone by, for the public has been educated up to a point where the crude productions of such would-be printers are rejected with contempt. It requires both experience and large facilities to carry on a job printing establishment nowadays, and both of these have had their influence in building up the large patronage enjoyed by Mr. Geo. A. Callahan, who is engaged in carrying on an enterprise of this kind at No. 21 Lisbon Street. This gentleman is a native of Lewiston, and began operations over a quarter of a century ago, having founded his business in 1862. He is a very well known and highly esteemed citizen and a member of the school committee. One floor measuring 85x35 feet is utilized, and three large presses operated, a four-horse engine furnishing the motive power. Both book and job printing are done in the very best style, and the resources of the establishment permit the assurance that only short notice is required for the furnishing of work in any desired quantity while the rates charged are low and equitable.

D. P. Field & Co., Dealers in Ice, Offices at 40 Hammond Street, P. C. Tarbox & Co.'s, Wm. Cloutier & Co.'s, C. H. Graffam's, A. L. & E. F. Goss', and E. H. Kimball's Coal Office, Lewiston; Stevens & Lord's, Knight & Chase's, A. M. Penley's, and A. B. Craft's, Auburn. "Keep cool" is excellent advice at all times and particularly so in summer when old Sol threatens to burn us all up. But, like most good advice, this injunction is much easier to give than to follow, and hence anything tending to make it less difficult must be held to be in the nature of a public benefit. In this connection let us call attention to the enterprise inaugurated by Messrs. D. P. Field & Co. in 1886, for these gentlemen are dealers in Ice, and are prepared to do their best toward keeping the whole community cool at the lowest market rates. Although only beginning, as we have said, in 1886, they have already built up a large trade, and this is not at all surprising to those who are conversant with the business methods they pursue. The facilities for leaving orders are numerous and wide-spread, there being offices established at Messrs. P. C. Tarbox & Co.'s, Wm. Cloutier & Co.'s, C. H. Graffam's, A. L. & E. F. Goss', and E. H. Kimball's coal office, Lewiston, and Stevens & Lord's, Knight & Chase's, and A. B. Craft's, Auburn. The firm is constituted of Messrs. D. P. Field, Hillman Smith and L. G. Lord, who reside in Auburn, although their business is largely done in Lewiston, their principal office being on Hammond Street. The gentlemen of the firm are well known to most of the citizens of our two cities. They are all members of the G. A. R., having cheerfully responded to their country's call for help in her hour of danger during the late rebellion, Mr. Field as a member of the 29th Maine Reg't, Mr. Lord as a member of the 12th Maine Reg't, and Mr. Smith as a member of the 8th Maine Reg't. Mr. Field, the senior member, has been especially honored by his townsmen, having been a member of the City Council of Auburn, and subsequently with the Board of Aldermen, and now being Representative to the Legislature. Messrs. Lord and Smith, the other two members of the firm, are old residents and quite well known, Mr. Lord being for many years a member of the wellknown firm of Stevens & Lord, blacksmiths, Auburn. Mr. Smith is the ex-Sheriff of our county, having filled the office for six consecutive years. Storage capacity of the amount of five thousand tons is had, and Androscoggin River Ice is handled at wholesale and retail.

LEADING BUSINESS MEN OF LEWISTON.

H. P. Dorman & Co., Dealers in Coal and Wood, office Cedar Street, near Lincoln, Lewiston. Among the minor evils and inconveniences which at times combine to make the householders lot far from being a happy one may be mentioned that of not receiving goods when they were promised, for it requires but experience to realize that the failure of dealers to keep their agreements in this respect may cause considerable bother and annoyance to say the least. Especially is this true as regards such bulky articles as coal and wood, for special preparations have generally to be made for their reception, and therefore we feel that we are doing our readers a service by directing their attention to an establishment where these commodities are not only supplied at the lowest market rates but where all promises made are strictly adhered to. We have reference to that conducted by Messrs. H. P. Dorman & Co., and are sure that practical trial of the advantages offered by this house will bear us out in all that we have said in its favor. Business was begun in 1878 by the existing firm which is made up of Messrs. H. P. Dorman and S. T. Woodward, the former a native of Bridgton and the latter of Bath. The premises utilized are sufficiently spacious to provide storage facilities for thirty-five hundred tons of coal and about one thousand cords of wood, and being situated on the line of the railway the expenses of handling are reduced to a minimum, thus allowing goods to be retailed at very low rates. The office is located on Cedar Street, near Lincoln, and orders will be given prompt attention.

Lincoln House, L. C. Dunham and C. F. Andrews, proprietors, Lewiston. One often hears the question asked, on the cars and elsewhere, "I am going to (such a place), where would you advise me to put up?" Now, such an inquiry is a very natural one to make, if a man has no previous acquaintance with the city or town which he proposes to visit, and as many come to Lewiston daily, for the first time, we wish to say right here, that if a hotel is sought that shall be complete in its appointments, convenient in its location and liberal in its management, we know of none better than the Lincoln House, conducted by Messrs. Dunham & Andrews. Under the name of "Lincoln Block," this was carried on as a boarding house up to 1886, when after extensive and thorough overhauling, repairing and renovation, the present name was adopted. The premises in use comprise five floors of the dimensions of 100x50 feet, there being one hundred guest rooms, which are conveniently arranged and very comfortably furnished. The table is supplied with excellent food, skillfully and carefully cooked, while the service is both courteous and prompt. Both the proprietors are very well-known gentlemen, and are also proprietors of the popular Elm House, Auburn, Mr. Dunham being a member of the Board of Aldermen. He is a native of Leeds, while Mr. Andrews was born in Greene. The terms are very reasonable, board being but one dollar per day, and a first-class livery stable is connected with the establishment, at which stylish and speedy teams may be obtained at low rates.

W. A. Libby, Contracting Mason, 26 Pine Street, Lewiston. Ordinary justice requires that in making mention of the leading business men of this section the name of Mr. W. A. Libby should not be omitted, for this gentleman is one of the most widely known of our citizens, and has established a reputation for probity and strict fulfillment of agreements that of itself would cause him to be worthy of a place in our pages. He is a native of Wales, Maine, and began operations here in the firm of W. A. Libby & Co., becoming sole proprietor of the enterprise in 1885. He is a member of the Free Masons, and it is most fitting that he should be, for he is one of the foremost contracting masons of this State, and is prepared to undertake operations of the greatest magnitude, and give satisfactory sureties as to responsibility, good faith, etc. But those who are familiar with his work in the past would not be apt to ask for such bonds excepting as a mere matter of form, for the reputation we have already alluded to is widely known in the community and the most utter stranger would have but little difficulty in soon arriving at a satisfactory conclusion as regards Mr. Libby's standing. He employs an average number of thirty assistants and occupies a spacious office at No. 26 Pine Street, where he may be seen by those desiring anything in his line.

George R. Page, Fine Millinery, 27 Lisbon Street, Lewiston. When Mr. George R. Page began business in Auburn twenty years or more ago, it is probable that he had not the slightest idea that at the present time he would conduct what is in all respects the leading establishment of its kind in Lewiston, but such has been the outcome of the unremitting efforts he has made to serve the public in the best manner possible, and it gives us pleasure to record success so worthily bestowed. "Smartness" and deceit may make a good showing for a time but in the long run genuine merit and honorable business methods afford the surest pathways to success, and the experience of Mr. Page is but further confirmation of this truth. He is a native of Winthrop, Maine, and is one of the best known of our merchants. The premises in use are of the dimensions of 75x35 feet, and are none too large to properly accommodate the heavy and varied stock carried which includes Millinery and Fancy Goods of every description, and which for "cleanness and general desirability is worthy of careful study and admiration. Employment is given to seven assistants, and the utmost willingness is exhibited in the showing of goods as Mr. Page invites all to inspect his stock and is anxious to facilitate such inspection by every means in his power. Low prices combined with first-class attractions are hard to resist, so that the heavy business done is only what is to be expected. The Custom Millinery department is one of the best equipped in the State, and those employed therein rank with the highest as regards taste and skill. Buying of the leading jobbing houses and manufacturers, Mr. Page's connection in New York and Boston markets together with the fact that all bills are discounted in ten days, customers are enabled to obtain the very latest and most desirable goods at the lowest possible prices.

LEADING BUSINESS MEN OF LEWISTON.

John Garner, Dealer in Fancy Groceries, Patent Medicines, Meats and Provisions, Passenger and Exchange Agent, 213 Park Street, Lewiston. This well-established Grocery and Provision House has a wide reputation for the fine stock of Staple and Fancy Groceries always to be found here. This house was established by its present proprietor in 1864, and for the past quarter of a century has enjoyed a large and lucrative wholesale and retail trade, extending among many of our leading families. The premises occupied for the business are located at No. 213 Park Street, and consist of one floor and basement each 95x18 feet in size, where a very fine and attractive stock of Groceries and Provisions is carried, including fine Teas, Coffees, Spices, the best brands of Flour, and Choice Meats and Provisions, also a full line of Patent Medicines. Mr. Garner is also the sole agent in this vicinity for the celebrated Fleischmann & Co's. Compressed Yeast, Agent for Hecker's Self-raising Flour, also Passenger and Exchange Agent. The steadily increasing trade of this house requires the services of five competent assistants, and the business is transacted in an energetic and enterprising manner. The store is finely arranged in all its departments, and the attention to customers is all that could be asked for,

these with the reliability of the proprietor tend to preserve a business so well conducted as this. Mr. John Garner is a native of England, and is one of Lewiston's most prominent citizens. He is one of the directors of the Peoples Savings Bank of Lewiston, and has been a member of the City Government four years as Alderman and Councilman. He is also the President of the Lewiston and Auburn Grocers Association and a Justice of the Peace. Mr. Garner also belongs to the Masons, Odd Fellows and Knights of Honor, and can honestly say that during the quarter of a century he has been in business he has paid dollar for dollar. If you intend visiting any part of the world, especially Europe, or sending for friends, or sending money to friends, buy your Passage Tickets and Drafts of John Garner.

Exchange Hotel, R. Young, proprietor, Lewiston. A hotel run expressly for the accommodation of business men should be spoken of in a businesslike manner, and we shall endeavor in this brief sketch of the public house, whose name leads this article, to state facts in a succinct and comprehensive manner, worthy of the careful attention of those for whose perusal it is specially intended. The Exchange Hotel is one of the oldest-established institutions of the kind in this vicinity, and under its present management it bids fair to attain a popularity beyond any it has ever known. The reason of this is not hard to guess, for since Mr. R. Young, who now owns it, assumed control, he has studied to please his patrons and to gain a reputation for his house that would assure it continued prosperity. He has succeeded in both these endeavors, and we can and do heartily advise those whom business or pleasure calls to this locality to make the Exchange Hotel their headquarters for the following reasons: 1, It is centrally located, being near to all stores and depots. 2, The accommodations are strictly first-class, the building being four stories in height, and 75x100 feet in dimension, and fifteen efficient assistants employed, enabling the wants of guests to be promptly and satisfactorily attended to at all times. 3, The terms are very reasonable, being but $2.00 per day, and very liberal arrangements are made with regular boarders. 4, The table is supplied with an abundance of nutritious and well-cooked food, which is promptly and neatly served. These four reasons might be greatly added to, but enough has been said to indicate what treatment the traveler receives here and to furnish cause to give this hotel the preference. Mr. Young is a native of Corinna, Me., and a member of the Knights of Pythias. He has hosts of friends, and will continually add to them as long as he adheres to his present liberal business methods. The facilities enjoyed by this hotel to cater to its guests are unsurpassed. This hotel is owned by its landlord, Mr. Young, who pays cash for everything required in running the house, thereby securing the best at the lowest possible price, which goes to the benefit of the guests in the reasonable rates charged them for *first-class* accommodations. Everything is systematized about this hotel, as one will readily see by taking a look about the house. In the basement, partitioned off, one notices almost a complete grocery. In another apartment a Fish and Meat shop, and in another apartment neatly packed, is a year's supply of kindling wood, shavings, charcoal, etc. In the kitchen, neatness and order prevail. A finely-equipped laundry is also a prominent feature of this finely conducted hostelry.

The Lewiston Commercial School, 149 Lisbon Street, Geo. E. Graham, Principal. It is but rarely that we have occasion to mention an enterprise that seems to us to be of such vital importance as is such an institution as the Lewiston Commercial School, of which Mr. Geo. E. Graham is the principal, and when we do, we can but regret the small space which the stern necessity of keeping this book within reasonable bounds limits us to. When we use the term "vital importance," we do so with a full realization of its meaning, for in the course of a somewhat extended and varied experience in all parts of this country with business men and business methods, we have come to have an appreciation of the priceless value the training given the conscientious student in so exceptionably well-equipped and managed an institution is to him. The Lewiston Commercial School is under the direction of George E. Graham, its talented principal. This gentleman brings to his chosen profession that mingled enthusiasm characteristic of the true teacher. This School is designed to qualify young ladies and gentlemen for business in a short time and at little expense. The instruction given is strictly individual, there being no classes whatever. By this system pupils of any grade may enter at any time. The school will be open every day and evening excepting Saturdays, thereby giving those who are employed during the day, an opportunity to acquire a business education without interfering with their daily occupations, as precisely the same studies are pursued evenings as are taken during the day sessions. The Business Course includes the following studies: Book keeping, Penmanship, Business Correspondence, Commercial Law, and the Solving of Arithmetical Problems by the Shortest and Most Practical Methods. Those who desire a thorough preparation for business can get it here in as short a time as possible, and at a very moderate expense. Terms: Day Sessions.—Full Business Course (six months), $25.00. Full Business Course (three months), $15.00. Evening Sessions.—Full Business Course (six months), $15.00. Full Business Course (three months), $7.50. Wedding, Address, and Visiting Cards and Penmanship of every description promptly executed at the schoolrooms. A specialty is made of teaching Penmanship exclusive of the business course. Day or Evening,—12 Lessons, $2.00. Hours, 9 to 12 A.M.; 2 to 5 and 7 to 9.30 P.M. The above prices include all stationery free of charge, and every effort is made to advance the pupils as fast as their abilities will permit.

A. S. Wright, 50 Lisbon Street, Lewiston. Dealer in Jewelry, Watches, Clock, Silver Ware. There are no Jewelry stores in this portion of the State that are better known than that carried on by Mr. A. S. Wright, at No. 50 Lisbon Street, and it goes without saying that this establishment is as favorably as it is widely known, for otherwise no such immense patronage would be enjoyed as is now the case. Mr. Wright is a native of Lawrence, Mass., and inaugurated the enterprise in question in 1883. The premises occupied are 65x30 feet in dimensions and contain a really magnificent stock of Watches, Jewelry, Silver-Ware, Clocks, etc., which is made up entirely of trustworthy goods and which is offered at the lowest market rates that can be quoted on standard articles of equal value. Employment is given to two courteous and efficient assistants and every caller is assured prompt attention and strictly honorable treatment. Repairing both of Watches and Jewelry is given special attention, and owners of fine chronometers may leave their timepieces here with the full assurance that they will be handled in a skillful manner and put into the best possible condition. All the standard makes of watches are sold, and bargains may be had either in the purchase of a cheap movement or in the most elaborate productions of the watchmaker's art. Clocks of many kinds are also extensively dealt in, and solid and plated silver ware is sold at the lowest market rates.

The DeWitt, H. A. Brick, proprietor, corner of Park and Pine Streets. It is much easier to describe an ideal hotel on paper than it is to realize that ideal in practical life, and indeed it is evident that even if a house were conducted in a manner perfectly satisfactory to one man, it would fall short in many respects of what was wanted by the remaining ninety-nine in the hundred. "Many men of many minds" are what the hotel keeper has to provide for, and it is but rarely that one meets with the success attained by Mr. H. A. Brick in his management of the DeWitt House. This popular hostelry is one of the oldest in this section of the State, having been originally founded close on to half a century ago. After various vicissitudes it passed into the hands of Messrs. Quinby & Murch in 1878, and in 1886, the present proprietor assumed possession. He is a native of Augusta and a member of the Knights of Pythias, and is one of the best-known of our Maine hotel men, being the Vice-president of the State Association as well as Vice president of the National Hotel Men's Association. We may say in passing, that the associations alluded too are of great value to the traveling public as well as to hotel proprietors and managers, as their chief aim is to improve the efficiency and reduce the needless expenses of hotel-keeping throughout the country. The DeWitt House comprises four floors, measuring 75x80 feet, and contains one hundred and twenty-five guest-rooms as well as a finely-equipped billiard hall, barber shop, etc. All modern conveniences and comforts are furnished to patrons, and we must make special mention of the table, as the most luxurious accommodations will fail to give satisfaction unless the "inner man" is properly looked out for, and we can assure our readers that more than one so-called "Metropolitan" establishment, located in Boston or New York, would have to lower its colors to the DeWitt in this respect. Employment is afforded to forty assistants, and the machinery incidental to the successful working of so elaborate an enterprise runs with that smoothness so grateful to those disliking the bustle always found in less ably managed houses. The terms are reasonable, and special rates are made by the week or month.

LEADING BUSINESS MEN OF LEWISTON.

Avon Mill, Quilts, Duck, Towels, etc., Lincoln Street, Lewiston. The old-fashioned quilt, made up of from hundreds to thousands of pieces and sometimes bearing designs which of themselves were enough to drive sleep from the pillow is rapidly becoming a thing of the past, and although the recent craze for patchwork resulted in many more monstrosities being put together, still this has already died out and the great factories are more than ever relied upon to supply the demand for quilts. The Avon Mill, located on Lincoln Street, in this city, produces an article in this line which meets with a large and ready sale as will be seen when we state that the annual output amounts to about one hundred and fifty thousand quilts, and this is all the more worthy of notice as the Mill only begun operations in 1882, and hence has by no means reached the full limit of its development. Light and heavy Duck are also manufactured very extensively three hundred and fifty thousand yards being made yearly, and Plain and Fancy Towels to the amount of eighteen thousand per week are produced in great variety. The buildings utilized comprise a Mill measuring 50x100 feet, a Bleachery of the dimensions of 24x50 feet. and a Dye-house 67x32 feet in size. Forty-four looms are in operation and a 135 horse-power water-wheel is required to furnish motive power. The company carrying on this important enterprise was organized some six years ago with a capital of $100,000, and is made up of residents of Lewiston and vicinity. The President, Mr. C. I. Barker, the Secretary and Treasurer, Mr. F. H. Packard, and the Agent, Mr. A. D. Barker, are all natives of this city. The company's interests are in good hands, it will be seen, and its future is apparently assured.

John B. Littlefield, Gunsmith, and dealer in Sporting Goods, Fishing and Shooting Tackle, 14 Main Street. Under the operation of the present game laws, Maine is coming more and more into prominence as a "sportsmen's paradise," and we are convinced that if the wise restrictions now placed upon the killing and capture of game are only faithfully adhered to, and all infractions of them surely punished, this state of affairs will not only continue, but in the near future some of the noble sport of days gone by can be had again. It only needs the co-operation of the people to make this result sure, and it seems to us as if the material advantages consequent upon attracting many strangers to the State during every "open season" must be apparent to all. Mr. John B. Littlefield, who succeeded Mr. C. F. Nason at No. 14 Main Street, is evidently determined to give such sportsmen from Boston and other large cities, as may give him a call, a favorable opinion of the goods supplied in Lewiston, for he carries a stock of Guns, Sporting Goods, Fishing Tackle, Bicycles, Etc., that would not disgrace a much more pretentious establishment, and what is more, he quotes prices on this assortment that cause many a visitor to open his eyes and wonder why he bought his outfit before leaving home. Mr. Littlefield is a native of Waterville, Me., and succeeded Mr. Nason in 1887, the latter gentleman having founded the business in 1852. One floor is occupied measuring 35x20 feet, and one assistant employed, repairing of all kinds being promptly and neatly executed and the manufacture of Nason's Patent Net Rings carried on. We advise sportsmen to give Mr. Littlefield a call, for he knows their wants and seeks to gratify them in a satisfactory manner. Mr. Littlefield is agent for the New Mail & Ival Safety Bicycles. He also deals in *all* kinds of New and Second Hand Bicycles, Buys, sells and exchanges.

J. N. Wood, 64 Middle Street, Lewiston. Dealer in Coal and Wood. Mr. J. N. Wood is the veteran Coal and Wood dealer of Lewiston. He commenced business twenty-three years ago. The coal consumed in Lewiston then was nothing when compared with the consumption at the present day. The sales were then meager, very few of the people at that time dared to leave the old black log for the black diamond— only about seventy tons of coal was sold the first season and that only by persistent push. Mr. Wood continued the business alone for a short time then joined partnership with Mr. Isaac Golder, and the firm thus continued until the death of Mr. Golder in 1875—during the eight years that Wood & Golder were in company they did a very prosperous business. They did not confine their sales to Coal and Wood but handled Lumber of all kinds and had quite an extensive trade in Hay. The "Grasshopper year", so called, was a lively one in the Hay market and Mr. Wood foresaw the inevitable and purchased all the standing grass possible. Hay that year sold in Lewiston at $40 per ton, and Wood and Golder had none to much to meet the demand. Since the decease of Mr. Golder Mr. Wood has continued the Wood and Coal business but has had little to do with Lumber and Hay. It is surprising to note the difference in the amount of Coal consumed in Lewiston today as compared with twenty-three years ago. By strict integrity, courteous demeanor and endeavoring by every possible means to meet the demands of his customers Mr. Wood has built up a business of gigantic proportions. Coal at the present writing is selling at $7.50 per ton, which is only fifty cents per ton above Portland prices. The highest that Coal has been sold in the city during the time that Mr. Wood has been in business was $16 per ton for Anthracite and $40 for Bituminous. The facilities for discharging and reloading Coal from Mr. Wood's yard are almost marvelous. He has sheds so located that a car of Coal can be unloaded in five minutes. The Coal is deposited in pockets from which it can be reloaded for delivery at very small expense. Mr. Wood uses a motor, power being furnished from the city water works. He has a splitter manufactured by Hildreth Bros., of Harvard, Mass., and with one man at the saw and two men at the splitter ten cords of Wood can be manufactured for the stove per day. Mr. Wood usually prepares his wood while it is yet green, piles it under cover during the early spring months, and in the autumn he has seasoned wood for delivery which cannot fail to please the most fastidious. He buys nothing but first-class coal and is always ready to guarantee sales as pertains to quality and quantity. Mr. Wood has one office in Auburn at the store of J. Dingley, on Main Street. In Lewiston he has an office at 170 Lisbon Street, and Wakefield Bros. Drug store. His yard and main office is at 64 Middle Street, near the upper Maine Central Depot. These offices are all connected by telephone, and all orders are sure to receive prompt attention. A few years since Mr. Wood erected buildings for storage purposes at the Maine Central upper station where he has the best of facilities for the storage of Flour and General Merchandise. Mr. Wood has traveled extensively and is well known. He is a very genial, public spirited man, always openly advocating enterprise for the public good, and as ready to denounce the shams of the present day. Be sure and call on him when in want of fuel of any kind and you will be so well treated that you will be more than willing to patronize him thereafter.

People's Savings Bank, Incorporated February 12, 1875. A "People's Savings Bank" that is true to its name, is what the most enlightened and prosperous community will welcome and what the most improvident and careless people cannot afford to be without. Many a man of middle age bitterly regrets that the saving habit he has been forced to form by the pressure of circumstances was not inaugurated by him of free choice when youth and freedom from responsibility combined to make life pleasant, so that now as family cares increase and occasional aches and pains remind him that he is not the man he once was, he would not have to fear that the grim specter of abject poverty would seize upon his family if he should be stricken down for a month or even a year. Moralizing is apt to be profitless work, and we are aware that it is especially so in these pages, but it is impossible for any thinking man to have the subject of Savings Banks brought before him without as a natural consequence being reminded of the bitter woe a proper use of these institutions might avert. No man worthy of the name wants to be dependent himself and much less does he want to have his loved ones dependent upon strangers for support and as long as present opportunities exist in this country, as long as health, strength and skill last no man should excuse himself from doing what even the "beasts that perish" have sense enough to do — provide in time of plenty for coming seasons of dearth and famine. No one can say "I know not whom to trust." The People's Savings Bank of this city has been in operation since 1875, it has time and time again vindicated the confidence placed in it, and a dollar confided to its custody is much safer than it would be in its owner's pocket. "Money breeds money" is a homely but expressive saying and it has one cardinal merit—it is strictly true. The first thousand dollars are always the hardest to save and no one need feel discouraged at the slowness with which this sum accumulates. Persevere and success is sure. The people now have deposits amounting to nearly $800,000 in this bank and are adding to them every month. The surplus is nearly $25,000. The President Mr. C. I. Barker, and Treasurer Mr. E. C. Wellman, are emphatically the right men in the right place, and with the Board of Trustees consisting of Messrs. C. I. Barker, A. B. Nealey, S. A. Cummings, John Garver, H. W. Maxwell, W. M. Chamberlin, A. R. Savage and D. B. Sawyer, may be depended upon to run the People's Bank in the interests of its namesakes. The institution deserves hearty encouragement and we are glad to see that it is receiving it.

Continental Mills, Manufacturers of Sheetings, etc., foot of Chestnut Street, Lewiston. As every well-informed person knows, it is principally on account of the enterprise of her people as manifested in manufacturing operations that New England has been able to retain her prominent position among the other sections of the Union, for the advantages denied to her by the comparative sterility of the soil have had to be compensated for by vigor and confidence in developing the resources found in her swift-running streams and thus enabling mighty factories to be run by purely natural forces. One of the most extensive and most elaborately designed of these manufacturing plants is that utilized at the "Continental Mills," located at the foot of Chestnut Street in Lewiston, and this enterprise is as well known as it is great in magnitude, for since its inauguration in 1864 its productions have found their way to nearly every quarter of the globe, and have established for themselves a reputation for even merit and desirability that has resulted in an immense and constant demand for them. To supply this call 1500 looms and 70,000 spindles are run and 1250 hands employed, 12 large buildings occupied and water-power equal to that of 1400 horses utilized. It goes without saying that the management of so colossal an industry calls for talents of a high order especially in these days of strict competition, and it is also evident that the Continental Mills must have been in good hands as otherwise they never could have attained their present position. The Treasurer is Mr. Geo. E. Towne of Boston, while Mr. R. C. Pennell is the Clerk and Paymaster, and Mr. E. S. Davis the Agent, the Directors being Messrs. Nathan Cushing, C. H. Wood, George E. Towne, L. Nichols, William J. Roteh, Nathaniel Thayer and John N. Graham. The Auditors are Messrs. A. M. Newton and H. C. Little.

H. B. Skinner & Co., Manufacturers of Bobbins, Spools and Skewers, also Dealer in Wood of all Kinds, Lewiston. Orders by Mail Promptly Attended to. Modern manufacturing enterprises are so dependent upon one another that prosperity and adversity are, as a general rule, experienced by practically all of them at the same time and as a consequence "hard times" in one branch of industry are soon felt in others that at first thought would seem to have no connection whatever with that originally affected. And, on the other hand, an important and prosperous line of manufacture like that devoted to the production of cotton and woolen goods, gives rise to numerous enterprises of less magnitude in supplying its requirements. For instance take the manufacture of Bobbins, these articles are of course indispensable to every mill engaged in the production of cotton or woolen goods and they are used in such enormous quantities that no small facilities will suffice those engaged in supplying the same. Probably one of the best equipped bobbin factories in this State is that conducted by H. B. Skinner & Co., at Nos. 2 and 4 Cross Canal, where two floors are occupied of the dimensions of 100x20 feet and all the necessary machinery is run by water-power. This enterprise was inaugurated over thirty years ago by a Mr. Drew, later by a Mr. Gilmer, twelve years ago by Messrs. L. E. Brown & Co., of which Mr. Skinner was the Co., and since passing into the possession of the present proprietors, H. B. Skinner and A. E. Madison, it has been greatly developed and extended. Bobbins, Spools and Skewers are very largely manufactured, employment being given to fifteen assistants and many wholesale dealers supplied. In addition to above three teams are used in their extensive Wood Business, this is sawed to order any length desired. Orders are promptly filled and the very lowest market rates prevail.

Calvert & Waldron, Publishers of the Lewiston and Auburn Daily and Weekly Gazette, Book and Job Printing, Waldron's Block, Lower Main Street, Lewiston. Messrs. Calvert and Waldron certainly require no introduction to many of our readers, for as the publishers of the "Gazette" their names have become familiar to the 3500 subscribers of the Weekly, and the 1800 subscribers of the Daily paper, and as it is estimated that there are on the average five readers to every copy issued it will be seen that about 26,000 at least must know of this well-established firm. But it is not so much the fact of their publishing the "Gazette" that we wish to call attention to as it is the superior facilities they have at hand for the doing of job printing of every description, for their work in connection with the paper mentioned speaks for itself, while there are many non-subscribers who frequently have occasion for good printing at fair prices, and who would best serve their own interests by patronizing the "Gazette" printing establishment. The business conducted by these gentlemen was inaugurated in 1872 by the late Col. W. G. Waldron, well-known as one of the good old war-horses of New England journalism, and the present firm-name was adopted in 1880. Mr. Thomas E. Calvert was born in England, Mr. Chas. W. Waldron being a native of Auburn. The premises utilized cover two floors of the dimensions of 60x50 feet, and three steam presses including a Campbell cylinder, enable the firm to fill all orders at the shortest possible notice. Employment is afforded to twelve assistants, and some of the best specimens of Book and Job Printing over seen in this city are turned out here in the ordinary course of business.

Hotel Rockingham, Lewiston, A. F. Irish Proprietor, R. C. Harmon Clerk. It is of course evident that no information can be of more interest to the majority of strangers visiting a community for pleasure or profit than that relating to the character of the hotels to be found there. What people want to know first of all is, where can I find a quiet home-like hotel, where guests are made to feel at home, and where comfort and convenience are carefully studied, at moderate expense and receive acceptable accommodations. The question is a natural one, and when asked in connection with Lewiston, the answer is easy to give. The Hotel Rockingham is a new house, each room being connected with the office by electric bells and speaking tubes, lighted by gas throughout and heated by steam; being seven miles drive to Poland Springs, three miles to Lake Grove, Horse Cars running to the foot of the Lake thence by steamer across the Lake to the Lake Auburn Hotel, also one mile to Auburn Crystal Springs. It has become a favorite with the "knowing ones." Its proprietor A. F. Irish, and the clerk, Mr. R. C. Harmon, are well known throughout the community. The Hotel Rockingham contains spacious and convenient rooms, and employment is given only to efficient assistants, and guests are waited upon with courtesy and promptness. The table and service of this house are all that one could ask for. Free sample rooms. First-class in every respect. Newly furnished throughout, heated by steam, Billiard room. No pains will be spared to make guests comfortable at reasonable rates. Hack and Livery Stable connected with the hotel. The prices are very reasonable for first-class accommodations. We therefore advise all visitors to Lewiston undecided where to stop, to try the Hotel Rockingham, as the facilities at his command enable the proprietor to offer first-class accomodations, and it is accordingly only natural that this house should be largely patronized.

HISTORICAL SKETCH

—OF—

AUBURN.

SOME cities are remarkable for the enterprise and progressiveness which characterizes their citizens; some for the natural commercial advantages which bring prosperity, and still others for a charming situation in the midst of many beautiful scenes of nature. Auburn is remarkable for all of these. The history of Auburn is of a quiet but suggestive type, marked by the features which have characterized the growth of the best towns and cities of New England. It was originally a part of a large section of the Pejepscot Purchase, which went under the name of Bakerstown and included present Auburn, Minot and Poland. The city as now composed has been a gradual assimilation of territory from other towns in the vicinity. Auburn village, the nucleus of all future growth, was first settled by Joseph Welch, in 1797. He erected a log hut near what is now Goff's Corner, and began to clear the ground. As other settlers came, they built around this clearing as a center. Mr. Doblmeyer put up the second house, which was a framed one, and he also built and ran a grist mill. The third settler in this vicinity was Solomon Wood. Near the present site of the Auburn depot, settlers had come a little earlier, among whom were Benj. True, Jabez, Levi and Daniel Merrill from Turner, and Jacob Stevens from New Gloucester. In 1791, Elias Merrill, of New Gloucester, bought up a large section of land here and took a prominent part in its settlement and cultivation.

One great feature of the early settlement of this region, was the bitter and prolonged litigation over land titles. In 1736, the General Legislature of Massachusetts had granted a large section of land to some officers and soldiers who had engaged in an expedition to Canada in 1690. These grants conflicted with the Prejepscot claims which went further, and the only result of long fighting was that the settling of the town was delayed many years. After the town had begun these, old disputes would arise like the ghost about the battle-field and caused many a scare, though perhaps not much damage. The action of the Massachusetts legislature was here very much at fault, as according to the best accounts they gave away, or sold, the same land three successive times. Undoubtedly, had it not been for this chaotic state of titles, Auburn would have been settled earlier, as this was one of the loveliest, healthiest and most fertile spots on the whole course of the Androscoggin. Col. Moses Little was one of the most prominent and influential men in the early affairs of Auburn, as he was of Lewiston. He was the agent of the settlers here, and owned much property himself, so he spent the most arduous endeavors in getting their rights and titles sustained, and induced many to settle, contributing a very marked share in the founding of the town. His two sons, Joseph and Edward, also did much to advance the town, the latter in particular, residing here and taking great and active interest in all local affairs. He was most influential in the establishment of the First Congregational Church and also the Lewiston Falls Academy, in 1835, of which he was an incorporator, and which afterward in honor of numerous benefactions was named for him.

From its late settlement, Auburn was not able to share in the honors or the toils of the Revolutionary War, and it was not until the effects of the war had been largely overpassed that it began to grow. Beside the Auburn village and depot settlement, there were two other village stations settled, which became a part of the latter town. One grew up about a mill erected by Jacob Mason, on the Little Androscoggin, in 1786. By 1789 there were seven families here, namely, the Small, Moody, Starbird, Bailey, Emerson, Coombs and Libby families. There were also four or five families settled at Young's Corner, on Wilson's Pond, now Lake Auburn. All these scattered settlements were gathered up into the town which was incorporated under the name of Poland, in 1798. In the following year the settlement began to show signs of rapid advance. Lots were surveyed and opened by Philip Bullen and Mr. Ballard. The town grew quite markedly up to the beginning of the nineteenth century.

In 1802, a part of the town which was rapidly progressing was set apart and incorporated under the name of Minot. This included all of primitive Auburn which was set apart when it was incorporated as a town. Among other very early settlers in this neighborhood, were James Perkins, Asaph Howard, John C. Crafts, Azee Kingsley. These, together with the families of James Parker, John Downing, Benj. Noyes, J. Nason, Mr. Bray and Mr. Verrill, built up a considerable settlement to the west of Wilson's Pond, which grew into the township of West Auburn. James Perkins, being a blacksmith and gunsmith, naturally took a prominent part in the affairs of this vicinity, as the services of such skilled mechanics were then very highly valued in all the pioneer settlements.

North Auburn, at the head of Lake Auburn, which has since gained a wide reputation as a summer resort, was first settled by Simson Caswell, in 1787, who came from Plymouth County, Mass. He built a mill, which greatly advanced the growth of the village now known as North Auburn. East Auburn, at the outlet of Wilson's Pond, about three miles from the falls, was first settled in 1797, by William Briggs, with a large family. Soon after, Benj. Pettengill, Joshua Taylor and Philip Peaslee, settled near by, and a mill erected by the first named, soon caused a considerable village to grow up in this part of the town.

One remarkable feature of the early history of Auburn, was the witch stories. These were rarer in Maine than in Massachusetts or New Hampshire. The wife of Johnny Merrill was supposed to be afflicted with this epidemic disease, but its effects do not seem to have been of a rare or peculiar order. Whenever Johnny did not do as Mrs. Merrill desired, trouble would ensue in the family log-cabin. A yoke of oxen which he sold to a neighbor once on a time, were found the next morning in that neighbor's barn dead on their backs. This, according to popular superstition, was Aunt Molly's work, feminine witches being supposed to care nothing for the strength of an ox when they had any purpose to fulfill. Another neighbor, Samuel Knox, borrowed a wagon of Johnny to drag home some grain in, but when he came to load it the trouble began. As fast as he put it in on one side it went out the other. Naturally, not understanding the law of gravity, he attributed it to Aunt Molly. These and other stories about Aunt Molly and other feminine disciples of Hecate went the rounds; but popular superstition did not go so far as in Massachusetts or the old counties, and happily no sanguinary results followed.

The early years of the nineteenth century were spent very quietly in the clearing of the ground and preparing for the farm, lands which have since been successfully developed. There were now no longer any French or Indians to trouble, so the good work went steadily on. At the time of the war of 1812 the town was yet too young to take any active part, but it shared in the privations and depressions which followed that financial mistake. An important domestic event occurred when Jacob Read opened the first store here in 1822 near Goff's Cor. He was the first trader here, and laid the foundation stone of the wide commercial business which has since cent'red in Auburn. The number of stores and traders kept constantly increasing, until at the time of the great fire of 1855 there were 25 business houses already established about Goff's Corner. Prominent in the early commercial history of Aub'rn was James Goff, who was an able merchant in the highest sense of the term, and whose financial and personal memory, of which he has left enduring testimonials, will long be cherished in this city of his adoption. The first hotel was opened here in 1822, by Jacob Reed, and long served as a way-inn on the stage route, one of the great features of life in this region before the establishment of the railroad.

In 1842, Auburn's separate career was begun, as it was then incorporated as a town, after long waiting and delays. The blessings of a magnificent situation and untiring energy now began to be most marked. In 1848, the opening of a railroad to Portland created a new financial epoch, and created a demand for the fine manufacturing facilities here enjoyed. Business continued steadily to expand and during the next decade assumed considerable proportions. The great fire of 1855 destroyed twenty-five or more buildings around Goff's corner, but as was experienced in other places, the people rose to the occasion and erected finer structures in every way than those that were burned. Though the loss could not immediately be recovered from, yet the great enterprise shown continued the advance of the town at a rapid pace. The following years, 1856–57, witnessed the erection here of the County Buildings, Court House and Jail at a cost of over $100,000. This fact reveals the

COUNTY COURT HOUSE AND JAIL.

position which Auburn had already taken in the county. In 1859 a part of the town of Danville was annexed to Auburn to meet the exigencies of the demand for land.

The civil war aroused all the energies, active and latent, in the town of Auburn. A most enthusiastic support was given to all measures in support of the government. Four hundred and twenty men were enlisted here, of which number only fifteen were drafted. Only once was a draft needed, and then only for a few hours. There were also seven Auburn volunteers in the navy. Thirteen men were killed in battle, and a very much larger number were lost by sickness or capture. The town paid large sums to the advance of the cause, $62,365 in bounties, and several thousand dollars for the support of soldiers and in private charities.

Among the talented and able officers who went from Auburn were Joseph S. Fillebrown who enlisted in and was made adjutant of the 1st regiment and was afterward lieut.-col. of the 10th; Chas. S. Emerson, a captain in the 1st, and afterward a lieut.-col. in the 29th; Lieut. Phineas Dill; H. L. K. Wiggins, surgeon; Jas. C. Felsom, 1st lieut. in 1st reg't; E. T. Luce, lieut.-col. in 23d, A. C. Pray, captain in 23d; Jos. Dingley, adj't of the 8th; Lieut. W. H. Chamberlain of the U. S. regulars; Lieut. Benj. M. Bradbury of the 10th; Granville Blake, captain in the 29th; Capt. Jos. Little of the 3d New Hampshire; Chas. B. Rounds, captain in 31st, and Rev. A. C. Adams, chaplain. This long and most honorable list of commissioned officers from Auburn, many of whom rose from the ranks, was complemented by the remarkable bravery and esprit shown by the uncommissioned soldiers, both of which render Auburn's soldiers' memories such as it may well be proud of, and has carefully preserved and commemorated.

The building of a bridge between Auburn and Lewiston, in 1823, was very beneficial to both, and opened up a great many advantages which contributed to its progress. The erection of the academy building, in 1835, was another evidence of the growth in size and refinement of the town. Mr. Edward Little gave nine acres, and considerable money to the academy, which was named soon after, "The Edward Little Institute."

At the close of the war Auburn continued its advance in all lines, and in 1868 had arrived at the dignity of a city charter, which was granted by the legislature. The people, however, seemed loth to give up their accustomed form of town government, and did not decide to accept this charter till the following year. Thomas Littlefield was chosen the first mayor in 1869. A police court was established the same year of which Nathaniel Finch was chosen judge. The city now contained all of the town of Danville, the remainder of which was annexed in 1867.

Since its incorporation as a city, Auburn has made marked advances in industrial, commercial and social lines, and has developed into a powerful and well-organized city. Its business interests have not been beyond the depressions which at times have swept over the country, but in the main have gone steadily forward. At the present time Auburn ranks in this respect among the first few cities of the state, and this is due, both to the great natural advantages, and the enterprising genius of her business men. Among the chief manufacturing and commercial enterprises now conducted are shoes, for which she has a national reputation, cotton and woolen goods, grain and produce, carriages, iron goods, brick and furniture.

The valuation of Auburn for 1887-88, was for real estate, $3,734,130; for personal property, $816,950; total valuation, $4,550,080. The total debt of the city is only $227,500, and is being steadily reduced. The tax rate is low, and advantages of situation for manufacturing, outside of the great water power of the river, are unusually excellent. The city officers for 1887-88 were Hon. A. W. Penley, mayor; John N. Foster, president of the board of aldermen; J. W. Mitchell, city clerk; N. M. Neal, president common council; D. W. Verrill, treasurer; Frank F. Goss, school commissioner; Thomas Littlefield, collector; and Geo. C. Wing, solicitor.

The modern city of Auburn is one of the most delightful for a summer sojourn. It contains about fifty square miles of beautiful residences, farm and woodland, interspersed with lovely lakes and charming rivers. It is on the west side of the great Androscoggin river with its tremendous water-power force, almost unlimited in its possibility of development. The Little Androscoggin river also runs through, affording several thousand horse power and good fishing and boating. Lake Auburn, the largest in the vicinity, containing eight or ten square miles, is a very popular summer resort. Two first-class hotels have been erected near the lake, and the outing privileges are widely famed and highly enjoyed. Poland Springs and Lake Maranocook are other noted resorts in the vicinity, easily and shortly reached. The drives through the city and country are exceedingly beautiful. The country is diversified with numerous romantic and delightful regions. It is an ideal summer home for a visitor desiring a quiet, satisfactory and recuperating enjoyment. After having known the charm of the region it lingers in the memory as an abiding pleasure.

The social, educational, and religious life of Auburn, is of a high tone, and admirably sustained. Ever since the early days of the town, the most careful and generous attention has been given to education, with the result that its twenty-four schools are maintained at the highest standard, and its beautiful high school, formerly the Edward Little Institute, is one of the most widely famed in the state. Its graduates enter Bowdoin and other colleges, where they rank among the first scholars. There are churches of the Baptist, Free Baptist, Congregational, Methodist and Universalist denominations here, and the religious activity in philanthropic work and in preserving the moral life of the city are very wide and effective. Though Auburn is not one of the oldest cities in the state, it has now reached a position where, for its good government and internal well-being, it is looked up to throughout Maine and well-deserves all the honor which has attended the efforts to beautify and uplift it of its good citizens in the present and the past.

LEADING BUSINESS MEN

OF

AUBURN, ME.

John F. Cobb & Co., Manufacturers and Wholesale Dealers in Boots and Shoes, 95-97 Main Street, Auburn. Boston office No. 301 Devonshire Street. Although there are some people, even at the present day, who affect to lament the decay of handicrafts and who sigh for a return to the "good old days" of hand labor and patient drudging, they are happily in a very small minority, and indeed it is not to be wondered at that they are, as such reasoning as theirs, legitimately and consistently carried out would result in the steamboat being abandoned for the row-boat on the ground that an oarsman must have skill while a steamboat passenger need have none. The trifling fact that if this were done there would be but very few travelers, does not seem to be worthy of their consideration any more than is the fact that the entire substitution of hand for machine labor in the shoe industry for instance would result in whole communities going barefoot. Machinery has undeniably worked wondrous changes in the manufacture of shoes, and a fine example of the perfection to which it has been carried may be seen in the establishment conducted by Messrs. John F. Cobb & Co., at Nos. 95 and 97 Main Street, in this city. Five floors are occupied of the dimensions of 42x70 feet, and three floors in addition 37x80 feet, making 22,500 feet of floor room, and a twenty horse-power is required to drive the ingenious and highly efficacious machinery in use, employment being given to one hundred and fifty hands. The enterprise now conducted by the firm mentioned was inaugurated more than forty years ago by Messrs. Harris and Cobb, who were succeeded by Cobb & Mills, then by Cobb, Robinson & Co., and they in turn by Mr. J. F. Cobb, who continued alone until 1869, when the existing co-partnership was formed by the admission of Messrs. John Pickard and in 1883, Chas. E. Cobb. The senior partner is a native of Sumner, Maine, and has long ranked as one of our representative citizens having been a member of the Board of Aldermen as well as holding other positions of trust and responsibility such as President of the Mechanics Savings Bank, Director and Vice-president of Shoe and Leather National Bank etc. Mr. John Pickard is a native of Lewiston, and Mr. Chas. E. Cobb of this city, and the firm is very extensively known among the shoe trade, etc., throughout the country, doing business in nearly every State in the Union from Maine to California. The firm carries on a Boston office at No. 301 Devonshire Street, and makes a specialty of the production of mens' fine and medium grade of boots and shoes, handling the same at wholesale and doing a large and growing business.

LEADING BUSINESS MEN OF AUBURN.

C. T. Nevens, Manufacturer and Dealer in Carriages and Sleighs, Wheels for Sale. Repairing of all Kinds, Junction of Turner and Pleasant Streets, Auburn. A carriage is one of those articles that look comparatively simple and easy to make when all done, but which really requires a high degree of skill and experience to manufacture successfully. A finished carriage is the result of the combined work of several trades, for the wood-work cannot be done by he who makes the iron-work, while the painting and varnishing are attended to by men who probably know nothing about "trimming" as the upholstery work on a carriage is called. Therefore as we have said, a well-made carriage is a production involving much skill and thought, and to produce such vehicles right along in the ordinary course of business is what few makers have gained so high a reputation for as has Mr. C. T. Nevens who carries on operations at the junction of Turner and Pleasant Streets. He is a native of Lewiston and founded his present undertaking in 1870 and some time since his productions were accepted as the standard of what such articles should be, a standard which he has rigidly adhered to. The manufacturing facilities are very extensive, there being seven floors utilized, measuring 60x45 feet and equipped with improved machinery, etc., including an elevator of sufficient capacity to convey the largest vehicle to the upper floors. Employment is given to twenty assistants and a very large wholesale and retail business is done, order work being made a specialty and turned out at short notice and at the lowest market prices for first-class articles. Farm wagons and carts are also made together with wheel-barrows, and these goods will be found as strong and durable as the carriages made are easy and elegant. Wheels are sold at low rates and repairing of all kinds is done in a thorough and workmanlike fashion that is bound to suit. Mr. Nevens carries a very extensive assortment of the leading makes and styles of carriages other than his own and no one wanting either carriage or wagon can afford to omit paying him an early visit.

Auburn Savings Bank, James Dingley, President, George H. Brown, Treasurer. In these days of education and culture there is a rule for everything, and whether a man wishes to win distinction in mercantile or professional pursuits, he is expected and advised to proceed according to certain arbitrary formulas laid down by those who consider themselves qualified to assume authority regarding such subjects. But to our mind there has as yet been no decided improvement made in the good old-fashioned receipt for getting on in the world, which was simply this: "Spend less than you earn." There is nothing very hard to understand about this advice, nothing, in fact, beyond the comprehension of the merest child, but still it is the master key by which all may open the door of prosperity and pass in, secure against the hardships and privations of those without. Don't be discouraged if your earnings are small, save money. Save a dollar a day if you are in a position to do so; save a cent a day if you can possibly do no better. The great thing is to attain the habit of saving, for with this five hundred dollars a year will offer opportunity to provide for the future, and without it a man earning ten times that sum is apt to die in a poor-house. Smile at these words if you will, but when you are through smiling look about you. Consult your own experience, and then if you consider them foolish and ill-advised treat them with whatever contempt you please. Don't hoard money up and keep it in the house, or bury it in the ground, but put it in the bank where it will work for you night and day and add to itself. What bank, you ask? Well, put it in the Auburn Savings Bank. You can do no better. It will be safe there. A liberal interest will be allowed on it, and you will find the officers of the institution ready to afford you any information you may wish for. Just a score of years ago this bank was founded, and the deposits now amount to over $700,000. A Reserve Fund and Undivided Profits, amounting to $24,000, show how the enterprise has been managed in the past, and we wish it still greater success in the future, for it has accomplished a grand work in the community and deserves the earnest, cordial support of every resident of this city. The President is Mr. James Dingley, the Vice-president, Mr. George S. Woodman, and the Treasurer is Mr. George H. Brown,—three names, of themselves enough to guarantee the high standing of the institution. The Trustees are Messrs. James Dingley, Geo. S. Woodman, Richard Dresser, Frank Bartlett, D. W. Verrill, Daniel Lara, John A. Morrill, A. M. Peables and Daniel Holland. In conclusion, let us say that as an undertaking of this kind is in a great degree a co-operative enterprise, it can offer greater advantages to many than to few, and hence the more it is patronized the better it is for depositors.

Stevens & Goss, Dealers in Groceries and Provisions. Flour a specialty, next to Goff Block, Main Street, near Court Street, Auburn. A reliable grocery store is one of the indispensable requisites of every community, since health, and perhaps life to some extent are largely dependant upon the vigilance and probity of the dealers supplying food for domestic purposes. In general esteem of consumers and dealers in Auburn, the house of Messrs. Stevens & Goss fully meets the requirements of the public in every regard. The business was established by this firm in 1886, and from the beginning has been conducted on a basis of the strictest integrity and fair dealing. The establishment is located at 94 Main Street, Phœnix Block. The premises comprise a store covering an area of 50x30 feet, and is well stocked with Staple and Fancy Groceries and Provisions of all kinds, a specialty being made of Flour and the most positive guarantee of excellence of merchandise is always given. The above-named goods are supplied by this firm at retail, at a fair price for the quality of goods, and prompt delivery is made free of charge to any part of the city. The individual members of the firm are Messrs. J. M. Stevens and H. A. Goss, both natives of this State, Mr. Stevens being born in Auburn, and Mr. Goss in South Paris, both enjoying in a full measure the confidence of the people of this city. Mr. Goss is a member of the Odd Fellows and Red Men, and Mr. Stevens of Masons, Odd Fellows and Red Men.

J. F. Atwood, Dealer in Boots, Shoes, Hats, Caps and Gents' Furnishings, 33 Court Street, Opposite Post Office, Corner of Main, Auburn. A careful review of the interests of Auburn develops the existence of a class of houses in every respect prepared to compete in the several lines they represent, with the rival establishments of any city. Their magnitude, ample resources, high commercial standing, and remarkable enterprise, are matters of which Auburn, has every reason to be proud. It is our mission to show to the outside world what this city produces, what it has to sell, the advantages possessed by it over many others, and the attractions it offers to capital for permanent investments, and to the trade as a purchasing center. In the especial branch of the retail shoe business, the house of Mr. J. F. Atwood must be awarded by the casual observer a foremost position. This establishment was founded by its present management in 1870, and from the first has ever maintained its present prosperous condition. Premises are utilized in Elm Block, opposite Post Office, comprising a store 80x22 feet in dimensions, and may be justly said to be one of the best appointed stores in this city. The energies of this house are devoted to the retail trade in Boots, Shoes, Hats, Caps, and Gents' Furnishings of which is carried the finest and most complete stock to be found in this section. Mr. Atwood is a native of Cape Cod, Mass., and too well known to this community and the trade to require from us any personalities, suffice it for us to say that his long experience in the business has given him a keen knowledge of what is demanded in the trade, and he is able to offer inducements to patrons, seldom if ever excelled.

O. A. Atkins, Dry and Fancy Goods, Dressmaking, etc., 23 Third Street, Barker Mill District, Auburn. Eligibly located in the Barker Mill District Auburn, Me., is the Dry and Fancy Goods establishment of Miss O. A. Atkins. Its prosperous career extends over a period of eleven years, and the fine assortment of goods constantly in stock, at most reasonable prices has done much toward establishing the enviable reputation it now holds. The original founders of this business were Dunn and Atkins who started in 1877, and in 1879, O. A. Atkins, assumed full management of the business. The premises occupied cover an area of 23x18 feet located at No. 23 Third Street. The store is fitted up with every facility for the prosecution of the retail trade, a specialty being made of Dressmaking, and the stock dealt in includes a varied assortment of Dry and Fancy Goods, Notions, etc., in great abundance which are offered at prices as low as they can be bought for elsewhere. Knowing as we do the reputation this house has gained, we can but feel that any further remarks at our hands would be superfluous.

H. Wesley Hutchins, Manufacturer of Patented Scale-Board Boxes, Auburn. Although inventions relating to any well-established manufacturing process are, as a general thing very difficult to introduce and firmly place in the market, still when an invention is perfected which is such a palpable improvement on anything that has preceded it that no proper comparison can be made, it only needs proper handling to make its way against whatever organized competition may be brought against it. Here we have the secret of the very exceptional degree of success attained by the Scale-Board Boxes of Mr. H Wesley Hutchins, for these articles are manufactured under patents issued to, and controlled by, that gentleman, whose productions are now sold throughout the country, as they are conceded by competent judges to be unrivalled for the purposes for which they are designed. The inception of this enterprise occurred in 1876, under the management of Messrs. Hutchins, Noyes & Co., and it has been carried on since by the New England Scale-Board Box Co. and the Boston Box Co., coming under Mr. Hutchin's sole control in 1880. He is the Inventor and Patentee of the Scale-Board Box, Box Machine, and Process of Manufacture, and the demand for the goods may be judged from the fact that the annual production amounts to about one million and a half boxes, six floors of the dimension of 130x 50 feet being occupied, and fifty hands employed to accomplish this result, and water power footing up to one hundred horse being utilized to run the highly ingenious machinery in use. This factory has only been occupied since February, 1887, and is arranged in the most improved modern style. Mr. Hutchins is a native of Minot, and is one of the best-known inventors and manufacturers in the country. He is a Mason of the highest degree, and is also prominently connected with the Odd Fellows. Few of our successful business men have so thoroughly deserved the appreciation of the public, and those most familiar with the obstacles Mr. Hutchins has overcome hold him the highest in their esteem.

George B. Attwood, Dealer in Boots, Shoes and Rubbers, No. 44 Court Street, Opposite Elm House, Auburn. There are certain houses in every city that enjoy an undisputed superiority in their several lines of trade, and this is as true of those in Auburn as in any other place. In the matter of fine shoes at retail this position is undoubtedly held by the establishment of Mr. George B. Attwood located at No. 44 Court Street opposite Elm House. Mr. Attwood learned the trade of bottoming shoes in 1857, and continued to work for Cushman & Merrill, then carrying on a business at West Minot until they dissolved partnership; he then worked for Ara Cushman until he moved to Auburn, after which he worked for Joseph Merrill until he moved to Mechanic Falls in the spring of 1865. After Mr. Merrill moved he opened a retail Boot and Shoe Store, running a custom and repair shop in connection at West Minot, and so continued until 1881, when he located at his present quarters, 44 Court Street, Auburn, and the result of his long engagement in the shoe trade, and the unusual ability and enterprise which he has shown in the management of his business is seen in the very large and increasing trade he now enjoys. A fine store, 45x25 feet in dimensions, is occupied and employment is given to experienced and able assistants. The entire establishment constitutes what is generally regarded as a fine appearing and first-class retail Boot and Shoe Store, and it is certainly a credit alike to its proprietor and the community in which it is located. The very complete stock on hand contains articles to suit every variety and gradation of taste, and although none but reliable goods are handled, there is a sufficient number of grades carried to permit all purses to be suited, and the general average of prices will be found very reasonable. Mr. Attwood has been Selectman of Minot and was City Treasurer of Auburn in 1886.

John Dingley & Co., Dealers in Groceries, Crockery, Oil-cloth, Lime and Cement, Phœnix Block, 86 Main Street, Auburn. A business enterprise which has been carried on for over thirty years in this city and which has from its inception been conducted in a manner both honorable and progressive can hardly fail to be a popular one, and such is the case with that we have now under mention, for the house of John Dingley & Co., is as highly respected as it is well known, and its patronage is not only very extensive but is continually increasing. The undertaking was inaugurated by Messrs. J. Dingley jr. & Co., this taking place as we have said over thirty years ago. The original firm was succeeded by Messrs. Dingley & Brewster, and this in turn by the present concern in 1886. Mr. John Dingley was born in Dunham, Me., and is connected with the Free Masons. He has, as a matter of course, a most thorough and perfect acquaintance with the many details incidental to the carrying on of such a business as his, and is consequently in a position to offer the public some very decided advantages at times when the market affords opportunity for foresight and resolution to assert themselves. The premises occupied are located at No. 86 Main Street, Phœnix Block, and comprise two floors measuring 35x55 feet, together with a storehouse of the dimensions of 30x40 feet. A very heavy stock is carried and an idea of its variety may be gained from the fact that it includes Groceries, Crockery, Oil-cloth, Lime and Cement.

C. J. Litchfield & Co., Carriage Manufacturers, Custom Work a specialty, Carriage, Sign and Ornamental Painting, Repairing of all kinds, Corner Turner and Pleasant Streets. The comfort of both horse and driver is dependent in a very considerable degree on the vehicles used and the importance of having a carriage made as light as is consistent with safety, and as easy riding as possible, can scarcely be overrated. Comparatively few people realize that the durability of a vehicle (other things being equal, is principally dependent on its springs, yet such is the fact, for experience and carefully conducted experiments, have shown that the sudden and violent shocks, a carriage or wagon receives when unprovided with springs, or equipped with those of inferior construction or design will destroy it much quicker than when properly made springs are used. The firm of C. J. Litchfield & Co., of this town have built up a large patronage, and high reputation, by the skill they have shown in turning out carriages, which are both durable and elegant in appearance, and a by no means unimportant factor in their success has been the fair and reasonable prices they have put on their productions which consist chiefly of Light Carriages, although they do manufacture some heavy wagons. This now extensive manufacturing and retail business was founded in 1885 by Mr. C. J. Litchfield, and in 1886 the firmname became C. J. Litchfield & Co. The premises occupied are located at the corner of Turner and Pleasant Streets and comprises four floors and a basement, each covering an area of 75x50 feet, where is conducted the carriage manufacturing business in all its branches. Employment is furnished to seven skilled and thoroughly experienced workmen, and a specialty is made of Custom Work and repairing of all kinds, also Carriage, Sign, and Ornamental Painting, is executed in the most satisfactory manner. The individual proprietors of this prosperous establishment are Mr. C. J. Litchfield and Mr. S. A. Miller, all thoroughly practical business men in a position to fully guarantee their productions. A full line of new sleighs is carried. Carriages of all kinds receive the same careful attention, and are supplied at the lowest market rates.

William A. Robinson, Druggist and Apothecary, Dealer in Trusses, Paints, Oils, Varnish, Paper Hangings, etc., Auburn. As the sick and the well, those who wish to avoid illness and those who wish to gain health, all patronize the establishment conducted by Mr. William A. Robinson in this city, it follows as a matter of course that he does a very large business, and also that as he is thus enabled to buy goods in large quantities and thus obtain them at the very lowest manufacturers' and wholesalers' rates, putting him in a position to offer special inducements to his customers both as regards the freshness of his stock and the low prices quoted on the articles constituting it. The enterprise we have under consideration was inaugurated in 1867 under the firm name of Robinson & Beedy, and came under the sole control of its present efficient manager and proprietor in 1884. Mr. Robinson was born at Vineyard Haven, Mass., but has been completely identified with the best interests of this community for many years. The premises occupied by him are of the dimensions of 70x30 feet, and employment is given to three highly competent and courteous assistants, such goods as Trusses, Paints, Oils, Varnishes, Paper Hangings, etc., being handled, as well as Drugs, Medicines and Chemicals of all descriptions. A specialty is made of the careful and accurate compounding of physicians' prescriptions and the facilities at hand to insure success and guard against error in this line are so complete and ingeniously devised as to make mistakes practically impossible. Mr. Robinson is also very favorably known in connection with certain Toilet preparations and home remedies which have proved themseves to be all that is claimed for them. Among them may be mentioned Robinson's Tonic Dressing for the hair, Bayleaf Lotion for the complexion, Shampoo Tonic for Dandruff, Robinson's Garget Remedy and Grandmother's Thoroughwort Syrup for coughs and colds.

C. H. Briggs, Truckman and Dealer in Hard and Soft Wood, Pressed Hay and Straw, Shavings in large or small quantities, Junction Pleasant and Turner Streets, Auburn. Everybody nowadays, at some time or the other, wants to secure the services of an expressman or teamster, and as a great deal of anxiety and annoyance may be saved by knowing where a perfectly reliable man may be found who is engaged in this business we need present no excuse for bringing to the notice of our readers so trustworthy an establishment as that conducted by Mr C. H. Briggs, located at the junction of Pleasant and Turner Streets, Auburn. The inception of this enterprise was in 1886, by its present able proprietor. A large and increasing patronage is enjoyed, the very best of accommodations being furnished, and all orders executed with a combination of speed and fidelity that would be hard to match elsewhere. Mr. Briggs was born in Turner, Maine, and is connected with the Free Masons and Odd Fellows. He employs six horses and seven large wagons, and two light wagons in his work, and five assistants are required to handle the volume of business transacted. Trucking for manufactories and teaming of all kinds will be done promptly and satisfactorily, and all directions carefully followed. In addition to the Trucking business Mr. Briggs deals very extensively in Hard and Soft Wood, Pressed Hay and Straw, also Shavings in large or small quantities. The premises occupied for the accommodation of the merchandise dealt in consists of three stories, each 55x25 feet in dimensions. We commend the enterprise of Mr. Briggs to our readers as one that occupies a prominence in the business community of Auburn.

H. R. Smith & Son, Dealers in Coal, Wood and Hay, 212 Court Street, next to M. C. R. R., Auburn. Although it certainly seemed at times during the past half year or so as if Coal was to become a luxury very desirable no doubt, but quite out of the reach of ordinary people, this

danger has happily been averted, and the question of fuel has returned to its proper position in the domestic economy. There is at all events a consolation in knowing that the supply at the mines is in no danger of exhaustion for generations to come, and if we can only induce those gentlemen who have devoted themselves to the handling of it to send along a proper quantity, there need be no alarm experienced regarding the possibility of keeping warm, and no experiments made in the line of accustoming ourselves to eat our food raw. But in all seriousness, no such mistake should be made as to ascribe the high prices that may be quoted on coal to the greed of local dealers, as these gentlemen would only be too willing to sell it at one-half the present rates even if they saw a fair and reasonable profit for themselves in doing so. Of course we speak of the standard and reputable concerns and one of the very best known of these is that carried on by Messrs. H. R. Smith & Son on Court Street, next to the M. C. R. R. This enterprise was inaugurated in about 1872, and in 1883 it came into the prossession of Mr. Chas. E. Smith, who in 1884 was succeeded by the present firm which is made up of Messrs. H. R. and S. B. Smith, the former is a native of Hallowell and the latter of this city. As Mr. H. R. Smith has acted as Mayor of Auburn as well as Representative to the Legislature, he is very widely known throughout this section and we may add, is as highly esteemed as he is well known. His son is also a prominent business man and the magnitude of the transactions carried on by the firm is indicated by the capacity of the storage facilities which is equal to the accommodation of 4000 tons of coal, and over 6000 are sold in the course of the year. Both a wholesale and retail business is done in Wood and Hay as well as in Coal, and employment is given to eight assistants, all orders being promptly filled at the lowest market rates.

Dingley, Foss & Co., Manufacturers of Boots, Shoes and Slippers, Auburn. Auburn contains more than one shoe factory of large extent and high repute but among them all it would be impossible to find any in which more pains were taken to produce goods fully up to the standard in all respects than is the case at that of which Messrs. Dingley, Foss & Co., are the proprietors. The undertaking carried on by these gentlemen was begun in 1875, and its present extent affords significant indication of the appreciation evinced by the public for the goods coming from this factory. As now constituted the firm is made up of Messrs. J. Dingley, jr., who is a native of this city, H. G. Foss, who was born in Wayne, E. G. Sprague, Green and E. M. Stevens, Auburn, all partners being well known, particularly Mr. Dingley who has officiated as Representative and also as State Senator. The premises now occupied for manufacturing purposes comprise a new factory off Hampshire Street, five floors of the dimensions of 154x40 feet, and are equipped with a thirty-horse engine, and of course with all the necessary improved machinery, etc., there being two hundred hands employed. The special line produced is Men's Fine Boots and Shoes, and considerable attention is also paid to the manufacture of Slippers, and Tennis and Base-Ball Shoes. There is an office maintained in Boston at No. 105 Bedford Street, corner of Lincoln, and the demand for the goods produced by this factory is a brisk and increasing one, for they have been found to stand the test of actual wear in a surprisingly satisfactory manner and are sold to dealers at very reasonable rates. They are such goods as may safely be "warranted" for the utmost care is used in their production.

J. H. Twombly & Co, Custom Tailors, Gents' Furnishing Goods, Opp. Y. M. C. A. Block, Court Street, Auburn. It is doubtless very true that a woman who feels herself to be well dressed is perfectly at ease as a general thing, even amongst the most imposing surroundings, but the same may be asserted with equal justice of ninety-nine men out of one hundred, or at least it may be said that the consciousness of being dressed as well as their neighbors is of the greatest value to about all men if they wish to meet those with whom they have dealings on equal terms and without the slightest embarrassment. Such being the case it needs no argument to prove that no one should be considered extravagant for dressing in accordance with the prevailing style and having his clothing made by a house that makes a specialty of fine and artistic work in this line, and in this connection we may well speak of the enterprise conducted by Messrs. J. H. Twombly & Co., on Court Street, opposite the Y. M. C. A. Block. This establishment was founded in 1885, and it has already become the headquarters for those desiring to inspect and select from the latest examples of Foreign and Domestic suitings, etc., for a large and full assortment of these goods is always to be found on Messrs. J. H. Twombly & Co's counters as well as an unusually varied collection of Gents' Furnishings of correct pattern. Messrs. J. H. Twombly and Geo. H. Cobb, who are both members of the Red Men, constitute the firm, and they are prepared to guarantee perfection of fit as well as of style to those who may favor them with orders for custom garments. Twelve skilled assistants are employed, and customers can be supplied at short notice.

Auburn Drug & Chemical Co., Court Street, Auburn. This company was incorporated in 1887 for the purpose of extending the sale of the Standard Remedies formerly prepared by H. C. Packard & Co. The capital is $50,000.00, and the directors comprise some of the leading business men of this section. The original firm was started in 1877, Mr. Packard coming from Readfield, Me. Owing to the rapid increase of business the present company was organized consisting of S. F. Merrill, President; N. W. Harris, Vice-president; H. C. Packard, Treasurer; W. B. Kilbourne, Secretary, and the trade, large as it was, has been extended. The preparations of this company are all made from tested prescriptions and care is taken that only the freshest and purest drugs and herbs are used in compounding them, and the same care is used in putting them up as when the sales were one-tenth of their present magnitude. An agent of the company drives through the several towns in this part of the State in a team costing almost $1,000.00. This is used in supplying the trade as the demand for these Standard Remedies is steadily extending and increasing. While the trade in the Standard Medicines is very large that is not the sole business. On the contrary one will find here an elegant and commodious drug store, fully stocked with everything in the line of Pure Drugs and Chemicals, Toilet Articles, Fancy Goods, etc.; a specialty is also made of the preparation of physicians' prescriptions. A number of careful and experienced assistants are employed who will give all orders prompt attention. The following are some of the preparations of this company: Pix Liquida Compound, a clean, bright, effectual cough cure, 35 cents; Kilbourne's Bismuth Mint Lozenge, cures sick headache and all unpleasant results of indigestion, 25 cents: Packard's Purity Powder, a Tooth Powder, which not only cleanses the teeth, but it disinfects the mouth, and is positively harmless, 25 cents; A. D. & C. Co.'s Best Honduras Sarsaparilla Extract, cleanses the blood, aids digestion, cures constipation, and does you good, 85 cents; Packard's Condition Powder is put up with as much care as if for man's use, instead of the horse he loves. You will find it the best powder for the least money. 1 pound boxes, 25 cents; Packard's Carbolic Ointment, the finest thing you ever saw in that line, just the thing for sunburns, or any other burn, sore, cut or eruption; Kilbourne's Pain Stop is a perfect thing in its line, good for internal use in small doses, and excellent for external use; Heave and Cough Capsules, sure cure for coughs of all kinds, and recent cases of Heaves, and will surely help all cases; Dr. Watson's Liniment. These may be ordered either direct of the company or through your nearest drug store in any place. Trade supplied by J. W. Perkins & Co., and Cook, Everett & Pennell, Portland. Retail orders should be sent to Auburn Drug & Chemical Co., Auburn.

Edwin T. Stevens, Dealer in Groceries, Meats and Provisions, No. 203 Turner Street. The Grocery and Provision establishment located at No. 203 Turner Street is not only already popular but is becoming more and more so, as the people get better acquainted with the business methods of its present proprietor, and have more of an opportunity to learn of the uniform merit of the goods handled and the low prices, at which they are sold. This enterprise was started in 1874 by S. Macumber, and since 1886 has been conducted by the present proprietor, Mr. Edwin T. Stevens. A fine store is occupied of the dimensions of 60x25 feet and the stock on hand includes everything in the fine Staple and Fancy Grocery line, together with Meats and Poultry of all kinds in their seasons also everything included in Provisions. Two reliable and experienced assistants are employed and the public has discovered that all representations made at this establishment can be implicitly relied upon, for it is the idea of Mr. Stevens to sell every article on its merits and not to take advantage of the inexperience of any buyer. The most fastidious will find themselves able to get choice cuts of Meats here, that will give complete satisfaction, and the choicest Family Groceries are also to be had at the lowest market rates. Mr. Stevens is among the most popular business men of Auburn. He is a member of the Free Masons and also is the present Commander of Burnside Post, G. A. R., No. 47.

J. E. Tibbetts & Co., Dealers in Flour, Corn, Meal, Oats, Wheat, Bran, Middlings, Cotton Seed and Linseed Meal, Hay, Straw, etc., Mill 33 Knight Street, Storehouse near Elm on M. C. R. R., Auburn. Among the more important articles of Merchandise handled in this city, due mention should be made of Flour, Corn, Meal, Oats, Feed and Pressed Hay, Straw, etc., as these staple products are in brisk demand, and quite a number of enterprising houses are employed in supplying them. One of the best known and most largely patronized establishments engaged in this trade is that now conducted by J. E. Tibbetts & Co., whose mill is located at the head of Knight Street, near Turner Street. The undertaking alluded to was established in 1861 by the senior partner of the present firm, and in 1883 Mr. N. S. Tibbetts was admitted to the firm, since which date the firm name has been J. E. Tibbetts & Co. They have built up a thriving and extensive business by means of intelligent management and close attention to the interests of their customers, as well as those of themselves. They are both natives of the State of Maine, and excellent judges of the articles in which they deal, and are in a position to accommodate all classes of trade by exercising judicious discrimination as to their respective needs. The Grist Mill occupied comprises four floors each 75x50 feet in dimensions and is supplied with every facility necessary for the conduct of the business which is operated by water power, and an extensive manufacturing wholesale and retail business is done. A large and complete stock is carried thus enabling all orders to be filled with celerity and accuracy, and in fact it is to this characteristic of their business that Messrs. Tibbetts & Co. owe no small part of the exceptional success attained. Mr. J. E. Tibbetts is a member of the city council of Auburn.

A. D. & E. F. Goss, Confectionery, Fruits and Cigars, 48 Court Street, Auburn. A popular house in Auburn concerned in those branches of business included under the above headings is that of Messrs. A. D. & E. F. Goss. This business was established in 1884 by Mr. A. D. Goss, and in 1887 Mr. E. F. Goss was admitted to the business since which date the style has been A. D. & E. F. Goss. The premises occupied cover an area of 45x20 feet, located at 48 Court Street. Which is well stocked with a complete and varied assortment of Confectionery, and Foreign and Domestic Fruits, also Cigars and Tobacco and in addition to the above-named lines of goods, the Messrs. Goss deal extensively in Soda Water and Ice-Cream, for which purpose their establishment is supplied with a fine Soda Fountain and Ice Cream Saloon, and altogether they conduct a first-class retail trade, and their stock of delicacies, are guaranteed always pure and fresh. Both Mr. A. D. Goss and Mr. E. F. Goss are natives of Danville, Me., and are in a position to offer the strongest inducements to patrons, and their retail trade is drawn from the best classes. Mr. A. D. Goss is a prominent member of the Red Men and E. F. Goss of the Knights of Pythias.

A. J. Verrill & Co., Marble Workers. Monuments, Tablets and Headstones on hand and made from the very best Italian and American Marble. Shop on Turner Street, Auburn. A statue, a monument, a tablet—in fact artistic stone-work of any description is quite beyond the power of words to give an adequate idea of and comes completely under the category of that which "must be seen to be appreciated." Therefore we will not waste our space or tire the patience of our readers by attempting a description of some of the productions of Messrs. A. J. Verrill & Co., but will simply say "visit their establishment on Turner Street, and see for yourselves." The firm in question is made up of Messrs. A. J. Verrill and F. A. Rendall, and begun operations in 1882. Mr. Verrill was formerly a member of the city council, and both he and Mr. Rendall are connected with the Odd Fellows, the latter gentlemen being also a member of the Ancient Order of United Workmen. Two floors are occupied of the dimensions of 50x55 feet, and the work done is not confined to marble alone but includes some granite as well, as for instance facades for buildings, etc. Employment is given to six skilled assistants, and the facilities at hand are ample to insure the prompt and thorough filling of orders. A very large and valuable stock is ready for inspection, particularly in the line of tablets and headstones, and those contemplating the purchase of an article of this description will find Messrs. A. J. Verrill & Co's goods satisfactory, not only from an artistic but also from a pecuniary point of view, as they are offered at surprisingly low rates and are fully guaranteed in every respect.

LEADING BUSINESS MEN OF AUBURN.

F. B. Bigelow, Dentist, 3½ Phœnix Block, Main Street, Auburn. While it is undeniably a fact that operations on the teeth are apt to be somewhat painful on account of the extreme sensitiveness of the nerves connected therewith, still it is also a fact that the great progress made in dental science, and in the perfection of dental instruments within the last score of years has rendered painless many operations which were formerly quite the reverse. Then again it may truly be said that the average of education and ability is much higher among the dental profession to-day than was ever the case before, and this also of course, tends to make it easier for those whose teeth require attention. As skillful and conscientious a practitioner as is found in this vicinity is Dr. F. B Bigelow whose office is located at No. 3½ Phœnix Block, and we voice the opinion of those most conversant with his abilities, when we say that it is impossible to find a dentist anywhere who is more anxious to fully satisfy his patrons, and who takes more pains to do good reliable, durable work. He makes a specialty of manufacturing artificial teeth. Dr. Bigelow is known to about everybody in Auburn and vicinity. He inaugurated the practice of his profession in Lewiston in 1870, where he served as State Liquor Agent in 1879. In 1876 he traveled extensively through South America. Since 1883 Dr. Bigelow has successfully conducted the dental profession at his present location in Auburn, 3½ Phœnix Block, Main Street. He has spared no expense in fitting up his operating rooms with the most improved and effective appliances, and keeps himself fully informed as regards the progress of Dental science, thus assuring his customers the most approved treatment. Dr. Bigelow is a native of Livermore and well known in this community. He has also been a member of the School Board of Lewiston. His rates for making artificial teeth are very reasonable, and all work is promptly done.

Arthur W. Penley, Dealer in Beef, Veal, Mutton, Lamb, Pork, Sausages, Vegetables, etc., No. 40 Main Street, Auburn. When Mr. A. W. Penley of Nos. 40 and 42 Main Street, began the sale of Groceries in 1887, he had already been engaged in the handling of Meats for some 22 years having inaugurated that business in 1865. The wisdom of his course in adding a grocery department soon became apparent for the public he had served so well in the matter of supplying Meats, etc., concluded that he would extend similar advantages in his new field of operations and they were not disappointed. Both Staple and Fancy Groceries are handled and the very lowest market rates possible on first-class goods are maintained. Mr. Penley was born in Auburn (formerly old Danville), and is a member of the Order of Red Men. He has many friends in Auburn and vicinity and his honorable business methods and strict adherance to all promises made have gained him the respect of all having dealings with him. The store occupied measures 25x40 feet and employment is afforded to five assistants. every order being given careful and prompt attention. Mr. Penley does a large business in Meats, and is prepared to furnish anything in this line in any desired quantity, and at positively the lowest attainable rates. Choice cuts are a specialty, and the most fastidious buyers are assured satisfaction.

R. S. Bradbury, Livery, Boarding and Feed Stable, Court Street, near the Bridge, Auburn. The man who can ride behind a spirited and speedy horse—see him fly along at a word or a sign from his driver, or slacken up in obedience to a command without a feeling

of exhilaration and light-heartedness has our profound sympathy, for the chances are that he is no longer able to extract enjoyment from anything. It is a pity that this form of relaxation is not made more general use of by our business men, for if it were there would not be so many mournful tales of premature old age extant—so many cases of brain disease and insanity brought about by over application and under recreation. Drugs are all very well in their place but at best they are but a makeshift and only do imperfectly what nature is willing and anxious to do perfectly if she is only allowed an opportunity. Fresh air, rapid motion, change of scene, cheerful conversation—all these are remedial agents more efficacious and infinitely more agreeable than any to be found in an apothecaries store, and they have one additional and pronounced advantage—they leave no bad effects behind. Perhaps we may be considered unduly enthusiastic on this subject, but this enthusiasm is the result of experience and observation, and is fully justified by the facts in the case. Of course to obtain the best results from driving, an easy carriage and a strong, kind and quick-moving animal are requisite, and so after seeking to inspire our readers with a desire for amusement of this kind, we can do no less than to inform them where such may be obtained at low rates. Fortunately this is easy to do for Mr. Russell S. Bradbury of this city is excellently prepared to suit the most critical of drivers, having a fine stable under his control, and the experience of over twenty years to guide him in the management of it. Four floors are utilized measuring 50x100 feet, and there are seven assistants employed, thirty horses and ten carriages being cared for. Carriages are furnished for any and all occasions, including weddings and funerals, two fine hearses being available, and many modern hacks and careful drivers. Orders are given prompt attention and no lower rates are quoted anywhere for similiar accommodations. Connection by telephone. Mr. Bradbury was born in Lewiston, and is a member of the Knights of Pythias and also of the Odd Fellows, being one of our best-known and most esteemed citizens. He has reason to be proud of his establishment which is really one of the finest in the entire State.

J. C. SYMMES, 56 COURT STREET, AUBURN.

J. C. Symmes, Dealer in Meats, Fish, Groceries and Provisions, Old Goff Market, No. 56 Court Street, Auburn. The commercial advantages of Auburn have brought men of enterprise and capital to establish themselves in our midst, and nearly every branch of industry is here carried on vigorously. The establishment popularly known as the Old Goff Market, and located at No. 56 Court Street, was founded in 1860 by Messrs. Symmes & Atwood, on Main Street, who were succeeded by Mr. J. C. Symmes in 1877, moving here in 1886. He has been engaged in the Meat and Grocery business for twenty-two years, and has a thorough and practical knowledge of all its details, to which he devotes his close personal supervision, thus insuring his customers every possible advantage to be obtained in the city. This market comprises one floor 45x25 feet in dimensions, which is well stocked with a choice selection of Meats, Fish, Groceries and Provisions and a specialty is made of Fruit. The extensive retail trade of this house requires the service of two experienced assistants, and all orders are promptly attended to and goods are delivered to any part of the city. Mr. Symmes is a native of Newfield, Maine, and a well known citizen of this community, and has been connected with the city government as both councilman and alderman. He is recognized not only as a liberal buyer, but as a man whose business management is honorable, and with whom business relations prove not only profitable but as pleasant and lasting.

Geo. M. Roak, Florist, 124 and 152 High Street. This is neither the time nor the place to indulge in a eulogy of flowers and flower-lovers, and indeed it is very unprofitable work at the best to endeavor to argue people into a fondness for and appreciation of these "smiles of nature" as somebody has called them, for if a person has not a love for flowers born in him, it is idle to seek to inculcate it by example or precept. In this article then we will treat the subject from its commercial side alone and that this is of great importance no one need be told who is at all familiar with the demands of custom and fashion as regards flowers and their uses. To begin with, it is impossible to conceive of articles better adapted to all occasions than are flowers for taste and custom sanction their use in time of joy and in time of sorrow, on the breast of the bride and on the bosom of the departed one. Flowers may be safely given when any other gift would be refused, and so wide is the range of their capabilities that either distant respect or fervent admiration may be expressed by them more eloquently than by words. Science has made possible many strange things but in nothing has she ministered more to the gratification of the wishes of cultivated people than in producing the most delicate flowers even at the height of our most inclement weather. Summer and Winter are much alike to the modern gardener in this—given the demand and he can supply about any blossom at any season. In Auburn and vicinity the trade in flowers is practically controlled by Mr. Geo. M. Roak, of Nos. 124 and 152 High Street, for this gentleman has such facilities and such skill as to render competition out of the question. He was born in this city and began business here in 1876, soon building up a large trade which has since steadily increased. Two large greenhouses are maintained, measuring 128x45 and 112x18 feet respectfully, and three skilled assistants are employed, flowers suitable for all occasions being raised in immense quantities. A specialty is made of Roses and the number and magnificence of the varieties shown of this royal flower are truly wonderful. Mr. Roak furnishes anything in his line at the lowest rates and is prompt in the delivery of all orders.

LEADING BUSINESS MEN OF AUBURN.

Peables & Garcelon, Dealers in Choice Groceries and Provisions, Phœnix Block, 70 Main Street, Auburn. In compiling the various industries of Auburn, the retail grocery and provision trade assumes a decided importance. Among those who supply Fresh Groceries and Provisions is the house of Messrs. Peables & Garcelon. Their store is located in Phœnix Block, 70 Main Street, and is well stocked with Staple and Fancy Groceries, Provisions, etc. This business was originally founded by L. F. Chase in 1865, and in 1871 Mr. Peables was admitted to the firm, and the business was conducted under the name of Chase & Peables till 1873, when it became Peables & Penley. In 1882 the title was again changed and became as at present, Peables & Garcelon. The premises occupied consist of one floor and basement each covering an area of 55x22 feet, which are admirably arranged for the extensive business transacted. Reliable clerks are employed, who wait upon customers in a polite and attentive manner, and all goods are delivered promptly as desired. This is one of the most reliable establishments in its line in Auburn, and the stock carried comprises everything usually to be found in a first-class Grocery and Provision establishment. Messrs. Peables & Garcelon are both natives of Auburn, Me. Mr. Peables is a member of the Odd Fellows, Free Masons and Knights of Pythias, and has been connected with the city government as councilman for three years. Both gentlemen are well and favorably known throughout this community, and number their friends by the score. Goods are sold in quantities to suit purchasers, and the prices will be found as reasonable as any in town for the same quality of goods.

Hill Brothers, Wholesale Fancy Goods, Hosiery and Small Wares, 57 Court Street. Auburn. Among the many wholesale houses located in this city there is not one which is more deservedly popular, or which gives promise of a more succesful future than that of which Messrs. Hill Brothers are the proprietors and which is engaged in the handling of Fancy Goods, Hosiery and Small Wares. Business was begun by present firm in 1882, but both partners were in same business in Lewiston and Auburn since 1868, but in present location since 1882, and as very superior inducements were offered to customers from the first, it followed as a matter of course that a large patronage was at once attained which has since been rapidly and steadily added to. The firm consists of Messrs. C. W. and B. J. Hill, both of whom are natives of Stetson, Maine, and very well-known citizens, Mr. B. J. Hill having been a Representative to the Legislature and now being a State Senator. The premises occupied are of the dimensions of 125x35 feet and are extremely well-stocked with Fancy Goods of various kinds, Hosiery, Notions, Laces, Gents' Furnishings, etc., employment being afforded to six assistants. It has been the experience of this house, at least, to be remarkably successful in "holding" their customers and we think that a careful comparison of the prices here charged with those of other establishments, not excluding some making far greater pretensions, will go far to explain this large trade.

F. Bartlett & Son, Dealers in Dry and Fancy Goods, Auburn. An establishment that is very widely known and most generously patronized by the ladies of Auburn and vicinity is that now conducted by the firm of F. Bartlett & Son. This highly popular house which deals in Dry and Fancy Goods was inaugurated in 1881 by Messrs. Bartlett & Jordan, and prosperously conducted under that title until 1884, when the firm's name was changed to its present style of F. Bartlett & Son. An extensive retail business is transacted, and a fine store is occupied covering an area of 70x25 feet with a large basement used for storage purposes. The elegant stock carried by Messrs. Bartlett & Son comprises a fine assortment of Dry and Fancy Goods of all kinds, including many fashionable novelties. Mr. Frank Bartlett the senior partner of this house has been engaged in this line of trade for the past twenty-five years, and is thoroughly conversant with all the details of the business. He is a native of Abbott, Maine, and his son Mr. Frank L. Bartlett, of Auburn, Maine. They are both well known and highly respected in social as well as business circles. Mr. Frank Bartlett is a member of the Odd Fellows, and a trustee of the Auburn Savings Bank, and has held the office of Councilman and Alderman. Mr. Frank L. Bartlett is a member of the Red Men.

Isaiah Mitchell, 211 Turner Street. Auburn. Dealer in Groceries and Provisions. It is a decided advantage to housekeepers to be able to put perfect confidence in the establishment from which they obtain their Groceries and Provisions, for they are often obliged to send their orders by those who are too young to be able to discriminate between that which is good and that which is not. Of course unsatisfactory goods can be returned even after a trial of them if their quality was misrepresented, but this proceeding at the best takes time and trouble and is one that no one likes to have recourse to, unless it is absolutely necessary. So it is that those dealers who have gained a reputation for reliability and honorable business methods enjoy the largest and most permanent trade, and one to be classed with these in Auburn, is Mr. Isaiah Mitchell whose establishment is now situated at 211 Turner Street. This enterprise was founded in 1879 by Messrs. Manly & Noyse, and since 1884 Mr. Mitchell has had sole control and management of the entire business, which has met with success from that date as it was bound to do under his skillful management. The premises occupied comprise a store 50x25 feet in dimensions, and are well stocked with a fine and fresh assortment of Groceries, Meats and Country Produce. Two experienced assistants are employed and all customers are insured prompt and courteous attention, and all goods dealt in are offered at the lowest market rates for first-class quality. Mr. Mitchell was formerly located on Spring Street, where he was burned out, losing every dollar, in 1877. Mr. Mitchell is a native of Durham, Maine. He is well and favorably known in this vicinity. He is a member of the Ancient Order of United Workmen and Sons of Temperance, and has held the office of Sheriff of Strong, Me.

J. Roak Pulsifer, Manufacturer of Leather Board Counters, Auburn. Push, energy, vim and determination are sure to win success where success is possible, and a shining example of the truth of this statement is to be seen in the rapid and steady extension of the business carried on by Mr. J. Roak Pulsifer, at No. 28 Miller Street. Mr. Pulsifer is a native of this city, and became sole proprietor of his present undertaking in 1886, the enterprise having been inaugurated by Messrs. Pulsifer & Fuller in 1877, and this firm was succeeded by Messrs. H. B. Pulsifer & Son, who in turn were succeeded by Mr. J. Roak Pulsifer. The premises utilized comprise three floors of the dimensions of 40x60 feet, and are equipped with a ten-house engine to drive the necessary machinery for the manufacture of Leather Board Counters, Pasted Heeling's, etc. Employment is afforded to sixteen assistants, and a large wholesale trade is carried on particularly in Massachusetts. The productions of Mr. Pulsifer's establishment are rapidly becoming known to the trade as being of remarkably even quality of great and durability, and as a consequence the demand for them is steadily and rapidly increasing. It is unfortunate that many concerns handling Leather Board pay more attention to cheapness than to quality for this material is susceptible of a wide range of uses if properly made, and the prejudice felt against it in some quarters is not due to any inherent defects in it but rather to the fact that only imperfect specimens have thus far been used therein. Mr. Pulsifer gives prompt and accurate attention to orders and guarantees his goods to prove just as represented.

Wood & Walker, Manufacturers of Harnesses, Dealers in Robes, Whips and Horse Clothing, Trunks, Bags and Umbrellas, Main Street, Auburn. The old rhyme which tells how — "for want of a nail the shoe was lost, for want of a shoe the horse was lost, for want of a horse the rider was lost, and all for want of a horse-shoe nail," conveys a moral regarding the importance of small things which is as worthy of attention as much now as ever, and which every runaway accident we hear of, resulting from some portion of harness giving way, or some other small breakage, give a new example of. Too much care cannot be put into either the manufacture or selection of a harness, for all considerations of safety and prudence demand that it be made of the best materials, by experienced hands. It is chiefly on account of their productions being fully up to the highest standard, that Messrs. Wood & Walker have built up so large a patronage during the past twelve years, that they have carried on this industry, for it is well known to their customers that they faithfully endeavor to combine strength with neatness, and durability with reasonable prices. This establishment was founded in 1867 by Messrs. Covill & Wood, and has been under the management of the present proprietors since 1876. The premises now occupied by them are located at No. 90 Main Street, and cover an area of 50x25 feet, where they manufacture all kinds of Harnesses, and deal in Robes, Whips and Horse Clothing, Trunks, Bags, Umbrellas, etc., and a fine retail trade, and custom and jobbing work, is transacted. Two experienced and careful assistants are employed, and the house has attained a high reputation for honorable and reliable treatment and fair prices. The individual members of this firm are J. C. Wood and W. S. Walker, both Maine men by birth and members of the Odd Fellows, and thoroughly experienced and practical business men, and highly esteemed citizens of Auburn.

S. L. Emerson, Livery, Sale & Baiting Stable, Opposite Roak Block, Main Street, Auburn. Extravagance is to be avoided of course, but if men confined to sedentary employments would as a general thing spend a larger proportion of their income on horse-hire

there is but little doubt that this procedure, although it might seem extravagant at the time, would eventually prove to be in the line of the strictest economy. How so? you ask. Well, let us answer that question in genuine Yankee fashion by asking others. Who among the workers in a community are most firmly in the grip of the demon of dyspepsia? Who are frequently obliged to force themselves to go through with their day's labor when every effort brings pain and can only be made at a destructive expenditure of vital energy? Who are most apt to suffer weeks of confinement in a sick bed put to great expense for doctor's bills and medicines and taught to consider themselves lucky if their positions are not taken from them during their illness? There can be but one reply—those engaged in sedentary employments, clergymen, lawyers, book-keepers, salesmen, clerks — all in fact whose work does not take them into the open air or expose them to the revivifying influence of the sunlight are living an unnatural life, are peculiarly subject to disease and unless they take advantage of such means of healthful and exhilerating recreation as is afforded by the livery stables they need not be surprised at the almost inevitable result, impairment of health. There are some good stables in this city, but there are none either in Auburn or its vicinity, that offer better accommodations than those of which Mr. S. L. Emerson is the proprietor located on Main Street, opposite Roak Block. Mr. Emerson is a native of Auburn and has been a member of the City Council. He founded his present business in 1883 and it has since been conducted in such a manner as to make the large business now done only the legitimate outcome of such honorable and liberal methods. Two floors are utilized measuring 125x65 feet and 35 carriages and 30 horses are at hand. First-class teams are furnished at reasonable rates for all occasions and liberal arrangements may be made for the regular hire of turnouts.

Auburn Marble and Monumental Works, End of Court Street Bridge, Auburn. Every intelligent person in the community has a tolerably correct idea of the value of articles in general use such as clothing, provisions, etc. but there is some information which is not common property such as that pertaining to the cost of Marble or Cemetery Work. From the very nature of things it is evident that the great majority of people can have but a hazy and imperfect idea of what should rightfully be charged for stone work, more especially for that designed as a memorial of the dead and it therefore becomes of importance when placing an order for anything in that line to patronize only such a reputable house as one can feel positively assured will not take advantage of the prevailing ignorance to fix exhorbitant rates on its productions. The residents of Auburn are fortunate in having an establishment located in their city, which is noted for turning out Marble and Granite Monument work unexcelled either for beauty of design or perfection of finish, and are especially to be congratulated on the fair and reasonable rates at which they may have their orders filled by the popular concern in question. We refer to that of which Mr. Geo. B. Smith is the proprietor, located at the end of Lewiston bridge and all that we have said in favor of this enterprise will be subscribed to heartily by those who have been familiar with it at any time since it was inaugurated in 1850 by Mr. H. R. Smith. The present owner has been in possession since 1884 and when we say that he has fully sustained the established reputation of the house for fair dealing and low prices we feel that further praise is quite uncalled for. He is a native of this city and is connected with the Knights of Pythias. The premises occupied measure 40x25 feet and employment is given to eight skilled workmen, all orders being filled at short notice. Some beautiful specimens of finished work are on exhibition and all interested should make it a point to give Mr. Smith a call. To parties desiring to have a Monument, Tablet, Headstone or Curbing placed in the spring or summer he offers extra inducements to order now. He manufactures them this winter, and places them in the cemeteries in the spring or summer at prices much lower than they can be made after the opening of the spring trade. He has the largest variety of designs to select from in the State. These works have been established nearly 40 years, and Mr. Smith is determined to keep up the reputation which they have gained for first-class work, low prices, and fair dealing with his patrons.

I. N. Haskell & Co., Dealers in Groceries, Meats and Provisions, Auburn. A finely appointed store devoted to the sale of Groceries and Provisions in this section of Auburn, is that of Messrs. I. N. Haskell & Co., whose commodious store is fitted up with every facility for the proper conduct of the extensive retail trade transacted. This house was established in 1879, by the present proprietors, and the premises occupied comprise one floor of the dimensions of 50x65 feet, which are finely fitted up and stocked with everything in the line of Groceries, embracing the finest quality of Teas, Coffees and Flour, besides a full line of choice and fresh Meats and Provisions of all kinds. Three polite and attentive assistants are employed, and orders receive prompt attention, goods being delivered to all parts of the city free of charge. In addition to the above-mentioned business Mr. Haskell is himself extensively engaged in the Poultry business raising fancy birds. He has about 500 fowl in his yard. All goods dealt in by this house are above comment, and all purchasers are well aware of their extra quality. The individual members of the grocery firm are Mr. I. N. Haskell, a native of Auburn, Maine, and Mr. A. W. Miller, of Oldtown, Maine. Mr. Haskell is a member of the Odd Fellows, and Mr. Miller has been councilman of Auburn and selectman of Oldtown. Both these gentlemen are thoroughly experienced in their business, and highly esteemed in this community.

Geo. B. Brooks, Dealer in Hardware, Iron and Steel, 10 Court Street, Auburn. A name which has long been identified with the best interests and most progressive commercial spirit of this vicinity is that of Mr. Geo. B. Brooks, the prominent dealer in Hardware, Iron and Steel, etc. The business was started in 1860, under the firm name of Barker Brooks, and since the death of Mr. Brooks senior in 1879, it has been under the sole control and management of his son, Mr. Geo. B. Brooks. A fine and extensive retail trade has now been built up in this city and vicinity, and the stock and dealings of this house are noted for their thorough reliability and liberal management. A fine store, with basement, each 50x25 feet in dimensions with plate glass front, located at 10 Court Street, is now occupied, and completely stocked with a fine assortment of Hardware goods, Iron and Steel, Farming Implements, Window Glass, and Cutlery, etc., which have a great patronage for their guaranteed reliability and the advantageous rates at which they are sold. A competent force of reliable assistants are employed to meet the growing demands of the trade. Mr. Brooks is a native of Auburn, and is among our most respected and successful merchants. He is a member of the Red Men, and exercises an unobtrusive yet powerful influence in the social affairs and life of Auburn.

Smith, Pray & Co., Manufacturers of Ladies', Misses' and Children's Fine Boots and Shoes, Nos. 166 to 172 Main Street, Auburn. It is unfortunate that so large a proportion of the public pay so small attention to what firm manufactures their boots or shoes, for the reason that on this account it is generally impossible to feel sure that the last pair bought are of the same make as those that gave such satisfaction before. For instance there is the firm of Smith, Pray & Co., that makes a specialty of the manufacture of Ladies, Misses' and Children's Fine Boots and Shoes. This concern bends all its energies to the task of producing superior articles of the kinds mentioned. It has every facility to turn out such goods at the smallest possible expense without sacrifice of quality; uses the best obtainable stock, the most effective machinery, employs men of experience and skill in every department and as a consequence produces Boots and Shoes that are unexcelled and in certain respects very hard to equal. Now if those who have worn these goods and appreciated them had made themselves familiar with the name of the firm manufacturing them can any one doubt that the business of Messrs. Smith, Pray & Co., large as it is, would be greatly increased? And can anyone doubt that the general result would be to improve the quality of boots and shoes of all kinds as their manufacturers saw that the public was noticing what they were doing? It is beyond question. The business carried on by Messrs. Smith, Pray & Co., was founded about a score of years ago by Foss & Smith, the present partnership having been formed in 1875. Mr. Smith is a native of Topsham and Mr. Pray of this city, the former being a member of the Odd Fellows and the latter of the Masons. Four floors are utilized, measuring 60x30 feet and 100 assistants are employed, the factory being located at Nos. 166 to 172 Main Street. A New York office is maintained at No. 104 Duane Street, and a very large business is done.

Atwood & Lowell, Dealers in Groceries, Meats and Provisions, Fresh Fish, Oysters and Clams, 220 Court Street. As desirable a place as we are acquainted with in Auburn at which to purchase fresh Groceries, Meats and Provisions in general, is that now conducted by Messrs. Atwood & Lowell, at No. 220 Court Street. Operations having been begun by J. Q. A. Atwood in 1873, and conducted under that name, until 1877, when the firm name became Atwood & Lowell. The premises occupied by them cover an area of 60x25 feet and the stock carried is one that must be seen to be appreciated, as in no other way can its many good points be properly understood. The line of Groceries dealt in is a very complete one, while Meats and Provisions of all kinds are constantly on hand. Particular attention is also paid to the handling of Fresh Fish, Oysters, and Clams, of which a fine assortment is always at hand to choose from, and offered at the lowest market rates. Employment is given to two well-informed and obliging assistants, who give prompt and polite attention to customers and see that every order is carefully filled and accurately delivered. A large business is done and the trade is steadily increasing. The individual members of this thriving firm are Messrs. C. S. Atwood and W. G. Lowell, both natives of Minot, Me., and well known in the social as well as business circles of Auburn. Both being members of the Odd Fellows and Red Men and Mr. Lowell is also connected with the Free Masons, and a member of the Knights of Pythias.

Wood, Robinson & Co., Paper Jobbers and Manufacturers' Agents, 101 Main Street, Auburn. Boston office, 13 West Street. Of all the materials manufactured at the present day there is probably not one capable of being put to more widely diverse uses than paper. And not only is it capable of a wide range of service, but it is actually employed in such, as may be seen from the fact that the wheels under a Pullman car and the sheet on which the lady of fashion inscribes her dainty characters are made of one and the same material—paper. It goes without saying that a product such as this must be sold in enormous quantities, and that its handling must have enlisted the services of many able men of business, for while there is no community so rude and uncultivated but what paper is of value to it, there is none so highly-civilized and advanced as to be able to dispense with it. One of the best-known houses in Maine engaged in the Paper Trade is that of Messrs. Wood, Robinson & Co., whose place of business is at No. 101 Main Street, and the celebrity these gentlemen have gained is principally due to the fact that, acting as Manufacturer's Agents, they have been able to offer exceptional inducements, more particularly to large consumers of paper. The enterprise they conduct was inaugurated in 1882 by Messrs. C. A. Robinson & Co., and a year later the present style was adopted, the partners being Mr. B. F. Wood, a native of Lewiston, and Mr. C. A. Robinson, who was born in Brasher Falls, N. Y. The former gentleman is connected with both the Odd Fellows and the Free Masons, and enjoys an extensive acquaintance among those interested in the production of paper, as does also Mr. Robinson, his associate in business. This firm have found it necessary to move twice to enlarged quarters. Three floors are now occupied, measuring 28x65 feet, and more room is now being provided. A specialty is made of the handling of Printing and Wrapping Paper, five assistants being employed, and a very large and rapidly increasing business is done as Jobbers and Manufacturer's Agents for the Sale of All Kinds of Paper.

Chase & Bean, Wholesale and Retail Dealers in Meats, Fish, Produce, Fruits, Canned Goods, etc. Oysters a specialty in their season, No. 108 Main Street, Auburn. An establishment that is capable of supplying a large share of household wants, is that of which Chase & Bean are the proprietors, and which is centrally located at 108 Main Street, Auburn. This establishment was founded twenty years ago and has been under the management of its present proprietor since 1888. Mr. Chase conducted the business alone from 1884 to 1888. They have established a reputation not only for the variety but also for the excellence of the goods handled that has resulted in the building up of a very large and growing trade. Mr. Chase is a native of Portland and a member of the Odd Fellows, and Mr. Bean a native of Auburn, both having many friends in this vicinity. The premises comprise one floor and basement each of the dimensions of 60x30 feet. They transact a large retail trade in choice family Groceries, Meats, Fish and Provisions, also handle a large quantity of Flour from the leading mills of the country, and a choice line of Foreign and Domestic Canned Goods; Fish of all kinds, and Oysters in their season are made a specialty. Employment is given to only courteous and efficient assistants, thus assuring prompt and polite attention to every customer. Some very superior inducements are offered in the particular line of goods dealt in. Perfect confidence may be placed in all representations made, as every article sold is fully warranted to be as described.

The National Shoe & Leather Bank, Ara Cushman, President, M. C. Percival, Cashier. Capital, $400,000. Mechanics Savings Bank Block. To so carry on a banking institution as to fully protect the interests of its stockholders, and at the same time exercise a wise liberality in the encouragement of deserving home enterprise, is a task for which very few men are really fitted, and, indeed, the more thought one gives to the subject, the more plainly it is seen that it is practically impossible to so manage an undertaking of this kind as to suit everybody, and the only wonder is that some banks come so near to the attainment of this impossibility. Take the National Shoe and Leather Bank of this city as an example. Here we have an institution that was founded in 1875, more particularly in the interests of the shoe and leather trades of this vicinity, as its name indicates. Mr. Ara Cushman, it's President, is universally known as one of the leading shoe manufacturers of the United States, and it is an open secret that much of the success which has generally attended the shoe trade of this section during the past dozen years or so has been brought about and rendered possible by the workings of the banking enterprise of which Mr. Cushman is the head. Yet for all this its benefits have been by no means confined to the shoe industry, and there is more than one business man in Auburn who can testify from his own experience to the truth of this assertion. Having a capital of $100,000 and a surplus of $40,000 the bank is in a position to afford great assistance in such cases as it may seem advisable so to do, and its management have never yet been found backward in extending aid to a legitimate object when such help was consistent with the maintenance of the prosperity of the institution under their charge. Indeed, an examination of the names of those acting as Directors — Ara Cushman, John F. Cobb, F. M. Jordan, R. C. Jewett, B. F. Briggs, Geo. C. Wing and M. C. Percival — is enough to inspire the fullest confidence in the bank and its methods, for these gentlemen are known to all in this vicinity, and we but do them simple justice in saying that they are as highly esteemed as they are well known.

F. H. Storah & Co., House and Fresco Painters, Paper Hangers, Grainers and Glaziers, dealers in Paints, Oils, Varnishes, Colors and Mixed Paints of all Kinds. Shop rear of Auburn Block, Auburn. One of the first proverbs to which the attention of children is called is "Practice makes perfect," and certainly it would be difficult to find one more thoroughly true in every respect. "Habit is second nature" is another saying in the same line, and daily experience demonstrates that in practical life nothing can take the place of prolonged practice. Therefore, when it is desired to have a thing done as it should be, it is an excellent idea to place the order with one who has had sufficient practical experience to be a master of the subject in all its branches. It is for this reason, among others, that the work turned out by F. H. Storah & Co. is so uniformly good, for these gentlemen have been engaged in business as Painters, Glaziers and Paper Hangers for many years. They have added to their stock a full line of Wall Papers, Ceiling Decorations and Picture Mouldings. Their goods are all new, and will be sold at lowest prices. They also employ a large crew of first-class Painters and Paper Hangers which will enable them to do any work in their line with neatness and dispatch. Their Paper Room will be open day and evening through the busy season. All orders by postal will receive prompt attention. They have been entrusted with the filling of many important commissions in their line of business, and their work is sure to be durable as well as ornamental, and the best of materials are used in the filling of orders. Messrs. Storah & Co. are prepared to undertake all branches of their business at short notice. Messrs. F. H. Storah and W. W. Pettingill are the members of this firm. Their charges are always reasonable, and estimates will be cheerfully furnished.

W. S. Morse, Plain and Fancy Job Printing, Main Street, Auburn. The fine Job Printing establishment of Mr. W. S. Morse has for many years been one of the most complete concerns of its kind in Auburn. The enterprise was inaugurated by the present proprietor about fourteen years ago, and from its inception it has been conducted with rare tact and energy and consequent success. The commodious office utilized by Mr. Morse is located at No. 88-92 Main Street, and is admirably equipped with first-class steam presses, type, lighted by electric lights from a plant located in the office, and has all the necessary appliances for the prosecution of fine, plain, and fancy job printing, experienced hands are employed in this establishment as compositors and pressmen, and every facility for executing orders for all kinds of job work at short notice and in the best style of the typographic art is possessed by the proprietor. Mr. Morse is an expert, practical printer. His aim has ever been to meet every want of his patrons, and to keep even pace with the improvements made from time to time in his art, and in these particulars he has been eminently successful. Mr. Morse is recognized as among the successful leaders in this line of industry in Auburn.

Albert M. Penley, Dealer in Staple and Fancy Groceries, 98 Main Street. The almost innumerable goods included in the term, Staple and Fancy Groceries are such as are to a great degree indispensable, and when the many millions of people in this country alone, which must be supplied with them, are brought to mind, it will be readily seen that an enormous business in these commodities must exist. Of the eastern houses engaged in the retail department of this trade, none bear a higher and more deserved reputation than does that of Mr. Albert M. Penley doing business at No. 98 Main Street, Auburn, for its operations extend throughout this vicinity, and it has been characterized from the first by the signal ability of its management and the perfect dependence which could be placed on its representations. This business was founded in 1883 by Mr. Albert M. Penley. He now occupies the spacious store located at the above-named address, which is completely stocked with a choice assortment of everything usually included in the line of fine Staple and Fancy Groceries. A full line of Meats, Vegetables, and Fresh Fish is also carried. The extensive retail trade transacted requires the services of three capable and efficient assistants, and every detail of the business is most ably handled. Mr. Penley is a native of Auburn, and despite the many cares and duties incident to an active business life, he has managed to discharge the duties of a member of the Common Council, in a manner highly creditable to himself and his constituents, and also to gain additional honors as a member of the Board of Aldermen, and at present he holds the honorable position of Mayor of Auburn.

Wise & Cooper, Ladies' and Misses' Perfect fitting Boots, Roak Block, Main Street, Auburn. It is well known that in no other section of the country is the manufacture of Boots and Shoes pushed to such a degree of perfection as in New England, and hence it follows that to excel amongst New England manufacturers is as high as it is well-earned and honorable. Messrs. Wise & Cooper inaugurated the manufacturing enterprise they now conduct in this city in 1863, and at the present time their productions take the very highest rank in the market against all competitors. They advertise to make perfect fitting Boots for Ladies and Misses, and that they carry out this announcement to the letter is proved by the fact of their goods being favorites with such ladies as have been afforded an opportunity to test their many good qualities. Any dealer who desires to increase his trade in the special direction mentioned would do well to secure a supply of Messrs. Wise & Cooper's Goods for they are *invariably* satisfactory and both as regards durability and style will meet every requirement, while they are supplied at such rates as will permit of an adequate profit on their handling. Mr. John D. Wise is a native of Haverhill, Mass., and is connected with the Free Masons, being one of the best-known men in the State engaged in the handling of shoes, while his partner Mr. A. H. Cooper was born in Richmond, Me., and is also a prominent figure in the shoe trade. Two floors are occupied, measuring 45x30 feet, fully supplied with steam power etc., and employment is given to thirty skilled assistants.

Geo. A. Allen, Dealer in New and Second Furniture, Carpets, Stoves, Glass and Crockery Ware, Chamber Sets and all kinds of Household Goods, No. 5 Roak Block, Auburn. One of the most necessary lines of trade engaged in, and one whose goods are in constant demand is that of the dealer in House Furnishing Goods, etc. One of the most complete establishments of this kind in Auburn, is that conducted by Mr. Geo. A. Allen, who engaged in this business in 1882, and from the inception has manifested marked business ability, and has been successful in building up a prosperous business, which necessitates the occupancy of a store covering an area of 60x30 feet in addition to a storehouse 25x30 feet in dimensions. The store is located at No. 5 Roak Block, Main Street, where a large stock of New and Second-hand Furniture may be found, also Carpets, Stoves, Glass and Crockery Ware, Chamber Sets, and all kinds of Household Goods, also Musical Goods, etc. In addition to this retail business, Mr. Allen acts as Appraiser and Auctioneer. The extent of this business requires the services of courteous and competent clerks, and patrons are assured of receiving prompt and gentlemanly attention while dealing at this house. One advantage offered by Mr. Allen is that of enabling patrons to secure first-class furniture at about one-half of its value, simply on account of its having been used for a short time. Also those contemplating breaking up house-keeping can dispose of their Furniture by calling on Mr. Allen who will be found liberal and just in his dealings. Mr. Geo. A. Allen is a native of Auburn and a member of the Free Masons. He is a thoroughly competent and practical man of business to which he devotes his personal attention.

Burt L. Alden & Co., Druggists and Apothecaries, Dealers in Drugs, Medicines, Stationery, Cigars, etc., Gents' Furnishing Goods, No. 10 Third Street, Barker Mill District, Auburn. One of the finest appearing Drug Stores in Auburn, is that conducted by Mr. Burt L. Alden, at No. 10 Third Street, Barker Mill District. This is not a case where appearances are deceitful either, for this establishment bears an enviable and well-earned reputation for the purity and freshness of its goods, and the prompt and courteous attentions paid to customers, so that even the most obstinate stickler to the old adage "handsome is that handsome does" cannot withhold his approval. The inception of this enterprise was in 1876, under its present title, and Mr. Alden has since carried on the business in a most successful manner being an educated and experienced druggist and apothecary, having cultivated a great amount of natural aptitude and ability by the most careful study and experiment. The store is 50x25 feet in dimensions, employment being given to only reliable and courteous clerks. The stock on hand is made up of a fine assortment of Drugs, Medicines, Chemicals, Fancy Goods and Toilet Articles, as well as a large and unusually complete selection of Stationery, Cigars, etc., also Gents' Furnishing Goods. Mr. Alden also manufactures a fine brand of Cigars. He is a native of Auburn, and well known in her social circles being a prominent member of the Free Masons, Knights of Pythias and Red Men.

LEADING BUSINESS MEN OF AUBURN.

S. A. Pollister, Fruit. Confectionery and Cigars, Stationery, Periodicals, etc. Daily and Weekly Papers a specialty, Court Street, Auburn. An enterprise of special interest to the people of Auburn, and one that will be of value to learn something about in this volume, is the Periodical and Stationery business of this city, and among the many houses engaged in this line is that of Mr. S. A. Pollister who has had sole control and management of this establishment since 1885. His store is located at 88 Court Street, where he transacts a large retail trade in Stationery and Periodicals, Fruits, Confectionery, Cigars, etc. The business of this house is steadily increasing, and its resources are ample to meet all demands made upon it, and its policy entitles it to the consideration of this community who will find assured advantages in dealing here. Mr. Pollister makes a specialty of all the Daily and Weekly Papers. His store is under able and efficient management, a full and complete stock of books and small fancy goods is carried, also a circulating library of four hundred volumes. Mr. Pollister is a native of Portland, Maine, a gentleman thoroughly conversant with the minutest detail concerning his business to which he gives his close personal attention, and our citizens are assured that they can obtain here the latest and most popular periodicals of the day, and we can commend them to no better house in Auburn, dealing in these lines of merchandise. Mr. Pollister has recently erected and now occupies a commodious three-story brick block the dimensions of store being 20x60 feet.

W. Pulsifer, Wholesale and Retail Dealer in Flour and Groceries, and Canned Fruits of all kinds, Main Street, opposite New Bridge, near Barker Mills, Auburn. One of the best known and largely patronized Grocery stores in this section is that carried on by Mr. W. Pulsifer, located on Main Street, opposite New Bridge, near Barker Mills, and it thus merits mention in a work treating of and seeking to encourage commercial enterprise and activity. This enterprise was founded in 1877 under the title of Pulsifer & Co., as a wholesale and retail store, and a year later the wholesale business was discontinued, the above firm continuing until 1883, when Mr. W. Pulsiver assumed full control of the business which he has continued up to the present time. Mr. Pulsifer was born in Poland, Maine, and few of our citizens are better known, and at the same time more generally esteemed, and his public spirit is generally acknowledged and appreciated. So far as circumstances have permitted he has striven to make his establishment a model of what such an undertaking should be, and though he has not made it perfect (and no one knows that such is the case better than he) he has no reason to be ashamed of the results of his labor. The premises occupied measure 50x30 feet, and a choice stock is carried and satisfaction is guaranteed (in every reasonable instance) to his patrons. The stock includes everything in the Grocery line besides Flour of the best brands, and Canned Fruits of all kinds, and the prices are guaranteed to be in accordance with the lowest in the market.

Revere House, corner Court and Main Streets, Auburn. A first-class hotel. Central location, steam heat, electric bells, electric light, hot and cold baths, and all modern improvements. Table and all appointments first-class. Hot and cold water on every floor. Terms, $1.00 to $2.00 per day. Mrs. S. P. Ryerson, proprietress. It is a good thing for any community to have a hotel carried on within its borders which can be confidently recommended as one where every reasonable provision is made for the comfort and well-being of guests, for the advent of strangers always has a tendency to stimulate trade, and there is no surer way to attract the best class of purchasers to a town than to provide for their hospitable entertainment when they get there. The Revere House, of which Mrs. S. P. Ryerson is the proprietress, has been carried on for several years, and its influence upon the development of Auburn's business interests has been by no means unmarked. Although this house does not pretend to vie with the first-class establishments in the large cities, as regards elegance of appointments, etc., it does endeavor to make its patrons feel at home, to give them all they want to eat, of excellent quality, and to provide them with comfortable rooms, and clean, easy beds; and that this endeavor meets with success is in our opinion beyond a doubt, being evidenced by the popularity of the Revere House with the traveling public. This popular house is located at No. 21 Court Street, and has gained a more than local reputation, and gives every sign of largely adding to it in the future, when its proprietress gains more experience and enlarges her facilities for carrying this pursuit. The table is supplied with the best the market affords, and the terms are very reasonable for first-class accommodations.

Henry Willis & Co., Manufacturers of Flour, and Dealer in Flour, Corn, Meal, Shorts, Oats, Cotton Seed Meal, Table Salt and Higgins' Eureka Salt, Wool Carding, 91 Main Street, Auburn. No doubt bread made of any other first-class flour would "rise" just as well and be as nutritious and palatable as though it were made of the special brand handled by Messrs. Henry Willis & Co. in this city, but nevertheless it would be hard to convince some of our older residents of this fact, for the reason that they have used this firm's flour for over a quarter of a century and have no desire to exchange what they *know* to be good for what may be worse and certainly cannot be *better*. Messrs. H. & M. Willis founded their business in 1860 and in 1865 Willis, Parsons & Co., which continued till 1882, then changed to H. & M. Willis. The firm is now H. Willis & Co. Both are Free Masons, and Mr. H. Willis has also been a member of the City Council and also of the Board of Assessors. Ware rooms are located at No. 144 Main Street, Roak Block, and comprise one floor, measuring 30x60 feet and a fine assortment is constantly carried of Flour, Corn, Meal, Shorts, Oats, Cotton Seed Meal, Table Salt and Higgins' Eureka Salt, also Higgin's English Dairy Salt. A force of four men is employed, and orders are given prompt attention, with the guarantee that all goods supplied will prove just as represented.

LEADING BUSINESS MEN OF AUBURN.

Chas. S. Emerson, Dealer in all kinds of Junk, also Ploughs, Harrows, Cultivators, etc., Main Street, opposite Maine Hotel, Auburn. Very few men can think of "junk" without also thinking of their boyhood days, for where is the boy who has not at some time begun a commercial career which perhaps in later years was to become a celebrated one, and involve transactions to the amount of thousands of dollars by negotiating for the exchange of various odds and ends such as bottles, old iron, copper, etc., for sufficient coin of the realm to enable him to defy the contingency of the home money market and enable him to pay his own way to see the circus he had set his heart on seeing? A boy who has not had this experience has been cheated out of a chief pleasure of boyhood, for the clown never looks as funny nor the animals so fierce as when seen through eyes that have grown keen searching for "unconsidered trifles" in every nook and corner. The Junk business is a great, yes, a tremendous industry. Hundreds of thousands of dollars are invested in it, and it has enlisted the services of some of the most energetic of our business men. Mr. Chas. S. Emerson of this city began operations here in this line of trade in 1877, and his establishment has for some years ranked among the most prominent in the State. He is a native of Litchfield, Maine, and has served for several years in our city council. Mr. Emerson saw some stirring times during the late Rebellion, and was commissioned as Lieutenant-Colonel of the 29th Maine Volunteers, and breveted Colonel in partial recognition of his services. He is now the highly popular commander of Burnside Post No. 47, G. A. R., and has literally "hosts" of friends in this vicinity. His store is located opposite the Maine Hotel on Main Street, and five assistants are employed therein. Ploughs, Harrows, Cultivators, etc., being largely handled, as well as junk of all kinds. A heavy stock is carried, and positively the lowest market rates maintained.

Garcelon & Hunton, Fire, Life and Accident Insurance and Real Estate Agents, No. 3 Phœnix Block, Auburn. The older the world becomes the wiser it gets, and with the passage of years there is a constant increase of more or less destructible property, so that the field for Insurance is constantly and rapidly widening. A large proportion of the many agents scattered throughout the country find ample employment in satisfying the popular demands for reliable insurance, and those doing business in this town are not a whit behind the rest in prosperity. One of the most popular and successful of our Auburn agencies is that conducted by Messrs. Garcelon & Hunton, at No. 3 Phœnix Block, and its total volume of business will to-day not suffer by the strictest comparison with that of some of the oldest of its competitors. There is nothing surprising in this as to begin with Messrs. Garcelon & Hunton are both energetic, enterprising men, and consequently well known and highly esteemed by many of our business men, and then again they have always made it a point to represent only such companies as are not only reliable but which settle losses promptly and do not put their policy holders to needless expense. Those familiar with the different Insurance Corporations will admit the truth of this after a perusal of the list of companies represented by them. Messrs. Garcelon & Hunton are also interested in the handling of Real Estate. In all the various branches of their business they consult the interests of their customers believing them to be identical with their own, and that this course is appreciated is proved by the many commissions executed by them.

Mark Morse, Manufacturer of Paper Boxes and Cartons, 28 Railroad Street, Auburn. Of course in a city where the manufacture of boots and shoes has assumed the dimensions and importance which it has in Auburn, it is but natural that numerous subsidiary enterprises should have sprung up which depend for patronage upon the greater industry carried on in this vicinity. Among these, one of the best-known and most deservedly popular is that conducted by Mr. Mark Morse, at No. 28 Railroad Street, for this gentleman manufactures Paper Boxes and Cartons, and as these are used by practically all shoe manufacturers, and those produced by Mr. Morse are all that could be desired as regards both quality and price, why it is by no means strange that a very large business should have been built up by him since beginning operations in 1881. Mr. Morse is a native of Gray, Me., and is a member of the American Legion of Honor, and has a large circle of friends in Auburn and vicinity. The premises utilized by him are of the dimensions of 50x80 feet, and comprise three floors, employment being afforded to from fifteen to twenty assistants. Five horse-power is required to run the machinery in use, and ample facilities are at hand to fill all orders without annoying delay, and at the very lowest market rates.

A. K. P. Gordon, Groceries, Flour, Grain, Meats and Fruits, 62 Spring Street, Auburn. Leaving the question of prices out altogether, one prefers to trade with a concern that he knows will give him courteous attention and fair treatment. It is natural that such should be the case, and so strong is this preference that a man will often patronize a firm that averages higher prices on its goods than some of its competitors, for no other reason than that given. Therefore when a house is found which combines both of these good qualities—which not only extends courtesy and fair dealings to all, but also quotes the lowest market rates on its goods, it is not surprising that its trade should be not only large already, but steadily and rapidly increasing. Such a position is that held by the enterprise carried on by Mr. A. K. P. Gordon, located at 62 Spring Street, Auburn, and its circle of patrons is consequently being constantly extended. The undertaking was started by Mr. C. Stackpole, and conducted by him until 1884, when he was succeeded by its present able manager and proprietor, Mr. A. K. P. Gordon. Mr. Gordon is a native of Durham, Maine, and is connected with the Free Masons and Odd Fellows, and has many friends in this community. A store is occupied 60x25 feet in dimensions, and a very complete stock is shown consisting of Groceries, Meats, Fruits, Flour and Grain. Two reliable assistants are employed.

LEADING BUSINESS MEN OF AUBURN. 97

Elm House, Court Street, Auburn, Dunham & Andrews, Proprietors. In commending this hotel to our readers it is perhaps well to begin by saying that those who prefer glitter and show to comfort and consideration, will not find it here. Those however—and we believe the majority of travelers are of this class, who enjoy a "good, old-fashioned inn"—will find as perfect an example as is in existence today, in the popular Elm House, which for twenty-nine years has been located on Court Street, Auburn. Here is the cozy office, with its open fire, around which can always be found, through the cool weather, a circle of arm-chairs. Then the dining-room, in which is served a most appetizing meal, with everything in plenty, and all cooked in "home" style, or as a traveling man very aptly expressed it, "as mother used to cook." The beds are clean, old-fashioned and comfortable, and when we add that the present proprietors, who have had a long experience in the business (as they have for some time conducted the Lincoln House, Lewiston) are not only retaining the old patrons of the house, as well as adding new ones, we think our readers will find they can at least do no better than to give this house a trial on their next visit to this section. Another feature which reminds one of the "days of long ago" is the sight of the stages starting for different towns off the line of the railroad. These stages make their headquarters at the popular Elm House, and those contemplating a stage journey will find this the most convenient house to stop at.

Barker Mills, A. M. Pulsifer, Treasurer, William Hayes, Agent, Manufacturers of Sheetings and Shirtings, Auburn. To say that the manufacture of cotton goods is an industry of national importance is simply to repeat what every schoolboy knows to be a fact, and that Auburn and Lewiston form the principal seat of cotton manufacture in this State is equally well known. We have no space to devote to a consideration of the reasons why Auburn offers special advantages to the textile manufacturer, but we may say in passing that the unfailing and abundant water-power available in this city is of the greatest importance in the successful prosecution of manufacturing operations. Taking for instance the Barker Mills as an example, we find that 400 horse-power is required to drive the necessary machinery, and that all this vast amount of force is furnished by the river. There are some drawbacks, to be sure, to the use of water-power, which partially compensate for its cheapness as compared with steam, but on the whole it must be reckoned as an important aid to the attainment of the highest economy. The Barker Mills were established in 1873, and are now known through their products in all parts of the country. Fine Sheetings and Shirtings are manufactured very extensively, just how extensively may be learned from the fact that 4,000,000 yards or 2,272½ *miles* of these goods were produced last year. Five floors are utilized, of the dimensions of 250x80 feet, and there are 275 operatives employed. As to the quality of the work turned out, no better evidence is needed than that afforded by the large and increasing sales, although it may be mentioned that goods from these mills received a high award at the Centennial Exposition in Philadelphia. The officers of the company are as follows: President, W. W. Bolster; Treasurer, A. M. Pulsifer; Agent, William Hayes. The Board of Directors is made up of Messrs. A. M. Pulsifer, W. W. Bolster, J. W. Kimball, R. B. Dunn, M. C. Percival, S. D. Bailey and Edward Robinson, all of which gentlemen are natives of this State, and widely-known citizens, the majority of them having held high public offices, and standing high in the esteem of the entire community.

Ara Cushman Company, Ara Cushman, President, Samuel F. Merrill, Treasurer, 209 Court Street, Auburn. Boston office, 128 Summer Street. That this is emphatically the age of machinery is a proposition that may well be called self-evident, for we are surrounded on every hand with plain proofs of it, and there is scarcely an article of food, drink or clothing but what owes some portion of its making, at least, to machinery of one kind or another. Associated with, and in some degree suggested by machinery, are immense manufactories, in which are employed hundreds of men, and by this means another important saving is made in the cost of production, as it is obvious that, other things being equal, two men can produce more than twice as much as one man, two hundred men a much larger proportionate amount than half that number, and so on, until, keeping within reasonable bounds, we may say that the larger the force employed, the more there is produced per man. Therefore when we find an establishment like that under the control of the Ara Cushman Company, equipped with the most improved labor-saving machinery, so arranged as to obviate unnecessary handling of stock or goods, employing six hundred to eight hundred hands, and run on a system so perfect that each department forms a part of a harmonious whole, thus doing away with friction and waste of energy, it may be concluded in perfect safety that goods are produced which combine a maximum of excellence with a minimum of cost, and on further investigation into the standing of the Company's productions in the market, it will be found that the conclusion arrived at is justified by the facts, for no house in the trade enjoys a higher reputation as regards both the lowness of its prices and the desirability of its goods. This great enterprise was inaugurated by Mr. Ara Cushman in 1854, and in 1865 the firm assumed the name of the Ara Cushman Co. The gentlemen associated with Mr. Cushman are Messrs. Samuel F. Merrill, John C. Hollis, Murray B. Watson, and Geo. E. Davis, all of whom are well-known and highly esteemed citizens. The senior partner is President of the National Shoe and Leather Bank. In the spring of 1888 the firm was changed to a corporation, under the name of the Ara Cushman Company, of which Ara Cushman is President, Charles L. Cushman, Vice-president, Samuel F. Merrill, Treasurer, Murray B. Watson, Clerk. A great portion of the output of this concern is disposed of through its Boston office, located at No. 128 Summer Street, and a heavy business is done.

Oscar Holway & Co., Flour, Grain and Grass Seed, 19 School Street, near Maine Central Depot, Auburn. Forty-one years ago the enterprise conducted by the house of Oscar Holway & Co. was inaugurated, today this concern stands at the head of the trade in Me., and ranks with the best known and most largely patronized in all New England. There you have in a nutshell the history of this popular undertaking, and it is one of which every public spirited citizen of Auburn should feel proud. The firm is made up of Messrs. Oscar Holway, Frank E. Tobey, Geo. P. Martin, and Chas. C. Holway, the first two gentlemen being natives of Fairfield, the third of Monmouth and the last of Augusta, Maine. All are well-known business men, and all are gentlemen whose integrity and ability in matters pertaining to the goods they handle have never been brought into question. The firm utilizes four buildings in this city, and also carry on an establishment at Augusta for the accommodation of their customers in that section. Employment is afforded to ten assistants here in Auburn, and a very extensive wholesale business is done throughout New England. Flour, Grain and Grass Seed are the great staples dealt in, and as we have before hinted no concern in the New England States is better prepared to supply goods of standard quality at the lowest market rates. Flour is made a specialty and is handled in all grades and the most popular brands at the smallest possible margin. Orders are attended to with celerity and accuracy, and the instructions of customers are carefully noted.

Park House, Mrs. S. C. Yeaton, Proprietress, corner of Main and Academy Streets, Auburn, two minutes walk from Grand Trunk Depot. Transients accommodated at reasonable rates. Experience will do wonders to smooth and make easy any undertaking or pursuit, and certainly traveling is no exception to the rule, some even going so far as to say that by the time a man learns how to travel properly he is too old to leave home at all, but however this may be, there can be no doubt that one of the fundamental rules of comfortable traveling is to know how and where to find the best hotels. It is by no means always the most pretentious or high-priced houses that are the most desirable or home-like, and a conspicuous example of this truth may be found in the case of the Park House, of which Mrs. S. C. Yeaton is the proprietress, located at the corner of Main and Academy Streets, two minutes walk from the Grand Trunk Depot. The accommodations for both transient and weekly boarders are eminently comfortable and complete. This house was first established in 1860, and has been under the able management of Mrs. Yeaton since 1883. It is a three-story house and covers an area of 50x60 feet, and contains twenty-five guest rooms and has four fine suites of rooms suitable for families. Mrs. Yeaton has established a reputation for low rates and unremitting efforts to please and satisfy her guests. She does a large business and fully deserves her success, as it is but the legitimate result of her liberal management and fair treatment. This hotel enjoys exceptional advantages as a summer resort, being close to Auburn Park and is delightfully situated, overlooking the entire Park and fronting the main street. Water is brought daily to the house from the celebrated Poland Spring.

Maine Benefit Association, of Auburn. Chartered March 5, 1885. The object of this Association is to furnish protection to the widows, orphans, or other dependents of its members, by the payment of a CASH BENEFIT to such dependents at the death of its members. This organization was chartered by the Legislature of Maine by an act approved March 5, 1885. By the terms of this charter the rights of members are protected and the perpetuity of the Association secured by the most carefully drawn provisions and safeguards. By the terms of the charter fifteen per cent of all death assessments collected is deposited in interest bearing securities with the State Treasurer as a reserve fund. This deposit, already large, is to be increased every year until it shall amount to one hundred thousand dollars, every dollar of which, with the income of the same, is absolutely and entirely for the benefit and protection of the members of the Association. There you have a clear, succinct and straightforward statement of what the Maine Benefit Association proposes to do; now for a necessarily brief consideration of the means by which they propose to do it. Persons between the ages of eighteen and fifty-five inclusive are eligible to membership under certain right and proper conditions, and after an examination by the Association's physician. The funds essential to the carrying on of the enterprise are secured as follows: *First,* By an Admission Fee, which is the same to all ages, and which varies from $5.00 where $1,000 insurance is wanted up to $15.00 where insurance to the amount of $5,000 is carried. *Second,* By an Annual Fee, payable semi-annually, and ranging from $3.00 to $5.00 according to the amount of insurance held. *Third,* By a series of assessments on the members, graded according to their age at the time of joining, and as frequent as circumstances require. Not one penny of the money collected by this third means can be used for expenses of management or anything else excepting the payment of death claims. A state of affairs that will be appreciated by those who know how to sympathize with the honest old sea captain who put a dime in the contribution box "for the heathen," and then added a dollar to "pay for getting it to them." THE ASSOCIATION IS PURELY MUTUAL. The members are the only stockholders, and as only sufficient money is collected to assure the payment of losses, there is no heavy surplus accumulated to tempt the cupidity of any one. Listen to these words from the Association's prospectus, and treasure them in your memory, for they are literally "as true as gospel." "Life Insurance, under any and all systems, consists in collecting from the living to pay the representatives of the dead." Remember this; and bear in mind also that anything more or less than this is not true Life Insurance. Those having direction of the Association claim that its system provides Life Insurance simply, directly and inexpensively, and in our deliberate opinion this claim is well-founded, and the Maine Benefit Association should be joined by every eligible person who cares for the future of those dependent upon him. Circulars giving all desired information can be had on application at the general office, Goff Block, Room 5. We present the names of the officers below, and feel that no stronger closing argument could be given to establish the reliable nature of the enterprise. President, George C. Wing. Vice-presidents, Wallace H. White, S. Clifford Belcher. Treasurer, Nathan W. Harris. Medical Director, Wallace K. Oakes, M.D. Secretary, S. Arthur Lowell. Manager, Milton F. Ricker. Directors, George C. Wing, Auburn; Charles H. Gilbert, Canton; George D. Bisbee, Buckfield; Seth M. Carter, Auburn; John B. Redman, Ellsworth; Nathan W. Harris, Auburn; Albert R. Savage. Auburn; Milton F. Ricker, Auburn; Wallace H. White, Lewiston.

Eureka Hosiery Co., Manufacturers of Cotton, Cashmere, All-Wool and Worsted Hosiery, Auburn. It is owing to the establishment and operation of such enterprises as the Eureka Hosiery Co., that the general average of Hosiery manufactured in this section of the country is so high, and when one comes to recall the old home-spun goods, and to remember the high price of handsome Hosiery at that time, some idea is gained of the benefits the community receive from the operation of accumulated capital. A manufacturing enterprise pays a dividend to its owners of course (or at least it should do so) but it also pays a dividend to the public, for if "a penny saved is a penny earned" we have all of us received many a liberal return from enterprises in which we have not invested a dollar. The Eureka Hosiery Co. is located at No. 103 Main Street, Auburn. It was established and incorporated in 1888, Geo. C. Wing, President, A. A. Waite, Treasurer and Manager, while the Directors are Geo. C. Wing, M. C. Percival, A. A. Waite, all gentlemen well known in business circles. Its works are equipped with the most improved machinery in use, and its productions are made from choice selected wool, entirely free from cotton, shoddy, or waste of any description. The colors are absolutely fast; they will not crock or fade, and are the most perfect fitting stockings in the market being knit in conformity with the foot, and are warranted to give entire satisfaction to the wearer. They also make to order children's stockings with double knees any size required, also lumbermen's heavy fulled socks for lumbermen and teamsters. The Eureka Hosiery Co. has had a most extended experience in connection with the manufacture of their goods, and take pains to maintain the reputation long since gained, and have every facility to assist them in so doing. These Hose are being sold by all first-class dealers throughout the country. Mr. A. A. Waite, the Treasurer and Manager, was for nearly fourteen years carder and spinner, in various cotton mills, in making plain and Ladies' dress goods. We print below a testimonial from Heselton Bros., the enterprising and successful Dry and Fancy Goods dealers in Skowhegan, as follows :—

"We guarantee the Eureka Hose to give satisfaction in every respect. Made from the best selected wool, entirely free from cotton, shoddy or waste of any description. Being knit in conformity with the foot gives them the desired shape. The colors are black, navy blue, drab, brown and scarlet.

C. A. Jordan, Carpenter and Builder. Jobbing of all kinds promptly attended to, and satisfaction given. Shop No. 14 Mechanics Row, rear of Auburn Hall. The services of a competent and reliable carpenter are pretty sure to be in active demand in such a place as Auburn, and not a few house-owners and others would like to hear of a carpentering establishment, where they could place their orders, with the positive assurance that they would receive prompt and careful attention. This business was started in 1878 by Paine & Jordan, succeeded by C. A. Jordan in 1882, and Jordan & Bond in 1884, and since 1887 the business has been conducted by Mr. Jordan. Not a great while elapsed after Mr. Jordan began operations here before considerable trade was built up, as all orders intrusted to him were carried out in the most satisfactory manner, and all agreements closely adhered to. This method of doing business has been steadily followed ever since, and as a result Mr. Jordan has an enviable reputation among those best acquainted with his work. Buildings from the hands of this firm, such as the Auburn High School, Stanley Dry Plate factory, Avon Mill, and residences of F. M. Jordan, Charles Gay, Fred Olfene, B. F. Briggs, Ara Cushman, F. H. Briggs, and many others, show some of the best examples of heavy framing and fine finishing to be found in the cities of Auburn and Lewiston.

A. B. Crafts, Dealer in Choice Family Groceries, Fine Teas, Coffees, Meats and Provisions, 178 Court Street, Auburn. A man who really makes a specialty of handling Choice Family Groceries, and supplies such goods at reasonable rates, is as sure to build up a large business eventually as he is to please his customers, and it is to be regretted, to say the least, that the feverish haste for wealth which actuates too many of those who have engaged in this line of trade, only results in their trying to dispose of second-class goods at first-class prices, with the legitimate conclusion that neither they nor their customers are satisfied. A proof of the soundness of our views on this subject may be found in the exceptional success attained by Mr. A. B. Crafts, of No. 178 Court Street, in endeavoring to do business in such a manner that no one concerned should have good reason to complain, for this gentleman has handled Choice Family Groceries from the inception of his undertaking, and has gained the good will, as well as the custom, of his patrons, by so doing. He began business in conjunction with Mr. Pulsifer, in 1877, under the style of Pulsifer & Crafts, but since 1881 he has carried on operations alone. Mr. Crafts was born in Hebron, Me., and is connected with the Odd Fellows and the Grand Army. He has gained the name of selling at a low price as well as of handling only reliable goods. A fine line of Fresh and Cured Meats is carried in addition to the complete assortment of Groceries in stock. Mr. Crafts has lately moved into his new quarters — a fine large store, built on the site of the old one,—with plate glass front, and all modern improvements, where he and his assistants will attend to the wants of customers, old and new, to their satisfaction.

HISTORICAL SKETCH

— OF —

AUGUSTA.

THE history of Augusta presents features of unusual interest even in this unusually interesting region of New England. Few spots in this country can trace back the advent of English influences to a more remote period, and few can show more glorious and worthy results evolved by more than two centuries and a half of growth from these original sources. Geographically, Augusta is nearly in the center of the Kennebec valley, and as such it was a favorite rallying place for the Kennebec Indians, by whom it was called "Cushnoc," the exact signification of which does not seem to have been yet discovered. Upon the site where now stands the fair city of Augusta, the Canibas tribe were often accustomed to meet both for purposes of peace and war, though they seem to have been a quiet, unaggressive people, as were most of their brethren of the Kennebec nation. For this reason, as well as for its fertility and accessibility, the Kennebec Valley was early chosen by the first colonists of New England as a trading center, and in 1629, before even Boston was founded, a trading-house was established here at Cushnoc by the Pilgrim Fathers of Plymouth. Probably not half a score of New England cities can trace their origin back so far as this. The trading-house continued here and prospered for about thirty years, and during that time was not seriously troubled by the Indians. In 1654, as the record shows, Lieut. Thomas Southworth was the Colonial Agent here. But about the end of this decade, a cloud arose in the shape of the Indian troubles which began to grow threatening throughout New England, and in 1660, thinking that this place was too near and open to attack from Canada, the Plymouth colonists withdrew and abandoned the trading-house to the mercy of the elements and more cruel aborigines. For about a century the place lay desolate, and no attempt was made to restore it, though traces of the old settlement were visible in 1692.

A more successful attempt to establish a settlement was made in 1754, though not primarily for that purpose. It was toward the end of the French wars, when the activity and spirit of that versatile but inconstant people were beginning to decline before the stubborn resistance of the more persevering English. As the latter kept driving the French further back, they reëstablished old settlements, and erected forts to maintain their conquests. One such, called Fort Western, was erected in 1754, on the ruins of the old trading-house at Cushnoc, by the Plymouth Colony, who still claimed the ownership of the region under their old charter. This fort was built very substantially and well garrisoned, as it was expected to protect the whole lower valley of the Kennebec, but no attack was made upon it during the war. In fact, Augusta never seems to have suffered at all from foreign invasion. Soon after the fort was completed, the fall of Quebec and the close of the war, removed all fears and restraints, and something more than a military settlement began to give signs of appearing. Houses were erected, clustering around the fort, most of the garrison, who were disbanded and might have departed, remaining and receiving choice lots of land for settlement. Other colonists commenced to come in, attracted by the fine soil, situation and the protection afforded by the fort, and within a decade quite a flourishing settlement had grown up here. The first record of a religious meeting being held, was in 1763, on the occasion of a visit of an English missionary named Mr. Bailey, who afterward settled further down the river, but made journeys occasionally through this region, and labored faithfully here, though most of the colonists were not in sympathy with the English church.

The land was formally and legally apportioned by the Plymouth owners to the garrison and other settlers in 1762, when fifty large and fine lots were surveyed and allotted on each side of the river, around Fort Western. The commandant of the fort, Capt James Howard, was a leader in the first settlement, and was allotted several large tracts of land. Benjamin Hallowell and Nathaniel Bowman also bought up large sections though not residents. Among the most prominent and active residents in these early days, were Ezekiel Page, Edward Savage, Ephraim Cowen, Josiah French, the first and only innkeeper for many years, and Pease Clark. Under able and far-sighted management, both at home and abroad, the place advanced rapidly in size and character, until in 1771 it was granted a town charter, and incorporated under the name of Hallowell, in honor of Benjamin Hallowell, Esq., who owned large sections of land here, and had done much to advance the town. By the time the Revolutionary struggle broke out, the town had advanced too far, and become too firmly established to be set back in its growth, but it did not do much more than maintain its own while the conflict lasted. Several military companies were raised here, and the town partook actively as well as earnestly in the maintenance of the great cause. The most direct touch of warfare it experienced was when Benedict Arnold with his small but heroic and devoted band marched through here in 1775, on the fateful expedition to Canada. Rumors of war, also, but little more came hither when the British invaded the Penobscot. Fort Western was repaired and strengthened, though never called into active demand, except for the quartering and training of volunteer troops. Although Augusta has never seen much bloody fighting, it has had more or less military aroma about its atmosphere, on account of the presence of soldiers and military buildings. The arrival of Samuel Cony, who came to Augusta from Massachusetts in 1777, has hardly been equalled in importance by the advent of any other one man, as he not only did much for the town himself, but founded a great family which has always been very active and generous in discovering and forwarding its best interests. The weary years of war and deprivation dragged themselves on until 1783, when the Declaration of Peace aroused great exultation and joy here, and again the town started on a rapid course of advancement.

The census of Hallowell, taken in 1784, showed a population of 692, and every year now brought large additions. As the people spread out and the farms grew through all the environing region, a movement sprang up and slowly grew stronger toward the formation of two separate towns. By 1796 this movement for division had grown importunate, and culminated in the following year in the separation from Hallowell of that part which is now Augusta. The new town, when first divided off, was called Harrington, in honor of Lord Harrington, a distinguished English patriot who had sympathized with the colonists during the Revolution, and who had evidently some ardent and influential admirers here. But this name seemed "too English, you know," to the large majority, and after it had been borne a few months, a spontaneous movement to change it sprang up, which resulted in the choice of "Augusta." There may have been some prescience in the minds of those far-seeing citizens of the importance the town would gain in after days, but if they had foreseen all its history they could not have chose a more stately and fitting name than Augusta.

The new town started on its independent career with a population of between eight and nine hundred, which had increased in 1798 to 1,140, and grew rapidly larger. Every augury was favorable, and the most promising sign was the dauntless and pushing spirit of its citizens, which has lain at the root of its great progress. A good evidence of this was shown in 1797 in the erection of the Kennebec bridge, which was the most extensive and formidable enterprise yet completed in Maine—no small tribute to one of its then smallest towns. But " coming events cast their shadows before." The progressive character of the town was early felt, for when Kennebec County was incorporated in 1798, Augusta was made the shire town, although one of the youngest, having only been formed the year before. The cause is shown however, in the fact that a large proportion of the County officers were from Augusta, such men as Joseph North, Daniel Cony, James Bridge, John Davis, Henry Sewall and Wm. Howard. Augusta has had good reason to know that a country's wealth is in its men, for though never one of the largest places in the State, it has exercised an ever-increasing influence, surpassed by no other city, in State affairs, because of the number and character of its truly great men. The last year of the eighteenth century was distinguished by the formation of a volunteer fire company, one of the earliest in the State.

The first years of the nineteenth century opened auspiciously, and steady expansion in all lines and departments of the town life was the order of the day. An evidence of its financial growth, was the establishment of the first State bank here in 1804. A movement of another but not less important character, resulted in the erection of the first church edifice here in 1809, at an expenditure of $8,000. With the vigor of mind and spirit which characterized all its endeavors, the citizens of Augusta early gave careful attention to military affairs, and in 1806 was formed the "Augusta Light Infantry Company, Captain Vose," one of the finest military organizations the State has ever known. It soon became famous through Maine for the perfection of its discipline, the beauty of its maneuvers and its thorough equipment in every particular. The enthusiasm shown in its establishment and maintainance was remarkable, and the laurels of glory which it won are yet fresh in the minds of many of the older citizens.

In the years 1808 and 1809, a series of remarkable disturbances occurred in this vicinity, which have had few parallels in the history of New England. Augusta, being the seat of the county jail, was naturally the center of the troubles, though its citizens, so far from being to blame for them, were largely instrumental in preventing their consequences from becoming momentous. A large part of the outlying districts of the Kennebec Valley had gradually become settled by squatters, without any claim to the land, not a few of whom were the reverse of mild in their dispositions. Consequently, when the owners sent surveyors through the region to lay out land for sale, and the sheriffs followed to maintain those who had bought land in their rights, the old squatter inhabitants were naturally "riled," and resisted to the best of their ability. Several sheriffs were severely handled and injured, and the excitement grew continually in intensity. A large number of arrests were made, and the old county jail house here was overstocked with unsavory inhabitants. But arrest only made the squatters more aggressive, and a large number of them rallied to the rescue of their imprisoned friends. The news of the approach of a considerable force was received in the town, and the militia was called out, but they were not strong enough to prevent the jail from being set on fire and burned to the ground, though they managed to keep their hands on the prisoners and prevented their release. The affair gradually blew over for a while, the guilty met their requisite punishment, and the course of law and order went steadily on through the county before which the lawless had inevitably to retreat. A new and stronger jail and court house was erected, which promised to stand the strongest attack. But even greater excitement ensued during the next year. A party of surveyors were working in the vicinity of Malta, when they were suddenly surprised and fired upon by a party of men disguised as Indians. One of them was so severely wounded that he died from the effect. Popular indignation caused a most thorough search to be made for the murderers, and nine of the old squatter inhabitants of the region were arraigned on this charge.

While these unique distractions were occurring at home, Augusta had also been troubled by events outside. The Embargo, first laid on our commerce in 1807, had gone on for several years, making things worse and worse, and Augusta suffered severely with the rest. Twice the citizens of Augusta drew up strong and pointed resolutions for the personal consideration of President Jefferson, and so powerfully were they put and difficult to answer, that the President wrote a personal letter which exists to-day in the city records, and in which he made important concessions from his policy. In 1810 the census showed an increased population of 1,805, and a total valuation of $178,064. In this year the Kennebec Bank was incorporated, with a capital stock of

$100,000. The sentiment of the town was strongly opposed to war, and in 1810 the Herald of Liberty, a Federalistic paper was started to represent that sentiment. But the war was declared, despite of them, in 1812, and foregoing private feelings and interests, the citizens joined with noble patriotism in the endeavor to maintain the national honor. Men and supplies were devoted to carrying on an undesired war, but when it was over none were gladder than the citizens of Augusta.

In 1815, Judge Cony, with his usual liberality, established an enduring monument to the city's and his own fame, in the founding of the "Cony Female Academy." At that time the subject of the education of women had received but a very small share of the attention it deserved, but under the leadership of Judge Cony, thoughtful men of Augusta made long advances on the old methods, and to the marvelous development which has attended this department of education in recent decades, the city of Augusta has contributed no small share. After the close of the war of 1812–15, the great question in Maine was its proposed separation from Massachusetts, and Augusta was strongly for separation. Under the first State census taken after the separation, the town in 1820 contained 2,457 inhabitants, and the valuation $282,549, both showing a large increase over the last decade. In this year $1,200 was appropriated for schools, $1,500 for the poor, and $2,300 for roads, which figures give a good idea of the town's progress and liberality.

In 1825 a movement of large importance to the interests of Augusta was inaugurated, resulting in the establishment in that year of the Kennebec Journal, than which there has since been no more reliable, progressive and valuable paper in the State. Its first proprietors were Eaton & Severance, and the Journal has gone on steadily increasing its circulation and power. The daily edition was first issued in 1870, and served to extend its already wide and marked influence. An event of great interest at the time, and large consequences since, occurred in 1826, when the steamboat "Legislature" came up the Kennebec to Augusta, from Boston via Portland. Since that time steamboat communication with Boston has constantly kept up and this has been a marked influence in the upbuilding of the commercial interests here.

The location at Augusta of the State Capital was a great benefit to its advance in many directions, and all items bearing on this point have a special interest. For over a decade after the separation, the State Legislature continued to meet at Portland, but it was obvious that this could not continue to be the favored spot, since it was indisputably too far from either the geographical or numerical center of the State to be considered. Many heated discussions were held in the early Legislatures on this important point, which was the rock on which one after another they all split. Each town which had a ghost of a show was very active and prominent in pushing its own claims, promising everything possible and impossible, if it were only made the favored spot. The first result which grew out of the discussions was that some place in the Kennebec Valley was undeniably considered by the majority as the most desirable spot. Then it came to a choice between a number of growing towns in this section, Hallowell taking the lead with Augusta a close second. A committee appointed by the Legislature, in 1821, reported in favor of the former place, but the decision was altered and deferred from year to year, until finally in 1827, after almost an interminable dispute and hard feeling, Augusta was chosen for the site. A large influence in deciding this choice was the quiet but powerful words and measures of the able men who now as always represented Augusta with unsurpassed devotion and talent, and also to the substantiality of the advantages which Augusta possessed. The great beauty and value of Weston Hill, which was offered by the town as a site, and where now the Capitol stands, was an inducement of great weight. The town also offered others of a monetary character, and being as near as possible to both centers, and the head of navigation on the Kennebec, it carried off the day with honors, and the wisdom of the choice has since been attended with increasing force as the years have clearly shown its advantages.

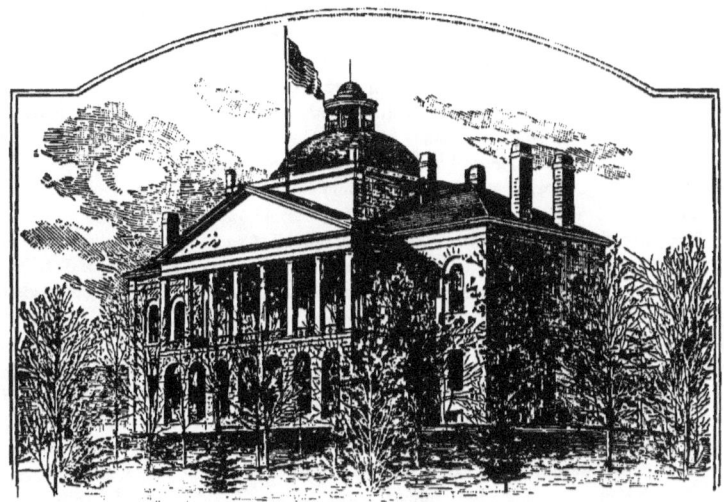

THE STATE CAPITOL.

Among other characteristic movements of the times was the erection of the United States arsenal in 1828. It was the greatest day the town had ever known, when, on July 4th, 1829, the cornerstone of the new Capitol was laid. An immense concourse witnessed the military display, which consisted of regiments from other States as well as almost all in Maine. Distinguished visitors from all parts of the country were present, and the services were very impressive and appropriate. The leaders of the day's celebrations were the able legislators of Augusta, who had done so much in securing the occasion, Nathaniel Weston, Reuel Williams, James Bridge and Henry W. Fuller. In 1830 the population had risen to 3,980, and there were already twenty-three members of the three leading professions situated here. The State House was completed in 1832, at a total cost of $138,991, to which Augusta contributed much more than its due share. In extent it is 150x54 feet, the wings being 33x54 feet, and the central portion 84x56 feet. It sets on a commanding position, and its front is beautifully finished off with an arcaded collonade of eight Doric pillars, 81 feet in height; the height of top of cupola is 114 feet from the base; the reception hall is handsomely finished off, and contains statues and paintings of some of Maine's greatest men; here also are the flags carried so honorably on many battle-fields by heroic soldier sons. The various department rooms and the two legislative halls are thorougly fitted up and models in their way. There is a large and valuable State library here under able and scientific management. The State House has listened to many powerful and noteworthy addresses, and has witnessed some remarkable occurrences. In front of it were stationed a large number of volunteer troops, and from its steps have been consigned stars and stripes, which were afterward baptized with fire and blood. A few years ago it witnessed a bloodless civil war between the two great parties represented in the State. One gained an apparent sweeping victory through the State and took possession of the State House. But charges of collusion were made and all the members-elect of, and those supported by, the other party, took up their headquarters on the State House green. By some inexplicable turning of the table after a few days the party inside was ousted and those outside got possession of the building in a body, and for the rest of that year this "anomalous legislature" was of one political complexion.

The year 1827 was not entirely fortunate, though Augusta gained the Capitol in that year, for the old Kennebec Bridge, which had stood so many freshets and storms, was burned, and a great conflagration causing much damage and loss to Augusta ensued. But measures of restoration were immediately begun and in the general rejoicing over the victory and the building of the State House, the minor loss was subordinate. The year 1834 witnessed the commencement of the building of the Maine Insane Hospital, which, in the choice of Augusta as Capital, naturally was located here. The work continued for six years, and in 1840 this noteworthy institution was completed. It has since been enlarged and improved; its methods have been broadened and made more scientific with the great advances made by mental science itself, and it now ranks among the best and most ably managed in this country. In this first year of its operation—1840—it treated one hundred and twenty-nine patients, and during the year 1887 some seven hundred and fifty-four patients enjoyed its privileges, which shows its great growth in the last half-century. The present superintendent is Dr. B. T. Sanborn, who has had long and thorough experience in the treatment of mind troubles, and has noticeably affected and improved the entire system here since he has taken charge; so that it is now in a most admirable state, and on a level with the most approved institutions of the kind.

The commercial interests of Augusta were largely interested in the building of the great dam, which was begun in 1835 and completed in the following year. It was a work of great magnitude and required a large outlay, but the value and necessity of the waterpower had already become evident, and neither the enterprise nor the faith of the business men of Augusta was wanting. It did require strong faith, however, to believe that a dam powerful enough to resist the tremendous spring freshets which occasionally occurred, could be built, and this faith has been tested many times. In 1839 occurred a great freshet, which broke and seriously damaged the dam in several places as well as considerable property near it on the banks. But this disaster did not discourage the people, and the dam was rebuilt stronger the following season. Another great freshet came in the spring of 1846, but the dam this time proved strong enough to withstand it, and less damage was done. A fire at the dam in 1850, changed its aspect somewhat, and in 1855 there was another freshet, which succeeded in breaking through in several places. But the greatest freshet ever known here since the dam was built occurred in 1870. It came with increasing force for several days and finally swept away the dam entirely. But it was rebuilt in the same year, the people rising to the urgency of the occasion, with greatly increased strength, and at a cost of $150,000. So thoroughly was the work done this time that though many times since the water and ice have risen high and strong against it, it as yet, has stood firm and steadfast. The railroad bridge which was also destroyed in 1870 was rebuilt at great expense and much more strongly.

The population in 1840 had increased to 5,314, and the next decade was one of the most prosperous in Augusta's history, the population in 1850 having come near its high-water mark, being 8,232, and the valuation $2,337,138, a remarkable increase. One great and helpful influence to Augusta's business interest during this decade, was the work done on the river, toward the broadening and deepening of its channel, which was begun in 1845 and has since been continued and renewed with good results. In 1848 the incorporation of the Augusta Savings Bank bore witness to the increase of wealth among the citizens. But a much more important incorporation occurred in 1849, when in response to an urgent appeal the Legislature granted a city charter to Augusta. After an interesting and protracted political struggle, General Alfred Redington was selected and elected as the first Mayor, and the new city government was inaugurated with the brightest auspices in 1850. In 1851 an event of incalculable importance to the city took place when the first railroad train came through, upon the opening of the road to Augusta in that year. Since that day the commercial life of Augusta, as well as its social and political life, have been most intimately connected with the railroad and has gained much profit therefrom. The year 1853 was marked by two important events—the occurrence of one of the greatest fires the city had ever known, and the arrival and settlement here of the Hon. James G. Blaine, who has since brought much fame to the city of his home, and who is greatly honored and beloved here. The year 1854 marked the close the first century of the city's uninterrupted life and growth, and was celebrated with appropriate ceremonies. The election of Governor Samuel Cony reflected honor on his native city. In 1858, in answer to a pressing need, the erection of a new, larger and stronger county jail was begun.

About the close of this decade the questions of slavery and secession were becoming topics of burning thought and discussion, and Augusta, naturally, as the Capitol, became the center of the State-feeling. All the measures of the National and State Governments were earnestly watched, and when the call to arms was made in 1861, this city was among the first and most generous. It became the central rallying place for the State forces and not only led, but heartily entered many movements for the advancement of the great cause. The first company here was raised April 22 1861, by Capt. H. G. Staples, and joined the third Maine Regiment, one of the earliest formed and sent to the field, in which there were two Augusta companies. A great bivouac and rendezvous camp for the volunteers was made on the State House Green, and here, among others, the 7th, 8th, 9th and 11th Regiments were enlisted and dispatched. Later, the 13th, 14th, 15th, 24th, 28th, 29th, 30th and 31st Regiments were all organized here and went forth to battle, in all of which and other State regiments were gallant sons of Augusta. The record of the city for generosity, the bravery and the genius of its officers and men was unsurpassed, and will ever form a bright

SOLDIERS' MONUMENT.

page in the military history of the State. Large sums were devoted to bounties, soldiers' families and supplies, and active and influential branches of the Sanitary and Ladies' Aid Societies were situated here. The honor and death list of Augusta was large, and heavy drafts were made upon her affectionate sorrow. The memory of the honored dead is preserved not only by a noble monument, but also imperishably in the hearts of the people. The city had hardly recovered from the immediate sense and experience of war and its bloody troubles, when, like its sister city, Portland, and soon after her, it also experienced a severe baptism of fire. It was in the night of September 7, 1866, that this greatest conflagration ever known in Augusta broke out, and it lasted through a large part of the following day. It originated in a large tenement building on Water Street, near Oak, and continued its rapid course until almost all the business portion of the city was laid in ruins, sweeping down both sides of Water Street and laying bare the west side of the city from Winthrop Street to Bridge. Every bank building in the city, every lawyer's office, as seems always to be the case, and almost every building used for business purposes, two large hotels, the Post-office and many dwelling-houses, were burned to the ground. In all, eighty-one buildings, forty-nine of them of brick, and valuable, were lost, and the total damage was estimated at about $500,000, only about half of which was insured. The fire-department worked most heroically and deserve the highest praise. With some of their apparatus destroyed and much impaired, they kept up a steady and gallant fight from the beginning of the fire to the end, and only by the most strenuous efforts could the fire be stopped where it was. They ventured on places where death seemed certain, and though help was gallantly afforded by surrounding towns, bore almost all the peril and exhausting toil and won the laurels of enduring praise. Although the firemen were of unsurpassed courage and skill, the test of the fire showed that some of the methods and appliances then in use were too antiquated, and these faults were so thoroughly remedied that the department now ranks with the highest in *morale* and efficiency. This fiery disaster was a great throw-back for the town, and one which, though met with great courage and energy, has never been entirely recovered from. The business men of Augusta immediately formed a committee, and in the extraordinary zeal and interest shown in the rebuilding of the burned district and the reëstablishment of business interests retarded, new avenues of industry were opened up and a more energetic spirit fostered, so that the balance of results of the fire was not entirely on the debit side. The business section, and Water Street in particular, was built up much more substantially than before, and Augusta is certainly a far handsomer city by reason of the fire. The extreme care and attention which have been brought about in this field by this great disaster, is the city's greatest safeguard and assurance against any repetition of it taking place.

An era of building, not confined to the parts visited by the fire, now set in and the year 1868 was marked by the erection of many new and beautiful structures. Another evidence of the expanding spirit of the city was shown in 1869, when the Free Bridge system was adopted and all the people's hearts gladdened by the removal of the tolls. Despite the great freshet of 1870, the city continued to advance through the following decade, though more slowly than before the war, and not without suffering severe depression through the great financial panics which swept over the country at this time.

In 1880 the population had become 8,666, and it has been increased somewhat more rapidly under the better prospects of the present decade, so that it is now in the region of 10,000. Liberal appropriations were made last year, and the policy of wise and economical generosity maintained. The school department received $20,781.59, which was carefully administered, and in every respect this department does credit to the long and unremitting efforts to perfect it, which have so generously been bestowed by the city and its leading men. There were 2,367 school children in the various districts of the city last year. There are twenty-three districts in all, and the teachers, buildings and facilities in each are all of a high order of merit. Especial attention is given by the school-board and the supervisor to the securing of first-class teachers, and the results as shown in the improvement of the pupils have been very satisfactory. The system of grading, and studies, are arranged according to the most approved educational methods adopted and used in this country. The high school has been named in honor of one of Augusta's most distinguished citizens and a liberal benefactor of its educational interests, the "Cony Free High School." It is under the able superintendence of Mr. Geo. B. Files, who, assisted by a talented corps of teachers, has raised it to the highest level of New England's famous public school standard. The curriculum is thorough, scientific and practical, fitting either for college or for business, and furnishing every ingredient of a good English education. Special attention is now being given to the scientific department, and the results attained both in the case of those who go directly from here to college, and those who take a general course as a preparation for business, are highly creditable to the school and to the city. The great wealth of Augusta, which has always laid in the character and ability of its citizens, will be powerfully conserved so long as the present efficient, inestimably valuable school-system is preserved.

The fire department has been constantly improved; it is now on a most efficient and admirable footing. Last year only $855.16 were needed to maintain it, yet it performed every duty with the utmost dispatch and effect, accomplishing a saving of many thousands of dollars to the city. The force consists of thirty-two men, (including the chief engineer, Henry T. Morse), divided into two steam fire-engine companies, with every modern and necessary appliance. There has been much discussion in recent years over the water question, and the Augusta Water Company has introduce its hydrants throughout the city. The completion of this water-work system, which draws its supply from the illimitable source of the Kennebec, will mark a great advance in the city's life, and contribute no small share to its further progress.

The sanitary preëminence of Augusta has been long and widely famed. Screened from the harsh east winds which devastate the Atlantic coast, it has other marked advantages in the great water-course which makes its soil salubrious and its drainage perfect. It has added much to the successful life of Augusta as a State Capital that it has always enjoyed such unusual health privileges. A local board of health keeps a constant watch-care over every possible invasion and spread of infectious diseases.

One noble institution, which cannot be passed without mention, is the New England branch of the National Military Asylum for disabled soldiers, located at Togus Spring, about four miles from Augusta. This was established by act of Congress and first opened here in 1866. Four large brick buildings (100x50) in the form of a quadrangle were erected here in 1868, and these have been much improved and enlarged since. Several hundred invalid veterans here find a quiet home under favorable surroundings, and every attention is shown to those who risked their all and sacrificed much of their life to the interests and safety of their country.

The social life of Augusta has peculiar features from the fact of its political character. Every other winter when the Legislature is in session, the season is a very brilliant one, and this gives a much wider and more varied social life than is enjoyed by most places of its size. From this fact, also, though there are a number larger, there is no city in the State that is better known than Augusta. The business streets and houses, public buildings and beautiful graded drives, all give one the impression of a large and prosperous city, and the visitor is surprised to learn that the population is no larger than it is. But, though Augusta has owed much to this periodical accession of influential visitors, it has owed far more of its internal development to the enterprise and foresight of its own able citizens. These have not spared any effort to develop its every resource to the utmost, and to give it every privilege enjoyed by the largest cities, and their efforts and sacrifices have been abundantly rewarded, in the growing fame, wealth and power of the city. Its handsome appearance and natural advantages make it no unworthy Capital for a great and growing State like Maine, and it will undoubtedly continue to advance in unison with the State. The business interests are now full of life and constantly expanding, and every line of the city's affairs are bright with promise.

AUGUSTA WATER WORKS.

IF there is any one desideratum for the prosperity and thrift of a city or town, it is a thorough system of water-works, furnishing an abundant and never failing supply of pure water for its inhabitants. Not only does it promote the industries and the business industries of the city, but as a sanitary measure alone, a water system is worth many times its cost. But to go still further there is no method yet discovered which is such an adequate protection to the ignitable property of a place as that furnished by well constructed modern water works. Augusta has but very recently completed a water system of which she is justly proud, as one of the most complete and honestly constructed of any in the country. Today we have a spacious reservoir, 24 miles of mains and a pressure of 125 pounds to the square inch on Water Street, throwing a stream over the tallest building which can be found on the street. The system was built between July and December, 1886, by the Augusta Water Company who contracted with Mr. Geo. P. Wescott and Mr. Joseph H. Manley of this city to construct the works. Over 700 men were employed in the undertaking, which was performed in the most thorough manner regardless of occasional drawbacks and obstacles, and is now, when finished, universally regarded as a credit to the city. The water is taken from the Kennebec river above the dam and is found upon analysis to be extremely pure. It is pumped into a reservoir upon Burnt Hill and thence distributed through the pipes as needed. The nature and extent of the works can best be understood by a detailed description of the main features of the system in order.

The pumps were manufactured by R. D. Wood & Co. of Philadelphia, and invented by A. Geyelin, a member of the firm. They required 40 tons of pig iron in their manufacture and are capable of pumping 2,000,000 gallons in 24 hours under an elevation of 300 feet, with perfect ease. The cylinders or valve chests are about five feet long, each has 96 brass valves 3 inches in diameter. They weigh about 10,700 pounds each, are double acting, pumping both ways of the stroke, which is 19 inches; and are both connected with a 12-inch pump. The large gear wheel weighs 4,600 pounds and is 96 inches in diameter. The running movement of the pumps is 25 strokes per minute, being capable of pumping against a pressure of 160 pounds to the square inch; and they lift 7 tons of water at every stroke. The 12-inch column of water in the pumping main travels at the rate of three feet per second. The turbine wheel which drives the pumps is supplied with power from the Edwards Company's canal. It is 72 inches in diameter with 30 phosphor bronze buckets and developes 175 horse power. A filtering house consuming some 90,000 brick, contains two circular wells in which is filter material sixteen inches thick, lying on a perforated copper plate, beneath which is a chamber receiving the filtered water in its course to the pumping well, surrounding the circular ones, or filterers. The water while filtering passes into the circular well above the filter bed, then down through and out into the pumping well and is taken from there and thrown into the reservoir. To cleanse the filter, the filter water is compelled by a system of gates to pass up and through the filter bed, washing out all sediment, and is then taken away by a pump erected for that purpose and thrown away. This process of cleansing continues until the water becomes clear. The filtering beds consist of gravel of different grades thoroughly washed before placed in position, and was obtained at the gravel bank at Cumberland Mills. The reservoir situated on the hill to the south and west of the Poor Farm, is 19 feet in height, a prominent object to one looking west from the north end or east side. It has a capacity of 8,000,000 gallons, and its bottom has an elevation of 307 feet above the Kennebec river below the dam, the top or crest being 326. Water is held at the elevation of 325 feet above the surface of the river below the dam, 200 feet above Water Street at the junction of Bridge, giving 125 pounds pressure to the square inch.

At the elevation of 325 feet the reservoir contains over 6,000,000 gallons, while the twelve-inch pipe that supplies it will deliver that and the capacity of the pump besides in less than twenty-four hours, if required. In the construction of the reservoir care was taken to make it perfectly water tight, and to do this some 7,000 cubic yards of clay were used. This clay started from a deep trench beneath the center of the embankment and rose to within two feet of the top, making a wall averaging five feet in thickness well puddled and rolled. Adjoining this at the surface of the ground, after sod and soil had been removed was a two foot thickness of clay passing to the inside slope and thence down the slope to another trench, which acted as a footing for the gravel and paving. Overlying the entire bottom, clay was puddled at different depths, according to the nature of the material beneath.

Inside this clay wall and lining and beneath the paving, above the original surface, was placed the best clay material the reservoir site afforded, rolled in layers of eight inches depth. The clay wall was rolled in six-inch layers, and not allowed to dry or crack in the sun. The poorer material was placed outside of this wall of clay, being intended to act as a weight, as it has no effect as a water-tight medium. Surrounding this embankment on top and the outside slope are some 2,000 cubic yards of loam covered with sodding, which is necessary to prevent washing by rains. There are now laid 6,830 feet of 12 inch pipe, 1,443 feet of 10 inch pipe, 59,589 feet of 8 inch pipe, 44,698 feet of 6 inch pipe, 9,616 feet of 2 inch pipe, 5,295 feet of 1 inch pipe, and there are 80 city hydrants and 12 private hydrants. The iron pipe is from the manufactory of R. D. Wood & Co., Philadelphia, and is prevented from rusting by a process which introduces tar into the pores of the iron under a high temperature.

The depth of mains below the surface is five feet and a half and is thus below the frost. There are gates at each end of the bridge and the 10 inch main which crosses can be emptied at any time. Gates are placed in the pipe so that the water can be shut off from certain sections and streets when necessary. The pipe is all tested at a pressure of 300 pounds to the square inch, and, in fact, the entire pumping main has that strength. The value and usefulness of these water works is now fully demonstrated, not only by the constant supply of pure water they afford, but also by the fact that they save our citizens $4,000 yearly for insurance premiums, reductions of rates having been made by the insurance companies in consequence of this increased protection these works bestow against fire losses. The works have also had their effect upon the city fire department, which has been enabled to dispense with its cumbrous and expensive engines and to substitute a hose carriage service, making use of the numerous hydrants of the water service.

KENNEBEC LIGHT & HEAT COMPANY.

THE Augusta Gas Light Company was incorporated March 9th, 1853. The city was first lighted with gas October 26, of the same year. The Hallowell Gas Light Company was incorporated April 8, 1854, the works were built by the same company which built the Augusta works, in 1855. The two companies were united under the name of Augusta and Hallowell Gas Light Co., and the company continued under that name until February 4th, 1867, when it was changed to Augusta Gas Light Co., and the Hallowell portion of the plant sold to private citizens. The streets of Augusta were first lighted with gas in 1859. The Legislature, in February 1887, chartered the Kennebec Light & Heat Co., and authorized the Augusta Gas Light Co. to sell its property and franchise to it. The legislature also gave the Kennebec Light & Heat Co. full authority to purchase the property and franchise of the Gardiner Gas Light Co., and gave it authority to furnish light and heat in Hallowell. The Kennebec Light and Heat Co. was organized in order to combine the lighting of Augusta, Hallowell and Gardiner by gas and electricity under one Corporation. The property of the several companies has been transferred to the Kennebec Light & Heat Co. Under the new management large sums have been expended in permanent repairs, and in a new gas plant. New main pipes for distribution have been laid in the principal streets and a new gas holder of 45,000 cubic feet capacity has been built. This holder was built in the most substantial manner of brick and iron. The company, also built four large purifiers of the most improved pattern. On the east side of the river, the Kennebec Light & Heat Co. have leased from the Edwards Manufacturing Co. power and erected a building to generate their electricity. The building is 60 feet in length and 36 feet wide and one story in height. Two large turbine wheels, constructed by Mr. P. C. Holmes of Gardiner, have been placed in one of the new flumes and furnish the power for the electric light station.

During the summer of 1888 a number of street electric lights were put up by the company, proving so satisfactory that in the following October a contract was made with the city government for 54 arc lights of 2,000 candle power each, to be placed at street corners. These lights are equal to 270 gas lamps, furnishing nearly twice the former amount of illumination. Besides these some dozen others are owned by private parties. Seven of the city lamps, on Water and Cony Streets burn all night, at a yearly cost of $125 each. The others burn from sunset till midnight, and cost $75 each per year.

The company propose to extend their lines, and string their wire so as to furnish electricity in Hallowell and Gardiner as well as in Augusta. Both systems of electric light are to be used, the arc and incandescent, and one of the most extensive electric plants in New England will be established.

LEADING BUSINESS MEN

OF

AUGUSTA.

E. E. Davis & Co., Clothiers and Hatters, under Cony House, Augusta. In no branch of business at the present day can a man afford to abate any appreciable degree of exertion to push to the front, for competition is brisk and enterprising, and if an undertaking, however well equipped and apparently secure is left to run itself, the consequences are very apt to be similar to those of a sailing vessel served in the same way,—ruin and destruction. This statement is more applicable of course to some business pursuits than to others, where there is not so much ability required, or where the field of operation is larger and less thoroughly worked, but of none can it be urged with more truth and force than in that relating to the handling of Clothing, etc., for in this there is apparently "war to the knife" declared between rival dealers. An establishment devoted to this trade in Augusta, which has met with an unusual degree of success in gaining the favor and patronage of the public, is that conducted by Messrs. E. E. Davis & Co., located on Water Street, under the Cony House. The inauguration of this enterprise was in 1879, and the rapid but steady increase that has characterized the extension of its trade cannot but be gratifying to its projectors, however well it may be deserved. The store utilized is of the dimensions of 27x60 feet, and is well fitted up for the display of an exceptionally varied and desirable stock of Fine Clothing, Hats, Caps, and Gents' Furnishing Goods, having the finest front and most attractive display windows in the city, if indeed they are equalled in the State. Four courteous assistants are employed, and garments unexceptional in cut and style may be had here, at surprisingly low rates. Especial attention is called to the make, trimming and fit of their clothing, the better grades being city SHOP made, and far superior in STYLE and FIT to garments usually offered by small manufacturers who are unable to secure the SKILLED help and overseers obtained in large cities, and he must be hard to suit indeed, who is not perfectly satisfied with some one of the many fashionable and beautiful fabrics from which these suits are made. New and nobby styles of head gear are on hand at all prices, and the line of Gents' Furnishings shown comprises all those numberless conveniences used by the most carefully dressed. Messrs. Davis & Co., are highly esteemed by the community for their ability and probity, and give their personal supervision to all the business of their establishment, thereby insuring perfect content on the part of their numerous patrons, who are drawn from within a radius of fifty miles of Augusta. The policy upon which their business is conducted is characterized by liberality and the careful fostering of the interests of their patrons, so that transactions once entered into with this house may be not only pleasant for the time being, but permanently. The individual members of the firm are Messrs. E. E. & W. H. Davis, the first having been engaged in the Clothing business nearly seventeen years, and the latter nine. Both are well known and highly respected citizens and business men of this city.

Lord & Lowell, Watches, Clocks and Jewelry, Water Street, Under Cony House. Among the best known and most reliable establishments of the kind in Augusta, is that now conducted by Messrs. Lord & Lowell, centrally located on Water Street, under the Cony House. This establishment has a well-earned reputation for the excellence of its wares, and the fidelity with which work entrusted to it is performed, hence its business is prosperous and steadily increasing. This house was first established in 1883 by Messrs. Wheeler & Lord and successfully conducted by them until 1887, when the firm-name was changed to its present style of Lord & Lowell. With the advancement of any community in wealth, intelligence, and culture, the fine arts of decoration and adornment prosper, and the skill and taste of the jeweler is brought more constantly and generally into requisition. Twenty years ago it would have been impossible to have found customers for that class of goods which are now really in the greatest demand. The stock carried by Messrs. Lord & Lowell, comprise the finest grades of Watches, Clocks, Silver Ware, and a beautiful and unique selection of Jewelry, calculated to please the most fastidious. The premises occupied comprise a store 20x50 feet in dimensions, a part of which is neatly fitted up as an optical room, where a fine stock of Spectacles, Eyeglasses, etc., is displayed. The entire management of both Jewelry and Optical departments is under the personal direction of the proprietors. Messrs. Lord & Lowell are both natives of Maine, and men of judgment and sound business principles, and of exquisite taste in the selection of their stock.

Daniel A. Cony & Co., Groceries, Corn, Flour, Hair, Lime, Cement, Hides, Wool, Wool Skins, Fertilizers, Grass Seed and Hay, Corner Cony and Bangor Streets, East Side. The number of concerns in this country engaged in handling what is known as "staple" commodities, is of course something enormous, for where there is a population of 60,000,000 souls to be fed, clothed and otherwise provided for, it is evident that there must be many hands to do the work. As a general rule the merchants of the United States are enterprising, sagacious and perfectly reliable, so that it requires a special degree of excellence to attain distinction when the average is so high, and therefore, those firms which have gained prominence are all the more worthy of mention. It is a well-known matter of fact, that so prodigal is Ceres in her bounty in the State of Maine, that there are many stores which are the rendezvous of the farmers with harvests of grain and produce. The prominent position which the house of Daniel A. Cony & Co., occupies among the representative firms of Augusta, deserves distinguished mention, and admirably supports the statement we have just made. No history of Augusta's more prominent business houses would be complete without mention of that conducted by the above named firm. The premises utilized comprise three floors of the dimensions of 22x65 feet, as well as three large storehouses; the stock always on hand being Groceries, Corn, Flour, Hair, Lime, Cement, Hides, Wool, Wool Skins, Fertilizers, Grass Seed and Hay. Employment is afforded to five efficient assistants, and both a wholesale and retail business is done, the transactions being by no means confined to this city alone, but reaching all over the entire county. The firm is made up of Messrs. Daniel A. and Frederick Cony, both of whom are too well known personally to require further mention. The advantages offered to purchasers are such as can only be extended by houses doing a large and growing business, and whether a large or small quantity of goods are wanted, it will be found advisable to deal with this enterprising concern, for orders are promptly, carefully and honestly filled, and the lowest market rates are strictly adhered to. Family Groceries are handled extensively, and the prices quoted on these goods, together with the excellent quality of the commodities furnished, have resulted in making this the most popular department of its kind in the city. Through strict personal attention to their business and liberal dealings with the public, this firm has acquired a reputation not to be equaled by any similar concern in the entire State.

VIEW OF WATER STREET, COR. BRIDGE STREET.

Chas. M. Sturgis, Furniture, Curtains, Curtain Fixtures, Coffins, Caskets and Robes, 173 Water Street, Augusta. This house was established in 1883, and from its inception has enjoyed a steadily increasing trade. The premises located at No. 173 Water Street, comprise three floors, each 25x65 feet in dimensions, with a basement of the same size, and a large storehouse outside, which are well arranged for the conduct of the business in all its branches. A large and well-assorted stock of Furniture is always to be found here, comprising Parlor, Dining-room, Chamber and Hall Furniture, Curtains, Carpets and Draperies, Curtain Fixtures, etc. These include new and original designs, and are elegantly finished and upholstered in costly and medium priced fabrics, comprising all the elements of attractive appearance, durability and usefulness. The large retail trade of this house requires the employment of thoroughly capable and experienced clerks. Mr. Charles M. Sturgis also deals in Coffins, Caskets and Robes of which he constantly carries a large and complete assortment. Mr. Sturgis is a native of Fairfield, Me., and is a member of the Free Masons and Knights of Pythias. He is a practical business man and gives it his close personal attention, a fact which insures all customers the most perfect satisfaction. This house occupies an important and well-recognized position in the trade, and as such we recommend it to our readers. Mr. Sturgis is polite and attentive to all and is well-fitted by long experience for successfully carrying on the business, and well deserves the confidence, consideration and esteem he enjoys, which has resulted in a large trade throughout this section.

F. W. Mathews, Hats and Furs, also a full line of Gent's Furnishing Goods. Trunks and Bags, Water St. A hat being as it were the finishing touch on a man's costume, naturally attracts a degree of attention out of all proportion to its apparent importance, and a person who would look well dressed with a "shocking bad hat" on would certainly merit a position in some museum as a *rara avis*. On the other hand, a fashionable and well-made hat will do much towards making any one presentable, and thus no portion of the costume merits more careful attention. In order to be sure of obtaining an article of head-gear suited to one's individual peculiarities, an establishment carrying a large and varied stock should be patronized, such a one, in fact as is conducted by Mr. Fred W. Mathews, cor. Water and Bridge Sts. This gentleman has conducted the enterprise in question since 1881, having assumed entire control of it on the retirement in 1884, of Mr. Upham. The premises utilized are 20x40 ft. in area, and the stock comprises Hats, Caps and Furs of all kinds, it will be found full and complete in all its branches, and the long established reputation of this house for handling none but reliable goods is sufficient proof, if proof be needed, that this is a most desirable place at which to trade. Mr. Mathews is one of our truly representative citizens, being a native of this city, and having a large circle of friends and patrons here. He transacts a large and ever-increasing business, a fact which enables him to keep his ever-changing stock replete with all the very latest styles and novelties. All callers may feel assured of prompt and willing attention and careful consideration of their needs.

H. S. Blaisdell, Dealer in Fine Ready-Made Clothing and Gent's Furnishing Goods, Under Hotel North, Augusta. First impressions are actually of much more importance than most people are willing to acknowledge, for although we all wish that others should believe us to be in the habit of forming an opinion of a person or a thing only after mature consideration, as a matter of fact, in the majority of cases our judgment is very apt to be considerably influenced by first appearances and first thoughts. Everybody knows that a well-dressed man can go where a badly dressed one would not be permitted, and as it is in this case, so it is in others, it is for the advantage of all of us to wear well-made and fashionable Clothing. But before it can be worn it must be bought, and one of the best places that we know of in this section of the city at which to procure anything of this kind is the establishment of Mr. H. S. Blaisdell, located Under Hotel North, Water Street, Augusta. Business was begun by this gentleman in 1884, and he has steadily increased the scope of his operations until they have reached their present magnitude. He is a native of Maine and well known in this city and vicinity. A store and basement are occupied, each of the dimensions of 25x60 feet and a very fine stock of Clothing is exhibited, also Gentlemen's Furnishing Goods, embracing all the latest fashionable novelties in these lines. Two experienced and polite assistants are at hand to serve customers with the utmost celerity, and every effort is made to satisfy all. The prices are very reasonable and the goods the best the market affords. Also a branch store in Skowhegan at 104 Water Street, next door to the Post Office.

Smith & Reid, State Book Binders, and Manufacturers of Blank Books Ruled to any Pattern, Magazines, Law and Library Books, Music, etc., Bound to Pattern Previous Volumes, Works of Art Bound in the Most Elaborate Styles if Desired, Allen's Block, Augusta. Book-Binding is much more of an art than the majority of people are aware of, but every lover of reading knows the luxury of using a volume that is bound as it should be, that is to say, so bound that it will stay open at any point, be durable and agreeable to the touch and capable of standing rough usage without serious injury. The firm of Smith & Reid, State Book-Binders, is doubtless one of the best known concerns in New England, engaged in this line of business, and since operations were begun in 1854, the firm name then being Hartford & Smith, a very important and extensive trade has been built up. The present firm has been in existence since 1880. Mr. Reid entering as partner in that year, and being the active member of the firm, having adopted this trade since he was a boy, and through hard work and perseverance has made an everlasting reputation as an expert Book-Binder. Both members of the firm are Free Masons and Odd Fellows, Mr. Reid also being an A. O. U. W., Knight of Honor, and a native of St. John, N. B. Mr. Smith was born in this city, having formerly been connected with the old dry goods firm of Fowler, Hamlen & Smith, till he severed his connection with the firm, going West, where he remained for two years. He returned to Augusta in 1885 and is one of the city's smartest and most popular business men. The premises utilized are of the dimensions of 40x65 feet, and the most improved and efficient machinery is employed, 4-horse power being required to run the same. Not only Book-Binding, but also Blank Book Manufacturing is extensively engaged in, and a specialty is made of the Ruling of Blank Books to order. Magazines, Law and Library Books, Music, etc., will be bound to correspond with previous volumes, and at rates that will bear the severest comparison with those of other houses. Mr. Reid is one of Augusta's most spirited and respected business men, and is also one of the city's officials, being a member of the City Council, and Director of the Building Association, has always in view everything pertaining to the welfare of this thriving place, is also a stockholder of the new Trotting Association, and is altogether a citizen who is counting his friends by the score, who is an honor to the city, and through his own exertions, "a self made man."

C. N. Hamlen, Dry and Fancy Goods, Corner of Bridge and Water Streets, Augusta. In every city and in every town, too, for that matter, there are certain houses, that are so well known in connection with special lines of trade, that a native or old resident cannot think of one without thinking of the others also, and it is just this knowledge, that the stranger in a city does not get, and is therefore under a disadvantage, when purchases are to be made. However, here in Augusta when one who is acquainted thinks of Underwear, Hosiery and Fancy Goods in general, the firm name of C. N. Hamlen, Corner of Water and Chestnut Streets, comes into his mind for the simple reason that the two are so intimately connected that this result is inevitable. This well-known house was established over fifty years ago by the father of the present proprietor, Mr. C. N. Hamlen, who assumed full proprietorship about ten years ago, and has continued the business in the same liberal manner. A large and thriving business has been built up by energy, enterprise, and a careful study of the public needs, and the trade is still increasing with the city's growth. The premises occupied cover an area of 25x55 feet, and employment is afforded to five courteous and efficient clerks. A large stock is on hand, comprising everything in the line of Dry and Fancy Goods, and these articles are sold at a very small margin. Mr. Hamlen, being a shrewd business man, knowing the Dry Goods business thoroughly, believes in "quick sales and small profits," and as a consequence the stock is constantly fresh and new. Mr. Hamlen was born in this city and, as might be supposed, being liberal in his dealings, genial and courteous to visitors, buyer or no buyer, he counts his friends and customers by the score, and his success in business is therefore justly deserved, as he always has given close personal attention to every detail of his business, thereby showing his ability and justly-won name as one of Augusta's most industrious business men and citizens.

A. L. Wells & Co., Dealers in Parlor, Chamber and all kinds of Common Furniture, Coffins, Caskets and Burial Robes a specialty, No. 7 Bridge's Block, Water Street, Augusta. For over half a century has the enterprise conducted by Messrs. A. L. Wells & Co., been in operation, and those at all familiar with the undertaking need not be told that it ranks with the most truly representative of our city houses. Founded in 1837, by C. R. & H. N. Wells, this business has steadily grown from small beginnings until now the premises occupied comprise five floors and a basement of the dimensions of 30x60 feet, and employment is given to eight assistants, both a wholesale and retail trade being carried on. Sept. 1st, 1888, the firm of C. R. &

H. N. Wells dissolved, and since then Mr. A. L. Wells, the present proprietor, has conducted the business under the firm name of A. L. Wells & Co. He was born in this city, and is too well known here personally to render any further comment necessary. He handles Furniture of every description, including Folding Chairs, Rattan Goods, Parlor and Chamber Sets, etc., and no house in this State is in a position to offer more genuine bargains, or is worthy of more absolute confidence. This may seem an unqualified endorsement, and so it undoubtedly is and is meant to be, for it is impossible for any fair-minded and unprejudiced person to investigate the past record and future prospects of this concern, without feeling that it is deserving of the most liberal support, and that the inducements offered by it are worthy the attention of every intelligent buyer. Besides handling Furniture, Mr. Wells is a competent Funeral Director, and extensive dealings are had in

Coffins, Caskets, Burial Robes, etc., a large stock of these goods being carried, and the prices on the same being placed at remarkably low figures. No 7 Bridge's Block. Water Street, is the address of Messrs. A. L. Wells & Co., and no one wanting anything in their line can afford to pass this establishment. Mr. Wells has been in the Furniture business since the end of the war, having been with the well-known Furniture house of Messrs Blake & Co., of Lewiston, Me., for sixteen years. He carried a gun in the war when only sixteen years old; he belongs to the G. A. R., and is also a member of the Free Masons and Odd Fellows. That he thoroughly understands the business is evident from the importance it has attained among similar enterprises in this section, and the prices quoted on the goods show that he is prepared to meet all competition. Patrons are assured prompt and satisfactory service.

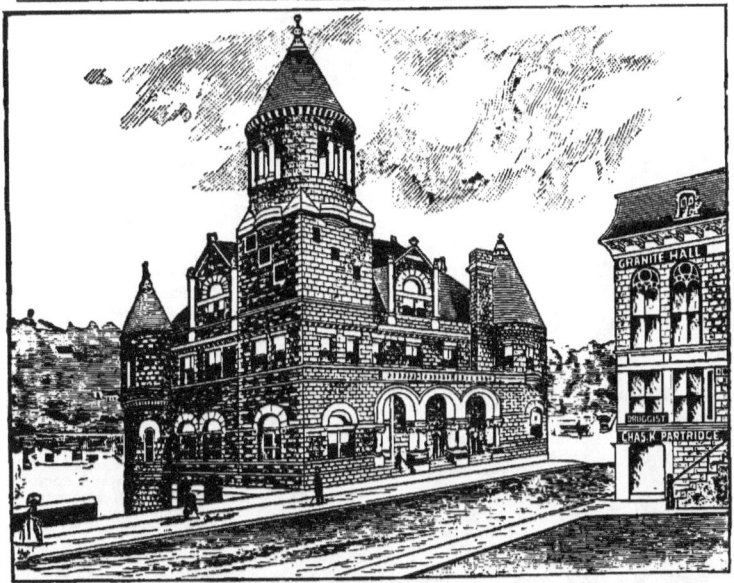

NEW POST-OFFICE BUILDING, WATER STREET.

Chas. K. Partridge, Druggist, Water Street, Corner Market Square, and Opp. New Post Office. This gentleman is one of the best-known pharmacists in the State, and the establishment conducted by him on Water Street at the Corner of Market Square, directly opposite the new Post Office building, is known as one of the best appointed in this section. He has worked hard to serve his patrons faithfully and well, has spared neither time nor expense in supplying the very best accommodations obtainable, and has succeeded in establishing a large trade which steadily grows from year to year. But what is even more gratifying than this liberal support is the entire confidence that is freely manifested in this establishment by those who are best acquainted with its resources, and the methods pursued in its management, which fairly justify the title of "Partridge's Old Reliable Drug Store." Mr. Charles K. Partridge bought in 1865 the old drug stand, established in 1828, on the opposite corner of Market Square, where now is located one of E. C. Allen's great publishing houses. The conflagration of that year swept away his store and stock but he secured a lease of his present store in Granite Hall Block, then in process of construction, temporarily locating his business in Bridge's Block until his new store was completed and ready for occupancy in the spring of 1866. In 1874 his brother was admitted to the business and the firm name became Partridge Brothers, but in 1887 Mr. C. K. Partridge again assumed full proprietorship, and the record of faithful and continuous service from the first is one of which he has every reason to be proud. The premises measure 24 x 70 feet and contain a heavy and varied stock of Drugs, Medicines, Chemicals, Proprietary Articles, Atlas Paints, Oils and Fancy Goods (for Toilet and similar purposes.) Mr. Partridge's prices are very moderate and his goods are sure to prove as represented in every instance. The facilities at hand for the prompt and accurate compounding of physician's prescriptions are hardly susceptible of improvement, and special attention is given to the filling of all such orders. The store and laboratory of Mr. Partridge are models of completeness and convenience. The valuable stock of fresh and reliable drugs, medicines and fancy articles is tastefully displayed, and an elegant soda fountain is a notable feature of the establishment. Experienced assistants are employed, the prescription department, however, being under the close personal supervision of the proprietor. Mr. Partridge is a well-known and life-long resident of Augusta. He was appointed by the Governor one of the three Commissioners of Pharmacy, on the enactment of the Pharmacy Law in 1877, and was first Secretary and afterward President of the Board until his resignation from the commission. Mr. Partridge prepares many specialties in Medicines of his own invention which are favorably known, among them the "U. S. Gold" Remedies.

Gay & Parsons, Manufacturers, Augusta Machine Works, Augusta. In the manufacture of hardware specialties this firm occupy so prominent a position as to demand more than brief notice in this work. The business was first commenced in 1879, and both gentlemen having a practical knowledge of the work, a persevering energy, and an ambition to succeed, have combined in making it a prominent factor of the business world. The premises occupied by this house are located on Rhines' Hill. Their buildings are fitted up with every convenience for the execution of the various manufactures, the machinery being all of the most approved designs. From twelve to fifteen hands are employed by the firm, many of whom are experts in their special branches of the industry. Two floors, 30x60 feet, are occupied. Specialties: all kinds of Machine Works, and have manufactured for the last ten years the "Double Action Ratchet Screw Driver," on that alone have sometimes employed thirty men. Have been located in Augusta in same business since 1870. The present shop, since 1888, has been located on Rhines' Hill. We desire to call special attention to some of the points of real merit that make the Ratchet Screw Driver a favorite with mechanics, amateurs, and all who have occasion to use similar tools. The ratchet mechanism consists of the well-known system of Square Toothed Ratchet and pawls, which has stood the test of ages, and has become the accepted and acknowledged standard wherever ratchet movement is required. In applying this principle to our Driver we have been able to arrange and proportion the various parts so as to combine the greatest possible Strength and Durability, and still retain that symmetry of form and elegance of style so desirable and necessary in first-class tools. Their ratchets and pawls are made from Bar Steel, and are Extra Long, giving a great length of bearing to resist strain and wear. The Blades are hand-forged from the best quality of steel, carefully tempered and tested. The best of material is used throughout. Geo. E. Gay was born in Thomaston, Me., and is a member of the United Friends. J. H. Parsons was born in Harrison, Me., and is a member of the Masonic Lodge and United Friends.

A. J. Hall, Merchant Tailor, 153 Water Street, Augusta. With a thorough knowledge of the business, and having acquired the reputation of expert, as a cutter of fashionable custom clothing, Mr. A. J. Hall has established, at 153 Water Street, what is now one of the most popular Tailoring establishments in the city. It is doubtless equal in every appointment to any other in this line in Augusta, and is well arranged for the display of stock. The line of goods carried is such as to meet the wants of the most fastidious and fashionable. The stock of woolens, both foreign and domestic, shown by Mr. Hall, is from the best manufacturers in America and England, and it embraces all the latest novelties. The business was established in 1883, by Mr. Hall, who has acquired a well-deserved reputation for strict attention to business, liberality in all dealings, and care in the fit and fashion of garments, which qualities are guaranteed perfectly satisfactory, this fact having had much to do with the success which he has attained.

C. B. Savage, Dealer in Fine Groceries, Flour of all Grades, Selected Teas, Coffees, Spices, Meats, etc., also the Celebrated Coburn Butter. Among the many houses in Augusta that carry a superior grade of Groceries and Provisions that now conducted by Mr. C. B. Savage, located on Cony Street, deserves special mention. This house was established in 1867 by Green & Haskell, and in 1887 Mr. C. B. Savage assumed full proprietorship and has by energy and perseverance, attained the position he now occupies among the business men of Augusta. The business premises occupied by him comprise two floors, each 20x60 feet in dimensions, and are admirably arranged for his trade, having all necessary facilities for carrying on the business. Courteous and obliging assistants are constantly employed, while the stock embraces all kinds of staple and fine Groceries, Flour of all grades, Selected Teas, Coffees and Spices, Fresh and Canned Fruits, Vegetables, Meats, etc. A specialty is also made of the celebrated Coburn Butter, his facilities for handling and furnishing choice goods being unsurpassed in this section of the city. Mr. Savage is an energetic gentleman of long experience in his business, to which he devotes his close personal attention thus insuring perfect satisfaction in all respects to his numerous patrons. Mr. Savage is a native of Augusta and well deserves the success he has attained.

The Fuller Drug Store, Established 1819, Frank R. Partridge, Apothecary, Augusta. As an important factor in the growth and general progress of the city, the drug trade has played no insignificant part as can be illustrated by the detailed history of the above house, which was established in 1819, by Mr. Eben Fuller, and popularly known as the Fuller Drug Store. Since 1887 this establishment has been under the management of its present proprietor, Mr. Frank R. Partridge. It is located on Water Street, Augusta, occupying the first floor, which is 25x60 feet, with a commodious basement for additional storage. He carries an extensive and complete stock of Drugs of all descriptions, pure and unadulterated Chemicals, Patent Medicines, Perfumery, Combs, Sponges, Brushes, Soaps, etc., etc., and a handsome and elegant assortment of Toilet and Fancy Articles, with all such goods as are to be found in a well-regulated establishment of this kind. There is also carried an assortment of Cut Flowers and Floral Designs for any occasion at short notice. Two clerks are employed and customers are served and orders filled with the most prompt and courteous attention. The most watchful care is exercised under all circumstances, and particular attention paid to compounding Physicians' Prescriptions, in the preparation of which the utmost accuracy and greatest care is shown, using only the purest Drugs and Chemicals, thereby enjoying the confidence of all the physicians in the city. Mr. Partridge is a native of Augusta, and a member of the Masonic Order. He is an experienced and practical apothecary, winning success by well-directed personal efforts and a determined endeavor to promote the interests of his patrons.

R. W. Soule, Commission Merchant and Auctioneer, Wholesale Dealer in Produce, Foreign and Domestic Fruits, Allen's Block, Water Street. Augusta. The swift and cheap transportation offered now by railways, steamboats, etc., has rendered possible and in fact common place many wonderful things, and not the least surprising of these is the bringing of many tropical fruits, and other productions, to our very doors. As such perishable articles require prompt and careful handling, in order to retain their marketable qualities, there has been gradually brought into operation a most admirable and complete system, which puts them before consumers with the greatest possible expedition and economy, but which our space forbids more than this allusion. Among the Wholesale and Retail Commission Merchants, Auctioneers, and Dealers in Produce, Foreign and Domestic Fruits, etc., in Augusta, the house of R. W. Soule holds a high position, and since its establishment in 1885 by its present proprietor it has built up a very extensive trade. Mr. Soule is a native of Maine and a prominent member of the Odd Fellows. The four floors and two basements, each 40x60 feet in size, occupied by Mr. Soule and located in Allen's Block, Water Street, is well stocked with a seasonable supply of Produce, etc., including immense quantities of Fruit in its season. Three experienced clerks are constantly employed and the house is in the possession of every facility for procuring and handling these delicacies, and customers are found throughout the entire State, and are being constantly added to, as the many advantages held by Mr. Soule are better understood and appreciated.

Lucius Hill, Dealer in Flour and Choice Family Groceries, Water Street, Augusta. As a source of food supplies of every kind, the city of Augusta will be seen through these pages to possess advantages equal if not superior to many cities of greater size. Among the numerous houses engaged in this line, we note that of Mr. Lucius Hill, which is located on Water Street, and which was established in 1886, by the present enterprising manager, and has since its start become well and favorably known throughout the community for the fine quality of its goods as well as the reasonable prices maintained. The store which is 20x60 feet in dimensions has a large basement for storage, and is admirably arranged for the display of goods dealt in, being finely and fully stocked with a carefully selected line of Choice Family Groceries and Flour. Families are supplied with Choice Butter, Fresh Eggs, Fine Teas, Pure Coffee and Spices, Sauces, Pickles, Preserves, etc. Two efficient assistants are employed to wait upon customers, and all orders are carefully filled and promptly delivered. Mr. Hill is a native of Vermont and a member of the Free Masons. We can commend his house to the attention of our readers believing as we do that his facilities, goods and terms, are sure to be found desirable, and highly satisfactory, and knowing him to be an honorable and liberal gentleman in all business transactions.

Johnson & Percival, Successors to Kennebec Confectionery Man'f'y. Manufacturers of, and Wholesale and Retail Dealers in Pure Candies, Plain and Fancy Cake and Ice Cream Made to order, No. 117 Water Street. Among the varied industries pursued in Augusta, the house of Messrs. Johnson & Percival, Manufacturers and Dealers in Pure Candies holds a prominent place in the trade centre. This establishment was first established under the title of the Kennebec Confectionery Manufactory, and so conducted until 1886, when Messrs. Johnson & Percival assumed full control of the business, and during the time since elapsed have most ably managed their establishment which is located at No. 117 Water Street and comprises three floors each covering an area of 20x60 feet. The extensive manufacturing wholesale and retail trade transacted by this firm requires the services of five very capable and thoroughly experienced assistants. The energies of the house are devoted to the manufacture of Pure Candies of every description, and Plain and Fancy Cake and Ice Cream are made to order in any quantity. Therefore we take pleasure in calling the attention of our many readers to this first-class and thoroughly reliable establishment. The proprietors are Mr. J. L. Johnson and Mr. H. W. Percival, both natives of Maine, and well known citizens of Augusta. Mr. Percival is a member of the United Workmen.

CLARK'S PATENT DROP AXLE DELIVERY WAGON,
Manufactured by HIRAM CLARK, Augusta, Me.

The advantage over all other low delivery wagons consists in the peculiar construction of the combination fifth wheel and the low straight line draft attachment, the Drop Axle and Fifth Wheel Combination being so arranged that the wagon can be turned around in a very small compass, while the shafts or pole are attached at such a point on the drop of axle that a low straight-line draft is obtained, which makes the wagon haul very light and easy. The body rests alike on both axles and only 24 inches from the ground, therefore it can be loaded and unloaded with very little lifting, also avoiding the tiresome necessity of climbing off and on a high wagon to deliver goods. In the manufacture of these wagons great care is taken in the selection of stock; nothing but the very best oak and hickory is used, and the iron work is nicely forged and fitted so as to obtain the greatest amount of strength and durability. The Drop Axle Delivery Wagon is the most desirable wagon for delivering goods ever offered to the public. Patented Jan. 31, 1888. Manufactured by Hiram Clark, 29 Water Street, Augusta, Me.

Geo. C. Libby, Dealer in fine Groceries and Provisions, Meats of all Kinds, Grain, Feed, Cordage, Lime and Cement, 131 Water Street, Augusta. The number of concerns in this country, engaged in handling what are known as "staple" commodities is, of course, something enormous, for where there is a population of over 60,000,000 souls to be fed, clothed and otherwise provided for, it is evident that there must be many hands to do the work. As a general rule the merchants of the United States are enterprising, sagacious and perfectly reliable, so that it requires a special degree of excellence to attain distinction, when the average is so high and therefore, those firms which have gained prominence are all the more worthy of mention. One of the foremost of these in this city is that now conducted by Mr. Geo. C. Libby, engaged in the retail trade of Groceries and Provisions, Flour, Grain, Lime, Cement, Field and Garden Seeds, at No. 131 Water Street, for the articles handled by him are "staple" in the full sense of the term, being uniformly excellent in quality, and such as are indispensable in every family. The enterprise now carried on by Mr. Libby was founded by B. Libby & Co., who gave place to the present proprietor in 1887. The premises utilized by him comprise two floors and basement each 22x60 feet in size, and are fully stocked with complete lines of the goods handled. Employment is given to a sufficient force of assistants, and the service is prompt and courteous. Mr. Libby is a native of Augusta, and so well known in this community as to hardly need personal mention at our hands. He is a prominent member of the Free Masons, and a thoroughly reliable and well-known citizen and business man of Augusta.

D. Knowlton & Son, Coffins and Caskets, Water and Oak Streets, Augusta. If any enterprise is entitled to prominence and confidence that of Messrs. D. Knowlton & Son can certainly make such claim, as it ranks among the most reliable Coffin and Casket Manufacturing establishments in this city. This business was established in 1822 by the senior partner of the present firm and during the sixty-seven years elapsed since then, this house has under its energetic and capable management enjoyed an uninterrupted success. The proprietors possess an extensive experience in all branches of their business, and by care and industry they have built up a large and steadily increasing retail trade in all styles of Coffins and Caskets. The premises utilized for this business are located on Oak Street, and comprise three floors each 60x25 feet in dimensions and are equipped with every necessary requisite for the proper conduct of the business. Every department of the enterprise is in fact well organized and under a thorough control. Mr. Chas. Knowlton is a native of Augusta and enjoys a high reputation as a citizen and reliable business man.

LEADING BUSINESS MEN OF AUGUSTA.

B. F. Parrott & Co., Wholesale Flour, Grain and Feed, Augusta. One of Augusta's old-established enterprises is that conducted by Messrs. B. F. Parrott & Co., on Water Street, for it is over 30 years since this undertaking was begun, it having been founded in 1858. The concern does a wholesale business, handling Flour, Grain, Corn, Oats, Shorts, etc., very extensively, and occupying two floors of the dimensions of 55x100 feet, respectively. A well appointed Grist Mill is run in connection with the enterprise, so that Messrs. B. F. Parrott & Co., are certainly in a position to supply anything in their line at manufacturers' prices. The flour produced by this house is in active demand among retailers, for they have found it to be a favorite article with their customers, who appreciate a fresh and pure article. Horse-owners, Stablekeepers, etc., also express a decided preference for the Feed coming from this concern as they say it is more uniform in quality than any they are able to obtain elsewhere. However this may be, it is at all events sure that Messrs. B. F. Parrott & Co., do a very large business, and spare no pains to give their customers entire satisfaction. Orders are filled at very short notice and the lowest market rates are invariably quoted at this establishment.

A. D. Ward, Formerly of Ward & Cogan, Plumbing and Steam Heating, Furnaces, Ranges and Kitchen Goods, Hardware, Iron and Steel, Paints, Oils and Varnishes, Carriage Stock, Agricultural and Carpenters' Tools, Cutlery, &c., 163 Water Street, Augusta. Mr. A. D. Ward needs no introduction to our Augusta readers for they will remember him as a member of the firm of Ward & Cogan as well as by the accommodations he has extended to the public since inaugurating his present enterprise in 1887. Mr. Ward was born in this city and is connected with the Free Masons. For a number of years he has been prominently identified with the Plumbing and Steam Heating business, and no man is considered a more competent authority on such subjects. His establishment at 163 Water Street comprises five floors of the dimensions of 20x55 feet, and contains an unusually heavy and complete stock of Furnaces, Ranges, Stoves, Kitchen Goods, Hardware, Iron, Steel, Paints, Oils and Varnishes, together with Carriage Stock, Agricultural and Carpenters' Tools, Cutlery, etc., not forgetting a full line of Plumbing and Steam Heating apparatus, Supplies, etc. Both a wholesale and retail business is done and employment given to twelve competent assistants, thus enabling Mr. Ward to promise prompt and skillful attention to orders, and the carrying out of the most difficult work in superior manner and at reasonable rates. Plumbing cannot be done too carefully or too thoroughly, and much annoyance and not a little sickness would be avoided if the public were to remember this fact and place their orders only at such reliable establishments as that conducted by Mr. Ward. Steam Heating plants will be set up and warranted to give entire satisfaction and save fuel, and in this as in other departments, the charges made are very moderate.

Henry W. Bicknell, Dealer in Tea, Coffee and Fancy Groceries, No. 158 Water Street, Augusta. While it is not the purpose of this book to praise one business enterprise at the expense of others, still the right has been exercised of calling attention to really meritorious establishments of all kinds, and it is in pursuance of this policy that we give space to a consideration of the enterprise of which Mr. Henry W. Bicknell is the proprietor, and which is carried on at No. 158 Water Street, Augusta. This gentleman is engaged in the retailing of Choice Family Groceries of various kinds and makes a specialty of handling of such staple products as Teas, Coffees, etc., and in addition to these goods Mr. Bicknell carries a fine line of Cigars and Tobacco. He began operations in 1881, and has built up a liberal degree of patronage, for his business methods are such as to inspire general confidence and he has invariably made it a point to practice none but legitimate means of extending his trade. The premises occupied are composed of one floor and basement, each 20x50 feet in size, and all the available space is taken up in accommodating the stock carried, for this is both large and varied and will compare favorably with that of more than one store of greater pretensions. The prices too are as they should be, and those who wish to deal at an establishment where fair dealing, and a liberal spirit are always observable, would do well to place a trial order at least with Mr. Bicknell, for we are assured that he stands ready to do his part toward establishing a connection that must of necessity prove pleasant and mutually profitable.

Bennett's Oyster and Dining-Rooms, 192 Water Street, Augusta. "Good Food, Neatness and Cleanliness," are about all the attributes to be looked for in a first-class dining-room and as these are made specialties at the establishment conducted by Mr. I. Bennett, at No. 192 Water Street, Augusta, it is not to be wondered at that this is one of the most popular restaurants in the city and is doing a business that increases as the reputation of the accommodations extended to guests become more widely known. The enterprise to which we have reference was inaugurated in 1868, and at once leaped into popularity as it was evident from the beginning that Mr. Bennett was determined to give his customers not fair but liberal treatment. He is a native of Augusta, and no man with whom we are acquainted has a more intimate knowledge of the business in which he is engaged. This restaurant comprises two floors, each 65x35 feet in dimensions, and its dining-rooms are tastefully and conveniently fitted up, for the comfort of its many patrons. Employment is given to three experienced and courteous assistants. Food is served promptly as well as temptingly and the prices are put so low that no one need go hungry against his will. A large trade is also carried on in Oysters which are served in all styles of cooking and may be had at all hours. The same qualities which have won popularity for Mr. Bennett's Dining-Rooms are manifested in this department of his trade. We commend this restaurant to all our interested readers as an honorably conducted and first-class establishment.

T. Fuller & Son, Wholesale and Retail Dealers in Groceries, Provisions and Country Produce, Lambard Block, Water Street. Largely engaged in the wholesale and retail branches of the Grocery and Provision business we would mention Messrs. T. Fuller & Son, who have for the past twenty-four years been recognized as among the prominent business men concerned in promoting the commercial interests of Augusta. This business was established in 1865 by Messrs. Fuller & Son, and from its inception gave promise of vitality, which the succeeding years have only rendered more apparent. The premises occupied for trade purposes comprise a store and basement, each 20x60 feet in dimensions, and is located in Lambard Block, Water Street. The stock is without exception one of the most complete in the city. They carry an immense stock of Groceries, Provisions and Country Produce, and are enabled to suit the large variety of tastes catered to, and everything is sold at the most reasonable market prices. The extensive wholesale and retail business transacted requires the services of four very capable assistants, and it may be safely asserted that in freshness, quality, and special variety, the stock carried here, has no superior in the city. Messrs. T. & A. T. Fuller are both natives of Augusta, where they are widely known and esteemed.

F. L. Hersey, Dealer in Boots and Shoes, No. 156 Water Street, Augusta. What was unknown to our ancestors is now an imperative necessity for us. We speak of the retail Boot and Shoe stores. Formerly the local shoemaker was the pride of St. Crispin for the whole parish, and all the people submitted their understandings to him. Now all average shaped feet are supplied from immense and economically managed boot and shoe factories. American machinery, particularly Sewing Machines, and American genius in meeting all difficulties and surmounting them, are responsible for the great and beneficial change. Among other enterprising business men engaged in the boot and shoe trade in this city is Mr. F. L. Hersey, who keeps one of the finest assortments of ready made Boots and Shoes, for Ladies, Gentlemen, Youths, and Children, and at prices sure to suit the times, and customers' pockets. This enterprise was established by its present proprietor in 1878, and is located at 156 Water Street, and consists of a store and basement, where is transacted a live business in the above named line of goods. Mr. Hersey is well known among the representative business men and citizens of Augusta. His establishment is known all over the county as the Boston Boot and Shoe Store. Prices the lowest, as this store is the only one of its kind which transacts a strictly *cash* business.

George S. Ballard, Dealer in Crockery, Glass, Plated and Britannia Ware, Manuf'r of all descriptions of Tin Work, Augusta. There is no house in Augusta with better facilities for supplying Crockery than that of Mr. George S. Ballard, No. 165 Water Street. The premises which are desirably located, comprise two floors, each 20x60 feet in dimensions, and the stock in trade is very complete, comprising everything beautiful and desirable in the wide range of Crockery, Glass, and Plated Ware, plain and ornamented in beautiful designs, and suited to all requirements of the general public. In quality, variety, and prices, Mr. Ballard may safely invite comparison with any competing house in this city. He supplies Britannia Ware, Plain and Japanned Ware, and Fancy Goods of every description. He is also a Manufacturer of all descriptions of Tin Work, and has by his square dealing and energy, established himself in a prosperous retail trade which is steadily increasing. Mr. Ballard is a native of Westbrook, Me., and has been established since 1857.

Philbrook & Leighton, Dealers in Foreign and Domestic Dry Goods, No. 172 Water Street. Among the prominent merchants engaged in this important branch of industry, we are pleased to call attention to Messrs. Philbrook & Leighton whose fine and complete establishment ranks among the leading houses of its kind in Augusta. This house was established by the above-named gentlemen in 1882, and has already gained a large share of public favor. They occupy two floors of the handsome building located at No. 172 Water Street, covering an area, each of 22x60 feet in dimensions. They carry a large and finely selected stock of Dry and Fancy Goods, consisting of the newest domestic and most popular foreign importations in the Dry Goods line. The extensive retail trade already acquired by this house requires the services of three thoroughly experienced assistants and the details of the business are most ably managed under the direct personal supervision of the proprietors. The individual members of the firm are Mr. A. W. Philbrook and Mr. W. B. Leighton, both natives of Augusta, and well and favorably known in social as well as business circles. They are men of rare natural ability and enjoy in a pre-eminent degree the respect and confidence of all who do business with them.

E. Stone, Dealer in Coal, No. 123 Water Street. If the public needed to be reminded how important Coal had become during the last 25 or 30 years, they certainly have been given that reminder by the numerous and serious labor troubles that brought about so pronounced a shortage in the supply last winter, and it is perfectly safe to say that more than one worried householder or manufacturer declared that if the time ever came when coal returned to its normal price, he would lay in a supply that would tide him safely over any such condition of affairs in the future. No house in Maine enjoys a better reputation as regards the handling of Coal in large or small lots, than does that conducted by Mr. E. Stone, at No. 123 Water Street, and nowhere else can orders be placed with a more well-founded assurance that they will receive instant and careful attention. Mr. Stone was born in Gardiner and is connected with the Odd Fellows. He has been identified with his present enterprise since 1884 and has built up an extensive and permanent trade of which he may well be proud. Both a wholesale and retail business is done and employment is afforded to eight assistants. All the standard grades of Coal are handled, and the very lowest market rates are quoted on all kinds and sizes.

LEADING BUSINESS MEN OF AUGUSTA.

Dirigo Business College, R. B. Capen, Water Street, Opposite Post Office, Augusta. That a prejudice exists against Business Colleges in some quarters is undeniably true, and that this prejudice is not entirely lacking in foundation, is also a fact that must be acknowledged however it may be deplored. But it should be remembered that the faults of some institutions of this character should not in common justice be visited upon others that are conducted on radically different principles, and if some Business Colleges are more theoretical than practical, there are others that bestow upon those attending them a valuable business training, unattainable by any other means than those provided by years of ill-paid drudgery at office-work. We speak with some earnestness, as our observations of practical business methods in this and in other States, have caused us to fully realize that a year spent under competent tuition will make a young man more valuable to his employers than an experience extending over four times that period in so-called "practical business life." The "Dirigo Business College," located on Water Street, opposite the Post Office, has been in operation since 1863, and doubtless many of our readers are by this time conversant with its merits. It is conducted by Mr. R. B. Capen, whose record as a progressive and conscientious educator is ample guarantee that the institution under his charge will not suffer for lack of skilled and painstaking direction. It is Mr. Capen's aim to prepare his pupils for the duties of commercial life, to ground them thoroughly in the principles and practice of correspondence, banking, etc., and in short to so equip them that they will be able to use their natural abilities to the best advantage and successfully engage in the grand "competitive examination" going on constantly in all parts of the civilized world. Nothing is neglected that can aid in securing this end and particular attention is paid to the teaching of the "New Short-Hand" for "time is money," nowadays, and a knowledge of the art of Short-hand means the ability to save your employer time, and consequently money. The terms of tuition are very reasonable and further information will be cheerfully given by Mr. Capen on application.

H. H. Hamlen, Harness Manufacturer and Dealer in Saddles, Harnesses, Blankets, Robes and Trunks. H. H. Hamlen at his store on Water Street, Augusta carries a large stock of Harnesses of all kinds, manufactured by himself. He sells at both wholesale and retail, and his trade extends throughout Maine and New England. He also carries a very large line of Fur Robes, Wool and Plush Lap-Robes, Horse Blankets, Whips and Horse Goods of all descriptions, also Trunks, Bags, Extension Cases, etc. Having been in business in Augusta, where he was born, more than thirty years, he is well known and has the confidence of the community.

Davis, Farr & Co. (Successors to Benjamin Davis & Co., Established 1817), General Insurance Agency, 129 Water Street, nearly opposite Post-office, Augusta. The amount of insurable property in Augusta and its immediate vicinity, reaches a very high sum total, and if it is not all fully covered by policies in reliable companies, it is not by any means the fault of our insurance agents, for no more active or energetic a set of men can be found in any business. Among those who have already attained a high position in this fraternity, are Messrs. Davis, Farr & Co., Fire and Life Insurance Agents, located at No. 129 Water Street, nearly opposite the Post-office. This agency was originally established in 1817 by Mr. Benjamin Davis, and conducted by him until 1879, when the firm name was changed to Davis, Farr & Co. These gentlemen announce that they are prepared to "place insurance in reliable companies at honest rates," and as no more than this can be asked by the most exacting customer, it is not surprising that they have found plenty of business to attend to. Prominent among the organizations represented are the Hartford, of Hartford, Phœnix, of Hartford, National, of Hartford, Home, of New York, Phenix, of New York, German American, of New York, Franklin, of Philadelphia, Fire Association, of Philadelphia, Pennsylvania, of Philadelphia, Royal, of England, Imperial, of England, Liverpool, London & Globe, of England, Mutual Life, of New York. These are noted throughout the country for their fair dealing and promptness in the settlement of losses. Mr. Farr is a native of Litchfield, Me., and well and favorably known in this community. He is a member of the Free Masons, Knight Templars, and Odd Fellows. He has also held the office of Town Collector and Supervisor of Schools in Litchfield.

Thomas M. Baker, Dealer in Groceries and Meats, Darby Block, Augusta. It is the opinion of experts that certain Augusta houses show as large and desirable variety of the goods in which they deal as is to be found in similar

establishments located in cities of much greater size and pretensions. For example they point to the store of Thomas M. Baker located at No. 1 Darby Block, Augusta, and ask where a finer assortment of Groceries of all kinds and Meats are to be found. The stock shown in the emporium is certainly a first-class and varied one, and it is hard to see what is lacking to make it perfect in all its details. This house was first founded by Messrs. Baker & Longfellow in 1877, and in 1882 the firm-name was changed to Baker & Yeaton, and in 1885 Mr. Thomas M. Baker, assumed full control. The present new premises occupied cover an area of 55x20 feet, and is finely stocked with a choice assortment of everything in the above mentioned line of merchandise. The services of two competent assistants are required to wait upon the many customers who daily throng this establishment. Mr. Baker is a native of Maine and all representations made by himself or his clerks may be confidently relied upon and accepted with the utmost confidence.

W. R. Stone, Dealer in Fine Boots, Shoes, and Rubbers, Repairing Neatly and Promptly Done, Darby Block, No. 189 Water Street, Augusta. As the boot and shoe trade of Augusta forms a significant element in the make up of the city's enterprises, in referring to the above house it may be stated that the special line to which its best energies are confined is the handling of medium and first-class lines of Boots, Shoes and Rubbers. He carries some of the finest goods manufactured in New England. This house was established in 1883, by Mr. W. R. Stone, since which date this gentleman has so successfully managed his large retail trade, that to-day his house ranks among the first in the city engaged in the shoe trade. Premises located at No. 189 Water Street, Darby Block, covering an area of 50x22 feet are utilized, and the assistance of experienced clerks are required, in addition to the close personal supervision of the proprietor. A specialty is made of repairing of all kinds included in this branch of business, which is neatly and promptly done. Mr. Stone is a native of Palermo, Me., well known in this city and a prominent member of the Masons and Odd Fellows. In conclusion we will remark, that while we do not indulge in laudation of any house in particular, it shall be within our province to state to the trade and our readers that if they would have their interests highly conserved the acquaintance of this house should be made.

H. L. Stone, Agent for Columbia Bicycles and Tricycles, 189 Water Street, Darby Block, Augusta. The ingenious and enthusiastic wheelman who divided cyclists up into two parts —"those who ride Columbias and those who would if they knew enough," might have been a little extreme in his statement, but he will be readily pardoned by those who have made practical trial of the famous Columbia wheels. From the "Mustang" of 1878 to the "Light Roadster" of ten years later, is a great stride, and yet the manufacture of the Columbia Cycles have not the least reason to be ashamed of the "Mustang" and "Standard Columbia" of the first-named date, for they were the embodiment of the most advanced ideas of the time, as the "Light Roadster" and "Expert" of the present day are. It is in this constant progression, in this never ending desire to produce the best wheel possible, that the chief element of the wonderful popularity of the Columbia Machines is to be found, and we honestly believe that to-day for use on American roads, and especially the hilly ones of this State, there is not a Bicycle or a Tricycle in the world that can compete with the Pope Manufacturing Company's production. Strength, rigidity, lightness, ease of propulsion, cheapness of repairing — all these are combined in these machines and we do not wonder that since Mr. H. L. Stone, the resident agent, began operations in 1885, he has been very successful in increasing the number of Columbia riders. His office is in Darby Block, No. 189 Water Street, and those wishing any information in the bicycle line would do well to give him a call, as he is very well informed on the subject and is willing to cheerfully give any information in his power. He can supply wheels at Boston prices and every one sold is fully guaranteed.

Oscar H. Groves, Manufacturer of Parlor Furniture, No. 207 Water Street, Augusta. It is hardly necessary to say that Parlor Furniture when it is ready for use looks decidedly different from what it does when in process of manufacture, but for all that, no one who has never visited such an establishment as is conducted by Mr. Oscar H. Groves at No. 207 Water Street, has any adequate idea of the many operations that must be gone through with before the finished product is ready for the market. Carelessness or undue haste in the carrying out of any of these operations may make a decided difference in the durability and real value of the article handled, and it is chiefly owing to the painstaking care that is observed in this respect that the Furniture produced by Mr. Groves bears so high and enviable a reputation among dealers and others acquainted with its merits. The gentleman alluded to was born in this State and is connected with the Odd Fellows, inaugurating his present enterprise in 1881. The premises utilized comprise two floors of the dimensions of 30x50 feet, and employment is afforded to seven skilled assistants. Mr. Groves' business is entirely manufacturing and wholesale, and he offers special inducements to dealers who will introduce his goods into new localities, guaranteeing that both the workmanship and the price of his furniture will be satisfactory.

Geo. O. Ayer, Photo. Artist, Corner Bridge and Water Streets, Augusta. Photography has come into great prominence of late years, and its application to the art of engraving and other industries has been of much service in facilitating work, and saving much unnecessary and wearisome detail. Although largely used for mechanical purposes, photography at its best is by no means a mechanical art, and the truth of this statement will, we think, be apparent to all after a little consideration. A successful and artistic photographer, must not only have an intimate and perfect acquaintance with the various processes necessary in obtaining a permanent and satisfactory picture, but he must also know under what conditions of light, etc., the exposure of the plate can best be made, and must arrange so as to secure these as nearly as possible. It is right here that the chief difference becomes apparent between an artist and a bungler, and it is right here that Mr. Geo. O. Ayer, at the corner of Bridge and Water Streets, this city, has clearly shown his superiority. He began business operations for himself in 1880, and conducted the business personally until 1885, when he bought out a Photographic Gallery in East Boston, at No. 74 Meridian Street, and has ever since, most of the time remained in that city. When this addition took place he left his gallery in this city in charge of Mr. J. F. Libby, who is considered as Augusta's most tasteful and skillful photographer. He is extremely courteous and accommodating, and enjoying the patronage of the elite of the city, and being a thorough artist, he has succeeded in making this place known all over the country. He is well assisted by Mrs. Ella Jones, a sister to Mr. Ayers, who is in charge of the printing department, and by viewing at the gallery the large variety of work done during the year 1887, and by closely inspecting the views of private residences, etc., taken by Mr. Libby, and ornamenting the cosy waiting-room, we are bound to acknowledge that by leaving this gallery in charge of such an able artist as Mr. Libby and his assistant, Mrs. E. Jones, that Mr. Ayer is a judge of true artists, and such a business conducted in such a courteous and artistic way is bound to succeed beyond the usual expectations.

M. S. Moulton & Co., Dealer in Fish of all kinds, Oysters a Specialty, Water Street, Augusta. In these days of rapid progress and forgetfulness, what was unheard of yesterday is practiced to-day and forgotten to-morrow, so that we accept quite, as a matter of course, things that to our ancestors, and even ourselves, at an earlier date would have been looked upon as the wild dreaming of a madman. Among these may be mentioned the system, now practiced as an ordinary function of the government, of stocking our ponds, rivers, lakes, and even the ocean itself, with fish. The importance of Fish as a food supply for the people is just beginning to be rated at its full value, and it is not too much to expect that under the influence of improved methods of fish culture, despite the increased consumption, fish will be cheaper and more plentiful in the future than has been the case in the past. A well-known house engaged in the fish trade in Augusta is that now conducted by M. S. Moulton & Co., retail dealer in all kinds of Fish, Oysters, Clams, etc. This enterprise was inaugurated in 1875 by B. S. Wright & Co., who were succeeded in 1881 by the present proprietor, who since that date has conducted the business under the style of M. S. Moulton & Co. Mr. Moulton was the Co., of Wright & Co., and managed that business since its inception in 1875. Mr. Moulton is a native of New Hampshire, and is a member of the Free Masons. The premises occupied cover an area of 20x60 feet and a large retail business is done, requiring the services of two thoroughly capable assistants. A large stock is constantly carried and goods are promptly supplied at rates that will compare very favorably with those quoted by other markets.

Augusta Marble Works, Robert Fox, proprietor, Cony Street, Augusta, Me. It is not to be wondered at that people are very apt to find themselves at a loss when suddenly called upon to place an order for a Monument, or for cemetery work of any kind, for knowledge of the most reputable and able house concerned in the production of such articles is not generally distributed, and hence it is hard to determine whom to patronize. If any of our readers are in this undecided condition, we feel that we are doing them a real service by calling their attention to the work turned out at the Augusta Marble Works on Cony Street, for Mr. Robert Fox, the proprietor of this establishment, produces Monuments, Gravestones, etc., that are fully equal to the best, and his prices are more moderate than those generally placed on work of the highest order of excellence. The enterprise to which we have reference was started in 1884, and soon received liberal and cordial support, as it was plainly evident from the start that Mr. Fox had no desire but to fully satisfy every customer. He shows a varied collection of beautiful and tasteful designs for Monuments, Headstones, and everything in that line, and will cheerfully give estimates of the probable cost of cemetery work of any kind, and guarantee that he can carry out the same to the satisfaction of his patrons. Three assistants are employed, and orders are filled at very short notice.

Pinkham & Sherburne, Props. of the Boston Branch Clothing House, 132 Water Street, Augusta. When the average citizen makes up his mind to buy anything, he wants to be convinced regarding the following points before placing his order: First, are the goods reliable. Second, are they of good style, and third, are they offered at the lowest market rates. No one wants to pay more for an article than it is worth, and certainly this is a very excusable feeling, for the most of us have to work hard enough for our money, and when we throw it away, we like to do so with our eyes open and not unwittingly. Now Pinkham & Sherburne, who carry on the Boston Branch Clothing Store at No. 132 Water Street, announce that they are prepared to supply anything in their line at the "lowest living prices," and as they sell not only Clothing but also Furnishing Goods, Hats and Caps, Underwear, Traveling Bags, Rubber Coats, Umbrellas, etc., it will be seen that their "line" is a tolerably extensive one. This business which was formerly conducted by E. G. Storer came into the possession of the present firm in Oct. 1888. They occupy premises measuring 20x40 feet and if they have any space to spare it escaped our attention, for it certainly seemed as if the stock covered everything. The business corresponds with their stock, for it is very extensive indeed and is increasing with steadiness and rapidity. This firm employ purely legitimate methods and have built up their present trade by hard work and good judgment. They buy cheap and sell cheap and always give an equivalent for every penny received.

J. M. Mixer, Druggist, No. 4 Bridge Block, Water Street, Augusta. No man can be engaged in any particular line of business for several years without becoming comparatively expert and well informed in it, and particularly is this the case with one who is well fitted naturally to conduct such an enterprise as he has chosen, and who has made a careful study of the theory as well as had a large experience in the practice of the line of trade with which he is identified. Mr. J. M. Mixer of No. 4 Bridge Block, 104 Water Street, needs no introduction to the residents of Augusta for he has carried on a first-class pharmacy in this city since 1886, and it is a very significant fact that those who are the most thoroughly familiar with his business methods speak in the warmest terms of the advantages of trading with him and "practice what they preach," by giving him their exclusive patronage in the purchase of Drugs, Toilet Articles, etc. The premises occupied by Mr. Mixer comprises one of the handsomest Drug Stores in Augusta, covering an area of 50x25 feet, and fitted up in the most approved style, with a fine high, frescoed ceiling and mosaic floor and the stock includes Drugs, Medicines and Chemicals of all descriptions and every facility is at hand to aid in the compounding of physicians' prescriptions, or family receipts. Two competent and courteous clerks are employed and this establishment is noted for the accurate and prompt manner in which all orders and patrons are served. Pure and fresh ingredients only are used, and no exorbitant prices are ever charged, while all annoying delays are avoided.

J. R. Manchester, House and Sign Painter, Grainer, Glazier and Paper Hanger, Dealer in Paints, Oils and Colors, Cony Street, Augusta. One of the well managed and thoroughly reliable Painting and Paper Hanging establishments in Augusta, is that conducted by Mr. J. R. Manchester located on Cony Street. It was founded in 1886 by its present proprietor, and since that time has won a wide custom and reputation for the finest work, as the fitting reward of business enterprise, and careful attention to the wants of patrons. The proprietor by long experience and thorough knowledge of every department of his business is admirably fitted to superintend the finest class of work, and is enabled to do this at unusually reasonable rates. He employs five thoroughly skilled assistants, and the large number of houses which he has painted and decorated in the most approved and beautiful styles, bear ample testimony to the high character of his work. He is prepared to fill all orders for House and Sign Painting, Graining, Glazing and Paper Hanging, and also deals in Paints, Oils and Colors of all kinds. He does the finest kinds of Graining and Wood-finishing and in every respect his work is first class. All patrons may place the most perfect confidence in his honorable dealings and skilled and satisfactory work. Mr. Manchester is a native of Augusta and takes an active and honorable part in the commercial and social life of the city.

Henry M. Faught, Manufacturer of and Dealer in every description of Cemetery Work in Marble and Granite, both Foreign and Domestic, Water Street, Augusta. The selection of an appropriate monument or headstone, is generally a task of no small magnitude and of no little delicacy, for the choice must be governed by so many considerations that each individual case demands individual treatment. Under some circumstances a tall slender shaft of marble conveys the proper effect, while under other conditions a massive block of granite is more satisfying and appropriate. In fact no general rule can be given, and the best that can be done is to visit an establishment where ample facilities are at hand for the supplying of anything in the line of Cemetery work and taking advantage of the opportunities there offered for study and comparison. Such an enterprise is that carried on by Mr. Henry M. Faught on Water Street, the premises utilized comprising two floors and a basement, of the dimensions of 27x53 feet, and an extensive stock of Marble and Granite, both Foreign and American, in the rough and finished, being at hand to select from. Mr. Faught has conducted his present undertaking since 1883 and does a very large business, both retail and contracting. He employs seven skilled assistants and there is no house of which we have knowledge that is capable of rendering more uniformly first-class and satisfactory service to its patrons. Enjoying special facilities as regards the purchase of Foreign and Domestic Marble and Granite, Mr. Faught makes it a point to give his customers the benefit of his favorable relations with producers and hence fixes his prices at remarkably low rates.

Chas. H. Nason, Merchant Tailor, Manufacturer of Fine Ready-Made Clothing and Dealer in Hats, Caps, and Furnishing Goods, 135, 137 and 139 Water Street. "Fine feathers" may not make "fine birds," but they are very apt to exert a powerful influence in that direction, and if the other old saying, "birds of a feather flock together," be considered, it will be seen that those who take no pains with their dress and are slovenly and unattractive in appearance are very apt to be classed on a plane below those who are more careful. It pays to dress well. This may be accepted as an axiom and, within reasonable bounds, no young man can spend too much on his clothing. But he can throw away money by not buying to the best advantage, and right here we want to say that no better establishment can be found to deal at than that conducted by Mr. Charles H. Nason at Nos. 135, 137 and 139 Water Street. This gentleman is a native of Hallowell, a member of the Free Masons and the Odd Fellows, and one of the most enterprising and at the same time reliable business men in Augusta. Two floors and a basement are occupied by him, the premises being of the dimensions of 50x60 feet and a magnificent stock carried consisting of Fine Ready-Made Clothing, Hats, Caps, Furnishing Goods, etc. Mr. Nason is a Manufacturer of Ready-Made Clothing and hence can offer such goods at bottom prices. He also does a very extensive Merchant Tailoring business, carrying a fine supply of Foreign and Domestic Woolens in stock, and making garments to order at but a slight advance over ready-made prices, perfection of fit and general satisfaction being guaranteed. Employment is afforded to 45 efficient assistants and orders can be filled at remarkably short notice, while the assortment of ready-made garments contains sizes and varieties to fit men of all figures.

James E. Fuller, Wholesale and Retail Grocer, 123 and 127 Water Street, Augusta. No matter what part of the country be visited, Maine or California, Minnesota or Texas — it will be found that the Grocery business is one of the most important branches of trade and that it absorbs a large share of the ability and capital of the community. Truly we must "eat to live" and the articles included under the general head "Groceries" are so many and so indispensable that existence would be practically impossible without them. Of course, then, Groceries are in great demand and establishments devoted to their sale are many and extensive, but few among them are worthy of more careful consideration than that conducted by Mr. James E. Fuller at Nos. 123 and 127 Water Street, for this is one of the most popular houses of the kind in Maine, and enjoys an extremely heavy and constantly increasing patronage. Seven floors are utilized of the dimensions of 22x60 feet, together with a store-house of ample proportions, and it is hardly necessary to add after calling attention to accommodations of such magnitude, that the stock carried is a very heavy one. Both a wholesale and retail business is done and employment is given to six courteous and efficient assistants. Buying in such large quantities, it of course follows that goods are procured at the lowest attainable rates and that all competition can be easily met. Orders are promptly and accurately delivered and every article sold is warranted to prove as represented.

Augusta Savings Bank, 174 Main Street, Augusta. It would be difficult to find an idea capable of working more mischief and at the same time more generally held, than that of making a fortune at a "jump." How many men there are who plod along taking no heed of the future but dimly believing that some time or other their time will come and they will find themselves raised in some mysterious way from poverty to wealth. How, they do not know; when, they do not know, but, nevertheless, they hold to this faith year in and year out, confident in the truth of the proverb that "Fortune knocks at every man's door at least once in a life-time," and relying like the immortal Mr. Micawber on something "turning up." Now this is no way to live at all. It is childish and foolish in the extreme, and those who allow themselves to be guided by such views will see youth slip away, middle-age come, and finally weakness and poverty assume chief control and land the believer in "luck" in the poor-house if not in a worse place. Provide in time of strength for time of weakness. You are now able to earn *more* than you need to spend, see that you insure against the time when the balance may be the other way. Small savings mount up wonderfully, and those who have noticed how soon the trivial sums expended here and there "spoil a ten-dollar bill," as the saying is, should bear in mind that this ratio of increase will be even added to, if such sums are deposited instead of being thrown away. Try it for a while. Open an account with the Augusta Saving's Bank and find out for yourself whether what we have said is true or not. Is not the plan worth trying? We do not ask you to *spend* a cent, quite the reverse in fact. If you find we have deceived you, that saving don't pay and that those who save are the ignorant and not the intelligent members of the community, you can withdraw whatever deposits you have made and proceed as before to wait for that marvelous event that is to put an end to all work and worry. But first, try our plan for a year at least. The Augusta Savings Bank has been in operation since 1848 and is as secure as such an institution can be. The gentlemen entrusted with its management are representative citizens, and are fully able as well as honestly anxious to protect the interests of depositors. The process of depositing and withdrawing money at this bank is very simple and involves but little delay and no annoying "red tape," and all business is transacted with courtesy and care. William S. Badger is President; William R. Smith, Treasurer; Edwin C. Dudley, Assistant Treasurer. Liabilities—Jan. 1, 1889. Deposits, $4,805,954.10; interest, $132,-318.34; reserved fund, $212,500.00; prem. ap., $1,010.74; total, $5,109,783.18. Resources—District of Columbia bonds, $31,000; public funds, $2,490,600; railroad bonds, $1,317,857.50; bank stock, 60,000; loans to National Banks, 24,000; loans to cities, 12,000; loans on mortgages, $129,933; loans on collaterals, $416,944.54; real estate and furniture, $10,600; premiums, $88,-435 42; cash, 596,412.72.

S. S. Brooks & Company, Dealers in Hardware, Iron, Nails, Glass, Carriage Wood Work, Paints, Oils and Varnishes, Manilla Cordage, Belting, Lace Leather &c., Central Block, opposite Post Office, Augusta. Such a number of articles have come to be included within the term "Hardware," that exceptional experience and ability are called for on the part of those undertaking to carry on an establishment successfully in which Hardware is given special prominence. That this experience, and this ability are fully possessed by the gentlemen constituting the firm of S. S. Brooks & Co., no one acquainted with the facts will deny, for this house has been identified with the Hardware trade for nearly half a century, having had its origin in 1842. The firm is made up of S. S. & W. H. Brooks, both of whom were born in this city. The premises occupied are very spacious comprising seven floors of the dimensions of 22x60 feet, and affording accommodation for the very heavy and complete stock that the immense business done compels the firm to carry. This business is both wholesale and retail, and the services of seven assistants are required to properly attend to orders. Iron, Nails, Glass, Carriage Wood-Work, Paints, Oils, Varnishes, Manilla Cordage, Belting, Lace Leather, etc., are to be had here in quantities to suit, and at the lowest market rates, and every article sold is fully guaranteed to be as represented. The store is located in Central Block, opposite the Post Office, and callers will receive prompt and polite attention, and will find that their orders will be carefully observed. Messrs. S. S. Brooks & Co., are in a position to guarantee their customers prices as low as the lowest, and have no trouble in maintaining their position among the leaders.

Steam Dye House, (a few doors south of R. R. Bridge), Emile Barbier, Proprietor. An Agency in every Maine Central station to Bar Harbor, and Knox & Lincoln Railroad station to Camden. These Steam Dye Works were established in 1867 in Augusta, by the present proprietor, Mr. Emile Barbier, and so encouraging has been his success, that to-day he is the proprietor of the large Steam Dye House located on Water Street, a few doors south of the R. R. bridge, and since it was thrown open to the public, twenty-two years ago, has met with universal approbation and a steadily increasing business. The premises occupy two floors, each 20x40 feet in dimensions. The Works are equipped with the latest improved machinery and every requisite for their operation. Four skilled hands are employed and all work is guaranteed satisfactory. A specialty of this house is the dyeing, cleansing and pressing of Ladies' and Gentlemen's Garments without ripping or taking off the trimmings; Lace Curtains are cleansed and finished to look as good as new; Kid Gloves cleaned and dyed black; Feather Beds and Pillows are thoroughly renovated by steam; general agency for the New England Crape and Lace Refinishing Co.; also, new goods or heavy cloth for stores, Dyed and Finished in the best manner at very low prices, and all work intrusted to this establishment will be done in the best manner, and the prices will be found as low as any similar concern. Mr. Barbier is an excellent business manager, whose qualifications have won for him a prominent position in this line of business. He is also highly esteemed as a citizen throughout the community.

Boynton & Farr, Dealers in Groceries, Provisions, Meats, etc., Flour of all grades, Fine Teas and Coffees, Edwards Block, Water Street, Augusta. When Mr. E. M. Boynton started the enterprise with which he is now identified, in Dec., 1887, it was with the determination to carry on a strictly first-class family grocery, and we are sure that none who have been familiar with the enterprise from its inception, will dispute that this resolve has been fully carried out. In March 1888 Mr. Boynton became associated with Mr. Farr under the existing firm name and the steadily increasing patronage the concern receive, is the best proof that their methods of doing business are honorable and enterprising. Mr. Boynton is a native of Liberty, Maine and is connected with the Free Masons, the Ancient Order of United Workmen and Seth Williams Post G. A. R., while his partner was born in West Gardiner. We spoke of the enterprise as a first-class family grocery, but in point of fact it is something more than that, as a full line of Provisions and Meats is carried, and thus practically all the food supplies required can be obtained here. Flour is one of the most important food staples, and the firm have taken special pains to build up a reputation in the handling of this commodity, dealing only in such brands as they can conscientiously recommend, and making their prices in accordance with the lowest market rates. Fine Teas and Coffees are always to be had at this popular store, and as "the proof of the pudding is the eating" we ask no stronger confirmation of the truth of this statement than that afforded by a careful trial of the goods offered. Staple and Fancy Groceries, Canned Goods, etc., in immense variety are always in stock, and bottom prices and polite treatment are assured to every customer.

A. J. Pierce, Successor to J. D. Pierce & Son, Importers and Dealers in Crockery, China and Glass Ware, French and Bohemian Fancy Goods, Silver and Nickel Plated Wares, No. 150 Water Street, Augusta. Among the enterprises of this kind in Augusta few establishments have greater prestige than the extensive retail Crockery, China and Glass house of Mr. A. J. Pierce. This house was established in 1842, under the title of J. D. Pierce & Son, and so conducted until 1880, when Mr. A. J. Pierce assumed full proprietorship. Its field of operations is by no means confined to the city, but extends throughout the trade radius of Augusta. Such a business as is here transacted was not built up in a day; it is the result of careful industry, a thorough knowledge of the wants of the trade, enterprise in procuring supplies at the fountain head, and handling them on small margins, and energy in maintaining a high standard of output and strict integrity and fair dealing. The premises utilized by Mr. Pierce are located at No. 150 Water Street, and consist of a store 20x65 feet in dimensions, and is fitted up with special reference to the business which involves the importing and retailing of Crockery, China, and Glass Ware, French and Bohemian Fancy Goods, Silver and Nickel Plated Ware, Table and Pocket Cutlery, Scissors, Tea Trays, Lamps, Chandeliers, etc., etc. Mr. Pierce is a native of Augusta and a member of the United Workmen. Even the most casual observer upon visiting his store cannot fail to be impressed with the system and completeness of the establishment, and which it may be safely asserted has no superior in this city.

Benj. Gardner, Dealer in Flour, Grain, Feed, Hay, Straw, Groceries, Provisions, and Country Produce, 42 and 44 Cony Street, East Side, Augusta. So prodigal is Ceres in her bounty in the State of Maine that there are many stores which are the rendezvous of the farmers with their harvest of grain and other produce. Augusta is particularly rich in first-class houses whose trade extends over the entire State. The house of Mr. Benj. Gardner is one of the most substantial and enterprising in the city, and carries a large stock of Flour, Grain, Feed, Hay, and Straw, also Groceries, Provisions, and Country Produce, at his premises, situated at Nos. 42 and 44 Cony Street, East Side, which comprises two stores of two floors, and each floor covering an area of 40x60 feet. This business was established by Mr. Gardner in 1880, who has since built up a flourishing retail trade, requiring the services of capable assistants. Mr. Gardner is a native and well-known citizen of Augusta, and a prominent member of the Odd Fellows. With capital ample for his requirements, and a thorough knowledge of all the details of the business, Mr. Gardner has met with success and prosperity hitherto, which will doubtless continue with him as long as he remains actively concerned in the trade.

Bangs Brothers, Manufacturers of Window Frames, Doors, Sash and Blinds, East Side Kennebec Dam, Augusta. A very busy establishment is that conducted by Bangs Brothers at the Kennebec Dam, for the productions of the mills carried on by them are in active demand, and no difficulty is experienced in disposing of all the work that is turned out. The business was begun in 1875, and it has steadily increased, until now fifty assistants, and a variety of improved labor-saving machinery are required to keep up with the orders received. Window Frames are a specialty with them, and they use their patented Packet-cap, which is extensively used in Boston and vicinity, with hard-pine pulley stiles. Doors and Door Frames are very extensively manufactured, and Windows, both glazed and unglazed, are largely dealt in, both a wholesale and a retail business being done. Band-sawing and Circle work are done to order at short notice, and Planing of all descriptions is also given particular attention. Messrs. Bangs Brothers enjoy special facilities for the successful carrying on of their business. The lumber (of which they use two million feet yearly) is left on a side track near their factory. Ample water power is available, and everything necessary to the filling of orders to the best advantage is at hand. The firm deal extensively in Hard Pine Lumber, and are prepared to furnish it at short notice in quantities to suit. The prices charged in every department will be found to agree with the very lowest market rates, and the character of the goods furnished speaks for itself.

Report of the Condition of

THE FIRST NATIONAL BANK
OF AUGUSTA, ME.,

At close of Business, Dec. 12th, 1888.

RESOURCES.

Loans and Discounts	$810,887.99
Overdrafts, secured and unsecured	2,328.56
U. S. Bonds to secure circulation	250,000.00
Other stocks, bonds and mortgages	27,940.00
Due from approved reserve agents	71,913.42
Due from other National Banks	1,829.32
Real estate, furniture and fixtures	200.00
Current expenses and taxes paid	2,799.49
Checks and other cash items	12,585.21
Bills of other Banks	10,406.00
Fractional paper currency, nickels and cents	101.08
Specie	22,623.00
Legal tender notes	4,000.00
Redemption fund with U. S. Treasurer (5 per ct. of circulation)	11,250.00
Total	$1,228,864.07

LIABILITIES.

Capital stock paid in	$250,000.00
Surplus fund	60,000.00
Undivided profits	31,542.95
National Bank notes outstanding	212,630.00
Individual deposits subject to check	658,090.54
Cashier's checks outstanding	1,648.01
Due to other National Banks	14,952.57
Total	$1,228,864.07

State of Maine, County of Kennebec, ss.:

I, C. S. Hichborn, Cashier of the above-named Bank, do solemnly swear that the above statement is true to the best of my knowledge and belief.   C. S. HICHBORN, *Cashier*.

Subscribed and sworn to before me, this 15th day of December, 1888.

J. R. GOULD, *Notary Public.*

Correct.—Attest:
D. A. CONY,
THOS. LAMBARD, } *Directors.*
OSCAR HOLWAY,

DIRECTORS.

D. A. CONY, *President.*
THOMAS LAMBARD.
OSCAR HOLWAY.
JAMES W. NORTH.
LENDALL TITCOMB.

D. A. CONY, *President.*
C. S. HICHBORN, *Cashier.*
C. R. WHITTEN, *Asst. Cashier*

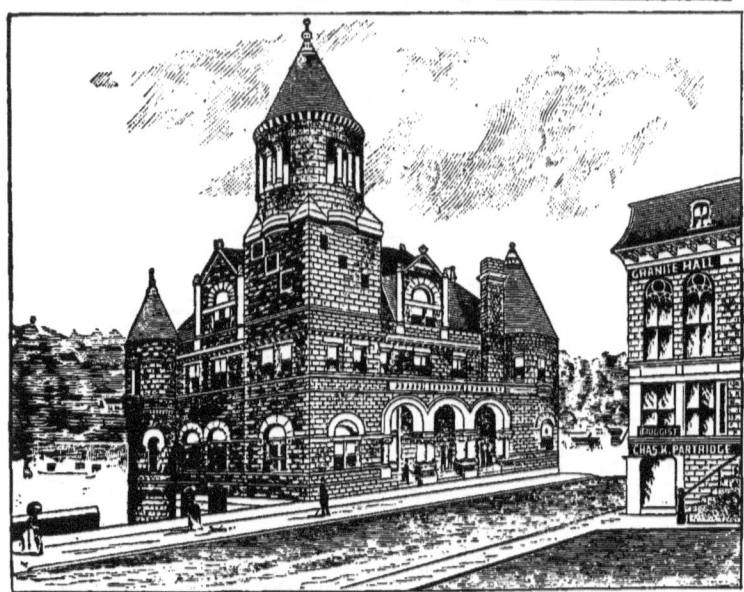

H. C. Caswell, Flour, Groceries, Provisions Beef, Pork, Mutton, Lamb, Poultry, Sausage, etc. Oranges, Lemons and Bananas, Tobacco and Cigars, No. 4 Granite Hall Block, Water Street, Augusta. Reliable goods, fair prices, prompt service, and courteous attention to customers,—these are the reasons for the liberal patronage bestowed upon the enterprise now conducted by H. C. Caswell, at No. 4 Granite Hall Block, Water Street, and our readers will admit that these are enough to gain success for any undertaking, and especially for one concerned in the handling of such indispensable commodities as Family Groceries, Provisions, etc. This establishment was inaugurated in 1884 by Messrs. Blackwell & Turner, who were succeeded by the firm of Webber & Co. In November, 1887, Mr. Caswell became sole proprietor. The trade is already a large one, and if the present rate of growth is continued, it will soon rank with that of the oldest established house of the kind in this section. The premises, occupied comprise one floor and a basement each of the dimensions of 20x80 feet, and contain a very carefully selected stock of goods including the choicest grades of Flour, as well as the best selections of Groceries and Provisions of all kinds, such as Beef Pork, Mutton, Lard, Poultry, Sausages, etc., also Oranges, Lemons and Bananas, and the best and most popular brands of Tobacco and Cigars. Low prices are quoted on all these articles and the most careful buyer will find that nothing is to be lost, and much to be gained, by placing their orders here. Three capable assistants are constantly employed, and every effort is made to serve customers promptly as well as politely, and orders are delivered without unnecessary delay. Mr. Caswell is a native of Augusta, and belongs to the A. O. U. W.

E. J. Roberts, D. D. S., Water Street, near Post-office, Augusta. In the rapid improvements of the last quarter of a century, every branch of business has seemed to move forward, but none more so than the dental art, which would seem to be at its height, especially as we view the appliances and improvements of our best dental rooms. Dr. E. J. Roberts is the leading man in this city engaged in this profession, and no pains or money is spared to provide every modern invention, and all branches of dentistry are conducted in an enlightened manner. Dr. Roberts occupies an elegant suite of rooms, handsomely furnished, and supplied with every convenience for the comfort of his many patrons. He is located on Water Street, near Post-office. Dr. Roberts founded his establishment in 1860, and has since that date obtained a reputation for first-class work and reasonable prices. He is thoroughly conversant with the dental art, and conducts it in all its varied and difficult operations. Dr. Roberts is a native of Maine, and well and favorably known in social as well as business circles of this community. We commend him and his establishment to the favorable notice of all the interested readers of this volume.

Geo. E. Macomber's Insurance Agency, Granite Hall Block, Market Square, Augusta. Fire, Life and Accident Insurance in the best American and English Companies. Capital represented, $50,000,000. Every man identified with the control of property, whether as owner, trustee or administrator, will recognize the importance of fire insurance. No man can lay any claim to business wisdom who disregards this duty, whether it be to himself or through himself to others. It of course relieves a business man of much anxiety to feel that his stock is fully covered by insurance; but care should be taken that this is placed in perfectly responsible and reliable companies, lest it should be discovered that the feeling of security was but ill-founded after all. As it is entirely out of the question for every man who desires insurance to personally investigate the solvency of the many companies now engaged in this business, the best plan, undoubtedly, is to intrust the placing of Insurance to some old-established, and well-known agency, which has served its customers well in the past, and has every inducement to continue to do so in the future. Life, compared to Fire Insurance, has to be looked upon in quite a different light. We have so often alluded to the importance of Life Insurance to the best interests of the community, that there is little more to be said to reinforce it. The most striking argument that can be offered for it is to be drawn from some one of the practical examples of "sudden deaths" that from time to time occur. We can quote instances where well-known parties have had their lives insured during the first days of a month, and who suddenly died but a few days later, their policy being $10,000. The shortness and uncertainty of life—how often do we read and hear the words, until they fall on the ear as a thrice-told tale, and, while we mentally give our assent to it, apply it rather to our neighbor than ourselves. It must come to us all, however, sooner or later, and the prudent man realizes that it is his duty, as well as his interest, to protect himself against the chance of an abrupt termination of his life. The satisfaction it affords in the feeling of security arising from the knowledge that no matter when the dread destroyer comes, your family is provided for, is of itself sufficient reason for insurance. In regard to accident policies, similar reasons could be argued in particular to the public who are travelling considerable, and to whom in such cases accidents are apt to take place at any moment, without warning, and even though taking all possible precautions. Any party representing such three lines as Fire, Life and Accident, may justly be called "a city's most important personage," and as this sketch is based upon matters of facts, and relating to Augusta, Me., Mr. Macomber is actually, in every way this city's principal Insurance man. Since 1876, Mr. Macomber has controlled this Agency, the companies he represents being the largest and soundest, are as follows: Ætna of Hartford, Conn.; Commercial of Hartford; Hanover of N. Y.; Insurance Co. of North America, Philadelphia; Insurance Co., State of Pa., Philadelphia; Continental of N. Y.; Springfield, Mass.; Niagara, N. Y.; First National, Worcester; New Hampshire, Manchester; Merchants, Newark, N. J.; Queen of England; London & Lancaster of England; Norwich Union of England; Citizens of Pittsburg; Granite State, Portsmouth, N.H.; Quincy Mutual, Quincy, Mass.; Lancashire of England; Holyoke Mutual, Salem, Mass.; Commercial Union of England; Peoples of Manchester, Eng.; Fireman's Fund of California; Traders & Mechanics, Lowell, Mass.; North British & Mercantile, England; Fire Insurance Association of England; Western of Canada; Northern of England; Ætna Life of Hartford, Conn.; Travellers' Life and Accident, Hartford, Conn.; Lloyds Plate Glass, N. Y.; the total amount being $100,000,000. Mr. Macomber is at present Mayor of Augusta, it being the third term he is serving in that capacity. Being highly respected, and taking a lively interest in the growth and welfare of the city, much of the prosperity of Augusta's flourishing business is due to its Mayor's high business qualifications and activity. He is well known, not only in this city and County, but through the entire State of Maine. Mr. Macomber solicits correspondence, and is ever ready to afford any additional information desired.

G. A. & H. Cony, Stable, Market Square, Augusta. The Livery and Boarding Stable carried on by Messrs. G. A. & H. Cony has long been known as one of the best appointed in the State, but since it was remodeled and enlarged in September 1888, it has held a higher position than ever, and the facilities for the accommodation of customers seem now incapable of improvement. There is a carriage-room on the first floor, measuring 50x110 feet, and a room of similiar dimensions on the second floor capable of accommodating fifty horses, there being five roomy and well-ventilated box-stalls and every provision made for the comfort and well-being of the animals cared for. Horses will be boarded by the week or month at very moderate rates, and we can assure our readers that the most valuable animals may be left here in perfect safety as the conveniences are first-class and kind treatment is invariably given. The upper story gives ample accommodation for thirty tons of hay, and the building also contains an elegant office with the toilet room, a parcel room, one for the storage of Robes, a Harness room, Hostler's room, etc. Business was begun in 1874 under the firm name of Cony, Farrar & Co., but since the death of Mr. Farrar in 1888, the present style has been adopted. The property has been owned from the first by the Messrs. Cony, Mr. Farrar simply having an interest in the livery stock. The location is remarkably central and convenient, being adjacent to the railway station and but half a block from the steamboat landing, and strangers in Augusta should by all means embrace the opportunity offered to drive about the city and vicinity—known throughout New England as among the most picturesque in the country. The firm are very liberal in catering to the public, and take pride in furnishing unexceptionable turnouts at low rates. Experienced and civil drivers will be supplied if desired, and we feel convinced that those who patronize this establishment on the representations here made will have reason to thank us for calling attention to the advantages offered.

"**The Bazaar,**" Gents' Furnishings, Umbrellas, Overalls, Jumpers, etc. Crockery, Glass and Tin Ware. 5, 10 and 25 Cent Goods. Novelties added weekly. Frederick H. Owen, Bazaar, Water Street, Augusta. Before paying 15 or 20 cents for an article elsewhere, be sure it is not on our 5 or 10 Cent Counters. If the word "Bazaar" be defined to mean an establishment where goods in great variety are sold at lowest rates we believe that no one familiar with the facts would question the justice of its application to the emporium conducted by Frederick H. Owen, at the Bazaar, Water St. This gentleman may be entitled one of the leaders in this line of trade in Augusta, and it would be difficult to find a man more thoroughly posted, or one more alive to the demands of the times. He began business in 1885 and during the time since elapsed he has built up a reputation for low prices and fair dealings. He is a native of this city and is one of the most widely known of our Augusta merchants. Two floors are occupied and a stock carried which is hard to parallel elsewhere either for size or variety. Among the more prominent goods handled are Novelties, Fancy Articles, Toys, Games and hundreds of other things which our limited space will not admit of mention. All these goods are classed and sold as 5, 10, and 25 cent goods. Three reliable and courteous assistants are employed and the entire business is conducted by Mr. Owen on a high plane of honor and fair representation of all goods and one price, that the lowest.

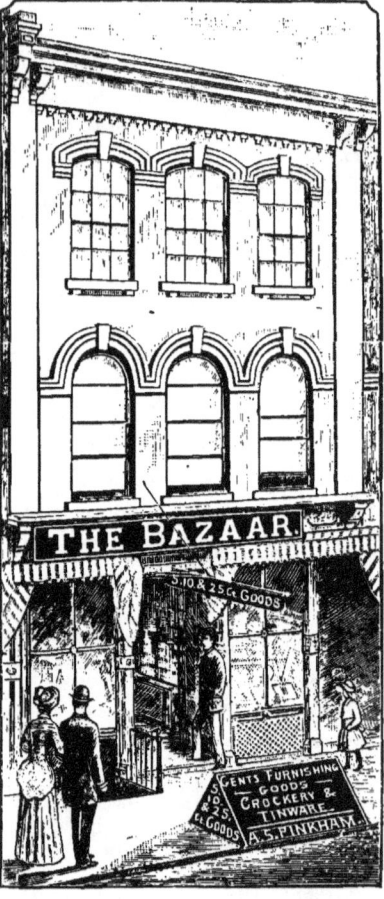

Miss L. M. Jordan, Millinery and Fancy Goods, No. 154 Water Street, Augusta. Among the many fine stores located on Water Street one of the most attractive in its line is that conducted by Miss L. M. Jordan. This establishment was founded in 1878 by its present proprietress, and from its inception has ranked among the first-class establishments in this line of trade in Augusta. The store covers an area of 20x50 feet, and is elegantly fitted up for the tasteful display of the large stock handled, which embraces a complete line of Millinery and Fancy Goods, and in fact everything usually called for in a first-class Millinery and Fancy Goods Store. Experienced assistants are employed and all orders are filled promptly. It is with pleasure that we recommend Miss Jordan and her establishment to the favorable attention of all our readers who have not patronized her; here they can obtain fresh goods of the latest designs and newest fashions at fair and reasonable prices. Miss Jordan is a native of Augusta and is thoroughly experienced in all the details of her business and well deserves the success she has achieved.

J. J. Maher & Co., Edward's New Block, North End Clothing House, Augusta. Travelers in this country from foreign lands, however much else they may see to admire, always find time to notice and to express their surprise at the well-dressed condition of the people here as a whole. There is no such attention paid to the wants of the people by clothiers abroad, as there is here, where the competition among those engaged in the business is so keen, that $2.00 is more often made on suits of clothes than $5.00, and where most of the dealers believe it is better to sell a large quantity at a small profit, than a small amount at a large profit. The clothing business is so arranged now that dwellers in the metropolis have no advantage whatever over those living in the surrounding smaller cities in the matter of purchasing clothing. It is a well-known saying, and one of no small amount of credence, that "the clothes make the man." But they must be good clothes, however, which is quite an-

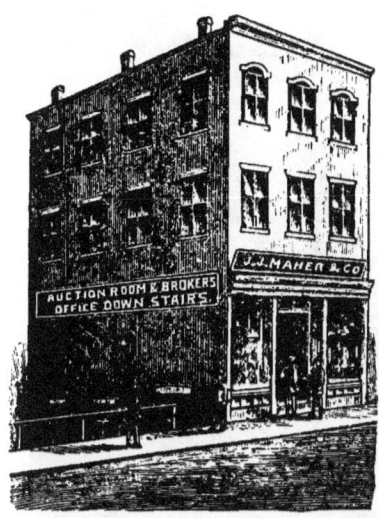

other thing, and the trouble is nowadays to find an establishment where garments suitable for the outer covering of a gentleman are made of good, honest material, which are of fashionable style, perfect fit, and last, but by no means least, at a reasonable outlay. This business of J. J. Maher & Co. was started Nov. 12, 1887. The store contains as full and as complete an assortment of clothing, Underwear, Hats, Caps, etc., etc., en fin, everything belonging to a first-class gents' furnishing goods store, as can be found in any store even in the metropolis. The store is well lighted, and measures 24x60 feet in dimensions. The policy upon which Mr. Maher conducts his business is characterized by liberality, and the careful fostering of the interests of his patrons, so that transactions once entered into with him may be not only pleasant for the time being, but of a permanent nature. Buyer or no buyer, every one is requested to inspect his assortment before making a bargain anywhere, and the general opinion has always been that J. J. Maher & Co., the clothiers, carry an A 1 complete assortment, and is invariably the cheapest in Augusta, which means a great deal. Beside clothings, Mr. Maher is manager of the firm of Dr. J. J. Maher & Co., the proprietors of the celebrated "Clover Bitters," "Clover Balsam and Relief Liniment," all of which are so well known all over New England that further recommendation of these celebrated medicines by our pen is entirely unnecessary. Mr. Maher was born in Springfield, Mass., is a prominent member of the A. O. U. W., was in 1887 elected overseer of the poor for a term of three years, and is today, through perseverance, honest dealings, and strict "personal" attention to his business, one of the city's well-known and highly-respected citizens, and is what may be termed "a self-made man."

Charles Bryant, Dentist, 140 Water Street, Augusta. American dentists have the reputation of being the best in the world, and certainly if they are not they should be, for they have an excellent opportunity to practice their profession on their fellow-countrymen, as the latter have the poorest teeth of any nation. Another advantage they enjoy is in the superior inventive talent of citizens of the United States, which has been used to such good purpose of late years in dentistry, that much of its attendant drudgery is now greatly lightened, and much trouble and expense are thus saved. Among the dentists who have gained the confidence of the public the establishment conducted by Charles Bryant holds a deservedly high position. This gentleman began the practice of his profession in Augusta, in 1884. His patronage is at present large and select. At this establishment one may have their teeth extracted, and artificial ones inserted. His operating room is supplied with all the latest modern instruments and facilities for thorough and artistic work, and all unnecessary display of them is carefully avoided, a point that will be appreciated by nervous or timid patrons.

D. P. Knowlton, Dealer in Picture Moldings, Oil Paintings, and Steel Engravings. Picture Framing a Specialty. Upholstering and Jobbing. 101 Water Street, nearly opposite Post-office, Augusta. The artistic taste of a community is a sure index of its refinement and culture, and we are safe in asserting that in no city of equal magnitude is this more evident than in Augusta. This city possesses, to a marked degree, in its establishments, every facility for fostering the æsthetic tastes of the community, and it is in a large measure due to a house like that of Mr. D. P. Knowlton, which serves as a prominent type that these to-be-desired results have been obtained. Mr. Knowlton has been established in this line of business in Augusta since 1881, and during the period elapsed this enterprise has steadily advanced in importance until it has attained its present position. The premises utilized for the business are located at 101 Water Street, nearly opposite the Post-office, and comprise two floors and basement, each 20x60 feet in dimensions, where is tastefully displayed the very fine and complete assortment of goods handled, which consists of a fine selection of Picture Moldings, Oil Paintings, and Steel Engravings. Employment is given to capable and reliable assistants, and the extensive retail trade, which is under the direct management of Mr. Knowlton, is most efficiently managed. Mr. Knowlton makes a specialty of Picture Framing, and in additon to the above-named line of business he is prepared to do Upholstering Work, and all jobbing in this line is promptly attended to. All work intrusted to his care is executed in the best manner possible, and patrons visiting this establishment will find many inducements to purchase; difficult to duplicate elsewhere.

Charles C. Hunt, Hallett & Davis Pianos, Augusta. The recognized superiority of the Hallett & Davis Pianos over many others in use has of late years created a demand for these instruments almost equal to the facilities for their productions, great as they are. Popular among the dealers who are agents for these instruments is Mr. Charles C. Hunt, whose establishment is located on Water Street, Augusta, and is so efficiently and ably managed by him. Mr. Hunt is acceded to be one of the ablest and most reliable judges of musical instruments, especially Pianos and Organs. The premises occupied consist of three floors, each 20x60 feet in dimensions, where many fine specimens of these popular instruments are displayed. The business transacted here comprises an extensive retail trade in Pianos, Organs, and Sheet Music, requiring the assistance of two thoroughly competent clerks, who are polite and courteous in their attention to visitors, who are invited to inspect the goods dealt in here, before purchasing elsewhere. Mr. Hunt is a native of Readfield, Me., and a member of the Free Masons. He is an efficient business man and in his keeping the interests of his patrons are admirably subserved.

George D. Haskell, Dealer in Choice Family Groceries, Wholesale and Retail, Provisions, Teas and Coffees, Cony St., East Side. We know of no more worthy example of the old and representative houses of Augusta than the popular establishment now conducted by Mr. Geo. D. Haskell, and located on Cony Street, East Side. This establishment was originally started under its present title of George D. Haskell. This house possesses a valuable and extended experience in the Grocery and Provision interest, and by liberal treatment of customers has rapidly advanced in public favor. Mr. Haskell occupies attractive premises, comprising three floors, each covering an area of 40x65 feet, which are well stocked and very conveniently arranged, and the trade is very large, both in wholesale and retail. Four very competent and experienced assistants are in attendance, thus insuring the patrons of the house prompt attention. A large and well-selected stock is constantly kept on hand, including the choicest Family and Fancy Groceries, Provisions and Meats. Also Fresh and Salt Fish of all kinds (the only Fish Market on the East Side), Glass Ware, Crockery, and Earthen Ware, Lamps, Flower Pots, Wooden Ware, etc. Mr. Haskell is also Agent for the Barton Cheese and Coburn Butter. No inferior goods are sold, and every effort is made to avoid adulterated articles. The low prices and fine assortment carried have given this establishment the large trade it enjoys. Mr. Haskell is a native of Augusta, and a member of the Odd Fellows, and is an active business man, enjoying the respect and esteem of this community.

O. Williamson, Manufacturer and Dealer in Furnaces, Stoves, Hardware, Tin Ware and Cutlery; Plumbing; also Coal Merchant. A full line of Agricultural Tools, Mowers, Horse Rakes, Plows, Plow Castings. No. 6 Union Block, Augusta. An Augusta business house, whose reputation is by no means confined to the city, or even the State, is that now conducted under the name of O. Williamson, at No. 6 Union Block, Augusta. Mr. Williamson, who is now the sole proprietor and director of this enterprise, is a native of Maine. This Manufacturing and Retail business in Furnaces, Stoves, Hardware, etc., was established twenty years ago, under the firm name of Williamson & Greenwood, and so continued until 1870, when the firm was changed to Williamson, Ward & Cogan, and in 1887 Mr. O. Williamson, the present proprietor, assumed the full control and management of the business. The premises utilized for Hardware and Plumbing comprises four floors of the building, each covering an area of 50x23 feet. He has also five floors devoted to Agricultural Implements, Seeds and Phosphate, opposite 6 Union Block. The energies of this house are devoted to the manufacture and retail branches of the above-named lines of business, giving employment to twelve thoroughly reliable and experienced assistants. The stock carried embraces Furnaces, Stoves, Hardware, Tin Ware, Cutlery, etc., and in the Plumbing department, Force

LEADING BUSINESS MEN OF AUGUSTA.

Pumps, Tubs, Copper Boilers, Stop-cocks, and Lead and Iron Pipes. Also Mowers, Horse-rakes, Plows, Plow Castings, and everything usually kept in a first-class agricultural store. A specialty is made of job work of all kinds, which is promptly attended to. Mr. Williamson is one of our prominent and well-known citizens, having been a member of the School Committee.

Edwards Manufacturing Company, Cotton Mills, Water Street, Augusta. For a good many years New England has maintained her supremacy in the line of Cotton Manufacturing, and the State of Maine has done its share toward securing this condition of affairs. Maine has always labored under some disadvantages as compared with her sister states, by reason of her comparative remoteness from the great centers of trade, but the natural advantages she possesses in the shape of valuable water-powers, etc., together with the enterprise and industry of her citizens, have done much to neutralize the offset referred to, and have led to the establishment within her borders of such mammoth undertakings as that carried on by the Edwards Manufacturing Company, on Water Street, by the Kennebec Dam. The plant utilized at this point is very extensive indeed, and yet is so far insufficient to supply the active and increasing demand for the companies goods, that there is being erected a large five-story factory, in addition to the buildings already occupied. These consist of three mills, comprising five stories and a basement each, and within these buildings may be found 1,500 looms and 60,000 spindles, employment being given to seven hundred hands, and the monthly pay roll amounting to $18,000. The goods produced are Prints and Shirtings, and the output of the Edwards Manufacturing Company is too well known to the trade in general to make it necessary for us to call attention to its superior and uniform excellence. The selling agents are Bliss, Fabyan & Co., 100 Summer St., Boston, and 71 Thomas St., New York, and the management of the Co.'s affairs is in the hands of the following well-known gentlemen:—President, Dexter N. Richards; Treasurer, Jacob Edwards; Agent, N. W. Cole; Clerk, Chas. B. Johnson; Directors, Dexter N. Richards, Jacob Edwards, Isaac Fenno, Chas. U. Cotting, J. H. Manley, J. Manchester Haynes, O. H. Alford.

J. A. Fairbanks, Dealer in Fishing Tackle and Fine Cutlery, Sewing Machines, Dog Collars, Whistles, Bells, etc. Roller Skates in great variety. Fine Breech-Loading Rifles and Double Guns a Specialty. Gun Store and Office, 111 Water Street, Augusta. One of the best stores in Maine for the purchase of Fishing Tackle, and everything used by sportsmen, is conducted by J. A. Fairbanks. He is well known among sportsmen, and his store is the headquarters for all kinds of Ammunition, Whistles, Bells, Roller Skates, etc. In addition, he sells Sewing Machines of popular makes, and all in want of one of these useful articles would do well to examine his stock. Too much cannot be put into either the manufacture or selection of a Gun, for all considerations of safety and prudence demand that it be made of the best material by experienced hands. It is chiefly on account of his productions being fully up to the highest standard, that Mr. Fairbanks has built up so large a patronage. Experienced and careful assistants are employed. Orders are given prompt attention, and Repairing is done in the best manner, at the shortest notice and lowest price. It is believed that no house can offer more liberal inducements, or is in any way better prepared to fully satisfy its patrons.

GRANITE NATIONAL BANK

OF AUGUSTA.

Designated Depositary of the United States.

Capital, $100,000.

Surplus, $25,000.

AUGUSTA, ME., Jan. 12, 1880.

OFFICERS.

PRESIDENT,	D. ALDEN.
VICE-PRESIDENT,	J. W. BRADBURY.
CASHIER,	TREBY JOHNSON.
ASSISTANT CASHIER,	ASA W. HEDGE.

DIRECTORS.

D. ALDEN,
J. W. BRADBURY,
JOHN W. CHASE,
HORACE H. HAMLEN,
TREBY JOHNSON.

Charles Jenkins, Dealer in Fresh, Salt, Smoked, Canned and Pickled Fish, Oysters and Clams, Opposite Kennebec Journal Office, Water Street. A very popular establishment in this city is that carried on by Mr. Charles Jenkins, opposite the Kennebec Journal office on Water Street, and this popularity is due not only to the business methods of the firm mentioned, but also to the nature of the commodity in which he deals, for everybody likes fish, and there is no house in the State that takes more pains to supply a good and reliable article, than that of Mr. Charles Jenkins. The premises occupied are of the dimensions of 18x40 feet and contains a stock made up of Fresh, Salt, Smoked and Pickled Fish, Oysters, Lobsters, and Clams. Pickles by the jar or gallon are also extensively handled and Oyster and Fancy Crackers are on hand in great variety. A popular feature of the enterprise is the free delivery of goods to any part of the city, and in fact the business methods throughout are as liberal as they are intelligent. This undertaking was founded in 1876 and during the past twelve years has become more or less familiar to every citizen. Therefore we need hardly say that it deserves hearty support, for the public have long since discovered that a due equivalent is given here for every penny expended and that the best of goods are supplied at the lowest market rates.

Parker N. Savage, Livery Stable, Cony Street, Augusta. Getting a horse at the average Livery Stable is a good deal like getting a wife — you may strike a good one the first time but the chances are all against you. Now on the goodness of the horse depends all the enjoyment of driving, for one can put up with ancient and springless carriages, rough roads, and even bad weather on a pinch, as long as they have a speedy and willing animal between the shafts; but the finest vehicle and smoothest roads are of no avail if the horse has to be "driven" in fact as well as in name. A Livery Stable which since its establishment in 1884, has gained a high reputation and a large amount of custom by the fine character of the turn-outs furnished by it, is that conducted by Mr. Parker N. Savage on Cony Street. This gentleman is a native of Augusta and widely known here. The premises in use by him comprise one building with all the facilities for a modern Livery and Sale Stable. A large number of Horses and Carriages are now accommodated here and those wishing to procure a stylish and elegant team at a reasonable price, should give Mr. Savage a call. Employment is given to capable assistants and all horses entrusted to this stable are assured the best of care and attention, and the kindest treatment.

F. L. Webber, Dealer in Choice Family Groceries, Fine Flours, Meats, Country Produce, etc., No. 4 Union Block, Augusta. It is useless to ask our readers if they wish to be assured of polite treatment and fair dealing when placing their orders for Groceries and Provisions, for everybody of course *does* have just this wish and is by no means always able to gratify it. However, we can afford some assistance at least to those who are not entirely satisfied with their present relations with grocers, etc., for we feel assured that Mr. F. L. Webber, of No. 4 Union Block, Water Street, Augusta, is in a position to satisfy all who may favor him with their custom, and we have no doubt but that those who have dealings with him will sustain us in recommending his establishment to all who appreciate reliable goods and courteous treatment. This concern was first established twelve years ago and after one or two changes in its management, came under the control of Messrs. Blackwood & Webber in 1875, and was successfully managed by them until 1882, when Mr. F. L. Webber assumed full proprietorship. The premises utilized by him are 65x20 feet in dimensions, and the stock on hand is sufficient to fill all the available space, being made up of Choice Family Groceries, Fine Flours, Meats, and Country Produce, etc., and being complete in every detail. Employment is given to three assistants, and Mr. Webber endeavors to handle no goods except such as he can recommend, and to place his prices at such figures that all will be satisfied. Mr. Webber is a native of Maine, and well known in social as well as business circles, being a member of the Masons, Odd Fellows, and United Workmen.

J. S. Hendee, Photographer, Augusta. Since the time that the great French artist discovered the art of daguerreotyping, photography has been making rapid and continual advances, until to-day it occupies a position of commanding influence. Mr. J. S. Hendee, opened his Photographing Studio here in 1859, and the popularity and success which have attended his subsequent progress speaks most conclusively for his skill as an artist, and the good taste of the people of Augusta. He occupies three well-fitted up rooms, each 22x72 feet in dimensions, and located on Water Street, and is prepared to offer all his patrons the most satisfactory work in the way of fine photography, and every facility is at hand in the way new and improved apparatus for the production of first-class work. An examination of his work and the testimony of his large circle of patrons will confirm all the claims for his talent and workmanship. Mr. Hendee is a native of Vermont and has made many friends in our midst by his thorough and uniform courtesy and trained skill as an artist. He is ably assisted in his Studio by the talented and popular Miss Juliet Bigelow, who is considered to be one of the finest retouchers in Maine.

A. C. TITCOMB,
SURGEON DENTIST,
DENTAL ROOMS,
Cor. Water and Bridge Sts.,

AUGUSTA, ME.

Cony House, G. A. & H. Cony. Proprietors, Water Street, Augusta. It is fitting and proper that in this review of the commercial interests of Augusta and vicinity, we should make prominent mention of such an establishment as the Cony House, for the leading hotel of the State's capital is certainly worthy of respectful consideration. This house has been conducted without change in ownership for nearly a score of years, in this respect standing alone among similar institutions in this city. The premises occupied comprise four floors of the dimensions of 90x60 feet, and are divided up into fifty rooms. Both Messrs. G. A. & H. Cony are natives of Augusta, and are so universally known here that further personal mention of them is hardly called for. Suffice it to say that although they take pride in the past record of the Cony House, they are by no means disposed to rest on their laurels, but on the contrary are ever on the alert to improve the character of the service offered to the public. Ten experienced assistants are employed and a careful supervision of the entire establishment is kept up, thus assuring that guests shall receive the attention and respect that are their due, and that the complete system in operation shall not suffer from neglect in any of its details. The table is supplied at all seasons of the year with the best that the market affords, and the bill of fare is sufficiently varied to suit all tastes. Cooking and serving will be found very satisfactory, for great pains have been taken in this department and the result is most gratifying and acceptable. The terms for regular or transient guests will compare favorably with those asked for decidedly inferior accommodations elsewhere, and in short liberality and experience are plainly observable in the management of this establishment from roof to cellar. A first-class Livery Stable is connected with the hotel, this being conducted by Messrs. G. A. & H. Cony, and having been in operation since 1874. Messrs. G. A. & H. Cony are natives of this city, and Mr. G. A., a member of the Free Masons, and Mr. H. Cony, an Odd Fellow, both gentlemen being well known about the city. Carriages will be furnished for any occasion at short notice, and experienced and careful drivers are furnished when desired. Single and double teams can be obtained here at very low rates, and horses suitable for ladies driving can always be supplied.

Augusta & Waterville Marble Works, W. H. Turner, Proprietor; Monuments, Tablets, and Grave Stones, of Italian and American Marble, also Scotch and American Granite Monuments, Bridge Street, Augusta, Main Street, Waterville. The enterprise known as the "Augusta and Waterville Marble Works," must be familiar to every resident of this city, for it has been carried on for nearly 40 years, having been inaugurated in 1850. A branch house is maintained in Waterville, on Main Street, and the premises occupied in this city comprise two floors 20x50 feet in dimensions together with ample yard-room, the establishment being located on Bridge Street. Monumental Tablets and Grave Stones of Italian and American Marble, are dealt in very extensively and will be made to order at short notice. Designs will be furnished on application, and Cemetery Work of all kinds done at the lowest market rates and in an eminently satisfactory manner. The proprietor, Mr. W. H. Turner, is a native of Augusta and a member of the Free Masons. He employs five experienced and skilled assistants and permits no work to leave his premises that is not fully up to the standard which the public have learned to expect in connection with orders filled at this old established concern. Both a wholesale and retail business is done and Marble is by no means the only material worked, for both Scotch and American Granite are handled to a considerable extent and some very tasteful and beautiful monuments are produced. The importance of combining good taste and fine workmanship in Cemetery work can hardly be over-estimated, and those having any orders to place in this line can do no better than to give Mr. Turner a call.

Bean & Hamlin, Pianos, Organs, and Sewing Machines, 123 Water Street, next to Kennebec Saving Bank, Augusta. A most desirable place in Augusta, for the purchase of Pianos, Organs and Sewing Machines of all makes is that of Bean & Hamlin located at No. 123 Water St. This representative firm was formed here in 1888, and has from the beginning met with decided and deserved success. The office and store room are located at the above address and are filled to the utmost capacity with the elegant assortment of Pianos, Organs, and Sewing Machines of all styles and makes. They supply everything in their line at the lowest prices, for first-class instruments, and all are warranted, and satisfaction always guaranteed. Both are natives of Maine, and well known in the business circles of this community. They have unsurpassed facilities for successfully conducting a large trade. They are reliable and responsible in business, and have won success in trade here because of their sterling worth and ability.

Bussell & Weston, Foreign and Domestic Dry Goods, under Cony House. Augusta being one of the most popular and enterprising cities of the State, it is not at all surprising that this city is also a great distributing point from which goods are sent to all the sections adjacent. There are many enterprising firms here engaged almost exclusively in this class of trade and among these none bears a higher reputation, not only for energy and shrewdness, but also for strict commercial probity, than does that known as Bussell & Weston, doing business on Water Street, under the Cony House. This enterprise was founded in 1881 by Messrs. Bussell and Weston. The house deals in Foreign and Domestic Dry Goods at retail, and occupies a store 25x40 feet in dimensions, for the accommodation of the heavy and complete stock which is constantly on hand. Large quantities of everything included in the Dry and Fancy Goods line are disposed of, and three very capable, and thoroughly efficient assistants are employed. The individual members of the firm are Mr. W. F. Bussell and Mr. N. Weston, both natives and highly respected citizens and business men of Augusta. Their trade is rapidly growing and they evidently have a bright future before them.

G. A. Bryant, Livery and Sale Stable, Bowman Street, Augusta. Of the many means of relaxation and recreation open to the people nowadays, few, if any, have that perpetual charm and infinite variety that characterize riding and driving. There is something in associating one's self with a good horse that almost invariably tends to drive away "the blues," and when gliding along behind a speedy stepper, the brisk motion, the fresh air, and the sense of power that comes when controling a spirited and powerful animal, all combine to make a man forget the rise in corn or the drop in wheat, and cause him to be happy and irrepressible for the time being. So it is no wonder that riding and driving are popular, and that Livery Stables increase and multiply. Of course to experience the pleasurable sensations hinted at above, you want a good horse, and one of the surest ways of securing one, if you propose to hire a turnout, is to call on Mr. G. A. Bryant, who conducts the Livery and Sale Stable, on Bowman Street, Augusta. This establishment was founded in 1883, by the present proprietor. Two stables are occupied, covering an area of 30x100 feet, affording ample room for the horses placed here on sale, in addition to those owned by Mr. Bryant. The business requires the services of very capable assistants. Mr. Bryant is a native of, and extremely well known in Augusta, and his intelligent efforts to provide a much more desirable service to his patrons than the average stable affords, have met with great success, and gained him many well-wishers. The prices for letting horses are as low as circumstances will permit, and carriages can be furnished for any occasion at short notice.

G. A. Bryant, Proprietor Franklin House, corner Cony and Bowman Streets. Augusta has many fine hotels, but few of them combine, in so satisfactory a manner, the comforts of a home and the conveniences of a public house, as does the popular Franklin House. It will be seen that the location of the house is central, and this fact, together with the liberal and accommodating manner in which the hotel is managed, have had much to do with the success of its enterprising proprietor, Mr. G. A. Bryant, who has conducted it since 1885. The hotel contains eighteen rooms, all of good size and well lighted. The closest inspection of the house, from roof to cellar, will only discover neatness and order, as the proprietor keeps a vigilant watch over the whole establishment, and not only requires his employees to keep affairs in that condition, but by personal superintendence satisfies himself that his orders are strictly complied with. The best of accommodation is furnished for either transient or regular boarders, at most reasonable rates, the best that the market affords being served to guests, and the large number that patronize the house shows how the treatment received is appreciated.

C. Beale & Co., House and Sign Painters, and dealers in Paints, Oils, Varnishes, Japan, Putty, Glass and Paper Hangings, No. 5 Union Block, Water Street. The work of the house painter is very important, combining as it does, utility and beauty, and it is becoming more and more important every year as the popularity of "Queen Anne," and similar styles of houses increases. The day has gone by when a square structure covered with white paint answered for a dwelling house, and nowadays we have cosy looking buildings with a bewildering confusion of angles, etc., painted in three or four colors and appearing as homelike without as they are inviting within. But to get the best effect from such dwellings it is essential that they should be painted by experienced hands, and not only that, but the material used should be first-class and able to stand the severity of our New England weather. Therefore houseowners will find it worth their while to take some little trouble to place all work of this kind in competent hands, and they can possibly do no better than to leave their orders with Messrs. C. Beale & Co., doing business at 5 Union Block, Water Street, Augusta, for this concern has been engaged in the painting industry since 1833, when it was established by Mr. J. Beale and continued by him until 1837, when Mr. Heath was admitted to the firm, and its style became Beale & Heath. In 1850 it was changed to Beale & Farnham, and so continued until 1873, when the present style was adopted of C. Beale & Co. They have gained a reputation second to none for durable, tasteful, and entirely satisfactory work. The individual members of the present firm are Messrs. C. Beale, F. H. Beale, and E. F. Blackman, all of whom are natives of Maine, and well-known and highly respected business men of this community. The business premises occupied by Messrs. C. Beale & Co., consists of three floors and basement of the building, each 60x22 feet in size, where in addition to custom work in House and Sign Painting they have a wholesale and retail trade in Paints, Oils, Varnishes, Japan, Putty, Glass, and Paper Hangings. Employment is given to a large number of thoroughly experienced and skilled assistants, and all orders in any of the above lines of business will be promptly filled and executed in the most satisfactory manner.

HISTORICAL SKETCH

—OF—

GARDINER.

IN this State of magnificent rivers, the Kennebec has been widely regarded as unsurpassed for its beauty, and the power and charms of the towns and cities which adorn its banks. Since the early days of the colony, Gardiner has always been among the most influential and prominent of the communities in this part of the State. With Hallowell and Augusta it gives a solidity and power to this heart of the State which makes it a great center of industrial and political interest. The Kennebec Indians were the first known human occupants of this vicinity. They have left traditions and memorials not loud but deep. The bones of their departed ancestors are occasionally discovered throughout this region. All evidences go to show that the tribe was powerful and advanced beyond the ordinary Indian standard. Their form of government and mode of life was nearly the best that has been discovered to exist upon the hunting stage. They had their councils and chiefs, their orators, political managers and medicine men. The fertility of the soil made them more than commonly agricultural in their tastes, so that they were in the main a peaceful tribe, and did not give much annoyance to the English, who first came into this region to form a permanent settlement about the middle of the 18th century, though there had been trading stations along the river before that time.

After various transitions of ownership, a grant of this region was made in 1729 to William Bradford, of the New Plymouth colony, the title later revoking to the colony itself. Through the "Kennebec Purchase," Dr. Sylvester Gardiner became a proprietor in the company endeavoring to colonize this region in 1754, and to him this region owes more than to any other man. Dr. Sylvester Gardiner was one of Boston's most talented, learned and able professional men. Greatly interested in the growth of this vicinity, he gave such earnest and energetic attention to its progress that a large grant of land here was awarded him for his services. In 1760, he sent out a little company of seven men and four women, with their families, who were landed at this point of the river, and laid the foundation of the town afterward named in Dr. Gardiner's honor.

In the following year Dr. Gardiner had a mill erected here, which was of great utility to the little but growing village. Among the earliest settlers were Thomas, Fitch, Lovis, Winslow, Davis, McCausland and Philbrook. The first white child born was Jonathan Winslow. Before the settlement advanced very far it was confronted with the intemperance question in the large importation of bad whiskey, etc., which obstruction to their progress was not removed until after a long and hard struggle. Benaiah Door, who came here in 1763, became influential in the early days of Gardiner.

Dr. Sylvester Gardiner, though very energetic and successful in the druggist business, where he made his fortune, had strong conservative leanings. He was one of the largest proprietors in the State of Maine, owning here over 100,000 good acres; but when the Revolution came on he gave them all up for the sake of principle and the mother country. As he espoused the British cause he was obliged to leave Boston and his great possessions behind. But through many litigations after the war, his sons managed to gain possession of their legitimate heritage, which gave immense returns for Dr. Gardiner's laborious efforts. After the war, Dr. Gardiner returned to Boston, and died at Newport in 1786.

THE "CASTLE," ONE OF THE OLDEST BUILDINGS.

The Revolution, however, found few Tories in this vicinity. Great enthusiasm was shown in the support of the principles and battles of the Revolution. By united action the settlers around were able to send a company of thirty men, under Reuben Colburn, to Cambridge in 1775. Others also enlisted in the disastrous expedition to Canada under Benedict Arnold, who passed through the Kennebec valley in the fall of 1775. The town contributed more than its due share, and took the deepest interest in the great cause; none rejoicing more heartily in the Declaration of Peace in 1783.

The closing years of the eighteenth and first of the nineteenth century were ones of marked progress. By 1803, this part of the region had so increased as to be set off from Pittston and incorporated as a separate town. Its original name was "Cabbassia," from the Indian, meaning "the place where sturgeon abound." At this time the population was estimated at about two hundred and fifty inhabitants.

The first town officers were as follows:—Moderator, Dudley B. Hobart; Town Clerk, Seth Gray; Selectmen, B. Gannett, D. B. Hobart and William Barker. Soon after this the primitive name was changed in honor of the family which had done so much to upbuild the place. The Gardiner Lyceum was founded in 1822, and was a strong influence in advancing the intellectual life of the place from that time on.

Among the most prominent citizens of Gardiner at this period was the Hon. Geo. Evans, who represented this District in Congress and was a leading man in State politics for many years.

An important commercial epoch was inaugurated in 1826, by the arrival of the first steamer run on the Kennebec, The Waterville. Since then the facilities for transportation on water have rapidly increased, and now constant communication by water is maintained with Boston and other great cities. This fact has been very helpful to our business interests, developing them and rendering Gardiner one of the choicest places for manufacturing settlement in the State. This place is now the practical head of summer navigation on the Kennebec.

In 1848, the beautiful Oak Grove Cemetery was completed and consecrated. In 1850, the arrival of the first telegraphic dispatch; and in 1851, the entrance of the first railroad train into Gardiner were events of deep and wide importance, whose

RESIDENCE OF MR. W. H. RING.

influence of upbuilding has been constantly felt up to the present time. Among the most remarkable men Gardiner produced in the first half of the century was William Burns, born in 1819, who achieved a great success, both in Boston and New York, as a leading journalist. The population of Gardiner in 1850 had arisen to 6,486, and its valuation was $2,098,000. In the same year it was incorporated as a city, the first mayor being Mr. R. H. Gardiner, and the city clerk John Webb. Since that time Gardiner has continued to develop its municipal government until it is so effectual and reliable that it is a model, and has been, to many new cities. The Kennebec river at Gardiner can easily float a vessel of 800 tons, and during the first half of this century the shipping interests of Gardiner were prosperous and progressive. The decay of this interest, and the separation from Gardiner of other towns, tended to retard its growth, but the introducing of manufacturing enterprises has neutralized it and inaugurated a great advance movement.

The military history of Gardiner has been honorable and energetic. A riflemen company was formed in 1813, which took an important part in the land troubles about Augusta in that year. In the Mexican war the city was represented by Col. F. T. Lally, Capt. Chas. N. Bodfish and other gallant soldiers. The duties involved by the civil war were discharged with eagerness and celerity. A full quota of men was sent, largely enlisted in the 1st, 3d, 9th, 11th, 14th, 15th, 24th, 28th and 29th State Volunnteer Regiments. Col. Geo. M. Atwood, of the 24th, and other gallant officers and men maintained the honor of the city, not without loss and death. The city contributed generously to all allied measures, and has not ceased to cherish the memory of its noble soldier sons.

GARDINER WATER WORKS.

The water supply of Gardiner is chiefly confined to the Cabossee Center river, though there is a possibility of vast power to be obtained from the Kennebec by wise utilization. On the former stream there are eight powers whose lowest possible value is 1200 horse, and which is capable of great advancement. The privileges for manufacturing here are of the finest, both as concerns the natural power and facilities of market. Among the chief interests are lumber, machines, iron work, furniture, grain, plaster, woolen goods, paper, carriages, axes, brooms and other utensils. No observant man can doubt that Gardiner is destined to great progress along these and other industrial lines.

Gardiner has always been famed for its refinement and high moral standard. The schools are liberally and wisely managed; the churches and all charities and benevolent work admirably sustained. The situation of the city is remarkably beautiful and healthful. All sanitary measures have received careful attention, and natural advantages improved by wise measures and works. The water supply is unsurpassed, and no luxury or utility necessary to a modern city is lacking. It is a most delightful spot for a long and delightful summer residence. The cool breezes from the river, the charming drives throughout the vicinity which contains many attractions, and the easy communications possible with the great cities, render it a favorite among summer visitors, who have come to see its advantages. Every year these become better known, and as the fame of the city spreads, there can be little doubt that the spirit

HISTORICAL SKETCH OF GARDINER.

which carried it forward in the past will continue its development until before many decades it takes its natural place among the leading social and industrial centers of the State.

From the commercial standpoint recent years have brought good results and promise of greater things in the immediate future. A more admirable situation to enjoy and share all the advancing prosperity of the Garden State could hardly be chosen. With the finest water and rail facility, being on the main line of the Maine Central railroad, and connected with Boston also by a steamer route making several round trips a week. Magnificent passenger steamers render this line a most enjoyable one during the season, and freight rates to Boston and the whole country

THE STAR OF THE EAST.

are reduced by the transportation of this excellent route. The large business development in many lines has served to advance the prosperity of the whole city.

The advantages of locating here for any manufacturer could hardly be over estimated. Great inducements are offered and the facilities and privileges here are unsurpassed. With the tested and reliable enterprise of its citizens, and the great opportunities now opening before the city, it is not unreasonable to expect that Gardiner is destined to sure and advancing prosperity, and that it will come to be one of the leading centers of the Kennebec valley, after all, and prominent among the largest and most influential cities of the State.

LEADING BUSINESS MEN

OF

GARDINER, ME.

Z. F. Little, Dealer in Dry Goods, Water Street, Gardiner. There are not a few people who have a preference for being served with promptness and politeness when purchasing goods of any kind, and such people are very apt to fail to see the advantages of dealing at an immense establishment, where there is so beautiful a "system," that while the customers are waiting for their goods so much time elapses that there is danger of their being out of style before they are received, and will not tolerate being obliged to waste time, as is frequently the case in larger stores — Boston and New York. Many shoppers know from sad experience what it is to make their way through a struggling crowd to some counter in an immense store, only to be told that the "department" of which they are in search is somewhere in the vicinity of a half-mile or so farther along, and finally, after having by persistent exertion reached the spot pointed out, had to wait anywhere from five minutes to half an hour before they transacted their business and received the goods. But those familiar with shopping at the dry goods establishment conducted by Mr. Z. F. Little, of Water Street, Gardiner, will, by entering this popular store, select his goods, pay for them, and be on the street again in less time than the first operation could be gone through with in some places. When hunting for "bargains," don't forget that "time is money," and few of us can afford to waste it. Without any exaggeration, this store may be considered as one of the largest and best conducted this side of Boston. It contains two floors, each 50x80 feet in dimensions, both splendidly lighted and well ventilated, divided into several departments, all of which are attended to by courteous assistants. The shelves are filled with a complete assortment of everything pertaining to a first-class Dry-Goods Store, and the counters always contain a great variety of "great bargains." Not only Dry and Fancy Goods are on hand, but also a select stock of Carpets, Wall Papers and Crockery. Mr. Little started in business in Gardiner, January 1, 1883, a few doors from his present store, but as the trade increased to such an extent that room for customers was sometimes at a premium, he was compelled to have an establishment built according to his need of space, which was done under his own directions, and on September 1, 1885, he removed into his present capacious emporium. Mr. Little is one of the shrewdest buyers, and dealing with the manufacturers directly, as he buys in quantities, he is enabled to defy any competitors, and his prices therefore are "bed rock." As a man of great business capacity, enterprising and courteous to all, Mr. Little has contrived to make his establishment the most popular one for miles surrounding, and is always willing to further the interests of the city by giving his personal support to any new enterprise. Mr. Little is looked upon as one of Gardiner's most energetic and honored business men and citizens.

J. C. Lander, Dealer in Hardware, Ship Chandlery, Crockery, Glass and Plated Ware, Paints, Oils, Cordage etc., 233 Water Street, Gardiner. Goods delivered free of charge. This year marks the 22d anniversary of the founding of the enterprise carried on by Mr. J. C. Lander at No. 233 Water Street, and it is fitting that this review of Gardiner's business interests should make prominent mention of the house in question, not alone from the fact alluded to above, but also because this enterprise is one of the most popular in this section of the State, and is generally recognized as being a truly representative undertaking. Operations were begun under the firm name of Tibbets & Lander, the present proprietor assuming sole control in 1874, or just eight years after the business was established. He is a native of this city, and is almost universally known hereabouts, having served in the City Government, and being prominently connected with both the Free Masons and the Odd Fellows. Mr. Lander occupies premises of the dimensions of 25x60 feet, comprising three floors, and also utilizes a spacious storehouse for the accommodation of a portion of his large and varied stock, which includes Hardware, Ship Chandlery, Crockery, Glass and Plated Ware, Paints, Oils, Cordage etc. These goods are offered at the lowest market rates, Mr. Lander enjoying the most favorable relations with producers etc., and hence being able to buy to the best possible advantage. He acts as agent for the sale of White, New Home and Remington Sewing Machines and does a large business in this department alone, as the inducements he offers are too exceptional to disregard. Orders are promptly filled and goods delivered free of charge.

A. C. Stilphen, Attorney and Dealer in Investment Securities, Gardiner. One of the best-known gentlemen in Kennebec County is A. C. Stilphen was born in Dresden, Lincoln County, Me., in 1842, coming to Gardiner in 1862, since which time he has been identified with its interests. During the late war, and for several years after, Mr. Stilphen held the position of deputy collector of Internal Revenue, much of the time acting as collector. In 1869, was admitted to the bar in Augusta, since which time he has practiced in Gardiner. Owing, however, to his large practice from corporations, and his interest in financial matters, he has withdrawn from general practice, confining himself to corporations only. He is a director in the Oakland Manufacturing Company, and was general manager for the first seven years. He is also director and general representative for Maine of the Commonwealth Loan and Trust Company, who negotiate and deal in First Mortgages on Improved Farm and City Property in Eastern Kansas and Western Missouri. Also in strictly first-class City, County, School and Water Bonds. We take the following from their circular:—

"The business of this Company is to obtain, by loans of money, first mortgages on improved farms and city property in Kansas and Missouri, in sums varying from $200 to $10,000, and offer the same for sale to Eastern investors. We do not loan money in the far Western and undeveloped counties of Kansas, Nebraska and Dakota. We prefer to accept a lower rate of interest than is obtained by some other Companies that loan there, and thereby save all doubts as to the character of our securities. We make loans in Eastern Kansas and Western Missouri (in the counties bordering on Kansas), where corn, cattle and hogs constitute the chief products of the farming communities, and are a never-failing source of profit to the farmer. We loan only on first mortgages, covering improved property valued at not less than three times the amount of the loan in each instance. The principal and interest of all our loans are payable at our Boston office (interest semi-annually). We deliver to each purchaser of a loan a full set of papers, viz., Mortgage Note or Bond, Mortgage Deed, Abstract of Title, and Insurance Policy when there is insurance on the buildings. We take care of every loan we sell until it is paid off — principal and interest. We collect and pay the interest, see that taxes are paid by the borrower on the property mortgaged, and that the insurance is kept in force. We watch the property to prevent strip or waste, or depreciation for want of proper repairs, and thereby save the investor all trouble and expense of looking after his security. We do not make a loan on any property until our inspector employed for this special purpose examines and reports all the facts respecting it, and such report has been approved by the Kansas City office. Our inspectors are salaried men, and the tenure of their employment with us depends upon the ability, accuracy and care they exhibit in making a thorough examination and conservative estimate of the value of the properties they inspect. Abstracts of title are examined with the utmost care by an attorney, with special reference to his competency to certify with absolute correctness the quality of every title submitted to him. The three rules to be observed as requisite to a good mortgage loan are the following, viz.:— *First,* Ample security in the value of the property mortgaged. *Second,* An absolutely perfect title. *Third,* Proper care and watchfulness of the property mortgaged as security, after the loan has been made to prevent waste and depreciation. We claim that every loan we make is, and shall be, founded upon an unqualified observance of the three rules above mentioned; and we further claim that our mortgage loans will bear the closest inspection by the most conservative investors; and to make valid and available this claim, this committee will repurchase any loan it makes and sells, if the purchaser of it, after an examination of the security, can demonstrate that the security was not exactly as we represented it to be when he purchased it. This is the plan on which the Commonwealth Loan and Trust Company does business, and we do not believe in any other plan. Intelligent Eastern investors buy Western mortgages of those companies, or persons, in whom they have personal confidence. Large capital stock and high-sounding phrases do not influence them. The absolute fact that the security is ample and the borrower a trustworthy debtor, are the business conditions that every investor should insist on. We secure these conditions, and can assure our customers that the principal of the loans purchased of us will be paid at maturity, and the interest promptly paid as it accrues. Our accounts are kept at the Boston office, and will show at any time the exact financial condition of the Company; and any of our customers or stockholders are cordially invited to call on us at any time, and receive a statement of our assets and liabilities. Interest coupons on all loans sold by us are cashed at our Boston office, 131 Devonshire Street. Funds may be deposited with us, at either of our Eastern offices, for investment, and interest at six per cent per annum will be allowed on the same from the date of deposit until placed in satisfactory mortgage loans and the loans delivered. At close of business, July 31, 1888, being the end of its first eighteen months business, the Company had deduced in dividends fifteen per cent on its capital stock, and had additional undivided profits amounting to fourteen per cent.

BOARD OF DIRECTORS.

Hon. Oscar H. Bradley...*East Jaffrey, N. H.*
Pres. Monadnock Savings Bank.
Geo. M. Woodward............*Taunton, Mass.*
Pres. Taunton Copper Mnfg. Company.
Geo. F. Baker................*Boston, Mass.*
A. C. Stilphen..............*Gardiner, Me.*
Counselor-at-law.
Edwin B. Rogers...........*Brookline, Mass.*
Treasurer Bay State Boot and Shoe Co.
F. H. Foster....................*Topeka, Kan.*
Counselor-at-law.
F. M. Hayward...............*Topeka, Kan.*
Counselor-at-law.
Dr. F. D'Obert.................*Topeka, Kan.*
C. A. Parks....................*Boston, Mass.*
W. W. Mason..................*Boston, Mass.*
L. R. Smith...................*Kansas City, Mo.*
Late Cashier Bank of Odessa.

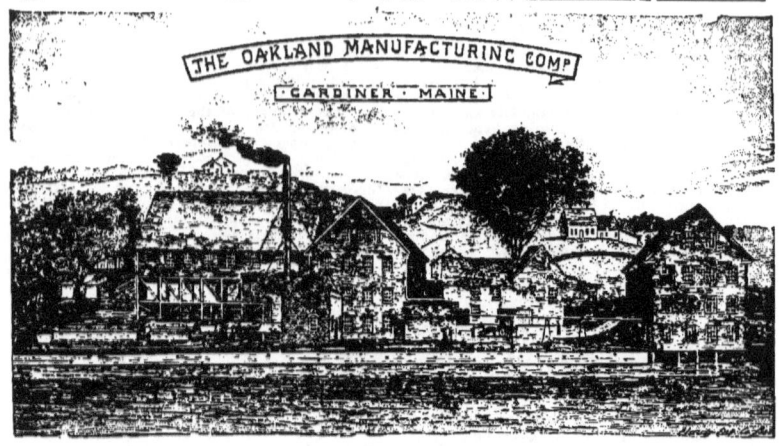

OAKLAND MANUFACTURING CO.,

Manufacturers and Wholesale Dealers in

Gutters, Conductors, Moldings, Bed Slats,

Spring Bed Stock, Broom Handles, &c.

74 and 96 Summer Street, Gardiner.

One of the prominent manufacturing enterprises that have done so much to give Gardiner the leading position it occupies, is that carried on by the Oakland Manufacturing Company, 74 to 96 Summer Street. This Company produces and sells at wholesale, Gutters, Conductors, Moldings, Bed Slats, etc., together with Broom Handles, Spring Bed Stock and other commodities of similar character. The entire plant utilized, covers an area of two acres of ground and includes five buildings, fitted up with improved machinery and supplied with 100-horse water power, in addition to that afforded by a 40-horse steam engine. The annual out-put of the works is very large, the company having prosecuted the enterprise in question for about seventeen years and built up a heavy and increasing demand for its productions. The success attained is of course due to various causes, but the chief element which has aided in bringing it about is the liberality and enterprise the company has shown in keeping itself fully up to the times as regards facilities for carrying on the business to the best possible advantage. By taking this course, it is enabled to easily meet all competition, either as regards the excellence or the cheapness of the articles handled, and thus add to its list of customers continuously. The President, Mr. J. Gray, and the Treasurer, Mr. A. E. Wing, are both well-known citizens who are highly esteemed in the community, and the works are under the immediate supervision of Mr. A. W. McCausland, the efficient Superintendent.

To meet all demands for large orders for quick delivery, they carry an immense stock of hard and soft wood lumber, which is kept in huge piles in their mills, stock-houses and yards. Their four dry-kilns are kept in constant use night and day, drying stock for different uses. All of their mills and yards are well protected from fire by eight hydrants, which are connected directly with the city water company's mains, and show a pressure of ninety-five pounds, thus requiring no other power to force an abundance of water to any point required. Adding to the above watchmen's clocks, electric alarms, etc., their customers can feel assured of prompt attention.

The work of such Mills has wrought a great change in carpentering, relieving it of the hard hand work formerly spent upon planing and jointing, tongueing and grooving, working gutters and moldings, sawing brackets, etc. The proprietors thoroughly understand their business.

C. E. WAKEFIELD & SON,

WATER STREET, GARDINER,

—DEALERS IN—

Fresh, Salt, Dry and Pickled Fish,

Beef, Pork, Lamb, Mutton, Poultry, Veal, Tripe, Salt Provisions, Sausages, Choice Brands of Flour, Staple and Fancy Groceries, Country Produce, Cigars, Tobacco, Fruit and Vegetables.

The first necessity of life is food. We may manage to do without proper clothing, and may retain health with perfect ease when dressed in rags, but no long continued abstinence from nutritious food is possible without its resulting in serious harm. Therefore the question of food supply is of prime importance, and the reason why we have given great prominence to the establishments devoted to furnishing the public with Groceries, Provisions, etc., becomes evident to all. The enterprise carried on by Messrs. C. E. Wakefield & Son, on Water St., is worthy of particular mention in this connection, and when we come to review the management given it during that long period of time, we have done much to explain the large measure of success attained. Judging from the results at hand, there seems to be no question but that from its inception this business has

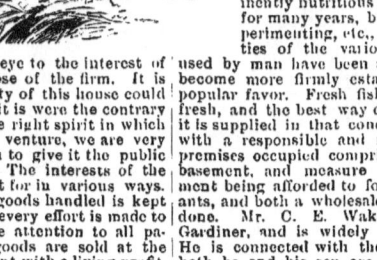

been carried on with an eye to the interest of patrons as well as to those of the firm. It is evident that the popularity of this house could not be nearly so great as it is were the contrary the case, and as this is the right spirit in which to conduct any business venture, we are very happy to be in a position to give it the public recognition it deserves. The interests of the customers are looked out for in various ways. First, the quality of the goods handled is kept as high as possible; then every effort is made to assure prompt and polite attention to all patrons, and finally, the goods are sold at the very lowest rates consistent with a living profit. These gentlemen carry a stock that is remarkable alike for extent and variety, and that,

taken as a whole, is hard to match in this city. It includes Fresh, Salt, Dry and Pickled Fish, Beef, Pork, Lamb, Mutton, Poultry, Veal, Tripe, Salt and Smoked Provisions, Flour, Staple and Fancy Groceries, Country Produce, Cigars and Tobacco, etc., and is offered at prices that have done much to build up the very heavy trade that this firm is engaged in. Deserving to rank among the "eally great inventions of the nineteenth century, is that by which food products may be perfectly and cheaply preserved for any period of time, for, by this process, a possible future shortage of the crops may be provided for, or those who would otherwise be deprived of the healthful influence of fresh meats or fresh vegetables, supplied with both these articles in first-class condition. There is an immense amount of capital engaged in the packing industry, and some brands of these goods have gained a world-wide celebrity; but for evenness of merit and fineness of flavor, there are none which deserve to be classed above those sold here. It has been well said by one who had made the subject a life-study, that the sea, barren and sterile as it appears, was nevertheless capable of producing more food to the acre than any species of soil, however fertile. The great value of fish, oysters, etc., as a cheap and eminently nutritious food, has been known for many years, but as by analysis, experimenting, etc., the peculiar properties of the various articles of food 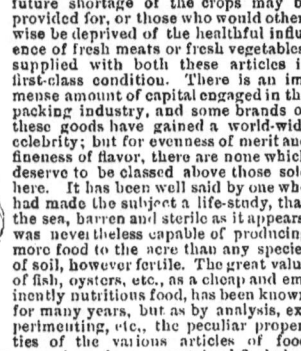 used by man have been ascertained, fish has become more firmly established than ever in popular favor. Fresh fish to be good must be fresh, and the best way of assuring one that it is supplied in that condition is to deal only with a responsible and reliable house. The premises occupied comprise two floors and a basement, and measure 20x60 feet, employment being afforded to four competent assistants, and both a wholesale and retail business done. Mr. C. E. Wakefield was born in Gardiner, and is widely known about town. He is connected with the Odd Fellows, and both he and his son are much respected for uniform fair dealing, and as enterprising and progressive business men.

J. A. Jackson, Druggist and Apothecary, wholesale and retail dealer in Patent Medicines, Fancy Goods, Paints, Oils, Dye Stuffs, Perfumery and Cigars, Corner Store, opposite Evans Hotel, Gardiner. It would be a strange omission did we not make mention of the time-honored establishment conducted by Mr. J. A. Jackson on Water Street, opposite the Evans Hotel, for this enterprise is a truly representative one in every sense of the word, and no review of Gardiner's business interests can be considered as complete unless it contains some account of the undertaking in question. Operations were begun in 1855, under the firm-name of J. A. Jackson & Co., and five years later Mr. Jackson assumed sole control, and has since retained it. He is a native of Pittston, and a member of the Odd Fellows, being known throughout the community. The premises utilized comprise two floors and a basement; the stock on hand is as varied as it is large, being made up of Patent Medicines, Fancy Goods, Paints, Oils, Dye Stuffs, Perfumery, Cigars and many other articles, a very extensive wholesale and retail business being carried on. Mr. Jackson employs two experienced and courteous assistants, and all callers are assured prompt and polite attention. The compounding of Physicians' Prescriptions is made a specialty, and great pains are taken to continue the high record this establishment has held for so many years in this department. The stock of Drugs, Chemicals etc., is very large and most carefully selected, and so far as experience and ability will admit, mistakes are made impossible. The charges will be found to be moderate and fair, and orders will be filled with the utmost celerity consistent with safety.

G. S. & G. L. Rogers, Jewelry and Silver Ware, Water Street, Gardiner. It is impossible to use too much care in the selection of Jewelry, for there is no article of personal wear that is looked upon as more accurately representing the taste and position of its owner. Richness is to be sought for, while showiness is of course to be avoided, and the most satisfactory method with which we are acquainted, to obtain jewelry that will please the eye and not offend the taste, is to visit such an establishment as that conducted by Messrs. G. S. & G. L. Rogers, on Water Street, and make choice from the many standard articles and fashionable novelties kept in stock. As this enterprise has been carried on for the last thirty-one years, its proprietors ought certainly to have a well-established reputation by this time, and such of our readers as live in Gardiner or vicinity need hardly be told what standing is held by Messrs. G. S. & G. L. Rogers, for this concern has ranked with the most reliable in the State for many years. The premises utilized are 20x60 feet in size, and the assortment of Jewelry, Silver Ware, etc., shown, is a most complete and varied one. This firm are in a position to meet all honorable competition, and while they pay more attention to the quality of their goods than to offering cheap articles, their prices will be found to compare favorably with those quoted at other establishments on goods of equal merit.

R. A. Sager, Manufacturer and Dealer in Harness, Saddles, Bridles, Collars, Whips, Robes, etc., 146 Water Street, Gardiner. Some horses are so intelligent that they can do about everything but talk, and it is to be regretted in some cases that they cannot do that also, for if they could, they would be able to express their opinion of the kind of harness they have to wear sometimes, and this opinion would be well worth hearing, you may be sure. It pays to get good harness every time. Your horse feels better, acts better, moves better, and looks better, and the expense of providing him with a first-class harness is not necessarily any more than the price that is often demanded for an inferior article. The whole secret is, — go to the right place. Mr. R. A. Sager, of No. 146 Water Street, has been known in connection with his present enterprise since 1848. He is, as may be supposed, a thoroughly expert harness maker, and allows nothing to leave his shop that is not done in a careful and workmanlike manner. Mr. Sager was born in Hallowell, Me., and is a member of the Free Masons. He is known throughout this section, and his work is even better known than himself, for it is in active demand, and is recognized as being of standard quality. The premises in use measure 20x50 feet, and five competent assistants are employed. Harness, Saddles, Bridles, Collars, Whips, Robes, and other horse goods, are kept in stock, and offered at bottom prices, and no one wanting a trustworthy article of this kind will regret placing their order with Mr. Sager.

J. B. Libby, Carriage and Sleigh Manufacturer, corner Church and Mechanic Streets, Gardiner. That it is always best to get a good article is a tolerably safe assertion to make, for the few exceptions that might be pointed out only serve to emphasize the rule. Particularly is this the case where Carriages and such light vehicles are concerned, for these articles have many severe strains, and much constant wear put upon them, and hence it is absolutely necessary that they be constructed of the best materials, put together in a careful and skillful manner. The Carriages and Sleighs made by Mr. J. B. Libby, at his establishment on the corner of Church and Mechanic Streets, serve to prove the truth of what we have stated, for these productions have gone into general use since Mr. Libby began operations in 1873, and their enviable record under the most unfavorable conditions, shows that selected stock and good workmanship can always be depended upon to win. The premises occupied comprise three floors, of the dimensions of 20x60 feet, and are fitted up with all the machinery, etc., necessary to carry on the manufacture of Fine Carriages and Sleighs to the best advantage. Particular attention is given to Order Work, and Mr. Libby is always ready to hear suggestions from his patrons as regards the style and arrangement of their vehicles, and to carry them, if practical, or show where they can be improved, if improvement is necessary. Repairing is also done with neatness and dispatch, at low rates, and seven competent assistants are at hand to fill all orders without delay.

A. L. Stephenson, Successor to J. W. Estes & Son, Boots, Shoes and Rubbers, 125 Water Street, Gardiner. There are probably very few of our readers but what have experienced more or less difficulty in getting foot-wear to suit them, for it is a well-known fact that boots and shoes are among the hardest of all articles of wearing apparel to select. The most successful dealer is the man who recognizes the diversity of taste among his customers, and acts accordingly. Therefore after inspecting the stock carried by Mr. A. L. Stephenson at No. 125 Water Street, one feels no surprise at the very extensive business carried on, for it is plainly evident that provision is made for supplying widely varying wants. Boots and Shoes for business, street and dress wear are included in the assortment offered, and by no means the least noticeable characteristic of this establishment are the bottom prices quoted in the various departments. Mr. Stephenson acts as agent for the celebrated "James Mean's Three Dollar Shoes" and also for the famous Howard Shoes, which take a high rank among the finest goods produced. He is also agent for the American Rubber Company, and always has a full assortment of the standard rubbers, overshoes etc., made by that well-known corporation. Mr. Stephenson is a native of Hingham, Mass., and is connected with the Odd Fellows and the Knights of Pythias. He succeeded Messrs. J. W. Estes & Son in the control of his present business early in 1888, and his reputation for enterprise and fair dealing is already firmly established. Customers not only know what they are getting, but also know that they are being supplied at the lowest market rates, and the stock is so large and varied that the most difficult feet can be fitted, while the latest novelties are always to be found therein.

William Jewell, Livery Stable, 61 Water Street, Gardiner. The person that doesn't go to ride more or less when in Gardiner or its vicinity, makes a big mistake, for if he or she is ill, it will do them good, and if sickness is not present, the invigorating motion, the pure air, and the enjoyment of the beautiful scenery will drive it farther away than ever. The man who told a friend that remonstrated with him for spending his money on horse hire, that he was "only paying his doctor's bill in advance, and getting a big discount," evidently knew just what he was talking about, for pure air and healthful diversions are the cheapest of drugs, and are all the more worthy of being taken advantage of because they are within the reach of all. A team can be hired for a very small sum of money, and if you don't believe that a good horse and carriage can be secured at a Livery Stable, just call on Mr. William Jewell, on Water Street, and see what he can do for you. Mr. Jewell only opened his stables in 1886, but he has already obtained a large circle of patrons, and owes the greater part of this success to his policy of furnishing first-class accommodations at reasonable rates. He was born in Topsham, Me., and has many friends in this city. The premises utilized measure 40x70 feet, and three competent assistants are employed, all orders being given prompt and painstaking attention.

Wadsworth Brothers, Manufacturers of Cherry, Imitation Cherry, Ash and Oak Chamber Sets, Water Street, Gardiner. No doubt most, if not all of our readers, have noticed the improvement in quality and reduction in price that have occurred in connection with the manufacture of household furniture of late years, and if so, some of them must have wondered how this condition of affairs was brought about. Well, it may be broadly said that the chief reasons are the general introduction of improved machinery, and the dividing-up of furniture-making into specialties. For instance, the well-known house of Wadsworth Brothers, doing business on Water Street, this city, makes a specialty of the manufacture of Cherry, Imitation Cherry, Ash and Oak Chamber Sets. The premises utilized comprise four floors of the dimensions of 40x70 feet, and two floors measuring 40x20 feet, costly and ingenious machinery being operated by water power, and employment being given to fifteen experienced assistants. This enterprise has been carried on for nearly a quarter of a century, having been inaugurated in 1865 by Messrs. Morgan & Sypher. The firm name was changed during the same year to L. W. Tibbetts & Morgan, and again in 1866, to Tibbetts, Morgan & Co. In 1868, Mr. M. C. Wadsworth, the senior partner of the present firm, assumed control, and in 1886, the existing co-partnership was entered into under the style of Wadsworth Brothers. Both members of the firm are natives of Pittston and members of the Free Masons, and Mr. M. C. Wadsworth has filled many public positions of trust, such as member of the city council and of the school committee, representative to the legislature for two years, etc., beside being connected with the Grand Army. He saw a good deal of active service during the Rebellion, going in as a private in Company B of the 16th Maine, and coming out as 2d lieutenant. Some of the most important engagements of the entire war were participated in by Mr. Wadsworth, for he fought at South Mountain, Fredericksburgh, Chancellorsville and Gettysburgh, being taken prisoner on that last historic field, and confined for twenty long months, during which time he saw the inside of Libby, Danville, Macon, Savannah, Charleston, and Columbia prisons. Both Mr. M. C. Wadsworth and his brother are very extensively known in Gardiner and vicinity, and in a business way are even more widely acquainted, shipping goods to nearly every part of the State, and carrying on a large and increasing trade.

A. Bailey, Fire Insurance, Depot Square, Gardiner. In spite of the fact that American fire apparatus is unquestionably the finest in the world, and that the Fire Departments of our large cities are made up of picked men, drilled with almost military severity, and capable of accomplishing astonishing results, fire losses in this country are greatly in excess of those occuring in other civilized communities, where the provision made for fighting fire is not nearly so elaborate or so effective. The explanation of this apparent contradiction lies in the difference between the method of building at home and abroad; the English or French Warehouses and other large structures being so arranged, and composed of such material that even should a fire break out in one room, it can generally be confined to the single apartment in which it started. Under existing American methods, the only wise thing for merchants and others to do, is to insure as completely as possible, for no matter how careful one may be to avoid setting fire to his own premises, they are apt to be consumed at any time by reason of the carelessness or ignorance of his neighbors. Fortunately there are plenty of facilities offered for the placing of Insurance in perfectly reliable companies, and among these may be mentioned the enterprise conducted by Mr. A. Bailey in Depot Square, of this city. This gentleman is a native of Gardiner and commenced operations in his present line of business in 1884. Owing to energetic and liberal business methods, he has already been instrumental in the placing of many policies, and the popularity of his agency is largely due to the standard character of the companies represented. They are as follows: Liberty of New York Mutual Life of New York, Hanover, New York, Phoenix, Hartford, Springfield, Springfield, North British and Mercantile, London, Royal Insurance Co., Liverpool, and Portland Marine Underwriter. Mr. Bailey is in a position to write policies in these well-known organizations at bottom rates, and gives prompt attention to all orders.

C. H. Harden, Dealer in Drugs and Medicines, Choice Perfumeries, Toilet and Fancy Goods. Prescriptions a Specialty. 165 Water Street, Gardiner. We are often told that confidence in one's physician is a most important aid to recovery, and the experience and commonsense of us all, combine to support the truth of this statement. But if confidence in one's medical adviser is so powerful an element in the regaining of health, confidence in the pharmacist who is called upon to compound his prescriptions, must also be no small service, for no physician, however skillful, can foresee the errors which may be made in the filling of such orders, and therefore the only thing to do is to have them carried out by some one who is known to be both competent and careful. It is hardly necessary for us to state that Mr. C. H. Harden, of No. 165 Water Street, is fully prepared to compound the most difficult prescriptions at short notice, and in a most accurate and conscientious manner, for this gentleman has been identified with his present enterprise for nearly a decade (having become connected with it in 1879), and has long since proved himself worthy of the fullest confidence. He was born in this city, and is a member of the Free Masons, being widely known here as a skillful pharmacist and an enterprising business man. The store he conducts has been in operation since 1830, but was never more completely stocked, or more capable of meeting all demands upon it than it is at the present time. Drugs, Medicines and Chemicals are on hand in great variety, and a most beautiful assortment of Choice Perfumeries, Toilet and Fancy Goods is also open to the inspection of the public.

Preble & Keene, Dealers in Furniture, Carpets and Bedding. Undertaking a specialty. Upper end of Water Street, Gardiner. That it is wise to make home as attractive as possible, we think no intelligent person will deny. A man owes a duty to his wife, to his children, and to himself in this respect, and the reasons must be very weighty that can excuse him from doing his utmost to furnish his dwelling to the best advantage. The expense is not necessarily great by any means, for furniture is now sold at remarkably low rates, and this cheapness is not attained by the sacrifice of durability, either. Of course we mean provided the furniture be bought at a reputable establishment, and in this connection we may well say a few words concerning the goods offered by Messrs. Preble & Keene, at their store on Water Street. To begin with, this firm succeeded, in 1882, Mr. James Nash, who began operations in 1870. Messrs. Preble & Keene have thus been before the public for about six years, and the unanimous verdict is that they give full value for money expended, every time. Furniture, Carpets, Bedding, etc., are very extensively handled, as may be judged from the fact that the premises utilized comprise seven floors, each of the dimensions of 50x50 feet, and is one of the largest establishments in Maine. Mr. Preble is a native of this city, and Mr. Keene was born in Randolph, Me., both gentlemen being members of the Odd Fellows. Employment is given to five assistants, and customers are promised courteous treatment as well as standard goods at low rates. Particular attention is paid to Undertaking, and the facilities at hand are all that could be desired, while no exorbitant charges are made.

C. F. Trask, Livery Stable, Water Street, Gardiner. Everybody is familiar with those people who are said to "enjoy life as they go along," and really such a disposition is to be envied, although of course in enjoying the present, the future should not be entirely lost sight of. Relaxation is as necessary to a hardworking man as it is to a steel spring, or to a piece of rubber, for although the spring may be kept bent and the rubber stretched for years, if necessary, still neither will last so long as it would under different circumstances. Many a man who found his head aching daily, and a generally uncomfortable feeling all over, has been made "as good as new" by a little riding in the open air, and in fact there is nothing that is more powerful in driving away the blues, and making a new man of one, than a brisk drive along a good road. If you don't believe it, just go to the Stable carried on by

Mr. C. F. Trask, on Water Street, and hire one of his stylish and speedy turnouts. Take your wife along, of course; or if you have no wife take an agreeable companion of some sort, and if you don't come home with an appetite like a horse, and with new strength and courage to take up your daily tasks again, why the only thing to do is to repeat the dose on the next pleasant day, and keep it up until health and cheerfulness are restored. Mr. Trask is very reasonable in his charges, and no expense is too great, anyway, where happiness is concerned. He is a native of Jefferson, Me., and is connected with the Free Masons, having a large circle of friends in town, and having been identified with his present enterprise since 1884. Mr. Trask's accommodations are always satisfactory, and it is not strange that his establishment is very liberally patronized.

B. W. Partridge, Merchant Tailor, and Dealer in Fine Ready-Made Clothing, Water Street, Gardiner. There are many things in which an American citizen can take honest pride, and one of the most gratifying of these is the generally well-dressed appearance of his fellow countrymen. In other lands the nobility, the so-called "upper-classes," enjoy almost a monopoly of handsome and comfortable clothing, but in the United States, rich and poor, old and young, dress neatly, tastefully and seasonably. Exceptions can be pointed out, of course, but these are by no means confined to any station in society, for we have fully as many rich men, proportionately, who wear shabby clothes as we have workingmen who do not care to dress as handsomely as their fellows. The general prosperity of this country, is, of course, the prime reason for this gratifying state of affairs, but there is another powerful factor that helps to make it possible, and that is the moderate price at which good clothing can be obtained. Let us, for instance, visit the establishment of Mr. B. W. Partridge, on Water St., and see what he has to offer in the way of goods and prices. We choose this establishment as it is one of the best-known in this section and is a truly representative one in every respect, having been founded over half a century ago by Mr. O. H. Partridge, the exact date being 1835. The present owner took control in 1887, and has fully maintained the ancient prestige of this time-honored house. He is a native of this city and a member of the Knights of Pythias. Two floors and a basement, of the dimensions of 22x65 feet are occupied, and employment given to fifteen assistants. Merchant Tailoring in all its branches is carried on, and a very heavy stock of Imported and American Suitings, is at hand for the inspection of customers, the goods being of late styles and guaranteed excellence, and garments being made from them at short notice and in a thoroughly first-class manner. A full assortment of Fine, Ready-Made Clothing is also constantly carried, and perfection of finish and generally honest workmanship throughout, make these garments very desirable and very cheap at the prices quoted on them. No one need to be ill-dressed while such an establishment is in operation, and we take pleasure in unreservedly commending it to our readers.

City Steam Laundry, Kenniston Block, 156 Water Street, L. B. Wing, Proprietor, Gardiner. Public Laundries have not been in general operation for a very long space of time, but nevertheless their sudden withdrawal would cause widespread and serious inconvenience to the community at large. People have to get accustomed to the idea of having their clothes washed away from home, just the same as they do any other novelty, but the family that abandons the practice after having once commenced it, is the rare exception, for its advantages far outweigh any real or fancied drawbacks. Not a few people are deterred from sending their clothes outside by the fear that such a course is very expensive, but really this fear has little or no foundation in fact, for if any of our readers will acquaint themselves with the price-list in force at the well-known "City Steam Laundry," No. 156 Water Street, Kenniston Block, they will find that the service rendered is as economical as it is efficient. The enterprise alluded to was started in 1884, and has already attained great popularity. Its proprietor, Mr. L. B. Wing, is a native of Gardiner and a member of the Odd Fellows, and has hosts of friends in this community. The premises occupied by him are 20x60 feet in size and include two floors, employment being afforded to seven competent and careful assistants. Mr. Wing guarantees that the work done here shall be first-class in every respect, and the arrangements for the prompt delivery of packages are very satisfactory.

G. E. Warren, Apothecary, Milliken Block, Gardiner. It is impossible to have extended dealings with Mr. G. E. Warren of Milliken Block, Water Street, without feeling that he thoroughly understands his business in every detail; and indeed it is no wonder that he is thoroughly acquainted with it, for, in addition to his five years' experience in this city, he conducted a similar enterprise in Hallowell for fifteen years. Mr. Warren was born in Farmingdale, where he was Town Clerk for some time. He is a member of the Free Masons, and has made many friends in Gardiner and vicinity since beginning operations here. The premises occupied measure 20x60 feet, and a heavy and most skillfully selected stock is carried, comprising Drugs, Medicines, Chemicals, etc., of all kinds. Mr. Warren spares no pains to make his establishment entirely trustworthy in every respect, and endeavors to give all customers complete satisfaction. That he has succeeded admirably thus far, is proved by the liberal patronage received, and there can be no doubt but that a continuance of the methods employed will steadily add to the popularity of his establishment. Prescriptions are compounded with the utmost care, and those who desire to feel assured that they can rely upon the manner in which their orders of this kind are filled, should, by all means, patronize Mr. Warren, as he is as skillful and experienced as he is careful, and so is especially well-equipped for the carrying on of work of this kind. His prices are very reasonable, and all customers are promptly served.

LEADING BUSINESS MEN OF GARDINER.

Josiah Maxcy & Sons, Insurance Agents and Brokers, 195 Water Street, Gardiner. The laws of man are constantly being changed, and are not infrequently violated with impunity by those whom they should bind, but not so the laws of nature. Natural law is unchanging and inviolable; if one goes against it, the consequences are sure, and ofttimes terrible, and as nature is no respecter of persons, all are equally forced to obey her behests. Gradually, but surely, the fundamental principles of existence are being discovered and acted upon, and it is owing to the great law of average that powerful companies can be formed to insure the community against loss by fire. Insurance is one of the great interests of the age. In money, power, and influence, it ranks with banking, railroading, mining and mercantile pursuits. The penniless and dependent are protected through its blessed influence. All over the globe the protecting power of this science is felt. The only question to be considered is, Which are the best conducted and safest companies in which to insure? In our day it is manifestly the part of prudence to "divide risks" when effecting a large amount of insurance, as the surest safeguard against loss is to obtain policies in a number of the best companies. But the facilities possessed by those desiring insurance, for ascertaining the status of companies doing business in their locality, are not always the best, and they largely rely on the underwriters having agencies in their midst. It of course relieves a business man of much anxiety to feel that his stock is fully covered by insurance, if care is taken that it is placed with perfectly responsible and reliable companies. As before mentioned, it is entirely out of the question for every person who desires insurance to personally investigate the solvency of the many companies now engaged in this business, and the best plan is therefore undoubtedly to intrust the placing of insurance to some old-established and well-known agency, which for years has served its customers faithfully, with every inducement to do so in the future. Such an agency is carried on by Messrs. Josiah Maxcy & Sons, 195 Water Street, Gardiner. It was established by Josiah Maxcy in 1860, who conducted it alone till 1873, when he admitted as partner his son, Josiah S., who has constituted one of the firm ever since, and in 1881, Mr. W. E. Maxcy entered the firm, the name remaining Josiah Maxcy & Sons. The integrity of this foremost of all insurance agencies in Gardiner is almost a proverb, and representing the most substantial and reliable fire insurance companies in the world, we may safely state that the bulk of all the insurance placed with any agency of this city goes to the oldest and best conducted, that of Messrs. Josiah Maxcy & Sons, and they represent the following well-known companies: Hartford Fire Insurance Company; Home, of New York; Insurance Company of North America, of Philadelphia; Fire Association of Philadelphia; Commercial Union of London; Imperial, of London; National, of Hartford. This enterprising firm also transact a general brokerage business, making loans on mortgages, and the members of the concern being young and energetic, taking active part in the furthering of this thriving city's welfare, the Messrs. Maxcy are considered as some of Gardiner's foremost merchants and citizens, and being leaders in society their names as business men and favorites of the inhabitants for miles surrounding, are so well known that comments from our pen are entirely unnecessary.

Brann Brothers & Co., Dealers in Groceries, Meats and Provisions, 97 and 99 South End Water Street, Gardiner. Among those Gardiner establishments which may well be called "popular" in every sense of the word, that conducted by Messrs. Brann Brothers & Co., at 97 and 99 South End Water Street, must be given especial mention. This firm handle Groceries, Meats and Provisions, and do a business that is increasing steadily, although it has been established about fourteen years, and is already very large. Two floors are occupied, measuring 25x60 feet, and a sufficient number of assistants is employed to permit of all orders being filled with promptness and care. The firm is constituted of Messrs. A. A. and W. E. Brann, and J. E. Cunningham, the two first-named gentlemen being natives of Gardiner, while the latter was born in Waterville. All are well known and highly esteemed in this city, Mr. A. A. Brann having an especially large circle of friends, as he served for two years in the city council. The stock on hand is composed exclusively of goods of standard character, as the firm cater to the best trade, and have no desire to handle other than satisfactory articles. The prices quoted are as low as can be named on such commodities, as the concern enjoys the best of relations with producers, wholesalers, etc., and is consequently able to buy to the best advantage. The assortment of Staple and Fancy Groceries is very complete, and includes full lines of Canned Goods, Relishes and other luxuries.

John C Houlehan, Dealer in Pure Drugs and Medicines, Select Toilet and Fancy Articles, Perfumes, Fine Cigars, at No. 142 Water Street, Gardiner. A Tasty Drug Establishment. During the past summer Mr. John C. Houlehan, who for over fifteen years had served in the capacity of chief clerk in one of the leading drug stores in Gardiner, decided to make a change, and go into the Drug business for himself, and accordingly leased the store No. 142 Water Street, which he proceeded to have fitted up, and about September 1st opened one of the prettiest and most convenient Drug Stores to be found in this section. The fixtures are of mahogany, and with plate glass windows and electric light, the effect in the evening is very telling. Mr. Houlehan handles everything connected with a first class Drug Store, using only the best of chemicals, dealing extensively in a certain Sarsaparilla and Spruce Gum Cough Syrup, both of which are not to be equalled anywhere, and enjoy a very large sale. Mr. Houlehan has a high reputation as a careful and reliable Druggist, and is fully acquainted with every detail of his trade. Being a favorite in society, counting his friends by the score, and being young and enterprising, he will no doubt soon succeed in ranking among the most prominent of Gardiner's business men.

WATER STREET, GARDINER, ME.

Bicknell & Neal, Clothing and Furnishings, Water Street, Gardiner. It is not necessary at this late date to call attention to the favorable manner in which ready-made Clothing compares with that which is made to order. Every intelligent person knows that the day of "slop-work" has gone by, and that ready-made garments are now produced that are undistinguishable from the best Clothing made to measure. Of course there are some Clothiers who cater to an inferior class of trade, or who depend on the inexperience of their customers to make a sale, but if an establishment similar to that conducted by Messrs. Bicknell & Neal, on Water Street, be visited, it will be seen that the garments in stock will bear the most severe examination and comparison. The firm alluded to began operations in 1885, and have established an enviable reputation for furnishing customers with stylish, durable, and perfect-fitting Clothing, at the lowest market rates. Of course, under the circumstances, their trade was bound to rapidly increase, and in point of fact there are few similar enterprises in the State that can show so great a development in the same length of time. One floor and a basement, measuring 22x65 feet, are occupied, and a fine stock is carried, comprising not Clothing alone, but also Gentlemen's Furnishing Goods of the latest patterns and most approved manufacture. A judicious buyer can make a small sum of money go a good ways, nowadays, in the Clothing line, and no better establishment is known to us at which to accomplish this than that carried on by Messrs. Bicknell & Neal.

W. H. Moore, Manufacturer of Bed Slats and Spring Bed Materials, Water Street, Gardiner. As a third of one's life is, or should be, passed in bed, it is not surprising that the demand for beds should be brisk and constant. The Spring Bed has been called "the index of civilization," and as a matter of fact we believe that Spring Beds are unknown in uncivilized lands. They have gone into universal use in this country, however, and the house without a Spring Bed is quite a rarity nowadays. Improved methods of manufacture have so lessened the cost of the luxuries that they can now be afforded by all, and one of the foremost of those who have brought about this gratifying condition of affairs is Mr. W. H. Moore, who has manufactured Spring Bed Material for the last score of years, having begun operations in 1868. The premises he utilizes are very spacious, the plant covering some half an acre of ground, and five buildings being occupied. Employment is afforded to twenty-five assistants, and a very large amount of material is annually produced. Mr. Moore is a native of Gardiner, and is well known in and about the city, having been elected to the Board of Aldermen. The manufacture of Excelsior from Spruce, which is by a new process, patented in March, 1888, forms a very important department of his business, and the demand for these goods is extensive and increasing. Mr. Moore makes it a point to exercise a close, personal supervision over the various details of his enterprise, and is thus in a position to guarantee that all articles leaving his factory are thoroughly and honestly made.

Joseph Perry, Machinist and Millwright and Manufacturer of Circular Saw Mills, Shingle and Clapboard Machines, Water Wheels, Shafting, etc. Mill Work and Jobbing done promptly. Circular Saws constantly on hand, Corner Bridge and Summer Streets, Gardiner. Wood-working machinery is naturally in active demand in a State so liberally endowed with lumber and with manufacturing facilities as is Maine, and of all the machinery of this kind placed upon the market, none bears a higher reputation, both for efficiency and durability, than that manufactured by Mr. Joseph Perry, at the corner of Bridge and Summer Streets. Mr. Perry should certainly produce a superior article, if experience has anything to do with it, for he has been identified with his present enterprise for over half a century, having inaugurated it in 1836. He is a native of Topsham, Me., and is a recognized authority in this city on municipal affairs, having been a councilman for three years, and a member of the Board of Aldermen for two years. Mr. Perry occupies premises comprising three floors, of the dimensions of 35x80 feet, and utilizes a twenty-five horse-power engine in the running of the necessary machinery. Employment is given to twenty-one assistants, and Circular Saw Mills, Shingle and Clapboard Machines, Water Wheels, Shafting, etc., are very extensively manufactured. Mill work and jobbing of all descriptions are done at short notice and at reasonable rates, and the past record of this establishment shows that all such orders are insured painstaking attention, and will be carried out in the most durable and workmanlike manner. Mr. Perry carries a complete assortment of Circular Saws constantly in stock, and offers the same at the very lowest market rates on goods of equal quality.

Bartlett & Dennis, Groceries and Grain, Water Street, Gardiner. Thirty years is a long time for any business enterprise to be continued, and considering that the firm of Bartlett & Dennis has been before the public for the period mentioned, it is not surprising that this concern should be one of the best known in the city, or that we should deem it worthy of special mention in a work that is intended to call attention to the most prominent and truly representative of Gardiner's mercantile undertakings. Messrs. Bartlett & Dennis operate a well-appointed Grist Mill, that is run by water-power, and that ofttimes finds its capacity severely taxed in meeting the demands upon it, and are also extensively engaged in the handling of Groceries, etc., conducting a spacious establishment, located at 210 Water Street, and comprising three floors and a basement, of the dimensions of 20x80 feet. Employment is afforded to six efficient assistants, and both a wholesale and retail business is done. Mr. Bartlett is a native of this city, and is very widely known here, as is also Mr. Dennis, who was born in Litchfield, and is connected with the Free Masons. The firm has established a most enviable reputation for progressive enterprise and strictly honorable business methods, and we take pleasure in making note of the success of so highly deserving a house.

J. R. Sawtelle, Wholesale and Retail Dealer in Lime, Plastering Hair, Hydraulic and Rosendale Cement. Wool, Hides and Wool Skins, Water Street, Gardiner. An enterprise which bids fair to attain extended proportions in the future, is that carried on by Mr. J. R. Sawtelle, on Water Street, and this fact is gratifying, not only to the gentlemen mentioned, but also to the public at large, for as Mr. Sawtelle deals chiefly in building materials, the prosperity of his business indicates corresponding prosperity in the surrounding community. He began operations here in 1882, and occupies premises comprising two floors, of the dimensions of 25x60 feet. Lime, Plastering Hair, Hydraulic and Rosendale Cement are among the more important commodities dealt in, and Wool, Hides and Wool Skins are also extensively handled. Mr. Sawtelle has had an extended experience in his present line of business, and understands it thoroughly in every detail. He has carried on operations in Hallowell for fifteen years or so, and is well known throughout the trade as a careful and discriminating buyer, who sells goods entirely on their merits, and hence exercises unusual care in the selection of the same. Employment is given to two efficient assistants, and every effort is made to give all orders prompt and painstaking attention, and supply goods of standard quality at the lowest market rates.

Geo. W. Brown, Successor to E. S. Brown & Co., Dry Goods, 185 Water St., Gardiner. "Brown's Dry Goods Store" has been widely and favorably known in this vicinity for over a quarter of a century, and no higher praise can be given Mr. George W. Brown, the present proprietor of this establishment, than to say that since he assumed control in 1880, the enterprise has become more popular and more largely patronized than ever before. The business was founded in 1860 by Messrs. E. S. Brown & Co., and was carried on under that style until the change mentioned above took place. The premises occupied are located at No. 185 Water Street, and comprise two floors, of the dimensions of 22x55 feet. A very heavy and varied stock is carried, made up of Foreign and Domestic Dry Goods of all descriptions, Dress Goods, Hosiery, Gloves, Corsets, etc. Special attention is given to the sale of Small Wares, and a very desirable selection of such goods is always at hand to choose from. Mr. Brown is a native of Gardiner, and is well known as an enterprising and progressive business man, who believes in and practices liberal methods. He employs five efficient assistants, and assures to all callers prompt and polite attention. The motto of this establishment has long been "Not to be undersold," and the present proprietor is certainly well fitted to so manage as to fully live up to it, for he is a careful and experienced buyer, and enjoys such relations with producers and wholesalers as to enable him to easily meet honorable competition at all times. Low prices, reliable goods, prompt service, courteous treatment — these certainly form a strong array of attractions, and fully explain the great and increasing popularity of the establishment we have noticed in this article.

C. A. Woodward, Dealer in Fine Watches, Clocks, Jewelry, Solid Silver & Plated Ware, No. 200 Water Street, opposite Post Office, Gardiner. Repairing promptly attended to. Since the birth of civilization, even in its lowest form, the love of the beautiful, as displayed in jewelry, has been a prominent characteristic of the race, and has only strengthened and grown with time; and with the advancement of any community in wealth, intelligence and culture, the fine arts of decoration and adornment prosper, and the skill and taste of the jeweler is brought more constantly and generally into requisition. Twenty years ago, it would have been impossible to have found customers for that class of goods, which is now really in the greatest demand. It is usually thought by the public, that large cities always contain the choicest articles from which to select, which was actually the case, perhaps ten years ago or so; but if the purchaser, in need of jewelry etc., would inspect the assortments kept in the stores of jewelers in cities like Gardiner, they would come to the conclusion, that the store kept by Mr. C. A. Woodward of 200 Water Street, can display as complete and as varied a stock of Silver Ware, Clocks, Watches, etc., etc., as any other store through the whole State of Maine. In regard to prices, we may safely state, that as Mr. Woodward receives his goods directly from the manufacturers, he is able to successfully compete with any jewelry establishment this side of Boston. Since Mr. Woodward started this business, June 1st, 1888, he has succeeded in building up as flourishing a trade as only energy, geniality and liberality can produce. Jewelry of every description is displayed in handsome show-cases, from the plated ware to the pure, eighteen carat, and with a choice assortment of Diamonds and Watches from the best manufacturers in this country, and imported French and Swiss ones, this store may safely be called the "palace of gems." Opera and Marine Glasses in large variety, Eye-glasses to fit everyone are always on hand, and the Repairing Department is paid extra attention, as Regulating and Repairing Jewelry of any description, and Watches in particular, is to-day considered as the most important one among the Jewelers. The store is handsomely fitted up. A full stock of Cutlery is another attraction of this well-kept and stocked "palace of gems." Mr. Woodward is constantly in attendance on the steadily increasing customers, whose verdict invariably has been, that the cause of success, which so far has and will pursue Mr. Woodward in this new enterprise of his is on account of honest dealings, and knowledge of the selection of his elegant, and complete stock. Mr. Woodward was born in Dresden, Maine, and although not having resided in Gardiner more than a year, he is well-known in society, counting his friends by the score, being one of this thriving city's most popular young men on account of his geniality and liberality. He is a member of the Masonic Lodge and Knights of Pythias.

S. N. Maxcy Manufacturing Co., Manufacturers and Dealers in Gutters and Moldings, Doors, Sash, Blinds, Door and Window Frames. Job Work of all kinds done promptly, Summer Street, Gardiner. One of the most completely equipped establishments in Gardiner, is that conducted by the S. N. Maxcy Manufacturing Company, on Summer Street, and the annual output of Gutters, Moldings, Doors, Sash, Blinds, Door and Window Frames, is very large indeed. This enterprise was inaugurated in 1865, and ranks with the most firmly-established in the State, the productions of the company being accepted as of standard quality, and the demand for them being brisk and continuous. The entire plant in operation covers an area of some two acres, and comprises several large buildings, some fifty horse-power being utilized. Employment is given to fifteen assistants, and no pains are spared to fully maintain the record long since established, of furnishing a uniformly superior article at the lowest market rates. Mr. Maxcy is a native of Gardiner, and is one of the best-known of our business men throughout this vicinity. The company with which Mr. Maxcy is identified makes a specialty of Gutters, Moldings, and House Finishing Materials, and is most excellently prepared to fill orders of this kind at short notice, and in an entirely satisfactory manner.

Hollingsworth & Whitney Paper Co., Water Street, Gardiner. The names of Hollingsworth & Whitney are too permanently identified with the manufacture of Paper in this country to ever be forgotten when that industry is under consideration, and some idea of the extent of the business carried on by the Hollingsworth & Whitney Paper Company may be gained from the fact that their mills in this city, large as they are and capable of turning out fourteen tons of Paper daily, are after all but a small portion of their entire plant, which includes one at Windsor, Conn., one at Watertown, Mass., and one at South Braintree in the same State. The Gardiner establishment covers five acres of ground and comprises eight buildings, two steam engines being utilized, of the power of one hundred and fifty and one hundred horse, respectively. Employment is given to one hundred men, and since operations were begun here in 1875, an enormous quantity of Paper has been produced and an amount of money put in circulation in this vicinity, which has been of great service in developing the business resources of the community. Gardiner has many advantages as a manufacturing center, and it is the successful operation of just such vast enterprises as the one under consideration that will go farther than anything else to make these advantages generally known, and cause them to be utilized to the mutual benefit of all parties concerned. The Hollingsworth & Whitney Company is under the immediate direction of Messrs. Sumner Hollingsworth, C. A. Dean and E. B. Eaton, the first-named gentleman occupying the position of President, the second officiating as Vice-president and Selling Agent, and the third discharging the responsible duties of manager. This is one of the leading industries of the State, and we take pleasure in giving it the prominence it deserves.

Charles R. White, Mercantile Printing, Office Supplies, Rubber and Metal Stamps, Stationery, Wall Paper, etc., 3 Depot Square, Gardiner. We can justly say that one of the most gratifying evidences of the increase of correct artistic taste among all classes of society is the great attention that is now paid in the beautiful designs in the way of Job Printing of every description. Our productions in this line are not surpassed by those of any other country in the world, and every year this gratifying feature becomes more marked, and there is plenty of work for those that turn out first-class jobs. We have here mentioned the merits of Printing, and representing in able manner this very important article in Gardiner, we call the reader's attention to one of this city's most promising young business men, Mr. Charles R. White, whose office is located at 3 Depot Square. This business was established by the present genial proprietor in 1886, and since its inception it has rapidly increased in patronage, Mr. White's motto being " Fair dealing, quick sales and small profits." His office contains a full supply and well selected stock of Office Supplies in all its branches. Bill files of all kinds and account books ready made or to order. Wall Paper is also extensively dealt in, as Mr. White deals directly with the most prominent manufacturers of this necessary article. As a specialty, he pays considerable attention to orders for Rubber Stamps, an article which for the last year or so has become an almost indispensable article, not only for the business community, but also for the household, as stamps for clothes are so cheap that few housewives can dispense with one. Orders for printing of all descriptions, as well as engraved work, such as visiting, wedding and invitation cards, are neatly executed, and the prices so low that competition from other parties is out of the question. Mr. White being born in Gardiner takes great interest in the welfare of this booming city, and being young, energetic and enterprising, a successful future business career awaits him, and he is today considered as one of Gardiner's promising leading young business men.

Gardiner Savings Institution, Water St., Gardiner, Although the city of Gardiner presents many an indication of prosperity and thrift, and the general appearance of its stores and other business enterprises clearly proves the existence of a progressive and enlightened spirit among those making up the population, still, to our mind, the very best evidence of all going to show that Gardiner is a desirable place to live in, is that afforded by the carrying on of such an institution as the Gardiner Savings Institution, and the remarkable financial showing made by that old-established enterprise. To successfully operate a Savings Bank, it is necessary, first, to put it under the management of men in whom the community has absolute confidence; second, to so conduct its affairs as to prove this confidence to be well deserved; and third, to bring forcibly before the minds of the people the many advantages consequent upon the formation of saving habits, and the comparative ease with which nearly every man can save a portion of his earnings if he really tries to do so. Man has been called "a bundle of habits," and in many respects such a characterization is correct. Comparatively few of our daily acts are performed entirely by the voluntary exercise of the will, and it is just as easy to get into the way of saving mechanically, as it is to follow the more general course and spend mechanically. Nor is any reasonable enjoyment lost by so doing. A man who puts money aside, who has a thoughtful care for the future, and who seeks to protect his family from prospective want by the exercise of present prudence, finds true and generous compensation for his self-denial, and takes satisfaction in the thought of the growing sum to his credit that is in no way tainted by any miserly love of money for its own sake. A saving community is a prosperous, peaceable, intelligent and cheerful one, and he who casts his lot with such a people has every reason to expect happiness and contentment. The Gardiner Savings Bank has been carried on for over half a century, its inception dating back to 1834. It has for officers, Mr. Weston Lewis, President, and Henry S. Webster, Treasurer, the Board of Trustees being composed of Messrs. Weston Lewis, Edward Robinson, David Dennis, L. D. Cooke, W. W. Bradstreet, Isaac J. Carr, Sanford N. Maxcy. No detailed individual mention of these gentlemen is necessary. They are known throughout this vicinity, and the fact that the institution under their charge has now deposits confided to it amounting to over $1,750,000, shows the esteem in which they are held. A reserve fund of $100,000 is carried, and certainly the Gardiner Savings Bank has no reason to fear comparison with any similar institution in the country.

J. S. & F. T. Bradstreet, Saw Mills, Water Street, Gardiner. Considering the large number of Saw Mills carried on in this State, and the immense capacity of many of them, it seems almost incredible that the supply of lumber should have held out to the present time, and still more surprising that those in a position to know should maintain that there is more merchantable standing timber in Maine today than there was a score of years ago. Those making this assertion explain it by saying that the former hap-hazard way of procuring lumber has for years been done away with, and that under present methods of lumbering the future is fully provided for. Some idea of the annual consumption of Maine lumber may perhaps be gained from the fact that a single establishment at South Gardiner turns out about 100,000 feet daily. This mill is run by Messrs. J. S. & F. T. Bradstreet, who have an office on Water Street. Operations were begun in 1878, and employment is given to 150 men, the entire plant in use covering an area of two acres of ground, and including a steam-engine of 350 horse power. Both members of the firm are natives of Gardiner, and the enterprise they conduct is one of the most important in the city, and has done and is doing much to extend the fame of Gardiner as a manufacturing center.

Kennebec Steam Towing Company, William Perkins, Agent, Water Street, Gardiner. The value of the services rendered by the steam towboats of the present day in extending the navigable area of rivers, and other confined and winding streams, can hardly be overestimated, and it is especially noticeable in this State, which ships enormous quantities of ice and other commodities, in a manner that would be impossible were it not for the numerous and powerful fleet of steam tugs maintained in this vicinity. The chief requisites of an efficient and satisfactory steam-tug service may be summed up as promptness, reliability, and the maintenance of moderate charges, and we need hardly say that the general popularity enjoyed by the Kennebec Steam Towing Company among ship-owners, consignors, etc., is largely due to the fact that this Company spares neither trouble nor expense to furnish just such a service as we have mentioned. Operations were begun in 1880, and a most gratifying change was soon noticeable in the management of our river traffic. Mr. William Perkins, the Gardiner agent, has an office on Water Street, and gives instant and careful attention to all orders received. The Company's charges are fair and reasonable, and the service is strictly first-class and entirely satisfactory.

E. D. Tasker & Co., Hack & Livery Stable, opposite Depot, Gardiner. First-Class Teams Furnished at all Hours on Reasonable Terms. During the ten years that the enterprise conducted by Messrs. E. D. Tasker & Co. has been carried on in this city, it has become one of the most largely patronized undertakings of the kind in this section, and it is but due to its proprietors to say, that every provision has been made to meet all demands in a first-class and liberal manner. The premises occupied, are located opposite the Depot and are 40x140 feet in dimensions, employment being given to three competent assistants. The firm announce that they are prepared to furnish Frst-class Teams at all hours on reasonable terms, and those who have made trial of their accomodations are foremost in proclaiming that this announcement is fully justified by the facts. Hacks will be supplied for Funerals, Parties, Weddings or other occasions at short notice, and careful and expert drivers are invariably placed in charge of such conveyances. The facilities for boarding horses are of the best, animals being assured proper care and comfortable quarters. Mr. Tasker was born in Randolph, while Mr. C. O. Turner, his associate in business, is a native of Wiscasset; both these gentlemen being connected with the Free Masons, and Mr. Turner with the Odd Fellows also. Sale Horses are constantly kept on hand, and we would most certainly advise those who wish to purchase a trustworthy animal, to call and see what this firm has to offer them. The advantages of buying of a reputable concern should certainly be apparent to all, and there need be no fear of imposition when dealings are being had with a house of such standing.

J. S. Lambard, Jewelry and General Variety, Auctioneer and Real Estate, 153 Water Street, Gardiner. Few, if any, of our Gardiner readers, need to be informed that Mr. J. S. Lambard is one of the best-known business men in the city, for this gentleman has carried on operations here ever since 1856, and has been prominently identified with Real Estate and General Commercial Interests for a number of years. Mr. Lambard occupies one floor and a basement, 22x65 feet, and handles Jewelry and General Variety Goods very extensively. The stock he offers is one well worthy of a much more detailed description than we can give it in these columns, and we should certainly advise any one who wants anything in the line of Jewelry, etc., to give Mr. Lambard an early call. His goods are all fully guaranteed to prove as represented, and his prices only need comparison with those of other houses to be appreciated. The high reputation held by this establishment is the best proof of the uniform excellence of the goods dealt in, and the services of two assistants are required to attend to the many orders received. Mr. Lambard was born in Gardiner, and is connected with the Free Masons. He is considered an authority on local Real Estate, as he has given close and long-continued attention to this subject, and has handled many valuable properties. As an Auctioneer Mr. Lambard is also most favorably known, and his services are frequently availed of in this capacity.

Gardiner Water Company, Gardiner. Although "doctors disagree" very frequently regarding minor points, there are certain principles which are unanimously subscribed to by physicians of all schools, and prominent among these is that relating to the paramount importance of a pure and abundant water supply. The painstaking and exhaustive researches into the origin and causes of the more prevalent and dangerous diseases, made by scientific men of late years, have resulted in the discovery of many startling facts, and it has been demonstrated beyond the possibility of a reasonable doubt, that some of the most destructive epidemics — epidemics which have swept away thousands of lives, and placed whole communities in mourning — would never have occurred had proper attention been paid to the water question. Not a few popular beliefs have been proved to be totally erroneous, and one of the most wide-spread of these (that well water is necessarily purer and more wholesome than that from ponds or rivers) is so far at variance with the facts that, generally speaking, it may be said, that a well is the worst possible source from which to obtain drinking water. Taste is of but little use in determining the true character of water, for careful analysis has demonstrated that filth and poison may be present without being detected by the palate or seen by the eye. Under these circumstances the beneficent effects of such an enterprise as that conducted by the Gardiner Water Company can hardly be overestimated, for leaving the question of protection from fire entirely out of the reckoning, the general health of the community cannot fail to be materially heightened by the opportunity presented of obtaining an unfailing supply of pure water at a comparatively nominal expense. These Water Works were built in 1885 by Messrs. Weston Lewis and Josiah S. Maxcy, the supply being taken from the Cobbossee river, at a point just above the stone dam erected by the company, and conducted through some fourteen miles of pipe to Gardiner, Farmingdale and Randolph. A powerful Blake pump elevates the water to a reservoir 230 feet above the Kennebec river, thus giving sufficient "head" for all purposes. There are now some seven hundred consumers on the company's books, and the demand for water service is steadily growing. As the Cobbossee river drains a chain of lakes remarkably free from chances of contamination, the water is admirably suited for domestic use, being pure, sweet and clear, and in short, ranking with the best in the country. Whatever the enterprise that Messrs. Lewis and Maxcy undertake, it is bound to succeed, as both gentlemen are considered to be the most active and most shrewd of Gardiner's business men, taking energetic measures, whenever an opportunity presents itself, to further the interests and welfare of this, one of Maine's most prosperous of cities. Both above-named gentlemen are highly honored and respected by all who have had business connections with them, on account of their square dealings and liberal methods of doing business. With such men as Messrs. Lewis and Maxcy the city of Gardiner may justly be proud and honored to count them in their midst.

P. H. Gilson, Manufacturers of Light Carriages and Sleighs, Heavy Wheels, Rims, Shafts, and Mortised Hubs for sale, 26-30 Maine Avenue, Gardiner. There is many a Carriage and many a Sleigh in this vicinity that came from the shop of P. H. Gilson, for this gentleman has been concerned in the manufacture of such goods for thirty-seven years, and has produced a large number of Vehicles during that time. He was born in Boston, Mass., and is a member of the Free Masons and also of the Knights Templar, having a very large circle of friends in Gardiner and vicinity. The premises occupied are located at 26-30 Maine Ave., and comprise four floors of the dimensions of 20x50 feet, there being a blacksmith, a paint, and a woodworking shop in operation, and employment being given to seven assistants. Light Carriages and Sleighs, Heavy Wheels, Rims, Shafts, and Mortised Hubs, are manufactured and sold at low rates, and the reputation this establishment has held for so many years, of turning out durable and trustworthy work, is as well deserved today as ever. Mr. Gilson takes pride in the record of his factory in this respect, as he has every reason to do, and gives close personal attention to the various processes of manufacture so as to assure a continuance of so desirable a celebrity. Selected stocks and the most improved methods combine to make the Carriages, etc., manufactured here fully equal to the best, and equal care is taken in the doing of Repairing, such orders being filled at short notice, in a thorough and neat manner.

A. H. Potter, General Truckman and Stevedore, and Dealer in Coal, Rogers' Block, Depot Square, under Journal office, Gardiner. It is just ten years ago that the enterprise known as the "Citizen's Coal Yard" was established in this city, and as Mr. A. H. Potter assumed control of the undertaking in 1885, he has had it under his management during about one-third of its existence. Under his liberal business methods the enterprise has become a popular and largely patronized one, and many of our citizens would never think of obtaining their supply of coal elsewhere. Mr. Potter has made it a rule from the inception of operations to handle only coal of standard quality, and hence he is in a position to guarantee satisfaction to all who may favor him with an order. Employing ten experienced assistants, he is also able to promise early and accurate delivery, and as a large supply of coal is generally on hand, orders for any kind or size can be filled without delay. The yard affords capacity for the storage of three thousand tons, and is very conveniently located. Mr. Potter's office is in Rogers' Block, Depot Square, under the Journal office, and favors left there or sent by mail will receive prompt and careful attention. A General Trucking and Stevedore business is also carried on by Mr. Potter, and he is especially well-prepared to undertake heavy jobbing at short notice and on reasonable terms. His teams are powerful and well-equipped, and are in charge of careful and experienced drivers. Mr. Potter is a Gardiner man by birth, and is a member of the Free Masons, being very widely and favorably known.

Gardiner Marble Works, (formerly works of Hiram Preble,) Gardiner, Monuments, Grave Stones, Tablets and everything in Marble or Granite Work. The enterprise now known as the "Gardiner Marble and Granite Works" was inaugurated just thirty years ago, its founders being Messrs. Preble & Johnson. Mr. Hiram Preble carried it on alone for an extended period of time, and finally, in 1882 the business came into the hands of Mrs. Emma J. Preble who has since had sole control. When this lady announced her intention of carrying on the undertaking, there were not a few who prophesied failure, and many, even of those who wished her every success, considered her chances dubious. But what has been the result? During the six years that have since elapsed the patronage accorded the enterprise has increased in no small degree, the character of the work turned out was never better than it is to-day, and in short the Gardiner Marble and Granite Works are fully prepared to meet all honorable competition, and to produce stone-work that cannot fail to satisfy any fair minded person. Monuments, Gravestones, Tablets etc., are made to order at the shortest possible notice, and Cemetery Work of all descriptions will be done in a prompt and painstaking manner. Mrs. Preble is prepared to give personal attention to the wishes of her customers, and those who wish anything in the line of stone-work are invited to notify her by mail, when she will visit them in person, show specimens of work etc., and give full information regarding prices. The advantage of dealing directly with the proprietor rather than with some irresponsible agent is obvious, and will be appreciated by all who are acquainted with business methods. Mrs. Preble employs seven experienced and skillful assistants and occupies premises on both Church and Bridge Streets. Her prices are as low as is consistent with good work and satisfaction is fully guaranteed.

Kane & Stuber, Cigar Manufacturers, Hats and Caps, Water Street, Gardiner. The firm whose card we print above, comprises two industries which are not frequently associated, but the results attained have been so gratifying that we need not say that their undertaking is a pronounced success. Operations were begun in 1876, and a very large business has since been built up, for exceptional inducements are offered in some respects, and the public are quick to take advantage of liberal methods and honorable dealing. Mr. Kane is a native of Wilmington, Del., while Mr. Stuber was born in Utica, N. Y., both gentlemen being intimately acquainted with the various details of their business, and giving close personal attention to the filling of orders. The premises occupied comprise one floor and a basement, and employment is afforded to five experienced and efficient assistants. The Cigars manufactured by Messrs. Kane & Stuber are noted for their uniform excellence, both of material and of workmanship, and it is not surprising that they should be in active and increasing demand. Hats and Caps of the latest and most fashionable patterns are also handled very extensively, and supplied at the very lowest market rates.

Arthur L. Berry, Insurance Agent and Broker, Water Street, Gardiner. Insurance has become so universally recognized a factor in modern business methods that the man who is not insured has become the exception rather than the rule, and we find the most intelligent and progressive members of the community taking the fullest advantage of the opportunities offered for the protection of their families and themselves. As it is convenient to place all policies, whether Fire, Marine, Accident or Life, through a single agency, it is not surprising that Mr. Arthur L. Berry, of Water Street, should find a brisk and continuous demand made upon his services, for he represents some of the strongest companies in the world, and can write Fire, Marine, Life or Accident Policies on the most favorable terms. He was born in this city, and has been identified with his present undertaking since 1882. Two offices are occupied, and two assistants employed, all callers being given prompt and courteous attention, and any desired information cheerfully afforded. As for the character of the Insurance offered, no further proof of its reliability can be required than the standing of the companies represented, a list of which is herewith given: German American, Phœnix, Queen, Guardian, New Hampshire, Lancashire, Merchants, New York, Peoples', Holyoke Mutual, Provident, Washington, Travelers' Life and Accident of Hartford, and the Equitable Life Assurance Society of New York. It will be seen that risks placed by Mr. Berry are widely distributed, and it would be difficult to make up a list that would combine more real advantages.

Smith, Tobey & Co., Commission Merchants, and Dealers in Staple and Fancy Groceries, all kinds Fresh Fish and Meats, Wholesale Fruits and Produce, 242 and 244 Water Street, Gardiner. The firm of Smith & Tobey began operations in 1882, and soon established a business that has steadily and rapidly grown, until now it will bear comparison with that of many houses of much greater age. Both partners are natives of Gardiner, and both are members of the Odd Fellows, being well known in the community as enterprising and progressive business men. The premises utilized are located at 242 and 244 Water Street, and comprise two floors, each of the dimensions of 50x83 feet. A very heavy stock is carried, and it is as varied as it is large, for it includes Staple and Fancy Groceries, all kinds of Fresh Fish and Meats, together with Fruits and Country Produce. The business done is both Wholesale and Retail, an important department of it being the selling of goods on commission, an industry for the successful prosecution of which this concern enjoys special advantages. Consignments are solicited, and returns will be made with promptness and accuracy. Employment is given to four efficient assistants, and the retail department of the establishment is most liberally patronized, for the public are quick to learn where to buy to the best advantage. Reliable goods and bottom prices are bound to tell, and the trade is evidently destined to continue to grow for some time to come.

Benjamin U. Dill, Dealer in Corn, Flour and Provisions, Ship Stores, West India Goods, New Bedford Cordage, Oakum, Bone and other Fertilizers, opposite Public Library, Gardiner. There is no need of our saying that the undertaking conducted by Mr. Benjamin U. Dill in this city is one of Gardiner's representative enterprises, for the fact is too well known to require argument or even statement. Mr. Dill was born in Gardiner, and began operations here in 1865. From 1865 to 1888, is a long period of time, very nearly a quarter of a century, yet during all that time the establishment with which Mr. Dill is identified has maintained its position as a leader among enterprises of a similar character. The premises utilized are located on Water Street, opposite the Public Library, and comprise two floors and a basement, of the dimensions of 25x70 feet. Corn, Flour, Provisions, Ship Stores, Family Groceries, etc., are handled very largely, and New Bedford Cordage, Oakum, Bone and other Fertilizers, are also extensively dealt in. As might naturally be supposed in the case of so old-established an enterprise, the most favorable relations are enjoyed with producers, wholesalers, etc., and as a consequence the inducements offered to customers are many and pronounced. A competent force of assistants is employed, and all orders are filled with the utmost promptness, the quality of the goods being in all cases guaranteed to prove as represented. Mr. Dill is thoroughly conversant with every detail of his business, and gives close personal attention to its supervision. As a member of the city council he has rendered valuable service, and is in every respect a truly representative citizen.

H. W. Jewett & Co., Manufacturers and Dealers in Lumber, Clapboards, Shingles and Laths. All kinds of Dimensions Sawed to Order. Bridge Street, Gardiner. No resident of Maine at least needs to be informed regarding the importance of Lumber as an article of commerce, for it is to her vast supplies of this material that the State chiefly owes her present position, nor is this supply so nearly exhausted as some people would have us think. On the contrary, it is asserted by those in a position to speak with authority, that there is actually more merchantable standing timber in Maine now than there was ten years ago, and they ascribe this fact to the more scientific methods practised by the lumbermen of today than were employed in the past. It is at all events sincerely to be hoped that this statement is justified by the facts, for Maine can poorly afford to lose the revenue brought in by the sale of Lumber. One of the best-known houses in this vicinity, handling this indispensable commodity, is that of Messrs. H. W. Jewett & Co., doing business on Bridge Street. This enterprise was inaugurated in 1863, and is of no small magnitude, the entire plant in operation covering an area of five acres of ground, and employment being afforded to ninety assistants. Lumber, Clapboards, Shingles and Laths are very largely manufactured, the works being run by water power, and about ten million feet of Long Lumber being produced annually. All kinds of Dimensions are Sawed to Order, and the facilities are such that such work can be done at short notice and most reasonable rates. Mr. H. W. Jewett was born in Alna, Me., and is known throughout the Lumber trade. The entire enterprise may be considered as a representative one, and is a credit to the locality in which it is carried on.

S. D. Warren & Co., Copsecook Mill. Paper Manufacturers, Water Street, Gardiner. There is not an article that is used so extensively and known so little about by the general public as Paper, and notwithstanding all that has been said and written on the subject, we question if one man in a hundred of those not directly acquainted with the business could give the least idea of the processes by which Paper is produced. Its uses we know more about. And even the fact that car-wheels and boats are made of this material, is a common matter of knowledge. As fine an example of a modern paper-mill as can easily be found is that afforded by the Copsecook Mill, conducted by Messrs. S. D. Warren & Co., on Water Street, and some idea of the magnitude of this enterprise, and of the ready market that is found for the product of the mill, may be had from the fact that the amount of paper daily produced is no less than four tons. This undertaking was founded in 1860, and has long ranked with the leading industries of Gardiner and vicinity. The ponderous machinery in use is run by water power, and employment is given to fifty assistants. The proprietor, Mr. Warren, is a Boston gentleman, but the establishment is under the immediate supervision of Mr. H. E. Merriam, who was born in Grafton, Mass., and who neglects nothing that would tend to improve the efficiency of the plant under his charge.

The Gardiner National Bank, of Gardiner. The Gardiner Bank, of which the Gardiner National Bank is the successor, was chartered as a State Bank by the Commonwealth of Massachusetts, in January, 1814, and has been in continual operation as a State and National Bank to the present time. In its three-quarters of a century of active business who can estimate the benefits that have been derived, directly and indirectly, by the community in which it is located? Who can tell how many local enterprises owe their present existence to this institution? Who can enumerate the merchants that have been aided, the manufacturers that have been assisted in time of trouble, the almost numberless cases in which temporary aid from the Bank has resulted in a crisis being successfully met, and future prosperity assured? "But all this help was given in the way of business," you say. So it was. But suppose there had been no bank to do this. Suppose dependence had to be placed on out-of-town institutions, managed by men who had no personal interest in Gardiner's prosperity, do you suppose that the results would have been the same, and our city just where it is today? The question answers itself. Certainly not. The officers and directors of the Gardiner National Bank are all well-known citizens, and a perusal of their names will serve to show

how deeply they are interested in the city's growth. They are as follows: President, Isaac J. Carr, Cashier, Everett L. Smith. Directors, I. J. Carr, P. G. Bradstreet, W. F. Richards, J. C. Atkins, Augustus Hopkins. The institution has a capital stock paid in of $50,000 and surplus and profits of $30,000, and is in a most excellent financial condition in every respect.

S. Soule & Son, Dealers in Boots, Shoes and Rubbers, Davis Building, Water Street, Gardiner. Men are as unlike in their desires as they are in their characters, as a matter of course; and then the difference in occupations comes in to still further increase the variety of conditions to be suited in the selection of goods. One man, for instance, wants his shoes easy and comfortable, another demands that his be snug and tight. A calls for heavy boots; B must have light slippers, while C scorns extremes and asks for a shoe that is stylish but easy, light but durable. To satisfy all these demands is, as may well be supposed, no light task, and it is owing to their having been so successful in accomplishing this result that the firm of Messrs. S. Soule & Son enjoys its present popularity and extensive trade. This concern began operations in 1875, and occupy premises of the dimensions of 28x40 feet in the Davis Building, Water Street. Boots. Shoes and Rubbers of all kinds, sizes and qualities are handled, and an important factor in the success attained, has been the magnitude of the stock carried, for this is always sufficiently great to allow of all tastes being suited and all purses provided for. Mr. S. Soule is a member of the Golden Cross and Mr. H. E. Soule is connected with the Free Masons and the United Workmen and the Knights of Pythias. Both these gentlemen have the respect and esteem of the community, and we can assure our readers that no other boot and shoe house in the city is in a position to guarantee more solid satisfaction to its customers.

Robbins & Sons, Foundry and Machine Shop, Gardiner. An enterprise which has gained a high reputation since it was inaugurated here ten years ago, is that carried on under the firm name of Robbins & Sons. As originally constituted, the firm was made up of Messrs. C. A. E. & A. A. Robbins, but since the decease of the first-named gentleman in 1886, the enterprise has been continued by Messrs. E. E. and A. A. Robbins, under the old style. Both the proprietors are natives of Gardiner, and are well-known citizens, the Machine Shop and Foundry they carry on ranking with the most reliable in the State. The premises utilized are spacious and well fitted up, and the facilities for filling all orders with promptness and accuracy are unsurpassed, a competent and careful force of assistants being employed, and no means neglected to insure the attainment of the best results. Enjoying many advantages, the firm are in a position to make their prices as satisfactory as their goods, and those who want anything in their line will best serve their own interests by learning what Messrs. Robbins & Sons have to offer.

George W. Cross, Gun and Lock Smith, and dealers in Guns, Pistols and Sporting Goods. High Explosive Powder for Blasting Purposes, Base Ball Goods, etc. Special Attention given to Repairing Clothes Wringers. Saws Hammered and Filed. No. 11 Depot Square, Gardiner. One of the busiest establishments that we know of in this city, is that of which Mr. George W. Cross is the proprietor, located at No. 11 Depot Square, and it is no wonder that this should be the case, for Mr. Cross not only deals largely in Guns, Pistols and Sporting Goods in general, but also in Locks, Knives, Razors, etc., and beside this, makes a specialty of Repairing; paying particular attention to Clothes Wringers. Saws are Hammered and Filed, Carpet Sweepers, Lawn Mowers, Sewing Machines, Paring Machines, etc., put in order at short notice, and in fact Mr. Cross announces that he is prepared to undertake the repairing of anything that may be brought to him. Pinking Irons, Knives and Blades, Shears and Small Tools in general, are offered for sale at the lowest market rates, and a full stock of ammunition is carried, including Powder, Shot, Shells, Wads, etc. Mr. Cross is a native of this city, and is connected with the Free Masons. He is also a member of the Grand Army, and served under Sheridan in that General's famous raid of which so much has been written and said. The premises utilized for the carrying on of operations, are 18x55 feet in size, and employment is given to two assistants, Orders are filled with the utmost dispatch, and particular attention is given to the fitting of keys.

Joshua Gray & Son, Manufacturers and Dealers in all kinds of Pine, Spruce and Hack Lumber, Clapboards, Shingles, Laths, Gardiner. Maine is so intimately associated with the minds of a majority of the people with lumber in one form or the other, that they find it impossible to think of the one without recalling the other also. As often as the figures have been made public, there are still very few who have any realizing sense of the amount of lumber that is annually produced in this State, but that this amount is something enormous, is to be seen from the fact that a single Gardiner establishment — that of Messrs. Joshua Gray & Son, located on Summer Street — turns out *six million feet* yearly. They own forty thousand acres of timber land. This is one of the oldest undertakings of the kind in this section, having been founded in 1847, and Mr. Gray has for many years been regarded as a representative citizen, having served in both branches of the City Council as well as in the position of Mayor. He is a member of the Odd Fellows, and is of course almost universally known and very highly esteemed. The firm of Joshua Gray & Son maintain a plant covering some five acres of ground, on which are located five buildings of varying size. Employment is given to fifty hands, and Pine, Spruce and Hack Lumber is manufactured and dealt in very largely, as are also Clapboards, Shingles and Laths. No concern enjoys better facilities, either for the obtaining of raw material, or for working it up into merchantable form, and no concern is in a position to offer equally desirable stock at lower rates.

LEADING BUSINESS MEN OF GARDINER.

J. L. Stoddard, Broker, Insurance Agent, and U. S. Claim Agent, Kennebec and Penobscot River Ice and Ice Stock, bought and sold on Commission. Pensions, Bounties, etc., procured. Office, Water Street, opposite Johnson House, Gardiner. The propriety and wisdom of securing a competent agent when seeking to bring about certain results, hardly needs to be mentioned in these columns, for it is to be presumed that all of our readers are intelligent people, and being so, they can require no argument to convince them of the advisability of such a course. This being the case, we need make no apology for calling their attention to the enterprise carried on by Mr. J. L. Stoddard, who has an office on Water Street, opposite the Johnson House, for this gentleman acts as Broker, Insurance Agent, and U. S. Claim Agent, and may be implicitly depended upon to protect the interests of his clients to the extent of his ability. Mr. Stoddard was born in Edgartown, Mass., and officiated for thirteen years as deputy clerk U. S. Internal Revenue, retiring on the first of June, 1886, and inaugurating his present enterprise the year following. He is a member of the Free Masons and G. A. R., and has a wide circle of friends. He represents the Fireman's Fund Insurance Company, of San Francisco, the Anglo Nevada, of the same city, the Sun of London Insurance Company of the State of Pennsylvania, and the Provident Aid Society, of which latter organization he was one of the incorporators. Mr. Stoddard can place Insurance at the lowest obtainable rates, and does a large business in this department alone. He is prepared to buy and sell Kennebec and Penobscot River Ice and Ice Stock on Commission, and enjoys very favorable relations with producers and the general business public. Especial attention is given to the collections of claims, and we believe there is no U. S. Claim Agent in this State who is in a better position to advance the best interests of those having occasion for the services of such a representative. Mr. Stoddard's charges are fair and moderate, and he is very prompt and painstaking in his business operations.

Fred Littlefield & Co., Manufacturers of and Dealers in Harness, Trunks, Bags, Whips, etc., Horse Clothing of every description, Harness at Wholesale and Retail, 211 Water Street, Gardiner. Our Harnesses are all hand-made (no factory work), and made from the very best Oak Tanned Stock. We make over fifty different kinds, and will send one to any address in the State, express prepaid, subject to examination, C. O. D., and if not perfectly satisfactory it may be returned to us at our expense. In ordering, please be very particular and state as near as you can the style of trimmings, heft of harness, style of reins, and about the price you wish to pay. Correspondence solicited. Water Street. It is a very costly mistake to assume that the harness worn by a horse has but little effect upon his capacity for work, and those who hold such a position are growing fewer in number every year. Just as surely as it is easier to cut with a sharp knife than with a dull one, can a horse accomplish more when provided with a harness suited to him than when he has to put up with one that is not, and therefore when buying a harness procure it at an establishment where skilled labor is employed, and where a large and varied stock is carried. Such an establishment is that conducted by Messrs. Fred Littlefield & Co., No. 211 Water Street, and those who will examine the assortment of goods shown by this firm will find that it includes not only Harness and Horse Clothing of every description, but also Trunks, Bags, Whips, etc. Mr. Littlefield was born in this city, as was also his associate in business, and has been identified with his present enterprise since 1875. Four floors, of the dimensions of 20x55 feet, are utilized, and six experienced and efficient assistants employed. Harness is manufactured and dealt in both at wholesale and retail, and the work done at this establishment is strictly first-class, being warranted in every particular. The lowest market rates are quoted in every department, and it is only natural that a very large business should be done.

A. Fuller & Son, Grocers and Flour Dealers, Gardiner. An establishment from which many Gardiner families procure their supplies of Groceries, etc., is that conducted by Messrs. A. Fuller & son, on Water Street; and this enterprise is deemed worthy of special mention, as it is a truly representative one in many respects, and is one of the most liberally patronized in this section. Business was begun in 1874 by Mr. A. Fuller, the present co-partnership being formed in 1886. Both members of the firm are natives of this city, and the senior partner has served on the Board of Aldermen, and is connected with the Golden Cross and the Grand Army. He was a member of the 11th Maine Regiment at the time of the Rebellion, and was stationed at Washington for a considerable period. The premises utilized for the carrying on of the business, consists of one floor measuring 40x38 feet, and a spacious storehouse. Doing both a wholesale and retail business, it is, of course, necessary to carry a heavy stock, and we believe that few similar establishments in the State contains a more carefully and skillfully selected assortment of the best Family Groceries, Meats, etc. It will be found to be complete in every department, made up of fresh and desirable goods, and offered at prices that would insure the sale of far less standard articles. Employment is given to four competent and polite assistants, and customers are promised prompt and courteous attention, while a full guarantee is given that goods shall prove as represented.

J. D. Hughes, Dealer in Pianos, Organs, etc. Tuning and Repairing promptly attended to. Orders by mail. Catalogues sent on application, Water Street, Gardiner. It is not our intention, and indeed this is not the place, to present an essay on the intimate connection between music and home, but all of our readers must have noticed how essential music of some kind is to a perfect home, and hence will support us in the assertion that no family circle is really complete unless it contains a musical instrument of one kind or another. Pianos and Organs are doubtless the most popular of all family musical instruments, for although their cost is greater than that of simpler and more-portable articles, still their advantages for what may be called "all 'round use"— dancing, playing, singing, etc.,—more than make amends for this one drawback. A good Piano or Organ will last a lifetime, and may be bought at a surprisingly low figure nowadays, if the right place be visited, and in this connection we wish to call attention to the establishment conducted by Mr. J. D. Hughes, on Water Street, for this gentleman can supply a Piano or an Organ at bottom prices, and since beginning operations in 1877, has built up a business that shows the public are quick to recognize reliable and liberal methods. The premises occupied measure 20x50 feet, and a fine stock of Pianos, Organs, and Musical Instruments in general is constantly carried. Mr. Hughes employs three competent and polite assistants, and all callers are assured prompt attention and uniformly courteous treatment. Any desired information will be cheerfully given, and we would advise all interested to give Mr. Hughes an early call.

John W. Berry, Fresco and Scenic Painter, Goodspeed Block, Depot Square, Gardiner. Our readers need not be told that the subject of Interior Decoration has received great attention of late years in this country, for the evidences of it are to be seen on every side, and there are several periodicals published which are devoted almost entirely to this art. That it is an art, no one will deny, and indeed so comprehensive is its scope that no one man can practice it in all its departments, and consequently it has been divided up into various specialties, of which that attended to by the Fresco Painter is one of the most important. The possibilities of Fresco Painting are almost endless, and a skillful and original designer of thorough technical training can transform a bare and ugly ceiling into "a thing of beauty" if not "a joy forever." The name of John W. Berry is so intimately associated with this branch of art in the minds of residents of Gardiner and vicinity, that the one cannot be mentioned without recalling the other. Mr. Berry is a native and a life-long resident of this city, and the fact that he is now serving his second term as mayor (he being the youngest mayor Gardiner has ever had), shows the estimation in which he is held here, and renders extended personal mention quite unnecessary. He began operations in 1869 as a Landscape Painter, but since 1879 has devoted himself to Fresco and Scenic Painting. Mr. Berry makes a specialty of original designs, so that it is not surprising that his work is quite devoid of that machine-like and monotonous character which has ever been the bane of American Fresco decoration. Among the more prominent buildings on which he has been employed are the Court-House in Augusta, the Soldiers' Home at Togus (in which he decorated General Franklin Hall), the chapel at the Insane Hospital, the hall of the Knights of Pythias in this city, and the new chapel at the National Home. Mr. Berry's place of business is in Goodspeed Block, Depot Square, and those contemplating having anything done in the Fresco-painting line would do well to give him a call.

W. B. Neal (Successor to B. A. Neal & Son), Insurance Agent and Broker. Fire, Marine, Life and Accident. Represent the largest companies in the World. Office over Brown's Dry Goods Store. Water Street, Gardiner. It is now over a quarter of a century since the insurance agency, conducted by Mr. W. B. Neal was founded, in 1862, it being carried on from that date up to 1887, under the firm-name of B. A. Neal & Son. Of course during its long and useful existence this agency has become known throughout Gardiner and vicinity, and the total amount of Insurance placed by it has reached enormous proportions. Representing the largest companies in the world, Mr. W. B. Neal is prepared to afford Insurance of the most satisfactory and reliable character, and is in a position to quote the lowest rates on Fire, Marine, Life and Accident risks. Mr. Neal is a native of this city, and a well-known business man. He is also secretary of the Board of Underwriters. Two offices, measuring 20x40 feet, are occupied at No. 72 Water Street, over Brown's Dry Goods store, and any of our readers wishing information relative to Insurance, would do well to give Mr. W. B. Neal an early call, for he is an authority on the subject, and is always ready to render any aid in his power. The following companies are represented:— Ætna, of Hartford; Liverpool and London and Globe, London; Northern London; Germania, New York; Niagara, New York; Union, Philadelphia; Orient, of Hartford; Employers' Liability, England; Mutual Life, New York. No stronger or more comprehensive list could be asked for, and merchants who want their stock protected, manufacturers who want their costly machinery covered, ship-owners, etc., who want their vessels and cargoes insured, professional men who want to provide against accident or death — all these will find unsurpassed facilities at this office for the transaction of such business.

Lawrence Brothers, Saw Mills, South Gardiner. In the preparation of a work of this kind, considerable difficulty is experienced in presenting an adequate idea of the comparative importance of the many business enterprises it treats of, for while some of these are of local celebrity, others are known throughout the State, and not a few are known all over New England, and in fact even outside of that section of the country. Among these latter concerns, prominent place should be given to the house of Lawrence Brothers, for the undertaking carried on by this firm has been in operation for twenty-two years, and is one of the most important of its kind in the State. The works are located at South Gardiner and include a Saw Mill and a Planing Mill, the entire plant covering an area of five acres of ground, and employment being given to seventy-five experienced assistants. The firm is made up of Messrs. C., H., S., and G. Lawrence, all of whom were born in this city. These gentlemen have one of the best-equipped Lumber Mills in Maine, and are in a position to offer decided advantages to those purchasing lumber in large quantities. Their sources of supply are unfailing and they are prepared to furnish any desired quantity at short notice and at the lowest market rates.

LEADING BUSINESS MEN OF GARDINER.

KENNEBEC STEAMBOAT COMPANY, O. M. Blanchard, Agent.

This Company is proprietor of the line of Steamers running from this city to Boston, and by connecting Steamer to Augusta. It originated in 1834, when the pioneer Steamer "McDonough" opened the business, not running direct to Boston, but making direct connection with other steamers at Portland. In 1836 she was succeeded by the New England, which was the first to run to Boston, and from which time the direct line has been maintained, she being followed by the Huntress, in 1838, the John W. Richmond in 1840, then by the Penobscot, the Kennebec and the Charter Oak, in turn, then by the Ocean in 1850, the Governor in 1854, the Eastern Queen in 1857, and the Star of the East in 1866, which is still running and one of the safest and best-managed Steamers sailing from Boston. Her commander, Capt. Jason Collins, was first employed on the line in 1836, and has been in the same employ—with the exception of about eight years spent on the Pacific Coast—from that time to the present. He became captain of the Eastern Queen in 1860, and was transferred to the Star of the East when she was built, in 1866, and stands to-day as one of the ablest and most popular steamboat captains in New England. This line has been largely instrumental in the prosperity of the Kennebec Valley, and always ready to meet all the requirements of the business public. They are now having built by the New England Co., at Bath, an elegant new steamer, to go on the route early this season, and run with the Star, giving greatly increased facilities for travel and freight carrying. The new steamer is to be 205 feet in length, and 62 feet in breadth, over all; is to be equipped with all modern conveniences, and with electric lights, electric bells and steam steering apparatus, and will be one of the most elegant steamers sailing from Boston. Among the early proprietors of this line, were the well-known names of Nathaniel Kimball, William Bradstreet and Isaac Rich; while among the present owners are found the members of the firm of which Mr. Rich was the head and the sons of Mr. Bradstreet, who are all most zealous in the work of the line, which came to them from so worthy hands. Among the heaviest stockholders stand also the names of James B. Drake of Bath, and E. C. Allen and Oscar Holway of Augusta. The old patrons of the line, as they go upon the steamers, find themselves carried back to their early years as they find the genial officers of twenty years ago the Pilots, Captains Baker and Peach; the Clerk, C. G. Wall, whose father was one of the first Clerks on the line; the veteran Steward, loved by all, Frank Dunphy; the Second Steward, C. H. Stetson; the Mate, Capt. C. E. Bradstreet, and many a waiter who has passed nearly his whole life in this service. Thomas A. Rich, of Boston, is President, and with him are associated Wm. H. West, of Boston; J. B. Drake, of Bath; E. C. Allen, of Augusta; and Capt. Collins, as Directors; and E. L. Smith, of Gardiner, is Clerk and Treasurer. O. M. Blanchard is Agent at Gardiner; W. J. Tuck at Augusta; the veteran General Eastern Agents, Hiram Fuller, at Hallowell; John T. Robinson at Richmond; G. C. Greenleaf at Bath; and Charles H. Hyde at Boston.

Evans Hotel, O. C. Rollins, proprietor, Water and Church Streets, Gardiner. It has long been our opinion that the services rendered any given community by the establishment and maintenance of a really first-class Hotel in its midst, are greatly underestimated in the majority of cases. No one who has given the matter any attention will deny that a liberally and intelligently managed Hotel will attract visitors to the city or town in which it may be located. The fact is notorious, how the class of people who patronize a first-class Hotel, as a rule have money to spend and do spend it freely, and there is not a merchant in town but what is benefited more or less directly by the presence of such visitors. It should therefore be a subject for congratulation among Gardiner business men that the Evans Hotel should be under its present management, for there is no denying that this is a first-class house, run in a first-class manner, and the effect of the liberal methods pursued by its proprietor is plainly to be seen in the character and extent of the patronage received. The Evans Hotel occupies three floors of the dimensions of 40x60 feet, and is most conveniently arranged and very completely fitted up. The proprietor of the establishment, Mr. O. C. Rollins, was born in Pittston, Me. He has made many friends since becoming identified with his present enterprise in 1867, for he is very solicitous of the comfort of his guests, and spares no pains to make them feel entirely at home while stopping under his roof. There are ten assistants employed, and prompt and polite service is guaranteed, both at the table (which is bountifully and tastefully supplied), and in all the other departments of the establishment.

Richards Paper Co., Water Street, Gardiner. The Manufacture of Paper forms, as most of our readers doubtless know, one of the most important of Gardiner's industries, and the advantages afforded by the natural facilities in and about the city were early recognized, as will be seen from the fact that one establishment now maintained here (that run by the Richards Paper Company), has been in operation for seventy-five years. About 1835, it became known as the "Richards Paper Mill," the proprietors being Messrs. Richards & Huskins, who were succeeded in 1858, by Richards & Co., and in 1884 the present company was formed, and assumed control. The President is Mr. J. F. Richards. The Treasurer and General Manager, Mr. Henry Richards, and the Superintendent Mr. A. McDermid. The entire plant in operation covers an area of three acres of ground, and includes costly and elaborate machinery of the most approved and efficient design. A one hundred and fifty horse-power steam engine is at hand to furnish motive power, either in connection with or independent of the large water power also available, and employment is given to seventy-five assistants, the total daily production of the establishment amounting to eight tons and the pay-roll footing up $2200 per month. The carrying on of such an enterprise cannot fail to be of great benefit to any community in which it may be located, and the citizens of Gardiner may well congratulate themselves on having so representative an industry connected with their city.

The Holmes Gear Works, P. C. Holmes & Co., Proprietors. Manufacturers of The Holmes Turbine Water Wheel. Accurately Spaced and Planed Gears, Shafting, Hangers Bridge Trees. Pulleys, General Mill Work and Castings, Water Street, Gardiner. We need not point out the establishment carried on by Messrs. P. C. Holmes & Co., as a representative one in many important respects, for the fact is too generally known to require further extension. This enterprise was inaugurated over a half-century ago, being founded by Messrs. Holmes & Robbins in 1837. The present firm-name was adopted in 1860, and the concern is now made up of Messrs. P. C., G. M., and P. H. Holmes, the first-named gentleman being a native of Kingston, Mass., and the two latter of Gardiner. The senior partner was formerly a Representative in the State Legislature, and all the members of the firm are too well known to require further personal mention. About one-half acre of ground is occupied by the plant in use, there being a machine-shop two stories in height, a foundry, occupying one floor, and a pattern shop, comprising three stories. A twenty-five horse-power steam-engine supplies the motive power, and a sixty-horse boiler is used in connection with it, employment being given to about forty men. The Holmes Turbine Water Wheel is the most important article manufactured, and orders for these appliances come in rapidly and steadily, as the Holmes Wheel is known to be one of the most economical and efficient ever produced. Accurately Spaced and Planed Gears are also extensively manufactured, as well as Shafting, Hangers, Bridge Trees, Pulleys, Castings, etc. General Mill work will receive prompt and satisfactory attention, and while skilled help and the best of material are employed, the charges made will be found reasonable and just.

Merchants National Bank, 166 Water Street, Gardiner. It is quite unnecessary for us to mention in detail the reasons for the establishment of the Merchants National Bank, which began operations in 1884. Suffice it to say that the liberal patronage accorded the institution has fully vindicated the judgment of its founders, and that no Bank in the State has a more prosperous future apparently assured to it. Of course a prime factor in the success of an institution of this kind is the establishment of confidence in its directing officers, and the Merchants Bank is especially favored in this respect, for the gentlemen identified with its management are universally known in this community, and are respected as substantial business men, who have the best interests of the city at heart. The President is Mr. David Dennis, and the Cashier Mr. Henry Farrington, the Board of Directors being made up of the first-named gentleman, together with Messrs. Charles Danforth, Joseph S. Bradstreet, Jason Collins, and Harvey Scribner.. Under their fostering care the Merchants National Bank has already established a prominent place for itself in the financial operations of this section of the State, and has proved itself to be in fact, as well as in name, a "Merchants" Bank. The institution has a capital of $100,000, and a surplus of $5,350, and is prepared to discount approved commercial paper, receive deposits, and in fact transact a general banking business. While striving to aid deserving local industries as much as possible, the management do not forget that their first and most important duty is to keep the Bank in a perfectly sound financial condition, and their record so far, certainly, shows them to be well qualified for the task they have undertaken.

SMITH & GARDINER,

MANUFACTURERS AND DEALERS IN

CARRIAGES AND SLEIGHS,

154 Church Street, Gardiner, Maine.

Smith & Gardiner, Manufacturers and Dealers in Carriages and Sleighs. Particular Attention paid to Ordered Work and Repairing done in the best manner at short notice. 152 and 154 Church Street, Gardiner. Those of our readers who have read (and what New Englander has not?) Dr. Holmes' description of the building of the "wonderful one hoss shay," will remember how many varieties of wood were named as entering into the construction of it. Ash, oak, whitewood, hickory — all these and some others were combined in that truly "wonderful" old vehicle that was "so built that it couldn't break down." When it finally went to pieces "All at once and nothing first, just as bubbles do when they bust," it was not broken down but simply worn out, in fact, it came to just such an end as its designer intended it should. Now although Carriage Building has not yet been reduced to such a science that "breaking down" is entirely done away with, nevertheless by the judicious selection of materials, and the exercise of skill and care in putting them together, some very durable vehicles have been produced, and those who want a Carriage combining elegance of design with thoroughness and strength of workmanship, can do no better than to place their order with Messrs. Smith and Gardiner, doing business on Church Street. This firm began operations in 1871, and their productions have for years been regarded as standard articles in every respect. They combine lightness with strength in a marked degree, and are fully warranted as regards perfection of workmanship and material. In addition to Building fine Carriages and Sleighs to order, This firm gives particular attention to making Express and Business Wagons and Pungs to order. Employing skilled workmen and having every facility for turning out first-class and durable work, it is no wonder that their trade constantly increases. At the beginning of the season, the owner of a Carriage or Sleigh usually finds that more or less repairs are necessary, either in the way of Upholstery, Painting or Varnishing even if nothing is broken. Instead of waiting until the last moment, the far-sighted individual will send the vehicle to Messrs. Smith & Gardiner some time before it is wanted. He thus gets it out of his dusty barn or carriage-house, and when the season opens is not obliged to wait his time for the Carriage to be finished, as is the case when all come at once. Sleighs or Carriages may be sent in at any time for repairs, and will be stored free until they are wanted, ample room being provided for their large trade. The premises occupied are 42x80 feet in size and comprise two floors, employment being given to seven assistants. Repairing is extensively carried on, and the charges in this department, as well as for new work, are moderate and satisfactory.

Oakland National Bank, Water Street, Gardiner. For nearly a quarter of a century has the Oakland National Bank been carried on in this city, and we question if the full magnitude of the service of this institution has rendered in building up Gardiner's business interests will ever be appreciated. From the inception of operations in 1865, the bank has been managed in a conservative, and yet liberal manner, and though making no great pretensions, still its record is one that might well be envied by many a much more aggressive and prominent institution. There is a wide difference between the meaning of the words "prominent" and "important," although they are frequently used in the same sense. And we know that those conversant with the facts will subscribe to our assertion that the character of the service rendered by the Oakland National Bank has been such as to make that institution of much more importance than prominence. The Bank has a capital of $50,000, surplus and other undivided profits $32,600, and is as sound as a rock financially, being most admirably prepared to maintain the honorable position it has held so long, and giving every promise of enjoying as bright a future as it has a past. The President, Mr. Joshua Gray, and the Cashier, Mr. S. Bowman, are well known and popular gentlemen, who are highly esteemed in Gardiner and vicinity, while the Directors are composed of such men as Joseph Perry, Myrick Hopkins, P. N. Barstow, and Charles Swett, in addition to Mr. Gray, the gentleman first mentioned. After presenting such a list of names, there is no need of dwelling further upon the solidity of the institution. Its affairs could not be in better hands, and success is assured under such circumstances.

William H. Ring, Dealer in Beef, Pork, Lard, Hams, Butter, Cheese, Poultry, Vegetables, Canned Goods, Tobacco, Cigars, Salt and Fresh Fish, Country Produce, Choice Groceries, and Fruits of all kinds, 141 Water Street, Gardiner. There are certain advantages which householders find in trading at the establishment conducted by Mr. William H. Ring, at No. 141 Water Street, which certainly go far to explain the exceptional popularity of the house in question. Mr. Ring sells so large a variety of food-products that it is possible to purchase all one's supplies of him, week after week, without sameness and monotony. Meats, Fish, Provisions and Groceries—all these are obtainable at his store, and that, too, at prices that will compare favorably with those quoted elsewhere on goods of equal merit. The premises utilized comprise one floor and a basement, and measure 25x60 feet. A large stock is carried, and Beef, Pork, Lard, Hams, and other Fresh and Cured Meats form a prominent part of it, while Fresh and Salt Fish are also extensively handled. Staple and Fancy Groceries, selected expressly for Family use, are offered at the lowest market rates, and Country Produce and Fruits of all kinds are also for sale at bottom prices. Especial attention is called to the Butter and Cheese handled at this establishment, for they are received direct from the best dairies, and are fully guaranteed. Mr. Ring employs three efficient and polite assistants, and all callers are assured prompt and courteous attention. He was born in this city, and is a member of the Knights of Pythias. Mr. Ring has been identified with his present enterprise for about seventeen years, and well deserves the success he has won.

E. E. Lewis, Architect, Water Street, Gardiner. There are few men but what make up their minds to build, sooner or later, for it is an inborn instinct in humanity to wish to own the roof over its head. Now a man who contemplates erecting a building of any great pretensions, of course always employs an architect, but it is often the case where only an ordinary dwelling is to be built, that the services of an architect are looked upon as unnecessary, and will be dispensed with in order to save expense. We believe such a course to be not only unwise but also un-economical, for the cost of drawing up the plans, etc., for an average dwelling-house is really very small, and the advantages of having specifications to go by are too numerous to allow of their being lightly set aside. Every man has his own ideas of how he wants his house built, and if a competent architect be engaged, these ideas may be put into practical shape; their mistakes corrected and their good points taken advantage of. Some pains should be taken, of course, to choose an architect who would heartily lend his co-operation in the attainment of satisfactory results, and in this connection we desire to call the attention of our readers to the record made by Mr. E. E. Lewis of this city. Since he began operations here in 1884, Mr. Lewis has shown himself to be a competent and original architect, who is not above receiving suggestions from his customers, and has gained no small degree of popularity by reason of the evident personal interest he takes in carrying out the commissions with which he is favored to the best advantage. His office is located at 161 Water St., and employment is given to two assistants, enabling him to produce plans, etc., at short notice, while his charges are, in all cases, moderate and equitable.

George McIntosh, Photographer, Water Street. Gardiner. We need not describe the various steps by which the art of Photography has reached its present perfection, for our readers are of course aware that great progress has been made of late, as shown by the results attained by Mr. George McIntosh, at his studio on Water Street, for this gentleman is an Artistic Photographer in every sense of the word, and the portraits produced by him will bear comparison with those coming from the most noted Boston and New York photographers. The premises utilized comprise a reception-room, of the dimensions of 20x20 feet, and three other apartments, having an area of 20x40 feet, every facility being at hand for the convenience of patrons, and also for carrying on operations to the best advantage. Mr. McIntosh was born in Hallowell, Me., and inaugurated his present enterprise in 1872. He has been favored with many orders, and the results have been so uniformly and highly satisfactory that a large and steadily-growing business has already been established.

Gardiner Beef Co., Commission Merchants in Chicago Dressed Beef, 69 Water St. We eastern people are apt to smile good-naturedly at times at the pretentious and "big" assertions of our fellow-citizens of the "boundless west," but nevertheless it must be confessed that in certain things they do indeed "beat the world," and one of the most important industries in which they excel, is the raising and handling of Beef. Since "Chicago Dressed Beef" began to be known in our eastern markets, there has been a long and bitter fight for the supremacy, but it is now, and has been for some time, settled that western beef is, on the whole, far superior to that of our own raising, and that "Chicago Dressed Beef" is as good as the best, and very hard to beat in any particular. This beef is sold all over the United States at the present time, and in some foreign countries, and we have yet to learn of an authenticated instance where it failed to give satisfaction to any reasonable purchaser. Appreciating the sharp competition which they have to withstand, they make it a point to handle only such an article as cannot fail to please. One of the most enterprising and largely patronized of the many houses dealing in this product, is that carried on by the Gardiner Beef Co., in this city, at No. 69 Water Street, and the volume of business done shows how abundantly the goods dealt in are appreciated.

HISTORICAL SKETCH
— OF —
HALLOWELL.

THE irony of history is well illustrated in the fortunes of the twin cities—Hallowell and Augusta. A century ago the former place seemed to have much the better prospects. Including all of the present territory occupied by both cities, it gave strong evidence of becoming the leading city of the Kennebec valley. But though that part of the original town set off and named Augusta, has had better fortunes than the rest, there is still much of great interest and historical value in the older city of Hallowell. The earliest settlement within the limits of old Hallowell was at Cushnoc, now Augusta. Here the Pilgrims built their block-house in 1629, and here in 1754 was Fort Western established by the Massachusetts colonists. Around this fort for several miles up and down, and on both sides of the river, the old settlement grew up until it was all incorporated, in 1771, under the name of Hallowell in honor of Benjamin Hallowell of Boston, a leading owner of real estate in the town. What is now the city of Hallowell was originall called "Bombahock," by the Indians. Among the earliest settlers at this point were Jonathan Davenport, who came in 1762, Samuel Bullen and Ezekiel Chase who came in 1783. When the town was incorporated in 1771, the settlers from this section took a leading part in the local government. In the following year there were ninety-six tax-payers within the limits of the town. The first religious meetings were held in the vicinity of Fort Western, and the first minister, Rev. John Allen, came in 1774.

The growing settlement naturally took a deep interest in the symptoms of war which now began to manifest themselves. Being of a liberty-loving, enterprising disposition, it immediately espoused the cause of its countrymen, regardless of evil consequences to itself; for, although the war greatly retarded its advancement, it never murmured or bated a jot of its strong endeavors to promote the struggle for victory. A committee of safety and correspondence was formed at Hallowell, among the earliest of the Revolutionary committees in the District of Maine.

In the early part of 1775, soldiers were sent to Boston and engaged with gallantry in the fighting around that city. Hallowell, itself, had a glimpse of the battle-field and of the stern-faced men who were engaged in the struggle, when Col. Benedict Arnold, with his heroic and unflinching band of volunteers passed through the town in the fall of 1775. Quite a number enlisted for the expedition from this town, and but few returned from the desperate, forlorn expedition. In the year of Independence, 1776, this little settlement subscribed the sum of £66 to advance the cause, an amount which at that time and place was equivalent to many thousands of dollars now. A company of volunteers was also raised.

The years of the war dragged slowly on, each one increasing the burdens on the people, yet evidently bringing the close and reward of the struggle nearer. The year 1779 was remarkable for the fact that an unusually large tax was raised, amounting to over $12,000. In that year fifty men were sent from Hallowell to engage in the unsuccessful expedition against the English posts at Castine and Bagaduce; the failure being due to the inefficiency of the leadership, and not to the gallantry of the soldiers.

The close of the war in 1783, not only caused great rejoicings, but also more practical fruit in an immediate resumption of the forward movement in size and wealth which the war had stopped. Business now began to expand; new settlers came and laid out farms, and especially around Fort Western. Every year witnessed marked changes, already foreshadowing a town of considerable size and importance. By the beginning of the next decade, both the "Fort" and "Hook" sections of old Hallowell were prospering and spreading widely through the surrounding country. A post-office had been established in each section and at the "Hook"; besides the mercantile stores were several flour and saw mills, a distillery and brewery. A meeting-house had already been built and opened, and in 1791 the "Hallowell Academy" was incorporated by the General Court of Massachusetts. At that time it was the highest institution in the District of Maine, and was the best in New England, north of Exeter, N. H. This fact well illustrates the leading position in the State, which Hallowell had so early taken, and also the cultivated character of its citizens. The population in 1790 had risen to 1194, and was increasing rapidly.

The year 1797 was marked by an event, than which hardly a more important one has taken place in the history of the town, namely, the separation of Augusta. This movement had caused much discussion for several years, the settlement at the "Fort" claiming a distinct name and government, and after much fighting they carried their point, inflicting a blow not yet overcome in the growth of the old town. After the separation Hallowell continued to advance, but slowly, up to the present century.

The first decade witnessed much growth in size and wealth, though the Emgargo had a paralyzing effect on commerce for a time. At the beginning of the war of 1812 considerable business interest was manifested here, but the war had a deadly effect, and it was long before it was recovered from. Although at much personal-loss and inconvenience, the people of Hallowell entered into the war of 1812 with patriotism and devotion.

The valuation of the town in 1830 was $315,000, and among its property were 3,916 tons of shipping, which showed that the town had already gained quite a marine interest. The decline of this and the cotton interest injured the growth of the town more than any other two agents, but other openings came to help supply their loss, and especially the great development of the granite business.

The Hallowell artillery, formed in 1821, was a great institution, the first, and best at the time in the State. Two brass six-pounders and a tumbrill formed the battery of this primitive organization, but it accomplished a good work, introduced a salutary discipline, and was a strong and healthful influence in the social and political life of the time and locality. Many anecdotes and reminiscences of this "ancient and honorable" body exist to the present day.

The history of Hallowell through the middle of this century was one of slow and natural development, unmarked by any striking events. A great tornado in 1846 caused a great deal of damage, but no loss of life. From 1850 on, the slavery question became more and more prominent and exciting, the sentiment of the town being strongly in favor of the abolition of slavery. When the civil war broke out a large number of its citizens were ready to offer their lives for the maintenance of the Union and the freedom of the slave. Considerable detachments from this town joined the First, Ninth, Eleventh, Thirteenth, Twenty-fourth, Twenty-eighth and Twenty-ninth Maine Regiments, and some soldiers from Hallowell, were in almost every regiment sent out by the State. Many gallant men and talented officers went from Hallowell.

Since the war the progress at Hallowell has not been so rapid as at an earlier period, yet sufficiently marked to be undeniable. Among other interests the granite resources of the town have been admirably developed, making the name of the town famous in many parts of the land, for the unusual density, durability and beauty of the celebrated rock found here. The name of the late lamented Governor Bodwell naturally suggests itself in connection with this interest, which he did so much to develop here. The late Governor was highly honored at his home in Hallowell, and his death, while occupying his responsible position, was a sad blow to numerous friends and sympathizers in this city.

The city government of Hallowell was incorporated in 1850, and has always been noted for the extreme care and honor with which its business has been conducted. All protective measures through the employment of trained and competent fire and police officers are carefully provided for, and every endeavor made so that an unusual degree of security is obtained for property and person. The sanitary standard is among the highest in this unusually salubrious State, and the death rate very low, hardly one in one hundred. A city physician is employed to exercise careful supervision over every health interest of the city. The moral standard also of the town is of a rare and lofty type, the slow growth of the city having prevented the introduction of influences which tend to break down the bulwarks of society. There are churches of almost every important denomination, which are largely attended and exert a wide and efficacious influence for the highest good of the citizens of the city.

LEADING BUSINESS MEN

OF

HALLOWELL.

Hallowell National Bank, Hallowell. The Hallowell National Bank is one of our city institutions, of which we may excusably feel a little proud, for although it may do business on a smaller scale than some of our other New England Banks, located in Boston and other large cities, still its record will bear comparison, when the field operated is taken into consideration, with that of any enterprise in the country of a similar nature. Business was begun in 1804 as the "American National Bank," and on the expiration of the charter in 1884, it was renewed, or rather re-issued, under the present name. Mr. John Graves, the President of the Bank, is a native of Kingston, N. H., while Mr. A. D. Knight, the Cashier, was born in Lincolnville, Me. He is judge of the municipal court, and is very popular with our resident business men, always being ready to grant any accommodation permitted by his duty to the Bank. The Assistant Cashier is Mr. W. H. Perry, who is also widely and favorably known, and the Board of Directors is made up of Messrs. John Graves, William Wilson, B. F. Warner, and A. D. Knight and David Elliott. The capital stock amounts to $50,000, there being a surplus of $12,500, together with undivided profits amounting to over $5,800. No better financial condition could be desired than this Bank exhibits. It pays a dividend of four per cent semi-annually, and its deposits have largely increased, not only on account of its being a local institution, but also because its management have always made it a rule to assist deserving Hallowell enterprises as much as possible, and the outcome is gratifying, insomuch as it proves that liberality pays, and that the confidence of the Bank in Hallowell's business men and business interests is fully justified by the facts. Mutual aid within reasonable limits is one of the essentials of success in any community, and it would be well if the example set by the Hallowell National Bank were more generally followed.

Northern National Bank, Water Street, Hallowell. Me. "Brilliant" financiering is all very well in its way, no doubt, and "young Napoleons of Wall Street," who make something out of nothing by the simple process of buying that which they have not the means to pay for, may be valuable men to have in the community; but many people are old-fashioned enough to think that solid merit is more to be desired than mere outer show, and that a successful gambler may make a very poor figure as a legitimate banker. To conduct financial operations in which large amounts are involved to the best advantage, requires a thorough business training and a judicious combination of conservatism and enterprise, and in practical life no "nerve" or "dash," or "inspiration," can take the place of such qualifications. The history of the origin and development of the Northern National Bank of this city, shows that it has, on the whole, been exceptionably fortunate in its managers, and the present condition and future prospects of this institution, gratifying as they are, have been hardly worked for and honestly won; not by "brilliant" methods, but by intelligent, honorable and progressive financiering. The inception of this enterprise dates back over half a century, for the Northern Bank was incorporated under State laws in 1833, becoming a National Bank in 1864. In 1884 its charter was renewed for another score of years, and none were better pleased at this than our resident manufacturers and merchants, for they have learned to appreciate the aid which this bank is able to offer. The President of the institution was Justin E. Smith up to January, 1888, when he retired on account of old age and ill health, when the present President, Mr. Jas. H. Leigh, succeeded him. Mr. Smith died in April, the same year. Cashier, Mr. George R. Smith, and the Assistant Cashier, Mr. George A. Safford. These gentlemen are natives of Hallowell, and require no introduction to our readers. The Board of Directors is composed of Messrs. James H. Leigh, Ben. Tenney, S. Titcomb, C. L. Spaulding and D. P. Livermore, and the present financial condition of the bank may be judged from its having a surplus of $25,000, with a capital of $100,000.

Lowell & Simmons, Dealers in Groceries, Meats, Vegetables, Grain, Provisions, etc., Perley's Block, Water Street, Hallowell. It is by no means an uncommon occurence for the inquiry to be made, "Where can I find a perfectly reliable Grocery and Provision Store?" and as a truthful answer to this question is bound to prove of interest to hundreds of our readers, we take pleasure in calling attention to the establishment conducted by Messrs. Lowell & Simmons, located in Perley's Block, Water Street, for if ever an enterprise deserved the name of reliable, it is certainly the one with which they are identified. This concern began operations in 1817, and hence has steadily served the public for seventy-one years, and the record made by it during this long period, is one of which its present proprietors may well feel proud, for it affords a guarantee not only of their reliability but of their enterprise, and will bear the severest comparison with that of any similar house in this city. This enterprise was originally established in 1817, by Mr. John Lowell, and conducted by him until 1867, when Mr. Jno. H. Lowell assumed control of the business and continued it alone until 1882, when Mr. G. F. Simmons was admitted as a partner, since which date the firm name has been as at present—Lowell & Simmons. The premises occupied comprise three floors and a basement, each covering an area of 65x45 feet, and an extensive wholesale and retail business is done. Three experienced and polite assistants are at hand to give prompt attention to every caller. The stock handled is a very large one, and every facility is at hand for the preservation of the same in the way of immense refrigerators, etc., and comprises Groceries, Meats, Vegetables, Provisions, Grain, etc. A specialty being made of Chicago Beef. Orders are delivered promptly and no pains spared to give complete satisfaction to every customer. Both members of the firm are natives of Hallowell and well-known and highly respected throughout the entire community. Mr. J. H. Lowell has been connected with the city government as Mayor, Alderman and Councilman; and Mr. G. F. Simmons as Alderman and Councilman.

S. Currier, Dealer in All Kinds of Coal, Wood, Hay, Flour and Feed. Agent for the best Fertilizers. Also connected a First-Class Livery Stable. North End of Water Street, Hallowell. An establishment that is highly esteemed and liberally patronized by the residents of Hallowell and vicinity, is that carried on by Mr. S. Currier, at the North End of Water Street. Mr. Currier has been in charge of the enterprise in question since 1873, it having been started in 1845 by Mr. Samuel Johnson. Coal, Wood, Hay, Flour and Feed, are dealt in very extensively, and the most approved Fertilizers are, also largely handled, Mr. Currier acting as agent for the manufacturers and being in a position to sell at the very lowest rates. He is one of the most generally known of our business men, and is a member of the City Council. The premises utilized include one building containing three floors, of the dimensions of 55x45 feet, and another with two floors, measuring 65x70 feet, together with sheds having a capacity 3,000 tons of coal and 800 cords of wood. Both a wholesale and retail business is done, and orders are filled without delay and always at the very lowest market price. A specialty is made of supplying family trade, and those who purchase their Fuel or Grain of Mr. Currier, may depend upon getting just what they pay for every time. A first-class Livery Stable is carried on in connection with the enterprise, and stylish and speedy teams may be hired for any desired time at fair rates. Hacks and Barges will be furnished for all occasions at short notice, and only experienced and courteous drivers are employed. The livery accommodations have proved the most popular feature of Mr. Currier's business, and he is always striving to make the service as perfect as possible. His horses are carefully selected and the vehicles are easy-riding and kept as neat as wax.

LEADING BUSINESS MEN OF HALLOWELL.

Hallowell Iron Foundry, George Fuller's Sons, Iron Founders and Machinists, Manufacturers of Iron and Brass Castings, Shafting, Hangers and Pulleys and General Mill Work. Dealers in Iron Pipe for Steam, Gas or Water. Steam and Gas Fittings constantly on hand, South End, Water Street, Hallowell. The Hallowell Iron Foundry may justly be regarded as one of the "institutions" of the city, for not only has it been in operation for many years, but its proprietors are recognized throughout the State as representative citizens, as well as enterprising business men. The undertaking had its inception just about half a century ago, its founder being Mr. J. P. Flagg, who was succeeded by Mr. W. R. Prescott. In 1850, the firm of Prescott & Fuller was formed, and ten years later, Mr. George Fuller assumed sole control, the existing firm, name "George Fuller's Sons" being adopted in 1878. The gentlemen associated under this [style, are all natives of Hallowell and are all brothers, the firm consisting of Messrs. Geo. S., W. H. H., J. W., B. F., and C. T. Fuller. It is very rarely that a family becomes so prominent in public affairs as this one has, but each member of it is a firm believer in Hallowell and her future, and is ready to do what he can at any time to advance or protect the city's interests. Mr. Geo. S. Fuller has been Alderman and Mayor. Mr. W. H. H. Fuller has served in both branches of the Council, and Mr. B. F. Fuller has been a Common Councilman, while Mr. J. W. Fuller has occupied the positions of City Clerk and Assessor and is now Mayor. The firm carry on a general business as Machinists and Founders; Manufacturing Iron and Brass Castings, Shafting, Hangers and Pulleys, and attending to Mill Work generally. A varied assortment of patterns for Building Fronts, Columns, etc., can be found at their works. Some of the most costly Iron Fronts in this part of the State can here be found. Fence and Railings can be manufactured at short notice. Iron pipe is dealt in largely, and Steam and Gas Fittings are kept always in stock. The works are located at the South end, Water Street, and are extensive and most completely fitted up, comprising various buildings which are occupied as Foundries, Machine shops, Pattern-shops etc. Employment is afforded to thirty experienced men, and a specialty is made of the production of Print Blocks for Oil Cloth, Paper Hangings, etc. This concern has unexcelled facilities for supplying anything in its line, and the magnitude of the business done is sufficient to test these facilities severely. Even excellence, is striven for in every department of the works, and the productions of Geo. Fuller's Sons are recognized as being of standard quality. They are so well known and highly regarded that they need no encomiums at this late day, and we will only remark that the same careful supervision is exercised in every department of the business as was the case when this house had a reputation to make, and with the same result—superiority and uniform excellence of product. The annual output of this concern is of great and increasing value. Orders are filled with the promptness and accuracy due to perfect system, and no enteprise is better prepared to furnish anything in this line at the lowest market rates.

Fuller & Co., Hallowell, manufacturers of Whiting and Putty; works on Litchfield road. Among those common articles of commerce, which are by no means imposing in appearance and of which but little is known by the general public, mention should certainly be made of Whiting and Putty, for these are used for a great variety of purposes, and it is hard to see how they could be dispensed with in the doing of certain kinds of work. The manufacture of Whiting is a simple operation, but like many other simple operations, there is a right way and a wrong way of doing it, and the quality of the product may be much impaired by improper handling. The residents of Hallowell have an excellent opportunity to gain a practical knowledge of Whiting and Putty manufacturing, for the firm of Fuller & Co. carry on a well-equipped factory on the Litchfield road, and the daily product reaches a very considerable amount. Some idea of the extent of the business done may be gained from the fact that the average annual manufacture of whiting is eight hundred tons. The chalk from which this is made is procured from the chalk cliffs of England. This is brought to New York by steamer or otherwise, and from there re-shipped by coasters to their dock in Hallowell. These works are run only during the spring, summer, and early fall—generally from the middle of April to the early part of November. This firm, we might state, by the way, is identical with that of George Fuller's Sons, the same gentlemen composing it, so that the Hallowell Iron Foundry and the enterprise under notice are under the same management. We have said that the manufacture of Whiting is a simple operation, and so it is, consisting merely of crushing chalk into an impalpable powder and then forming the same into lumps; but those having occasion to use Whiting for polishing or other purposes, will confirm our statement that there is considerable difference observable in that offered in the market, some containing a much greater proportion of "grit" than others, and consequently much more apt to scratch and otherwise injure smooth surfaces. The out-put of Fuller & Co.'s Works is of uniformly superior quality, for great care is exercised in the selection of stock, and the details of pulverizing are given close and skillful attention. As a consequence the demand for the product of this factory is constantly increasing, not only so far as the Whiting is concerned, but also in the case of the Putty, which is made by the mixture of Whiting and Linseed Oil in proper proportions, the compound being thoroughly combined by agitation, and so packed as to remain moist for a long period. The firm have excellent facilities and can furnish goods at the lowest market rates. Several vessels are employed in the transportation of the product, and there is also a considerable amount sent to customers by rail. Perfect order and system are observable in every department of this mammoth enterprise, and no pains are spared by the firm to keep the goods fully up to the high standard their patrons have been taught to expect from them. They are in a position to supply the public, either at wholesale or retail, at the lowest rates, and fill all orders promptly and accurately.

Edwin H. Atkins, Boots and Shoes. Fine Custom Work and Repairing, Water Street, near Bank, Hallowell. It is said by those who have given the matter careful study, that there is not the slightest need of anybodys having corns or bunions, and that in the cases where such are present, it is only because ill-fitting or badly-shaped shoes have been worn. Now, although many, and in fact most of the sufferers from corns, etc., will stoutly deny that they have ever worn shoes too small for them, still it should be remembered that although a shoe may be plenty large enough, taken as a whole, still it may press so hard upon a certain portion of the foot as to cause serious inconvenience, and finally to bring about the formation of the painful excrescences we have previously alluded to. The remedy is simple. Purchase your boots and shoes from a house that carries so large and varied a stock as to enable all feet to be perfectly fitted, and that includes the productions of some of the best makers known. It is just such an assortment as this that is offered by Mr. Edwin H. Atkins, on Water Street, near Bank; and although the enterprise conducted by Mr. Atkins was inaugurated only about 13 years ago, a very large and rapidly increasing patronage has already been attained. Mr. Atkins was born in Kennebunkport, Me., and is a member of the Odd Fellows, and very well and favorably known here. Realizing that there is a continuous demand in this vicinity for durable and thoroughly made foot-wear, at fair prices, he has endeavored to fully meet it, and his success is a matter of general comment. His store is 75x22 feet in size, and two efficient and polite assistants are in attendance, and all visitors are assured prompt and courteous attention. A specialty is made of Custom Work and Repairing of all Kinds.

A. C. Harrington, Dealer in Groceries and Provisions, Water Street, Hallowell. Included under the heads of Groceries and Provisions are such a variety of staple and indispensable articles that it is a matter of course, that any house prominently engaged in handling them, must, of necessity, do an enormous business, and such is the case with the popular concern of A. C. Harrington, to a brief mention of which this article is devoted. The enterprise in question was inaugurated by its present proprietor, in 1878, and has fairly won the prosperous position he now holds, for he has spared no pains to furnish his customers with just what was ordered by them, and has made it a point never to allow himself to be undersold, but to promptly meet all honorable competition. Mr. Harrington is a native of Topsham, Me., and ranks with the truly representative business men of this city. He has been connected with the city government of Hallowell as Councilman and is Past Master of the Masons. The business premises occupied comprise two floors, each covering an area of 55x30 feet, and a large retail business is done, and two efficient assistants are employed. The store is located on Water Street, and the choice stock handled includes a complete and desirable assortment of Staple and family Groceries; also Fresh Provisions of all kinds, and those who place their orders with this house are assured of getting them promptly and satisfactorily filled.

D. H. Johnson, Dealer in Stoves, Ranges, and Furnaces, Japan, Tin and Sheet Iron Work and Plumbing. Sole agents for the celebrated Magee Furnace Co's. goods, Hallowell. It is said that the man who has traveled the most and seen much of the world is much more apt to be contented and settle down in one spot, than he who has not had his advantages; and it may also be said with perfect truth, that the surest way of obtaining an article that will give enduring satisfaction is to visit an establishment where about all varieties are kept, and selecting it from amid an abundance. Take it for instance in the case of one wanting a Stove, Range or Furnace, if a call is made at the establishment of Mr. D. H. Johnson, and his mamouth assortment inspected, it will be strange indeed, if nothing can be found which will prove satisfactory, both as regards capacity and price. The business now conducted by the gentleman above named, was inaugurated many years ago by Mr. James Atkins, but since 1884 Mr. Johnson has had sole control. He is a native of Hallowell and a member of the Masons, and ranks with the most enterprising and highly esteemed of our men of business. The premises utilized comprise one floor of the dimensions of 50x25 feet, and a stock is carried consisting of Stoves, Furnaces and Ranges. Mr. Johnson is sole agent for the celebrated Magee Furnace Co's., goods. Particular attention is paid to Japan, Tin and Sheet Iron work. Also Jobbing and Plumbing Work. All orders will be filled in the best manner at short notice and reasonable rates. Employment is given constantly to two efficient workmen, and anything offered for sale or manufactured at the establishment is guaranteed to give perfect satisfaction.

LEADING BUSINESS MEN OF HALLOWELL. 177

J. Q. A. Hawes, M. D., Druggist & Apothecary, Hallowell. The carrying on of such an establishment as that conducted by J. Q. A. Hawes, M.D., is not a task to be assumed lightly by any means, for it involves great responsibility, and the person who essays to fill the position satisfactorily, must have the assistance of a liberal education and a careful practical training. Very few men could be found who are better fitted to conduct such an enterprise than Dr. Hawes, for he is not only an educated physician and a thoroughly competent Druggist, but also has had abundant opportunity to put his knowledge to practical use, not only in civil life, but as Surgeon in the 19th Maine Volunteers during the Great Rebellion. He is a member of the Grand Army, and no man in this city is more generally known and esteemed. He has served as City Clerk and also as Alderman of Hallowell, and is a member of the School Board and also of the Grand Commandery of Maine, Free Masons, besides being a Commissioner of Pharmacy in the State of Maine. The enterprise with which Dr. Hawes is now identified was inaugurated in 1820 by a gentleman named Fales who was succeeded in 1867 by Messrs. Warren & Hawes, Dr. Hawes becoming sole proprietor ten years later. He is a native of Lovell, Maine, and handles Drugs, Medicines. Chemicals. Druggists' Sundries etc., very extensively, employing competent and careful assistants. Dr. Hawes is very reasonable in his prices, particularly in his Prescription Department, to which especial attention is given. No trouble is spared in the compounding of such orders, and the implicit confidence shown by the public in Dr. Hawes facilities and skill, is amply justified by the facts.

Day & Co., Corn, Flour, Plain and Fancy Groceries, Crockery, Lamp Ware, Cutlery, Plated Ware, &c., Water Street, Hallowell. Of course it would never do to pass over such an establishment as that carried on by Messrs. Day & Co., on Water Street, without mention, for this undertaking is in many respects a representative one, being of very long standing and being controlled by representative men. It was inaugurated in 1841, under the firm name of Day & Co., and in 1845 the style was changed to F. J. Day. Ten years later, the original and present firm name was re-adopted, the proprietor now being Mr. C. A. Cole. This gentleman was born in this city and is too well-known to require personal comment. Mr. Cole is connected with the Masonic Order. The firm occupy three floors of the dimensions of 32x50 feet, and carry an immense stock of Corn, Flour, Staple and Fancy Groceries etc., together with complete assortments of Crockery, Lamp Ware, Cutlery, Plated-Ware etc. Employment is given to several efficient and courteous assistants, and customers are served with a promptness and politeness that are as gratifying as they are unusual. Mr. Cole handles only reliable goods, but for all that, the prices are as low as the lowest and no greater bargains are obtainable anywhere. Doing a large business and being well-known to producers, wholesalers etc., the firm is enabled to purchase on the most advantageous terms, and it is the policy of Mr. Cole to share these benefits directly with customers. As a consequence, the public have long since decided that this is a good store to patronize, and this decision is confirmed by the every-day experience of each customer.

Sidney T. Preble, dealer in Fancy Goods, Hosiery, Corsets, Gloves, Ribbons, Ladies' Merino and Cotton Underwear. Neck Wear and Laces a Specialty, Hallowell. One of the most varied, and at the same time one of the cleanest stocks with which we are acquainted, is that carried by Mr. Sidney T. Preble, of Hallowell. As some of our readers may not know just what is meant by a "clean" stock, we will explain that when an assortment of goods is composed entirely of fresh and desirable articles that are reasonably sure to be in active demand, and contains no old-fashioned or unseasonable goods to amount to anything, it is technically called "clean." Such is the stock we have referred to, and therefore it is but natural that it should meet with a ready sale, and that the establishment in which it is found is very popular. Mr. Preble began operations in 1887, and occupies a fine store 20x35 feet in dimensions. Among the articles handled may be mentioned Fancy Goods, Hosiery, Corsets, Gloves, Ribbons, Ladies' Merino and Cotton Underwear, Small Jewelry and Cutlery, a specialty being made of Neck Wear, and Lace, which are handled in great variety, and offered at prices much below those quoted at many establishments supplying no better or more fashionable goods. Employment is given to a sufficient force of assistants, and courteous attention is assured every caller. Mr. Preble is a native of Sullivan, Me., and highly respected in the social and business circles of this community, and is a member of Ancient Order United Workmen.

Eagle Iron Works, McClench & Co., Proprietors, Hallowell. The "Eagle Iron Works" are very extensively known throughout this State, and indeed it would be surprising if such were not the case, for they have been carried on for nearly half a century, having been founded by Mr. McClench in 1836. The present proprietors are McClench & Co., the firm being made up of Messrs. Geo. B. McClench and W. A. Winter. Mr. McClench being born in Mt. Vernon, Me., and Mr. Winter in Hallowell. Mr. McClench was alderman for two years and councilman for five years. Mr. Winter was formerly a member of the Board of Aldermen and Assessor, and both he and Mr. McClench are very generally known. The premises utilized comprise a foundry, of the dimensions of 30x80 feet, and a blacksmith shop, measuring 25x30 feet, employment being given to ten competent assistants. Both steam and water power is made use of, and General Foundry work is done, orders being promptly filled in a manner only possible where ample facilities are combined with skill and experience. A specialty is made of the manufacture of Oil-cloth Machines, and the many commissions executed in this line show the esteem in which the work done at the Eagle Iron Works is held by those in a position to judge intelligently. The prices quoted by Messrs. McClench & Co. are as low

LEADING BUSINESS MEN OF HALLOWELL.

as could be wished, for although the employment of inferior material or of incompetent workmen is carefully avoided, the experience of years and the possession of a complete and effective plant put the firm in a position to meet all competition and guarantee complete satisfaction.

H. D. Pinkham, dealer in Beef, Pork, Lamb, Mutton, Poultry, Veal, Tripe, Salt Provisions, Sausages, Country Produce, &c.; also, Fruit and Vegetables in their season, No. 1 Perley Block, Water Street, Hallowell. The gentleman whose card we print above, has been identified with his present enterprise for very nearly a score of years, it having been founded by him in 1869. In 1870 the firm name became Pinkham & Small, but in 1871 the original style was resumed, and Mr. Pinkham has since carried on operations alone. He is a native of Hallowell and was formerly a member of the city government, being connected with the Common Council. The premises occupied comprise two floors and a basement, measuring 55x35 feet, and being located at No. 1 Perley Block, Water Street. Beef, Pork, Lamb, Mutton, Poultry, Veal, Tripe, Salt Provisions, Sausages, &c., are kept in stock at all times and very extensively handled; while Country Produce, Fruits and Vegetables are also largely dealt in. Mr. Pinkham employs two capable assistants, and makes it a point to see that his customers get prompt and polite attention. As for the quality of the goods handled, that is best attested by the character of the patronage, it being conceded that no similar establishment in the city caters to a higher class of trade. Low prices are quoted on everything in stock, and some of the choicest cuts of beef, etc., to be found anywhere, may be obtained at this highly popular store. Special pains are taken to insure accuracy in the delivery of goods, and one of the most gratifying characteristics of the management is the faithfulness with which all promises made are lived up to.

Alden A. Heath, Apothecary, Water Street, Hallowell. As useful, and in fact indispensable, as physicians are to a community, they are hardly more so than are well-managed drug stores, for it is on them that physicians must depend for much of their success. Of course it is possible, and was once the universal practice for the village "doctor" to supply his own drugs, etc., buying them at wholesale, and compounding the medicines himself, but this style of doing things had many serious disadvantages, not the least of which was, that by the time the stock on hand was exhausted, of any particular drug, its virtues were apt to be greatly impaired by age and other causes. But all this has gone by in localities of any importance, and in fact it has been about fifty years since Hallowell was without a first-class Apothecary Store, as that of which Mr. Alden A. Heath is now the proprietor was founded as many years ago by Mr. Samuel Page, Mr. Heath having assumed full control of the business in 1877, and has since conducted it with ever-increasing success. This gentleman was born in Whitefield, Me., and has been a resident and prominent business man of this town so long a time that he has become a Hallowell man by adoption, at least. He is a member of the Masons and Odd Fellows, and of course is very widely known, and is as highly esteemed as he is well known, for he has given abundant evidence in the fact that his chief aim is to serve the public in the best manner possible, and although his trade has long been a large one, he has steadily continued his efforts to please. The premises occupied are located on Water Street, covering an area of 60x30 feet, comprising a fine Drug Store, well stocked with a fresh and reliable assortment of Drugs, Chemicals and Medicines of all kinds. Also a fine assortment of everything included under the head of Druggists' Sundries. The public are assured the most reliable goods, and skilled and efficient service when patronizing this house.

HISTORICAL SKETCH
—OF—
SKOWHEGAN.

THE oddity of its old Indian name has secured to Skowhegan a wider celebrity beyond the borders of the State than most towns of its size enjoy, but in the beauty of its situation, the character and refinement of its people and the solidity of its interests, this enterprising town is worthy of all and even more fame than it has received. It is situated thirty-three miles from Augusta, and can be reached directly by a branch of the Maine Central Railroad, of which it is the terminus. Sheltered by lovely hills, with fine water privileges, a fertile soil and salubrious climate, this beautiful town near the center of Maine is one of those delightful spots which sometimes surprise an experienced traveler with glimpses of charms he has never seen before, and remain one of the most treasured of memory's bright pictures. The name of the town was about the only thing bequeathed to it by its earliest inhabitants, who were quite famous for inventing odd cognomens of this character, and who seem to have exhausted most of their inventive talent in this way. It does not seem to have had the distinction, shared by most of the towns on the Kennebec River, of having been a national burying-ground for the untold number of ancestors of that powerful tribe, but rather to have been one of the earliest summer resorts of this Garden State. The Kennebec pronunciation of the same was "Skoohegan," and meant "the place to water." Hither the worthy warriors of the Kennebec tribe, with their families, used to come in the spring and stay till autumn, the great attraction being the salmon fishing which was largely indulged in. The king of fish was very numerous here at that time, and could be caught, by wading into the stream, in great numbers. This favored spot seems to have been the chief fishing resort of the Kennebec tribe, other varieties beside the salmon being very plenty. When this region of Maine was first settled in the latter part of the last century, the present town of

HISTORICAL SKETCH OF SKOWHEGAN.

Skowhegan was then a part of Canaan; the beauty of the place suggesting to the original Puritan settlers the thought that it was not unworthy of being associated, at least by name, with the promised land. Its individual history began with its separation from Canaan and incorporation in 1823, but the first settler of Canaan, named Peter Hayward, had planted the little log cabin that grew into a prosperous town

WATER STREET, SKOWHEGAN.

near Skowhegan Falls as early as 1771. For a number of years growth was unusually rapid, and sufficient to allow this region to furnish about one hundred men to the advancing of the cause of independence during the Revolutionary War. Despite the set-back given by the embargo and war of 1812, the growth of the town went on steadily up to the time of its incorporation in 1823. The first officials of the town were as follows: Moderator, Joseph Patten; Town Clerk, Samuel Weston; Selectmen, Benjamin Eaton, Joseph Merrill, Samuel Weston, Josiah Parlin. When the town was incorporated it went by the name of Milburn, but the majority of the people preferred to keep the ancient name of the place, and, as is generally the case, they had their way, and the name was changed back again to Skowhegan. The town contains 19,071 acres of valuable territory, forming the best part of the old town of Canaan. Though the town pursued its unbroken path of progress quietly and steadily, it yet took a deep and hearty interest in the great questions which agitated the whole country from 1850 to 1860, and when the war broke out in 1861, it had many loyal sons ready at once to offer their lives and their fortunes for the sake of the country. Enlistments were made in one of the first regiments to leave the State, the

Second Maine Volunteers, Col. Jameson, from Bangor. Other Skowhegan men went out and performed gallant service, chiefly in the ranks of the Sixth, Ninth, Fourteenth, Eighteenth, Twenty-eighth and Thirty-first Regiments. Of over a hundred who enlisted, at least a third were tenderly and deeply mourned by those who could ill spare their generous, noble lives, and no fitting commemoration of their memory has been spared. The quarter of a century which has elapsed since the war, while witnessing no remarkable changes, has seen steady progress and evolution in every department of town life. The germs of prosperity have been carefully nurtured, and are springing up with promise of large harvests. The sanitary, educational, and religious interests have received general and careful attention. In two lines, especially during the present decade, when the greatest progress has been seen, namely, the commercial and summer tourist interests have marked advances been made.

Situated on an advantageous portion of the great Kennebec, the possibilities of development of water-power at Skowhegan have long attracted the attention of careful observers, but only in recent years have they received a tithe of the improvement which they deserve. The most noted of these powers is situated at Skowhegan Falls. At this point there is a natural fall of twenty-eight feet in half a mile, almost all in perpendicular sections, and the power obtainable can be further increased by dams so as to be practicably unlimited. The bed and banks of the river, as well as an island in the center of the channel, are all of solid rock, so that admirable sites can be obtained, and the present "North" and "South Channel" dams are rendered of impregnable strength. The bulk of the manufacturing interest is situated here at the "Falls," and largely on the channel island, where the opportunities for an advantageous site are unsurpassed. There is another immense power lower down the stream, at what is known as the "Basin," and a great fortune here awaits the skilled eye and experienced management of some enterprising merchant who may develop it. There are also two other good privileges on the Wesserunsett Stream, which empties into the Kennebec at Skowhegan. Not only the fact that there is such a vast water-power here, but its situation as the natural and controling center of trade for all upper Somerset, and parts of Franklin and Piscataquis Counties, the great quantities of lumber available here, and the advantageous privileges of site and exemption from taxes given to manufacturers, render this a peculiarly favorable location for commercial enterprises. The business of Skowhegan has considerably increased during the present decade, and is undoubtedly destined to undergo great development in the not far distant future.

Skowhegan has also enjoyed no small share of the swelling tide of summer visitors every year. The drives and walks through the surrounding country are unsurpassed, the hunting in the forests and fishing in river and lake are excellent, and the facilities for quiet, homelike board render the pleasant old town of Skowhegan one of the most satisfactory places to spend a summer vacation in the State.

LEADING BUSINESS MEN

OF

SKOWHEGAN, ME.

Dr. S. F. Conant, Inventor and Proprietor of the Health Restorer and Life Preserver, Compound Vapor Bath, Elm Street, Skowhegan. Truly "the world moves," and the methods and practices of one age are superseded by the more intelligent operations of a succeeding one. This is not the place (even if we had the requisite space) to enter into a discussion of the old methods of healing disease. Everybody is more or less familiar with their general principles, and everybody is aware that they often fail to have the desired effect. The propriety of filling an already weakened stomach with nauseous and sometimes poisonous drugs, is questioned by some of the foremost thinkers of the day, and the "regular" physician who confessed that every dose of medicine was "a blind experiment," only voiced the inward conviction of many of his brother practitioners. It is generally conceded now that *nature* really effects the cure, when one is wrought, and that the true province of the physician is to use his skill to assist nature as much as possible. It is on this great principle that the highly-valuable invention of Dr. S. F. Conant acts, and it was only after a most thorough and exhaustive study of the subject that the doctor brought his invention to its present perfection. Briefly speaking, it is an air-tight receptacle in which the patient is placed, the head alone remaining outside. When in this position the patient is given what is known as the "Compound Vapor Bath," the result of which is to disinfect poison and expel disease. In the first place let us remember that if our body secretes its own wastes faster than it excretes, it must necessarily become diseased. Now, then, what is to become of the body when thus charged, if those wastes are retained until they become tainted or decomposed? Disease in some of its forms is inevitable; and show me the person so scientific as to be able to inform us where it will manifest itself or what form it will take. Now Dr. Conant declares that a pure blooded body cannot become diseased while pure, or free from poisonous deposits. And furthermore, that upon these elements deposited, all disease, regardless of the names invented for the various symptoms, finds a basis. Consequently, if we would respect the demands of mother nature, we must take measures to unload the blood and tissues of these deposits, instead of undertaking to coerce by drugging the dyspeptic stomach. He is often accused of promising to cure everybody by the C. V. Baths; while the truth is he claims to cure no one. But whatever name is given to the disease, if the vital organs are not already fatally destroyed he declares his ability to extract all movable deposits, and by permeating the veinous or capillary system by these purifying fumes, the entire system is disinfected in a prompt and effective manner, thus inviting nature to the restoration of physical power. Such a thing as a healing remedy has not, as yet, been invented outside of nature; and all that any reasonable man can claim is to aid nature by removing the embargo that her work may go on unobstructed. No one will dispute the person who declares his ability to smoke a ham to the marrow in a few hours. Then why dispute his ability to smoke the entire body through much quicker while he has the absorbents actually at work, by the increased circulation of the veinous blood as a vehicle of transportation? Were it not for this veinous distributer does anyone suppose that morphine would ever be injected through the skin for the purpose of bringing the system under its paralyzing influence? It is too definitely established now for anyone to dispute his ability to feed the blood by this method, as he is armed to-day with thousands of positive witnesses who have dared to take his advice with the treatment and adhered to the work until the body has been unloaded of these elements of disease. His failures have been almost universally from those chronic invalids who have been led to believe that there was no reason why they should not be cured by as few Baths as their neighbor had been. No one can tell how many loads there are to be hauled away, but patiently back up the little cart so long as there is any poisonous rubbish to load on, is his advice. As a matter of course there are cases so fatally advanced as to render it impossible for nature to get in her work after renovation. And there are other conditions where the patient has not vitality enough left to go on with the work; but in each and every case injury is out of the question, and he hereby challenges any practitioner, by any method, to compare with his average, even with the most chronic invalids who are entire strangers to him, but have followed his advice with his method in their homes. He cordially invites all who are suffering from disease in any of its forms, to investigate the results of this principle in their own behalf. We might enter into elaborate explanations, showing that the thing is possible; that through the numberless pores of the skin, action and re-action can take place,—disease going out and health and life coming in, —but for what purpose? No more convincing proof can be asked by the most skeptical than that many serious symptoms of disease *have* been cured in this way, and this fact can be easily verified by proper inquiries. Dr. Conant calls the Compound Vapor Bath a "Health Restorer and Life Preserver," and it certainly deserves its name. He is a native of Topsham, Maine, and a member of the Odd Fellows, being one of the best-known residents of Skowhegan. His rooms are located on Elm Street, four apartments being utilized and every necessary facility provided. Callers will receive polite and considerate treatment, and all desired information will be cheerfully given.

E. F. Fairbrother & Co., Wholesale and Retail Dealers in Furniture, Carpets, Bedding, etc., Nos. 65 and 67 Water Street, Skowhegan. There is many a home in Skowhegan and vicinity that is wholly or partially furnished from the establishment of E. F. Fairbrother & Co., and the fact that this is the case, and that those who have patronized this concern in the past are most enthusiastic in its praise at the present, speaks louder and more eloquently than words can, regarding the resources of the house and the treatment accorded customers. Business was begun in 1877 by Mr. E. F. Fairbrother, who afterward took Mr. Geo. C. Fairbrother into partnership, under the firm-name of E. F. Fairbrother & Co. This association continued until terminated by the death of the junior partner in July, 1887, and Mr. E. F. Fairbrother has since retained sole control. He is a native of Skowhegan, and few of our business men are better known, none being more thoroughly respected. Mr. Fairbrother is very upright in his dealings, rejecting even the appearance of anything wrong, and the public have long since learned that all goods coming from his store are sure to prove as represented every time. His experience of ten years, from 1867 to 1877, in the Wholesale Furniture business in Boston, has been of great advantage to him in buying goods, and in many other ways. The premises occupied comprise four floors, measuring 30x122 feet, and contain a very heavy and valuable stock of Furniture, Carpets, Bedding, etc. They are located at Nos. 65 and 67 Water Street, and are well worthy of a visit from any one who contemplates buying anything in the House-furnishing line. The assortment contains the most fashionable novelties as well as staple goods, and is fresh and desirable in quality, as Mr. Fairbrother does not believe in letting his stock mold on his hands, and puts his prices at such figures that a brisk business is always carried on. Both a wholesale and retail trade is transacted, and employment is given to four competent and polite assistants. Orders will be promptly delivered, and the goods are sure to suit the most fastidious.

Weston & Brainard, Manufacturers of Hard and Soft Wood Lumber, Island Avenue, Skowhegan. There are few houses engaged in a similar line of business, and located in this State, that are in a position to fill orders more promptly and satisfactorily than that carried on by Messrs. Weston & Brainard, on Island Avenue. Lumber has been manufactured on this water power for nearly one hundred years, but not till 1880, when the present firm was formed, had it been attempted on a large scale. Mr. Weston is a native of Skowhegan, while Mr. Brainard was born in Columbia, Cal., this latter gentleman being connected with the Odd Fellows. Both members of the firm are thoroughly acquainted with the Lumber business, and not a small part of the efficiency of their mills is due to the close personal supervision constantly exercised. The manufacture of Hard and Soft Wood Lumber is carried on very extensively, the plant covering an area of three acres of ground, and comprising three buildings beside numerous storage-sheds, etc. Both a wholesale and retail business is done, employment being afforded to fifty men or more, and the most improved labor-saving machinery utilized. The past year machinery for baling sawdust and other waste material has been put in. This, while quite a departure from ordinary saw mill methods, promises to prove a successful venture. All orders are filled at the lowest market rates, and large or small commissions are executed with equal promptness and care.

Dr. H. Leavitt & Son, Dentists, Water Street, Skowhegan. Undoubtedly the best way to preserve the teeth is to take proper care of them in the first place, but as unfortunately most of us have so abused our teeth when young as to cause them to show unmistakable symptoms of decay by the time that we have arrived at years of discretion, it becomes necessary to call in skillful professional aid, in order to prevent matters becoming any worse. It is well for the community that there are many competent Dentists ready to undertake the care of the teeth at moderate charges, but it is very bad for the community that there are a few ignorant and dishonest practitioners, who profess to be masters of the science of Dentistry, but who are unfit to treat anything more delicate than the teeth of a saw. Be sure therefore that you visit a competent operator, and if you decide to avail yourself of the accommodations offered by Dr. H. Leavitt & Son, doing business on Water Street, you may congratulate yourself on having escaped all danger of receiving any but the most skillful and honorable treatment. The senior member, Dr. H. Leavitt, is a native of Athens, Me., and is a member of the Free Masons, and Frank A. is a native of Dover, Me. Dr. H. Leavitt opened his present office here in 1867. The premises occupied are conveniently situated and appropriately fitted up, comprising two rooms, of the dimensions of 20x30 feet. Drs. Leavitt are prepared to fill all orders in the line of operative dentistry, and the work they have done in the past speaks better than words could, concerning what may be expected in the future. Their charges are fair and moderate, and callers will receive prompt attention.

LEADING BUSINESS MEN OF SKOWHEGAN.

Estes & Ward, Clothing, Hats and Caps, Water Street, Skowhegan. There are two ways of finding out anything. One is by persistent inquiry, and the other by careful observation. For example, suppose a stranger in Skowhegan should want to know where he could buy a suit of Clothes, a Hat, Underwear—in short, a whole outfit—to the best advantage. Well, he might go about asking those whom he thought would be able to tell him, or he might observe what establishments offered the most attractions and seemed to be doing the largest business, but in either case he would probably find himself at the end of his investigations in the store carried on by Messrs. Estes and Ward, on Water Street. The senior member started in 1861; this firm has been in operation since 1883, but they have the faculty of "getting there" very strongly developed, and offer advantages that many a much older house cannot equal. Mr. Estes is a native of Durham, Me., and Mr. Ward of Skowhegan. Both partners are personally well known here, both in a business way and socially. The premises utilized, comprise one floor and a basement of the dimensions of 20x100 feet, and as fine a stock of Ready-Made Clothing, Hats and Caps, Men's Furnishings, etc., is carried as can be found in this section of the State. Three efficient and courteous assistants are employed and customers are waited upon with celerity and politeness. "Call once and you'll call again," is a safe thing to say when talking about this establishment, for it is the almost invariable rule with those who give Messrs. Estes & Ward a trial order. Prices are very low and only reliable goods are handled.

White & Wildes, Dealers in Dry Goods, Water Street, Skowhegan. The feminine passion for shopping is often made sport of by the lords of creation; but if every store were conducted on the same principles that are noticeable in that carried on by Messrs. White & Wildes on Water Street, there would certainly be no need of offering any explanation of a fondness to visit them. The establishment to which we refer was opened in 1879, and few, if any, of our local business enterprises, have become so firmly implanted in the favor of the public, during the past ten years. Both members of the firm were born here, and both are thoroughly familiar with the details of their business, and are determined to carry their store as near to perfection as circumstances will allow. The premises in use comprise one floor and a basement, and are of the dimensions of 22x125 feet. Both a wholesale and retail business is done, and employment is given to twenty assistants, orders being filled without delay and with the most gratifying care. The assortment of Foreign and Domestic Dry Goods carried is very complete, for it includes all the latest and most popular novelties as well as full lines of those standard goods that are always in request. Trimmings, Laces, Embroideries and Notions, are also largely handled, and the prices quoted in every department are such as to make it well worth one's while to pay this store a visit. Dressmaking is extensively carried on, and no better work is done in this section of the State. The facilities at hand are excellent, and complete satisfaction is assured.

Bixby & Buck, Wholesale and Retail Dealers in Books, Stationery, Wall Papers and Fancy Goods, 78 Water and 30 Russell Streets, Skowhegan. It would certainly be an unpardonable omission did we fail to make mention of the enterprise carried on by Messrs. Bixby & Buck, at 78 Water and 30 Russell Streets, for this is a representative house of its kind, and ranks with the most prominent in this section of the State. Operations were begun in 1865, under the existing firm name, the partners being Mr. A. R. Bixby, a native of Norridgewock, and Mr. F. R. Buck, who was born in Bucksport. This latter gentleman is connected with the Odd Fellows and both are members of the Free Masons. A large wholesale and retail business is done, and Drugs, Books, Stationery, Paper Hangings, Picture Frames and Fancy Goods are extensively handled. The premises utilized comprise two floors and a basement, measuring 20x100 feet, together with a storehouse of ample proportions. Where so varied a supply of articles is carried, it is impossible in a notice so brief as the exigencies of space require this to be, to make proper detailed mention of the many commodities contained within it; but it may be broadly stated, that whatever the firm of Bixby & Buck offer to their customers, is sure to be reliable, and fully worth the price set upon it. Their stock of Drugs is noted for its freshness and purity, and not a few people make it a rule to have all their prescriptions prepared at this establishment. The Books handled are varied in binding as well as in subject, and not only is a fine assortment of the most popular works carried, but orders will be taken for any desired book, the volume being supplied at the regular market price. Some beautiful patterns are shown in Wall Papers and Picture Frames, and choice designs are also offered at low rates.

A. A. Pierce, Dealer in Meat, Fish and Vegetables, Skowhegan. Many a housekeeper is looking for just such an establishment as that carried on by Mr. A. A. Pierce, on Water Street, and we take pleasure in commending this enterprise to such inquirers, for we know that Mr. Pierce's methods are bound to please, and we know that those who have business dealings with him are outspoken in their approval of the accommodations he offers. Operations were begun in 1886, and the trade has since been steadily increasing. Mr. Pierce is a native of Portland, and a member of the Knights of Pythias, and has a large circle of friends in this vicinity. The premises utilized are of the dimensions of 20x40 feet, and the stock on hand is not only large but unusually varied as well, as it includes Meats, Fish and Vegetables. It will be seen that the greater part of the household food supply may be obtained of Mr. Pierce, and as his prices are all that could be reasonably desired as regards fairness, etc., it is well worth while giving him a call. The Meats on hand comprise Beef, Mutton, Veal, Lamb, Pork, etc., and either Choice Cuts or Soup Stock are to be had at all times. The Fish handled are various in kind and fresh in quality, while the Vegetables, received direct from the producers, are quoted at prices as low as the lowest.

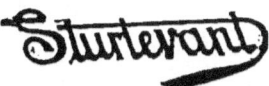

E. E. Sturtevant, Portrait and Crayon Artist. Life-size Crayon Portraits a specialty. Studio, Madison Street, Skowhegan. We take great pleasure in calling attention to the facilities provided by Mr. E. E. Sturtevant for those who wish to obtain accurate and artistic portraits, for a really first-class portrait is a treasure that improves with age, and will be cherished long after other things would be cast aside and forgotten. The ordinary photograph is very unsatisfactory to those who are acquainted with what has been accomplished in the photographic line, for the common photograph does not give one the real expression of the face it purports to represent, although it may be a "striking" likeness for all that. Mr. Sturtevant is wonderfully successful in the posing of his sitters, and as all his work is very carefully finished, one may visit more than one of the celebrated Boston and New York studios before obtaining equally gratifying results. This we know from personal experience, and to all who wish to get portraits of real interest and value, we would say, "Go to Sturtevant's." Mr. Sturtevant is a native of Milo, Me., and is connected with both the Free Masons and the Odd Fellows. He began operations here in 1882, and has built up a large and increasing patronage by strictly legitimate methods. The premises occupied comprise three apartments of the dimensions of 30x40 feet. A specialty is made of Life-size Crayon Portraits, and those who know what wonderfully life-like results have been attained by Mr. Sturtevant, will not be surprised to learn that this is one of the most popular branches of his profession. His prices are moderate, and all should visit his studio.

Mrs. B. R. Flagg, Millinery and Fancy Goods, Madison Street, Skowhegan. An establishment which deserves special and flattering mention, is that carried on by Mrs. B. R. Flagg, on Madison Street. It is deserving of this treatment on many accounts, among which may be noted the fact of its long-standing, for it was founded over a quarter of a century ago, operations having been begun in 1860. Mrs. Flagg is a native of Newcastle, Me., and few ladies of this place are better-known or more generally esteemed. Her store has long been a favorite resort with those seeking Millinery and Fancy Goods that could be depended upon, and the enterprise shown in obtaining the latest novelties in these lines, is fully noted and cordially appreciated by the public. The store is 20x30 feet in size, and the stock on hand is worthy of much more than a passing glance. Mrs. Flagg's exceptional experience, combined with natural good taste, enable her to offer valuable advice in regard to the selection of Millinery Goods, etc., and she is ever ready to offer suggestions to such as may desire a little help in determining what is best suited to them. Custom Work is attended to at short notice and low rates, and Millinery Goods of all kinds are at hand for customers to choose from.

W. H. Fuller, Druggist and Apothecary, 23 Madison Street, Skowhegan. We doubt if we could name a single enterprise in Skowhegan that is more generally or favorably known, than that conducted by Mr. W. H. Fuller, at No. 23 Madison Street, nor is there any reason for surprise that this should be so. The enterprise in question was inaugurated very nearly thirty years ago, having had its inception in 1859, and during all this time has been a great public accommodation, so that its popularity is perfectly natural. Mr. Fuller is a native of Readfield, and is personally very extensively known throughout Somerset Co. The premises utilized by him measure 20x50 feet, and the stock on hand comprises Drugs, Medicines, Chemicals, etc., in great variety, a full assortment of fine Toilet Goods, etc., being also at hand, and the fitting of Trusses a specialty. Employment is given to two assistants, who will be found courteous and careful in their filling of orders, and the means at hand for the quick and accurate preparation of physicians' prescriptions are believed to be as complete and as well advised as any to be found in this section. A specialty is made of this branch of the business, and no pains are spared to insure satisfaction to every customer. The charges are reasonable and right, and so numerous and well considered are the precautions taken against error, that it is apparently impossible for any serious mistake to go undetected.

Thompson & Howes, Dealers in Fresh Meats, Fish and Vegetables. South Side Market. The "South Side Market" has "got on the right side" of many of our most experienced householders, for the inducements offered to customers are hard to resist, and the quality of the goods handled is always first-class. One thing that strikes a stranger doing business with this house for the first time, is the cheerfulness and alacrity with which he is waited upon. Nothing is more exasperating than to go into a store and have to wait around until some one sees fit to attend to you, and yet this experience is the rule rather than the exception in some establishments that could be named. The proprietors of the South Side Market—Messrs. Thompson & Howes—don't do business that way, and callers at their store may feel assured of being served at the earliest possible moment. The result of this and other popular features of the management, is to be seen in the large business that has been built up since operations were begun in 1886. The premises occupied are 20x40 feet in size and the assortment of goods on hand comprises Fresh Meats, Fish and Vegetables, in great variety. Employment is given to two efficient and polite assistants, and as no pains are spared to facilitate operations as much as possible, and the system of delivery is prompt and accurate, a good deal of business is done with very little fuss and trouble. The firm consists of Mr. Frank Thompson and Mr. Fred Howes, both being natives of Skowhegan, and the latter a member of the Odd Fellows. The firm is a popular one, and its members give close personal attention to business.

R. T. Patten, Registered Pharmacist, 43 Water Street, Skowhegan. One generally feels considerable hesitation in giving advice as to what physician shall be consulted, or at what Pharmacy prescriptions shall be compounded, for the consequences of advising wrongly in either case are too grave to be lightly assumed. Still we feel perfectly sure that all who may patronize the establishment conducted by Mr. R. T. Patten, at No. 43 Water Street, will have no reason to regret having done so, for we know that the stock of Drugs, Medicines and Chemicals there carried is full and complete, and we also know that Mr. Patten may be depended upon to compound every prescription with which he is intrusted with care. He is a Skowhegan young man, and is connected with the Masons, is a prominent officer in the Wheel Club and Athletic Association, and is the champion bicyclist of Maine, and opened his present store in 1887. He is always ready to aid the furtherance of business or pleasure. The premises occupied are of the dimensions of 20x50 feet, and are well arranged and fitted up for the purposes for which they are used. Mr. Patten endeavors to handle only Pure and Fresh Drugs, etc., and secures that end so far as possible by procuring his supplies from the most reputable sources, and manufacturing most of his preparations from the crude drugs. He is very moderate in his charges, and employs sufficient assistance to enable him to fill all orders without undue delay.

H. D. Patterson & Co., Fancy Grocery, Tea and Coffee Store, 143 Water Street, Skowhegan. An establishment that has come to the front rapidly since it was opened in 1886, is that carried on by Messrs. H. D. Patterson & Co., at No. 143 Water Street. This firm is what is known in some parts of the country as a "hustler," and when it sets out to accomplish a thing, it takes no half-way measures, but just works for all it is worth, until the desired end is attained. When the business was started it was with the idea that there was room here for a first-class Fancy Grocery and Tea and Coffee store, and the result has proved that this idea was entirely correct. The firm are jobbers of Teas, Coffees and Flour, and run two large stores, giving their retail customers the full advantage of dealing with a house that does business on a large scale, and gets corresponding reductions in rates. Mr. Patterson is a native of Belfast, Me., and is very thoroughly acquainted with the Grocery business, both in its wholesale and retail forms. He is a fine judge of Teas and Coffees, and the goods offered by the firm are remarkable for their rich and delicious flavor no less than for the low prices at which they are quoted. The premises utilized comprise two floors, measuring 20x100 feet, and we can assure our readers that none of this large amount of space is wasted, for the immense stock carried occupies all the available room. Those doing business here may depend upon being treated with courtesy, and above all, with that fairness and liberality that distinguish an honorable house from one that is of the opposite character.

N. S. Hawkes, Photographer, Water St., Skowhegan. Few people, aside from those connected with the profession, have any idea of the number of things that must be attended to in order to produce a good photographic likeness, and if more were generally known regarding the difficulties that must be met and overcome, there would be much less surprise expressed at the rarity with which a really good photograph is met with. Among the best-equipped artists in this line that we know of in this section, is Mr. N. S. Hawkes, whose studio is located on Water Street, over Skowhegan Market. Mr. Hawkes was born in Auburn, and began operations here in 1885. Three apartments are occupied and every attention is paid to the comfort and convenience of patrons, prompt attention being given to every caller and every needful facility being at hand to enable orders to be filled at short notice, in an eminently first-class manner. The work done at this studio is very carefully finished, and especial attention is given to securing a perfect likeness, and at the same time preserving that softness of outline so indispensable to a really artistic picture. Mr. Hawkes is remarkably low in his prices and is straightforward and courteous in his dealings, so that it is a pleasure to do business with him. He is a member of the Grand Army and has a war record of exceptional interest, as he took part in some of the most famous engagements of the Rebellion; among these were: Second Bull Run, Gettysburgh, Fredericksburgh, etc., and while a prisoner in the hands of the enemy, Mr. Hawkes saw the inside of Andersonville and Richmond.

E. B. Carter, Custom-Made Clothing, Water Street, Skowhegan. There are certain subjects which every man feels an interest in as a matter of course, and one of the foremost of these is that pertaining to Clothing, and how to buy it to the best advantage. It is unnecessary here to point out the advantages of being well-dressed. Every thinking person is aware that, — other things being equal,— a well-dressed man will meet with better treatment, make a more favorable impression, be able to transact business to better advantage, and in short be superior in about every respect to a man who is handicapped by shabby garments. Therefore we will only say, that none but the rich can afford to dress poorly, and even then they lose more than they gain by so doing. A call at the establishment of Mr. E. B. Carter, on Water Street, will convince the most obdurate that dressing well need not necessarily cost a great deal of money, for Mr. Carter produces Custom-Made Clothing at remarkably low prices, and he guarantees fit, goods and making to be what they really are—first-class. This establishment was opened in 1885, and it is a great favorite with those aware of its merits, for at few places can so liberal a return be obtained for every dollar expended. Premises measuring 20x40 feet are occupied, and employment given to from 8 to 15 assistants. Mr. Carter carries a fine assortment of Foreign and Domestic Fabrics to select from, and makes up garments in the very latest style at short notice.

Heselton Bros. & Co., Dealers in Fancy Dry Goods, Corsets, Ladies' Underwear, Linen Goods, etc.; 5 and 10 Cent Goods a specialty, 137 Water Street, Skowhegan. There is not a doubt but that many of our lady readers, residing in Skowhegan, know much more about the establishment carried on by Messrs. Heselton Brothers & Co., than we do, for the character of the goods by this firm is such as to appeal directly to feminine trade, and as the enterprise has been in operation since 1881, abundant opportunity has been afforded to judge of the business methods of the concern and the extent to which it is entitled to the patronage of the public. That those most familiar with the enterprise fully share our opinion concerning it, we know, for otherwise no such extensive business could be carried on as is now the case. Fancy Dry Goods, Corsets, Ladies' Underwear, Linen Goods, Hosiery, Laces, Ribbons, etc., are some of the more prominent articles handled; and extensive dealings are also had in 5, 10 and 25 Cent Goods, these being made a specialty and given particular attention. The premises occupied are located at No. 137 Water Street, and are of the dimensions of 40x75 feet, with plate glass front. The store is one of the best arranged for the business carried on by this firm of any to be found on the Kennebec river. Ladies accustomed to trade here speak in the highest terms of the celerity and willingness shown in serving them. The prices will bear comparison with those quoted at any similar store, quality considered, and goods are never misrepresented in the least degree. M. B. Heselton, senior member of this firm, is a member of Carrabasset Lodge, No. 34, I. O. O. F., of Parmenas Encampment, No. 18, I. O. O. F.; also of the Grand Lodge and Grand Encampment, I. O. O. F. of Maine, and D. D. Grand Patriarch of the 14th District of Maine. He has held the office of Scribe of the Encampment for six terms.

H. W. Chaney, Carpenter and Builder, Russell Street, Skowhegan. It would be an excellent thing if every man could own the house he lives in, and it is to be regretted that so many who *could* have homes of their own if they chose, are content to live in hired houses, and every ten years or so pay the price of a building for the mere privilege of occupying one. The cost of a comfortable and convenient dwelling-house is considerably less than what many people think, for although it is of course easy to spend $10,000 on an edifice of this kind, still one-tenth of that sum will build a cozy and comfortable home. Should you feel disposed to question our figures, or if you are interested in the subject, and disposed to learn more regarding it, just call on Mr. H. W. Chaney, doing business on Russell Street. He is a native of Skowhegan, and has carried on operations here since 1884, and as a carpenter and builder ranks with the foremost in this vicinity. Mr. Chaney thoroughly understands his business, and always having the interests of his patrons at heart, can offer some valuable suggestions to intending builders. He occupies two floors, measuring 20x30 feet, and employs six competent and experienced assistants. Estimates will be furnished on application, and every facility afforded for the ready and satisfactory dispatch of business. Jobbing orders are also given prompt attention, and Repairing will be attended to without delay and at moderate rates.

Doran Furnace Company, Madison St., Skowhegan. The question whether Stoves or Furnaces afford the best means of heating a house, is to be decided entirely by a consideration of the circumstances in the case; but it may be truthfully said that very few people who have once experienced the conveniences of a Furnace, are content to go back to Stoves again. By the use of the Doran Wood Furnace,

those living where wood is plenty, can get any required amount of heat at a very small expense, either of time or money, for this Furnace is very economical of fuel, and is simple in construction and most effective in action, requiring very little care. The patentee, Mr. W. Doran, is a native of Augusta, and a member of the Free Masons. He carries on business on Madison Street, and deals in Furnaces, Stoves, Tin Ware, Plumbing Materials, etc. Business was begun in 1856, this establishment having been for years one of Skowhegan's representative business-houses. The premises utilized comprise two floors and a basement, and measure 30x80 feet. Both a wholesale and retail trade is carried on, and the advantages enjoyed are such that bottom prices are quoted on all the goods handled. Jobbing orders are given immediate and painstaking attention, and Plumbing of all kinds will be done in the most thorough and satisfactory manner, at low prices. Mr. Doran employs four competent assistants, and guarantees that every article bought of him shall prove as represented. Callers are assured courteous attention, and the establishment fully deserve its unquestionable popularity.

Hotel Heselton, Bath-room and Billiard Hall, Livery and Sale Stable connected. Headquarters for the Forks, Athens, Canaan and Mercer Stages, F. B. Heselton, proprietor, Water Street, Skowhegan. The man who can put up at the "Heselton," partake of its accommodations, experience its hospitality, and then go away unsatisfied, is to be pitied, for he will find it impossible to get suited anywhere. This probably seems a somewhat strong statement to those unacquainted with the hotel to which we refer, but we have no fear but what those in a position to speak from experience will be practically unanimous in indorsing what we have said. The Hotel Heselton was built in 1881, has been newly furnished throughout, and has every "modern convenience," in the full sense of that much-abused term. It is heated by steam and lighted by electricity, and is so constructed and arranged as to provide for an abundance of fresh, pure air in summer time. The building is of very pleasing design, and contains four floors, there being seventy-five guest-rooms. A thoroughly appointed Bath-room and Billiard Hall are to be found on the premises, and the Livery and Sale Stable connected with the House is first-class in every respect, and fully deserving of the liberal patronage it receives, Teams being furnished at all hours at very moderate rates. This Hotel is the Headquarters for the Forks, Athens, Canaan and Mercer Stages, and is one of the most popular in the entire State, with travelers who have experienced its accommodations. Mr. Heselton, the genial proprietor, is a native of Skowhegan, and a member of the Odd Fellows. One of the most popular features of his management of the House is that connected with the character of the *cuisine*, for the table is supplied with the best that the market affords, and a pleasing variety is practiced in the Bill of Fare. Employment is given to twenty-five efficient assistants, and the service is prompt, polite, and in short such as would be expected in so well-managed an institution.

R. S. Hillman, Wholesale and Retail Dealer in Tea, Coffee and Spices. Also Dealer in 5, 10 and 25-cent Goods, Peddlers' Supplies, Glass, Tin, Crockery Ware and Notions. No. 39 Water Street, Skowhegan. Tea, Coffee and Spices are articles that are sold at almost innumerable stores; but for all that it is by no means easy to find a place where fine quality is combined with low price. In some establishments, doing a small trade in this line, the goods themselves are all right when first placed in stock, but they are disposed of so slowly that they become deteriorated by age and are then distinctly inferior to what they should be. Therefore, it is well to buy such articles of a dealer making a specialty of handling them, and we know of none more worthy of patronage than Mr. R. S. Hillman, whose store may be found at No. 39 Water Street. This gentleman was born in Troy, Me., and is connected with both the Free Masons and the Odd Fellows. He founded the establishment to which we have reference in 1885, and the extent of his present trade is sufficient indication of how the inducements he has to offer are appreciated. One floor and a storehouse are occupied and a large stock is carried, which is as varied as it is large, for it comprises (besides Tea, Coffee and Spices), 5, 10 and 25-cent Goods, Peddlers' Supplies. Glass, Tin, Crockery Ware and Notions, etc., etc. Employment is given to four competent and obliging assistants, and no pains are spared to please and satisfy every customer, the goods being reliable and the prices low. Mr. Hillman also handles Old Junk and Paper Stock, and, in fact, is one of the busiest men to be found in this locality.

LEADING BUSINESS MEN OF SKOWHEGAN. 189

Mrs. H. H. Bigelow, Millinery, Madison Street, Skowhegan. Just what that quality is that enables the person possessing it to beautify a thing with a few deft touches, is a question that has puzzled many a head beside our own. Call it "good taste," and you have not described it, for not a few have unexceptionable taste, and yet lack this power of which we speak. But no matter what it is called, it is indisputable that it exists, and a large share of the pronounced success that has been won by the enterprise carried on by Mrs. H. H. Bigelow, on Madison Street, is due to her possession of this "extra sense." The lady alluded to began operations in 1887, and has proved herself to be particularly well fitted for the carrying on of such an enterprise. She carries a fine stock of Millinery Goods, which although not so large as some, is selected with such excellent taste and skill that it embraces articles suited to all ages, conditions and preferences. Mrs. Bigelow employs three competent and polite assistants, and is in a position to turn out custom work at short notice, and in the most satisfactory manner. Trimmed and untrimmed hats and bonnets, in the latest shapes, are offered at the lowest market prices, and the most popular novelties in the millinery line are always to be had here on favorable terms.

Woodbury, Morrill & Gage, Flour, Grain, Groceries and Provisions, opposite the Depot, Skowhegan. Cash paid for all kinds of Produce. The establishment carried on by the well-known house whose card we print above, is a noteworthy one in many respects, and is so managed as to make it one of the most popular enterprises of the kind in this vicinity. Business was begun in 1878, and has been successfully carried on. This concern spares neither time nor trouble in improving the efficiency of its service, and as a consequence, not only carries on one of the most liberally-managed establishments in Skowhegan, but is constantly adding to the claim it already has on the patronage and cordial support of the public. Mr. Woodbury was born in Farmington, Mr. Morrill in Hartland, and Mr. Gage in Salem. Messrs. Woodbury and Morrill are both members of the Odd Fellows and Free Masons. Premises measuring 125x100 feet are occupied, opposite the Depot, and a large and finely-selected stock is carried, comprising Flour, Grain, Groceries and Provisions. Both a wholesale and a retail business is done, and employment is afforded to two competent and polite assistants. Country Produce is made a specialty, and cash will be paid for all commodities of this kind. The assortment of Flour handled is an unusually desirable one, and being made up of goods selected especially for family use, it is well worthy the careful inspection of householders. Decided inducements are also offered in the purchase of Grain of all kinds, while tho the line of Groceries handled is very complete, and embraces both Staple and Fancy Articles in great variety. They are also one of the largest Wool buyers in Somerset County. Customers are assured of perfectly fair dealing at this establishment, and as the prices are very low, no better place can be found at which to leave orders.

Horatio W. Cushing, Apothecary and Druggist, Water Street, opposite Post-office, Skowhegan. Although there are not a few people who consider that Apothecaries, as a rule, have a remarkably easy time of it, still we question if there is another business or profession — call it what you will — where the responsibilities assumed are graver, and the average reward more insignificant. To establish a modern Apothecary store calls for no mean sum of money; the fixtures are numerous and expensive, the stock must be large, and must contain goods subject to deterioration, and the competition is sufficiently keen to reduce profits to a minimum. But after all, the chief point to be considered is the responsibility. Intrusted with the dispensing of the most deadly agents known to chemistry — agents as sure and almost as swift in their action as a lightning-stroke — the apothecary must fill prescription after prescription, must combine all possible ingredients, and if one small mistake is made, who can foresee the result? In a well-managed Drug store, however, no mistakes are made, and a fine example of such an establishment is that carried on by Mr. Horatio W. Cushing, on Water Street, opposite the Post-office. This undertaking has been carried on since 1873, and is one of the best known in this vicinity, for the methods displayed in its management have met with the favor of the public, and have resulted in a large business being built up. Mr. Cushing is a native of this place, and is connected with the Odd Fellows. Premises of the dimensions of 20x60 feet, are occupied, two competent and careful assistants employed, and especial attention paid to the accurate compounding of prescriptions at short notice.

E. L. Walker, Painter and Paper Hanger, Water Street, Skowhegan. It is wonderful the change that can be made in a house by the proper use of Paint and Wall Paper, and if some people only realized how much can be done in this line for a little money, they would no longer be content to allow their premises to remain shabby and worn. There are very few but what can afford to keep their house well-painted, and, indeed, it is the truest economy in the long run to do this, as the weather soon rots and destroys unpainted wood-work. The skillfulness with which paint is applied has much to do with its lasting powers, and in order to get the best results in this respect, it would be well to employ the services of Mr. E. L. Walker, who has had a large experience in such work, and who has every facility at hand to fill orders promptly and cheaply. Mr. Walker is a native of Skowhegan, and started his present enterprise in 1880. He employs ten efficient assistants, and occupies premises located on Russell and Madison Streets, and measuring 24x50 feet. Orders for Painting, Paper-hanging, etc., are attended to at once, and we can assure our readers that they will have no reason to regret favoring Mr. Walker with an order. His charges are moderate, and as he uses selected stock and employs skilled assistants, durability is assured.

George D. Arnold, Dealer in Flour and Groceries, Country Produce, Oranges, Lemons, Figs, Raisins, Canned Goods, etc., etc. Cash paid for Eggs, 51 Water Street, Skowhegan. It is frequently remarked by those doing business with Mr. George D. Arnold, at No. 51 Water Street, that he is a good man to deal with, and indeed, as one becomes familiar with his methods, no surprise is felt, either at his personal popularity or the magnitude of his trade. He was born in Skowhegan, and is a member of the Odd Fellows, inaugurating his present enterprise in 1880. The premises utilized by Mr. Arnold comprise two floors and a basement, and measure 20x90 feet. Flour and Groceries of every description are handled, and when we come to add to these Country Produce, Oranges, Lemons, Raisins, Figs, Canned Goods, etc., it will be seen that it is necessary to have rather spacious accommodations. The quality of the goods dealt in here is uniformly first-class, and it is to this that the store owes much of its popularity. When you buy a thing of Mr. Arnold, you know what you've got, and you may always depend on every representation that may be made by him or his assistants, as all goods are guaranteed, and no false statements are made concerning them. The line of Flour for Family use that Mr. Arnold carries is a complete and skillfully selected one, and those wishing a bag or barrel of this indispensable commodity would do well to place their orders right here. Goods are promptly delivered, and polite attention assured to all. He also deals largely in Vermont Cheese (Sage and Plain) and Butter. Also receives Fleischmann's Yeast Cakes *three* times per week *direct* from the *Factory*, saving twelve hours delay in Portland.

George Cushing, Retail and Jobbing Druggist and Apothecary, Bookseller and Stationer, 31 Water Street, Skowhegan. Also Agent for American Express Company. The establishment conducted by Mr. George Cushing, at No. 31 Water Street, is one of the best known in this section, not only on account of the many years the enterprise has been carried on in the town of Skowhegan, but from the reason of its being the pioneer Drug and Book house in Somerset County. Business was begun over half a century ago by Mr. William Dyer, this gentleman founding the enterprise in 1837. In the fall of 1860 the firm-name became Dyer & Cushing, and in 1880 the present proprietor assumed sole control. Mr. Cushing is a native of Skowhegan, and is connected with the Free Masons. The premises utilized by him comprise three and one-half floors, of the dimensions of 24x72 feet, and an immense stock is carried, both a wholesale and retail business being done. Drugs and Medicines, Books and Stationery, Wrapping Paper and Bags, Fancy Goods, Art Goods and Materials, Cutlery, Bird Cages, Trusses, Confectionery and Fruit, are very largely handled, and employment is given to three competent and courteous assistants, who give prompt attention to customers. The supply of Drugs and Medicines on hand is an exceptionally complete one, and every facility is enjoyed for the filling of orders with accuracy and dispatch. Prescriptions compounded at this establishment are assured the most careful and intelligent handling, and the charges made are reasonable and fair. The supplying of physicians with pure Drugs in quantities is a specialty with this house. Mr. Cushing is Agent of the American Express Company, and the business has his personal oversight. Mr. Cushing also deals largely in Spruce Gum of the very best grades, and sends to dealers in all parts of the State and country. Samples are sent with prices on application. In the month of December a very extensive stock of fine Christmas and art goods is carried, and his store is the most attractive one in all these parts. This is a progressive house, and Mr. Cushing keeps ahead in all the various departments of his business.

M. J. Allen, Mill-Wright, Sawing, Planing, etc., Island Avenue, Skowhegan. Time is money, as everybody knows, in this age of progress, and the amount of time—and consequently of money—that is saved daily by such establishments as that conducted by Mr. M. J. Allen, on Island Avenue, is almost inconceivable. Mr. Allen does Sawing, Planing, Turning, etc., to order, at the very shortest notice, and as his shop is equipped with the latest improved wood-working machinery, and he has ample water-power available to keep things moving, he is in a position to rush orders through with great speed, and to meet all demands that may be made upon his resources. He is a native of Skowhegan, and is very well-known in that vicinity, having inaugurated his present enterprise here in 1874. He is a member of the Ancient Order of United Workmen. The premises utilized are of the dimensions of 50x250 feet, and an adequate force of experienced and skillful assistants is at hand. Mr. Allen is very reasonable in his charges, and as his work is uniformly accurate and satisfactory, it is not surprising that he does a very large business.

E. S. Prescott, Dealer in all kinds of Fancy Groceries, 51 Water Street, Skowhegan. The term "Fancy Groceries" means much more now than it used to, for one article after the other has been put upon the market, until the complete list is a very extensive one, and the business of handling the goods mentioned in it has become a special branch of trade. Certainly one of the best known and most successful establishments, devoted entirely to the sale of Fancy Groceries, is that of which Mr. E. S. Prescott is the proprietor, located at No. 51 Water Street. This enterprise had its inception in 1877, and the rapidity with which it has developed and increased only shows that it has been skillfully and liberally managed. Mr. Prescott is a native of Vassalborough. He employs two efficient and polite assistants, and utilizes premises of the dimensions of 20x50 feet. Fancy Groceries of every description are kept in stock, and callers will find a most complete assortment of choice Canned Goods, Pickles, Relishes, Condiments, Jams, Preserves, and in short everything that properly comes under the head of Fancy Groceries. Mr. Prescott is very reasonable in his prices, for he buys in large quantities, and gives his customers the benefit of the saving made by so doing. Orders are promptly filled.

L. W. Chase, Livery and Sale Stables, Also Dealer in Carriages, Harnesses, Robes, Whips, etc., Water Street, opposite Hotel Heselton. The establishment is well worthy of a visit from all interested in Good Horses or Fine Carriages, for at this place one can either buy or hire anything in this line, and is sure of getting his money's worth in either case. Mr. Chase was born in York, Maine, and is connected with the Odd Fellows. He inaugurated the enterprise to which we have reference in 1885, and has already raised it to a leading position among undertakings of a similar nature in this section of the State. The premises in use comprise two floors of the dimensions of 50x200 feet, and employment is given to three efficient assistants, orders being attended to without delay and in the most satisfactory manner. A good horse and comfortable, stylish carriage, will be supplied by Mr. Chase at a very low price, and strangers in town who wish to get an idea of the lay of the land, can find no more agreeable and economical way in which to do it than by hiring one of his turn-outs for an afternoon or so. Some fine animals are always on hand for sale purposes and those who are wise enough to buy their horses of reputable parties, would do well to note what Mr. Chase has to offer. Carriages, Harnesses, Robes and Whips, are also sold at the lowest market rates, and everything will prove as represented.

FAIRGRIEVES RESTAURANT
10 & 12 Madison St.,
SKOWHEGAN, - - MAINE.

HISTORICAL SKETCH
—OF—
DEXTER.

DEXTER is one of the most enterprising and important towns in the northwestern part of Penobscot county. It is reached directly by railroad, branching off from the main line of the Maine Central at Newport, and is situated about thirty miles from Bangor. It lies in the midst of a fertile and beautiful rural district, and contains about 20,370 acres of valuable territory. The town owes its growth and prosperity, not only to the favorable situation it possesses, but also to the efforts of generations of pushing and honorable men who have made it their home. It was first prospected and surveyed in 1772 by interested owners of the land, who thought this an advantageous spot, and wanted to lay out a town here; but the outbreak of the Revolutionary war delayed matters, and it was not actually settled until about thirty years later.

In 1801 the long-talked-of and proposed settlement was made, so that the town dates its birth back almost to the beginning of the century. The first settler was Ebenezer Small, who hailed from Gilmanton, N. H. Soon after he had broken soil for his cabin and farm, a man named Elkins arrived, who was long a leading light in the dark, early days of Dexter. So much so, in fact, that the place was popularly known as "Elkinstown" up to its incorporation under its present name in 1816.

Among other early settlers were Joseph Tickler, Seba Smith, Wm. Mitchell, Simeon and John Stafford, Jeremiah Abbot, and Shepley Smith and Maxwell with their families. These energetic and courageous men (for it required some courage to push thus far out into the wilderness in those days, as it was not a pleasure excursion) were all farmers by birth and education. The place was located as township No. 4, fifth range, one of the "no-name townships." The early settlers received grants of good land, and improved them so rapidly that the fame of the town spread through the State and attracted many new-comers. By 1813 the boundary lines throughout the town had been established and all the land was taken up by the settlers. A township charter had been granted in 1804, and so quickly did it grow up that within ten years a movement was started for incorporating it as a town, which resulted in the granting of a town charter by the Legislature on the 17th of June, 1816, the place being named in honor of the Hon. Samuel Dexter of Boston, who was a large owner of real estate here, and prominent in the up building of its interests.

The population which in 1810 was 136, had risen in 1820 to 461, and the valuation in that year was $27,391. The first church edifice here was erected by the Universalists in 1829, and this was followed in 1834 by the church of the First Congregational Society. The population in 1830 was 885, and had increased to 1,464 during the next decade, so that it was evident that the town was making steady progress.

Dexter from its age and situation, was not able to take much part in the war of 1812, but when the British sent their invading fleet up the Penobscot in 1814, fifteen Dexter men volunteered as militia and joined the American forces, many of whom after the repulse, escorted them all the way from Bangor home in unusually quick time. Some of the demoralized forces did not even stop here, but started off in the direction of Moosehead Lake.

An event long remembered in Dexter was the "Great Tornado" of 1848, when the force of the wind tore up great trees by the roots, leveled barns and houses to the ground, and not only created great damage, but endangered many lives. Old people used often to say, and perhaps say still, that there was never seen anything like the "great storm of '48."

In 1850 yet further progress was revealed by the census, the population being 1,948. During the next decade nothing of particular note happened to the town, and while deeply interested in the slavery troubles in other parts of the country, it continued on its way of unchanged growth at home, and in 1860 numbered 2,365 people, with a total valuation of $465,023. The town entered into the civil war with the utmost patriotism and devotion. A large number of its leading citizens and strong young men enlisted in the Union army, most of the volunteers going to the Second, Sixth, Eighteenth, Twenty-fourth and Thirty-first regiments. The town showed great liberality throughout in its appropriations of money and supplies, and the Ladies' Aid Society was very active and generous in its services.

During the first few years after the war the town felt the effects of the "boom" which spread all over the country, so that it grew and prospered rapidly until, in 1870, the population was 2,875, and the valuation, $1,006,966. After this came the great financial depressions throughout the country, and Dexter again felt the effects and fell away some, though only a little, and the old spirit still remained ready to revive

HISTORICAL SKETCH OF DEXTER. 193

at short notice. The population in 1880 was 2,563, and the valuation $963,029. In the present decade a revival of business and general interest has taken place, and greater advancement has been made than for many years past. The manufacturing interests have extended rapidly, and now includes lumber, grain, boots, shoes, carriages and furniture. The population is in the region of 3,000, and the valuation has risen to over a million dollars.

STREET IN DEXTER.

The opening of the branch of the Maine Central from Newport, was a great thing for Dexter, and has contributed much to its wealth and growth. While the business affairs have been prospering, other interests have not been neglected. Education has received the careful attention which the mind of New England has always discerned as extremely important. The schools are conducted liberally and well, and maintained at a very high standard. There is a fine public library here, containing several thousand of carefully selected and valuable books; and in matters relating to intellectual advancement the citizens of this progressive town are well and thoroughly posted. In religious affairs the town is unusually active; there is a representative church here of almost every prominent denomination.

Through the railroad Dexter is coming in for its share of the annual tide of summer visitors to this "Garden State," and moreover is proving itself well worthy of the honor. A quiet and beautiful town, situated in a delightful region, where everything that can charm the eye and nourish the tired frame back to vigorous health is found in abundance, it is no wonder that its fame grows with every passing year.

LEADING BUSINESS MEN

OF

DEXTER, ME.

Amos Abbott & Co., Woolen Manufacturers, Grove Street, Dexter. The manufacture of Woolen Goods is one of Maine's great industries, and it is one that is destined to develop wonderfully, if not interfered with by mistaken legislation. There are many woolen mills carried on in this section of the State, but among them all it would be hard to find another one with a record similar to that held by the undertaking carried on under the firm-name of Amos Abbott & Co. This famous enterprise was inaugurated in 1825, and was the first Woolen Mill in Maine to ship goods to the Boston and New York markets. It has exerted a most powerful influence in extending the celebrity and advancing the true business interests of the town in which it is located. Amos Abbott, its founder, was born in Andover, and Messrs. J. and G. A. Abbott, who now carry it on, are natives of Dexter. The plant utilized covers an area of three acres of ground, and includes seven buildings in addition to a spacious storehouse. The machinery in use is of the most improved description, and is run by waterpower, employment being given to fifty hands. It seems idle for us to refer to the business methods of the gentlemen conducting this time-honored enterprise, for they are already well known, doubtless, to the majority of our readers. The goods made by this Mill are accepted by those in the trade, as the standard by which others may be judged. No pains are spared to make the product fully equal to the reputation so long held by it, and the admirable system in operation at this Mill, permits of every detail of the manufacture being closely scrutinized. Skilled hands are employed, and the pay-roll amounts to some $1,500 per month.

S. D. Fish & Son, Harness Manufacturers, Grove Street, Dexter. Everybody knows that some men can get a great deal more speed or a great deal more work out of a horse than others can, and that, too, without injuring or overworking the animal. Now what is the reason of this? Well, a good part of it is, these men thoroughly understand their business. They have made a study of horse-flesh, know the habits of the animal perfectly, and make it a rule to get acquainted with the individual peculiarities of every horse they handle; for horses have their peculiarities the same as men. Then they have the harness especially suited to the animal that is to wear it, and here is an important point that everybody can appreciate, but that is too often neglected. Messrs. S. D. Fish & Son, doing business on Main Street, are well-qualified to render efficient aid in the selection of a proper harness, for they are manufacturers of skill and experience, and give careful, personal attention to every order. Premises of the dimensions of 30x60 feet are occupied, and employment given to two efficient assistants, thus enabling the firm to turn out Order Work or Repairing at short notice. Only the best of material is used; and the work done here is as remarkable for its strength and durability as it is for its neatness and fine finish. There is carried in stock a fine assortment of Harnesses, Horse Furnishings, etc., and the prices quoted on the same will be found to be "right" in every respect. Messrs. Fish & Son also deal in New and Second-hand Carriages, which they claim to sell very low for cash, or on easy terms. They are also ready at all times to exchange carriages to the mutual satisfaction and benefit of both parties concerned. In fact, to deal with all justly, so that they will come again and influence their friends to call, not only for Carriages, but Harnesses of their own manufacture as well.

Dexter Machine Company, Main Street, Dexter. The position held by Dexter as a manufacturing center, is so prominent that the great majority of our readers are doubtless aware of the many advantages the town offers to those desirous of establishing mechanical industries. Besides being so situated as to afford excellent facilities for the reception of raw materials and the shipping of finished goods, Dexter affords ample and unfailing water-power, a point which is greatly appreciated, as it reduces the cost of production and puts the manufacturer in a position to be quite independent of coal-handlers' strikes and such serious interruptions to business. One of the latest enterprises of magnitude to be inaugurated in this town, is that establised by the Dexter Machine Company, Builders of Machinists' Tools in 1887. This starts out under the most favorable auspices, for it is under the management of able and experienced men who have already given decided proof of their fitness for the position they occupy. The President of the company is a Dexter man by birth and is well known in this vicinity, we refer to Mr. F. E. Burger who also acts as Superintendent. The Secretary and Treasurer is Mr. J. B. Haskell, and the general foreman, Mr. C. S. Kinney. The plant utilized by the company, is of modern construction, and embodies the latest improvements, thus enabling orders to be filled at short notice and at bottom rates. Employment is afforded to ten skilled assistants.

B. L. Call, Photographer, Grove Street, Dexter. To hear the extravagant claims made by certain parties, one would really think that a monopoly of artistic photography was held by them, and that no one else could accomplish satisfactory results. But are these claims well-founded? No, fortunately not; nor is there any prospect of their being, so long as the same sun shines for all, and the same opportunities are open to all who are not afraid to work. Mr. B. L. Call doing business at No. 1 Grove Street, does not profess to be the only Photographer in the State capable of making satisfactory likenesses, but for all that, is able to produce as faithful and finely-finished pictures as anybody could desire. He has carried on his present establishment since 1886, and has built up a liberal and increasing patronage by keeping all promises made to customers, and furnishing first-class work at moderate rates. Mr. Call is a native of Exeter, being thoroughly acquainted with the many details of the business. The premises utilized, comprise two floors of the dimensions of 30x50 feet, and contain the latest improved apparatus, and all other necessary facilities. Pictures, Frames and Moldings are carried in stock, and are offered for sale at the lowest market prices. All orders will be given prompt and careful attention, and those wishing anything in the Picture line should certainly pay the firm a visit.

C. P. McGrillis, Groceries and Feed, at the Depot, Dexter. Considered from some standpoints, 18 years is a very long time, while from others it seems but a brief period after all. But however long or short a time it may seem, the fact remains that few business enterprises attain so high a position in the esteem of the public in 18 years as has that conducted on Main Street, at the depot, by Mr. C. P. McGrillis. This gentleman was born in Dexter, Me., and founded the undertaking with which he is now identified, in 1870. He has resorted to no illegitimate or questionable methods to build up his business, but has proceeded from the first, on the good, old-fashioned principle of giving a dollar's worth for a dollar, and assuring equal and equitable treatment to all. The premises utilized comprise two floors, measuring 40x100 feet, and the stock on hand is made up of Choice Staple and Fancy Groceries, selected especially for family trade, together with Flour, Corn and Feed of all kinds; also dealer in Potatoes and Country Produce. Mr. McGrillis employs three assistants, and supplies Goods in quantities to suit, doing both a wholesale and retail business. He endeavors to fill orders promptly and accurately, and so far as care and hard work can assure this being done, customers of his may depend upon it. The prices quoted on the many articles handled, are as low as can be named by any dealer in similar goods, and no trade is sought for by misrepresentation and deceit.

S. S. Ireland, Dealer in Dry and Fancy Goods, Carpets and Woolens, corner of Main and Grove Street, Dexter. Perhaps there are still a few ladies residing in Dexter or vicinity, who are not thoroughly acquainted with the inducements offered at the establishment conducted by Mr. S. S. Ireland, at the corner of Main and Grove Streets, and if so, we can do them no more genuine service, than to earnestly advise them to visit the store in question, and see for themselves, Mr. Ireland is a Newport man by birth, but has carried on business in this town for nearly a score of years. He occupies premises of the dimensions of 25x60 feet and handles Dry and Fancy Goods, Carpets, Woolens etc., in immense variety. No one can be in business, without gaining a pretty correct idea of what the public really want, and it is often remarked by visitors to Mr. Ireland's store, that they are sure to find there just the styles and goods they are looking for. His prices too, are very acceptable, for he manages business on the "quick sales and small profits" principle and so is always offering some noteworthy bargains. The carpets exhibited at this establishment, are well worthy of the examination of not only those who wish to buy, but also those who wish to keep informed regarding the latest fashionable novelties. Employment is afforded to two competent and courteous assistants, and callers are invariably given prompt and polite attention, and furnished all desired information. In short, Mr. Ireland's store is conducted on liberal and far-sighted principles, and amply deserves its great popularity.

LEADING BUSINESS MEN OF DEXTER.

Springall & Co., dealers in Pure Drugs, Chemicals, Medicines, Toilet Articles, Books, Stationery, & Fancy Goods, Sheet Music and Musical Merchandise, Main Street, Dexter. There are many reasons why the enterprise carried on by Messrs. Springall & Co., on Main Street, should receive special consideration, for not only is it of old establishment, but it is also of prime importance to the community at large. It is over a quarter of a century since operations were begun, for the house of Barron, Springall & Co., became known to the public in 1860. Fifteen years later, the present firm-name was adopted, and the business has steadily developed with the growth of the town in which it is located. Mr. Springall was born in Dexter, and is a member of the Knights of Pythias. He is known throughout the community, and is looked upon as being one of the most thoroughly competent dispensing Chemists in this section. The firm make a specialty of the handling of Pure Drugs, and being very careful as to where they obtain their supplies, are in a position to speak with confidence concerning the Chemicals, Medicines, etc., which they carry in stock. Accuracy in Dispensing is a fundamental principle of the business, and those having physicians' prescriptions can certainly do no better than to have them compounded at this popular establishment, such work being done at short notice, and at low prices. Toilet Articles, etc., are dealt in largely, and a fine line of Books, Stationery, and Fancy Goods is at hand to select from, at rates as low as can be named anywhere. Sheet Music and Musical Merchandise are offered in great variety, and two competent and polite assistants give prompt attention to all.

Leighton & Haines, Groceries and Crockery, Agents for American Express Company, Main Street, Dexter. All housekeepers are aware that there are a variety of articles, which, while included under the head of Groceries, are still not to be bought to advantage in every grocery store. These goods are generally called "Fancy Groceries, and include the latest novelties in Relishes, Condiments, etc., as well as Canned Goods, Jams, Preserves, etc. A house, which while dealing in all descriptions of Family Groceries, still makes a specialty of Fancy Articles, is that of which Messrs. Leighton & Haines are the proprietors, located on Main Street. This enterprise was inaugurated in 1880, and the public were quick to appreciate the advantages attendant upon dealing with this firm. The premises in use are 20x60 feet in dimensions, and contain an attractive stock, attractively arranged. Both partners give close personal attention to the business, and being well posted in its various details, are able to maintain the high standard of efficiency this house long since established. Employment is given to two experienced and polite assistants, and callers are in all cases shown due consideration, and assured being waited upon at the earliest possible moment. In addition to the Staple and Fancy Groceries handled, considerable of a trade is carried on in Crockery, a fine and varied selection of these goods being always on hand. Purchasers may depend upon the articles bought, for no misrepresentation is allowed here, and the prices are always low.

John W. Springall, Watchmaker and Jeweler, Dealer in Watches, Clocks, Jewelry, Silver Plated Ware, Spectacles and Eye Glasses. Agent for the American Watch. Grove Street, Dexter. The man who has once carried a really accurate watch, will never be satisfied afterward with a time-keeper that is not to be entirely depended upon. There is a peculiar satisfaction in owning a watch that you can "swear by," known only to those who have experienced it, and if any of our readers should be about to purchase a Watch, we would most certainly advise them to pay a fair price and get a reliable article. Those living in Dexter or vicinity, can do no better than to place their order with Mr. John W. Springall, doing business on Main Street, for this gentleman makes a specialty of fine Watches, and is in a position to offer unsurpassed inducements to purchasers. He was born in this town and is a member of the Knights of Pythias, and since opening his present store in 1884, has built up a large business by close attention to his patrons and fair dealing with all. Mr. Springall warrants the Watches he sells to give entire satisfaction, and knowing how much depends on the care they receive, he gives certain directions to watch-owners on his business card that are worthy of a careful observance. Condensed they are as follows: "Keep the Watch free from dust, dampness and extremes of heat and cold; have it cleaned annually; don't let it run down; wind at regular intervals with a perfect-fitting key and hold it still while doing so; hang it up when not in use, and buy a *good* Watch to begin with." If these simple rules are followed, the result will be gratifying enough to pay for the trouble many times over. Mr. Springall makes the Repairing of Fine Watches a specialty and does such work at short notice and at low rates. He carries a fine stock of Clocks, Jewelry, Silver Plated Ware, Spectacles, Eye Glasses, etc., and offers these goods at most reasonable rates. One assistant is employed and callers are assured prompt and courteous attention as well as fair dealing, and desirable goods at low prices.

F. J. Fogg, Dealer in Family Groceries, Meats and Fish. Prominent among the well-known establishments in the Grocery and Meat business in Dexter, is the house of F. J. Fogg, which since its inception has ever maintained a high reputation for integrity and honorable business dealings. The premises utilized for the transaction of business consist of a fine store and basement, where is handled one of the most complete stocks of groceries and provisions carried in Dexter. The stock embraces everything included in the line of choice family groceries, meats, and, in fact, all the condiments and delicacies usually carried by a first-class house of this kind. Prompt attention is given to all orders, which are accurately filled and delivered to all parts of the town. The proprietor is an active business man, who gives close personal attention to all branches of the establishment, especially to the purchasing and selection of the goods, which are guaranteed to be the best the market affords. None in this line of trade in Dexter enjoy a higher reputation for reliability, and the success of this house is as well-merited as it is prominent.

W. E. Brewster, wholesale and retail dealer in Corn, Flour, Oats, Shorts, Cotton Seed Meal, and Fine Groceries, Dustin Block, Main Street, Dexter. Everybody has use for Flour, and a great number have use for Oats, Shorts, and Feed in general, so that we feel sure that a few words concerning where all these articles can be bought to the best advantage will prove of interest. By calling on Mr. W. E. Brewster, doing business in Dustin Block, Main Street, you will find a heavy stock of such goods as we have mentioned; and what is more, you will find that the prices are away down to the lowest notch, for Mr. Brewster makes a specialty of the sale of Corn, Flour, Oats, and Shorts, giving particular attention to the two first-named articles, and is prepared at any time to supply customers, either at wholesale or retail, with any desired quantity. He is a native of Parkman, is connected with the Free Masons and the Odd Fellows, and inaugurated his present enterprise in 1887, having already built up a large and growing trade. The premises utilized comprise three floors and a storehouse, and are of the dimensions of 25x60 feet. Cotton Seed Meal is handled quite extensively, and Fine Groceries of all descriptions are dealt in largely, and guaranteed to prove as represented every time. Mr. Brewster gives close personal attention to his business, and employs sufficient assistance to enable him to fill all orders without delay.

Dexter Gazette, Day & Bunker, Proprietors; E. Bunker, Manager, Dustin Block, Main Street, Dexter. It is a quarter of a century since the *Dexter Gazette* was established, and some very radical changes have taken place in the town since this enterprise was begun. It is said that few papers survive more than a year, fewer still five years, and when we come to reckon up those that have existed over a score of years, we find that they form a very small percentage of the whole. The *Dexter Gazette* has lived and prospered all this time, simply because it was liberally managed and ably edited, and as these characteristics distinguish it now as much as ever, it is only natural that its popularity should be growing daily. Broad in its views and catholic in its ideas, the *Gazette* has always striven to advance the best interests of Dexter, and though there may have been errors of judgment at times, no one can honestly question the purity of its motives. Mr. E. Bunker, the Manager, is a young man of energy and unquestioned business ability, a member of the F. & A. M., and also belongs to the I. O. O. F. He is too well known to render it necessary to make further personal mention of him. The same may be said of the Editor, Mr. H. F. Day, a graduate of Colby University, and a member of this wide-awake firm. Mr. Day works hard to keep his paper in the front ranks, and has reason to congratulate himself on the success he attains. The premises occupied measure 31x63 feet, and comprise two floors, the necessary presses, etc., requiring ten horse-power to run them. The typographical appearance of the *Gazette* is very neat, and the paper is as attractive to the eye as it is to the intellect. The proprietors make a specialty of Job Printing in all its branches, and the quality of their work is widely acknowledged to be unexcelled by any printing establishment outside the large cities. The *Gazette* job-print is widely known among theatrical managers as the only establishment in Maine with facilities for doing their class of work, and it is continually in receipt of large orders from all parts of the country.

N. L. McGrillis, Clothing Manufacturer, Upper Main Street, Dexter. The manufacture of Clothing has reached enormous proportions of late years in this country; first, because the number to be clothed has largely increased, and second, because the tendency has been toward the wearing of ready-made garments, and the centralization of its making into large shops where the various processes could be more economically carried on. Take, for instance, a single establishment in this town—that of Mr. N. L. McGrillis, located on Upper Main Street. This gentleman is a native of Skowhegan, and is connected with both the Free Masons and Odd Fellows. He became identified with his present enterprise in 1874, and some idea of the magnitude of his business to-day, may be gained from the fact that employment is given to two hundred hands. The premises occupied are of the dimensions of 25x70 feet, and are fitted up with the most improved facilities, etc., for the carrying on of operations to the best advantage. Mr. McGrillis does a strictly wholesale business, and his productions are well known to the trade in general, being in constant demand, owing to their uniform excellence and the low figure at which they are quoted. He gives prompt attention to every order and his trade is consequently increasing.

Morse & Bridges, Manufacturers and Dealers in All Kinds of Cemetery Work; Scotch Granite a specialty. No. 19 Grove Street, Dexter. Branch Shop at Newport. An enterprise which, having its origin in the centennial year, has steadily grown in public favor up to the present time, is that carried on by Messrs. Morse & Bridges, at No. 19 Grove Street. This firm is prepared to undertake Cemetery Work of all descriptions, and certainly has ample facilities to enable it to meet all honorable competition and attain results that cannot but be satisfactory. Mr. Morse was born in Augusta, while Mr. Bridges is a native of Dexter. The former is connected with the Knights of Pythias and the latter with the Odd Fellows, both being extremely well-known in this vicinity. A branch shop is maintained at Newport, but the headquarters of the concern are at No. 19 Grove Street, where premises of the dimensions of 30x60 feet are utilized, and many beautiful specimens of finished work shown. Scotch Granite is made a specialty by Messrs. Morse & Bridges, and those at all familiar with this ornamental and durable stone, will recognize at once its peculiar fitness for use in Cemetery Work. A great variety of chaste designs are open to the inspection of patrons, and those wishing any information relative to the cost, or advice regarding the style of any proposed monument, headstone, or similar article, will be cheerfully furnished with it on application.

LEADING BUSINESS MEN OF DEXTER.

H. A. Blethen, Watches, Clocks, Jewelry etc., special attention given to Repairing, Main Street, Dexter. No thinking person needs to be told that it is of the first importance, when purchasing anything in the line of Watches, Jewelry, etc., to patronize a strictly reliable house, yet an opposite course is occasionally pursued by those who ought to know better, and the result is uniformly — dissatisfaction. There is no excuse for allowing one's self to be imposed upon, for the reliable jewelry houses of a community are easily found, even by a stranger, if trouble is taken to make a few inquiries, and it is safe to say that if such inquiries were made in Dexter, about the first establishment pointed out would be that of Mr. H. A. Blethen, located on Main Street. Certainly the residents of the town have had abundant opportunity to judge concerning the reliability of the enterprise in question, for it was inaugurated over a quarter of a century ago, its inception occurring in 1861, under the firm name of H. A. & A. G. Blethen & Co. Mr. H. A. Blethen became sole proprietor in 1876, and the last decade has added largely to the reputation and patronage of the establishment. Mr. Blethen is a native of Dover, and is connected with the Odd Fellows. The premises occupied are of the dimensions of 20x50 feet, and the stock on hand is sufficiently large to enable all the available space to be fully utilized. Watches, Clocks, Jewelry, Silver Ware and such goods are dealt in largely, and Mr. Blethen is prepared to meet all honorable competition in the way of furnishing standard articles at low prices. He employs three careful and polite assistants, and gives special attention to Repairing; Watches, Clocks, Jewelry, etc., being put in order at short notice, and in a neat and durable manner at a low price.

Charles T. Moses, Packer of "Royal Brand" Sugar Corn, Main Street, Dexter. Factories at Dexter and Corinna. The discovery of the process by which vegetables, meats, and other perishable products can be preserved for an indefinite period, must be accepted as one of the great events of the century, for it has resulted in the building up of a vast industry, and in making it possible to provide in time of plenty against prospective famine. Seamen and other travelers can now enjoy a healthful and refreshing diet at all times, and by the proper use of Canned Vegetables, Fruits, etc., entirely avoid that terrible scourge — scurvy. Sugar Corn is one of the characteristic productions of this continent, and we are all too familiar with the many ways in which this nutritious food can be utilized, to render it necessary to speak at length concerning its great and abiding popularity. Fresh from the field, it is a delicacy that it is hard to equal, and by improved methods of canning, and careful selection of the corn handled, some of our Packers succeed in wonderfully preserving the desirable qualities of the fresh Corn. None have been more successful in this respect than Mr. Charles T. Moses of this town, and his Factory on Lower Main Street is a scene of bustling activity during the canning season. Two floors, measuring 50x60 feet, are occupied, and employment is given to 130 assistants. The finished product is shipped to all parts of the country, and is in demand wherever an honestly put-up article of the kind is appreciated. Mr. Moses was born in Standish, Me., and is to be congratulated on having built up so flourishing a business.

Levi Bridgham, Registered Apothecary, 21 Bank Block, Main Street, Dexter. It would be difficult to find an establishment of more genuine value to the community than that carried on by Mr. Levi Bridgham, Bank Block, Main Street. This undertaking was founded in 1872, and has since largely developed as its influence to the public became more plainly manifest. Drugs, Medicines and Chemicals are supplied in quantities to suit, at the lowest rates that can be named on first-class goods; and as the filling of Prescriptions is given especial attention, customers may feel assured of their favors being appreciated, and of their orders being handled with that skill and accuracy so desirable in this connection. Every precaution is observed that will tend to reduce the liability of error to the smallest possible amount, and every facility is at hand that can aid in attaining this result. Mr. Bridgham is moderate in his charges, and certainly has solved the problem of combining reliable service with popular prices. The sale of Books, Fancy Goods, etc., forms another important department of his business, and is conducted on the same liberal scale that characterizes the management of his Drug Trade. The Stock carried is fresh, varied and acceptable, and customers are treated with a courtesy and consideration that are delightful and unusual.

G. W. Lincoln, Custom Clothing, Main Street, Dexter. It may safely be said that 99 men out of 100 would have their clothing made to order were it not for the additional expense of so doing. Every man likes to wear a good-fitting suit, and it stands to reason that one made to order is much more apt to fit as it should, than one ready-made. Now so far as the expense is concerned, many people make a big mistake. There is not really much difference between the price of a custom-made garment and one that is not made to order; that is, provided the goods, trimmings, etc., are the same; and right here comes in the reason why many ready-made suits are sold cheap, — they are made cheap and have defective trimmings. Call on Mr. G. W. Lincoln, at his store on Main Street and see what he can do for you in the way of furnishing a suit to order at a low figure. Mr. Lincoln is a native of Waterville, and has been engaged in his present line of business for more than thirty years, so that he certainly ought to understand it thoroughly by this time. Premises measuring 20x60 feet are occupied, and employment given to ten efficient assistants. Orders will be filled at short notice, and satisfaction is confidently guaranteed, both as regards fit and finish. Mr. Lincoln's prices are invariably moderate, and considering the superior durability of the garments made at his establishment, it is doubtful if they are actually more expensive than ready-made clothing.

FAY & SCOTT,
MACHINISTS AND FOUNDERS,
DEXTER, MAINE.

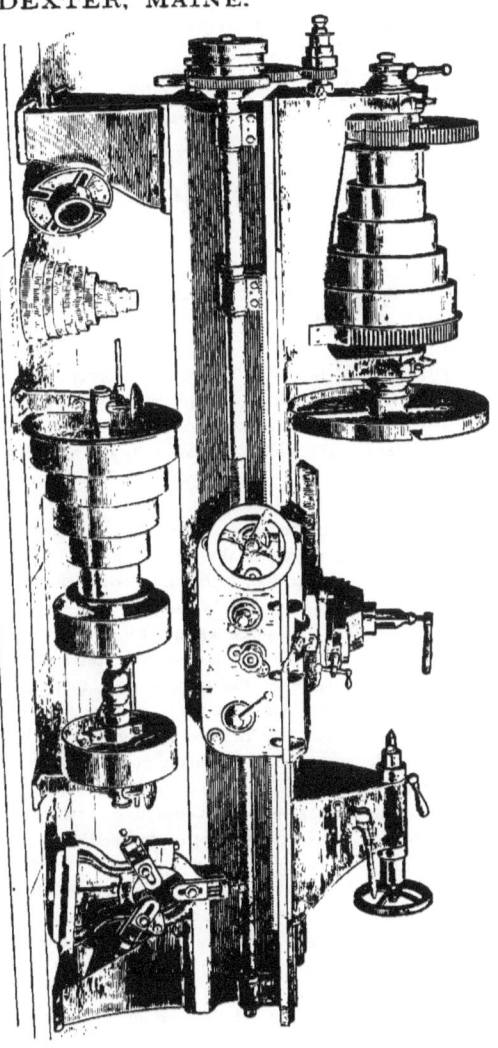

Fay & Scott, Machinists and Founders. Manufacturers of, and Dealers in, Machine Tools, Machinery, etc., Spring Street, Dexter. Nowadays, when Machinery plays so important a part in production, and when the margin between the cost price and the selling price of most manufactured articles is so narrow, it is of the highest importance to every manufacturer to equip his works with the most improved machinery and to keep a sharp watch, lest the progress of invention should leave him in the rear, with an equipment that forbids his competing with other houses in the same line of trade. Not only machinery but machine tools, are constantly undergoing improvement, and there is no house in the State that gives more careful attention to furnishing its customers with the best there is to be had in this line, than that of Fay & Scott, doing business on Spring St. Business was begun in 1881, and as manufacturers and others were quick to recognize the genuine character of the advantages gained by those leaving their orders with this concern, a large and growing trade has already been established. Mr. Fay was born in Massachusetts, and is an Odd Fellow, while Mr. Scott is a Maine man by birth, and a Mason, both being well-posted in every detail of their business and giving it their close personal attention. In this way, not only their interests but also those of their customers are fully protected, and the firm stands ready to guarantee that every Machine and every Tool they sell, shall prove as represented. Iron Working and Special Machinery of all Descriptions are Manufactured and Dealt in, employment being given to 25 assistants; and premises of the dimensions of 40x80—Machine Shop, two stories; and Foundry 30x80 feet occupied. Ample water-power is at hand to drive all necessary machinery.

E. A. Flanders, Lumber, Box-Shooks, Spool Stock etc,, Dexter. Wood-working is without doubt one of the most important industries in the State, and not the least important division of it, is that devoted to the production of Box-Shooks, Spool Stock, Cloth Boards etc. The active and constantly increasing demand that exists for these articles, makes the field a promising one for those who are possessed of the necessary enterprise and "push" to cultivate it successfully, and a proof of this is to be found in the rapid development of the enterprise carried on by Mr. E. A. Flanders since he inaugurated it in 1880. The premises occupied, measure 30x60 feet, and employment is given to ten assistants. Mr. Flanders, who is a native of Dexter, does both a wholesale and retail business and is well prepared to furnish anything in his line at the lowest market rates. He deals largely in Lumber and is in a position to meet all honorable competition, as he enjoys the most favorable relations with producers and has all necessary facilities to fill orders promptly, accurately and in short, satisfactorily. Standard grades of material are used at this establishment, and they are worked up in a careful and thorough manner.

HISTORICAL SKETCH
—OF—
WATERVILLE.

THE early history of Waterville is inseparably connected with that of Winslow, of which it was for many years a part. The former place was settled about the middle of the eighteenth century, and underwent the usual experience of a tiny frontier colony in this region, harrassed by the French and Indian war. As a necessary protection a fort, or more properly, perhaps, a block-house, was erected at Winslow in 1754; and around this as a nucleus, the embryo town slowly and painfully grew up. After the French wars with their attendant fears and perils were safely over, the great attractions of the Kennebec valley soon made it a favorite with settlers who soon began to flock hither in ever-increasing numbers. The Indian name for that part of Winslow, now Waterville, was Tacconet, which has since been corrupted to Ticonic. This place was a great center of the Kennebec tribe of Indians. Their greatest orator and the great warrior, Bomazeene, beside other leading men of the nation, lived here. At Tacconet tribal gatherings were frequently held, and one of the great reasons which drew them here was the fact that this was the great burial-ground of the tribe. The Indians themselves have long since disappeared from this region; but the ancient bones of many generations remain, and will remain for centuries to tell the sad tale of a departed race.

At the time of the Revolution Winslow was too small and unimportant to take any noticeable part in the struggle, but several settlers from the vicinity were participants, and the region was not entirely unacquainted with the taste of battle, as the passing through of Arnold's expedition, and the invasion of the British up the Penobscot, both affected it directly. After it was all over the valley settlements again began to grow, and up to the beginning of the present century a most prosperous period was enjoyed.

In 1784 the first mill was erected at Ticonic Falls by Samuel Redington, and this represented the growth of a new settlement on the opposite side of the river from the old town. So rapidly did this section grow that by 1802 it was large enough to be set apart from Winslow as a town by itself under its present name, derived from its magnificent water supply. After it began its separate existence it grew even more rapidly for a while, as the establishment here of a Baptist Seminary in 1813 is ample testimony, showing that it had become the center and most eligible site of all this portion of the valley. But the influences set at work by the embargo in 1807, and the war of 1812, spread all through New England, affecting her growth and commercial prosperity; and they did not spare Waterville, which up to the middle of the century underwent the alternate times of "booming" and depression which were the usual experience of the towns in the State. In the war of 1812, the young town took a deep interest, and sent quite a number of its young men down the river as participants in the cruises of the famous Yankee privateers. When the British again invaded the Penobscot valley in 1814, it was near enough to witness some of the effects of the defeat and flight of the Americans. Though not directly affected by the decay of American shipping, it yet suffered indirectly by the general commercial depression which resulted therefrom throughout Maine and New England.

The opening of the railroad, about the middle of the present century, was a most important event for Waterville, and marked the opening of a new epoch in its history. Its commercial prospects were immediately brightened, independent of the important industry which was opened by the establishment of the railroad machine and repair shops here. The magnificent water privilege here, now for the first time, began to be appreciated and it has since received increasing attention. Manufacturing, to which evidently a large part of Waterville's progress has been and must be due, now began to assume considerable proportions, and the consequent benefits have been very extensive.

During the civil war the town performed its duty in a most patriotic and generous manner. A goodly number of its sons and maturer citizens responded to the call for volunteers, and throughout the struggle it never failed to fulfill every request

THE OLD FORT BUILT IN 1754,

for men and money immediately and ungrudgingly. In the First, Second, Fourth, Sixth, Fourteenth, Fifteenth, Eighteenth, Nineteenth, Twenty-First, Twenty-Fourth, Twenty-Eighth and Twenty-Ninth volunteer regiments of Maine, were noble representatives of Waterville's best families, and not a few of these were called upon to sacrifice a member to the nation's weal. This period, though far from prosperous materially, is the most honorable and glorious in the history of the town.

Since the war the progress of the town in all lines has been steady and marked. The population in 1870 had risen to 4,852, and the valuation was $1,904,017. Part of the town was set off in 1873, but nevertheless the population in 1880 was 4,672, while the valuation had arisen to $2,612,496; both these figures have since been increased by at least one-half, as the present decade has been one of marked advancement. The expansion of commercial interests and rise of real-estate values have been the most important characteristics of recent years. The valuable manufacturing privileges at the Ticonic Falls have received attention, and are now undergoing a development which must contribute largely to the material growth of the town. Cotton mills, woolen mills, saw-mills, are already well under way here, and the prospect of the town's becoming a leading manufacturing center seems assured. Among other prominent industries, the tanneries, machine and iron foundries, and furniture manufactories, deserve attention. The machine shops of the Maine Central railroad have grown steadily with the growth of the road itself, and are now of considerable extent and first importance. The depot here is one of the most beautiful and convenient of any on the road.

Opposite the railroad station stand the dark-gray, handsome buildings of COLBY UNIVERSITY, in the midst of a fine campus, with greensward and magnificent elms in abundance. This is one of the leading Colleges in the State, and was organized and incorporated in 1813 as a Seminary, especially with the idea of training ministers, by the Baptist denomination of Maine. It was first called the Maine Literary and Theological Institution, and the first President was the Rev. Jeremiah Champlin, D.D. In 1820 it was granted collegiate powers by the State Legislature at its first meeting, and the name was changed to "Waterville College." At the same time important donations of land were made. The first graduates after it became a college were George Dana Boardman and Ephraim Tripp. The former was the great Baptist missionary to the Karens in Burmah. The growth of the College through the middle period of the century was gradual and slow, yet steady. At the time of the civil war it had already become a marked force in the life of the State, and contributed some of its best and most brilliant members to the Union cause. Among other celebrated alumni of this period was Gen. Benjamin F. Butler. Twenty of Colby's sons served in various ways during the war. The beautiful Memorial Hall was erected in honor of those who fell in the service.

In 1867 the name of the institution was changed to Colby University, in honor of Gardiner Colby, Esq., of Boston, Mass., who became a very large contributor and benefactor. Its influence in the State and New England has always been strongly Baptist; but it has always welcomed students of other denominations, and its courses are thoroughly scientific and unsectarian. It has now about two hundred students and is accomplishing a strong and most useful work. The curriculum is high, many talented instructors are connected with the institution, and the presiding administration is vigorous and progressive. It has become a vital force in the State, and is not only destined to grow continually with it, but beyond it, extending its influence ever wider through the country, and advancing the interests both of Waterville and of Maine.

The social life of Waterville is in no small degree affected by the fact that it is a college town. Not too large to be thoroughly permeated by this academic spirit, the town is heartily in sympathy with the life and aims of the college. The social season practically begins with the college year and closes at its end. Many students enter the general society of the town and that of the various churches, and are often its active life. The culture and refinement of the town is consequently of a more than usually advanced type. As the college acts upon the town, increasing and uplifting its intellectual standards, so the town reacts upon the college, adding the charms of social life, and these are often among the pleasantest memories of graduates. It is

still an open question among educators whether the greater quiet and freedom from many temptations which the colleges situated in the country and smaller cities enjoy do not more than counterbalance the advantages which come from being situated in a great city, and an interested student will find all the great privileges and beauties of the former class at the highest point of development in Colby University, here in the delightful town of Waterville.

The immense advances made by the State of Maine as a summer resort have been, and will continue to be an even more advantageous influence to Waterville. Situated in the center of a most charming district, and itself possessed of many attractions for the tourist and summer resident, the advancing years will only serve to increase and enhance these. The Maine Central Railroad, which has already done so much in advancing the town, as its great business increases, makes it better known and more appreciated, and every year is marked by a larger number of visitors. The drives in and about the town are very beautiful, unsurpassed anywhere in the State. Outside of the five handsome buildings of the college and its campus, there are many handsome buildings and grounds. Many charming spots of natural interest and beauty are in the immediate vicinity; and in every direction, whether by rail, stage-coach or ordinary carriage, the country opens up great attractions, many of which are not yet widely known. The Kennebec and Messalonske rivers, beside the other beautiful streams and lakes, offer the best facilities for boating and all kinds of aquatic sports.

The streams and ponds on all sides abound in black and silver bass, and also gamy trout, and partridges, quail, woodcock and other game can be found by the enterprising sportsman in considerable numbers and not far away. Even deer have been known to venture down near the town, and some have been shot near by in recent seasons. No more quiet, restful and attractive spot for a delightful and recuperative summer vacation could be discovered. Its convenience to the railroad, and yet unsurpassed attractiveness in all the delights of country life, are great points in its favor, and will gain in influence every year as they become better known. It is also a great railroad center, and this contains great promise of growth. The branch of the Maine Central to Skowhegan, the two main lines through Lewiston and Augusta, and those going via Bangor to Belfast, Bar Harbor, Moosehead Lake and Canada, all meet here and make it one of the most traversed spots in the State. Even short acquaintance shows one that as a commercial, social and tourist center Waterville has a great future before it, which before many decades have passed will make it one of the leading cities in the State. And not the least satisfactory consideration is that by reason of its location and character, its natural and sanitary advantages, and its cultured and progressive people, it is fully worthy of all the prosperity which the great development of Maine has and will bring to it.

LEADING BUSINESS MEN
OF
WATERVILLE, ME.

L. A. Presby & Co., Wholesale and Retail Dealers in Dry and Furnishing Goods, Small Wares, etc. Rubber Goods of All Kinds a Specialty. Dunn Block, Waterville. An establishment which every resident of Waterville has reason to be honestly proud of is that conducted by Messrs. L. A. Presby & Co., in Dunn Block, and we only regret that the necessity of keeping this book within reasonable bounds compels us to forego giving this enterprise the extended notice its merits and comparative importance demand. Business was begun in 1884, and the rapid growth of the trade to its present imposing dimensions shows that the public have been quick to appreciate the advantages of dealing with this house. The firm is constituted of Mr. L. A. Presby, a native of Boston, and Mr. R. W. Dunn, who has passed most of his life in Waterville, and is a graduate of Colby University. Both a wholesale and retail business is done, and six stores are occupied, having total dimensions of 150x75 feet. The department devoted to Dry Goods is of course a special favorite with the ladies; and they have reason to feel pleased at the inducements offered them, for no house in the county is in a position to place a greater variety of seasonable goods before its patrons, or to name lower prices on standard articles, since they manufacture many of their goods, and receive them first hand. Everything in the Dry Goods line is handled by this concern, and whatever representation may be made concerning the articles on sale may be strictly depended on, for no statements are allowed to be made by salesmen that are not precisely in accordance with the facts. This, of course, has exercised a most powerful effect in bringing about the present feeling of confidence that is manifested by the purchasing public regarding this concern, and this feeling is also sustained by the fact that the various announcements made from time to time respecting special sales, etc., have always proved to be justified by the actual facts. Furnishing Goods and Small Wares are handled very largely, and Rubber Goods and Boots and Shoes are made a specialty — all descriptions being dealt in, and only the productions of reliable makers offered. Employment is given to eight courteous and efficient assistants, and all orders, whether large or small, are given prompt attention.

LEADING BUSINESS MEN OF WATERVILLE.

E. N. Small, Merchant Tailor, Dealer in Clothing and Gents' Furnishing Goods, Main Street, Waterville. "It takes all sorts of people to make up the world," so everybody admits, but at the same time, how few of us can allow a man to suit his own taste in matters of dress. etc., if it happens to run contrary to our own; Some men prefer Ready-made and some prefer Custom-made garments, and in the large majority of cases, every man has good reason for whatever preference he may have. It may be stated as a general truth, that any individual knows better what is suited to him than any other party possibly can, and the wisest course to pursue is to do as Mr. E. N. Small does, and stand prepared to furnish customers either with Custom or Ready-made Clothing, as they may choose. Mr. Small was born in West Vernon, and began operations in his present line of business in 1876. He occupies one floor of the dimensions of 25x75 feet, and has ample facilities at hand to accomodate his customers in the best possible manner and without delay, employing eight assistants, and positively guaranteeing that every garment leaving his hands shall prove as represented. Under these cirumstances it is hardly necessary to add that Mr. Small's business is thriving and that his list of both old and new customers is constantly increasing. He is connected with both the Free Masons and the Odd Fellows and is also a member of the Grand Army, having formerly served as Orderly Sergeant in Co. A., of the 16th Maine, and afterward as a commissioned officer in the Cavalry. He was present at Gettysburg and Fredericksburg, and certainly has no reason to be ashamed of his record. We heartily commend his enterprise for we know that its management is characterized by honesty and fair dealing.

D. Gallert, Dealer in Dry Goods, Main St., Waterville. There is no use in trying to carry on a Dry Goods Store nowadays so as to supply the best of goods at the lowest market rates, unless considerable experience has been had in this line of trade, for the competition is so keen that the margin between profit and loss in the sale of Dry Goods is very narrow indeed. Those who have have had dealings with Mr. D. Gallert at his establishment on Main Street, will fully agree with us when we say that he offers bargains in many lines that it would be hard to find equalled elsewhere, and in his case we have a good example of what experience can do, for he has been engaged in his present enterprise for a quarter of a century, having inaugurated it in 1862. He is a native of Prussia, and a member of the Free Masons, and the establishment occupied by him comprises two floors of the dimensions of 25x75 feet. The stock on hand is so varied and extensive that it is impossible to give any adequate description of it here, and we can only advise our readers to call and see for themselves, as the assortment is not only extensive but is offered at prices that cannot fail to be appreciated by all careful buyers. Both Fancy and Staple articles are handled, and five assistants are at hand to give customers that prompt and polite attention for which Mr. Gallert's establishment has long been noted.

George W. Dorr, Druggist and Apothecary, also a full line of Fancy Goods, Cigars, etc., Main Street, Waterville. An establishment which contributes its full share to the mercantile activity of Waterville is the Drug Store of Dr. G. W. Dorr, which is located on Main Street. This house was founded by Dr. Dorr in 1850. As a Druggist and Chemist of experience and practical knowledge he is maintaining a first-class position in the profession, and holds the esteem and confidence of the entire community. His handsomely appointed store is well stocked with pure and fresh Drugs, all the standard Proprietary Medicines, and the best Chemicals, as well as Perfumery, fine Soaps and other Toilet Articles. The Prescription Department is under the trustworthy management of the proprietor and two assistants, who carefully and conscientiously prepare physicians' prescriptions and family recipes at all hours, using only pure drugs, and allowing no substitution in compounding the same. The store covers an area of 20x60 feet, and has ample accommodations for transacting the large and prosperous retail business. The most desirable inducements are offered to the public, both in excellence of goods and economy of prices. Dr. Dorr is a native of Augusta, and a member of the Free Masons, and has the requisite talent, training and good judgment to win the highest success as a thorough master of his profession. He also prepares the following specialties: proprietor of Dorr's Wild Cherry Bitters; Dorr's Fragrant Odozone for the Teeth; Dorr's Compound Syrup of Tolu, Tar and Wild Cherry, for Coughs, etc.; Dorr's Instantaneous Cleanser,—knocks the spots out of all kinds of goods, and Dorr's Condition Powders.

W. M. Lincoln, Dealer in Groceries, Provisions and Meats, Main Street, Waterville. It is almost an invariable rule that in all centers of business, there are certain houses in each line of trade that stand pre-eminent, and have, by close attention to the wants of their customers, a thorough knowledge of the business and purchasing goods direct from first hands, built up a trade that goes ahead of that of many of their contemporaries. Such an establishment in Waterville is the Wholesale and Retail Grocery, Provision and Grain House of W. M. Lincoln. This house was founded in 1857, and has, for the past thirty-one years, been the center of a first-class trade, which both in extent and quality has few, if any, successful rivals in Waterville. The premises occupied for the business are located on Main Street, and comprise two floors, each 40x60 feet in dimensions, with an additional outside storehouse. At the store will be found a full and choice assortment of Staple and Fancy Groceries, also Provisions and Meats, which embraces everything usually handled by a first-class house in this line of trade, and are guaranteed to be the best goods to be obtained in the market. Constant employment is given to two experienced clerks and all orders are promptly attended to. Mr. Lincoln is a native of Waterville and a member of the Free Masons. His high personal character is a sufficient guarantee of the substantial and reliable manner in which all business is transacted.

LEADING BUSINESS MEN OF WATERVILLE.

F. A. Wing & Co., Commission Merchants and Wholesale Dealers in Foreign and Domestic Fruit, Common Street, Waterville. Although it is very true that under certain circumstances even the most enterprising and liberal business methods will fail to bring about satisfactory results, still it is an undeniable fact that the prosperity of any community depends largely upon the character and energy of those carrying on mercantile operations within its boundaries. Taking this view of the subject, it is evident that the commission merchants of this country have done much to establish the reputation enjoyed by Americans in general for shrewdness, foresight, and the early adoption of the most improved methods, for there is no class in the mercantile community that is more distinguished for the possession of just these qualities than that mentioned. The house of F. A. Wing & Co., located on Common Street, has only been before the public in its present form since 1887, but it has already built up a very thriving patronage, and may be considered as having "come to stay," in good earnest. Mr. Wing was born in Fayette, Me., and is a member of the United Workmen. Foreign and Domestic Fruits of all kinds are very extensively handled at Wholesale, and the premises occupied comprise one floor and a basement of the dimensions of 40x65 feet, together with a spacious storehouse. The facilities enjoyed for the procuring and handling of the commodities dealt in are of the very best, and no concern in this section is in a position to offer more favorable terms to those who may favor it with an order. Superior advantages are also enjoyed in the line of Selling Goods on Commission, and those consigning articles to Messrs. F. A. Wing & Co. may depend on receiving prompt and satisfactory returns. Much is already done in the commission line, and the business is as yet but imperfectly developed.

Percy Loud, Dealer in Boots and Shoes, Main Street, Waterville. No two individuals are exactly alike in the matter of general appearance, and when we come to particularize and compare details, we find even an increased dissimilarity. The consequence is, of course, that what may suit one will be far from suiting another; and so we find that if a large custom is to be had in any business relating to the supply of articles of personal wear, for instance, a sufficiently large and varied stock must be carried to supply widely varying tastes. It is probably owing to his appreciation of this truth that one of our Boot and Shoe merchants, Mr. Percy Loud, has met with such gratifying success, for at his establishment, located on Main Street, may be seen about every imaginable style and kind of footwear, both for the house and street use. This gentleman, who is a native of Massachusetts, began his business operations in Waterville in 1872, and during the sixteen years he has been before the public, he has established a reputation for furnishing reliable goods at low prices. The premises comprise a store and basement, each 20x55 feet in dimensions, so that it will seen that there is ample space to accommodate the large retail trade enjoyed. The general prices of this establishment will be found as low as is compatible with the best of stock and workmanship.

O. E. Emerson, Dealer in New and Second-Hand Stoves, Furniture, Crockery Ware, Tin Ware, etc., 21 Main Street, Waterville. There can be but very few of the many keeping house in Waterville, that have not heard of the establishment conducted by Mr. O. E. Emerson at No. 21 Main Street, for this gentleman began business in 1867, and has dealt in House Furnishing Goods so long and offered so many attractive inducements in the purchase of such, that his customers are now numbered by the thousands, and are to be found throughout Waterville and its vicinity. Mr. Emerson was born in Bangor, and is a member of the Free Masons. The premises utilized by him comprise four floors of the dimensions of 25x70 feet, and two floors measuring 25x40 feet, an immense stock being carried of New and Second-Hand Stoves, Furniture, Crockery Ware, Tin Ware, etc. This stock has been selected with all the intelligent judgment that an experience of about twenty-one years allows Mr. Emerson to exercise, and both as regards variety and completeness it would be difficult to improve upon it. Stoves of every approved pattern and of all capacities for cooking or heating. New and Second-Hand, are offered at prices that are bound to attract attention, while in the line of Furniture an assortment is shown that embraces all grades and kinds of articles, and includes those designed for kitchen, dining room, parlor or bed-chamber. Some very decided bargains are to be had in this department, and also that devoted to the sale of Crockery Ware, while in the way of Tin Ware there is to be had all of the one hundred and one articles required in modern housekeeping at bottom prices. Three courteous assistants are employed and customers given prompt and polite attention.

Edwin Towne, Dealer in Flour, Tea, Coffee and Spices, No. 17 Main Street, Waterville. An accommodating spirit and a determination to do the fair thing in every transaction are very powerful aids to success in any business enterprise, and they have not failed to exercise their usual effect in the case of Mr. Edwin Towne who began operations in Waterville in 1880. At his store, No. 17 Main Street, Mr. Towne carries on a thriving trade in Groceries and Provisions, and has many regular customers who have tested by years of experience the genuineness of the bargains and the uniform excellence of the goods he has to offer. He is a native of Winslow, and a member of the Free Masons; also a member of A. O. U. W., and is widely known in the community as an enterprising and reputable merchant who neglects no honorable means to extend his business operations. Mr. Towne claims to have the best line of Flour, Tea, Coffee and Spices in the place, and certainly the assortment he exhibits of these goods is admirable not only for its completeness but also for the standard character of the articles composing it. The premises utilized comprise one floor and a basement, and measure 22x80 feet, and everything is so arranged as to permit of the prompt and accurate filling of all orders. "Edwin Towne's Best American Soap" is very extensively handled at this establishment, and those who want a superior soap at a low price should give it a careful trial.

Learned & Brown, Plumbers and Steam Fitters, Dealers in all kinds of Plumbing and Steam Fitters' Supplies, 27 Main St., opposite Post-office, Waterville. The importance of having such work as Steam and Gas Fitting done by experienced and skillful hands only, would seem to be sufficiently obvious to need no particular mention were it not for the fact that hardly a day passes but what news is circulated of some accident happening, owing to steam or gas piping being improperly done. Now there is no necessity for such occurrences, as there are concerns that are possessed of both the experience and the ability to fill all orders for Piping and Plumbing in a thoroughly satisfactory and durable manner, and one of the best-known and oldest-established of these is that of Learned & Brown, doing business at No. 27 Main Street; also branch on Bridge Street, Fairfield, under the superintendence of John Green. The enterprises carried on by this firm were inaugurated in 1865, and has for many years occupied a leading position among similar undertakings in this section. Mr. Learned is a native of Winslow, Me., and Mr. Brown was born in Boston. The premises utilized are 25x60 feet in dimensions, and a large stock is carried of Steam, Gas and Water Pipes and Fittings of every description, these goods being sold at bottom prices and guaranteed to be of standard quality in every respect. Orders for Piping and Plumbing will be given prompt and careful attention at all times, and as three efficient assistants are employed, and the most improved tools and appliances at hand, the most difficult jobs can be undertaken with a guarantee of complete satisfaction. Mr. Learned belongs to the Masons, and Mr. Brown belongs to the Odd Fellows.

C. Shorey & Co., Livery and Boarding Stable, rear of Corner Market on Temple St., Waterville. It would be a shame indeed, if there were no way by which strangers in town, or others not owning horses could not take advantage of the many beautiful drives in the vicinity of Waterville, but fortunately abundant opportunity is offered to enjoy the drives mentioned, as one of the best equipped Livery Stables in this section of the State is carried on by Messrs. C. Shorey & Co., in the rear of the Corner Market on Temple Street, where two floors are utilized of the respective dimensions of 40x70 and 20x30 feet. This enterprise was inaugurated in 1886 by Mr. C. Shorey, who became associated a year later with Mr. L. W. Rollins under the present firm-name. Both these gentlemen are natives of Albion and members of the Free Masons, and they both endeavor to serve the public in the best possible manner. As a consequence, their establishment is a very popular one, and we can unreservedly commend it to our readers, for we know that all patrons are assured courteous treatment, and that the teams furnished are neat, stylish and satisfactory in every respect. Horses will be taken to board and given the best of care and accommodations, and any special directions given will be conscientiously observed. The prices are extremely reasonable, and no one entering into business relations with this firm will have reason to regret it.

The Waterville Grist Mill, which has been run since May 1, 1888, by Mr. W. S. B. Runnels, has been thoroughly repaired and enlarged, and an addition of one "run" of stone has been made by him, also a machine for cleansing grain before ground, so that now the already well-earned reputation of this establishment will be enhanced under the management of Mr. Runnels. It is very evident to all who will take time to observe the bustle and other signs of activity about the premises, and it is a pleasant and agreeable task for us to chronicle this success, for the reason that it has been brought about by purely legitimate means, and has been won by hard, earnest and intelligent work. The new proprietor, Mr. Runnels, was born in Vassalboro, and is a member of the Ancient Order of United Workmen, also of the Masonic Order. The establishment of which he is proprietor occupies two floors of the dimensions of 85x30 feet, and is equipped with new machinery which is now run by water power. Both a wholesale and retail business is done, and Flour, Corn, Meal and Feed are sold in quantities to suit at positively the lowest market rates. That Flour, Meal, etc., are much more valuable and nutritious in a perfectly fresh condition than when they have been carried in stock for weeks and months is known to all, and one of the reasons of the popularity of this establishment is to be found in the fact that being a manufacturer, he is able to furnish these indispensable commodities fresh ground. A heavy trade is also carried on in building materials, such as Lime, Cement, Plaster, etc., only standard articles being handled, while Salt, Hay and Straw are very extensively dealt in and carried in stock at all times. Prompt and courteous attention is given to customers by Mr. Runnels or his two efficient assistants, and bottom rates are named on every article.

Geo. F. Davies, Carriage and Sign Painter. First-Class Repair Shops Connected. Savage's Hall, Mechanic Square, Waterville. Among the successful business enterprises in Waterville, the Carriage and Sign Painting establishment of Mr. George F. Davies, occupies a prominent position in this line. He commenced business in Waterville in 1884, and has, through his native ability, energy and perseverance, built up his present desirable business. The premises utilized are located in Savage's Hall, Mechanic Square, and are equipped with every facility for the execution of Carriage, Sign and Ornamental Painting. Mr. Davies is also prepared to do Repairing in this line and has a first-class Repair Shop in connection with his other premises. He is doing a flourishing business in his different branches, and guarantees satisfaction to every patron. Mr. Davies is thoroughly conversant with all the details of his business, having been engaged for eleven years in Augusta, Me., in the same line of operations. Mr. Davies is a native of Sidney, Me., and belongs to the Masonic Order and the Knights of Pythias. He is prompt and reliable in all his engagements, and has, through these important qualifications, laid the foundation for a prosperous and enviable business career in this vicinity in the near future. Mr. Davies is a gentleman well-known and highly respected in social and business circles of this community.

C. G. Carleton, Photographer, 66 Main Street, Waterville. Probably in no branch of the arts have more improvements been made during recent years than in that of photography; and the avidity with which the inventions of late days have been availed of by the profession, is a convincing proof of the spirit of enterpise which has been a distinguishing feature of those concerned in the business. Mr. C. G. Carleton has been established here since 1862,

as a Photographic Artist, and has a long and practical experience. His Studio is located at 66 Main Street, and comprises Reception and Operating Rooms, covering an area of 25x100 feet, which is considered one of the finest and largest in the city. Mr. Carleton is an example of a painstaking, thorough artist. A visit to his Studio will amply repay the lover of the beautiful and artistic. Mr. Carleton is a native Whitefield, N. H.; well-known in social as well as business circles of this community, being a member of the Free Masons. He has achieved most honorable distinction as one of the finest and best-known Photographic Artists of this State.

S. A. Dickinson, Harness Manufacturer and Dealer in Whips, Robes, Blankets, Bells, Trunks, Valises, etc., etc. Rubber Boots for Wagons. Horse Covers, etc., cor. Temple and Main Sts., Waterville. The only way to make a good and satisfactory Harness is to combine thorough workmanship with the best of materials, and he who attempts to do

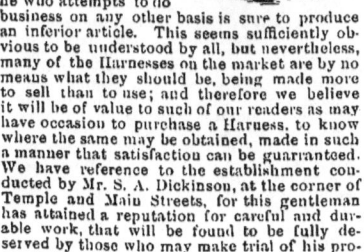

business on any other basis is sure to produce an inferior article. This seems sufficiently obvious to be understood by all, but nevertheless, many of the Harnesses on the market are by no means what they should be, being made more to sell than to use; and therefore we believe it will be of value to such of our readers as may have occasion to purchase a Harness, to know where the same may be obtained, made in such a manner that satisfaction can be guarranteed. We have reference to the establishment conducted by Mr. S. A. Dickinson, at the corner of Temple and Main Streets, for this gentleman has attained a reputation for careful and durable work, that will be found to be fully deserved by those who may make trial of his productions. Using strong and standard material, and paying strict attention to every detail of the manufacture, Mr. Dickinson is enabled to fully guarantee that his Harnesses shall stand every proper test to which they may be subjected, while he supplies them at the lowest market rates. Mr. Dickinson is a native of Wiscasset, Me., and has been engaged in the Harness business about sixteen years; his father being in the same business in Wiscasset for twenty years. Therefore he is thoroughly conversant with every detail of the business, and warrants his goods to stand hard and constant usage.

J. H. Wood, Dealer in Jewelry, Watches, and Silver Ware, Main St., Waterville. Among the many prominent concerns engaged in this line of business is that of Mr. J. H. Wood. This house was established by Mr. Wood in 1862, and since that date he has achieved gratifying success, and is now the proprietor of the attractive establishment located on Main Street. This establishment comprises a store 15x50 feet in dimensions. Here can be found a stock of Jewelry, Watches and Silver Ware of the finest workmanship and most artistic design and finish, and everything in the Jewelry line that is to be found in a first-class and thoroughly-equipped establishment of this kind. Mr. Wood is a native of this State, and is a prominent member of the Free Masons. He is an enterprising and reliable business man, well-known throughout the community as he has been so long engaged in this business and so well known to the trade. We are not called upon to make any personal comments. In general regard his house is one with which it is desirable to maintain business relations.

L. H. Soper, Dry Goods, 54 Main Street, Waterville. It is to the fair sex that the dealer in Dry Goods looks for the bulk of his patronage, and as this is the case, it is evident that among the ladies can the popularity of an establishment of this kind be best ascertained. Abiding by the verdict there obtained, we have no hesitation in according a prominent position to the enterprise carried on by Mr. L. H. Soper, at 54 Main Street; for this undertaking must be well worthy of patronage or it would never receive the many warm commendations we have heard bestowed upon it. Mr. Soper was born in Oldtown, and begun operations here in 1877. The premises utilized by him consist of two floors, measuring 25x75 feet and fully occupied with a heavy and skillfully selected stock of Dry Goods of standard quality, embracing many of the latest and most fashionable novelties of the day. In the line of Dress Goods alone, such decided inducements are offered as to more than repay the trouble of a visit, and we need not remind those who have had dealings with Mr. Soper, that every article leaving his store is sure to prove just as represented. Employing six efficient and always courteous assistants, he is able to assure all callers quick and polite attention, and, as is well known, makes it a point to allow no one to undersell him, the quality and style of the goods offered being taken into consideration.

Colby University, President, Rev. G. D. B. Pepper, College Street, Waterville. From the landing of the Puritans up to the present day, New England has always provided the best possible educational facilities, and the wisdom of this course, even from a strictly utilitarian point of view, has been the theme of many an orator and writer. The mental training acquired in our schools and colleges has done much to enable New Englanders to deserve the reputation for culture, enterprise and progressive ideas that they hold throughout the civilized world, and the idea that education unfitted a man to engage in the struggles and combats of mercantile life has long since been abandoned by all save a few determined enemies to progress of any kind. One of Waterville's most popular institutions, and one whose influence is much more powerful and far-reaching than many people suppose, is that known as Colby University, located on College Street. This was chartered in 1820, and was known as the "Waterville College" for many years, assuming its present title in 1867. The President, Reverend G. D. B. Pepper, D.D., LL.D , ranks with the best-known and most successful educators in the country, and those who have the advantages derived from the training received at the establishment under his charge have reason to congratulate themselves on the perfection of their equipment. We might present a long list of distinguished graduates of Colby University, but refrain from doing so, as however interesting such a list might be, it might convey a wrong idea of the aims of the institution. Its management conscientiously endeavor to fit the pupils under their charge for the all-important duties of American citizenship, and however gratified they may be when some of their students attain distinction, they find their best reward in the thought that the educated, earnest men who graduate from the University cannot fail to exert a pronounced influence in the happy settlement of the many important questions now crowding upon us as a people. There are eight buildings occupied and about one hundred and twenty students are in attendance. We would like to give a detailed description of the various departments of the University, but space forbids and we will simply state that every provision is made for careful and thorough instruction, and the health of the pupils is zealously guarded.

George Jewell, Proprietor Elmwood Hotel and Silver Street Livery, Hack and Boarding Stables, Waterville. There is no disputing the fact that the "Elmwood" Livery, Hack and Boarding Stables occupy a leading position among similar establishments of the kind in Waterville; and it is perfectly natural that such should be the case, for their proprietor is one of the most experienced stable-keepers in the State and spares no expense to afford his customers every accommodation. The enterprise under his charge was inaugurated in 1858, and we are happy to say that never before in its history did its future look more prosperous, and never before was Captain Jewell better prepared to serve his patrons in a thoroughly

LEADING BUSINESS MEN OF WATERVILLE.

first-class and satisfactory manner. He is a native of Waterville and a member of the Free Masons, also Odd Fellows and is one of the representative men of this community, having a very large circle of friends and being very popular both socially and in a business way. The "Elmwood" Stables, are located at the Elmwood Hotel and on Silver St., and are the most extensive as well as the best appointed in Waterville, employment being given to ten assistants. Captain Jewell gives personal attention to the Letting and Boarding of horses and is consequently enabled to guarantee prompt attention and efficient service to such as may favor him with their patronage. His establishments are well supplied with horses, carriages, etc., intended for letting purposes, so that the large livery trade carried on can be fully accommodated, and we can assure those who have not yet made trial of Captain Jewell's facilities that they are equal to the best and are in fact far superior to those of the average livery stable, while his prices are low and equitable. Hacks will be furnished for all public occasions such as Funerals, Weddings, Parties, etc., and commodious and easy-riding barges together with experienced and careful drivers, will be supplied to large excursion parties, etc. All of the horses, vehicles, harnesses, etc., used in the Elmwood stables are kept in first-class condition, and as a consequence the most fastidious customers can find no reasonable ground for complaint.

F. J. Goodridge, Manufacturing Jeweler and Dealer in Watches, Clocks, Jewelry and Silver Ware; also Diamonds and Optical Goods, Main Street, Waterville. Among Waterville establishments which have great and deserved popularity, that of Mr. F. J. Goodridge, located on Main Street, deserves prominent mention, for although this enterprise was only inaugurated in 1880, it has long since gained the full confidence of the public. Mr. Goodridge, who is a native of Dexter, and a member of the Knights of Pythias, is a Manufacturing Jeweler and Dealer in Watches, Clocks, Jewelry and Silver Ware, and being thoroughly acquainted with the practical details of the manufacture of jewelry and similar articles, he is able to intelligently recommend to his customers such goods as he deems adapted to their use. By liberal and strictly honorable dealing, he has gained the entire confidence of those who have done business with him, and everything coming from his store may be implicitly depended upon in every respect. One floor, 24x65 feet in size, is occupied, and the assortment of goods shown is noteworthy both on account of its extent and its completeness. Watches in Gold and Silver cases are offered in great variety, at bottom prices, and Mr. Goodridge is prepared to furnish a perfectly reliable time-piece at an extremely low figure. In Clocks also, some surprising inducements are extended, and in the line of Silver Ware he shows the latest productions of the most popular manufacturers. Diamonds and Optical Goods are given particular attention, and Mr. Goodridge has some beautiful brilliants in stock, set in the most fashionable manner and offered at prices as low as can possibly be afforded.

Low Brothers, Star Laundry, Main Street, Waterville. New England people as a general thing are rather conservative, and are not given to making changes without some good reason exists for doing so; but on the other hand, they are quick to recognize genuine merit, and hence may be depended upon to patronize any really worthy enterprise to which their attention may be called. As a case in point, let us refer to the high degree of success attained by the popular "Star Laundry," of which Messrs. Low Brothers are the proprietors, located on Main Street. This enterprise was inaugurated in 1885, and some little time elapsed before any considerable amount of business was done, but as soon as the fine character of the work turned out became known, and it was learned that the prices were as reasonable as the work was satisfactory, a large patronage was accorded the firm, and this has steadily and rapidly increased up to the present time. Both members of the firm are natives of Belfast, and to both must due credit be given for the establishment of an industry so useful to the community, for both have worked hard and earnestly to keep all promises made, and to thoroughly cleanse the finest fabrics without injuring them in the slightest degree. The public has long since discovered that the cock and bull stories circulated by certain interested parties, calculated to convey the impression that goods intrusted to a public laundry would be soon destroyed, were entirely unworthy of credence, for however it may be with other concerns, the Star Laundry employs no agents or machines that could possibly harm the articles treated by them.

Lowell & Putnam, Manufacturers of Fine Havana and Domestic Cigars; Private Brands a Specialty. Dealers in Chewing and Smoking Tobaccoes, Pipes, Cigarettes, etc., etc., corner of Main and Common Streets, Waterville. We know that smokers who are not yet acquainted with the establishment conducted by Messrs. Lowell & Putnam, at the corner of Main & Common Streets, will thank us for advising them to make trial of some of the fine brands of Cigars and Tobacco there obtainable, for the firm mentioned is really offering some superior and exceptional inducements to users of Tobacco, and by so doing have already built up a very large trade, although business was not begun until 1887. Mr. Lowell is a native of Lewiston and Mr. Putnam of Lewiston, the former being an Odd Fellow and the latter a member of the Knights of Pythias. The store occupied measures 18x35 feet, and contains a very extensive and intelligently selected stock of Chewing and Smoking Tobaccoes, Pipes, Cigarettes and Smokers' Articles in general, together with a magnificent assortment of Cigars made by this concern, and including articles made of the finest imported stock as well as those of choice domestic material. Messrs. Lowell & Putnam are able to quote very low prices on Cigars, as they save one profit by retailing their own goods, and depend more on the magnitude of their business than anything else to repay them. Customers are given courteous and prompt attention, and the list of regular patrons is already a large one.

LEADING BUSINESS MEN OF WATERVILLE.

F. A. Robbins, Harness Maker and Upholsterer, Furniture, Sleighs and Carriages Upholstered. Harnesses made to order and kept constantly on hand. Head of Silver Street, Sign of the Big Whip, Waterville. Those who have made trial of the productions of Mr. F. A. Robbins, doing business at the head of Silver St., (Sign of the Big Whip) need no urging to patronize him in the future, for such uniformly excellent work as he turns out is not so common as to excite no comment or admiration. Mr. Robbins is a native of Skowhegan, and is connected with both the Odd Fellows and the Order of United Workmen, having carried on his present undertaking since 1876, and being among the best and most favorably known of the merchants of Waterville. He is extensively engaged in the manufacture of harnesses, and as he has always endeavored to use only reliable material and put the best of work into such articles, it is not surprising that his reputation in this line of manufacture is an unusually high one. A fine assortment of single and double harnesses is kept constantly on hand, and the facilities for the turning out of order work are such that these goods can be made to order at very short notice, when desired, and at the lowest market rates. Much is also done in in the Upholstering line, he carrying a full line of Upholstery Goods, and a specialty is made of the upholstering of Furniture, which is attended to in the most careful and artistic manner and all work warranted to be satisfactory. Mr. Robbins employs two skilled assistants and occupies premises 22x45 feet in size. Fair dealing is assured to all customers and we can heartily recommend this establishment.

W. E. Chadwick, Dealer in Pianos, Organs and Sewing Machines, Main Street, Waterville. A well-established and highly-regarded business enterprise in Waterville, is that conducted by W. E. Chadwick, at No. 37 Main St., for the sale of Pianos, Organs and Sewing Machines. Its inception was in 1884, and since that date the present proprietor has had sole control. As is well-known, it is particularly desirable when purchasing a Piano, Organ or Sewing Machine, to be sure that you will receive honorable and liberal treatment, for certain unscrupulous manufacturers have produced such close imitations, as regards appearance, etc., of standard and popular articles in this line, that no one who is not an expert in judging such goods can be assured that they will not be deceived. Mr. Chadwick is a graduate of Bryant & Stratton's Business College of Boston, and was, for a number of years after leaving that College, employed by the New England Organ Co., of Boston. The experience which he had with this large house, together with that which he has had since, in business for himself in Waterville, has made him perfectly familiar with the almost endless varieties of Pianos, Organs and Sewing Machines on the market at the present time, and one buying of him may rest assured that the purchase will prove strictly as represented in every respect. A large assortment is on hand to choose from and the lowest market rates prevail. Mr. Chadwick is a native of Waterville and one of our best-known business men. He is a member of the Free Masons and Odd Fellows.

Henry A. Taber, Plumbing and Steam Heating. Agent for the Gorton Steam Heating Boiler. Water Street, Augusta; Branch Store on Temple Street, Waterville. The importance of the work done by the Plumber is so evident that even the least observing cannot fail to appreciate it, partially at all events; and it is on account of its importance that we feel sure that our readers will be interested in learning of a Plumbing Establishment which stands second to none in the character of the work done and the fair treatment extended to every customer. We refer to that conducted by Mr. Henry A. Taber, on Water Street, Augusta, and Temple

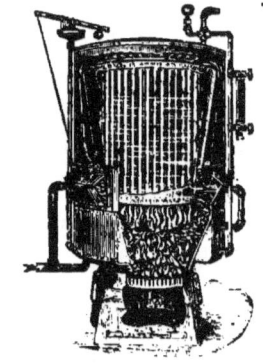

Street, Waterville. We feel confident that the closest investigation and most careful trial will only serve to confirm the good opinion which we hold of the enterprise. It was established in Augusta in 1878, and in Waterville in 1887. A fine stock is carried of Plumbing Materials of all kinds, which are offered at the lowest market rates. Mr. Taber is most excellently prepared to fill all orders with the least possible delay, for he gives employment to eight skilled and experienced assistants, and has every facility at hand to aid him in turning out the best of work. He gives close personal attention to the many details of his business, being a practical Plumber himself, and the result of his endeavors to please his customers is to be seen in the trade carried on, which is already extensive and is steadily increasing.

G. S. Flood & Co., Shippers and Dealers in all kinds of Anthracite and Bituminous Coal, Wood, Lime, Cement, Hair, Pressed Hay, Straw and Drain Pipe. Coal Yards and Office, corner Main and Pleasant Streets; Down-Town Office, Marston Block, Waterville. The residents of Waterville are to be congratulated on having so enterprising and honorable a house of which to procure their supplies of coal, etc., as is that conducted by Messrs. G. S. Flood & Co., having their yards and up-town office at the corner of Main and Pleasant Sts., and also maintaining a down-town office in Marston Block. This enterprise was started by Mr. E. C. Low in 1875, and passed under the control of Mr. G. S. Flood a year later. The present firm was formed in 1882, and has met with great success in its efforts to extend and develop the trade now enjoyed. Mr. G. S. Flood is a native of Clinton, and both he and his associates in business are very widely known throughout this section. The coal yards of the firm cover about an acre and a quarter of land, and eight buildings are utilized in the carrying on of the business, employment being given to ten competent hands. Anthracite and Bituminous Coal of all kinds are handled very largely, both at wholesale and retail, and the relations had with producers are such that customers of this firm are assured the lowest market rates, whether large or small quantities are ordered. Prompt delivery is another popular feature of the management of the business, and no pains are spared to insure satisfaction. Wood, Lime, Cement, Hair, Straw, Pressed Hay, and Drain Pipe are also dealt in in quantities to suit, and fair dealing and courteous treatment may be confidently expected by all doing business with this popular concern.

J. G. Darrah, Crockery and Glassware, General Variety. Main Street, Waterville. It is very nearly a score of years since the enterprise conducted by Mr. J. G. Darrah on Main Street, was inaugurated, and as may be supposed from the fact that "experience teaches" he is now better prepared than ever to supply the public with anything in his line at the most satisfactory prices, and when we speak of "anything in his line," we are aware that we are covering a wide ground, for Mr. Darrah handles a general variety of goods, besides giving particular attention to the sale of Crockery and Glassware. Two floors are occupied, of the dimensions of 30x45 feet and the stock carried is a very heavy one, comprising every staple article in the commodities handled as well as many of the latest and most fashionable novelties. Mr. Darrah is a native of Richmond, and is connected with the Knights of Pythias. He gives employment to three assistants, who will be found courteous and well informed, and strives to give every customer, not only perfectly fair and equitable treatment but also prompt and painstaking attention. A large business has been built up by the steady employment of such methods, and as Mr. Darrah's prices are always as low as the lowest while his goods are uniformly reliable, his trade is sure to grow as long as he serves the public so faithfully and intelligently. Mr. Darrah has also a branch store on the old Post Office Stand with the largest stock of Fancy Goods in the State.

F. M. Hanson, Livery and Boarding Stable, Silver Street, Waterville. The establishment conducted by Mr. F. M. Hanson, on Silver St., and popularly known as a First-Class Stable, was founded by him in 1882, and is one of the best public Stables in Waterville. The premises utilized measure 90x23 feet, and comprise two floors, there being a number of stalls and accomodations for several Carriages. Mr. Hanson employs only competent and reliable assistants, and spares no pains to keep at the "top of the heap," as regards the accomodations he offers his customers. He does not proceed on the principle that apparently actuates many stable-keepers—giving the least possible service for the greatest possible sum—but on the contrary, realizes that the same laws that govern success in any other legitimate business are applicable to his own, and that a satisfied patron is not only apt to come again, but to induce one or more friends to follow his example. As a consequence, Mr. Hanson's business is an increasing one, and those favoring him with an order may depend upon its being promptly and satisfactorily filled. Those wishing to board their horses will find this Stable to possess every facility requisite for the good care and comfort of horses, and would do well to give it a trial. Mr. Hanson is a native of So. Windham, Me., and a highly respected resident of Waterville. He makes his charges as low as the proper maintenance of his plant will permit, and they will bear comparison with those asked for far inferior accomodations.

S. S. Vose & Son, Photographers, Main Street, Waterville. Although it is unquestionably correct to speak of Photographs as "sun-pictures," and to say that they are produced by the action of light upon a surface made sensitive by proper treatment, still the sun does not do everything by any means, for if it did there would be no good photographers and no bad ones and one man possessed of the necessary apparatus could do just as good work as another. This we know is not the case, and it is therefore evident that human taste and skill enter largely into the bringing about of satisfactory results, and that to procure a good picture one must patronize a competent artist. Since Messrs. S. S. Vose & Son began operations here, in 1880, they have often proved their ability to turn out portraits equal to the best, and we have no hesitation in advising any of our readers who may desire a faithful and life-like representation of themselves or of a friend to give this popular concern a trial. It is made up of Mr. S. S. Vose, a native of Cape Cod and a member of the Odd Fellows, and Mr. E. A. Vose, who was born in Turner and is connected with the Knights of Pythias. The former gentleman is also a member of the Grand Army; and as a private in Co. I, of the 16th Maine, he fought in the great Rebellion, was taken prisoner at the Battle of Gettysburg, and only released after 10 months and 20 days of captivity. The premises occupied as a studio, reception room, etc., comprise two floors, of the dimensions of 20x60 feet, and are conveniently fitted up for the comfort of patrons and the doing of the best work. Sittings will be given until satisfaction is attained, and very low prices are quoted on all classes of work.

C. A. Hill, Livery, Boarding and Sale Stable, Main Street, Waterville. Although the day of stages has passed away, the demand for the Livery Business has only increased with advancing wealth and refinement, and the first-class Livery Stable is now, as much as ever, and it will continue to be, a practical necessity in every cultivated community. The Livery Business of Mr. C. A. Hill of this place, was established here in 1872, and has continued uninterruptedly since then to meet all demands upon its services in the most prompt, courteous and satisfactory manner, being without a superior in this vicinity, and ranking with the best city stables. The fine Stable now occupied and used, is located on Main Street, and covers an area of 50x60 feet, and is fitted up and stocked in the most appropriate style. Horses and Carriages are kept constantly in readiness, and the most satisfactory and agreeable arrangement can be made at any time for any of the requirements of a first-class Livery Stable. The public will also find the best opportunities here for boarding and the sale of horses. The advantages of this stable and the liberal and reliable methods of its able proprietor are too well known to the residents of Waterville to need any commendation. Mr. Hill is a native of Skowhegan, a member of the Odd Fellows, and is universally awarded a place among our most honorable and representative citizens.

Fred. Pooler, Dealer in Groceries, Water Street, Waterville. In compiling the various industries of Waterville, the Retail Grocery trade assumes a decided importance. Among those who supply fresh groceries is the house of Mr. Fred. Pooler. His store is located on Water Street, and is well stocked with choice Staple and Fancy Groceries of every description. This business was established by Mr. Pooler in 1863, having been under its present management for the past twenty-five years. The store is 23x65 feet in dimensions, and is admirably arranged for the extensive business transacted. Courteous clerks are employed, who wait upon customers in a polite and attentive manner, and all goods are delivered promptly when desired. This is one of the oldest establishments in its line in Waterville. Mr. Pooler is a native of Waterville. He is well and favorably known throughout the community, and numbers his friends by the score; and his prices will be found as reasonable as any in town for the same quality of goods.

Spaulding & Kennison, Carriage, House and Sign Painters, West Temple Street, Waterville. House and Sign Painting and Ceiling Decoration, are three different trades, each requiring special practice and skill, and it is comparatively seldom that a concern is found that is prepared to execute orders in any or all of these lines at short notice, and with a guarantee of satisfaction. Such, however, is the position held by Messrs. Spaulding & Kennison, doing business on West Temple Street; and we can assure any of our readers who may wish anything done in their line, that they cannot possibly do better than to favor the firm alluded to with their orders, as every facility is at hand and skilled labor available to give every commission prompt and painstaking attention. The enterprise conducted by Messrs. Spaulding & Kennison, was started in 1875 by Mr. S. D. Savage, but for a considerable time has been under the control of its present proprietors. Mr. Spaulding is a native of Waterville, while Mr. Kennison was born in Norridgewock; the latter gentleman being a member of the Knights of Pythias. One floor is occupied of the dimensions of 30x85 feet, and a full assortment of Paints and Painters' Materials is carried, thus enabling all orders to be filled without delay. The work done will be found to be both durable and elegant in appearance, while the lowest rates consistent with the employment of first-class materials are maintained.

Waterville Water Company, Waterville. The idea of Waterville without a water-supply is hardly consistent with the name of that thriving town, and we are happy to say there is a water-supply, and a most excellent one, too; for since the Waterville Water Company put in the present system in 1887, this town has no reason to fear comparison on this score with any of its neighbors. As a matter of fact, this is one of the largest systems in the State of Maine, as it supplies both Waterville and Fairfield through some twenty miles of capacious cast-iron mains. It is a great convenience to manufacturers, of course, and is well appreciated by them, the immense car shops of the Maine Central Railroad, for instance, being supplied by the Company; but after all the best reason why its introduction should be a cause for rejoicing, is the powerful influence it will exert on the prevention of disease. One of the most celebrated physicians the world has ever seen has declared as the result of his life-experience, that "dirt and disease are inseparable," and the dictates of common sense echo the sentiment. Without wholesome drinking water, no community can be healthful, for pure air, pure food and good habits, powerful as they are in warding off disease, are all of no avail when the system is being poisoned by the use of water containing organic and refuse matter. The surprising, but well-authenticated cases of chronic disease which have been brought about by the continuous use of certain mineral waters, are too well known to require detailed mention here, but it may not be generally understood that the virtue of these waters is not so much owing to their "mineral" character as to their freedom from animal or vegetable contamination. "Sulphur Springs" are all very well, but the same water with the sulphur removed would be still more efficacious, excepting perhaps in the treatment of diseases of the skin. The water supplied by the Waterville Water Company is taken from the famous Messalonskee Lake, at Crummett's Mills, and is forced by the most powerful steam-pump in the State into a capacious earth reservoir, lying some two miles west of the Kennebec, at an elevation of 225 feet. No expense has been spared to make this system fully equal to the most extraordinary demand that will be made upon it, and so far as human foresight can provide for the future, the customers of the Company are assured a constant and adequate supply.

E. Gilpatrick, Carpenter, Water Street, Waterville. In spite of the fact that many serious objections have been raised to contract work, it is indisputable that these have been due to abuses of the system and not to any inherent fault in the system itself, as we think is fully proved by the fact that in the proper hands, contract work invariably proves satisfactory and advantageous to all parties concerned. We believe that all contracts made with Mr. E. Gilpatrick, the popular Carpenter and Builder, doing business on Water Street, will be carried out to the satisfaction of all reasonable persons, and our reason for this belief is to be found in the record made by the gentleman alluded to since he began operations in 1870. He is a native of Washington, Me., and since the inception of his business has executed many commissions in the carpentering and building line, in a manner that has conclusively proved his fitness for his chosen occupation. The premises occupied are of the dimensions of 30x70 feet, and employment is ordinarily given to about ten assistants, although this force can be quickly and largely added to should occasion require. Mr. Gilpatrick is prepared to contract for about everything in the line of house-building, and his experience and facilities are such that we can and do, most heartily, advise those of our readers who want anything of the kind done to call and see what he has to offer.

George H. Wilshire & Co., Dealers in Carriages of All Kinds, and Sale Stable for Horses. Gentlemens' Driving Horses Always on Hand and for Sale. Repository on Union Street, near Elmwood Hotel, Waterville. An establishment which can be unhesitatingly recommended to those wishing to purchase anything in the line of Carriages, Horses, or Horse Furnishings of Any Kind is that carried on by Messrs. George H. Wilshire & Co., on Union Street, near the Elmwood Hotel. Although there is popularly supposed to be more danger of imposition in buying horses than there is in the procuring of almost any other article of trade, still we think that this belief is but ill-founded, for it has been our experience that honorable men practice honorable methods whether it be horses or houses that they sell. At all events, the reputation of the firm we have mentioned is too high to allow of the least doubt of the integrity of the gentlemen constituting it, and those who may do business with them may rest assured that every article sold will prove just as represented. The concern is made up of Messrs. George H. Wilshire and J. M. Bunker, the former a prominent Free Mason and a native of Waterville, and the latter of Dover, N. H. Business was begun in 1882, and the many decided advantages offered to customers soon built up a large trade which has continued to steadily and rapidly increase. The repository occupies two floors and a basement, 40x60 feet in size, and contains a large and unusually varied and complete stock of Carriages of All Kinds, Sleighs, Harnesses, etc. Special attention is given to the supplying of Gentlemens' Driving Horses, and a desirable selection of such animals is always to be found here. This firm is known to be particularly interested in this line of business by all of those in the vicinity who handle horses for the market, so that the best driving horses are to be obtained of Messrs. G. H. Wilshire & Co., as they have their pick of what are offered for sale. Any required information will be cheerfully given, and intending purchasers cannot afford to let this establishment remain unvisited.

F. A. Lovejoy, Jeweler, 100 Main Street, Waterville. Waltham Watches a Specialty. No man can afford to be without a watch nowadays, for in the first place they are sold at a very low price, and then again it is generally considered that a man who has no watch, cannot set much value upon his time anyway. It is not necessary for us to speak in praise of Waltham Watches. They are known throughout the civilized world, and are as highly regarded as they are well-known, for their sterling qualities have been often proved, under all conditions and in every variety of circumstances. Therefore we will simply state that Mr. F. A. Lovejoy of No. 100 Main St., makes a specialty of Waltham Watches and is prepared to furnish them in all grades and in all cases, at prices varied enough to permit of all purses as well as all tastes being satisfied. He carries a fine assortment in stock and anyone wanting a good, reliable and handsome time-keeper, should most certainly make him an early call. He does not confine his business to the sale of Watches, by any means, however, and offers some decided inducements in the way of Jewelry, Silver Ware, etc. One floor is occupied, measuring 22x40 feet, and the assortment carried is displayed to excellent advantage. Mr. Lovejoy warrants his goods to prove as represented, and the most inexperienced may buy of him without the least fear of imposition. He a native of Bath, Me., and founded his present undertaking in 1884. Mr. Lovejoy is a member of the Free Masons and has a large circle of friends throughout this vicinity.

Paul Marshall, Dealer in Groceries and Provisions, Water Street, Waterville. Among the many fine establishments located in Waterville and utilized by their proprietors for the prosecution of the Grocery and Provision business, it is with pleasure that we call attention to the one now conducted by Mr. Paul Marshall. This house was established in 1882, by its present able proprietor, who now conducts a popular and first-class Grocery and Provision establishment. The premises are located on Main Street and comprise a store 25x60 feet in dimensions, which is fitted up with every necessary requisite for the proper conduct of the business. Mr. Marshall deals in every description of goods in the Grocery and Provision line, embracing both staple and fancy Groceries and choice, fresh Provisions. The steadily increasing retail trade necessitates the employment of two experienced clerks, and the details of the business are most ably handled. Mr. Marshall is a native of Waterville, and a live, active business man, and few stand in advance of him in the commercial circles of this city.

L. W. Rogers, Proprietor of the Waterville Tea and Coffee Store, and Dealer in Fancy Groceries, Wholesale and Retail, Waterville. It is pleasant to be able to call attention to an enterprise which one feels will be found wanting in nothing that would add to its facilities for serving the public; and therefor it is an agreeable task to allude to the undertaking carried on by Mr. L. W. Rogers, under the name of the Waterville Tea & Coffee Store, for this enterprise is lacking in nothing that should be found in a first-class, modern Grocery and Tea House, and the high record it has made in the past is ample guarantee that it will be conducted in the most liberal and accomodating manner. It was founded in 1880, and has steadily and rapidly increased in importance. The premises occupied comprise two floors and a basement, of the dimensions of 37x80 feet, and employment is given to five efficient and polite assistants. The assortment of Teas and Coffees on hand is remarkable alike for the variety and general excellence of the goods, and Mr. Rogers deals so largely in them he is enabled to quote very low prices for strictly reliable articles. Both a wholesale and retail business is done, and all orders are attended to with promptness and accuracy. Both staple and fancy Groceries are handled, and a full supply of everything required for family use is at all times on hand. Mr. Rogers was born in Oldtown, and is one of the best-known of our men of business.

A. Otten, City Bakery, Temple Street, Waterville. We are desirous of calling the attention of our readers to the well-known Bakery, located on Temple Street, which has been from its inception successful in building up an extensive wholesale and retail trade in Bread, Cake, and Pastry. This establishment was started in 1883 by Mr. A. Otten, who is its present and sole proprietor. The premises occupied and known as the City Bakery comprise two floors, each 22x70 feet in dimensions, which are fully equipped with all the necessary requirements for the successful conduct of the business, the extent of which gives constant employment to six thoroughly experienced assistants. Mr. Otten carries a fine stock in all branches of his business, and is prepared to supply customers at short notice with any goods in his line of manufacture, and perfect satisfaction is guaranteed as to both quality and price. This establishment is largely patronized by families throughout the city, who appreciate first-class Bread, Cake and Pastry of all kinds. Mr. Otten is a native of Cologne on the Rhine. He is a man of excellent business qualifications and high standing in this community.

Morse & Cannon, Dealers in Groceries, Meats and Fish, Main Street, Waterville. This firm have—since 1887—conducted a flourishing Grocery and Provision trade in Waterville, and their store, located on Main Street, is one of the popular sources of food supply in this city. The store is commodious and attractive, having a frontage of 22 feet and a depth of 70 feet, and is a model of completeness and convenience in appointments and arrangements. The stock is uniformly first-class and complete, comprising a full assortment of choice, fresh Groceries, staple and family. Also a large assortment of Meats and Fish of the finest quality. The firm make a specialty of supplying all merchandise of a superior quality, at low prices, guaranteeing satisfaction in every particular. Two capable assistants are employed, and all orders are promptly filled and delivered, free of charge, to all parts of the city, and the worth and methods of these reliable merchants inspire the fullest faith and confidence. Messrs. Morse & Cannon are Maine men by birth; the latter is a member of the Knights of Pythias, a member of the City Council and last year was Alderman, and both are widely known and universally esteemed.

George Stackpole, Dealer in Cigars, Tobacco and Confectionery, Main Street, Waterville. Among the fine stores and plentifully stocked establishments in this section of Waterville, is the house of Mr. George Stackpole, dealer in Cigars, Tobacco, Confectionery, etc. This establishment was founded by its present proprietor in 1871, who, by long experience, is thoroughly conversant with all the details and requirements of the business. His business premises are located on Main Street, and cover an area of 20x40 feet. The storeroom is neatly fitted up, and filled with as complete, varied and choice stock of goods, in his line, as can be found in this part of the city. His stock is frequently replenished with all the best brands of Cigars, Tobacco and Smokers' Articles in general. He also deals in Confectionery, which is guaranteed to be pure and fresh. Mr. Stackpole is a native of Waterville. He has met with success and prosperity, which will doubtless continue with him so long as he remains engaged in commercial pursuits. An attractive stock and liberal prices, together with reliable and courteous dealings, have gained this gentleman the esteem and confidence of the community.

Gilbert H. Carpenter, Dealer in Organs, Pianos and Music; also Ladies' Patterns, 146 Main Street, Waterville. An establishment which is familiar to the many music-lovers of Waterville and vicinity, is that so successfully conducted by Mr. Gilbert H. Carpenter, at 146 Main Street. This gentleman began business in the year 1852, and during the thirty-six years since elapsed, has built up a retail trade of prosperous proportions. He carries a complete assortment of Organs, Pianos and Music, and also deals in Ladies' Patterns. The premises occupied comprise a store 20x60 feet in dimensions. The services of two assistants are required, who are familiar with all the new and popular musical publications. Mr. Carpenter deals in the productions of the most successful and reliable manufacturers, and an instrument warranted by him may be purchased in the full assurance that it will prove to be precisely as represented. Mr. Carpenter is a native of Guilford, Vermont. His house is, perhaps, as widely and favorably known as any in Waterville, in its special line, and offers inducements to purchasers not easily duplicated.

A. E. Davis, Insurance Agent, 79 Main St., Waterville. People are beginning to realize more than ever before the necessity of placing their insurance in reliable companies, and in this connection we would especially direct our readers to a gentleman who represents some of the strongest Fire, Life and Accident companies in this country. We refer to Mr. A. E. Davis, having an office at 79 Main Street, and well known in this vicinity, being a native of Waterville and a prominent member of the Knights of Pythias. Mr. Davis gives every care to the writing of Fire Insurance, and those having property to insure may feel confident that their interests will receive his personal attention.

Dolloff & Dunham, The One-Price Clothiers. Fine Ready-made Clothing, Hats, Caps and Gents' Furnishing Goods, No. 40 Main Street, Waterville. There is a certain feeling going with the consciousness of being well-dressed, that has often been remarked upon, and which none of our readers can fail to be familiar with. It is neither pride nor self-satisfaction, but invariably makes the subject of it more self-respecting and respectful to others, and hence is deserving of the utmost encouragement. Messrs. Dolloff & Dunham, of No. 40 Main Street, are certainly doing all in their power to encourage the wearing of fashionable and tasteful apparel, for since they opened their present establishment, in 1887, they have offered such pronounced and unusual inducements in the way of Clothing for men, youths and boys, that hundreds have taken advantage of the opportunities extended to buy durable, stylishly-cut and reasonable garments at really remarkably low rates. Mr. Dolloff is a native of Mt. Vernon and is connected with the Knights of Pythias and the Odd Fellows. Mr. Dunham being also a member of the latter organization and a native of West Paris. The premises in use are of the dimensions of 25x85 feet. Strict personal attention of both members of the firm is given to their patrons. Fine Ready-made Clothing, Hats and Caps, are on hand in great variety, and a most extensive and skillfully-selected assortment of Gents' Furnishings is offered, comprising many English novelties, and marked at prices that insure its early sale.

Dow & Green, Dealers in all kinds of Coal and Wood, office on Main Street, near Freight Depot, Waterville. The serious troubles which have so long continued in the coal regions, and the consequent interruptions that have occurred in the supply of the "dusky diamonds," have given our local dealers a chance to show how they are prepared to meet unforseen contingencies in their line of business, and whether they are disposed to take advantage of circumstances to impose on the public or not. We are happy to say that our coal dealers as a body, have shown themselves to be public-spirited citizens as well as enterprising merchants and no firm amongst them has gained a more enviable reputation in this respect than has that of Dow & Green, having an office on Main Street, near the Freight depot. This firm succeeded Lawrence & True, and is composed of Messrs.

William H. Dow and S. A. Green, the former being a native of Vassalboro and the latter of Fairfield, Me. Mr. Dow is connected with the Odd Fellows and both he and Mr. Green are well and favorably known throughout this vicinity. The premises occupied comprise an area of about one acre of ground on which are located five buildings, used for storage and other purposes. Both a wholesale and retail business is done, and Wood and Coal of every description are very extensively handled. Employment is given to seven assistants and orders are filled without delay and at prices that are always as low as the market will permit.

Hayden & Robinson, Contractors and Builders, Mechanic Square, Waterville. Reputation is a very essential thing to every business man or firm, and it should not be confounded with credit, as it is something quite different from that although it may be influenced by it to a considerable degree. A firm may have the best of credit and a very indifferent reputation, or the reverse may be the case, although as a general thing good reputation accompanies high credit. It is particularly important that an excellent reputation should be held by such concerns as are engaged in Contracting and Building, and in this connection mention should be made of the firm of Hayden & Robinson, having headquarters in Mechanic Square, for since the inauguration of the enterprise conducted by these gentlemen in 1875, they have built up a reputation for conscientious work and strict adherence to all agreements, that has served to win them a deservedly high place in the confidence of the public. Both members of the firm are natives of Waterville, and rank with the best known and most highly esteemed of our citizens. Two floors are occupied, having the dimensions of 20x40 feet, and employment is given to twelve competent and skillful assistants. Estimates will be made on any proposed line of work coming within the scope of the firm's operations, and they are prepared to undertake anything in their line, with the assurance of satisfaction, both as regards the results attained, and the cost of the same, compared with that of similar operations conducted by other houses.

Ira H. Low, Apothecary, 68 Main Street, Waterville. The position of the Apothecary unites the requirements and responsibilities of both the professional and the business man, and as is always the case, it thus involves peculiar fitness and the combination of rare and opposite characteristics of mind, which we seldom find in one individual, in order that the duties and cares may be properly and successfully met. To the fact that these conditions of scientific knowledge and business enterprise have been exceptionally well-filled, is chiefly owing the marked and increasing success which has attended the business of Mr. Ira H. Low from the start, forty-two years ago. The business was established in 1846, under the title of I. H. Low & Co., and so conducted until 1876, when Mr. Lowe assumed sole proprietorship, and has always shown peculiar capabilities for his work and a thorough reliability, which has won the confidence of the public. His premises comprise a store and basement, each 20x70 feet in dimensions, which are well-stocked with a complete and valuable assortment of Pure Drugs and First-class Druggists' sundries. Two talented and experienced assistants are employed, and special attention is given to the Prescription Department, which is managed with unusual accuracy. Mr. Low is a native of Fairfield and is one of our most successful and popular Apothecaries, and has justly earned the esteem and appreciation of his fellow-citizens.

O. J. Pelletier, Dealer in Groceries and Dry Goods, Water Street, Waterville. With characteristic energy and consequent success, Mr. O. J. Pelletier has, for the past eight years, carried on a large and growing Grocery, Boot and Shoes and Dry Good business in Waterville, and the house at this writing is one of the first-class concerns in this field of trade in the city. Mr. Pelletier occupies for business purposes a fine storeroom, 25x40 feet in dimensions, located on Water Street, and carries in stock a large and select assortment of merchandise. The finest and freshest family and fancy Groceries, and a full line of Dry Goods and Boots and Shoes are always to be had of this house at lowest current prices, and the honorable and square dealings of the proprietor, justify unqualified faith in the standard quality of the merchandise. Mr. Pelletier employs two capable assistants, and has the best possible facilities for meeting all the requirements of his customers, and orders are promptly filled and goods are delivered to all parts of the city. Mr. Pelletier is a native of Canada and is justly esteemed in this community for his integrity and liberal dealings.

HISTORICAL SKETCH
—OF—
OAKLAND, ME.

THE enterprising town of Oakland, Maine, is one of the suburbs of Waterville of which city it was formerly a part. It is in the extreme south of Somerset county, sixteen miles north of Augusta, and seventy-seven from Portland, reached directly via. the Maine Central Railroad. It is also a terminus of the Somerset Railroad. Its early history is identical with that of Waterville. It was one of the first sections of that city to be settled, mainly on account of its attractive location and fertile soil; and during the early years of the century a few enterprising farmers laid the foundation here for the present prosperous community, undergoing the usual wants and fears of the times, the restrictions of the Embargo, the scarcities in the war of 1812, and the various financial panics in the first half of the present century. It was deeply interested and patriotic in action during the great civil war though all the achievements of its sons were credited in general with those of the men of Waterville, of which it was then a part. Most of the soldiers who enlisted from Oakland joined the Second, Sixth, Ninth, Eleventh, Eighteenth, Twenty-Fourth and Twenty-Eighth Maine Volunteer Infantry Regiments. The town was generous in the sacrifice of material goods as well as in the priceless blood of its sons. All demands upon it were met promptly and generously, supplies furnished and much private benevolence was rendered, chiefly through the Ladies' Aid Society, Christian Sanitary Commission and such noble institutions. A number of the town's gallant sons fell while in the service, and their loving sacrifice has been tenderly and long commemorated.

The great advance of the town has been made since the Civil War. The expansion of business interests and the stimulation of new lines of activity have rapidly made it a prominent and prosperous commercial center. The financial panics which have swept over the country have affected it but slightly, and it has kept steadily on its upward way. It was set off from Waterville and incorporated as West Waterville, February 26, 1873. Since that time its progress has been marked and continuous. Its great advantages have attracted new business men and enterprises, and as it has become better known its commercial activities have correspondingly increased. It has continued to offer special facilities to large enterprises for settlement, in the way of exemptions from taxation, and other privileges, which are of an exceptionally fine character, and deserving the attention of all business men thinking of making a new settlement. At the present time the business interests of the town are largely concerned with the canned goods trade in all its departments, carriage-making, furniture and upholstery, agricultural implements, and all kinds of tools, machinery, woolen goods, granite-quarrying, lumber, coffins and shoes. These interests are expanding yearly and new ones being constantly inaugurated. The agricultural resources abound. The soil is fertile, and under the careful methods of scientific farming, great results are obtained. Fruits and vegetables abound, and considerable attention is given to grazing and dairy-farming. The population in 1880 was 1646, it has since increased, being now around 2000. The valuation in 1880, was $661,157. This also has advanced, and is now in the vicinity of a million dollars. The Selectmen of the town for the past year were the following: O. E. Crowell, Stephen C. Watson, C. M. Crowell; Town Clerk, H. G. Winslow; Treasurer and Supt. of Schools, Geo. W. Field.

The town has always been noted for its fine educational facilities, and the attention given to this important department. Being contiguous to one of the best colleges in the State has undoubtedly had a tendency to raise its standard. Appropriations have been ample, the teachers and officers. carefully selected, have been noted for their ability and efficiency, and the results as shown in the education of the younger generation most satisfactory. The moral and religious tone of the town also have always been high. Church and benevolent work have been earnestly and effectively carried out. There are five churches in the town, two Baptists, one Free Baptist, one Universalist, and one Methodist. These all are active and progressive, and are heartily supported by the people.

The sanitary advantages of Oakland are of the most satisfactory kind. The drainage is rendered almost perfect by the proximity of the river, and pure and abundant water is obtained. The conveniences of modern life, as gas, electricity, etc., are provided for, and the proximity of the railroad makes traveling easy and delightful.

The advantages of Oakland from the standpoint of the summer tourist are too many to admit of rapid specification. Situated near the river, with the neighboring hills, the air is rendered pure and cool. The pleasure of wood and water, hunting, fishing, boating and sailing, can all be participated in. The usual advantages of country life in the way of out-door exercises, fine drives and walks, which are especially beautiful in this region, the plenteous supply of country-produce, fruit and vegetables at low rates, and the general moderate cost, render Oakland especially worthy of consideration by those planning for a summer in the State of Maine. Its proximity to Augusta and Waterville, and the ease of communication by railway, are important points. The great promise of Oakland in the future lies in its business development, and it will some day be one of the best-known and important commercial centers in the Kennebec valley.

LEADING BUSINESS MEN
OF
OAKLAND, ME.

Dunn Edge Tool Co., Manufacturers of Scythes, Hay Knives, Axes and Grass Hooks, Oakland. An enterprise which has been the means of favorably introducing the name of Oakland in many localities where it would not otherwise be known is that carried on by the Dunn Edge Tool Company. The productions of this company are conceded by good judges to rank with the best in the markets of the world, and goods bearing the trade-mark of this concern are unquestionably accepted as the standard by those who have had the uniform excellence of such products proved to them by the test of practical use. Mr. R. B. Dunn began business in North Wayne, Me., in January, 1840, and seventeen years later the present corporation was formed. This proved a wise proceeding, for having ample capital at its command, the company was able to extend the manufacturing facilities in every way, and to rapidly build up the reputation of its products. A liberal course has been pursued from the first, and neither labor nor trouble has been spared in constantly improving the goods and diminishing their cost to the consumer, the most improved labor-saving machinery being utilized throughout the extensive works. The materials used are selected with great care, many of them being imported expressly for the company, and every process of their working up is carefully carried on under strict supervision. No "guess-work" is allowed in this company's shops, and under the rule that "equal causes produce equal effects," the uniform superiority of the articles produced is easily accounted for. Wherever the Dunn Edge Tool Company has exhibited its products in competition with others, it has been awarded the medals and diplomas granted for excellence; and such competition has been confined to no section, for it has been entered into at home and abroad; in London, in Philadelphia, in New York, in Maryland, in Massachusetts, and in New Orleans, so that rival concerns have been successfully coped with on their own grounds. Among the more important articles manufactured may be mentioned Scythes, Hay Knives, Axes and Grass Hooks, and no section of the country is neglected in the getting up of special styles, for patterns suitable for use under all conditions are turned out. The Improved "Cyclone" Hay Knife, made by this company is without doubt the most efficient tool of the kind made, each being sharpened ready for use and capable of cutting hay in mow, stack or bale with unequalled rapidity. Peat and turf are cut with equal facility, and no more useful device for the stock-farm can be found. The Dunn Edge Tool Company's goods are handled by all prominent retailers and are sold under a full guarantee of excellence. Quantity considered, they are at least as cheap as any in the market, and we are convinced that such of our readers as may once give them practical trial will indorse all we have said regarding their unusual merits. The personal history of Mr. Reuben B. Dunn may be studied with profit by every young man who has his way to make in the world, for not only is it a more valuable "Guide to Wealth" than any of the many books published under that title, but it also shows how a man may advance the best interests of the community at the same time that he is carving his own fortune. Mr. Dunn early cultivated the habit of close observation, and to this, together with an independence and promptness of action that characterized him, he owes much of the abundant success he has attained. Quick to see an opportunity, he is equally prompt in taking advantage of it, and once embarked in an undertaking, no difficulties or discouragements can deter him from pushing it to a successful conclusion if such an ending be possible. Mr. Dunn is an excellent judge of men, and is ever ready to show appreciation of faithfulness and zeal on the part of his agents. "Credit where credit is due" is one of his guiding principles, and he frequently remarks that no man has been more favored than he with intelligent and conscientious assistants. The business now carried on by the Dunn Edge Tool Company is a monument to his far-sightedness in commercial affairs, and his services in connection with the management of the Maine Central R. R. (of which he was formerly President), have been of a character to earn for him the gratitude of every public-spirited citizen of this State.

Dustin & Hubbard Manufacturing Co., Engineers, Machinists and Iron Founders. Specialties of Machinists' Tools, Water Wheels, Steam Engines, Saw Mill Machinery, Steam Heating, Shafting and Pulleys, Heavy Gearing, Grist Mill Machinery, Fire Pumps and Friction Gears, Oakland. We know of no more striking example of prompt success in a business venture than that afforded by the enterprise carried on here by the Dustin & Hubbard Manufacturing Company. This Company began operations in 1887, and have so rapidly increased their sales that figures that are authorative today, would be of but little value in indicating the true magnitude of the business done a month from now. Such a showing at a time when many manufacturing enterprises are not doing so well as usual, is more eloquent than words in pointing out the advantages derivable from placing orders with this concern, and as a matter of fact, no one wishing anything in the line of Machinists' Tools, Water Wheels, Steam

Engines, Steam and Hot Water Heating Apparatus, Shafting and Pulleys, Heavy Gearing, Pulp Mill Machinery, Fire Pumps or Friction Gears, can afford to allow the opportunities offered by this company to go unimproved. The "Risdon" Turbine Water Wheels, the "Dustin" Machine Tools and "Pine Tree Pulp Grinder," are among the most valuable of the specialties manufactured, and the record these articles have made in practical use, is enough to fully explain their abiding popularity. Mr. J. U. Hubbard, the President of the Company, is a native of Oakland and a member of the Free Masons, while the Superintendent, Mr. F. E. Dustin, was born in Dexter, and is connected with the Odd Fellows and the Knights of Pythias. Mr. G. H. Bryant, the Treasurer, has resided in Oakland twenty-four years; he is a native of Dorchester, Mass., and is a member of the Ancient Order of United Workmen, also the Masonic Order. All these gentlemen are well-known in this vicinity, and their undertaking is looked upon as one of the most important in town. Employment is given to fifty-four assistants, and the works contain some 50,000 feet of floor space, the plant in operation being very extensive. The Company fill orders without delay, and can quote the most favorable terms, as its facilities are equal to the best.

A. W. Leonard, Groceries and Provisions, Oakland. It is hardly necessary to state that the Grocery and Provision trade is one of the most important in the country, for this fact can not fail to be evident to all readers. An enormous amount of capital is invested in it, and considering the population of the place, Oakland has no reason to fear comparison with any other community, in the character of the concerns engaged in this line of trade within her borders. One of the best known of the establishments alluded to, is that of which Mr. A. W. Leonard is the proprietor. This was opened in 1885, and has met with great success, for Mr. Leonard has carried it on on liberal principles from the first, and the public have appreciated his straight-forward and honorable methods. He was born in Belgrade, Maine, and is a member of the Free Masons. The premises made use of comprise four rooms, each being 70x25 feet in dimensions, and employment is given to two efficient assistants. Customers receive immediate and polite attention, and orders are promptly and accurately delivered, both a wholesale and retail business being done. Mr. Leonard deals very extensively in Grain as well as in Groceries and Provisions, and those wanting anything in the line of Flour and Feed, would do well to give him a call.

LEADING BUSINESS MEN OF OAKLAND.

Mr. and Mrs. B. F. Frizzell, Dealers in Fashionable Millinery, Medicines, Stationery, School Supplies, Confectionery, Cigars and Yankee Notions, Rubber Stamps, Door Plates, Pillow Sham Holders, etc., all of which will be sold cheap for cash, Church Street, near the Depot, Oakland. The establishments conducted by Mr. and Mrs. B. F. Frizzell, although different in their character, should properly be considered together, as the stores are connected, being located side by side on Church street. Mrs. Frizzell, who commenced in Millinery in 1868, deals extensively in Fashionable Millinery and Fancy Goods. Also material for Fancy Needle Work. The writer being "only a man," must confess his ignorance of the mysteries of Millinery, but he has heard enough from Mrs. Frizzell's patrons to warrant the assertion that those leaving orders with her are assured complete satisfaction, and will be supplied with stylish goods at bottom prices, all commissions being executed at short notice, and in workmanlike manner. Mr. Frizzell handles Medicines, Stationery, School Supplies, Confectionery, Cigars and Yankee Notions as well as Rubber Stamps, Door Plates, Pillow Sham Holders, and many other articles too numerous to mention. A specialty is made of Sewing Machines and Supplies, such as Attachments, Needles, Shuttles, Bobbins, Oil, Oil Cans, Screw Drivers, etc., for every description of machine. Both New and Second-hand Machines are dealt in, and particular attention is given to Repairing. Mr. Frizzel having been in this business for nearly twenty years and fully warranting all his work. He invites all having ailing or broken machine heads to bring them to his store, where he will "doctor" them up and restore them to perfect order at low prices. Second-hand machines may be bought or rented of him, and no one in want of an article of the kind, can afford to neglect taking advantage of the unusual opportunities he offers.

James T. Flinn, Carriage Jobbing and Repairing, Oakland. It is no doubt true that the manufacture of Carriages has been brought to a higher stage of perfection in the United States than anywhere else in the World. Mr. James T. Flinn, of Oakland, Me., has attained no little reputation in the line of Carriage Work, among those who have been in a position to judge of his skill; and it is the general opinion among those who have done business with him, that no Jobber and Repairer in Oakland, turns out more desirable or durable work. The premises occupied by Mr. Flinn are 20x28 feet in dimensions. He is a native of Oakland, and has conducted the enterprise in question since 1887. The assistants employed are experienced and careful workmen and as only standard and approved materials are used in the filling of orders, it is not surprising that the results are uniformly satisfactory. Particular attention is given Repairing and Jobbing of every description and every facility is at hand to enable orders of this kind to be filled at the shortest notice and the lowest possible rates. Neatness and strength are combined in the repairs made here, and we can heartily recommend this establishment to our readers.

J. B. Clair, Dealer in Boots, Shoes and Rubbers. Custom Work a Specialty; Church Street, Oakland. It hardly needs demonstration that a man who has been in the handling of certain articles of commerce for a number of years, should be tolerably familiar with the same, and in a position to offer customers special inducements as regards their purchases; but if such demonstrations are needed, they may be had by inquiring as to the experience of the patrons of Mr. J. B. Clair, who founded his present business in Oakland in 1882, and has attained the large patronage he now enjoys by giving value for money received in every case. He is a native of Burlington, Vermont, and belongs to the Ancient Order of United Workmen, and is one of our highly esteemed and best-known residents. Mr. Clair manufactures a very fine class of mens' and women's Boots and Shoes, only manufacturing sewed work. He also runs a cosy and first class Shoe Store, keeping nothing but the best of goods for style as well as durability. We can assure our readers that goods suited to their peculiar needs are obtainable here, for everything in the way of first-class Boots, Shoes and Rubbers is offered by Mr. Clair, and his goods are always sure to prove as he represents them to be, and Custom Work in this line is made a specialty. All tastes and purses are provided for, and the latest fashions are obtainable here.

McLure & Danforth, Dealers in Flour, Grain, Feed, Salt, Groceries and Provisions, Oakland. The firm of McLure & Danforth begun operations in the summer of 1885, succeeding A. J. Libby & Son in the Grocery business. In 1887 they succeeded S. Blaisdell in the Grain and Milling, doing all kinds of Custom Grinding, also wholesale and retail dealers in Flour, Grain and Feed. Mr. D. F. McLure is a native of Skowhegan, while Mr. G. H. Danforth was born in Boston, and both are connected with the Odd Fellows. Mr. McLure being also connected with the Masons. Groceries, Provisions, Flour, Fresh and Salt Meats, etc., are very largely dealt in, and it would be impossible to find a store in this vicinity in which lower prices are quoted on goods of equal merit. Messrs. McLure & Danforth make a specialty of handling Teas and Coffees and are in a position to offer decided inducements to users of these popular commodities. They guarantee the purity of their goods, and their excellence of flavor commend them to every discriminating purchaser. Fine family Flour is offered in quantities to suit, and the firm possess peculiar advantages in the handling of this staple, as they carry on an extensive Grist Mill in connection with their store and can consequently guarantee the quality and quote bottom prices on Flour and Feed in general. Fresh and Salt Meats of all kinds may be had here at the lowest market rates, and choice cuts of Beef and Mutton are kept in stock for the accommodation of fastidious patrons. Vegetables of every variety—in their season—are also largely dealt in, and in fact there is a comprehensive assortment of food supplies for family use constantly kept on hand. All goods are delivered free, and customers are assured polite and prompt attention.

Hubbard & Blake Manufacturing Company, Manufacturers of Edge Tools, Oakland, (Formerly West Waterville), John U. Hubbard, President and Superintendent, Nathaniel Meader, Treasurer. The history of the enterprise carried on by the Hubbard & Blake Manufacturing Company, is well worthy the careful study of those who would achieve success in business, for it proves that genuine merit is sure to triumph in the end, and that a determination to produce the best possible articles for which a market can be found, will find its legitimate reward at the hands of a discriminating public. The enterprise to which we have reference, was inaugurated a quarter of a century ago, by Messrs. Hubbard & Blake, the present company having been incorporated in 1875. It consists of Messrs. Hubbard, Blake, Meader, Smith and Ray, and has one of the finest Edge Tool manufacturing plants in the world, employing one hundred assistants and shipping goods to nearly all parts of the continent. The plant is divided into what are known as the Upper and "Lower" works, the former comprising a "Hammer Shop" 100x40 feet, and a Grinding, Polishing and Finishing Shop of the same dimensions, three stories in height. The Lower works include a Hammer Shop, measuring 300x40 feet, and a Grinding and Polishing Shop, two stories in height, and 60x40 feet in size. There are thirty trip-hammers and eighteen Grind-stones in use, and Axes, Hatchets, Hay-knives, Scythes, Grass Hooks and other Edge Tools, are very extensively manufactured. The "King of the Forest" and "Forest Clipper" Axes have gone into general use, and no more valuable or celebrated goods are found in the market today. They are made in a variety of patterns, including the Maine, Vermont, Wedge, Jersey, Western, Double Bitt, Michigan, etc., and quality considered, are probably the cheapest and most efficient that can be bought. Boy's axes are also very largely manufactured, and a specialty is made of Hunting Hatchets and Camp Axes, with Crosby's Patent Covers, which make their transportation perfectly safe under all circumstances and can be removed in an instant. These hatchets are made in weights varying from one to four pounds, and those wishing full information should send for descriptive circular, which will be mailed on application. Mr. John U. Hubbard is President and Superintendent of the Company, and the position of Treasurer is filled by Mr. Nathaniel Meader.

Mills Brothers, Livery and Boarding Stable, Main Street, Oakland. It is fitting that we should make special mention of the establishment located on Main Street, for several reasons, some of which are that this is one of the best known enterprises of the kind in Oakland, that it has a reputation second to none, and equalled by but very few. The Messrs. Mills Brothers, the proprietors of the Livery and Boarding Stable to which we have referred, established their present enterprise in 1886, and are both natives of Oakland, and very widely known throughout the vicinity. The premises utilized by them comprise two floors. Seven fine turnouts are kept at this stable and every facility is at hand to fill orders for all kinds of first-class teams at short notice, and as their carriages are kept in strictly first-class condition, it is not surprising that their facilities are made constant use of. Teams will be supplied to those who wish to enjoy a drive and handle the "ribbons" themselves, and ladies will find special provision made for their accommodation, as the Mills Brothers have some horses that are good roadsters and yet are gentle and fearless, hence being particularly adapted to ladies use. Easy-riding carriages are on hand in considerable variety and all the facilities for a most enjoyable excursion are afforded here at moderate rates. Horses will be taken to board and assured the best of care and the premises are always kept in neat and healthful condition.

Stephen Blaisdell, Marble and Granite Works, Oakland. The gentleman whose card is printed above has not carried on his present enterprise for a very long time, but, nevertheless, has already built up a business of extensive proportions. Operations were begun here in Oakland in 1885, and in the fall of 1886, a branch was opened in Waterville, on Mill Street. Marble and Granite are dealt in to a considerable extent, and Building and Cemetery Work is done at short notice in a uniformly superior manner. The Oakland establishment is devoted principally to Polishing, and in both shops every detail of the work is carefully carried out by skilled hands. Mr. Blaisdell is a native of Rome, Me., and thoroughly understands every department of his business. He uses this knowledge to good effect in avoiding all unnecessary sources of expense, and the large business done is principally due to this fact, for though his work is equal to the best, his prices are remarkably low, as the public have learned from experience. Employment is given to twelve assistants, and quite a variety of finished work of various kinds is kept in stock, the assortment being worthy of careful inspection. Order Work will be attended to at the shortest possible notice, and designs will be cheerfully shown on application, estimates of cost, etc., also being carefully made, and all desired information promptly given.

Dr. M. L. Damon, Dentist, Oakland. The popular dental establishment of Dr. M. L. Damon, located on Main Street, Oakland, deserves particular notice in a volume of this character. He has been established in this locality since 1887, and has gained a high reputation. The location is convenient and the premises commodious comprising four large rooms. The reception rooms are handsomely and appropriately furnished, while the operating rooms are provided with the best known appliances for the rendering of satisfactory services. Dr. Damon attends to all branches of Dentistry, Extracting and Filling Teeth, and also the manufacture of Artificial Teeth, and employs his talents in all directions where skill is necessary. His work is always of the most perfect character. Dr. M. L. Damon will be found reliable, prompt and accurate in the fulfillment of orders, and his prices are very moderate and are suited to the means of all. He is a native of Pittsfield, is a graduate of Baltimore College of Dental Surgery, and is well-known throughout this vicinity and is a gentleman of enterprise and energy.

Greenleaf T. Stevens, Attorney-at-Law, Oakland. The time-honored saying to the effect that a man who is his own lawyer "has a fool for a client," looses none of its truth with the progress of time, but on the contrary gains more force as more instances are afforded of the practical effects of such attempted economy. The Law is one of the noblest of professions, and this fact is not to be gainsaid because there are a few engaged in it who think more of personal advancement than of honor and probity. Honorable Lawyers are quite as common as honorable physicians, clergymen, etc., and no one need lack proper legal advice by reason of the difficulty of obtaining such. Among those who have gained the respect and esteem of the public in this line of effort, mention should be made of Mr. G. T. Stevens, for during the score of years that this gentleman has practiced his profession, he has built up a most enviable reputation, not only for knowledge of the law, but for what is still more important—complete devotion to his clients' interests. Mr. Stevens was born in Belgrade, Maine, and received his education at the Litchfield Liberal Institute. He is a graduate of Harvard University and holds the degree of LL.D. from that institution. Mr. Stevens has an exceptional war record, having served in the army for three years and seven months. He was Captain of the 5th Battery, Mounted Artillery, Maine Volunteers, from May 3d, 1863, and the character of the service he rendered in that capacity, is evidenced by his appointment as Major by Brevet for gallant and meritorious conduct at the battles of Cold Harbor, Winchester and Cedar Creek. He is a member of the Maine Gettysburg Commission, and is widely-known in Grand Army circles. Mr. Stevens was elected to the Maine House of Representatives in 1875, and was a member of the State Senate in 1877 and 1878, the latter year being Chairman of the Committee on Judiciary. He is one of our representative citizens and is very popular, both in and out of his profession.

J. Bachelder & Son (Abram Bachelder, proprietor), Manufacturer of Wood Seat Chairs, etc., Oakland. There are comparatively few enterprises that are continued by members of one family for nearly half a century, yet such is the case with that carried on by Mr. Abram Bachelder in this place. The inception of the undertaking in question was in 1842, the founder being Mr. Joseph Bachelder who continued alone up to 1867, when Mr. Henry A. Bachelder was admitted to the firm. This gentleman retired ten years ago, and since then the present proprietor has had sole control. Mr. Joseph Bachelder was born in Gardiner, Henry being a native of Waterville. Mr. Abram Bachelder is very widely known in this vicinity, not only on account of his prominence as a business man, but also by reason of his connection with the principal fraternal organizations. The factory carried on by him comprises three floors of the dimensions of 30x75 feet, and employment is given to seven competent assistants. The most approved labor-saving machinery is utilized, and abundant water-power is at hand to furnish all necessary motive force. Wood-seat Chairs and Settees are manufactured in large quantities, and a ready market is found for these articles, for the productions of this shop bear an unsurpassed reputation for honesty of workmanship. Mr. Bachelder can meet all honorable competition in the way of prices, etc., and is prepared to fill orders of any magnitude at short notice.

Emerson & Stevens Manufacturing Co., Manufacturers of Scythes and Axes, Oakland. Edge-tools differ from most other articles in one important respect—it is generally practically impossible to judge of their merits by any examination, however thorough. There is but one way to test them, and that is to apply them to the uses for which they are intended. This is particularly true concerning Scythes and Axes, for although the shape of these articles has much to do with their effectiveness, and of course this can be seen before purchasing, still, after all, the most important point is their cutting qualities, and this is only revealed by practical use. Farmers, lumbermen, etc., cannot afford to throw money away on inferior articles. A poor Scythe or a poor Axe is worthless, for it is not only a continual source of exasperation, but it is always having to be ground, and soon causes the loss of enough time to pay for the finest tool of the kind in the market. The only way to be reasonably sure of getting the best, is to learn of some concern making a uniformly first-class article, and insisting upon being supplied with goods of their manufacture. Those having occasion to use Scythes and Axes, generally understand that the productions of the Emerson & Stevens Manufacturing Co. are unsurpassed for uniform excellence of quality, for since these articles were put upon the market, in 1870, they have been severely tested under all conditions, and have proved equal to the best. The present company was incorporated in 1885, consisting of the gentlemen who had founded the enterprise—Messrs. L. D. Emerson, J. F. Stevens, W. R. Pinkham and G. W. Stevens. A spacious factory is occupied, 11,544 feet of floor space being utilized, and employment being given to forty-eight hands. A great variety of styles are turned out, suited to different sections of the country, etc.; but all of them are characterized by the excellent qualities of tempering, etc., that have given the company's productions their enviable reputation.

J. M. Field, Drugs, Watches and Jewelry, Junction Main and Water Streets, Oakland. Agent for Augusta Steam Dye House. The man that can't afford to own a watch nowadays must be pretty "hard up," as the saying is, for when Geneva, Waltham and Elgin Watches are offered in the market for $5.50, and an imitation Waltham Watch may be bought for $3.75, even the poorest can buy. But "you never saw them quoted at such prices," you say. Well, that is because you have not visited Mr. J. M. Field's store, at the junction of Main and Water Sts. Mr. Field invites everybody to call, examine and get prices, for he considers it no trouble to show goods and has a stock of Watches, Clocks, and Jewelry, fresh from Boston, of which he is justly proud. It is his desire to put watches within the reach of all, and the prices we have quoted are only to be found at his popular establishment. Spectacles and Eye Glasses in Gold, Steel, Celluloid and Rubber, are also offered at bottom rates, and the famous "Rogers Bros." Knives, Forks and Spoons and Reed and Barton's, Hollow Ware may be bought of him at the most reasonable prices. Drugs are also dealt in to a considerable extent and goods are received for the Augusta Steam Dye House, of which Mr. Field is agent. He is a native of Cumberland, Maine, and is a member of the Odd Fellows. Operations were begun by him in 1866, and no local business man is more generally known and respected. Particular attention is paid to Repairing of all kinds, and orders will be attended to without delay.

C. Marshall, Manufacturer of Shovel Handles, Oakland. Regarded from any point of view, the enterprise conducted by Mr. C. Marshall, in Oakland, is one of great importance, and it must be evident to any observer that it could never have attained its present magnitude had it not been most skillfully and intelligently managed. Mr. Marshall was born in North Anson, Maine, and is a member of the Masonic Order, and has been so continuously before the public that he is one of our best-known business men in town, and is highly esteemed for his reliable business methods and his readiness to do all in his power to advance the interests of this section. Mr. Marshall began operations in Oakland in 1887, and also owns one-half interest in the Shovel handle Factory at Auburn, Maine, and the goods manufactured by him have long since gained the distinction of being accepted as the standard without question by those who have learned by practical experience the absolute reliability of every article warranted by Mr. Marshall. The premises comprise two floors, each covering an area of 30x50 feet, and a large business is done in the manufacture of Shovel Handles of every description, and employment is constantly given to fifteen thoroughly competent workmen. While quickly responding to every call of his customers, Mr. Marshall assures all that he only makes such articles as will prove their value in actual service, for he has had sufficient experience to know that many an appliance which looks pretty "on paper," utterly fails to give satisfaction when put to actual service. His prices are as low as the use of first-class materials and the employment of skilled labor will allow, and orders for any quantity are always promptly filled.

A. A. Johnson, Merchant Tailor, Ricker's Block, Main Street, Oakland. It is very hard to define just what "extravagance" is, for what seems extravagant to one person seems entirely proper to another, and of course circumstances alter cases very materially. But it is to be doubted if much that is commonly called extravagance is really deserving of such characterization. For instance, take the subject of dress. Very often we hear that a young man is "foolishly extravagant," spends all that he earns on his back, etc. Now this is possible, of course, and some few do spend too much on clothing, but the majority go to the other extreme. "The apparel oft proclaims the man," said the poet, and that is as true today as in Shakespear's time. A good appearance is largely essential to business success, and well-made clothes exert a most powerful influence over anybody's appearance. Besides, two suits costing $20.00 each are as expensive as one costing double that amount, and the latter will generally wear as long as both the cheaper articles. One should use discrimination in choosing a Tailor, and should give the preference to one who is prepared to supply goods of all desirable varieties, and in this connection we wish to call attention to the establishment conducted by Mr. A. A. Johnson, in Ricker's Block, Main Street, for here may be found an extensive assortment of Foreign and Domestic Woolens, carefully selected for the most fastidious trade. Premises measuring 60x20 feet are occupied, and employment is given to five assistants; orders being promptly filled, and a satisfactory fit, etc., being guaranteed. Mr. Johnson has built up a large business since beginning operations in 1887.

H. A. Benson & Co., Manufacturers of Carriages, Buggies, Sleighs; also of the Celebrated Timkin Spring Buggy. Special attention paid to Order Work and Repairing; Oakland. A well-designed and constructed Carriage is a fine piece of workmanship in more ways than one, and is well worthy of admiration on account of the skillful manner in which strength is combined with lightness and symetry with durability. In purchasing a vehicle it should be borne in mind that "the best is the cheapest" in the long run, for though an inferior article may be had at a slightly lower price, when the cost of repairing, etc., is figured up it will be found that no real saving has been made. A firm which has built up an enviable reputation for handling Carriages that not only look well but wear well, is that of Messrs. H. A. Benson & Co., and as this firm is satisfied with a fair profit, and charges no exhorbitant rates, it is not surprising that a thriving business should be done. Operations were begun in 1880, by Mr. H. A. Benson, he becoming associated with Mr. Edward Wing two years later, under the present firm name. The former gentleman is a native of Oakland, and the latter was born in West Sidney. A factory measuring 30x45 feet, also a spacious storehouse are utilized, and employment given to three efficient assistants. Carriages, Buggies and Sleighs are manufactured; special attention being given to ordered work, and no pains spared to fully satisfy every customer. The firm make a specialty of the well-known Timkin Spring Buggy, and their vehicles contain all the modern improvements, being both stylish and comfortable. Repairing is done at the shortest possible notice, and at rates that cannot fail to be satisfactory.

E. M. Stacy, Dealer in Books, Fine Stationery, Wall-paper, Curtains and Fancy Goods, Church Street, Oakland. This popular Bookseller and Stationer, during the three years he has been established here, has attained a prominent position among Oakland's business men. He occupies a store 23x30 feet in dimensions, located on Church Street, which contains a fine selected stock of Books, Stationery and Fancy Goods. This business is an old and long established one, and under the management of Mr. E. M. Stacy has been greatly extended and become the local headquarters for Paper Hangings, Curtains, and other staple goods. In addition to doing a live business in the above-mentioned line, Mr. Stacy makes a specialty of Holiday and Fancy Goods, and shows marked taste and judgment in their selection and display. Capable and reliable assistants are constantly employed. The store is neat and attractive in all its appointments, and customers are treated in a polite and attentive manner, and the wants of the public are studied in every respect. Mr. Stacy is a native of Benton, Me., and a gentleman combining business talent with fairness in all his dealings. He is well qualified to push his business to still greater usefulness and importance. Besides his prominent position as a business man, Mr. Stacy combines withal the duties of Agent for the American Express Company and Operator for the Western Union Telegraph Company, positions in which these great companies find their interests well cared for and the public served in an attentive and respectful manner. Mr. Stacy is thus well known throughout this vicinity and is regarded as a reliable and representative business man.

Ayer & Greeley, Dealers in Coal and Wood, Oakland. It is both gratifying and convenient to have orders for Coal and Wood filled with the utmost promptness, for the majority of people wait until the last moment before ordering their fuel, and consequently are liable to be seriously discommoded by delay in receiving the same. A house dealing extensively in Coal and Wood, and enjoying an exceptional reputation for keeping strictly up to its agreements regarding the delivery of goods, etc., is that of Ayer & Greeley, which has now been in operation about six years—having been founded in 1882. The firm consists of Messrs. W. M. Ayer and H. W. Greeley, the former a native of Bangor and the latter of Belgrade. The senior partner has held the office of High Priest of Drummond Royal Arch Chapter. Being succeeded in that position by his present business associate, Mr. Greeley. Mr. Ayer is Superintendent of the Somerset R. R., and both he and Mr. Greeley are very generally-known throughout this section as energetic business men, who neglect no honorable means of advancing Oakland's best interests. The Concern utilizes a coal-shed measuring 420x26 feet, and a wood-shed of the dimensions of 120x25 feet, a very heavy stock being constantly carried, and large or small orders being given immediate attention. Unexcelled facilities are controlled, and no house in this vicinity is more favorably situated to supply uniformly satisfactory goods at bottom prices.

F. H. Gilman's New Drug Store, Physicians' Prescriptions a Specialty, at lowest prices; Oakland. The residents of Oakland and vicinity have reason to congratulate themselves on the existence in the community of such an enterprise as that carried on by Mr. F. H. Gilman, for a really first-class Drug Store is almost as useful as a skillful and experienced physician and indeed the usefulness of the latter may be heightened by the aid that such an establishment can afford. Mr. Gilman was born in Manchester, Maine, and is a member of the Knights of Pythias. It was in 1887 that he opened his present store, but already a large trade has been attained, and the patronage is steadily increasing as the manifest advantages of dealing here become more generally known. The store is of the dimensions of 60x18 feet, and contains an exceptionally large and varied stock of Drugs, Medicines, Chemicals, Fancy and Toilet Articles, etc., making the preparation of Physicians' Prescriptions a specialty. Mr. Gilman strives to insure absolute accuracy in this highly important department, and in view of the precautions taken it certainly seems as if serious error were impossible. The Drugs supplied by him are fresh and of the best quality to be found in the market, and the prices quoted in the Prescription Department are positively the lowest consistent with the use of such ingredients. Customers are promptly served and uniform politeness is shown to all. He also prepares Gilman's Throat and Lung Balsam, warranted a sure cure for Coughs, Colds, Sore Throat, Bleeding and Soreness of the Lungs, Croup, and all Diseases leading to Consumption.

C. W. Folsom, Dealer in Hardware, Iron, Steel, Stoves, Tinware. Paints, Oils and Varnishes. Glazed Sash, Doors and Blinds. Agent for Walter A. Wood's Mowing Machines, Church and Water Streets, Oakland. Among those Oakland business establishments which may justly claim to be entitled representative, that carried on by Mr. C. W. Folsom, on Church and Water Streets, deserves special and prominent mention. This enterprise was begun over a quarter of a century ago, under the firm name of Blaisdell & Folsom, the date of its inception being 1862, and about two years later the present proprietor assumed full control of the business. Mr. Folsom is a native of Monmouth, Maine, and a member of the Free Masons. Of course a merchant of such long standing is almost universally known throughout this section, and Mr. Folsom's store has long been regarded as one of the most desirable to trade at in Oakland. That this statement of it is well-deserved, a personal visit will prove to the satisfaction of any intelligent and unprejudiced individual, especially if he be well-acquainted with the value of Hardware, Iron, Steel, Stoves, Tinware and similar articles. Four floors are utilized, each 24x40 feet in dimensions, besides a Tin Shop adjoining. In the heavy stock carried, Hardware, Iron, Steel, Stoves and Tin Ware, of every description is given particular attention; but a large business is also done in Paints, Oils, and Varnishes, Glazed Sash, Doors and Blinds of all kinds. Considering the reputation this establishment bears, it is unnecessary for us to say that no misrepresentation is practiced or permitted; but we may call attention to the fact that quality for quality no other dealer can undersell Mr. Folsom. He is in a position to buy as low as anybody can, and his prices will be found to rule as low as the lowest in every department. Mr. Folsom is also agent for Walter A. Wood's Mowing Machine. Mr.

Folsom is also owner of the royally-bred Percheron stallion, Capt. Pulley—2,664, Percheron stud book of France. Three years ago, when Messrs. Blaisdell & Folsom purchased this horse in New York, and put him in the hands of Mr. Herrick, the step was considered visionary by many, but time has silenced all doubts and proved its wisdom. The illustration which we present is not a fancy picture, made to order, as are so many, but rather a faithful representation of the horse as he is, the electro being reproduced from a pen and ink sketch made by a well-known Maine artist, William Sturdivant, of Fryeburg. An examination of it will indicate at once the strong points of the valuable stock horse. Capt. Pulley was foaled in the district of Alencorn, department of Orne, France, April 4th, 1883, and imported to New York, by John W. Akin, in August of the same year; was bought of him and brought to Oakland, by Blaisdell & Folsom, in June, 1885. He was got by LeDuc, dam by Poule by Papillion, he by Moutard. He stands 16¼ hands high, weighing 1,700 pounds; is black in color, with fine glossy coat, has a thick curly mane, and very heavy tail, a fine clean head, which he carries very high; arching neck, deep broad chest, long quarters and wide flat legs, with the very best of feet; he has been successfully bred to mares ranging in weight from 805 to 1,500 lbs., of nearly every shade of color, producing stock either bay, brown or black, with hardly an exception. The colts have been rapidly picked up at prices perfectly satisfactory to the breeders. Although but three years in the State his popularity has steadily increased, farmers returning their mares the second and third season.

George W. Goulding, Pharmacist, Main Street, Oakland. Prompt attention to customers is one of the chief elements of success in the carrying on of any business, but particularly is this the case with the retail Druggist. He is often called upon to compound prescriptions or to perform some other responsible and delicate duty at the shortest notice, and it is therefore necessary for him to combine skill, experience and good judgment, with coolness and self possession, if he is to be prepared to properly meet all the demands made upon him. The pharmacists of Oakland as a class, need not fear comparison with those of any other city, for they are extremely well-informed men, and strive to protect the interests of their customers at all times. Where the average of excellence is high, comparisons are more than ever odious, but without seeking to draw a comparison, we may at least call attention to a Pharmacy which is thoroughly well managed in every respect. We refer to that located on Main Street and conducted by Mr. George W. Goulding. This gentleman is a native of North Wayne, Me., and has had the management of this business since 1868. He was connected with the Legislature as Representative of Waterville and West Waterville for two years, and is Grand High Priest of the Grand Royal Arch Chapter of Maine. His store has a convenient and accessible location opposite the Maine Central Depot, and the premises occupied comprise three floors, each 40x65 feet in size, and a large and varied stock is handled of Drugs, Medicines and kindred goods with a well-chosen assortment of Toilet and Fancy Goods. Polite and efficient assistants are employed and no pains are spared to assure customers prompt attention, and the prices are low and reasonable in every instance. Mr. Goulding also runs a store in Madison, Me., the stock consisting of Ready-Made Clothing, Gents' Furnishing Goods and Paper Hangings.

James B. Redmond, Carriage and Sign Painter, Oak Street, Oakland. Notwithstanding that there are many Carriage and Sign Painters in Oakland it is sometimes rather hard to satisfactorily place an order for work of this kind as, of course, everybody desires to patronize a reliable concern, and many people are ignorant of the respective standing of the different houses engaged in this line of business. We can assure our readers that they need feel no hesitation in intrusting Mr. James B. Redmond with any commission of this nature, for he is exceptionally well prepared to give satisfaction to every customer and will do either Carriage or Sign Painting at short notice and in first-class style. Mr. Redmond's place of business comprises four floors, each covering an area of 22x29 feet, and employment is given to a sufficient force of assistants to enable him to "rush things," when hurry is required, without injury to the quality of work done. He inaugurated his present enterprise in 1885, and has since built up a thriving and growing patronage. Fancy and Plain Sign Painting will be produced at the lowest market rates, and Carriage Painting of all kinds will also be done at low prices and in durable and workmanlike style. Mr. Redmond is a native of Solon, Me., and a member of the Odd Fellows, also the Grange, and is highly esteemed by all who know him.

A. Swain, Dealer in Boots, Shoes and Clothing, Oakland. To know of a reliable establishment at which to purchase Boots, Shoes and Clothing to the best advantage, is, by no means, an unimportant piece of knowledge, and we take great pleasure in making mention of the store carried on by Mr. Albert Swain in this connection, for we are sure that those who may visit it on account of this notice, will have reason to thank us for calling their attention to its many merits. Mr. Swain is a native of Skowhegan, and began operations here in 1884.

He is a member of the Free Masons and is too well-known to require extended personal mention. The store occupied is 70x25 feet, and contains a most carefully-selected stock of Boots, Shoes and Pants of all kinds. There are two assistants in attendance who will be found courteous and obliging, and extremely well-informed concerning the articles they handle. The Boots and Shoes dealt in are from the most reputable manufacturers, and are warranted to prove as represented in every respect. All grades and styles are kept in stock, and equal inducements are offered in street and dress Shoes. Hats, Caps and Gents' Furnishings are also handled largely; the latest novelties in Neck Wear, etc., being shown, and all at bottom prices. Mr. Swain is heavily interested in the Barrel Hoop industry, and last year he handled 1,700,000 of these articles.

W. H. Wheeler, Manufacturer of and Dealer in Furniture, Coffins and Caskets, Oakland. Successor to Wells & Wheeler. A piece of furniture may be strong and well made, of the best material, but even all this will not insure it against needing repairs at times, for "accidents will happen in the best regulated families," and even when nothing of the kind occurs, the progress of age is sure to show itself in one way or the other. Now it is obvious that a man who makes a specialty of manufacturing as well as repairing furniture is able to give work of that kind more skillful and careful attention than one who does not, and, therefore, we take pleasure in recommending to our readers Mr. W. H. Wheeler, on Church Street, Upper Village, Oakland. The business he now conducts was established in 1884 under the firm name of Wells & Wheeler, and after about one year, Mr. W. H. Wheeler assumed full control and management of the business, and has executed many difficult commissions with perfect satisfaction to all concerned. He is a native of Waterville, and has a very large circle of friends and patrons throughout this vicinity. The premises occupied are utilized for the Manufacturing, Repairing and Upholstering of Furniture, and also for dealing in Furniture, Coffins and Caskets. Competent assistants are employed, so that orders can be turned out at remarkably short notice when desired. Mr. Wheeler is too widely known as a skillful and faithful Mechanic and dealer to render it necessary for us to extend him any further personal mention, and we will simply add that the character of his work speaks for itself, and needs no eulogy.

Mrs. Julia A. Farnham, Millinery and Dress Making, Church Street, Oakland. The truest economy is that gained by judicious expenditure, and those who have learned this lesson will never make the mistake of loosing money by not spending it. This may seem a contradiction of terms, but, nevertheless, it expresses what is done by many people over and over again, and we therefore think that some consideration of how to avoid this practice in one important branch of expenditure, at least, may prove of interest. Everybody will agree that the most fashionable and the most costly fabrics will not look well unless they are made up skillfully, and in style suited to the wearer; and as very few are able to secure these results by their unaided exertions, it follows that the employment of a competent Milliner and Dress Maker becomes necessary, and is in the line of strictest economy. As really superior Milliners and Dress Makers are, by no means common in Oakland, we take pleasure in commending to the favorable attention of our readers, the establishment conducted by Mrs. Julia A. Farnham, located on Church St., for we feel confident that all orders placed there will be executed to the complete satisfaction of customers, and at prices that cannot fail to be acceptable. The enterprise was inaugurated in 1886, and has already gained a high reputation in the vicinity. The lady mentioned carries a stock of goods that is carefully and skillfully selected, and she supplies anything in these lines at the lowest market rates. Efficient assistants are employed, and work is satisfactorily executed at reasonable prices and at short notice.

HISTORICAL SKETCH
— OF —
FAIRFIELD, ME.

AMONG the most delightful features of a journey through the State of Maine, the observing tourist must estimate highly the pleasure which is not infrequently occasioned by coming across those charming towns and villages which nestle cosily among the hills, sloping gently to the banks of the mighty rivers, and enlivened by the social amenities and industrial enterprises which render it a real *microcosmus* of our American life. A few miles above Waterville, on the Kennebec river, is one of the most beautiful and charming of those towns in Maine. We refer to the progressive town of Fairfield. This is the southern-most town of Somerset county, about twenty-six miles north of Augusta, and is remarkable both for its scenery and the enterprising genius of its people. It contains about forty-two square miles of territory, and at this part of the river is one of the most valuable water-powers on the Kennebec. When the town was first settled, in 1774, it received its name from the "fair appearance" of its situation, and it would never have seemed to have forfeited the distinction. Its growth was not rapid, and was marked by the various disturbances and obstacles which beset the towns of this vicinity, yet has been decidedly uniform, and since the manufacturing privileges of the water-power supply have been improved it has made marked progress. The first Congregational church was founded here in 1815. The town was incorporated in 1788, the years immediately following the Revolutionary war being unusually marked by prosperity and growth. The embarrassments of the Embargo in 1807 and 1808, and the war of 1812, as well as the panic of 1832, were serious set-backs; but by the middle of the century the population had become 2,482. During the next decade it rose to 2,753.

The people of Fairfield entered into the great struggle against slavery with enthusiastic generosity and devotion. They spared neither men or money in their patriotic service, and the achievements of their sons, and the tender memorials of lost heroes have ever since been zealously guarded and honored. Since the war the advance of the town has been steady and marked. The population in 1870 had risen to 2,999, and in 1880 to 3,044. The valuation in the latter year was $1,283,582. The town officers for 1888 were as follows: Selectmen, F. E. MacFadden, C. J. Greene, N. Howe; Town Clerk, F. E. MacFadden; Treasurer, E. G. Pratt. Since 1880 the population and valuation have been both increased largely. The water-power at Fairfield is practically inexhaustible. There is a fall of thirty-four feet within a short distance at the falls, and over this for eleven hours a day there is a constant run of 117,300 cubic feet of water per minute. This is equivalent to 7,540 horse or 300,000 spindles. This great power, moreover, can be increased by various improvements if the demand should be extended.

Though not one of the largest, Fairfield is certainly one of the most enterprising towns in this State of business genius. Its industrial spirit penetrates many varied lines, and is alike successful in all. Among the chief lines of business enterprise are those of lumber, furniture, frames, carriages, machinery, canned goods of all kinds (this being an industry in which great success has been achieved), boxes, grain and produce, shoes, and tools of all kinds. The mill industries at the various villages are centers of population and commercial advancement. The out-put of two of these mills alone is over $350,000 a year. In the lumber business there are eight saw-mills. The chief centers or villages of the town, chiefly divided according to commercial enterprises, are as follows: North Fairfield, Fairfield Corner, Fairfield Village (the largest center, including Kendall's Mills), Somerset Mills, Blacknell's Mills and Winslow Mills. Fairfield has also a First National Bank, and Fairfield Savings Bank. "Fairfield Journal" is an enterprising local weekly, of an independent and lively spirit, and furnishing news and entertainment to many readers. Such is the great resource of water-power at Fairfield that her manufacturing industries admit of great expansion, and as they became more widely known, and the privileges of location offered to manufacturers are realized, there must be a great source of wealth and progress coming to Fairfield in this line, for there are few towns or cities that have been more abundantly enriched by the bounty of nature's gifts than she. At the present time there are six physicians, five lawyers and six clergymen located here. There are six churches,—one Baptist, three Methodist, one Free Baptist, and one Universalist. The religious life of the people is progressive and wholesome, the moral standard of a high stamp, and the interest in charity and benevolence wide-spread and earnest. Great attention is given to educational matters, and the public schools of the town are liberally and well conducted. The social life is quiet and retired, yet is marked by the refining and charming influences which the country towns of New England peculiarly possess. The beauty of the surrounding country and the unusually healthful situation are advantages not to be lightly regarded. Nor are the attractions to tourists and summer travelers unworthy of attention.

Situated on the great Kennebec, and the main line of the Maine Central Railroad, it is easily reached both from Portland and Bangor, and possesses both the advantages of suburban and country life. Its ancient beauty still attracts, and will, many delighted tourists every year. Sportsmen find good opportunities for sport with rod and gun through the surrounding country, and tired families can nowhere obtain better accommodations, with such recuperation and enjoyment at such small expense.

LEADING BUSINESS MEN

OF

FAIRFIELD, ME.

Kennebec Framing & Lumber Co., Mills at Fairfield, Maine. Boston office: 7 Exchange Place. Lumber; Buildings Framed by Machinery. Moldings and Finish Worked to Architect's Designs. Doors, Sash, Blinds and Window Frames. The rapidity with which a frame building can be erected nowadays is simply marvelous, and reminds one of the Arabian Nights' tales of stately palaces being erected in a single night. Nor is this rapidity gained at the expense of solidity. It is simply the result of the intelligent employment of ingenious and

powerful machinery, and so accurate and efficient is this that the framing for a vast building may be made here in Fairfield, shipped hundreds of miles, and put together with the absolute certainty that the pieces will join as perfectly together as though shaped slowly and laboriously on the spot by the most skilled mechanics. Practically all buildings of any size are now wholly or partially framed in this way, for hand work cannot compete with that done by machinery, either as regards economy or accuracy. The Kennebec Framing and Lumber Company is one of the best-known and most successful concerns in the country devoted to this branch of industry, and some idea of the extent to which its facilities are availed of may be gained from the fact that some six hundred carloads of Frames will be shipped during the present year. The inception of the enterprise occurred in 1873, Messrs. Smith & Mendes being its founders; and in 1881 the Kennebec Framing Company was incorporated, its name being changed to the Kennebec Framing and Lumber Company, in 1887. A Boston office is maintained at No. 7 Exchange Place, and orders are received from every part of New England. Three mills are in operation, covering three-quarters of an acre of ground, and employment is given to seventy assistants, the motive power being furnished by a one hundred and twenty-five horse Corliss engine. The machinery in use is of the most improved design, and the work turned out is spoken of in the highest terms by architects and builders, who find it unsurpassed for accuracy and beauty of finish. Doors, Sash, Blinds and Window Frames are extensively manufactured, and Moldings and Finish are worked to architects' designs. No lower prices are quoted on work of equal merit than those named by this company, and no concern can fill orders with greater promptness. The officers and directors are as follows: President, J. M. Lasell; Treasurer, G. L. Briggs; Agent, L. L. Parsons; Directors, J. M. Laselle, G. L. Briggs, L. L. Parsons, C. W. Lasell, G. M. Whitin.

Fairfield Furniture Company, Manufacturers of Pine, Ash and Basswood Furniture. Boston Salesrooms, 31 Dunstable Street, Charlestown, Mass. Principal Office and Factory, Fairfield. Among those lines of manufacturing most extensively carried on in this State, that of Furniture is worthy of particular attention, for this industry affords employment to hundreds of skilled workmen, and is bound to develop steadily with the progress of time. Indeed the changes which have occurred in it even during the past decade, are by no means inconsiderable, and the tendency is steadily in the direction of producing superior articles at lower prices. It was in 1876, the centennial year, that Messrs. J. F. and E. P. Kenrick founded their present enterprise, and the Fairfield Furniture Company, under which style business is carried on, has since made its influence felt throughout the New England Market. Both members of the firm are natives of China, Me., and both are widely known in Fairfield and vicinity. Mr. J. F. Kenrick being one of the Trustees of the Fairfield Savings Bank, while Mr. E. P. Kenrick is a Director of the First National Bank, of the same town. The principal office and factory are located here. Boston salesrooms being maintained at No. 31 Dunstable Street, Charlestown District. The factory comprises three floors, measuring 117x50 feet, and is run by water power, there being employment given to forty assistants. The secret of the success with which this enterprise has met, may be explained in three words—thoroughness of manufacture. Nothing is left to chance, and "luck" does not enter into the means depended on to dispose of the goods turned out. The stock used is carefully selected, perfectly seasoned and skillfully handled. The percentage of waste is reduced to a minimum, the workmen are encouraged to do their best, and are furnished with the most improved tools and machinery. New methods which give promise of being valuable are given early and exhaustive trial, and in short no pains is spared to keep the factory up to the highest point of efficiency. Pine, ash and basswood furniture in the white is manufactured, and the prices are put at the lowest rates consistent with the production of articles that are made to wear as well as sell. On this solid basis is the reputation of the Fairfield Furniture Company established, and it is not to be wondered at that its goods are in active demand, the annual production footing up about ten thousand chamber sets. True merit is sure to win appreciation, and no one can envy success so honorably attained.

N. Totman & Sons, Manufacturers and Dealers in all kinds of Pine and Spruce Lumber, Clapboards, Shingles, Laths, Pickets, etc. Dimensions sawed to order. As vast as the Lumber interests of this State are, there are certain houses which are of such prominence as to be easily distinguishable among their fellows, and especially is this true of that of Messrs. N. Totman & Sons, which has been carried on under its present name since 1873. The undertaking had its origin in 1835, Messrs. E. & N. Totman being the proprietors, and the principles which have governed its prosecution up to the present time, have resulted in placing it among the representative enterprises of the State. Messrs. N. Totman & Sons are manufacturers of and dealers in all kinds of Pine and Spruce Lumber, Clapboards, Shingles, Laths, Pickets, etc., and the premises utilized, comprise two floors of the dimensions of 100x76 feet. A very complete and costly plant of machinery is in operation, ample water-power being available to furnish motive force. There is every facility at hand that experience can suggest, and employment is given to fifty men the year round. Some 5,000,000 feet of Lumber is annually manufactured for Maine and Massachusetts markets, an important branch of the business being the sawing of dimensions to order. No house is more favorably situated as regards its ability to furnish prompt and reliable service to customers, and the prices quoted are consistent with the unexcelled facilities enjoyed. The firm as now constituted, consists of Messrs. N., F. M., and L. Totman, the first-named gentleman being a native of Abington, Mass., and two latter of this town. The senior partner was a member of the State Senate in 1878, and is now President of the First National Bank. Messrs. F. M. and L. Totman are connected with the Free Masons, and are very generally known throughout this section. Fairfield has profited much by the existence of this enterprise in its midst, and no sketch of the business interests of the town would be complete without mention of this leading firm.

J. A. Cilley & Co., Manufacturers of and Dealers in Pine, Ash, and Basswood Furniture of All Kinds, Fairfield. Salesrooms 339 Medford Street, Charlestown. The manufacture of Furniture by machinery has reached a high stage of perfection at the present time, and results are now attained that would have been looked upon as impossible comparatively few years ago. By the aid of machinery, it is possible to produce furniture at prices the poorest can afford, and it is a fact that many a workingman has his house furnished in a manner that would bear comparison with that only shown in the homes of the rich in by-gone days. There have been many changes in methods of manufacturing since the house of J. A. Cilley & Co. was founded, in 1864; but the firm have always been among the first to adopt desirable improvements, and, in fact, were the first in Maine to manufacture Shooks and Fine Furniture for the Boston market. Their salesrooms are at No. 339 Medford Street, Charlestown, Mass., and they also have a factory in that city, besides their extensive works here in Fairfield which occupy three floors of the dimensions of 120x50 feet, and are run by water-power. Employment is given to thirty men, and Pine, Ash and Basswood Furniture of All Kinds is very largely manufactured, a business of from $40,000 to $50,000 per annum being done. Every detail of the work is intrusted to experienced and skilled operatives, and as the system in operation in the factory permits of the closest inspection at all stages, the concern is able to fully warrant its productions in every respect, and to quote prices that will bear the severest examination. As now constituted, the firm is made up of Messrs. J. A., A. E., and E. A. Cilley, and was never better prepared to carry on operations to the best advantage. Its goods are accepted as the standard in the Boston market, and although competition is strong in this line of trade, meet with a ready sale among discriminating buyers everywhere.

A. H. & C. E. Duren, Manufacturer and Dealer in Pine and Spruce Lumber, Laths, Shingles, Clapboards, Pickets, etc. Dimensions Sawed to Order. Special attention given to Clapboards and Shingles. Office on Water Street, Fairfield. It would be difficult to find an enterprise that has done more to bring Fairfield into prominence as a manufacturing center than that conducted by Messrs. A. H. & C. E. Duren, for since this undertaking was founded, in 1873, it has developed until it has become one of the most extensive in this portion of the State. Both members of the firm are natives of Canaan, and Mr. A. H. Duren has served on the Board of Selectmen of Fairfield, as well as Assessor of Corporations. No thinking person can visit the mills without being impressed with the evidences of careful and thorough preparation everywhere manifest, for it has been the policy of the firm from the first to hold itself in readiness to fill the most extensive orders at short notice, and the plant operated is most admirably adapted to secure that result. Two large buildings are occupied, measuring 115x65 and 150x32 feet respectively, with ample water-power available to run the necessary machinery. The works have a capacity for the production of 8,000,000 feet of Long Lumber, 5,000,000 Shingles, 500,000 of Clapboards and Laths, Staves and Pickets to the amount of about 4,000,000, employment being given to eighty men. Dimension Lumber is sawed to order at short notice, and special attention is given to Clapboards and Shingles; Pine and Spruce Lumber, Pickets, Laths, etc. being also very largely dealt in. The office is located on Water Street, and the facilities for shipping goods are of the most satisfactory character. This enterprise is a truly representative one, and the residents of Fairfield may well congratulate themselves on its unsurpassed standing in the mercantile world.

Stephen A. Nye, Manufacturer and Dealer in Long and Short Lumber, Spruce, Pine and Cedar; Fairfield. The gold mines of California never produced so much wealth as the forests of Maine, and it is difficult to justly estimate the importance of the Lumber interests of this State. We may obtain the figures showing the annual production of manufactured lumber, the number of men employed, the amount of wages

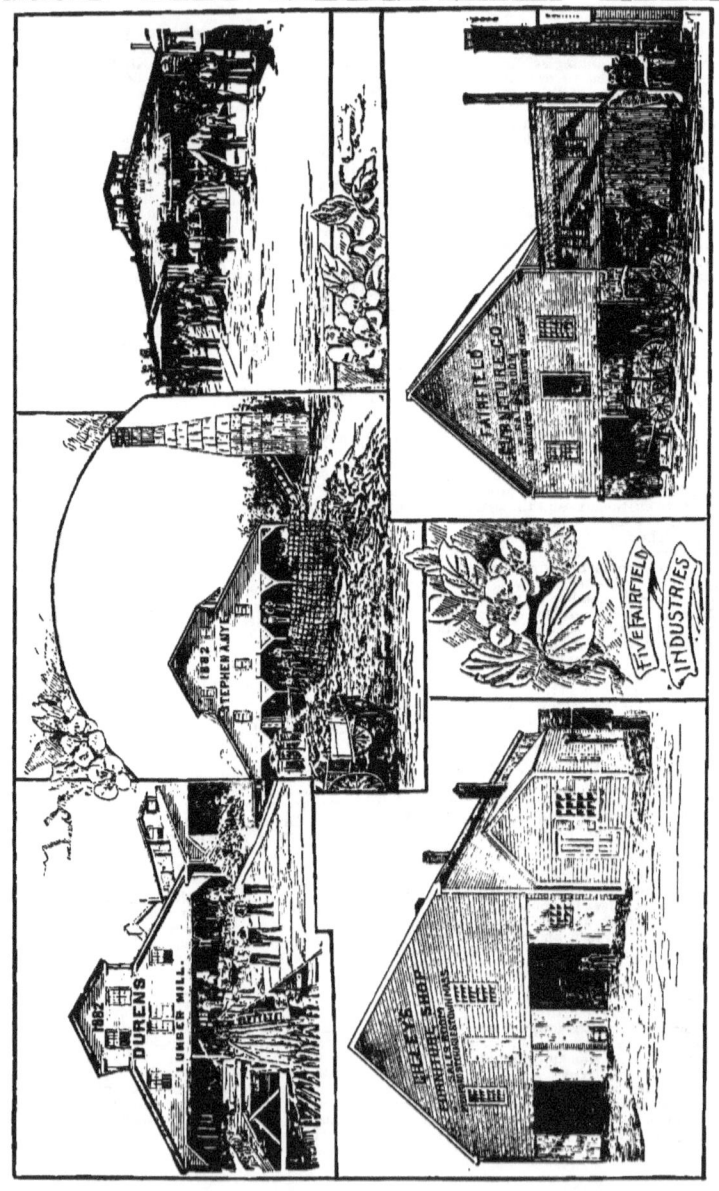

paid, etc., but still we will have but an imperfect idea of the true condition of affairs, for the indirect good done by this vast industry, the hundreds of enterprises tributary to it, will not show in the account at all. Without doubt, one of the best-known manufacturers of Long and Short Lumber in the State is Mr. Stephen A. Nye, for not only is his establishment one of the best-equipped to be found anywhere, but his public services have caused him to be known, by reputation at least, throughout this section. Mr. Nye is a native of Fairfield, and is very prominently connected with the Free Masons, having held a very high office in that ancient order. He was Representative to the Legislature in 1882, and served in the Senate in 1884. Business was begun in 1873, by Nye, Fogg & Co., the present proprietor assuming entire control in 1877. The premises utilized comprise two floors, each of the dimensions of 100x100 feet, and the elaborate machinery in use is run by water-power, employment being afforded to one hundred assistants. As may be imagined, the capacity of such a plant is very great, amounting to 8,000,000 feet of Long Lumber, 5,000,000 shingles, 800,000 clapboards, and from 3 to 4,000,000 each of Laths, Staves and Pickets. Such facilities enable Mr. Nye to fill orders without delay, and he is in a position to meet all honorable competition and hold his present place among the leaders of the Lumber Trade.

S. H. Blackwell, Hardware, Cutlery, Nails and Glass, Doors, Sash and Blinds, Farmers' and Mechanics' Tools, Kitchen Furnishings, Artists' Materials, Paints, Oils, Varnishes, etc., Fairfield. The Hardware trade is of necessity one of the most important carried on in this country, for an immense variety of articles are included within this term, and "Hardware" is coming to mean more every day; "Builders' Hardware," "Piano Hardware," "Saddlery Hardware," and many other special branches of the business are followed, but in none of them is a more intimate knowledge of the goods handled required than is called for from those dealing in "General Hardware." Mr. S. H. Blackwell has been identified with the last-named branch of the trade for several years, having begun operations in 1882. He was born in Oakland, Me., and is a member of the Masons, Odd Fellows, A. O. U. W. and the Grand Army. He is also Vice-president of Fairfield Board of Trade, and is one of the best-known of our local business men. Mr. Blackwell utilizes two floors, of the dimensions each of 55x35 feet, and the immense stock carried includes not only Hardware, Cutlery, Nails, Doors, Sash and Blinds, Farmers' and Mechanics' Tools, Artists' Materials, Paints, Oils, Varnishes, Glass, etc., but also a general assortment of Kitchen Furnishing Goods are at hand to select from, and the prices in this, as in other departments, will be found to be as low as the lowest, while the quality of the goods is unexcelled. The store occupied since 1886 is located on Main Street, corner of Bridge Street. Employment is given to competent and attentive assistants. Orders are filled at the shortest possible notice, and whether a large or small quantity of goods be desired, every effort will be made to so supply the customers that perfect satisfaction will be the result.

Fairfield House, Fairfield Hall, A. S. Pease, Proprietor; also livery stable; Fairfield. We are by no means sure that regular patrons of the house we speak of will thank us for extending a knowledge of its merits among the general public, for selfishness is unfortunately a pronounced characteristic of human nature, and all of us when we get a good thing are too apt to strive to keep it to ourselves. But as we are bound to bring forward the worthy and representative institutions of Fairfield in this book, we feel under obligations to mention this enterprise, knowing that if by so doing we are incurring the displeasure of one class, we are certainly putting ourselves in a position to earn the gratitude of a much larger portion of the people at large. Therefore, we would advise those desiring hotel accommodations for a long or short period in this town to make a trial of the Fairfield House, feeling very sure that they will find there many of the comforts of a home combined with the convenience of a public house. Mr. A. S. Pease, the proprietor of the establishment, is a native of North Anson, Me., and has been concerned in the present enterprise since 1880. Mr. Pease formerly kept the Evans House, in Gardiner, Me., and also carried on the Livery Business there for twenty years. The Fairfield House is three stories high, and with the stable and yard room, altogether cover an acre of ground. The table is supplied with a variety of food, only limited by the condition of the market. Mr. H. B. Bradstreet is clerk, and the service is prompt, courteous and willing. Ten assistants are employed, and every effort is made to make the guests feel at home, and satisfy them in every reasonable respect.

Frank J. Savage, Custom Miller and Dealer in Phosphate, Flour, Grain, Meal, Feed and Grass Seed, Lime, Hair, Cement and Glazed Tile. Manufacturer of Ground Plaster, Fairfield. One of the first uses to which water-power was put, was the grinding of wheat, etc., and the majority of the grist mills in use to-day, are run by this means. Great improvements have, of course, been made in the methods of utilizing and applying this power, and also in the character of the flour, etc., produced, and a mill embodying about all that has been done in these lines is that carried on by Mr. Frank J. Savage, in Fairfield. Business was rbegun by him in 1882, and as the superior character of the articles produced soon became manifest, a brisk trade was soon established, and has since continued to increase. The premises occupied comprise two floors, the Plaster and Feed room measuring 20x25 feet, and the grinding room 40x40 feet; and a large custom and retail business is done. Mr. Savage is a native of Anson, Maine, a member of the Masons and the A. O. U. W., and ranks among our best-known business men. The goods handled include Phosphate, Flour, Grain, Meal, Feed and Grass Seed, Lime, Hair and Cement, and Glazed Tile, together with Ground Plaster. Prices are in accordance with the lowest market rates, and orders will always receive immediate and careful attention. Custom grinding is done without delay and carried out in a superior manner. Four competent hands are constantly employed and patrons receive polite and courteous service

LEADING BUSINESS MEN OF FAIRFIELD.

E. Totman & Co., Manufacturers and Dealers in Lumber of all kinds, Fairfield. No work treating of Maine's prominent business enterprises, would be complete did it not contain extended reference to the Lumber trade, for, as all our readers know, this is one of the most flourishing industries in the State. Where so many large concerns are engaged in a certain line of effort, it is often difficult to single out those worthy of special mention, but no such difficulty is met with in the case of Messrs. E. Totman & Co., as it is universally conceded that no Lumber House in this vicinity holds a higher position than that referred to. The enterprise with which it is identified, was inaugurated over half a century ago, operations having been begun in 1835, under the style of E. & U. Totman. Mr. E. Totman died in 1881, and since that date, the business has been continued by his sons, Messrs. C. G. and A. H. Totman. Both members of the original firm, were born in Abington, Mass., and the present proprietors are natives of Fairfield. Both are connected with the Free Masons, and Mr. A. H. Totman, also belongs to the Odd Fellows. The mill is located on the Island, an area of four acres being occupied and employment given to from forty to fifty men. Lumber of all kinds is manufactured and dealt in very extensively, both a wholesale and retail business being done, and large and small orders given equal consideration. Having the prestige arising from over fifty years successful establishment, and enjoying the most complete facilities for the obtaining of raw material, and the economical working of it, it would be strange if the firm were not in a position to offer unusual advantages to its customers. That these advantages are perceived and improved, may be easily seen from the fact that the annual sales amount to above $100,000. Goods are promptly shipped, and the prices quoted are such as could only be named by a house occupying as advantageous a position as the one in question.

Wiggin & Nye, Dealers in Meats, Vegetables and Groceries. Teas and Coffees a Specialty. Highest Cash Prices Paid for Country Produce. Fairfield. If there is any one branch of trade in which the general public may be reasonably expected to take a special interest, it is certainly that carried on by the Grocer and Provision Dealer, for there is no other branch so intimately connected with every-day life. A modern store of this kind is well worthy of careful study in more respects than one, for it contains a stock gathered from the four quarters of the world; and there is not a climate, and hardly a country, that is not represented more or less largely. It is owing to this immense variety in the articles handled that the business of the Grocer and Provision Dealer embraces such a vast amount of detail, and the responsibility felt is by no means lessened by the fact that the customer who comes in and asks for five cents' worth of the only article you happen to be out of will invariably henceforth regard you as behind the times, and spread that opinion abroad, quite forgetting the thousand and one *other* articles that you had in stock and were ready to furnish. As may be imagined, it is no easy task to hold a leading position in the retail trade for year after year, but such is the record made by a few houses, and prominent among such is that conducted by Messrs. Wiggin & Nye in this town. Everybody in this vicinity knows this concern, and well they might, for it has served the public in an honorable and upright manner since its inception which occurred in 1887. Spacious premises are occupied, covering an area of 50x75 feet, and every provision made for the carrying on of operations to the best possible advantage, for the proprietors know that the public demand prompt and accurate service, as well as perfectly reliable goods, and stand ready to meet all reasonable expectations. It would be useless to attempt even a partial description of the stock on hand, so we say "go and see for yourself." It is varied, large, well-selected and fresh, and comprises Staple and Fancy Groceries, Meats and Vegetables. These goods are high in grade but not in price, and the most economical buyer can trade here to advantage. Mr. I. B. Wiggin and Mr. W. W. Nye are both natives of Maine and members of the Odd Fellows.

D. W. Foye, Dealer in Confectionery, Ice Cream, Fruit, Cigars, etc., Fairfield. One of those places which it is both agreeable and profitable to visit, is that conducted by Mr. D. W. Foye, located in this town. This opinion is doubtless held by hundreds of others besides the writer, for the patronage accorded the enterprise is very generous indeed, and is steadily increasing from year to year. The inception of this popular undertaking occurred in 1881, its founder being Mr. G. A. Savage, who was succeeded by the present proprietor in 1885. This latter gentleman is a native of Palermo, Maine, and is well-known throughout Fairfield, both in a business and social way, being connected with the Masonic Order. The premises made use of comprise one floor of the dimensions of 60x20 feet. Confectionery, Ice Cream and Fruit are largely handled, together with a fine assortment of Cigars, etc., of the best foreign and domestic makes. Mr. Foye puts his prices at very reasonable figures, and as his goods are first-class there is no occasion for surprise at the magnitude of his business.

G. T. Piper & Co., Dealers in Dry and Fancy Goods, Fairfield. There is a certain air about a popular and well-patronized establishment of any kind that is easily distinguished by a careful observer, and although it would often be difficult to define just what is meant by an "air of prosperity," still it is impossible to mistake such an appearance after once becoming familiar with it. If any of our readers wish an example of what we mean, let them visit the establishment conducted by G. T. Piper & Co., and they will find one of the most popular Dry and Fancy Goods stores in this section of the State. Mr. Piper was born in Livermore, Mo., and inaugurated the enterprise in question in 1887. The premises occupied comprise one floor of the dimensions of 20x75 feet, and afford opportunity for the display of one of the most varied and desirable assortments of Dry and Fancy Goods in Fairfield. Employment is given to three competent and polite assistants, and in every department of the store the same scrupulous attention to details is noticeable, the result being that customers are always assured prompt and courteous attention, and that the goods offered are both fashionable in style and low in price. Mr. Piper is fully aware that close personal supervision is essential to the maintenance of the admirable system in force in his establishment, and may be depended upon in the future as in the past to give his best efforts toward assuring satisfaction to every customer. No misrepresentation is allowed, and prices are made as low as possible. Mr. Piper is a well-known member of the Free Masons and Odd Fellows.

G. C. Philbrook, Manufacturer of Harnesses of all Grades, Robes, Blankets, Whips, etc., Bridge Street, Fairfield. Harness Goods, etc., are difficult things to buy unless you know just whom you are trading with, for it is hard to judge of the true value of such articles, simply by personal inspection. Nothing can equal the test of actual wear, of course, but one thing can be done at all events, and that is to deal with a house that is unquestionably reliable and unquestionably moderate in its prices. No better example of such a concern could be wished for than that afforded by the enterprise conducted by Mr. G. C. Philbrook, on Bridge Street. This has certainly been carried on long enough to enable some insight to be gained concerning its characteristics, for it was inaugurated in 1887. Mr. Philbrook was born in China, Me., and is a member of the Free Masons. Owing to his upright business methods, he is very generally known in this vicinity, and is as generally respected as he is known. The premises made use of, measure 20x36 feet, and employment is given to two assistants. Mr. Philbrook manufactures Harnesses of all grades,and deals in Robes, Blankets, Whips, etc., and is in a position to supply a standard article at the lowest market rate. Every article sold by him, is warranted to prove as represented, and integrity and honor are the distinguishing characteristics of his business methods. Custom work is promptly and skillfully attended to, and particular attention is paid to Repairing, such work being done neatly, but as strongly and durably as possible.

F. M. Cotton, Drug Store, Fairfield. Perfect neatness and order are of course expected in every pharmaceutical establishment and are almost invariably present; but even these qualities, admirable as they unquestionably are, cannot compensate for want of experience and skill, and, therefore, we think the public will be interested in learning of a pharmacy where all these desirable attributes are assured, and where strictly reliable goods are to be had at the lowest market rates. We have reference to the establishment carried on by Mr. F. M. Cotton, and are sure that our favorable opinion of its merits is fully supported by the facts and indorsed by those who have had an opportunity to judge of its correctness from personal experience. Mr. Cotton is a native of Fairfield, and inaugurated the enterprise alluded to in 1888. There are utilized one floor and a basement of the dimensions of 28x50 feet, which are well stocked with Drugs of All Kinds, Books and Stationery, and Fancy Goods. Although at some city drug store there may be larger stocks carried than that shown by Mr. Cotton, still it would be difficult to find one more varied and at the same time composed of more first-class materials, and it is to this variety and completeness of the goods on hand that the establishment under notice owes much of the reputation attached to it for accuracy and celerity in the compounding of prescriptions. The facilities at hand in this department are of the very best and most approved description, and nothing is left undone to secure reliable and satisfactory results.

John Green, Steam Piping and Plumbing, Fairfield. It is a very useful thing to know of a good plumber who may be depended upon to give prompt attention to orders, for waterpipes have a way of busting without notice, and other repairs in the plumbing arrangements are constantly having to be made, so that such information is pretty sure to be often made use of. He has built up an enviable reputation since he founded his present undertaking in 1887, and we feel that we can give our readers no better advice than to direct them to intrust this gentleman with such repairing or other work in his line that they may wish to have done. The premises occupied comprise one floor, which is well supplied with all necessary requisites for the proper conduct of this business. Employment is given to competent assistants and orders for Plumbing and Steam pipe Fitting of every description, will be given instant attention and faithful and thorough work is guaranteed. Also special attention given to drainage and ventilation. Customers will find that their interests are given careful consideration and work of all kind will be finished in a durable and workmanlike style. Mr. Green is a native of Portland, Me., and served in the Mexican and Civil wars. He is a thoroughly skillful and practical plumber, fully deserving the favorable reputation he has already attained in this vicinity.

U. G. Salley, Fine Custom Tailor and Dealer in Woolens, Fairfield. The rapidity with which the enterprise conducted by Mr. U. G. Salley, has reached its present dimensions, has occasioned no small amount of comment among those conversant with the magnitude of the business now done, but it is easily understood after careful consideration of the methods by which it has been brought about. Mr. Salley, who is a native of Madison, Maine, begun operations here in 1886, and it soon became manifest that he was exceptionally well-prepared to cater to the most fastidious trade. It has been his aim from the beginning, to thoroughly satisfy every customer, and the present wide popularity of his establishment, is but the legitimate result of such a policy. The premises occupied, comprise two floors of the dimensions of 60x40 feet, and afford accommodation to one of the finest lines of Suitings to be found in the State, as Mr. Salley is a large dealer in Woolens and handles the productions of some of the most celebrated Foreign and Domestic mills. It is largely owing to the latitude of choice his stock allows, that his ability to satisfy every patron is due, for the goods offered at his store comprise the latest fashionable novelties, as well as full lines of staple suitings, and are adapted to all ages and habits. Employment is given to twelve assistants, and orders are filled with the utmost celerity, although care is taken to attain uniform excellence of finish, and perfection of fit is guaranteed. Mr. Salley is reasonable in his prices, for his trade is so extensive as to warrant his depending upon the *number* of his orders for a fair profit on the capital invested, rather than on a high margin on comparatively few commissions.

W. S. Miller, Dentist, office hours, from 8 to 12 A. M., 1 to 6 P. M. Anæsthetics administered at usual rates. Rooms in Burgess Block, cor. Main and Bridge Streets, Fairfield. Few things are more difficult for the average man to bring himself to do than to visit a dentist's rooms, and it is just on this account that a great deal of the pain suffered in such places is due. When attended to in time, operations on the teeth are entirely painless; and in cases where decay is just beginning it can be arrested and the tooth preserved for many years, perhaps for life, by proper treatment. Yet how many people see their teeth decaying, know that they are growing worse daily, know that a competent dentist could obviate further destruction of them, and yet let week after week go by, until the only thing left to do is to extract the tooth, and thus loose a faithful servant that might have been kept for years. Such conduct is certainly foolish, yet it is the rule rather than the exception. Residents of Fairfield certainly have no excuse on the ground of there being no competent dentist near by, for Dr. W. S. Miller is known to be a skillful and conscientious practioner, who gives his best efforts to his patrons and neglects no means of attending to their best interests. He was born in Searsport, Me., and has practiced his profession here since 1887. His dental rooms are located in Burgess Block, corner of Main and Bridge Streets, and cover an area of 25x15 feet, and are conveniently fitted up for the purpose for which they are utilized. Dr. Miller is moderate in his charges as well as thorough in his work, and gives prompt attention to every caller. He has every method for the Painless Extraction of Teeth, including Ether, Nitrous Oxide Gas, Electricity and Local Anæsthesia, or Freezing the Gums as it is usually termed.

Tuttle & Frazier, Dry and Fancy Goods and Millinery, Fairfield. Some of those people who are so fond of declaring that it is only by confining himself to the sale of one particular line of articles that a man can quote low prices on the same ought to visit the establishment of Messrs. Tuttle & Frazier, in this town, and thus learn by a careful examination into goods and prices how mistaken they have been in making any such assertion. In theory they may have been correct, but as practice and theory are often widely divergent, it is always well to look into the former before having a great deal to say about the latter. The firm which we have mentioned began operations in 1888. Dry and Fancy Goods and Millinery Furnishing Goods are among the chief articles handled, and no better commeutary can be made on the methods employed in the buying and selling of the same than to state that no concern in Fairfield is prepared to offer more genuine inducements in any or all of the articles mentioned. The store is 25x36 feet in dimensions, and affords an excellent opportunity for the display of the goods handled. Staple and Fancy Dry Goods in all the standard and popular materials, shades and makes are shown, and in this line alone such bargains are offered as to well repay a visit, while a beautiful assortment of Millinery Goods at the "people's prices" furnishes additional incentive, if such be required. Two polite and competent assistants are employed, and all visitors to this establishment are promptly and courteously served. The individual members of the firm are Mr. C. W. Tuttle and Mr. Abner Frazier. Both gentlemen are well-known and highly respected in this community.

D. W. Allen & Co., Dealers in Hardware, Iron and Steel, Paints and Oils, Stoves and Tin Ware, Doors, Glazed Sash and Blinds, Wheels and Spokes, Mill Supplies, Cordage, Agricultural Implements, Wooden Ware and Oilcloths. Tin and Sheet Iron Work, Piping and Plumbing, Done to Order; Fairfield. The firm of D. W. Allen & Co. has only been before the public since 1887, but the enterprise with which it is identified is of much longer standing, having been inaugurated in 1872, by Messrs. Allen & Totman. Mr. Allen is connected with the Free Masons and with the Odd Fellows, and is associated in business with Messrs. V. M. Mayo and Walter Tozier. Spacious premises are utilized, three floors of the dimensions of 80x75 feet being occupied, and an immense stock is carried, comprising Hardware of all descriptions, Iron and Steel and Paints and Oils, together with Stoves and Tin Ware, Doors, Glazed Sash and Blinds, Wheels and Spokes, Mill Supplies, Cordage, Agricultural Implements, Wooden Ware, Oil Cloths, etc. Tin and Sheet Iron Work is done to order at short notice, and Piping and Plumbing are attended to in the most careful and satisfactory manner at reasonable rates. Both a wholesale and retail business is done, and employment is afforded to four competent assistants. The assortment of Agricultural Implements shown, is particularly large and well-selected, and farmers will find all the most improved appliances offered at the lowest market rates. Durability is a most important factor in the value of anything in this line, and it is therefore best to buy of a house whose warrant may be depended upon. The stock of Paints and Oils is also very complete, while that of Stoves and Tin Ware is worthy the attention of every housekeeper, as it includes goods embodying the latest improvements, and is sufficiently varied to meet the wants of all tastes. Prices are low in every department, and customers are assured prompt and polite attention.

Amos Learned, Dealer in Fruit, Confectionery, Nuts, and Choice Brands of Cigars and Tobacco, Fairfield. Good nature being a most desirable quality, and good living largely promoting good nature, it follows that Mr. Amos Learned is in some respects a public benefactor, insomuch as he furnishes his customers with excellent living and therefore if they do not all become good natured, it is plainly no fault of his. Information as to the whereabouts of a first-class and liberally managed Eating and Oyster House, is by no means to be despised, and as this is just the description of the enterprise carried on by the gentleman before named, we take pleasure in informing our readers, that it is located on Main Street. Here are occupied three floors, each of the dimensions of 90x24 feet, and includes a fine Billiard Hall. Everybody who wants a good, substantial, well-cooked and well-served meal, at a low price, should by all means give Mr. Learned a trial. He has carried on operations here since 1880, and is constantly increasing the desirability of his establishment. Close personal attention is given to the details of the business, and every effort made to continue the excellent record thus far established. Mr. Learned was born in Clinton, Me., and is connected with the Odd Fellows. He gives employment to three assistants, and deals largely in Fruit, Confectionery, Nuts and Choice Brands of Cigars and Tobacco, etc., and in this, as in the other branches of his business, gives a full equivalent for every cent received.

Everett F. Files, Dealer in Dry and Fancy Goods, Millinery, etc., Fairfield. Among the Dry and Fancy Goods Stores to be found in this section—and they are many in number and generally excellent in character—we know of none more worthy of liberal patronage than that located on Main Street, and carried on by Mr. Everett F. Files. This establishment was founded in 1853, by Miss M. M. Owen, and in 1876 the present proprietor was admitted to the firm, and in 1880 assumed the full control of the business, and the many opportunities since had for testing the inducements it offers to the public, have resulted in its attaining the high position it now holds. Dry and Fancy Goods, both imported and domestic, are very largely dealt in, and a specialty is made of Millinery, etc. The latest fashionable novelties in this line being obtained as soon as placed on the wholesale market, and the prices being such as to make this store a favorite resort with ladies who are aware of its advantages and who desire to dress stylishly at a small expense. Mr. Files is by no means content to rely on the reputation his store has already gained, but is ever on the alert to offer even more decided inducements.

HISTORICAL SKETCH
—OF—
FARMINGTON.

IN a secluded, yet easily accessible region of the Garden State, lies one of the most beautiful and attractive towns of New England. Farmington has long been known and sought by lovers of nature for its rare and unique charms. Situated in the southern part of Franklin County, of which it is the shire town, it is reached directly by the Maine Central Railroad, of which it is the terminus, being about ninety-five miles distant from Portland. It is also the southern terminus of the Sandy River Railroad, being the central station and starting-place for all the lovely region between it and the Rangely Lakes. It is a large town, being about ten miles in length and seven in breadth, containing twenty-seven thousand square acres of unusually fertile soil. When it was first settled it received its name Farmington because of its great fertility of soil and great advantages for farming. The chief products of the soil, since an early period, have been hay and wool. The Sandy River runs through the town almost north and south, dividing it in the center, the most populous part of the town being to the east of the river. The most prominent elevation in the town is called "Powder House Hill," and is a favorite resort for those seeking and delighting in the magnificent prospect of the surrounding country which it affords. The town is famed for its broad, smooth streets, beautified by double rows of magnificent shade trees, and the charming residences along many of them. One most striking feature of the town is the number and excellence of the educational institutions which it possesses, rendering it in this respect unusually advanced, even for New England. The "Willows, Young Ladies Seminary," "Western Normal School," "Little Blue School," and "Wendell Institute," are some of the best known of these, which are all marked by the beauty of their buildings and grounds, their fine facilities and scholarly curriculum and management. The town was first explored, with a view to settlement, in the great year of American Independence. In 1776, Stephen Titcomb, Robert Grover, James Henry, Rob-

A STREET IN FARMINGTON, 1889.

ert Alexander, and James MacDonald, all from Topsham, Me., arrived here, and took a long and careful survey of the land. By making a line out of pieces of bark joined together, they measured off the land, and laid out settlements for each, deciding that the richness of the soil and advantageous situation made settlement a most obvious and fortunate enterprise.

The land which was taken up by the Farmington settlers, belonged to William Tyng & Co., of Massachusetts, having been granted to William Tyng in 1703, on account of services rendered to the State. It was accordingly first called "Tyngtour," being also known as "Plantation Number One," and "Sandy River Plantation." The settlement continued to grow steadily, though slowly, during the Revolutionary War, and in 1780, a survey of the land was made by Col. Joseph North. In 1794, the town had grown sufficiently to obtain a charter of incorporation, on demanding it. Three years later, in 1797, a post-office was opened here, and communication with the outside world well established by the opening of the regular stage route. That the early settlers were of an unusually cultured type is shown by the marked and intelligent attention which they gave to educational matters from the beginning. In 1798, Farmington was first represented at the General Court of Massachusetts, by Hon. Supply Belcher. Among the eminent citizens who have honored Farmington with their admiration and interest in their residence here have been

A STREET IN FARMINGTON, 1889.

Jacob and John S. C. Abbott, the well-known authors, Hon. Hiram Belcher, the founder of the "Willows," (which was for years one of the most beautiful Young Ladies' Seminaries in the State), Hon. Robert Goodenow and others. In addition to the libraries of the educational institutions there is a fine circulating and a social library in the town. The public schools, also, as well as the private academies, are conducted with great ability and most satisfactory results.

During the war of 1812, the town was too small, and remote from the seacoast, to contribute much to New England's great achievements for American Independence at that time, but in the Civil War it took a most earnest and glorious share. It sent nearly one-tenth of all its inhabitants, two hundred and sixty-eight men, to the war, of whom fifty-seven were sacrificed to the maintenance of the great cause, and lost to many mourning friends at home. The town also contributed generously of its wealth to the government and soldiers.

The growth of population in Farmington has been steadily continuous, after the substantial, good old-fashioned way of sturdy country towns, whose strength and life are more highly developed by being slow and long in growth. In 1850, it was 2,725, in 1860, 3,106, 1870, 3,251, 1880, 3,353. In 1880, the valuation of the town was $1,601,271. Since 1880, the growth of the town has been somewhat more rapid, and now its population is nearly 4,000, and its valuation in the region of $2,000,000.

The great fertility of the soil makes farming particularly advantageous, and the wool industry is especially developed, this being one of the largest wool-producing towns in New England. Among the leading business industries are carriage-making, hardware, and tools of all sorts, grain and produce, wool, baskets, bricks, lumber, wood-turnings, etc. The business enterprise of the citizens of Farmington have accomplished great results against many obstacles, and the introduction of the railroad has been an inestimable boon to the commercial affairs of the region. The manufacturing interests of Farmington have made marked progress in recent years, and with the improvement of transportation facilities there can be no doubt that great material results can be reaped in this department of industry, in which, indeed, lies the great hope and promise of all New England's industrial progress. Especial privileges are offered by the enterprising citizens to manufacturers who will locate here, and such as are worthy of the careful attention of all meditating a change of business or the starting of a new manufacturing industry.

The social life of Farmington is marked by the refinement and culture of an old New England town. The great care taken in providing the best and broadest education, and the high moral tone of the community, unite in making the social charms of residence here in harmony with the beauties of nature which environ it. The people are distinguished for their liberality and generous kindliness in hospitality, and in every good work and word. Literary topics naturally form a great feature of social gatherings, and inspire much attention and interest among both young and old. For all who experience the delightful charms of life and society amid these pleasant surroundings, the reminiscence is always one of the most bright and fascinating of all past experiences.

It would be impossible to describe within our brief space the advantages of this region from the tourist standpoint. The immediate vicinity contains all the attractions which make every year larger numbers of delighted visitors flock to the inland resorts of the Garden State. The river, on which the light canoe can penetrate far into the deep forest, and through still secluded ponds, offers fine attractions to the sportsman. It is a favorite center of lovers of the rod and gun in all seasons. Many ponds in all directions open up an almost inexhaustible field of sport to the fisherman, and the gunner does not have to go far before he comes upon the flocks of piping partridges and the tracks of deer and caribou. Through all this region up to the Rangeley Lakes and beyond, is a veritable sportsman's paradise, which is becoming widely famed throughout the United States, and of this great region Farmington is the natural center and basis of supplies. In addition, the opportunities for rest and recreation, which, in the nervous hurry of our American life, are becoming more and more a supreme necessity to our physical well-being, are here afforded in abundance.

LEADING BUSINESS MEN

OF

FARMINGTON, ME.

People's Trust Company, Farmington. Capital, $100,000. Geo. W. Wheeler, President. Daniel M. Bonney, Treasurer. Transacts a general Banking Business. Acts as Trustee for Railroads and other Corporations. Legal depository for Administrators, Executors, Trustees and Assignees. Interest allowed on Deposits. The People's Trust Company transacts a general Banking Business, but it is with its record and facilities as Trustee that the present article has chiefly to deal, as our readers are more directly interested in that department of its business. The company was incorporated in 1885 with a capital of $100,000. It was the belief of its founders that there existed a demand in this community for increased facilities for the safe deposit of Trust Funds and other moneys, in the disposal of which absolute safety of the principal was of more importance than the amount of the income received therefrom. This belief has been proved to have been well founded, for the opportunity offered by the company has been widely availed of by Administrators, Executors, Trustees and Assignees, for all of which the company is legal depository. Railroads and other corporations have also made use of the company as Trustee, and the manner in which the interests of all parties concerned have been protected by the management is evidenced by the statement of Fred E. Richards, Bank Examiner, under date of April 18, 1888. We present this statement in full, as it tells better and more forcibly than mere words could the exact financial condition of the institution, and its worthiness of the great confidence reposed in it. RESOURCES: Loans and Discounts, $234,606.92; Stocks and bonds, $176,106.50; Real Estate, $31,553.33; Furniture and Fixtures, $3,404.12; Expenses, $1,534.28; Taxes Paid, $1,050.56; Cash, on Hand and Deposited, $23,746.94; total, $472,002.65. LIABILITIES: Stock, $100,000; Surplus, $5,000; Unpaid Dividends, $819; Deposits, $361,253.75; Undivided Profits, $4,929.90; total, $472,002.65. This must certainly be considered a gratifying showing, and the indications are that now the enterprise has got fairly started, and the great capacity for usefulness has been made widely and plainly manifest, its progress will be more pronounced than ever, and its position become even more prominent than before. Interest is allowed on deposits, and the motto on the seal — "Fidelity Security" — is lived up to strictly in every respect. Mr. George W. Wheeler, the President, is a widely known business man, whose fitness for his present position was conceded even before he had opportunity to make it practically manifest, while Mr. Daniel M. Bonney, the Treasurer, has proved emphatically "the right man in the right place." The People's Trust Company's building is an elegant structure throughout. It is very centrally located, occupying the corner of Broadway and Main Streets. The banking rooms which are on the first floor are so elegantly fitted up and appointed that one on entering can almost imagine he is in some banking institution of a large city.

H. Ramsdell, Dealer in Dry and Fancy Goods, Small Wares, etc., Belcher Block, cor. Main Street and Broadway, Farmington. There are undeniable advantages to be gained by choosing from a large stock, no matter what kind of articles are wanted; but this is especially the case when anything in the line of Dry and Fancy Goods is to be purchased, for there is so much difference in taste where these goods are concerned, that satisfaction can only be had by selecting from a very extensive assortment. The Dry Goods establishment conducted by Mr. H. Ramsdell, in Belcher Block, corner of Main Street and Broadway, has long held a leading position in this section of the State, and this prominence is due not only to the variety and completeness of the stock offered, but also to the unusually desirable character of the articles composing it. Mr. Ramsdell certainly does not lack experience in his chosen line of business, for the enterprise to which we refer was started in 1864, under the firm-name of Hutchinson & Ramsdell, and for the past 20 years has been under the sole control of the present proprietor. This experience enables him to cater intelligently as well as liberally to the wants of his customers, and the result is to be seen in the great and still growing popularity of the undertaking. A double store and basement are occupied, each measuring 70x34 feet, and employment is afforded to four efficient assistants, both a wholesale and retail business being done. Callers are assured immediate and polite attention, and every article is sold under a guarantee that it will prove as represented, while the prices are as low as can be quoted on goods of equal quality anywhere, as no concern enjoys more favorable relations with producers.

LEADING BUSINESS MEN OF FARMINGTON.

George McL. Presson, Dealer in Watches, Clocks, Jewelry, Silverware, Spectacles, etc. Fine Watch and Clock Repairing done to order, Farmington. The stock carried by Mr. George McL. Presson, is worthy the careful inspection of all who contemplate the purchase of anything in the line of Watches, Clocks, Jewelry etc., for the assortment shown is unusually complete in every department, and what is more, the prices quoted are remarkably low, considering the quality of the goods. Mr. Presson was born in Farmington, and is extremely well known here, being prominent in Masonic circles as a member of the Blue Lodge and Chapter. He started the enterprise he now conducts, in 1885, and occupies premises of the dimension of 45x15 feet. Some very beautiful designs in Silverware are offered to select from, and the most fastidious cannot fail to find articles to please them at this establishment, for not only a full line of staple goods is carried but also many of the latest and most fashionable novelties in Jewelry, Clocks, Watches, etc., while especial attention is paid to the quality of the optical goods dealt in, eye glasses, and spectacles suited to all defects of vision, being always on hand. Particular care is taken to make no representations that are not fully justified by the facts, and hence the most inexperienced buyer may trade here with the assurance of obtaining just what he pays for. Fine Watch and Clock Repairing is made a specialty, and those who have a valuable and delicate time-piece which needs cleaning or repairing, will find Mr. Presson prepared to do the work in a perfectly satisfactory manner at a moderate charge.

J. F. Prescott, Lumber Dealer and Manufacturer of Clapboards, Floor Boards, Matched Boards, etc., Farmington. It is over a score of years since Mr. J. F. Prescott inaugurated his present enterprise, and it is well deserving of mention as a representative undertaking in every sense of the word, for the plant in use is of the most improved description; the product enjoys high popularity by reason of its uniform excellence, and the prices quoted are always in accordance with the lowest market rates. Mr. Prescott is a native of Farmington and is connected with the Free Masons. He deals extensively in Lumber, and manufactures Clapboards, Floor Boards, Matched Boards; also Hard Wood Flooring a specialty, his factory, comprising three floors and measuring 40x60 feet. During his long business career, Mr. Prescott has steadily pursued the policy of dealing honorably by all, so it is not to be wondered at that the public express the utmost confidence in everything coming from his establishment proving strictly as represented. Employment is given to six competent assistants, and orders can be filled at short notice, while the smallest commissions are given immediate and careful attention. The Clapboards, Flooring, etc., produced at this mill, are made from well-seasoned stock, and will consequently give much better satisfaction than those sometimes to be found in the market, while the prices quoted are equally low. Both a wholesale and retail business is done, and the trade is steadily increasing. Mr. Prescott also saws and furnishes White Birch Spool Stock, a business added to the above during the last two years. Mr. Prescott being advanced in years, will sell the herein described business property at a great bargain to some young and enterprising party, who can take in the future prospect of a paying business.

Franklin County Savings Bank, Organized 1868; Joseph W. Fairbanks, President, I. Warren Merrill, Treasurer; Farmington. Life would be but a dull thing without ambition to enliven it, and such enterprises as encourage the forming of a reasonable and worthy ambition, are deserving of the highest commendation. In this connection let us call attention to the work done by the Franklin County Savings Bank, for this institution has aided many a man in carrying out one of the noblest and worthiest resolves that can be made—that of securing his family against want in time of sickness or other emergency. There are very few men but what can save something from their daily earnings if they really wish to do so, and many a man who now spends every cent he receives, would lay a portion of his wages aside if some one in whom he had confidence would come to him and offer to care for all he could save, and to allow him a fair rate of interest on the principal. This is precisely what the Franklin County Savings Bank is prepared to do, and the security it affords is much greater than that any private individual could possibly offer, for the investment of the funds placed in its care is controlled by carefully considered laws, drawn up solely in the interest of depositors, and the system of frequent and exhaustive examinations carried on by the State authorities renders evasion of those laws practically impossible, even were the management of the bank disposed to attempt it. But the reliability and good faith of the institution can be more pleasantly and conclusively proved in another way. Operations were begun in 1868, so that ample time has elapsed to compare the performance with the promise. From the statement made over the signature of Fred E. Richards, Bank Examiner, September 6, 1888, we learn that the deposits held at that time amounted to $396,928.03, while the Reserved Fund was $18,100. There are now more than $400,000 held on deposit, and the gradual but steady increase to be noted in this respect from year to year, is the best possible proof of the faithfulness with which the interests of depositors are guarded. A glance at the list of officers and trustees shows the enterprise to be in the hands of representative citizens, who have proved their business abilities in other fields of action, and who must be known either personally or by reputation to nearly all our readers. The names are as follows: President, J. W. Fairbanks; Treasurer, I. Warren Merrill. Trustees, J. W. Fairbanks, F. C. Perkins, D. V. B. Ormsby, J. C. Holman, S. C. Belcher, H. Ramsdell, J. H. Waugh. This Banking Room is one of the most elegantly fitted up and appointed of any in the State, being beautifully finished in cherry and richly ornamented in the most modern and approved style; has large Fire-proof Vaults and contains one of Damon's best safes, with Automatic Bolt Work and Time Lock.

LEADING BUSINESS MEN OF FARMINGTON. 245

E. G. Blake, Wholesale and Retail Dealer in Watches, Clocks, Jewelry, Solid Silver and Plated Ware, Spectacles, Eye Glasses and Cutlery. Fine Watch Repairing a Specialty; established 1855; No. 40 Main Street, Farmington. There are but few business enterprises carried on uninterruptedly by one proprietor for a third of a century, and hence the undertaking conducted by Mr. E. G. Blake, at No. 40 Main St., is worthy of especial mention, if for no other reason than it was inaugurated by its present owner in 1855. But there *are* other and important reasons for giving it particular prominence in these columns, not the least noteworthy of which is the fact that no more reliable establishment can be found in the State. When one makes a purchase of Mr. Blake he knows just what he is buying. It may be a Watch, it may be some article of Jewelry or of Silver Ware, or it may be something in the line of Optical Goods; but whatever it is, it is sold simply on its merits, and is sure to prove just as represented in every detail. Then another thing, Mr. Blake has, as we have stated, been in business a good many years, and it is fair to presume that he is in a position to sell as low as anybody. That he *does* do so, many of our readers know from experience, and this being the case we need hardly add that his store is very liberally patronized, especially as the stock on hand is so large and varied as to allow of all tastes and purses being suited. It includes Watches, Clocks, Jewelry, Solid Silver and Plated Ware, Spectacles, Eye Glasses and Cutlery, and contains the latest novelties as well as full lines of standard goods. One floor and a basement, measuring 24x68 feet are occupied, and employment is given to two efficient and polite assistants. A specialty is made of Fine Watch Repairing, the work being first-class, the charges moderate and the results uniformly satisfactory. Orders will be filled at short notice, and the most expensive and delicate foreign or American Watches are successfully treated. A specialty is also made of Fine Engraving; this being the only establishment in Franklin County where Artistic Engraving is executed. Mr. Blake is a native of Salem, Me., and is very widely known in Farmington and vicinity. He is prominently connected with the Odd Fellows, having been Treasurer of that order for the past twelve years. Mr. Blake's store is one of the finest in this part of the State, and compares favorably with those in the cities. Elegant Show Windows of French Plate Glass and of mammoth size adorn the front.

The most modern and beautiful show-cases on either side, and extending nearly the full length of the store, filled with choice and elegant goods, which together with the rest of the stock combined, presents a very attractive and pleasing appearance; and last, but by no means the least what is also pleasing about this establishment, is in the following two words, Low Prices.

Hotel Willows, Will. H. McDonald, Proprietor, Farmington. The residents of Farmington have good reason to be proud of the new but already famous "Hotel Willows," for this palatial public house surpasses any other in Sandy River Valley as regards size, location and convenient and elegant appointments, and indeed will compare favorably with any establishment in the State in every essential feature going to make up a strictly first-class hotel. It was erected at a cost of over thirty thousand dollars, and first opened its doors to the public March 3, 1888. Its sight has many advantages both from an asthetic and a practical point of view, for it is one hundred feet above the picturesque Sandy River, and thus gives the eye a large extent of beautiful country to roam over, while the elevation permitted the construction of a drainage system which trained and competent judges declare simply perfect. An unfailing supply of Pure Spring Water is drawn from a source beyond all possible chance of contamination, seventy feet above the house, and the situation of the hotel assures an abundant supply of fresh, pure air at all seasons of the year, while the complete steam-heating plant on the premises is capable of maintaining an equable and comfortable temperature in every room during the severest winter weather. The building is four stories in height, with a French roof, has fifty elegant guests-rooms and handsome parlors, and is supplied with hot and cold water. The dining-halls are commodious and well lighted and ventilated, and are fitted up with rare taste in accordance with the most approved methods, rendering them highly attractive to the most fastidious persons. As for the *Cuisine*, it can hardly be too highly praised, for it is made a matter of special pride by the management, who find themselves well repaid for the trouble and expense gone to, by the surprised and delighted exclamations of tourists from the great cities, who find it hard to realize that they are not at "Young's" or "Parker's" in Boston, or at some other equally famous metropolitan establishments. Many of them however need no further explanation when they consider that the proprietor is Mr. Will. H. McDonald, for during the eight years that that gentleman conducted the United States Hotel in Portland, he gained a reputation for lavish and skillful providing that placed him high among the leading hotel men of this State. He has been connected with the National Hotel Association for a number of years, and is Secretary and Treasurer of the Maine Hotel Association. Mr. McDonald is a native of Windham, Maine, and is identified with various leading secret fraternal orders, such as the Masons, Odd Fellows and Knights of Pythias. He is especially prominent in the latter organization, having occupied various offices of trust among which may be mentioned that of Chancellor Commander. He is now a member of the Grand Lodge of Maine. We are sure there is not a more truly popular hotel proprietor in the State, and those conversant with the trouble that Mr. McDonald takes to make his guests feel at home and to have them redeem all the promises made or implied in connection with his beautiful hotel, will agree with us that his popularity is thorougly well deserved. Hotel Willows has a fine Livery connected, and teams may be had at all hours at reasonable rates. Barges and coaches connect with every train, and commercial men, as well as sportsmen and tourists, will find every convenience that could be wished, while the terms are uniformly moderate.

The Hiram Holt Company, Sole Manufacturers of The Lightning Hay Knife, Farmington. Farmers have discovered that labor-saving machinery is at least as essential to the successful carrying on of their occupation as it is to the manufacturer, and, as a consequence, the market is filled with agricultural machinery of more or less value. Many of these devices are of little practical use, not because they lack ingenuity, or because they will not do excellent work under favorable conditions, but because they are complicated or weak in construction, and are sure to fail just when their aid is most needed. In refreshing contrast to such as these is the long-celebrated "Lightning" Hay Knife, for not only does this highly popular machine do its work with the rapidity signified by its name, but it is always "*ready for business*," requires no coaxing to induce it to take hold, and, with decent usage, will last for years, making it the cheapest as well as the best Hay Knife ever produced. Some idea of the favor with which it is regarded by those familiar with its merits may be gained from the fact that from four to five thousand dozen of these knives are made annually, and the demand is still increasing. The sole manufacturers of this indispensable farmers' implement are the Hiram Holt Co., whose works are located at East Wilton, the plant covering an area of about four acres, and employment being given to twenty-five assistants. The company in question was formed in 1887, succeeding Hiram Holt & Co., who began operations as scythe manufacturers in 1864 as successors to Mr. Calvin Keyes, who commenced business in 1856. The manufacture of Hay Knives was begun in 1871. Mr. Hiram Holt was born in Weld, Me., and is the President of the present company, the Secretary and Treasurer being Mr. A. D. Parsons. Goods are shipped throughout the country, and no precautions are neglected to insure a continuance of the reputation for careful manufacture the Lightning Hay Knives have so long enjoyed. We here show a cut of this knife, on which is their "trade-mark," "Lightning," that farmers may not be in doubt to know what kind of knife to buy, and we feel warranted in saying that any one keeping only a horse and cow to feed will find it pays well to use one of these knives to cut and feed from the side of the mow where the hay is always fresh, rather than pitch from the top where it is continually drying up. It is useful in cutting clingy clover hay on the rack, that it may be pitched off more easily. And its merits are also shown in cutting sods and ditching, cutting through tough grass and bush roots easily. Farmers that are using this Knife say they would not do without one for many times its cost.

D. H. Knowlton & Co., Farmington, Publishers of The "School World" and "School Days," the best and cheapest supplementary reading; also The Excelsior School System, Excelsior Spelling Blanks, Excelsior Report Cards, Model Report Cards, Excelsior Questions in Civil Government, Excelsior Questions in Arithmetic, Picture Aids to Composition, Young Folks' Speaker, etc. **Knowlton, McLeary & Co.**, Steam Book and Job Printers, Farmington. There may be no "royal road to learning," but still it is unquestionably a fact that the scholars of today have many of the stumbling blocks which harassed their predecessors removed, and that the obtaining of an education is easier and pleasanter now than was ever the case before. The work done by such publications as the "School World" and "School Days" can hardly be too highly commended, and that they furnish the best and cheapest supplementary reading is testified to by many prominent educators and by the increasing army of subscribers, a monthly edition of seventy thousand copies being now required. Messrs. D. H. Knowlton & Co., the publishers of the periodicals mentioned, also issue the popular "Excelsior" series of educational supplies, comprising the Excelsior Spelling Blanks, Excelsior Report Cards, Excelsior Questions in Civil Government, Excelsior Questions in Arithmetic, etc., as well as the Model Report Cards, Picture Aids to Composition, Young Folks' Speaker, and other works well-nigh indispensable to every schoolroom. Mr. D. H. Knowlton is a native of Farmington, and began operations in 1871. Ten years later he became associated with Mr. McLeary, under the firm-name of Knowlton, McLeary & Co., the concern now doing a very large business as Steam Book and Job Printers, as they have unsurpassed facilities and are in a position to fill the most extensive orders at very short notice and at the lowest market rates. The premises occupied comprise three floors, of the dimensions of 30x70 feet each, and employment is afforded to eleven assistants. Mr. McLeary is a native of this town and is connected with the Odd Fellows, Mr. Knowlton being a member of the Free Masons and having held various responsible public offices among which may be mentioned that of County Treasurer. The firm is a representative one, and occupies a leading position among similar houses in this State.

LEADING BUSINESS MEN OF FARMINGTON.

S. Clifford Belcher, Attorney and Counselor-at-Law, Farmington. We believe there is not a more popular or more generally-known man of affairs in Farmington than Mr. S. Clifford Belcher, for this gentleman has carried on his profession here for nearly 30 years, and is highly esteemed in legal, commercial and social circles. His influence is felt in more than one field of effort, and his judgment is regarded with great respect, even by those who may differ from him in matters of public policy, for his experience has been long and varied, and he never hesitates to give utterance to his real opinion, even though it may be opposed to the drift of popular sentiment. Mr. Belcher was born in this town, and at the time of the Rebellion was active in encouraging the organization of military forces. He held a commission as Major of the 16th Maine, and in 1879 was appointed Inspector General of the State Militia. He is very prominent in Masonic circles, being High Priest of the Chapter, and has done much to bring the ennobling principles of Free Masonry home to the community. Mr. Belcher's reputation as an Attorney and Counselor-at-Law is wide-spread, and the success he has won in his profession is due at least as much to the study of men as to the study of books. He is a profound student of character, and ranks with those Lawyers who prepare a case carefully before entering court, but still are able to entirely change the line of its conduct without the least confusion should future developments render such a course advisable. But, after all, the successful Lawyer wins his greatest triumphs out of court, and the number of suits prevented by wise and temperate Counsel from legal advisers, would surprise those who believe Lawyers set up strife. Mr. Belcher has peculiar qualifications as a Counselor, and many of his clients consult him in this capacity alone.

G. C. Stewart, Millinery and Fancy Goods, 39 Main Street, Farmington. There is not a better or more favorably-known establishment of the kind in Franklin County than that conducted by Mrs. G. C. Stewart, at No. 39 Main St., and this is not to be wondered at, for the enterprise referred to was inaugurated in 1870, and has held a leading position for nearly a score of years. Mrs. Stewart occupies premises of the dimensions of 20x42 feet, and carries a stock of Fine Millinery and Fancy Goods that contains the latest Parisian and London novelties, while the prices quoted are at least as low as those named elsewhere on articles of equal merit. Particular attention is given to order work, and care is taken to avoid annoying delay. While Mrs. Stewart's experience and taste enable her to guarantee satisfaction to her customers in every instance. Trimmed and untrimmed Hats and Bonnets are carried in stock in great variety, together with a full line of Imported and Domestic Millinery Trimmings of the latest and most Fashionable Designs. Customers may depend upon receiving immediate and courteous attention, and goods will be cheerfully shown, every opportunity for careful selection being given. This store may properly be called the headquarters for Fashionable Millinery, for leading styles are frequently received in advance of any other establishment in this vicinity.

T. O. Trask, Cabinet Maker, Farmington. Repairing of all kinds neatly done. Everybody who has a hobby for collecting certain things, as, for instance, coins, stamps, minerals, insects, eggs, cards, stuffed birds, etc., will be interested in knowing where a thoroughly competent Cabinet Maker may be found, for two-thirds of the value of such collections is lost unless the objects composing them are properly stored and displayed, and every individual has his own ideas as to the proper way of securing this important point. Many are restrained from having cabinets made to order by their belief that the cost must necessarily be beyond their means, but if they will call on Mr. T. O. Trask, we think they will find themselves mistaken on this point, for Mr. Trask is very moderate in his prices, and don't assume that every collector is a millionaire and must be made to pay accordingly. He was born in Freeman, Me., and began operations here in 1884. One floor, measuring 65x15 feet, is occupied, and Cabinet Making of all descriptions is extensively carried on. Mr. Trask's work is made to wear, and not merely to "look pretty," and those who are used to the ordinary furniture of the day, made of half-seasoned material stuck together with cheap glue, will be surprised to see how that made at this shop will compare with it. Mr. Trask gives particular attention to Repairing of all kinds, filling orders promptly and at low rates. Neatness and strength are the characteristics of his work, and it is bound to suit the most fastidious.

J. D. Hardy, Dealer in Stoves, Tinware, Cutlery, Pumps, Hardware, Nails, etc., Farmington. Some of the stoves to be seen in the market nowadays make very handsome parlor ornaments, but so far as giving out heat is concerned they can only be regarded as dismal failures. This is all the more to be regretted from the fact that purchasers of these goods are very apt to become prejudiced against all "art stoves," and to declare that in the future the old-fashioned kind will be good enough for them. There are certain styles, however, which combine beauty and efficiency, and to be sure of getting one of these no better advice can be given than to call at the establishment carried on by Mr. J. D. Hardy, and choose from his extensive stock. Mr. Hardy knows all about stoves, and he will sell you one suited to your needs, at least as low as you can get it anywhere. He began operations in 1881, and was originally associated with Mr. W. B. Fletcher, but since 1884, he has been sole proprietor. Mr. Hardy was born in Wilton, and is a member of the Masons. He deals in the latest improved Cook-stoves and Ranges, and also handles Tinware, Cutlery, Pumps, etc., very extensively, together with Hardware, Nails, and a full line of similar goods. Prices rule very low in every department, and prompt attention is given to customers, goods being delivered at short notice. In company with Mr. J. J. Towle, Mr. Hardy manufactures the celebrated "Champion Creamer," these gentlemen being agents for the whole of Maine, excepting York, Cumberland and Oxford counties. This famous dairy appliance has proved itself fully worthy of the name it bears, and is now used in some of the best-known creameries in New England.

Abbott Family School, For Boys, Little Blue, Farmington. That every parent owes it to his children to give them as complete an education as circumstances will permit, requires no demonstration, for it is obvious that, having brought a child into the world, a moral obligation is incurred to spare no pains to develop whatever capacity he or she may have to become a well informed and useful member of society. Boys, being from the very nature of things, much less constantly under the mother's watchful care than are girls, are especially apt to acquire bad habits during the critical period when the character is being formed for life, and for this reason it seems to us that such an establishment as the Abbott Family School at Little Blue, can hardly be too highly praised or too liberally supported, for the training there given is moral as well as intellectual, and the government combines firmness and gentleness to a degree seldom attained at similar institutions. Unfortunately the restrictions of space forbid our making detailed mention of the policy pursued at this old and famous school, but we hope to interest our readers sufficiently in its methods, to induce such of them as have boys who stand in need of the training it so successfully gives, to investigate for themselves, the task being an easy one, as the Principal, Mr. Alexander Hamilton Abbott, takes pleasure in affording inquirers every facility to form a personal and unbiased judgment of every detail of the work. It being well known to every student of men and of affairs, that the character and usefulness of such an institution as this are directly dependant upon the fitness and capacity of its Principal, (the stream never being able to rise higher than its source). We need make no apology for presenting the following notice of Mr. Abbott, it being taken from the Memorial Edition of "Abbott's Young Christian," published by the Harpers, 1882: "The Little Blue establishment on the removal of Mr. Jacob Abbott to New York, was leased by his youngest brother, Rev. Samuel Phillip Abbott, then settled in the ministry at Houlton, Maine, for the purpose of a family school for boys, which was opened on the 19th of February, 1844, and which is still in active operation. On Mr. S. P. Abbott's death, in 1849, the school was taken by Mr. Alexander Hamilton Abbott, an accomplished graduate of Bowdoin College, who, though a native of Farmington, represents another line of the Abbott family. In his hands, the establishment of which he was soon the owner, has been greatly enlarged, and the school, of which he is now the active principal, has won a distinguished reputation and exerted a wide and commanding influence. The house has been greatly changed, and the grounds around have undergone many improvements; but the old outlines are still to be traced, and the spot holds its own as the foremost attraction of the village." After such commendation, any further personal mention may seem superfluous, but we beg leave to add

THE SCHOOL HOUSE.

that Mr. Abbott, is evidently—to use a common and expressive phrase—"in love with his work," and shows that fresh and inspiring enthusiasm, so potent in enlisting the sympathy of the most careless and indifferent pupil. The sanitary conditions of the school and its surroundings

THE POND.

are faultless, and many a delicate child has grown strong in body here, even before his mind had opportunity to show marked development. The terms of tuition, etc., are moderate, and the advantages offered, are, in our opinion at least, simply inestimable.

LEADING BUSINESS MEN OF FARMINGTON.

E. O. Greenleaf, Attorney-at-Law and Notary Public, Masonic Block, Farmington. We take pleasure in presenting this necessarily brief sketch of that able, genial and popular lawyer, Mr. E. O. Greenleaf, for this gentleman has gained the prominent position he now holds in his profession in the face of discouragements and reverses which would have disheartened a less determined man; and it may truthfully be said that all that he now has he owes to his own exertions, for he began the practice of law with no capital beyond that of energy and brains. Mr. Greenleaf was born in Stark, Somerset Co., Maine, in Dec., 1853, and graduated in 1875. The next four years were devoted to the reading of law in the office of Judge Bonney, of Portland, and in that of G. C. Vose, of Augusta, and in 1879 Mr. Greenleaf began the practice of law on his own account, having—as we have stated—only his ability to back him. He worked hard, and put his whole heart into every case intrusted to him, no matter how trivial it might be, and the consequence was that he gradually established a practice, got together an extensive and valuable legal library, and fitted up his office with all the necessary conveniences. Then came the destructive fire of October, 1886, and the library and the office furniture so patiently worked for went up in smoke. The task of replacing them was comparatively easy, however, for Mr. Greenleaf had, by this time an extensive practice, and his suite of rooms, now one of the best in Masonic Block, will compare favorably in point of equipment, with any law office in this vicinity. He is a member of the Democratic State Committee, and never hesitates to define his political position when occasion requires, but is not one who deems all the virtue confined to one party, and respects the views of others as he wishes his own respected. Mr. Greenleaf was formerly Supervisor of Schools, and now holds high offices in fraternal orders, being Senior Warden in Maine Lodge and King in Franklin Chapter, F. & A. M. Mr. Greenleaf is interested in education, and, in fact, any matter which is of general benefit to the town and county. His practice, which is rapidly extending, is not confined to Farmington or the county, but extends throughout the State, his services having been secured in many important cases where large amounts were at stake. In fact, he is very popular in and out of the profession, and owes no small portion of his success as a lawyer to the habit of thorough preparation which he has always adhered to. Knowing his profession so thoroughly, it is very difficult to surprise or disconcert him, and he may always be depended upon to fight for the interests of his clients to the very last extremity.

Byron Farrar, Harness Maker, and Dealer in Harnesses, Blankets, Robes, Trunks, Valises, Whips, Lap Dusters, Wool Mats, etc., 35 Broadway, Farmington. No harness can combine strength and beauty unless it be carefully made from selected material, and the most of the so-called "cheap" harnesses are cheap only in as regards first cost, the expense of keeping them in condition soon more than making up the difference in price between them and a really good article. Mr. Byron Farrar, doing business at No. 35 Broadway, carries a fine assortment of harnesses of all descriptions and quotes some very low prices, considering the quality of the goods offered. He has carried on his present enterprise since 1877, and has built up an extensive trade by supplying reliable articles at fair rates. The stock on hand includes Blankets, Robes, Whips, Lap Dusters, Wool Mats and Horse Furnishings of all kinds, together with Trunks, Valises, Traveling Bags, etc. Mr. Farrar is a native of Buckfield, and resided for some years in Phillips, being very prominent there in town affairs. He was a member of the Board of Selectmen, and also held the position of Town Treasurer, and officiated as Postmaster for five years. He is a practical harness maker, and is prepared to do such work to order at very short notice and at moderate rates. Harnesses will be oiled and repaired without delay, and as only skilled help is employed. Mr. Farrar is prepared to guarantee that all work done at his establishment will give complete satisfaction.

C. A. Allen, General Agent for Ivers & Pond Pianos; also New England, Worcester, Burdett, and and other First-Class Organs; also Strings for Violin Guitar, Banjo, Violincello, of the Finest Grades, at low prices. Farmington. A man who has been identified with the manufacture and sale of Musical Instruments for over thirty years, may reasonably be expected to know something concerning them, and when he gives his verdict in favor of a certain Piano, and accepts the General Agency for its sale among his friends and neighbors, the presumption is strong that the Piano in question is equal to any in the market. Well, those who have used the Ivers & Pond Piano need not be told that it is unexcelled in any of the essential points that go to make up a strictly first-class instrument, and the fact that one hundred and ten of them are used in the New England Conservatory (the largest Musical College in the world) is proof positive that their merits are conceded by trained musicians as well as by the people in general. Mr. C. A. Allen was born in Industry, Maine, and began operations in 1856. He is a member of the Odd Fellows and is, without doubt, one of the best-known men in his line of business in the entire State. Mr. Allen no longer manufactures Musical Instruments, but deals in them very extensively, and gives particular attention to repairing, the facilities at his command enabling him to do such work in first-class style at short notice and at moderate rates. A fine stock is carried, comprising Ives & Pond Pianos (for which Mr. Allen is General Agent), Burdette, Worcestor and other First-Class Organs, which are sold on very liberal terms. Violin, Guitar, Banjo and other Musical Strings of the finest grades, and similar Musical Merchandise. Very low prices are quoted on all these goods, and satisfaction is guaranteed, all orders being promptly filled. Mr. Allen has been President and Director of the Franklin County Musical Institute for more than twenty years, and has had charge of the advanced Music in Farmington State Normal School for fourteen years or more.

Levi G. Brown, Horseshoeing and Jobbing, Farmington. Among those enterprises which, by general consent, are given a leading position among the business undertakings of Farmington and vicinity, mention must be made of that conducted by Mr. Levi G. Brown, for there are none too many establishments in this State where strictly first-class horseshoeing is done, and it is the general opinion among those in a position to speak from personal knowledge, that the service afforded at the shop in question is worthy of unstinted commendation. Mr. Brown is a native of Abbott, Maine, and founded his present business in 1875. He is extremely well known throughout this vicinity and is very prominent in Masonic circles, being connected with the Royal Arch Chapter, and having held many important offices in the Blue Lodge. He was formally Deputy Sheriff of Franklin County, and is now Supervisor of Corporations, which office he has held for six years, and the record he has made in this capacity renders any words regarding his fitness for the position entirely unnecessary. The premises utilized by Mr. Brown for the carrying on of his business are 45x22 feet in dimensions, and employment is given to two careful and experienced assistants. The facilities at hand enable orders to be promptly filled, and no trouble is spared to maintain his reputation of the establishment for skillful and thorough work. General Jobbing is given immediate and painstaking attention, and as dependable materials are used and each job given careful consideration, the results attained are characterized by neatness and durability, while the charges made are uniformly moderate.

J. W. Hines, Wholesale and Retail Dealer in Dry Goods, Groceries, Boots and Shoes, Flour, Grain, Produce, etc., Farmington. There are very few business enterprises of a similar nature, that can show so rapid a growth as has been enjoyed by that conducted by Mr. J. W. Hines, and it is gratifying to be able to state that the development of the undertaking in question has been brought about by strictly legitimate means, and is consequently as well-deserved as it is unusual. Operations were begun by Messrs. J. W. Hines and A. F. Gammon in 1875, the latter gentleman retiring in 1881, since which time the present proprietor has carried on the business alone. He is a native of Hartford, Me., and is connected with the Free Masons. The premises in use comprise three floors, each of the dimensions of 50x40 feet, and there are also two storehouses utilized one measuring 20x50 feet and the other 24x40 feet. As may be supposed from these figures, an immense stock is carried, it being made up of Dry Goods, Groceries, Boots and Shoes, Flour, Grain, Produce, etc. Both a Wholesale and retail business is done, and employment is given to three assistants, all orders being promptly and carefully filled. The reputation which Mr. Hines holds for selling dependable goods at bottom prices, is the natural result of the policy he has steadily pursued, and is so wide-spread as to bring him in a constantly increasing patronage. Detailed mention of the special attractions offered in the various departments of his store is impossible for lack of space, but the statement may be truthfully made that no more advantageous inducements to the public are held out by any store in this section, for not only are the prices low, but the goods are such as cannot fail to satisfy the most critical.

L. A. Smith, Wholesale and Retail Dealer in Stationery, Fancy Goods, Musical Instruments, Sewing Machines, Crockery, China, Lamps of all description, also Tinware, Household Goods, etc., in great variety, Masonic Block, 47 Main Street, Farmington. One of the most interesting establishments to visit of which we have knowledge, is that conducted by Mr. L. A. Smith, in Masonic Block, No. 47 Main Street, for the extent and variety of the stock offered here must truly be seen to be appreciated. It comprises Crockery, China, Glass and Tinware, Stationery, Fancy Goods, Albums in great variety, Musical Instruments, Sewing Machines, Household Goods, etc. The finest Hanging Lamps in the State, as well as all other kinds, are found at this popular store. The stock is remarkable alike for its completeness in every department, and for the low prices quoted on the various articles. Mr. Smith has carried on the enterprise under consideration, since 1875, and has built up a reputation for uniformly fair dealing, which is as high as it is well-deserved. He is a native of New Vineyard, and is connected with the Free Masons, ranking with the most prominent of our representative business men. The premises in use consist of two floors, each measuring 22x75 feet, and both a wholesale and retail business is done, employment being given to two assistants. In the line of Stationery, inducements are offered to all classes of purchasers, for the assortment on hand includes a fine stock of standard goods, together with the latest fashionable novelties, and the prices quoted are sufficiently wide in range to suit all purses. The same may be said of the Fancy Goods, Crockery, China, Glass and Tinware, Lamps of all kinds, and House Furnishings dealt in, and those who buy anything in these lines without paying Mr. Smith a visit, are simply neglecting their own interests. The Musical Instruments sold at this store are from the most reputable manufacturers, and are sure to prove as represented in every respect, although no fancy prices are named on them, while the advantages offered to purchasers of Sewing Machines are too generally known to require detailed mention. Mr. Smith carries an immense stock, in fact, one that would do credit to a large city, and his beautiful store, with its immense Plate-Glass Show Window, is only in keeping with the large and elegant stock that he carries. Mail orders in any of the departments carried here, from either wholesale or retail purchasers, will be attended to personally by Mr. Smith, and are always as carefully selected as though the party were there in person, and the prices charged will always be the lowest market rates. Satisfaction in both quality and price is always guaranteed, and parties in any part of this county where this book may land, will do well to give Mr. Smith a trial order. He is headquarters for Genuine "Maine Spruce Gum," which he sends by mail and express to all parts of the land.

F. N. Harris, Wholesale Butcher and Dealer in Cattle, Sheep, Lambs, Veals and Woolskins, West Farmington. A review of the leading business men of Farmington and vicinity, which did not contain mention of Mr. F. N. Harris, would be sadly incomplete; for if there is an enterprising man of business in this section who is deservedly popular among all having dealings with him and who is equally prominent in commercial and social life, it is certainly the gentleman we have named. Mr. Harris is a native of New Sharon, Maine, and founded the industry he now conducts in 1876. He is a very extensive dealer in Live Stock, and his operations are profitable to the farmers located in this section as well as to himself, for he receives Sheep from every town in the county, and also from points outside its limits.  In connection with this portion of his business, it is but simple justice to make mention of one of Mr. Harris' most valuable assistants, "Dick." Dick is a full-blood Scotch Shepherd, between eight and nine years old, and was bred by Gen. Tilton of the Soldiers' Home. Mr. Harris has trained him from a pup, and should any of our readers want to buy him they would find it a somewhat expensive purchase, as an offer of $500 cash would be laughed at. Dick will take a flock of sheep that has been made up in the country and alone and unaided will drive them to Mr. Harris' yard at West Farmington. If the distance is too great to be covered in one day, he will sleep with the flock and be up with the lark in the morning ready for business, and those who insist that no animal can reason, ought to see Dick "on the road," for the combination of persuasion, strategy and assumed ferosity by which he keeps the flock under control, is simply wonderful. Mr. Harris has a commodious and well-equipped Slaughter-House on his premises, and Butchers every year from 200 to 300 head of Cattle, and from 5,000 to 8,000 Sheep, besides a large number of Hogs and Calves. The Hides and Pelts secured, find a ready market in Lewiston, Portland and Boston. The total amount of business done will average about $35,000 per annum. Mr. Harris served in the Second Maine Cavalry during the Rebellion, and has long been very prominently connected with the Grand Army, holding various important offices and being elected Commander of J. F. Appleton Post in 1887. He is Commander-in-Chief of the Franklin Veteran Association and is conected with the Odd Fellows' Encampment. One of the most striking proofs of Mr. Harris' personal popularity among all classes of citizens, was given in 1886, in which year he was nominated for Sheriff by the Democrats. Although defeated in the election, it was by a very small majority, for, though his party was hopelessly in the minority, his friends rallied around him so enthusiastically as to cause him to run nearly 400 votes ahead of his ticket. Mr. Harris is one of the busiest men in the community, for his affairs are of such a nature as to call for close and persistent attention; but he is always approachable and good-natured, and in this respect furnishes an excellent example for imitation to certain men who, because they sell two or three thousand dollars' worth of goods a year, consider themselves far above ordinary people.

C. F. Packard & Co., Manufacturer of the Packard Wagon, West Farmington. "The proof of the pudding is the eating," according to the old proverb, and the proof of the statement made by Messrs. C. F. Packard & Co., that the Packard Wagon is the best-built vehicle of the kind in the State, is to be found in the record it has made during the sixteen years that it has been in service. The first premium has been awarded it at four Maine State Fairs, and this judgment has been indorsed by practical men who have become convinced of its soundness by the experience they have had with the Packard Wagon under all conditions of service. The manufacturers have issued a circular which should be read by every man who contemplates buying a wagon, for it is straight, business-like and to the point, and contains information, the truth of which we can vouch for, and which, indeed, bears the evidence of reliability on its face. Among other things, the circular says that those who offer to sell a Wagon for from $60 to $85, and to warrant it for one year, run but little risk in so doing, for it must be a poor vehicle indeed that would not last for that length of time, when protected by a thick coat of paint. It is year after year of hard use that tests the value of a Wagon, and Messrs. C. F. Packard & Co., show the confidence they have in their productions, *not* by warranting them for one year, but by guaranteeing to make good any fault in stock or workmanship at *any* time, free of cost, upon demand. That they live up to this guarantee, their customers and their agents will cheerfully testify. The Packard Wagon is sold at a moderate price, and it is a positive fact that the percentage of profit upon it is a great deal smaller than on those vehicles which are offered at from $60 to $85. The firm began operations in 1872, and occupy two buildings, the plant covering an area of 2,800 feet of floor-space. Excellent facilities are at hand for the doing of Repairing at short notice, and the scale of prices is just and reasonable. Mr. Packard is a native of Norway, and holds a commission as Justice of the Peace. He is connected with the Knights of Pythias and is very widely known in the community where his straight-forward business methods have gained him many friends as well as a large and growing trade.

Titcomb & Cole, Dealers in Furniture and House Furnishing Goods, Farmington. It is always well to bear in mind when furnishing a house that the goods bought for that purpose are intended for permanent use, so that when choosing the same, the truest economy is served by purchasing durable and well-made articles. Those taking this view of the subject will thank us for calling their attention to an establishment where thoroughly dependable goods are handled, especially when we add that the prices quoted there will bear the severest comparison with those named anywhere on articles equally desirable. The firm of Titcomb & Cole occupy premises comprising four floors, each measuring 34x64 feet, and do an extensive wholesale and retail business in Furniture and House Furnishing Goods of every description. The enterprise carried on by them has been in operation some years, but the existing co-partnership was formed in 1888, the members of the firm being Messrs. G. W. Titcomb and G. W. Cole. Mr. Titcomb was born in New Hampshire, and is a member of the Odd Fellows, while Mr. Cole is a native of Massachusetts, and is connected with the Free Masons. This concern manufactures many of the goods they sell, and hence are in a position to speak with confidence concerning their quality. It is a rule that is rigidly observed here never to misrepresent an article in the slightest degree, and consequently the most inexperienced purchaser has only himself to blame if he buys goods unsuited to his wants. There is a noticeable absence of that "red-tape" so prominent in most large establishments, and any desired information can thus be easily and promptly obtained, while large or small orders are given immediate and careful attention. The senior member, G. W. Titcomb, also carries at No. 46 Main Street a large stock of Books, Stationery and Fancy Goods, Toys, Games, etc., all of which are sold at a small margin, and purchasers needing anything in the above line can do no better elsewhere, and they will make no mistake if they first make their call at Mr. Titcomb's establishment.

Elm House, Mrs. W. T. Locke, Proprietor, West Farmington. There are some people who prefer "style" to comfort and a fashionable location to a healthful one, but such people are happily in the minority, and should any of our readers be classed among them, we can simply say that they will find no attractions at the "Elm House." But to the large majority who enjoy home comforts, plenty of nutritious food, good air and well kept premises, we have a different story to tell, for all these advantages are to be had at the hotel in question, which is managed more on the plan of a strictly first-class Boarding House than anything else. The owner and manager of the Elm House is Mrs. W. T. Locke, who began operations in 1888, and has already built up an enviable reputation for the hotel. The house is a three-story structure, very pleasantly located, the grounds connected with it covering an area of about two acres. This House is not surpassed for Summer boarders. Mrs. Locke is a native of Strong, Maine, and has a large circle of friends in this section. She spares no pains to make her guests comfortable, and is ever on the alert to improve the service afforded in every practicable manner. The sleeping apartments are light and pleasant, and are kept in the best of condition, being supplied with comfortable beds and furnished with all necessary conveniences. Employment is afforded to four competent assistants, and polite treatment is accorded every guest under all circumstances. Mrs. Locke sets an excellent table and the service is prompt and obliging, while the terms of the house are remarkably low, considering the accommodations.

Farmington Chronicle, [Established 1840.] A Thirty-six Column Paper devoted to the interests of Franklin County. John M. S. Hunter, Editor and Proprietor, Farmington. It is not necessary to call our readers attention to the Farmington Chronicle, for that excellent newspaper has a habit of calling attention to itself, by means of the variety and value of its contents, and its circulation of nearly 3,000 copies is equivalent at a very conservative estimate, to from 10,000 to 12,000 readers. But it is a pleasant and grateful task to make appropriate mention of an enterprise so liberally and wisely conducted, and to note how fully the mission of the Chronicle, as indicated by its publisher and proprietor, is carried out — a paper devoted to the interests of Franklin County. Just how much it has advanced those interests, cannot of course be expressed in words or figures, but those who know how powerful is the influence for good exerted by an ably, energetically and clearly conducted newspaper, will join with us in declaring the Chronicle a great benefit to the community. It was established in 1840, by Mr. J. S. Swift, and since that date, has been carried on by Messrs. Sprague & Swift, Messrs. Prescott & Swift, Mr. A. C. Phillips, Mr. A. H. Davis, Capt. C. W. Keyes, U. S. A., Messrs. C. W. Keyes & Co., finally coming into the hands of the present Editor and Proprietor, Mr. John M. S. Hunter. This gentleman is a native of Farmington, learned the printer's trade in the Chronicle office, twenty-one years ago, and is too well known to the majority of our readers to render extended personal mention of him necessary. He was formerly Deputy U. S. Consul at Fort Erie, Ontario, and is high in Odd Fellowship, holding a leading office in Franklin Lodge, No. 58. Mr. Hunter is a hard worker, and has a fashion of putting his ideas into words which leave no room for doubt as to his meaning. The Chronicle is a four page, thirty-six column Weekly, Republican in politics, but above all, *American*. It gives great prominence to local news, and though conducted with force and ability, and very out-spoken when frankness is called for, it is pre-eminently a newspaper for the *family*, and never contains an item or an article unfit for home reading. We are glad it is appreciated as its circulation shows it to be, and the greatest prosperity we can wish its proprietor, is that all who would be benefitted by reading it, would subscribe without delay.

L. G. Preston, Dealer in Beef, Pork, Chicken, Lamb, Corned Beef, Canned Fruits, Provisions, Fresh and Pickled Fish, Choice Tobacco and Cigars, 41 Broadway, opposite Post-office, Farmington. Such of our readers as are fond of good living, and wish to know where to purchase good food supplies to the best advantage, should make an early call at the establishment conducted by Mr. L. G. Preston, at No. 41 Broadway, opposite the Post-office, for this gentleman carries one of the heaviest and most carefully-selected stocks to be found in Farmington and vicinity, and whether you want Groceries, Meats, Fish or Vegetables, he is prepared to furnish first-class goods at the lowest market rates. Mr. Preston is a native of this place, and founded the undertaking of which he is now proprietor in 1873. The store is 22x35 feet in dimensions and no room is wasted, for each department of the stock on hand is kept well-supplied, and as a consequence all orders can be promptly filled. Beef, Pork, Lamb, Corned Beef, Chicken, etc., may be bought here in any desired quantity at bottom prices, and choice cuts are made a specialty, Mr. Preston being prepared to suit the most fastidious customer. Fresh and Pickled Fish are also handled extensively, together with Canned Fruit put up by the most popular and reliable packers. The assortment of Tobacco and Cigars is made up of carefully-chosen goods, that are offered at very low rates, and a full supply of all kinds of Vegetables—in their season—is also at hand to select from. Customers are assured polite attention, and all goods may be depended upon to prove as represented.

Exchange Hotel, S. Knowlton & Sons, Proprietors, New House, Newly Furnished, Stable connected with House, Farmington. The Exchange Hotel is one of those public houses to a stay in which the traveler can always look back with satisfaction, for there is nothing more gratifying when on the road than to put up at a hotel which combines the comforts of a home with the conveniences of a public house. Guests at the Exchange are well housed and well fed, and those who have done much traveling need not be told that this combination is not very often afforded, even at houses of much greater pretensions where much higher rates are in force. The building utilized is three stories in height and measures 40x60 feet, there being an ell attached of the dimensions of 25x20 feet, and the guest-rooms are so arranged as to provide an abundance of light and air, the entire house being well-heated and well-kept, there being employment given to ten competent assistants. There is a first-class Livery connected with the establishment, and teams may be had at any time at reasonable prices. The table is supplied with an abundance of carefully selected and well-cooked food, which is served promptly and neatly, and if there was no other reason for the popularity of the Exchange, the excellence of the *Cuisine* would amply justify it. Operations were begun in 1880, by Mr. S. Knowlton, the firm of S. Knowlton & Sons being formed in 1886. The house has recently been newly furnished, and the proprietors spare no trouble to supply first-class accommodations at very low rates.

F. A. Bangs, Billiards and Pool, Confectionery, Tobacco and Cigars, Farmington. It seems impossible for some people to see the great difference between playing Billiards and Pool amid objectionable surroundings, and playing the same games in a perfectly respectable place, and therefore they denounce the recreation as "evil," and think that there must be something wanting in the morality of those who engage in it. This view of the matter is as foolish as it is exasperating, for as a matter of fact, no more innocent and enjoyable games have ever been invented than Billiards and Pool, and it would be well if many an overworked business man would dismiss care from his mind by the magic of the cue. There is a very considerable amount of exercise to be obtained in this way, and just enough excitement to relieve all monotony, and make one feel young again. Of course a good deal depends upon the character of the accommodations furnished, and for this reason we take especial pleasure in calling attention to the establishment of which Mr. F. A. Bangs is the proprietor, for everything there is kept in first-class condition, and there is nothing to be complained of in or about the place. Both billiard and pool players will find excellent facilities for engaging in their favorite games, and the character of the trade noticeable at this establishment is excellent proof that our best people enjoy "rolling the ivories." Mr. Bangs was born in Freeman, Me., and became connected with his present enterprise in 1888. One floor, measuring 60x22 feet, is occupied, and a choice stock of Confectionery, Tobacco, Cigars, etc., is on hand to select from, the goods being offered at the lowest market rates.

E. H. Lowell, Dealer in Produce, Flour, Groceries, Dry and Fancy Goods, Boots and Shoes, Tin, Crockery, Glass and Hardware, Lime, Hair and Cement, West Farmington. There are few establishments more interesting to visit than those commonly known as "General Stores," for the extent and variety of the stock, is so great as to make it attractive to all tastes. One of the best examples of this kind of which we have knowledge is that conducted by Mr. E. H. Lowell here in West Farmington, the undertaking to which we refer having been founded by Mr. H. W. Lowell in 1873, and coming into the possession of its present owner in 1887. One floor and basement are occupied, each of which measures 80x34 feet, together with two storehouses of the dimensions of 45x30 and 30x20 feet respectively, the smaller one being used for the storage of Hair, Lime, Cement, Shingles, etc., in which Mr. Lowell deals largely. He also handles Produce, Flour, Groceries, Dry and Fancy Goods, Boots and Shoes, Tin, Crockery, Glass and Hardware, doing both a wholesale and retail business, and employing two efficient assistants. Mr. Lowell was born in Farmington, and is well and favorably known throughout this section. The secret of the success he has met with in developing his present enterprise is probably to be found in the close personal attention he gives every detail of the business, for by so doing he is enabled to guarantee satisfactory service to his customers, and to supply them with the best goods the market affords at the lowest possible rates.

James H. Waugh, Wholesale and Retail Grocer and Flour Dealer, Dolbier and Waugh Block. Broadway, Farmington. One of the handsomest and most striking business blocks to be found in this section, is that located on Broadway, and occupied in part by Mr. James H. Waugh. This block was erected in 1882, and is most admirably adapted for the purposes for which it is used, as well as being an ornament to the thoroughfare on which it stands. The portion occupied by Mr. Waugh, comprises one floor and a basement, of the dimensions of 100x25 feet, and affords excellent accommodations for the heavy and varied stock carried by him, consisting of Staple and Fancy Groceries and Flour, in which he deals both at wholesale and retail. He is a native of Starks, Maine, and founded the undertaking he has so largely developed in 1871. There are two assistants employed, and customers are served with a courtesy and promptness that go far to explain the great popularity this enterprise has attained, while the prices quoted afford the best possible evidence that Mr. Waugh enjoys the most favorable relations with producers, and is in a position to supply first-class goods at the very lowest market rates. It would be simply impossible to give a detailed description of the articles comprising the immense stock within reasonable limit, and, therefore, we will simply say that it is exceptionally complete in every department, and is made up of goods selected from the most reliable sources. Special attention is given to the handling of Flour, and all the most popular grades for family use are supplied at bottom prices, orders being promptly delivered.

E. R. Starbird, Portrait and Landscape Photographer; Copying and Enlarging. Broadway, Farmington. Nothing is easier than to tell whether a portrait is satisfactory or not, but very often nothing is harder than to express just *why* one portrait is to be preferred to another. Probably all of our readers have seen Photographs which were good likenesses, and were well-finished perhaps, but still somehow failed to give entire satisfaction. The popularity which the establishment conducted by Mr. E. R. Starbird has attained since it was opened, in 1882, is due to the fact that this gentleman has the art or "knack," or whatever you may please to call it, of producing Photographic portraits which invariably please, and as his prices are very reasonable, it is not to be wondered at that an extensive business has already been built up. The premises occupied are located on Broadway, and measure 30x37 feet, being supplied with improved apparatus for the carrying on of Photography in all its branches, including Copying and Enlarging. Mr. Starbird is a native of Freeman, Maine, and is connected with the Odd Fellows. He has produced some beautiful work in the line of Landscape Photography, and the specimens to be seen at his studio are well worth the critical attention of lovers of nature, for they have an out-door effect seldom accomplished without the aid of colors, and embrace a large variety of picturesque and attractive scenes. Especially noticeable among the Landscape productions of this establishment is a large series of views of the sporting regions of Northern Franklin County, embracing the entire Rangeley Lake system and Parmachence Lake; also Tim Pond and the Seven Ponds, Round Mountain Lake, Chain of Ponds, King and Bartlett Lakes, Spencer and Kibbey Streams, etc. Mr. Starbird has several hundred negatives of these delightful summer resorts, and sells several thousand views to the sportsmen each year. Orders through the mail receive prompt attention, and satisfaction is guaranteed in this as in every other department of the business.

A. C. Norton, Retail Remnant Store, Dry Goods, etc., Farmington. Every lady who ever goes "shopping"—and where is the one that does not?—knows what a "Remnant" is and also knows that by keeping a careful watch for desirable articles of this kind some very decided bargains may be made. But the search for remnants is apt to be long and tiresome, and a good deal of ground has generally to be gone over and many establishments visited before a suitable article is found. Therefore it was a happy thought that caused Mr. A. C. Norton to open the "Retail Remnant Store" with which he is now identified, for by visiting this establishment one may have an excellent opportunity to examine remnants of all kinds, and to purchase standard goods at remarkably low prices. Mr. Norton is a native of this town, and began operations in 1888. The public have been prompt in realizing the advantages offered and as a consequence a large trade has already been built up, which may be expected to continue to increase, for the more extensive the business done, the more chance Mr. Norton has to establish favorable relations with those by whom his supplies are obtained. Dry and Fancy Goods are carried in stock in great variety, and all that bottom prices and fair dealing can do towards assuring satisfaction to customers, is done at this enterprising and justly-popular establishment.

J. W. Carsley, Harness Maker, Robes, Blankets, etc., Farmington. There is a good deal in knowing that the harness you are using is thoroughly and skillfully made from honest material, for when a man is sure that such is the case, he is much less apt to get excited and nervous when he finds himself in a "tight place" on the road, and, consequently, it is much pleasanter for him and for any companions he may chance to have. In order to obtain such a harness you must patronize a reputable dealer, and we know of none more worthy of every confidence than is Mr. J. W. Carsley, carrying on business right here in Farmington. This gentleman was born in Pownal, Me. The premises made use of by him measure 40x20 feet, and contain a very desirable and varied stock of Harnesses, Robes, Whips, Blankets, and other articles for the use of horses and horsemen. Mr. Carsley is a Harness Maker of experience and ability, and allows no work to leave his establishment that can fail to satisfy any reasonable customer. He makes Harness to order at short notice, and gives special attention to repairing in all its branches, using selected stock and taking care to do the work durably as well as neatly. Very reasonable prices are quoted, and a steadily increasing business is done.

Charles S. Wait, Dealer in Groceries and Grain, West Farmington. Although Mr. Charles S. Wait only inaugurated his present business in 1887, he has already built up an extensive trade, and it may be safely predicted that if he adheres to the principles which have thus far governed his management of affairs, the present steady and rapid increase of patronage will continue for some time to come. People like to have a large and varied stock of Groceries to choose from, and also like to feel sure that whatever they buy will prove as represented, and both these desires can be gratified by dealing with Mr. Wait, as many of the residents of West Farmington have already learned. The premises made use of comprise one floor and a storehouse, each of which measures forty feet square, and the assortment offered includes Choice Staple and Fancy Groceries of all descriptions, which are quoted at the lowest market rates. Flour and Grain are also handled very extensively, and orders are filled with a promptness and accuracy very pleasant to see. Mr. Wait is a native of Vienna, Maine, and is connected with the Odd Fellows. He wants the patronage of the public and is willing to work to get it, being confident that those who once open dealings with him will have no reason to regret having done so. Callers at this store are attended to courteously as well as quickly, and care is taken to give no one any reasonable cause for complaint.

G. L. & A. S. Riggs, Sheep Skin Tanners, and Manufacturers of Black Stock and Russet Linings. Tanneries at Farmington and Chesterville. Probably but a very small portion of the many thousands of people who make use of Sheepskin in one way or another, ever give a thought to the manner in which it is prepared for the market, and yet there are a good many processes to be gone through with before it is fit for use, and some of these operations are as interesting as they are ingenious. One of the best-known Sheepskin tanneries in this State is that carried on by Messrs. G. L. & A. S. Riggs, here in Farmington, and this firm ranks with the leading Tanners of New England, for they also conduct a tannery at Chesterville, whose capacity is even greater than that of the Farmington establishment. Operations were begun just twenty years ago, and the brisk demand which exists for the products of this firm is the best evidence that can be given of the character of the plant in use and the uniform excellence of the goods produced. The stock worked up in these Tanneries comes from Boston and New York, and all the finished products are shipped to the former city, some idea of the magnitude of the business done being afforded by the fact that the Farmington establishment is capable of turning out 250 dozen per week, while that in Chesterville has a capacity of 300 dozen in the same time. The firm only tan pickled skins, and are extensively engaged in the manufacture of Black Stock and Russet Linings. Both partners were born in New Sharon, Maine, and are very widely-known throughout this portion of the State. Mr. G. L. Riggs is connected with the Masons and formerly occupied the position of Deputy Sheriff of Franklin County. Mr. A. S. Riggs is one of the pioneers in music in the County, being one of the first members of the Franklin Musical Institute, an old teacher of singing, and was always considered one of the best directors of class singing.

Miss K. F. Wilder, Dress-maker, Teacher of the American Square, Farmington. Not every lady is in a position to make her own dresses, and therefore the opening of a well equipped dress-making establishment may well be considered a subject of public interest to the feminine portion of the community at all events. Miss K. F. Wilder inaugurated an enterprise of this kind in 1888, and has already built up a gratifying amount of trade, for she thoroughly understands her business in every detail, and is possessed of an unusual degree of taste which is generally appreciated among those who have seen evidence of her ability. Miss Wilder is a native of Temple, Maine, and has a large circle of friends in Farmington and vicinity. She occupies premises measuring 44x21 feet and employs two competent assistants, being in a position to fill orders promptly and to guarantee satisfaction to her customers. No small part of the exceptional success she has in fitting the most difficult forms, is due to her use of the well known "American Square" which simplifies operations wonderfully and enables the greatest accuracy of measurement to be easily accomplished. She gives instruction in the use of this ingenious and efficient system, and those who wish to become proficient in the art of cutting and fitting, can find no better or more thorough teacher.

M. C. Hobbs & Co., Manufacturers of Turned Wooden Goods, West Farmington. The establishment carried on by Messrs. M. C. Hobbs & Co. is a very interesting place to visit, especially for those who are desirous of learning to what perfection the manufacture of wood-working machinery has been brought, for this factory is fitted up with one of the most complete plants of the kind in the State, no expense having been spared to provide every facility. The enterprise had its inception in 1860, under the direction of Mr. Amos Hobbs, who carried it on alone until the firm of Amos Hobbs & Son was formed, this firm being succeeded by the present proprietors in 1888. These consist of Messrs. M. C. Hobbs and H. W. and P. A. Carter, Mr. Hobbs being a native of East Livermore, while both his associates were born in Carthage. The senior partner is connected with the Free Masons, and is also a member of the Patrons of Husbandry. The firm occupy premises comprising three floors and a basement, and consist of a main building, measuring 38x42 feet, and a wing 28x45 feet in dimensions. A specialty is made of the manufacture of Rakes, but all kinds of Novelty Wood Turning are done at very short notice. The Rakes made at this factory have gone into such general use and are so familiar to the public, that it is hardly necessary to say that they are unsurpassed by any in the market and in fact are unequalled in certain important respects, notably uniformity of excellence. Every operation connected with their manufacture is carefully carried out, and selected stock is used for each, the result being an article that will stand hard usage, although it is sold at a low figure.

The Farmington Manufacturing Co., Manufacturers of Greenwood's Champion Ear Protectors, Patented in United States and Canada; Farmington. No man who has once froze his ears, as the saying goes, is at all anxious to repeat the experience, for even a slight frostbite on that tender portion of the body is attended with pain of no small intensity, not to mention the fact that one's personal appearance is not materially improved by having one or both ears swollen and black for a week or so. The only practical way to keep the ears from freezing when exposed to such weather as all the northern states are liable to at certain seasons, is to cover them up; but this is easier said than done, or at least it was until Greenwood's Champion Ear Protectors were invented, for the articles previously on the market intended for a similar use, were so objectionable and uncomfortable that most men preferred to wear a fur cap, or else trust to luck and friction. The beauty of the Greenwood device is that it may be carried in the pocket without the least inconvenience, and when occasion requires it can be placed in position instantly, *and stays where it is put,* although there is no disfiguring elastic below the chin to make a man look like an overgrown school boy, and to interfere with the surface circulation so important in cold weather. That these advantages are appreciated, the remarkable demand for this invention proves, for the Farmington Manufacturing Company, which produces these Protectors, ship them all over the cold part of this country and throughout British America, and is obliged to employ twenty assistants in order to keep up with the rapidly growing demand. This company was formed is 1888, but the Protector has been on the market since 1873, having been introduced by Mr. Chester Greenwood, who is Treasurer of the present organization, the President being Mr. J. Currier Tarbox. Both these gentlemen are natives of Farmington, as are also the remaining members of the Company—Isabelle W. Greenwood and J. C. Holman. An exclusively manufacturing and wholesale business is done, and all orders are given prompt and careful attention.

Chester Greenwood, Machinist, and Dealer in Pipe, Valves, Packing, Steam Guages, Water Glasses, Babbit, Cap and Set Screws, Twist Drills, Chucks, Files, Pipe Wrenches, etc.; Plumbing, Steam and Hot Water Heating properly done; Farmington. There is no longer any dispute among those acquainted with the facts, that Steam Heating is by far the most economical means of supplying artificial heat, and the only objections that amount to anything made to this method, are based upon the danger that is supposed to accompany it. As a matter of fact, this is one of the strong points in favor of Steam Heating, for no safer system could possibly be devised, as the chances of accidental fire are reduce to a minimum, and a well-constructed Steam-Heating plant can no more explode than a tea kettle with the lid off. We say a *well-constructed* plant, and this expression refers to Boilers and Piping that are not only well-made of suitable material, but are set up as they should be, for it is just here that the explanation may be found of why damage is occasionally caused by the failure of Steam-Heating Apparatus. Mr. Chester Greenwood has given his attention to the manufacture and putting up of Steam-Heating Plants, since 1886, and we have yet to hear of a case where his work has failed to give satisfaction. The reason is obvious. He understands his business and is therefore competent to redeem the prom-

ise he makes that Steam and Hot Water Heating shall be properly done. He is sole agent for Franklin Co. of the "Florida" Steam Heater, a descriptive catalogue of which will be sent free on application, and is prepared to fill orders for Plumbing, etc., at short notice. His shop is supplied with steam-power, and Machine Jobbing of all kinds is promptly attended to at moderate rates. Every facility is at hand for the doing of hoisting work safely and satisfactorily, and Machinists' Supplies, such as Pipe, Valves, Packing, Steam Gauges, Water Glasses, Set Screws, Twist Drills, Files, Chucks, Pipe Wrenches, etc., are handled largely, low prices being quoted and only standard goods furnished. Mr. Greenwood is Agent for the Florida Steam Heater, and manufactures the Greenwood Steam Heater for wood, which is the best Heater made for all places where wood is cheaper than coal. Mr. Greenwood also manufactures the Greenwood Pipe Vise.

Farmington State Normal School, Farmington. The idea that it is necessary to "teach people how to teach" in order to obtain satisfactory results, was once received with derision, but the importance of professional training has been so often and so fully demonstrated that it is no longer a suitable subject for debate among persons of intelligence. Teaching being now regarded as a profession, it is natural that those who have been specially trained to follow it should be preferred when there are vacancies to be filled, and a significant indication of public sentiment in the matter is afforded by the fact that the Farmington State Normal School is unable to honor one-half the demand made upon it for trained teachers. This institution was formerly known as the Farmington Academy, its first principal being Mr. A. P. Kelsey. In 1864 its name was changed to that which it now bears, and in 1885 the present principal, Mr. George Colby Purington, assumed direction of the enterprise. This gentleman is a native of Embden, Maine, and graduated from Bowdoin College in 1878, fitting himself for admission to that institution while teaching in Hebron Academy. He was principal of the Brunswick High School until the summer of 1881, when he resigned to accept the principalship of the Edward Little High School at Auburn, remaining there up to the time of resigning in order to accept his present position. He is a member of the Free Masons and is Chief Engineer of the Farmington Fire Department and Foreman of Steamer Co. No. 1. He has also been recently elected President of the Maine Pedagogical Society. Mr. Purington is associated on the Board of Instruction with Mr. J. R. Potter, A.B., and the following ladies: Hortense M. Merrill, Lillian I. Lincoln, Lutie F. Luques, Harriet P. Young, Ardelle M. Tozier, Julia W. Swift. The purpose of the school,—briefly stated,—is to train teachers for their professional labors, and incidental to this work a course of study is pursued which includes the common English branches in thorough reviews, and such of the higher branches as are especially adapted to prepare teachers to conduct the mental, moral and physical education of their pupils; the art of school management having a prominent place in the daily exercises and the school being open (in accordance with the Legislative act under which it is conducted) to persons of different religious connections on terms of perfect equality." The course of study is arranged for two years of three terms each, and to meet the demand for high school teachers, there is an advanced course of one year, open to the *graduates* of this and other Normal Schools of the State. This course is purely optional, but is taken by many who desire the responsible and remunerative positions for which it fits them. The Farmington State Normal School was never in a more prosperous condition than at present, and the residents of the town have excellent reason for the pride they freely show concerning the institution. They have done much to promote its welfare, and give those coming here in order to attend it, a spontaneous and cordial welcome. We give below a list of the Normal School Trustees: Gov. Edwin C. Burleigh, Ex-officio; Hon. Nelson A. Luce, State Superintendent of Common Schools, Ex-officio; I. Warren Merrill, Esq., Farmington; Hon. Luther G. Philbrook, Castine; John A. Hinkley, A.M., Gorham; James O. Bradbury, Esq., Hartland; Stephen A. Lowell, Esq., Auburn.

LEADING BUSINESS MEN OF FARMINGTON. 259

FARMINGTON STATE NORMAL SCHOOL.

Dr. B. M. Hardy, Dentist, cor. Broadway and Main Streets, Farmington. The familiar axiom, "prevention is better than cure," applies with peculiar force to the care of the teeth, as many have learned to their sorrow, when it was too late to profit by the knowledge. We often hear it remarked how sensitive the teeth are, and how easily they may be seriously injured; but those who have made a study of the subject are very apt to hold quite an opposite opinion, for their experience teaches them that the majority of people abuse their teeth habitually from youth to middle age, and that the wonder is not that they finally give out, but that they last as long as they do. Undoubtedly many are restrained from consulting a Dentist by a nervous fear of the pain some consider inseparable from dental operations; but as a matter of fact, such fear is usually groundless, for if the proper steps be taken in time, before the nerve is exposed, a tooth may be worked upon without the slightest suffering, or even unpleasant sensation being caused. Modern Dentistry has reduced pain to a minimum, not alone by the use of anæsthetics, but by the introduction of improved appliances and methods of operation, which save much time and accomplish more perfect results. There are many skillful and experienced Dentists in this section of the State, and there is certainly no excuse for permitting one's teeth to suffer from lack of proper attention. One of the best-equipped Dental establishments of which we have knowledge is that carried on by Dr. B. M. Hardy, over the Peoples' Trust Company, cor. of Broadway and Main Streets, and it is natural that such should be the case, for Dr. Hardy is President of the Maine Dental Association, and of course makes use of the latest devices science has provided. He was born in Portland, Me., and is connected with both the Masons and the Odd Fellows. Dr. Hardy began the practice of his profession here in 1876, and has, for some years, held his present leading position. He owes no small part of his popularity to the thoroughness with which he carries out every operation intrusted to him, and especially to the gentleness which characterizes his methods. In view of the office he holds in the Dental Association, it would be as presumptuous as it is unnecessary for us to speak in detail of his abilities as a practical operator, so we will simply say that his charges are moderate and that previous appointment is necessary to assure prompt attention.

Stoddard House, Broadway, Farmington, Davis & Pierce, proprietors. Sample room on first floor. Free Carriage to and from Trains. If a jury of experts were to be chosen to decide which hotels in each community were most deserving of patronage, it would certainly be made up of commercial travelers, for what they don't know about hotel accommodations nobody knows. We have little doubt what the decision would be so far as Farmington is concerned, for it is easy to see that the Stoddard House is a favorite with the "knights of the road," and we must confess that they show their usual appreciation of liberal treatment in making such a choice, for the hotel in question is one of the most home-like in the State, and is managed with a constant and careful regard for the comfort and well-being of its guests. The present proprietors, Messrs. Davis & Pierce, assumed control January 1, 1889, and have already given evidence of their intention to make the Stoddard House more popular than ever, if enterprise, liberality and courtesy can accomplish that end. Mr. Davis is a native of Farmington, and is widely known in this section, having served in the Legislature in 1884, and being a popular member of the Grand Army. He is connected with the Free Masons, as is also Mr. Pierce, who was born in Houlton, and has had five years' experience in the hotel business. During the season of 1888 Mr. Pierce was clerk at the Mooselucmaguntic Hotel, the largest in the Rangeley Lake region, and made many friends by the genial and accommodating spirit with which he discharged the responsible duties incidental to such a position. Mr. Pierce certainly "knows how to keep a hotel," and now has an excellent opportunity to put that knowledge to practical use. The premises occupied are three stories in height, and comprise a main building measuring 60x40 feet, and an ell of the dimensions of 20x60 feet, there being forty guest-rooms. The house has recently been greatly improved, refitted and refurnished, and contains a convenient sample room on the first floor, there being a free carriage to and from trains. From eight to ten assistants are employed, and the service is prompt and courteous, the table first-class, and the terms remarkably reasonable for either transient or permanent guests.

M. P. Tufts, Dealer in Choice Groceries, Canned Fruit. Flour, Corn, Meal, Grain, Country Produce. Choice Tobacco and Cigars, etc. Broadway, Farmington. It is becoming generally understood nowadays, that the food we eat has more to do with our bodily health than any other one thing. Disorders and even diseases that were once treated with powerful drugs and medicines, are now corrected and cured almost entirely by careful attention to the diet, and it is conceded that the man who most perfectly suits his food to his temperament and his occupation, will, other things being equal, enjoy the best health. Therefore it is of the highest importance to know where reliable food-products may best be obtained, and we are happy to be able to call the attention of our readers to so deserving and well-managed an establishment as that carried on by Mr. M. P. Tufts, at No. 14 Broadway. The proprietor is a native of this place, and is connected with the Masonic Order. He began operations in 1886, and has already built up a very large trade, requiring the occupancy of one floor and a basement measuring 50x22 feet, and a storehouse of the dimensions of 35x35 feet. An extensive stock is carried, consisting of Choice Family Groceries, Flour, and Canned Fruit, Corn, Meal and Grain, together with Country Produce and Choice Tobacco and Cigars. Mr. Tufts obtains his goods from the most reliable sources and therefore is in a position to guarantee that they will prove as represented. Catering expressly to family trade, he spares no trouble to satisfy his customers, and quotes the lowest market rates on standard goods, filling all orders promptly and carefully. Aside from this business, Mr. Tufts is a Breeder of Pure Breed Hereford Cattle of the best quality.

LEADING BUSINESS MEN OF FARMINGTON. 261

S. O. Tarbox, Dealer in Groceries, Flour, Drugs, Medicines, Paints, Oils, Glass, Paper Hangings, Broadway, Farmington. One might search Franklin County from end to end, without finding a better known or more popular enterprise than that carried on by Mr. S. O. Tarbox, here in Farmington, for this undertaking was inaugurated in 1871, and has since gained an enviable reputation by reason of the methods which have characterized its management. Operations were begun by J. C. Tarbox & Co., and in 1876 the firm name was changed to Tarbox Brothers, Mr. S. O. Tarbox becoming sole proprietor in 1887. The premises utilized are located on Broadway and comprise one floor and a basement, each of which measures 22x70 feet. An immense stock is carried, consisting of Groceries, Flour, Drugs, Medicines, Paints, Oils, Glass, Paper Hangings, etc., and the quality of the goods composing it, is in every case precisely what it is represented to be—a fact which is appreciated by the public, as the popularity we have before noted proves. Mr. Tarbox is in a position to quote the lowest market rates on the goods he handles, and to fill orders as soon as received. The Medicines and Drugs contained in his stock are selected from the most reliable sources, and their purity and freshness may therefore be confidently counted upon, while the Canned Goods in the Grocery Department will be found far superior to the average, as they are freshly put up and bear the stamp of the most reputable packers.

F. E. Voter, Insurance Agent, No. 21 Broadway, Farmington. Good intentions, never carried out, are a fruitful source of annoyance and loss, and the man who makes a practice of putting off the accomplishment of an undertaking after once making up his mind to engage in it, can hardly expect to attain any decided success. This is proved by every-day experience, and it is a common thing to hear that so-and-so was going to take out an insurance policy on his house, but before he "got round to it," a destructive fire saved him the trouble. By making use of such facilities as are afforded by Mr. F. E. Voter, No. 21 Broadway, the trouble of placing Insurance is reduced to a minimum, and the expense is cut down to its lowest terms also. Mr. Voter acts as Agent for the following companies, and it would be difficult to make out a stronger and more generally desirable list: Fire—Commercial Union, of London; New Hampshire, of New Hampshire; Union, of Pennsylvania; Dwelling House, of Boston; Granite State, of New Hampshire; Peoples', of New Hampshire. Life and Accident—Mutual Life, of New York. the largest and best company in the world; Employes' Accident, of New York. These corporations have records that are easily accessible, and the more thoroughly they are studied the greater the confidence that will be reposed in them. Mr. Voter is prepared to write policies on the most liberal terms, and places a large portion of the Insurance carried in this vicinity. He was born in Farmington and is extensively well-known here, being Secretary of the Odd Fellows' Lodge with which he is connected, and having been Messenger in the State Senate for three years.

Hatch Brothers, Boots and Shoes, Farmington and Readfield. The boot and shoe store carried on by Hatch Brothers here in Farmington was not opened until 1887, but it leaped at once into the favor of the public, and a steadily increasing patronage is accorded it. The firm are no novices at the business, for in 1877 they started, and still carry on, a similar enterprise in Readfield, and the reputation gained there had much to do with the cordial reception given the later undertaking. The Readfield store is 30x60 feet in dimensions, while that in this town is 22x45 feet in size, and the stock carried is so large, so complete, and so desirable that young and old, rich and poor, married and single can all find goods therein suited to their needs at prices equally suited to their means. Customers don't have to wait around until they forget what they came for, but are served promptly and politely, given an opportunity to make a deliberate choice, and correctly informed as to the merits of the articles concerning which they inquire. In short, the poetical promise made by the proprietors is fulfilled to the letter, and just what this promise is, the following lines will tell.

The Boots and Shoes that here you buy,
Will fit the Foot, and please the Eye,
If satisfaction they do not give,
We'll make it right, as sure's you live.

There are three brothers in the firm, all of whom are natives of Jefferson, Me., two being members of the Ancient Order of United Workmen. The very lowest market rates are quoted, and the goods handled are durably as well as neatly made in every respect. Their stirring business maxim allows us to say there is no weather too hot, too cold, too wet or too dry to cause dull business at either of their stores.

Dr. E. C. Merrill, Dentist, No. 11 Main Street, Farmington. The advance and rapid progress of the arts and sciences excite the admiration of all, and nowhere is the progress more marked than in Dentistry. The mission of which is to repair and replace the teeth, one of the most important organs of the body. If the teeth, the instruments of mastication, are decayed or gone, the food cannot be properly prepared for the digestive organs, which become impaired, causing one of the most distressing diseases, and with much discomfort and pain, endanger the health. The greatest boon of the human race. The wonderful improvements that have marked the progress of both operative and mechanical Dentistry, has placed the profession beside that of medicine, in alleviating human suffering, and aiding personal adornment. With the present advanced treatment, decayed teeth can be saved for a life time, or they can be replaced, either singly, or in parts, or whole sets, in a manner that almost rivals nature in appearance, and performance of their functions. Dr. Merrill's fine office at No. 11 Main Street, is fully equipped with the latest and most approved appliances for operations of all descriptions upon the teeth, and an extended and growing patronage fully attests, to the careful and skillful treatment, and thorough and competent manner, that all operations are performed at his office.

David H. Chandler, Attorney-at-Law, Farmington. The gentleman whose card we print above, is doubtless known by reputation at least to many of our readers, for he has been prominent in the community for some years, and his position in the legal profession is a high and assured one. It is not our purpose to dwell at length on his capabilities as a lawyer, for these are generally known, and the estimation in which they are held is significantly indicated by the appointment received in 1882 as Judge of the Municipal Court — a position which is still occupied by Mr. Chandler. A work which treats of the leading business men of a certain section, must necessarily treat of those prominent in professional life as well as of those who have achieved success in mercantile affairs, and the zeal which Mr. Chandler has exhibited in advancing the best interests of the community by every means in his power, affords ample reason for presenting this sketch of his career in a review of the salient points of Farmington's commercial history. He was born in Temple, Maine, and was elected to the State Legislature from Chesterville in 1857. In 1879 Mr. Chandler was a member of the Board of Trustees of the Farmington State Normal School, and we may say in passing that he has always shown great interest in educational matters, and has used his influence to promote the free dissemination of knowledge by all practical means. The duties of Clerk of Courts for Franklin County were discharged by him during the term extending from 1880 to 1883, and we have already mentioned his appointment as Municipal Judge in 1882. His attention being occupied in the Municipal Court, his legal practice at the present time is not very extensive, but no Lawyer in the State gives more careful attention to the interests of his clients.

Chas. E. Wheeler, Manufacturer of Split Bamboo Fishing Rods, Broadway, Farmington. The delights of fishing are by no means easy to express with pen and ink, and unless the writer has a genius similar to that of the famous old Isaak Walton, the results of trying to do so are very apt to be decidedly unsatisfactory. The true fisherman has his love for the sport born in him, and it is useless for a man who has no taste in that direction to try to understand the fascination some find in making war upon the finny tribe. Scientific angling has always been a fruitful source of enjoyment among cultivated people, and of late years it has rapidly gained in popularity in this country, many a business man finding the few weeks he can spare each year to this pursuit, something to be looked forward to with eagerness, and improved as only such rare pleasure can be improved. The Rod comes first in importance in the fisherman's outfit, and unless this be made as it should be, half the enjoyment is lost. The perfect Rod combines strength and lightness in the highest degree, and to produce one that is first-class, requires ability and skill as well as long experience. Split Bamboo is the material most perfectly adapted to the manufacture of Fine Fishing Rods, and each of the many pieces going to make up the finished Rod must be carefully selected, shaped and adjusted, in order that the strain may be properly distributed. Mr. C. E. Wheeler has manufactured such articles for a full score of years, and his Rods are now preferred by many of the best-known amateur fishermen. He was born in Farmington, and is widely-known throughout this section, especially among those interested in field sports. Two floors, measuring 25x40 feet, are occupied on Broadway, and employment is given to six competent and careful assistants. Mr. Wheeler strives to furnish the best possible article for the lest possible amount of money, and his Rods are sold at remarkably low figures, considering the quality of the goods; orders being promptly filled.

Mrs. Wm. Randall, Fashionable Dress Making, Chronicle Office Entrance, Knowlton Building, Farmington. All of our lady readers, and not a few of those belonging to the sterner sex, can doubtless call to mind instances which have come under their observation where the most costly costumes, made from the richest and most fashionable materials, utterly failed to produce a desirable effect by reason of the incompetency or carelessness of those who were intrusted with their making. The handsomest and most tasteful fabrics may easily be rendered quite unattractive by improper treatment, and the advantages to be gained by making use of the services of an experienced and skillful Dress Maker, are too evident to render it necessary for us to dwell upon the importance of securing such aid. It is the general verdict among the ladies of Farmington and vicinity who have examined specimens of the work done at the establishment of Mrs. William Randall, that the results there attained are exceptionally satisfactory, and there has been ample time to form a complete judgment regarding the matter in question, for Mrs. Randall began operations in 1880, and her business has since rapidly and steadily developed. Four rooms are occupied in the Knowlton Building, and the premises may be reached by means of the Chronicle Office entrance. Employment is afforded to from four to six experienced and painstaking assistants, and orders can therefore be filled at short notice, the charges made being uniformly moderate. Mrs. Randall gives personal attention to the executing of every commission, and we have no hesitation in guaranteeing complete satisfaction to the most fastidious customer.

E. V. Varney, Horse Shoeing and Jobbing. All kinds of Repair Work promptly attended to. Farmington. Many people have discovered that it don't pay to give a high price for a horse and then have him injured or ruined by improper Shoeing, so that nowadays a good deal more discrimination is used in choosing a Horseshoer than was formerly the case. It is generally acknowledged that Mr. E. V. Varney does as good work of this kind as any man in this section of the State, and therefore it is not surprising that the services of two assistants are required in order to attend to all the business brought to his shop. Mr. Varney was born in South Durham, Maine, and inaugurated his present enterprise in 1878. He is very widely-known in Farmington and vicinity, and is connected with the Knights Templars and Odd Fel lows' Encampment. The premises made use of measure 35x40 feet, and are supplied with every facility for the doing of General Jobbing and Repairing. Horses can be Shod here at very short notice, and the owners of valuable animals may safely intrust them to the hands of Mr. Varney and his assistants, for no rough dealing is practiced, and the individual requirements of each horse are carefully studied and attended to. Repairing is done neatly and strongly at the shortest possible notice, and the charges made for this and all other work done here, will be found fair and reasonable in every case.

C. E. Marr, (Successor to P. W. Hubbard), Druggist and Apothecary; Manufacturer of Hubbard's Home Favorite Cough Syrup and Peoples' Favorite Tonic Bitters, 62 Main St., Farmington. Among such business enterprises as deserve particularly prominent mention, that conducted by Mr. C. E. Marr, at No. 62 Main Street, holds a leading position, for a first-class Pharmacy is a benefit to any community, and the establishment in question is first-class in every sense of the word. Mr. Marr is a native of Canaan, Maine, and is connected with the Masonic Commandery, and also with the Odd Fellows. He is successor to Mr. P. W. Hubbard in the ownership of his present undertaking, and is Manufacturer of Hubbard's Home Favorite Cough Syrup and Peoples' Favorite Tonic Bitters—two preparations which are "favorites" in fact as well as in name, among those who have tested their merits. The premises occupied comprise two floors, one measuring 44x22 feet and the other 20x22 feet, a very extensive assortment being constantly carried, of Drugs, Medicines, Chemicals, etc., together with a full line of Fancy and Toilet Articles, including the latest and most popular novelties in these goods. Mr. Marr carries on a large retail business, also supplying some of the trade of the neighboring towns at wholesale, and places his prices at the lowest figures consistent with the quality of the commodities furnished. The Prescription Department is given special attention, and every precaution is taken to make the service as reliable as that afforded by any similar establishment in the State. Orders are filled at short notice, and every caller is assured uniformly courteous treatment. The location on which Mr. Marr's store now stands is the original spot on which was located the first Drug Store of John W. Perkins, the extensive wholesale dealer now of Portland.

L. E. Witham & Co., Dealers in Meats and Provisions, No. 29 Broadway, Farmington. It is what we eat that enables us to work, and a man might as well expect to keep up a working pressure in a steam boiler by burning nothing but ashes, as to maintain his own health and strength by the consumption of improper food. It is very poor economy to cheat one's stomach, and we are happy to say that Americans, as a rule, spare no reasonable expense in providing for the table. But a high price does not always mean a good article, and, therefore, we desire to call the attention of our readers to an establishment where Provisions of all kinds are sold at reasonable rates, and where the quality of every article sold may be depended upon to prove as represented. The store in question is that located at No. 29 Broadway, opposite Stoddard House, and conducted by Messrs. L. E. Witham & Co. This firm was formed in 1888, and consists of Messrs. L. E. Witham and John Kern, the founder being a native of Starks, Me., and the latter of Switzerland. Mr. Witham was a member of the Starks Board of Selectmen for three years, and both he and Mr. Kern are well known in this vicinity. Premises measuring 75x24 feet are occupied, and a large and varied stock is carried, comprising Groceries, Meats and Poultry, Game, Venison, Fresh and Pickled Fish, Provisions of All Kinds, Canned Fruit, etc., together with a full assortment of seasonable Vegetables. All classes of trade are catered to, and uniform politeness is shown to every customer, while the service is prompt and accurate, orders being filled and delivered at short notice. A fine line of Canned Goods is included in the stock, and bottom prices are quoted in every department. Messrs. Witham & Kern's market is finely fitted up with modern improvements, and contains one of the best "refrigerator" rooms to be found anywhere. It is "The" Market of Farmington, where everything that its name implies is to be found in its season. The firm are very popular with the public, and their success is already established.

H. H. Rice, Dealer in Dry and Fancy Goods, Broadway, Farmington. Branch store at Madison. There is no more elegant store in Farmington than that occupied by Mr. H. H. Rice, in the Dolbier and Waugh Block on Broadway, and what is still more gratifying to his customers is the fact that the stock it contains is well suited to the store, being one of the most carefully selected assortments of Dry and Fancy Goods to be found in this section. Mr. Rice was born in Farmington, and founded his present business in 1881. He carries on a branch store at Madison, and from the very magnitude of his trade, is able to offer his customers inducements which it would be very hard to parallel elsewhere. One floor and a basement, measuring 100x25 feet, are occupied, and the different departments of the stock are so arranged as to make selection comparatively easy. Foreign and Domestic Dry Goods of guaranteed quality are offered at prices that assure a rapid disposal of the stock, for Mr. Rice prefers the "nimble penny" to the "slow sixpence," and hence takes measures to sell goods quickly, making room for a fresh supply. Staple articles as well as fashionable novelties are on hand in great variety, and some of the Fancy Goods offered at this store could not be found elsewhere in this vicinity, for Mr. Rice keeps a sharp eye on the market, and is ever on the alert to procure specialties suited to his class of trade. Both a wholesale and retail business is done, and the services of two competent and polite assistants are required to give callers the prompt attention they are accustomed to receive at this popular establishment, and business relations entered into with them are certain to prove not only pleasant, but advantageous.

E. Gerry, Dealer in Groceries and Flour, 41 Main Street, Farmington. That it is poor economy to use poor Groceries, will be readily agreed by all experienced housekeepers, and the importance of discrimination in the selection of these goods is due, not alone to this fact, but also to the influence of the food upon the health, an influence which is now conceded to be much stronger than would once have been admitted. Fortunately the residents of Farmington and vicinity need have no difficulty in securing reliable Groceries, for there are many honorable dealers in such goods to be found here, and one of the most prominent of them is Mr. E. Gerry, doing business at No. 41 Main Street. This gentleman began operations in 1872, under the firm name of E. Gerry & Son; but since 1880 the enterprise has been conducted by him alone. He was born here in Farmington and has long been considered a representative citizen, having served as Assessor of Corporations for three years, and being connected with both the Free Masons and the Odd Fellows, occupying the position of District Deputy Grand Master of Lodge, also of Encampment of the latter order. The premises utilized by Mr. Gerry consist of two floors and a basement, and measure 26x45 feet. He acts as Agent for the American Express Company, and is prepared to receive and forward goods to all points reached by that Company and its connections. The stock of Groceries, Flour, etc., on hand is large and varied, composing a full selection of Fancy and Staple products especially adapted to family use. The Teas and Coffees are of exceptionally fine flavor, while the assortment of Canned Goods is made up of the productions of the most reputable and popular packers. All the favorite brands of Flour are offered at the lowest market rates, and orders are delivered promptly, every article sold being guaranteed to prove as represented.

T. H. Adams, Dealer in Carpetings. Also Undertaking and Embalming done. 33 Adams Block, Main Street, Farmington. It being not far from thirty years since Mr. T. H. Adams began operations in this vicinity, it is not surprising that he and his establishment should be very widely known hereabouts. Mr. Adams was born in Farmington, and inaugurated his present enterprise in 1861. He occupies premises of the dimensions of 24x60 feet, at No. 33 Adams Block, Main Street, and deals largely in Carpetings, besides carrying on an extensive Undertaking and Embalming business. Window Shades and similar articles are also dealt in to a considerable extent, and Mr. Adams acts as Agent for the Monumental Bronze Company, of Bridgeport, Ct., manufacturers of White Bronze Monuments and Tablets. These articles are practically indestructible, even when exposed to our New England weather, and are coming into general use as their merits become more widely appreciated. They are furnished in many beautiful and appropriate designs, and at a remarkably low figure. We need not refer to the quality of the service Mr. Adams is prepared to furnish in the line of Undertaking and Embalming, for it is universally conceded that his facilities are unsurpassed, while his long experience has fitted him to meet all contingencies that may arise. His charges are uniformly moderate, and orders are given immediate and careful attention. Mr. Adams occupies the position of County Coroner, and discharges the responsible duties of that office in such a manner as to elicit the unstinted commendations of those conversant with his work.

H. L. Goodwin, Book, Card, and Mercantile Printer, 70 Main Street, Farmington. The old merchant who was asked to give the secret of his wonderful success in business, said it was owing to his taking the "printers into partnership," or in other words, he did not begrudge money spent on printer's ink. That many men fail because they take no pains to reach the public ear is undeniable, and even if the business be such that newspaper advertising is unadvisable, there can still be powerful help given by the printer, in the shape of attractive business cards, bill heads, circulars, etc. But the work must be first-class. Poor printing is as cheap and worthless a thing as could easily be named, and a slovenly printed card is about the worst recommendation a firm could have. First-class work may be easily assured by patronizing a first-class establishment, and no better one can be found in this part of the State than that conducted by Mr. H. L. Goodwin at No. 70 Main Street. Book, Card, and Mercantile Printing are done at short notice, and the mechanical excellence of the work is noteworthy and unusual. Mr. Goodwin has a finely-equipped Job Printing Office, and is prepared to issue tasty and dainty Circulars at low rates. Everything in this office is entirely new, and much of the type used was selected especially for Mercantile Printing, and some of the neatest cards and bill-heads we have seen were printed at this establishment.

George W. Ranger, Saw and Grist Mill, Dealer in Lumber, Fairbanks, Me. Mr. George W. Ranger should most certainly receive prominent mention among the leading business men of this section for he has done much to develop the national resources of the State, carrying on an extensive Lumbering business and employing fifteen men about six months in the year. He maintains a well equipped Saw and Grist Mill in the town of Fairbanks, two and one-half miles north from Farmington, and cuts 500,000 ft. of Lumber annually, besides 200,000 Shingles. The premises utilized comprise three floors, each of which measures 30x70 feet, and are fitted up with improved machinery throughout. Mr. Ranger is highly and deservedly popular in the community, and has a very extensive circle of friends, having occupied the position of Postmaster for the past eight years. He is a member of the Free Masons, and is a public spirited citizen who may always be depended upon to advance the best interests of the community by all honorable means. He founded his present business in 1872, and has built up the large wholesale and retail trade he now enjoys, by giving close personal attention to the management of affairs and by earnestly striving to deal honorably by all. The reasons of his success are very generally understood throughout this vicinity, and it is the common verdict that such a policy and such industry are deserving of every encouragement and commendation.

Miss M. N. Welch, Fashionable Dressmaker. It is said by those who should be authority, that our American ladies are the best-dressed in the world, and that one reason why this is the case, is because they not only know how to choose their costumes but how to wear them. There is no doubt that the art of Dress Making is much further advanced in this country now than it was a few years ago, and this is due principally to the effect of those who combine a thorough knowledge of the subject with natural taste and ability. In calling attention to the facilities possessed by Miss M. N. Welch, for the doing of Fashionable Dressmaking at short notice, we feel that we are rendering a real accommodation to our readers, for this lady has amply proved her entire fitness for the task she has undertaken, and those who make use of her services will have reason to congratulate themselves on having done so. Miss Welch keeps herself thoroughly informed concerning the latest novelties in the Dress Making line, and spares no pains to give her customers the full benefit of such knowledge. She is ready and willing to offer any suggestions her experience and study may prompt, if such assistance be desired, and her charges are extremely reasonable, considering the quality of the service rendered, orders being delivered promptly when promised.

Ranger & Butler, Wholesale and Retail Dealers in Flour, Corn, Meal, Feed, Lime, Salt, Groceries and Country Produce, Bonney's block, opposite Maine Central Depot, Farmington. Flour has risen so much in price within the last few months that housekeepers have good reason to be more careful than ever in placing their orders for this indispensable commodity, and it is well for those residing in Farmington and vicinity that they have so reliable and enterprising a house as that of Ranger & Butler to deal with, for this concern is prepared to meet all competition so far as the handling of Flour and Feed is concerned, and can quote the very lowest market rates on anything in this line. The premises in use give some idea of the magnitude of the business done, for they are 150x35 feet in dimensions, and there is a storehouse utilized which measures 50x40 feet. Flour, Corn, Meal, Feed, Lime, Salt, etc., are supplied in quantities to suit, at the very shortest notice, both a wholesale and retail business being done, while Staple and Fancy Groceries and Choice Country Produce are also dealt in largely. The firm is made up of Messrs. G. W. Ranger and F. L. Butler, the former being a native of Massachusetts and a member of the Free Masons, while Mr. Butler was born in this place and is connected with the Odd Fellows. Business is carried on in Bonney's Block, opposite the Maine Central Depot, and despite the many orders received, customers are given prompt and courteous attention, a sufficient number of assistants being employed to serve all immediately and carefully. This firm is entitled to be ranked among the leading business houses of the kind in the State, their business amounting to nearly $75,000 yearly, and we are pleased to note a popularity so richly deserved.

G. Drake, Manufacturer of Agricultural and Factory Baskets, all sizes, West Farmington. People are so accustomed to using Baskets for a great variety of purposes, that they seldom stop to think what would be the result did the supply suddenly cease. Of course substitutes for baskets could be found, but they would all be more or less clumsy and costly, for nothing in the shape of a receptacle combines strength, lightness and cheapness in so high a degree as a well-made basket. In connection with this line of manufacture, it is appropriate to mention the establishment carried on by Mr. Gardner Drake, for this gentleman is one of the best known Basket Makers in the State, having inaugurated his present enterprise more than a score of years ago, and conducting it steadily ever since. He is a native of Sharon, Mass., and is exceptionally well known hereabouts, having been Postmaster of West Farmington for eleven years. The premises made use of by Mr. Drake are 20x36 feet in dimensions, and are well adapted to the purpose for which they are employed. Agricultural and Factory Baskets of all descriptions are very extensively manufactured, and the largest orders can be filled at short notice. Mr. Drake's productions will bear the most severe comparison with those of any other maker, for they are carefully constructed of selected material, being put together by skilled hands. All sizes of Baskets are made, and the lowest market rates are quoted on large and small lots.

C. A. Gould, Manufacturer and Dealer in Lumber, West Farmington. No careful review of the lumber trade of this section, its rise and progress, would be complete without special reference to this widely known and reliable concern, now conducted by C. A. Gould, and in this connection it may be as well to call attention to the fact that few branches of trade in the United States are of greater importance than the handling of lumber, and few demand more ability, foresight, and close discrimination to attain successful results. The company in question succeeded the old established house of Joseph Gould, and no house in the trade maintains a higher reputation, or has rendered more uniformly satisfactory services to those having business relations with it. The business, which is both wholesale and retail, is very extensive, is steadily increasing, and affords constant employment to quite a large number of hands. Mr. Gould has every advantage necessary to furnish lumber of standard excellence, in any quantities, and for any desired purpose. His promptitude in filling orders, dispatch in delivering and forwarding, and honorable methods command the confidence of his trade, and have made this house a desirable one with which to deal.

HISTORICAL SKETCH

—OF—

MECHANIC FALLS.

THE enterprising village of Mechanic Falls is composed partly of the territory of Poland and Minot, and its history is largely contained in that of the two latter. The Minot part was first settled in 1836, by Dean Andrews, who was shortly followed by Peter Thayer, Amos Chapman, Eli Washburne and others. This section grew up very rapidly, owing to its fine soil, and the mercantile and manufacturing privileges afforded by the river. The Poland section was first settled in 1830, by Mr. Jordan, who began to utilize the great timber resources of the region for his logging business. He was soon followed by Isaiah Perkins and others. The Little Androscoggin runs through the town, dividing it in two, and from the beginning has been a great advantage and stimulator of growth. Since the Grand Trunk Railway was built, running through the village, growth in all directions has been very marked. The expansion of business interests in the last few decades has been continuous and rapid, as the great water privileges and other local attractions have become more widely known. At the present time the leading business enterprises are in the line of canned goods, paper manufacturing, bricks, novelties, confectionery, corn packing, carriages, tools, machines, steam engines and boilers, beside the retail trade in dry and staple articles. The present local government is divided between that of Poland and Minot, the nucleus and center of the commercial interests of this locality being situated at Mechanic Falls. For Minot section the following were in 1888 the town officers: Selectman, O. N. Bailey; Town Clerk and Treasurer, C. H. Dwinall. For the Poland section: Selectman, Charles E. Stevens; Town Clerk, Treasurer and Collector, Zenas Lane. There are two churches in Mechanic Falls, one Congregationalist and the other Universalist. The religious and benevolent interests of the town are carefully and generously supported and provided for. The educational interests also receive the thorough and adequate attention they deserve, the schools being maintained at a high standard, and having a wide reputation for their efficiency and success. The town, also, has two lawyers, who take charge of the legal affairs of this vicinity. The sanitary condition of the town is exceptionally good, and the great

VIEW OF THE FALLS.

natural advantages which Mechanic Falls possesses render its business success and advancement assured. As its opportunities and attractions become more widely known to the business men of New England, it is sure to increase what is already widely admitted, that it is among the most prominent and promising of the progressive, enterprising towns and villages of Androscoggin County.

Since the War the material progress of the town has been continuous and marked. The business interests of the town have been developed and now promise richer returns in the immediate future. The water-power of the town is good and will admit of large development beyond the present need and utilization. All the departments of the town life are vigorously and well conducted, the local government and officials are characterized by efficiency and reliability; all measures for local improvement are rapidly and thoroughly executed. The sanitary condition of the town is most satisfactory, the educational interests are also administered with customary care and good results, and the social life of the town is characterized by the purity, refinement and hospitality of the ideal New England town. The religious life is also active and successfully engaged in every kind of good work.

The town offers many attractions to the summer visitor. Situated in one of the quietest and most beautiful regions of the State, easily reached by railroad, with all the facilities of the post-office service, pure country air, and other advantages, it presents the conveniences of city life in union with those of the country. Its streets are broad and shady, the surrounding country full of charming retreats and able to provide plenty of occupation for the rod and gun. The rates are of the moderate type, and we cannot doubt, as the annual tide of summer visitors over the Garden State increases, a larger number of them will come this way.

LEADING BUSINESS MEN

OF

MECHANIC FALLS.

J. A. Bucknam & Co., Dealers in Dry Goods, Clothing, Boots and Shoes, Fancy Goods, Trimmings, Room Paper, Carpets, Hats, Caps, Gent's Furnishing Goods, Groceries, Crockery, Flour, Pianos, Organs, Sewing Machines and Fire Insurance, Mechanic Falls. In reviewing the many industries of the New England States, we have never found so large a business conducted by one firm in a town of this size as that known as J. A. Bucknam & Co., of Mechanic Falls. Their business is so extensive and is divided into so many branches that to give each department the extended notice it deserves, would require more space than we have at our disposal; we will, however, endeavor to give a brief description of the various departments, trusting that those who visit the place will inspect the many bargains offered in detail. The business was started in 1843, by Mr. J. A. Bucknam, and in 1863 Mr. F. H. Cobb became a partner with Mr. Bucknam, under the firm-name of J. A. Bucknam & Cobb; but in 1864 Mr. H. L. Jones was admitted, and the firm-name changed to Bucknam, Cobb & Co. In 1866 Mr. Cobb retired and C. H. Dwinal, Joseph and W. B. Bucknam were admitted, under the firm-name of J. A. Bucknam & Co., which style has continued to the present time. In 1870 Mr. Jones retired and Mr. E. A. Gammon, the present junior partner of the concern, who has almost entire charge of the vast business, entered the firm. Mr. Joseph Bucknam died in 1870, and in 1879 C. H. Dwinal and W. B. Bucknam retired. Mr. Gammon had been with the house previous to becoming a partner—since 1861—and has an intimate knowledge of every detail of the business. The store on Main St., is a large brick building, and is divided into several departments. The stock of Dry Goods to be found here is very extensive, and comprises all the new goods as fast as they appear in the Boston or New York markets. A full line of Fancy Goods, Trimmings, etc., is also carried, and should the article desired not be in stock the firm are pleased to procure it at short notice. Mr. Gammon makes frequent trips to Boston, and is often enabled to offer new bargains. Boots, Shoes, Hats and Caps, Custom and Ready-Made Clothing and Gent's Furnishing Goods, are also carried in great variety, at city prices. In the basement a fine assortment of Choice Family Groceries and Crockery is kept. An Insurance Agency is established for the convenience of those wishing to place insurance in reliable companies, and policies are written in the North British and Mercantile of London, and the Home of New York. Those who are furnishing a house will find Carpets, Wall Paper, Pianos, Organs and Sewing Machines, all sold on very reasonable terms, and part pay taken in work if desired. Speaking of work reminds us that we have not alluded to the principal business carried on by this firm—the Manufacture of Ready-Made Clothing. Recognizing the fact that there were many ladies in the surrounding towns who had time at their disposal in addition to their household duties, they determined to offer them remunerative employment. They therefore began in a small way the manufacture of Ready-Made Clothing for Boston houses, and from a small beginning the business now requires four double teams, which carry the cloth (and calling for it when put together) to upwards of 1,000 houses, scattered throughout Oxford, Androscoggin and Cumberland Counties. In addition to this force employed in their own homes, Mr. Bucknam & Co. have a three-story factory run by steam power, where the pressing, finishing and packing of Clothing is done. They manufacture 100,000 garments a year, and do an annual business of about $100,000. Both members of the firm are well-known and representative citizens. Mr. Bucknam has been Representative to the Legislature and has been prominent in town affairs, holding many offices. Both he and Mr. Gammon are members of the Masons and Odd Fellows.

LEADING BUSINESS MEN OF MECHANIC FALLS.   209

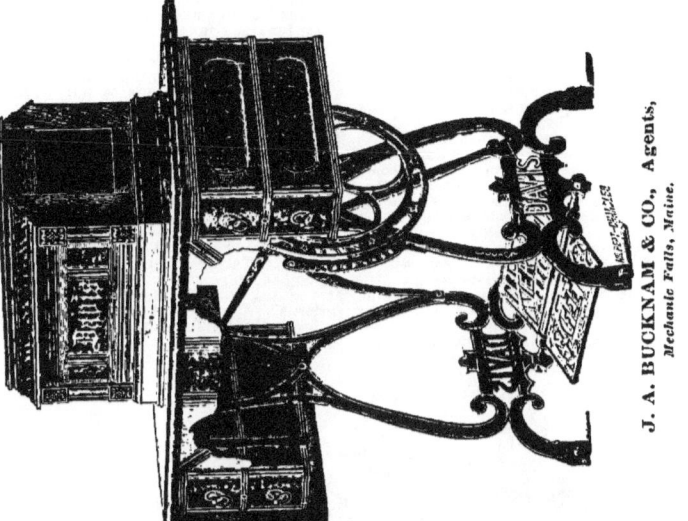

J. A. BUCKNAM & CO., Agents,
Mechanic Falls, Maine.

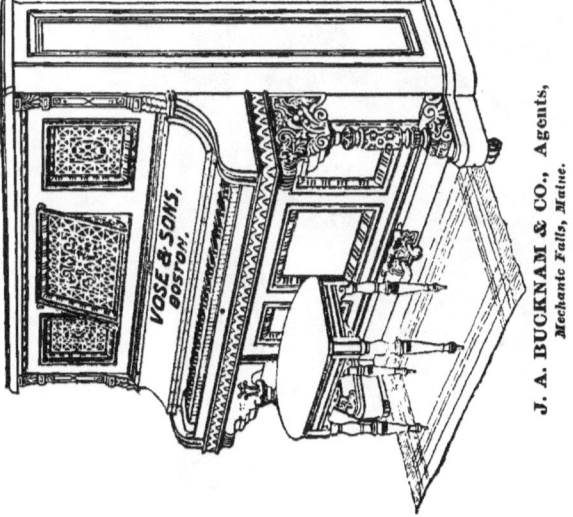

J. A. BUCKNAM & CO., Agents,
Mechanic Falls, Maine.

D. B. Perry, Manufacturer and Dealer in Furniture, Carpeting, Picture Frames, Guns, Revolvers, Ammunition, etc., Coffins, Caskets, and Burial Robes, constantly on hand, Mechanic Falls. When a man marries and "settles down" as it is called, it soon becomes apparent to him that truly "there is no place like home." To make his home as pleasant, cheerful and comfortable as his circumstances will allow, should be the aim of every good citizen, and it is really surprising to see how much can be done in this way, even by a person of very small income. House Furnishings were never so cheap as they now are, and if a little patience and determination be exercised, even a small sum of money can be made to go a surprisingly long way. Of course you must make your purchases at the right kind of an establishment if you wish to get genuine bargains, but there is but little danger of the residents of Mechanic Falls going to the wrong place, for the store conducted by Mr. D. B. Perry is too well known to be passed by. This enterprise was established twenty-eight years ago under the title of Perry & Merrill, and has been under the sole control of Mr. Perry for many years. The premises occupied by him comprises three floors each 50x50 feet in dimensions, and is one of the most popular in this vicinity, for the people have discovered that very superior inducements to purchasers are here presented, and they are not at all backward in taking advantage of the same. Furniture, Carpeting and House Furnishing goods in general are on hand in such variety that nobody can fail to find what they want somewhere about the store. Picture Frames, Guns, Ammunition, etc., Coffins, Caskets, and Burial Robes in all departments are as low as it is possible on reliable and standard goods. Mr. Perry is a native of Turner, Maine, and well known throughout this section. Was representative at Augusta, and is Treasurer of Masonic Relief Order; also a prominent member of the Odd Fellows, Knight Templars and Knights of Pythias.

J. A. BUCKNAM & CO.,

Agents,

Mechanic Falls, Maine.

LEADING BUSINESS MEN OF MECHANIC FALLS. 271

J. C. Walker, Apothecary, Mechanic Falls. There are certain lines of business in which enterprise and energy are more highly regarded than reliability, and which may be carried on to about equal advantage by almost anybody possessing the attributes mentioned; but there are others in which reliability ranks first, and which bring the public ask regarding those engaged in them, not are they enterprising or "smart," but are they strictly reliable? Occupying a most prominent position among such business enterprises stands that of the Apothecary, and it must be admitted that while energy and shrewdness are excellent things to put into enterprise, still there are other qualities that must be held superior to them when the handling and sale of medicines and drugs are concerned. If there is one Apothecary store in Mechanic Falls that is worthy of and which receives the confidence of the public, it is that conducted by Mr. J. C. Walker. This establishment which is located on Main Street, was founded by its present proprietor in 1878 who for ten years previous had occupied a store in another part of the village. This fine block is built of brick with granite front, is four stories high, the interior of the store being finished in ash and walnut. Mr. Walker is a native of Kennebunk, York County, Maine, and is well known throughout this community as a thoroughly reliable Apothecary. For over twenty years Mr. Walker has discharged the difficult and delicate duties of his position to the satisfaction of all with whom he has had to deal. The premises occupied cover an area of 25x45 feet, and employment is given to two capable and thoroughly skilled assistants; and so perfect are the facilities at hand for the putting up of prescriptions, and so large and complete is the assortment of drugs, chemicals, etc., on hand that no Apothecary in Mechanic Falls is better able to undertake the filling of such orders. A fine stock of Fancy Goods and Toilet Articles are also carried, and all patrons are served in a prompt and polite manner. Mr. Walker also runs a Drug Store in Biddeford, at 221 Main Street, in which, as at his Mechanic Falls establishment, a fine and complete stock is carried.

O. B. & C. H. Dwinal, Dealers in Ready-Made Clothing, Hats, Caps, Gent's Furnishing Goods, Boots, Shoes, Rubbers, Wall Papers, etc., Mechanic Falls. Within the last ten years the cost of clothing has been very materially decreased in this country, and without entering into a discussion of the cause of this state of affairs, we may say that the enterprise and energy of clothing retailers have had much to do with it. Among Mechanic Falls dealers there is none more deservedly popular than Messrs. O. B. & C. H. Dwinal. The enterprise conducted by them was inaugurated ten years ago, and has been under their continuous management since its inception. Messrs. O. B. & C. H. Dwinal are both natives of Minot, Maine, well known and highly respected throughout this community, Mr. O. B. Dwinal being a Constable and Collector, and Mr. C. H. Dwinal, Town Clerk, Treasurer, and member of the Odd Fellows. The business premises occupied by them cover an area of 30x50 feet, and a stock is carried such as only gentlemen of their experience and ability could get together. It includes about everything in the line of Men's Furnishings, the more prominent items being Ready-Made Clothing, Hats, Caps, Boots Shoes, Rubbers, etc., also a full line of Room Papers are constantly kept on hand, and the prices of all goods handled are put away down to the lowest notch, and no pains spared to give every purchaser complete satisfaction. The most fastidious dressers will not regret making Messrs. Dwinal a call, for their goods are not only low in price but fasionable in cut and make, and are warranted to prove as represented every time.

The Elms, H. S. Jordan, Proprietor. Situated Near the Depot, Heated by Steam, Livery Connected, Mechanic Falls. It would be well if all our hotels were run on the same general principles that characterize the management of The Elms, for if this were the case, traveling would be robbed of half its terrors and life would be a hundred per cent more enjoyable for those whom business calls "upon the road;" and by the way, when you see travelers patronizing a certain house almost exclusively, you can make up your mind without further investigation that *that* is one of the very best hotels in that section, for Commercial men make a science of traveling and what they don't know about the hotel accommodations on their routes, is not worth knowing. The Elms is carried on by H. S. Jordan, who is one of the best-known and most popular men in Mechanic Falls. He was employed in various capacities at the Block Island hotels for ten seasons, having learned the hotel business at that place, was engaged as clerk at the leading hotels there also at Hamilton Hotel, Washington, D. C. He is ever solicitous as to the comfort of his guests and is ever ready to heed any reasonable suggestion that will tend to enhance their enjoyment. The Elms has accommodations for sixty guests. The rooms are large and elegantly furnished, and are conveniently and pleasantly arranged, and heated by steam, the various apartments being kept in most excellent condition and everything in and about the premises showing prosperity and thrift. The table is supplied with the best that the market affords at all seasons, and the employment of capable assistants enables orders to be promptly filled, while uniform courtesy is shown to all. The Elms has a fine lawn in front and is pleasantly situated, near the depot. A well-appointed Livery Stable is maintained in connection with the establishment. The Elms is, beyond doubt, one of the most deservedly popular public houses in this section of the State. The terms are very moderate, and many a hotel charging much higher rates gives much less satisfactory accommodations. Mr. Jordan is a member of the Knights of Pythias.

Waterman & Jordan, Feed, Sale, Boarding and Livery Stable, also connected with the Elms Hotel, Pleasant Street, Mechanic Falls. There are not a few Boarding and Livery Stables in this vicinity which bear an excellent reputation, and we have no desire to exalt one at the expense of others; but still we may at least say that we know of none more deserving of the liberal patronage it receives than that conducted by Messrs Waterman & Jordan, on Pleasant Street. This Stable was established in 1875, and is excellently appointed, and is so carried on that the proprietors can be assured that their patrons are having their interests carefully looked after. They employ trustworthy men, and as they give close personal attention to the details of their business, they are in a position to at once detect and remedy any carelessness or wrong doing. Some valuable horses are quartered at this stable, and their owners speak in the highest terms of the accommodations given. Messrs. Waterman & Jordan are moderate in their prices, and any special directions concerning the diet or treatment of a certain horse will be conscientiously observed. Fifteen fine livery teams are owned by the proprietors, and those wishing to hire a turn-out will find what they want at this popular establishment. Mr. Waterman is a member of the Grand Army, and both members of the firm are highly respected throughout Mechanic Falls and vicinity.

Dirigo Laundry, D. B. Morse, Proprietor, Main Street, Mechanic Falls. The time has gone by when it was necessary to explain why people should patronize a public Laundry; such establishments have most certainly come to stay and the best reasons that can be given for their success, are that they fill a place that can be filled in no other way, and turn out work that proves its superiority by its appearance. Of course we are speaking of the first-class laundries, those that are intelligently and liberally managed for an example of this type, we need go no further than the widely-known Dirigo Laundry, of which Mr. D. B. Morse is the proprietor. This popular enterprise is located on Main Street, Mechanic Falls, Me., and since 1885, has been under the able management of its present proprietor. Many of our readers are doubtless familiar with the kind of work done here, and hence need no arguments to persuade them to patronize the establishment, but to others, we would say that no better work is done anywhere, and that the prices are as low as the lowest. The continual increase of business since Mr. Morse became manager of this Laundry, speaks of his ability to do first-class work better than we can. He has agents in the following places, where work can be left each week and returned without extra charges, the same as though it was left at the Laundry. Hebron, F. A. McCann or F. R. Glover; Buckfield, Stanley Bisbee; Canton, N. Reynold, (druggist); Dixfield, F. H. Keene; Welchville, Roscoe Staples; and once in two weeks at West Paris, N. G. Hollis; Island Pond, Vt., C. A. Volle or J. C. Rawson, (druggist). In places where he has no agent work by mail or express will receive prompt attention, and will be returned the same week if arriving before Thursday. The work is all done by hand and is done about the same as if it were done at your own house. All ladies work is under the entire charge of lady assistants. Clothes in fair weather are all dried out of doors, which makes them look better and is more healthful, than though they were dried by steam and under cover.

L. J. Morton, Dealer in Fruit, Confectionery, Cigars, Tobacco, etc., West End Bridge, Mechanic Falls. There is no possible harm in eating fruit provided it be ripe and in good condition, but on the contrary it may often be the greatest benefit to the health if used with the prudence and common sense, that should characterize the actions of all sensible people. More and more quantities of fruit are being consumed every year, and the demand is one that shows no signs of diminution, although the tendency is to require the furnishing of the choicest varieties as the public become more acquainted with them. As good a place to procure anything of this kind as is to be found in this vicinity is the establishment conducted by Mr. L. J. Morton, and located at the West End of the bridge. This gentleman does not deal in fruit alone, but also handles a superior assortment of Confectionery, Cigars, Tobacco, etc. This enterprise was originally established and managed by Mr. C. B. Adams, and later by E. J. Marston, and in 1885 the present proprietor, Mr. L. J. Morton, assumed the control of the business and soon attained a considerable patronage, which has rapidly developed as the merits of his goods become more generally known. One floor is occupied of the dimensions of 14x25 feet, and capable and polite assistants are employed. Mr. Morton was born in Poland, Maine, and is well known in this vicinity. Those fond of fruit and confectionery should visit his establishment, as he always carries a choice and fresh assortment of both, as well as the best brands of foreign and domestic Cigars and Tobacco, and smokers' articles in general.

Hiram Perkins, Boarding and Livery Stable, Mechanic Falls. The first problem and indeed the most important one that confronts him who would maintain a private equipage, is, "where shall my horse and carriage be kept?" for of course in the majority of instances it is quite out of the question to think of keeping them on one's own premises. Every one at all acquainted with horses, knows that not only the comfort of the animal, but also the enjoyment of his master depends in a great measure on the way in which the horse is fed and otherwise cared for, and therefore, as we say, the question of how to secure to him proper treatment and food becomes of paramount importance. There are doubtless many reliable establishments in Mechanic Falls where horses and carriages will be properly used, but we are sure that there are none in which more pains are taken to satisfy patrons than in that conducted by Mr. Hiram Perkins. This enterprise was inaugurated over twenty-five years ago, and has met with a high degree of appreciation, for the honorable and liberal methods of the proprietor quickly became manifest and the result is a large and growing business. Mr. Perkins is a prominent member of the Odd Fellows having been through the encampment. He is well known as a good judge of a horse and as a man who will not stand by and see one abused if he is able to prevent it. The premises occupied measure 92x38 feet, there being accommodations for a large number of horses and carriages.

J. W. Penney & Sons,

Engineers and Machinists, Manufacturers of Steam Engines and General Machinery, Mechanic Falls. The present century is clearly and distinctly the century of steam and steam machinery, whether the 20th will be the century of electrical machinery, remains to be seen. That the evolutions of the steam engine has played an all important part in the developments of our present civilization, cannot be doubted, considering the fact that steam machinery has made our modern cities and large business enterprises an established certainty. The history of a representative manufacture of steam engines possesses peculiar interest. Such an establishment is that of J. W. Penney & Sons of this town; founded in 1872, it has grown to its present magnitude, by the reputation it has established for first-class machinery. The materials used in the construction, and care taken that every piece of machinery, engine or boiler coming from this house shall be found perfect and durable, has resulted in the present large business which gives employment to a large number of experienced men. The works consist of a machine shop, blacksmith shop, foundry, pattern shop, pattern house, storehouses, etc. Each department is supplied with all the facilities and modern tools necessary to produce first-class work. A thorough test only establishes more firmly the value of the engines coming from these works, and the large number of them now running in different parts of the country, is the best testimonials to the appreciation they have received. All classes of engines are manufactured here and are classed as follows: — horizontal, upright, portable and yacht, plain slide valves and automatic. They also manufacture passenger and

Plain Slide Valve Engine.

Automatic Engine.

Automatic Elevator Hoist.

freight elevators with automatic safety appliances. Finley paper cutters, heavy paper machinery, shafting, pulleys, hangers, etc. The firm handles Allen & Sons boilers and the Wainwright Mnfg. goods exclusively in this State and are agents for all first-class steam engineering appliances. The business was established by Mr. J. W. Penney, in 1872, the firm assuming the present title by the admission of Messrs. A. R.

Steam Pump.

and S. R. Penney in 1884. Mr. J. W. Penney is a native of New Gloucester, Me., A. R. Penney was born in Minot, and Mr. S. R. Penney in Poland. They are all well and favorably known as representative manufacturers.

M. N. Royal & Co., Manufacturers and Dealers in Chocolate and Confectionery, Mechanic Falls. As fine an example of a business enterprise, having a gradual, sustained and extensive growth, as we know of in this vicinity, is that afforded by the undertaking conducted by Messrs. M. N. Royal & Co. This firm ranks with the leading manufacturers of Chocolate and Confectionery in Maine, and have gained their present prominent position from small beginnings, the enterprise being inaugurated in 1883. The premises utilized are located on Elm Street, and comprise one floor and a basement, each 32x70 feet in dimensions, being admirably adapted to the carrying on of the extensive Wholesale and Retail business transacted, which necessitates the services of four skilled assistants and a double team on the road. These facilities, taken in connection with the other advantages enjoyed, and the enterprising business methods employed, put the firm in a position to successfully meet all competition, and push its specialties with vigor and to the complete satisfaction of customers. The individual members of the firm are M. N. and C. W. Royal, both natives of Danville, Maine, and well-known in this community, and bear an honorable and enviable reputation for the invariable employment of strictly legitimate business methods as well as for the accuracy and promptitude with which orders intrusted to them are filled. This firm should certainly be able to produce a standard article as low as any house in the business, for they have the facilities and the experience, and the will is assuredly not lacking. Mr. M. N. Royal is Constable and a member of the I. O. of G. T., and Mr. C. W. Royal is a member of the Free Masons.

W. C. Bridge, Dining Room, also Dealer in Fruits, Confectionery and Cigars, Mechanic Falls. Mechanic Falls is known as one of the most active and most enterprising communities in the State, and her merchants are celebrated for their readiness to adopt uniform methods and their desire to give their customers every possible accommodation, so that to excel in any line of business amid such surroundings, is a difficult task, but when such superior excellence has been attained, it should certainly be given due appreciation; and, therefore, we take great pleasure in commending to the attention of our readers, the establishments of which Mr. W. C. Bridge is the proprietor. The Dining Room conducted by this gentleman is justly entitled to the leading position it is generally accorded. The premises occupied as a Dining Room cover an area of 15x50 feet, and three competent assistants are employed, there being facilities at hand to give customers prompt and polite attention at all times, while the bill of fare is as varied as the wide experience of the proprietor and the state of the market can make it. Mr. Bridge also runs a large Boarding House, and has earned the gratitude of his patrons by making it a rule to supply them with the best of food, well-cooked, and no efforts are spared to make the service as prompt and efficient as the food is acceptable. Mr. Bridge carries a fine assortment of Fruits, Confectionery and Cigars. Very low rates are charged and it would be hard to find similar establishments in Mechanic Falls more truly worthy of patronage and appreciation. Mr. Bridge is well-known in social as well as business circles, being a member of the Knights of Labor and Grand Army.

Poland Paper Co., Mills at Mechanic Falls, Me., Manufacturers of News, Fine M. F. Book, Extra S. C. Book Papers. Treasurer's Office, 24 Plum Street, Portland, Me. Among the various interests which diversify the industries of Mechanic Falls, none deserves more prominent mention than that of the manufacture of Paper. It is one that gives employment to a large number of operatives, and in many ways forms an important item in estimating the manufacturing and commercial importance of this enterprising and thriving town. The Paper Mills are located on the river. They are very spacious, and are admirably equipped with all the latest improved appliances, apparatus and machinery necessary for the systematic conduct of the business. Upwards of three hundred hands are employed in the various departments, and the total daily capacity of the mills is several tons. The officers of the company are gentlemen widely known and highly regarded in manufacturing and financial circles for their sound business principles, integrity and ability. Mr. C. R. Milliken being also prominently identified with the Portland Rolling Mill and the celebrated White Mountain Hotel, the Glen House.

F. H. McDonald Co., Dealer in Choice Family Groceries, Mechanic Falls. Among the many Grocery Dealers, Mr. F. H. McDonald occupies a prominent and leading position. Success seems to have attended the store from the first. That the articles sold are choice is proved by the character of the trade, and that the prices are reasonable is shown by the manner in which he has not only held his own, but constantly augmented the trade in spite of the sharp and enterprising competition which he is naturally obliged to meet. Assistants are on hand to attend to the wants of customers, and they will be found active, intelligent and obliging by all who have dealings with them. The goods in stock are very tastefully arranged in the store, and exquisite neatness is the rule throughout the establishment. Groceries of all kinds are received fresh daily, among which will be found Choice Teas, Coffees, Spices, Sugar, etc. It is safe to assert that this is one of the most popular stores of its kind in town, and we prophesy a brilliant future for the house if it continues under the fine management it now enjoys.

HISTORICAL SKETCH
— OF —
SOUTH PARIS.

SOUTH Paris is the most prominent section of the town of Paris, the county seat of Oxford County. It it reached by the Grand Trunk R. R., and is the commercial and social center of this part of the State. The whole town comprises about seventy-two square miles. The surface of the country is uneven, with large hills and fertile valleys intermingled. Streaked Mountain is the highest eminence in this vicinity; there are, also, numerous other high hills in the town, among which are Spruce, Jump-off, South Singlepole, Cable and Number Four. The Little Androscoggin river runs through the town, and in the southern part, well-known as South Paris, Stony Brook, a stream with considerable power, flows into the former. The scenery throughout this region is very beautiful and diversified. The town itself is a model of a quiet country town, with its broad, elm-arched streets with many spacious and elegant residences along them, and opening out into delightful regions on every side. Every enjoyment and advantage of country can be obtained here, and it is becoming very popular with discerning summer visitors.

South Paris is more essentially the business portion and is rapidly developing into the activity and proportions of a city. It is reached by the Norway branch of the Grand Trunk. It has a large supply of water-power and offers many advantages to manufactures which have been more recognized in recent years. As a result, its business interests have been, and are continually expanding. They chiefly consist now of flouring and lumber mills, barrel-machinery making, iron foundries, machine shops, and retail lines of staple goods. The enterprise of South Parisians has been the great element in the development of the material interests of the town and has proved a most efficient kind of capital.

South Paris has had a long and interesting history. The township was granted to Capt. Joshua Fuller of Watertown, and sixty-four privates of his company, in 1771, for gallant services during the French and Indian Wars. The first settlement was made in 1779, on Paris Hill, by John Daniels, John Willis, Joseph Willis, Benjamin

HISTORICAL SKETCH OF SOUTH PARIS.

Hammond, Lieut. Jackson and Uriah Ripley, all from Middleborough, Mass. Daniels payed the Indians in the vicinity an iron kettle for about all the land now contained in the town. In 1795 the First Church, the Calvinist Baptist, was organized here and its first meeting-house was erected in 1803. The first pastor was Elder James Hooper of Berwick. In 1793 the place was incorporated as a township, under the present name, and when Oxford was organized in 1850, it was made a shire town. The town was intensely interested and honorably represented in the War of 1812,

SQUARE IN SOUTH PARIS
IN 1889.

the Mexican War and the great Civil War. It was the birth-place and early residence of Hon. Hannibal Hamlin, Governor of Maine, United States Senator and Vice-President under Lincoln. The Hon. Sidney Perham, prominent in State and National politics, also resides here. Among the town's other prominent citizens have been Hons. Leon Hubbard, A. K. Paris, Enoch Lincoln, Thos. J. Carter, Rufus K. Goodenow and Charles Andrews. Few other places in the State have had the honor of having so many governors of Maine, it having had four. The local officers for the past year were the following: South Paris Village Corporation; A. C. T. King, Clerk; N. D. Bolster, E. F. Stone, F. A. Thayer, Assessors; H. W. Bolster, Treasurer; E. Shurtleff, Chief Engineer. The town has made most progress since the War. The population in 1870 was 2,065; in 1880, 2,930; the valuation in 1870 was $977,935; in 1880, $985,274. At the present time the population is a little over three thousand, and the valuation over a million.

South Paris has always been greatly interested in educational matters. One of the earliest and best institutions of its kind in the State was the Oxford Normal Institute, which is still flourishing and enjoys a high reputation. The other schools are also admirably conducted and liberally supported. In religious interests also the town is well represented, having one church each of the Baptist, Congregationalist and Methodist denominations. In all benevolent and charitable work the greatest care and generosity are shown. The townspeople have a great reputation for hospitality, and the town is well known through the State as a social center. Both in the summer and winter seasons there is much social activity, and the town is a most delightful place to visit.

LEADING BUSINESS MEN

OF

SOUTH PARIS, ME.

Paris Manufacturing Company, Geo. B. Crockett, Treasurer; O. A. Maxim, Agent. Manufacturers of Children's Sleds and Sleighs, The Comet Toboggan, Boys' Carts, Wagons, Wheelbarrows, etc.; also folding Laundry Benches, Tables and Chairs, Step Ladders, The Garfield Cot Bed, etc., South Paris. One of the most extensive and important enterprises carried on in the State of Maine, is that conducted in this town by the Paris Manufacturing Company. This Company was transferred to its present quarters in 1885, it having been started in West Sumner, Maine, in 1863, by Mr. H. F. Morton. The President, Mr. George A. Wilson, is a well-known man of affairs, who has served in the Legislature and as Judge of Probate, and who has been Treasurer of the South Paris Savings Bank since its organization. Mr. Geo. B. Crockett, the Treasurer of the Company, is also a leading citizen. Among the more important articles produced, may be mentioned Children's Sleds and Sleighs, the Comet Toboggan, Boys' Carts, Wagons, Wheelbarrows, etc., together with Folding Laundry Benches, Tables and Chairs, Step Ladders, etc. One of the most popular products of the company is the famous Garfield Cot Bed, this having gone into general use, not only on account of the ingenuity of its design, but also by reason of the thoroughness of its constrstruction—this being a distinguishing characteristic of all the company's manufactures. An exclusively wholesale business is done, and goods are shipped far and wide, one branch office being maintained in Boston, at No. 151 Congress Street, and another in New York, at No. 21 Park Place. Dealers report a brisk and increasing demand for the various products of the company, and it is gratifying to note this as an instance of the public's appreciation of goods made from selected material in a thoroughly workmanlike fashion. The annual sales amount to some $125,000, and employment is given to 150 assistants, 100-horse-power being required to drive the machinery in use. The company are prepared to fill orders at the shortest notice, for their facilities are unsurpassed, and goods can be furnished at the lowest market rates.

N. Dayton Bolster, Dealer in Dry Goods, Groceries, Crockery, Wall Papers, Paints, Oils, etc., South Paris. An establishment which is clearly entitled to a position among the leading and representative houses of this section, is that conducted by Mr. N. Dayton Bolster. This gentleman has carried on the enterprise in question since 1871, it having been founded by his father, Mr. Otis C. Bolster. The present proprietor is a native of Rumford, Maine, and is connected with both the Odd Fellows and the Good Templars. He is personally one of the best known of our merchants, and has held the position of Town Treasurer for eleven years. Mr. Bolster carries on a very large business, involving a vast amount of detail, and requiring unusual skill and intelligence to manage it successfully. The premises occupied comprise one floor and a basement, and their dimensions are 100x35 feet. So varied is the stock on hand that it would be idle for us to attempt to mention the almost innumerable goods contained in it, but it includes Dry Goods, Groceries, Crockery, Wall Paper, Paints, Oils, etc., and will be found as desirable as it is varied. Mr. Bolster is a careful and far-seeing buyer, and his experience enables him to judge very accurately what his customers need. The many fashionable novelties to be found among his Dry and Fancy Goods, show that he keeps a sharp eye upon the market, and equal enterprise is exhibited in keeping all the other departments fully up to the times. Prices are placed as low as the market will allow, and three competent assistants are at hand to serve customers promptly.

LEADING BUSINESS MEN OF SOUTH PARIS.

F. C. Briggs, Tea and Coffee Store, Dealer in Flour, Groceries, Meats and Provisions, Fruit, Tobacco and Cigars, Hides, Tallow, etc., Manufacturer of Sausage, South Paris. There is no better place in South Paris or vicinity at which to obtain household supplies, than at the store of Mr. F. C. Briggs, for there may be found as full an assortment of Family Stores as is to be seen in these parts, and the prices quoted are always as low as the lowest. Among the more important goods carried in stock may be mentioned Flour, Groceries, Meats and Provisions; and Fruit; Tobacco and Cigars are also extensively dealt in. Mr. Briggs is a manufacturer of Sausages, and also carries on a Fish Market, so that his facilities for furnishing food supplies of all kinds are very hard to match. He is largely interested in the live-stock trade and deals heavily in Cattle, Sheep, Veal, Calves, Hogs, etc., as well as in Hides and Tallow. The stock of Choice Family Groceries offered by Mr. Briggs includes both fancy and staple goods, and gives signs of great care in its selection, for it is made up of productions of standard merit and is bound to give satisfaction. In Teas and Coffees, special inducements are held forth, the purity and fineness of the goods being beyond suspicion. The rates at which the very best brands of Tea and Coffee are offered may seem surprisingly low, but it is Mr. Briggs' policy to be content with a small profit and to thus increase his sales to the fullest possible amount. Customers are attended to with courtesy and promptness, two efficient assistants being employed, and orders are assured early and accurate delivery.

S. Richards, Watch Maker and Jeweler; Repair Work a Specialty, South Paris. It is unfortunate that with the great increase of the number of Fine Watches in general use of late years, there has not been a corresponding increase in the number of those capable of repairing the same, for as matters now are, the better a Watch is the more liable its owner is to experience difficulty in having it repaired properly. That this is a correct statement of the case, no one acquainted with the facts will dispute, and, therefore, we feel that in directing our readers to an establishment where the best of work is done in the Watch Repairing line, we are giving them information which may save them time, money and trouble. Mr. S. Richards, the proprietor of the place to which we have reference, is a native of Oxford, Maine, and has had a long and varied experience in the Repairing of Watches of all kinds. He guarantees his work, and those who have a fine Watch which is not doing itself justice, or which needs attention in any way, will find their own interests best served by making Mr. Richards an early call. He gives personal and special attention to Repairing in all its branches, and his prices are moderate as his work is first-class. Mr. Samuel Richards, Jr., was born in Oxford, Maine, July 30, 1832; served three years' apprenticeship with Simeon Walton, of Norway, and became established at South Paris in 1856. Mr. Richards has had thirty-five years' experience in fitting Spectacles and Eye Glasses, using the most approved method for the detection and correction of visual imperfections. He has been called upon at different times to adjust a large number of fine Watches for wholesale dealers. This delicate work is performed by very few workmen. Mr. Richards is very successful in all kinds of Watch Repairing. The Repairing of Jewelry is also skillfully done at short notice, and a well-selected assortment of Jeweler's Goods is always at hand to choose from, together with Watches in Gold, Silver and Nickel Cases. Mr. Richards is believed to be the only Jeweler in Oxford County who served a full term of apprenticeship, and has continued in business since 1856.

F. A. Shurtleff, Drugs, Medicines, Chemicals, Books, Stationery, Toilet Articles, etc., South Paris. An establishment which well-deserves special mention in a book intended to be distributed among the people, is that carried on by Mr. F. A. Shurtleff, at South Paris, for this establishment is one of the most reliable Pharmacies to be found in South Paris. Mr. Shurtleff began business at his present location in 1887, and has since built up a large trade, not only in the immediate vicinity, but also for quite a distance around, for the care and skill shown in the compounding of Physicians' Prescriptions (of which a specialty is made) have excited no little favorable comment, and has resulted in Mr. Shurtleff's name being placed among the best-equipped dispensing Chemists of this town. He has the assistance of a competent clerk, and the details of the business are most ably managed. One floor, 90x25 feet is utilized, and as might be expected where so much prominence is given to the Prescription Department, an unusually large and varied assortment of Drugs, Medicines and Chemicals is carried; also Books, Stationery, Toilet Soap, Sponges, Brushes, Combs, Perfumery, etc., etc., are to be had here, and as the store is centrally located, our readers should make it a point to call and test the resources of this deserving establishment. Mr. Shurtleff is a native of South Paris and a prominent member of the Odd Fellows.

A. C. Jones, Machinist, all kinds of Tools and Machinery neatly and promptly repaired, dealer in Iron Pipes, Fittings and Valves, South Paris. The difficulty of getting Tools and Machinery properly repaired at short notice, is one that is well-known to every manufacturer, and it is often the case that serious delay and considerable pecuniary loss are caused in this same way. It is therefore important to know of a shop where a specialty is made of Repairing in all its branches, and where every effort is made to fill orders not only promptly but satisfactorily in other respects as well. Mr. A. C. Jones began operations here in 1879, and now carries on one of the best-equipped establishments of its kind in this section. He is a native of Levant, Maine, and is acknowledged to be a thorough Mechanic who allows no inferior work to leave his shop if he can prevent it. Two floors and a basement are utilized, and all the necessary Machinery is at hand, ample steam power being available. Mr. Jones is very reasonable in his charges, and spares no pains to deliver all jobs at the time promised. His work is as neat as it is strong and durable, only experienced assistants being employed. Quite a trade is carried on in Iron Pipes, Fittings and Valves; these articles being kept on hand in great variety, and offered at the lowest market rates.

C. R. Smith, Manufacturer and Repairer of Boots and Shoes, South Paris. The first thing to do when trying to find a thing is to learn where to look for it, and as many of our readers are doubtless trying to find reliable Foot Wear at bottom prices, we can give them a valuable hint by telling them to look among the goods made to order by Mr. C. R. Smith, of South Paris. This enterprise was started in 1865, by Mr. Smith, who formerly conducted an extensive manufacturing business in Mechanic Falls for fourteen years. Mr. Smith is a Vermont man by birth, and is well-known in the trade circle of this community. He understands the Boot and Shoe Manufacturing and Repairing business pretty thoroughly, and the reason why he can offer his customers the many unqualified bargains that he undoubtedly does in Order Work, is simply because he watches the market closely, and being acquainted with the true value of all standard materials, is in a position to know an opening when he sees it, and is prompt to take advantage of it. The premises utilized are 12x24 feet in size, where are Repaired and made to Order, Boots and Shoes in all the fashionable and desirable styles. Customers are given prompt and polite attention, and their needs carefully studied, and all transactions guaranteed perfectly satisfactory. Mr. Smith is a member of the Masonic Order and was Post-master at Mechanic Falls for eight years under President Buchanan.

H. N. Bolster, Variety Store and Wholesale and Retail Dealer in Country Produce, Market Square, South Paris. That it requires special ability to successfully carry on a Wholsale and Retail Variety Store at a time when competition is so sharp as it is nowadays scarcely needs demonstration, for even the least observant can hardly have failed to notice that the margin of profit on Dry Goods and Groceries have been reduced to a very low figure, but, however, what is the dealers loss is the public gain, and after all it is not the enterprising dealers that are complaining, but only those who have not the energy or the ability to meet the demand of the people for reliable goods at low prices. As popular an establishment as we know of in this vicinity devoted to the sale of Dry Goods and Groceries, is that carried on by Mr. H. N. Bolster. on Market Square, and this popularity is all the more noticeable because as this gentleman has been in the business since 1864, he must be thoroughly well known to the people by this time. Mr. Bolster is a native of South Paris, Maine, and a member of the Masons. One floor is utilized measuring 80x24 feet, and employment is afforded to two competent assistants. Dry Goods and Groceries of all descriptions are constantly carried in stock, and patrons will find that Mr. Bolster is excellently well prepared to supply their wants, and that he sells goods of standard quality at prices as low as can be obtained anywhere.

S. P. Maxim & Son. Glazed Windows, Blinds, Brackets, Molding, Inside Finish and Building Material of all Kinds, South Paris. This firm began operations here in 1880, doing a small business in their line of Builders' Finish and General Jobbing, but the demand for their work has increased so that from time to time it became necessary to enlarge their facilities, by adding new machinery and auxiliary steam-power, until at present they have one of the best factories of the kind in the State, being equipped with about twenty-five different machines of the most approved kind, the entire plant, including storehouses, having about 11,000 feet floor space. A large business is done in the manufacture and sale of Building Material of all kinds, including Doors, Glazed Windows, Blinds, Brackets, Moldings and Inside Finish; also Glass, Sheathing Paper, Window Weights and Builders' Hardware, are furnished at lowest market rates. Special attention is given to Jobbing of all kinds. The firm are Agents for the celebrated Cleveland Rubber Paint, they having sold over five thousand gallons, all giving the best satisfaction. A book containing colored plates of house elevations and sample colors, will be mailed to any address on application. This firm are quite extensive Contractors and Builders, and in connection with the manufacturing facilities, have the advantage over most others, and being practical Architects and Designers, their services are in demand, as the numerous edifices in town will testify. Mr. Maxim, senior, has several desirable building lots for sale, and those contemplating locating here would do well to examine them. The firm consists of S. P. Maxim and W. P. Maxim, both of whom are natives of Paris; the senior partner being a member of the Masonic Order and P. of H., while his son is connected with the I. O. O. F.

Andrews House, W. M. Shaw, Proprietor; A Good Livery Connected; Free Carriage to all Trains; South Paris. A true test of hotel keeping is to be found in the atmosphere which surrounds the house. If this be comfortable and home-like, then success has been attained, but if the contrary be the case, then the most carefully fitted-up hotel is going to prove a failure, no matter how elaborate may be the accommodations offered. Since Mr. W. M. Shaw assumed control of the Andrews House, in 1886, that hotel has gained high favor with the public, and we feel confident that such of our readers as may have experienced that gentleman's hospitality will join us in saying that this popularity is well deserved. Mr. Shaw is a native of Portland, and has already made many friends for himself in this vicinity. It is a great advantage to a community to have a first-class hotel in its midst, and the residents of South Paris have good reason to be grateful to Mr. Shaw for his unremitting efforts to keep such a house as shall suit the most fastidious. Elmer E. Thomas, the popular and efficient Clerk, is always on hand to attend to the wants of guests. Mr. Thomas is a Clerk who is universally liked. The hotel is a three-story structure and contains many pleasant and conveniently arranged apartments. It is furnished throughout in most comfortable style, and the table is one of its chief attractions; being always fully supplied with the best that the market affords. Employment is afforded to six competent and accommodating assistants, and guests may depend upon having their desires promptly attended to. A strictly first-class Livery is connected with the establishment and teams may be had at all hours at moderate rates. A free carriage is run to all the trains, and the terms of the house are liberal and just.

A. C. Dyer, Dealer in Flour, Groceries, Canned Goods, Fruit, Confectionery, Tobacco and Cigars, Lime, Hair, Cement. Store opposite Grand Trunk Ry. Depot, South Paris. There are many establishments of a somewhat similar character to the one now conducted by Mr. A. C. Dyer, located in this vicinity, but there are few of them that combine so many advantages as the one in question. This view of the case is evidently held by many others besides ourselves, for the business done at this establishment is very large and is steadily increasing at a most gratifying rate. The enterprise in question was first started by Mr. R. Smith about twenty-five years ago, and after several changes in its management came under the control of Mr. A. C. Dyer in 1888. Such success as he has attained is not gained without reason, and if any of our readers are desirous of ascertaining the reason why this establishment is so popular, let them visit the store in person and leave a trial order. They will find that prompt and polite attention is given to all, that the prices are in accordance with the lowest market rates, and that the goods are in every instance just what they are represented to be. Is it any wonder then that this house is so popular? The proprietor, Mr. Dyer, is a native of Webb's Mills, Me., and a member of the Odd Fellows. He has given his business the most careful personal attention from the start, and has certainly worked hard enough to amply earn even the liberal return he has received. The premises occupied consist of one floor and a basement, each covering an area of 40x40 feet, and contain a very heavy and varied stock consisting of Flour, Groceries, Canned Goods, Fruit, Confectionery, Tobacco and Cigars, Lime, Hair and Cement. Efficient and polite assistants are employed, and orders are delivered with accuracy and care.

Excelsior Picture Frame Co., Manufacturers and Wholesale Dealers in Every Variety of Picture Frames, Paintings, Engravings, Chromos, Panels, Easels, Fancy Cabinet Ware, Stereoscopes and Views, Looking Glasses, etc., F. A. Millett, President, No. 1 Odd Fellows' Block, South Paris. But few people really know how important it is to have a Frame especially adapted to the picture which it is to inclose, for the most of us hold that a picture is a picture, no matter how it is framed, or indeed, even if it is not framed at all. But no observing person can visit an art gallery without becoming impressed with the variety of frames there present. Some pictures are given a broad margin of smooth gold, others are set in narrow but deep frames, while still others are framed as simply as possible in natural wood. Now there is a reason for all this, and it would surprise the visitor to see the change that would be made by substituting one frame for another. As good a place to study Frames and their effects as anywhere, is at the establishment carried on by the Excelsior Picture Frame Co., near the R. R. depot. Two floors are occupied, of the dimensions of 44x20 feet, and as both Frames and Pictures of all kinds are to be found on the premises, every opportunity is had to make satisfactory and instructive tests. This enterprise was inaugurated by Messrs. Millett & Farrar, in 1884, and since 1885 business has been conducted under the present style, Mr. F. L. Millett being President of the Company. He is a native of Norway and is connected with the Free Masons. A beautiful and complete assortment of Paintings, Engravings, Chromos, Panels, Easels, Fancy Cabinet Ware, etc., is kept in stock, and Stereoscopes and Views, Looking Glasses, etc., are also largely dealt in. Frames of every description will be made to order at short notice, and the facilities of the company are such that it is enabled to confidently guarantee satisfaction, both as to work and to prices.

A. H. Dunham, Carriage, Sign and Ornamental Painter, Shop near G. T. Ry. Depot, South Paris. The large cities, such as New York, Boston, Portland, etc., show marked changes of late years in the character of their signs, and, generally speaking, the more progressive and important the business house, the more ornamental and striking its sign. Some very beautiful work in this line has been turned out, and enterprising merchants do well to keep up with the procession and show themselves capable of having as handsome a sign as anybody. The cost of a large, modern sign is considerable, but when well-painted, it is as durable as it is handsome, and may be considered an excellent investment, for it attracts trade and proves that its owner is up with the times. Mr. A. H. Dunham has done some extremely good work in this line, and those who are familiar with the thoroughness with which everything is done at his establishment, need not be told that his productions are durable as well as beautiful. He is a native of West Minot, and has been located in South Paris since 1888, having removed there from Mechanic Falls, where he began operations in 1886. His shop is near the Grand Trunk Depot, and is 75x30 feet in dimensions. Mr. Dunham is connected with the Odd Fellows, the Knights of Pythias and the Red Men, and is well-known socially as well as in a business way. He is prepared to fill orders for Carriage, Sign and Ornamental Painting at short notice, and fully warrants all work leaving his shop. Only selected stock is used, and every effort is made to fill orders in a style that cannot be surpassed, at prices that will be sure to give satisfaction.

A. M. Gerry, Druggist, South Paris. One of the best-patronized establishments to be found in this vicinity, is that carried on by Mr. A. M. Gerry, the Druggist, for the stock handled by him not only contains a full assortment of Pure Drugs and Medicines and Choice Toilet Articles, but also Sporting Goods in great variety as well as School Books, Stationery, etc. Mr. Gerry strives to have his stock complete in every department, and puts his prices so low as to remove all danger of goods accumulating on his hands. He was born in Lovell, Me., and is a member of both the Free Masons and the Odd Fellows. One floor and a basement are occupied, measuring 45x18 feet, and sufficient assistance is at hand to allow of all customers receiving prompt and courteous attention. Mr. Gerry has carried on his present enterprise since 1875, and his policy of supplying customers with none but Pure and Reliable Goods, has resulted in the building up of an extensive business. The Cigars sold by him are deservedly popular among smokers, for the goods offered are made from selected stock, and are decidedly superior to the average. Shot-guns, Rifles and Revolvers, may be bought here at bottom prices, and should any of our readers think they can do better elsewhere, we would certainly advise them to carefully examine what Mr. Gerry has to offer in the line of Fire-arms and compare his goods and prices with those to be found elsewhere. Patent Medicines of all kinds are largely dealt in, and everything in the line of Druggists' Sundries may be bought here at reasonable rates, some special attractions being offered in the shape of Choice Perfumery at bottom figures.

Dr. J. W. Davis, Dentist, Filling Natural Teeth a Specialty. Ether and Pure Nitrious-Oxide Gas administered when desired, South Paris. If people could only be taught that Dental operations do not necessarily cause pain, many a set of teeth would be saved that are now allowed to go to ruin. A partially decayed tooth can often be filled without its owner suffering more than during the process of hair-cutting, and it should be remembered that when taken in time, the teeth may be put into shape by a skillful dentist without the patient suffering a single twinge. Even sensitive teeth need not cause much suffering if treated in accordance with modern methods, and everyone should see that the dentist patronized has ample facilities and knows how to use them. Dr. J. W. Davis is of course already known to many of our readers, for he has practiced his profession here for some years and has established a well-earned reputation for thoroughness and skill. He is a native of Woodstock, Me., and is a very prominent Odd Fellow, having taken all the degrees in that order. He is also a member of the Golden Cross. Dr. Davis has his office fitted-up for the practice of Dentistry in all its details, and his tools and appliances embody all the latest improvements. A specialty is made of the Filling of Natural Teeth, and Extracting is quickly and painlessly done; Ether and pure Nitrious Oxide Gas being administered if desired. Plate-work of all kinds is also given prompt attention and Artificial Teeth are offered in a variety of grades, the best work being fully warranted and the prices as low as the lowest. Difficult operations upon the natural teeth performed in skillful manner. Roots crowned and made to do good service for years. Do not have your teeth extracted because they give pain, but have them treated and put in a healthy condition and filled.

W. J. Wheeler, dealer in Pianos, Organs, Stools, Piano Covers and Musical Merchandise, also Fire, Life and Accident Insurance Office, leading Foreign and American Fire Insurance Companies, South Paris. There are a great many Pianos and Organs in use in this country, but still there are many families yet unsupplied, and extensive as the trade in Musical Instruments has become, it is as yet but in its infancy. Although the cost of a first-class Piano or Organ is considerable, some dealers, by the employment of liberal "installment plans," so divide up the payments as to make it an easy matter to meet them, and one purchasing in this way becomes the owner of an instrument before he knows it. Mr. W. J. Wheeler is known as one of the largest dealers in Pianos, Organs, Stools, Covers and Musical Merchandise in general, in this section of the State, and his prices, for cash or on installments, are so low as to explain in a great measure the magnitude of his trade. All instruments are warranted for five years, and a sufficient variety is offered to allow of all tastes being suited. Mr. Wheeler is a native of Dixfield, Maine, and begun operations in this town in 1871. He is prominently connected with the Free Masons, Odd Fellows and Knights of Pythias, and is actively engaged in the Insurance business, representing some of the leading Foreign and American Companies and writing Fire, Life and Accident Policies. No agent offers greater inducements and none is more zealous in guarding the interests of his clients. Mr. Wheeler controls a fine stock farm situated about three miles from the village, and raises some excellent horses, those now on hand being valued at $3,000

Kenney & Plummer, Dealers in Boots, Shoes, Clothing, Hats, Caps, Gent's Furnishing Goods, etc., South Paris. It is really surprising how intimately we come to associate people with the Clothing they wear, for a little thought will prove to any one that he recognizes his friends almost as much by their garments as by their faces. A uniformed company of soldiers look very much alike, and it is very hard to pick out even a well-known face from such an assemblage. Therefore, as our clothes form so great a part of ourselves, it is important to choose such clothes as are specially adapted to our needs. Cheap, trashy garments are dear at any price, but excellent clothing can now be bought very low at certain stores, and among these none is more worthy of patronage than that carried on under the firm-name of Kenney & Plummer. Mr. J. F. Plummer, the present proprietor, is a native of Sweden, Maine. The premises utilized measure 60x30 feet, and employment is given to one active and accommodating assistant, in the person of Mr. O. R. Bean, who is always on hand to attend to the wants of their customers. A heavy and varied stock of Clothing is always to be found here, and it will bear the most severe examination, for it is made up of standard goods, thoroughly put together. The cut and "hang" of these garments are sure to give satisfaction, and the prices named on them are very low. Boots and Shoes may also be bought here to excellent advantage, as may Hats and Caps of all kinds, suitable for all ages. A fine line of Gentlemen's Furnishings is at hand for inspection.

Miss N. E. Dean, Fashionable Millinery and Fancy Goods, South Paris. Nothing so much points to the advance in the æsthetic taste and requirement of a community, as the establishment within it of houses devoted to the sale of goods comprised under the title of Fashionable Millinery and Fancy Goods, and in the possession of the above house South Paris is to be congratulated as having one of the most complete establishments in this line of trade in this section. This store was established by Miss N. E. Dean in 1884, and has since that date been conducted in an energetic and enterprising manner. The premises utilized for the business, comprise one floor 12x30 feet in dimensions, and contain an elegant assortment of Fashionable Millinery and Fancy Goods of every description. Two experienced assistants are employed and patrons are served in a polite and attentive manner. Miss Dean is a native of Buckfield, Me., and is conversant with every detail of her business, and to her house is due to a large extent, the fostering and education of the tastes of the community as regards the art of select and artistic Millinery, as well as a fastidious taste in the line of Fancy Goods.

Richardson & Libby, dealers in Hardware, Stoves, Furnaces, Ranges, Portable Ovens and Tin Ware, Springs, Axles, Carriage Wheels, also Iron, Steel, Horseshoes, Nails, Bolts, Etc., South Paris. That the United States produces more and better stoves, than any other nation on earth, is only another proof of the ingenuity of our inventors and the skill of our mechanics; and so far are our stoves and furnaces ahead of those manufactured abroad, that the latter could not be sold here at all unless for old iron. A good opportunity to become familiar with the very latest novelties in the stove line, is that afforded by Messrs. Richardson & Libby, for this firm deals very extensively in such goods, and handles only those embodying the latest improvements, carrying a stock complete in every department. Portable Ovens and Tinware are also to be had here at bottom prices, together with Springs, Axles, Carriage Wheels and Carriage Woodwork and Hardware of all descriptions. Iron and Steel, Horseshoes, Nails, Nuts and Bolts are also kept in stock, and both large and small orders can be filled without delay. The firm is made up of Messrs. J. P. Richardson and F. P. Libby, both of whom are connected with the Masons and the Odd Fellows. Mr. Richardson was born in Turner while Mr. Libby is a native of Harrison, and the enterprise they conduct has been in existence about a quarter of a century, it having been started by Mr. S. Richardson in 1864. The premises utilized comprise two floors and a basement, and are 75x45 feet in dimensions. A very valuable and varied assortment of goods is always to be found therein, and customers are assured immediate and courteous attention, there being three efficient assistants employed.

W. B. Royal & Co., Manufacturers of Royal's Dump and Mining Barrows, South Paris. A Wheel-barrow is not an especially attractive or interesting article so far as appearances go, but for all that there are very few vehicles to which the world owes more. Simple as a Barrow is, it combines efficiency and strength to a very high degree, and hundreds of thousands of dollars have been saved by its use, in the construction of railways, the working of mines and many other labors calling for the removal of large amounts of material. It is said that when Wheel-barrows were introduced into Cuba, the negroes insisted upon carrying them, load and all, on their heads, as that was the way they had always borne heavy burdens; but when the use of the wheel was explained to them, they finally saw its advantages. Large shipments of Wheel-barrows have been made from New England to Cuba and to points still further south. Messrs. W. B. Royal & Co., of this town having shipped ten tons at one time, to a South American port. This firm carry on a very thoroughly equipped factory; the log which goes in at one end of the works, coming out at the other a finished barrow. The premises are three stories in height and measure 40x80 feet. Royal's Dump and Mining Barrows are among the best-known in the market, their manufacture having been begun in 1853, by Messrs. W. B. and B. T. Royal. At the death of the latter gentleman, Mr. W. B. Royal's son and son-in-law, were admitted to partnership, and business has since been conducted under the present style. A great many Barrows are produced here annually and a ready market is found for them.

W. A. Porter. Dealer in Fruit, Confectionery, Tobacco and Cigars, South Paris. The Fruit business is rapidly becoming one of our most important industries, and it is well that this should be so, for nothing is healthier than fruit in the way of food, and many people have discovered that fruit is also useful as a medicine. As long as common sense is used no one need fear being hurt by eating ripe fruit of any kind, and the surest way of making sure that you will be furnished with ripe fruit, is to patronize a reputable and well-known establishment, such a one for instance as is conducted by Mr. W. A. Porter, at South Paris, Me. This gentleman was born in South Paris, and succeeded to the business he now conducts in 1887, it having been originally founded by Mr. G. H. Porter. He thoroughly understands the Fruit business, as he had a large and varied experience in it, and is therefore able to furnish his patrons with the very best goods at the very lowest prices. One floor is occupied, of the dimensions of 65x18 feet, and a large stock is carried comprising Foreign and Domestic Fruits of all kinds in their season, together with choice confectionery of the very best make, also Tobacco and Cigars. Mr. Porter has built up a very large trade, for he has always tried to satisfy his customers, so that those who have bought of him once are sure to come again. He employes competent assistants and can assure every caller prompt and polite attention. Mr. Porter is a member of the Free Masons and is well known in this community.

C. W. Bowker & Co., Cloaks, Dress Goods, Corsets, Laces, Hamburgs, Kid Gloves, &c., Housekeeping Goods, South Paris. South Paris business-men have a well-earned reputation of their own for liberality and enterprise, and those located here are not a whit behind their associates in other portions of the State. In fact in the opinion of not a few observers, some of them are just a little ahead of their neighbors as regards the inducements offered, and we may justly place among the leaders in this line, the well-known house of C. W. Bowker & Co. This concern began operations in 1886, so that for two years its efforts to serve the public have been open to inspection and have doubtless been judged on their merits.

The result is, that a large trade has been built up—a trade that is still steadily growing and that apparently is as far from having attained its full development as ever. The nature of the goods handled is such as to make the demand for the same almost infinite, for among the articles in stock may be mentioned Dry and Fancy Goods of all kinds, Cloaks, Dress Goods, Corsets, Laces, Hamburgs, Kid Gloves etc., as well as Housekeeping Goods. Mr. Bowker is a native of Paris, Me., and those who have made trial of the capabilities of his establishment need not be told that the results attained are unsurpassed by any other in the same line of trade in this vicinity.

J. D. Williams, Manufacturer of and Dealer in Harnesses, Saddles, Bridles, Collars, Whips, Robes, Blankets, Brushes, Combs, Harness Trimmings, Fly Nets, Trunks, Bags, &c., South Paris. Any man that owns a good horse, wants a good harness, and in fact we may go even farther and say that every horseowner wants a good harness, whether his horse is a good one or not, for the poorer the animal, the less he can stand being handicapped by being obliged to work in a poor harness. A call at the establishment of Mr. J. D. Williams will demonstrate the fact that a most excellent harness can be bought nowadays for a small sum of money, for that gentleman carries a complete assortment of such goods in stock, and offers them at bottom prices. Mr. Williams is a native of Houlton, Maine. He bought out his present enterprise in 1866, from S. M. Newhall, who had occupied the same shop and was engaged in the same business 27 years. An extensive business is carried on in Harness, Saddles, Bridles, Collars, Whips and Robes; and Blankets, Brushes, Combs, Harness Trimmings, Fly Nets etc., are also largely dealt in, together with Trunks, Bags and Valises. Repairing is given prompt and skillful attention, and jobbing of all kinds can be done at short notice. Mr. Williams is also a dealer in Mowing Machines and Harvesters, and these aids to the farmer may be obtained of him at bottom prices. He only handles such goods as have proved their superiority under the test of practical farm-work and he can therefore guarantee satisfaction to every purchaser.

HISTORICAL SKETCH

—OF—

NORWAY, ME.

THE growth and present prosperous condition of Norway reveal the distinguishing characteristics of a typical and model New England town. Within a little more than a hundred years worthy results have been obtained which merit great admiration. The town was first settled in 1786, though explorations, surveying and clearing had begun during the two last previous years. The first settlers were Joseph and Jonas Stevens, George Lessley, Jeremiah and Amos Hobbs, Nathan Noble and their families. The soil was very alluvial, fish and game plenty, wood abundant, so that the first few years were not marred by want, though they had most of the usual trials and hardships of pioneer life. These first settlers were of the sturdiest, most progressive New England type, and set to work with a fire and perseverance that soon told perceptibly on the wilderness around them. In the first year, 1786, also came Benjamin Herring, Dudley Pike, John and Wm. Parsons who also added force and wisdom to the rough pioneer work. A little later Lemuel Shedd, Jonathan Stickney and Nathaniel Stevens moved in and augmented the number of stout-hearted workers. The first child, Sarah Stevens, daughter of Jonas Stevens, was born October 17, 1787. The former name of the town was Rustfield, by which it was known for sometime after its settlement. A saw and grist mill was set up in 1789, which added greatly to the comfort and progress of the place. Benjamin Witt, a skilled blacksmith, also came and was gladly welcomed during the first few years. The first shoemaker was Peter Buck who moved here from Paris in 1790. From this time on people began to come in with constantly increasing numbers each year until the population in one decade had increased to five hundred in 1797, in which year the town was incorporated under its present name. The reason for the name is not recorded or apparent. By 1800, at the beginning of the century, the population of the town was six hundred, and through the various difficulties of the embargo, etc., the town continued to grow steadily. In 1810, the population had reached one thousand and ten, and to one thousand three hundred and thirty in 1820. Through the intermediate decades of the century its advancement continued, though not without some set-back; but the population had reached one thousand nine hundred and sixty-

HISTORICAL SKETCH OF NORWAY.

three in 1850. The town took deep interest in the struggle of the Rebellion and contributed liberally of its best men and substance. The volunteers from Norway served mostly in the First, Ninth, Eleventh, Twenty-first and Twenty-fourth Maine Infantry Regiments, and fought with a gallantry and devotion most honorable to their native place. The memory of those who fell in the great struggle has been and ever will be most tenderly cherished. After the war, for awhile the recovery from

STREET IN NORWAY, ME.

the financial strain and depression was not rapid. But after 1870, the town began to go forward with its old spirit and success. A shoe-manufactory established here in 1872 gave added impetus to the business interests of the town. About the most important event in the town's history, from a material standpoint, was the opening of the Norway Branch R. R., opened between this town and South Paris in 1879. The valuation of the town, which in 1860 was $450,000, has increased steadily, until now it is over $1,000,000. The annual business of the town is valued at more than $2,000,000. The population at the present time is a little over three thousand. The town debt is very small, only $5,041.07, and the taxes are therefore correspondingly light.

The attractions and excellencies of Norway are too extended to receive adequate treatment in this brief sketch. The business interests of the town are conservative, yet progressive. Being the center of a large growing district of the State, these are continually advancing. The advantages offered to manufacturers for settlement are of the first order. The schools and general culture of the town are at the high standard of which New England is so proud, and receive thorough and appreciative attention. The Norway Public School Building is a fine piece of tasteful architecture. The churches are strong and active; the religous and moral tone of the community is very high and active. All generous and noble works of charity receive merited attention. The sanitary condition of the town is unusually good, and the Water Supply Company is very satisfactory. Considering all these and other facts, it is not surprising that Norway has made a greater gain in population and valuation during the last fifteen years than any other town of the same kind in the State.

LEADING BUSINESS MEN

OF

NORWAY, ME.

Norway Tanning Co., Wax, Kip and Split Leather, Norway. The magnitude of the business carried on by the Norway Tanning Company cannot fail to be gratifying to every public-spirited resident of the town, for this industry is one that had small beginnings, and its pronounced success proves that those who chose Norway as a desirable point at which to establish a Tannery, made no mistake in their calculations. To Mr. J. L. Horne must be given much credit for the development of this enterprise, as he came into possession of it in 1852 and carried it on alone for a quarter of a century, taking his son, Herman L. Horne, into partnership in 1877. Business was conducted under the style of J. L. Horne & Son, until the latter part of 1885, when this company was incorporated. As now constituted its officers are: President, Edwin Wallace; Treasurer, Herman L. Horne. The President is prominently identified with the Tanning industry, being a member of the firm of E. G. & E. Wallace of Rochester, N. H. Mr. J. L. Horne is a heavy stockholder in the company, which maintains a plant capable of turning out 2000 finished hides per week, or 204,000 per annum. When Mr. Horne first took charge of the works, their capacity was hardly one-twentieth what it now is. The specialties of the Tannery are Wax, Kip and Split Leather, most of the products being utilized in the manufacture of brogans. The greater part of the out-put is shipped to the Boston market, where it is in active demand, as its even excellence is much appreciated by shoe-manufacturers. A 200-horse-power engine furnishes the motive power for the works, and a large force of experienced assistants find plenty to do in keeping up with the orders received.

Elm House, W. W. Whitmarsh, Proprietor, Norway. The Elm House is one of Norway's most deserving institutions, for not only is it of old establishment, but is also one of the most liberally and intelligently managed hostelrys in the State. The present proprietor, Captain W. W. Whitmarsh, came into possession of the property in 1866, succeeding Mr. Josiah Carpenter. He is a prominent figure in town affairs and served as Town Clerk from 1878 to 1886. He was Representative to the Legislature in 1884, was elected County Commissioner in 1885, is also Treas. of the Norway Water Co., and is a valued member of the Republican party. Captain Whitmarsh is a native of Norway and was connected with the Norway Light Infantry from 1850 to 1861. This company has the honorable record of being the first in the State to tender its services to the Government at the outbreak of the Rebellion, and as First Sergeant, Mr. Whitmarsh accompanied the command when it left town in April, 1861. He served with distinction in this and other companies and finally received a commission as Captain of Co. G., 29th Maine Volunteers. He saw much active service and officiated as Assistant Provost Marshal in the South during the last part of the war. Captain Whitmarsh has proved himself possessed of no small share of executive ability in peaceful as well as in war-like pursuits, for he has greatly improved the interior arrangements of the Elm House, and has made its name a synonym for hospitality among travelers. The accommodations provided are strictly first-class and the terms are very reasonable. No one who ever stopped any length of time at the Elm House, would consider a notice of that institution complete did it not contain mention of "Tim." Mr. Timothy Smith is that gentleman's whole name, but to his hosts of friends he is only known as "Tim." For thirty-five years has he been connected with the establishment as hostler, and the Elm House without "Tim," would be much like the play of Hamlet with Hamlet left out. Everybody knows him and everybody likes him, for he has the gift of making friends and is always ready to do what he can to make life pleasant.

Bearce & Stearns, Attorneys and Counselors-at-Law, Savings Bank Building, Main Street, Norway (Oxford County). Competent legal advice is of the greatest value to all active business men, for it is oftentimes very important not only to know what to do, but what *not* to do, also. Residents of Norway and vicinity are fortunate in having so reliable a firm to apply to as that of Messrs. Bearce & Stearns, for these gentlemen are exceptionally well-versed in the Law, both theoretically and practically. They became associated in December, 1883, and the union has doubtless been of mutual advantage. A very extensive practice is carried on, for a large proportion of the more important legal business in this section is intrusted to their hands. Mr. H. M. Bearce is a native of Hebron, and received his education in Maine institutions. He entered Waterville College, but during his senior year left that institution to enlist as private in Co. D. of the 23rd Maine. After serving as First Sergeant, he was promoted to the rank of First Lieutenant, and held that position when he received an honorable discharge. Subsequently he rejoined the army as Second Lieutenant of Co. B. of the 32d Maine, and was again promoted to a First Lieutenancy. He took part in the many fierce engagements occurring in the Wilderness and at Spottsylvania, Cold Harbor and Petersburg, and was captured on the last-named field of battle and confined in Columbia, S. C. Finally he was released on parol at the expiration of Sherman's March to the Sea. After receiving a diploma from Waterville College he read law with the Honorable Alvah Black, of Paris Hill, being admitted to the bar in September, 1866. Mr. Bearce does not confine himself entirely to legal business, being actively and extensively engaged in real estate operations, agriculture, stock raising, etc. He is President of the Norway National Bank, of which he has been a Director since its organization. He is also Treasurer of the Norway Savings Bank, and was Post Master of this town for thirteen years, receiving his appointment from General Grant. Mr. Bearce was a State Representative in 1883 and a Senator in 1885. As a member of the Commission for the Revision of the Statutes, he rendered most efficient service, and his labors in that capacity will not soon be forgotten. Mr. Seward S. Stearns was born in Lovell, Maine, and graduated from Bowdoin College in 1879, taking a high rank. After reading Law with Judge Walker, he was admitted to the bar in 1882, and after about two years of practice at Waterford, Maine, he came to this town and formed his present connection. Perhaps the most valuable public service that Mr. Stearns has ever rendered, is that given in connection with the organizing of our Public Library. To him and to Judge Whitman are the many who have profited by that beneficent institution, under great obligations, for these gentlemen spared neither time nor labor in making the library an accomplished fact. Mr. Stearns is President of that institution and may safely be depended upon to make it of the greatest educational value, and to preserve it in its integrity as a library for the people. Mr. Stearns has always been interested in politics, being now a member of the Second District Republican Committee from Oxford County.

G. P. Downing, Commission Merchant, and Dealer in Fruits both Foreign and Domestic, Country Produce, etc., Norway. The fruit trade of this country is assuming enormous proportions, for the public at large are beginning to appreciate the advantages attendant upon a liberal consumption of fruit of good quality and to learn that a dollar spent in this way may save several times its amount in doctor's bills. Among the best known handlers of Foreign and Domestic Fruit in this section must be mentioned the enterprising house of G. P. Downing, for although of quite recent origin, its methods are such as to have already given it a place in the front rank. Operations were begun by S. H. Billings in the early part of 1888 and shortly afterward Mr. G. P. Downing became associated with him. Early in 1889, Mr. Billings retired and it is now conducted by Mr. Downing alone. The premises utilized are located in the basement of the Masonic building and measure 60x38 feet, employment being given to two assistants. Every facility is at hand to carry on the business to the best possible advantage among which may be mentioned a large room devoted to the storage and ripening of bananas, this apartment being constantly kept at a certain temperature. A strictly Wholesale and Commission Business is done and special pains is taken in the handling of Country Produce, etc., returns being promptly made to consigners. Mr. Downing is in a position to quote bottom prices, and dealers would do well to investigate the advantages he offers.

Mrs. F. E. Chase, Dealer in Millinery and Fancy Goods, All Orders Promptly Attended to, 100 Main Street, Norway. The difference between the manner in which some persons push trade and others engaged in the same line of business allow things to drift along, without making an effort to do anything, is one that must have been remarked by all our readers, for it is plainly perceptible, and one does not have to go outside of Norway to find example of it. Take the enterprise conducted by Mrs. F. E. Chase, for instance, whose place of business is located at No. 100 Main Street. This lady began operations in Lincoln in 1864, removing to Waterville in 1875, and from there to Norway in 1877, having had a continuous business experience of twenty-four years. She has established a position for herself among the ladies in her line of trade, and how? Simply by offering reliable and fashionable goods at bottom prices and letting the public know of the fact. Premises measuring 40x20 feet are occupied and a large and varied stock is carried, comprising Millinery and Fancy Goods in all the latest and most fashionable styles. Mrs. Chase announces that her store is the headquarters for low prices on all kinds of goods, and after examining her stock and learning her prices, one cannot help agreeing with her. A specialty is made of Order Work, which is promptly attended to. Four courteous and experienced assistants are employed. The Trimming Department is under the immediate supervision of Miss L. F. Danforth, who has had many years experience in that line, and all careful dressers would do well to examine the stock offered by Mrs. Chase before purchasing Millinery and Fancy Goods elsewhere.

C. B. Cummings & Sons, Manufacturers and Dealers in Heels, Heelings, Inner Soles, Pasted Taps; also Shoe Boxes, Norway. **Chas, S. Cummings,** Dealer in Furniture of all kinds, Rattan, Parlor and Chamber Sets, Easy Chairs, Lounges, Spring Beds, etc., etc., Norway. In compiling a history of this kind, one has frequently reason to regret that the necessity of keeping it within reasonable bounds, renders it impossible to give adequate space to a consideration of some of the more important enterprises, but it is seldom that this is so forcibly brought to mind as in the case of the industries carried on by Messrs. C. B. Cummings & Sons. No man can estimate the benefit these industries are to the community at large, and still less can it be told how much encouragement to industrious young men has been afforded by the widely-known career of Mr. C. B. Cummings. Beginning with nothing but a capacity for hard work and a firm determination to succeed, Mr. Cummings has now reached a position of wealth and influence; and as the way he trod is open to all, no young man of spirit can hear the story of his life without feeling that pluck, brains and energy are sure to be rewarded. He was born in Norway, in 1834, and after living some years in Bethel, returned here when twenty years of age, to make his way in the world. No honest labor was despised by him, and finally, after learning the trade of cabinet making, he set up in business for himself, making the furniture with which he began housekeeping, and manufacturing by hand the orders he received from his neighbors. In 1861 he moved to more commodious quarters, and four years later erected the building now occupied by Mr. Chas. S. Cummings, his son. Subsequently he became interested in the manufacture of clothes-pins, and also in the production of all kinds of Lumber, Boxes, Staves, etc. Heels, Heelings, Inner Soles, Pasted Taps, etc., are also manufactured very extensively at one of his factories, some seventy hands being employed. Much valuable timber land is owned by him, and he is one of the largest real estate proprietors in this section of the State. A well-appointed Grist Mill is one of the numerous useful enterprises with which he is identified, and the Furniture Store under the immediate charge of Mr. Chas. S. Cummings, is known to be one of the best-stocked in the State; the goods being sold at low rates and an immense business being done.

Howe & Ridlon, Dealers in Dry and Fancy Goods, Carpetings, Feathers, Groceries, etc., Norway. In collecting information relating to the leading business men of Norway, it very soon became manifest that Messrs. Howe & Ridlon would have to be included in any account of such, for evidences were found on every side to indicate that these gentlemen were fairly entitled to the honor, and that as regards enterprise and popularity, they occupy a leading position in the trade circles. The enterprise now conducted by them was originally established in 1860, by Mr. E. W. Howe, and in 1883 Mr. C. F. Ridlon was admitted to the business, since which date the firm-name has been Howe & Ridlon. A most extensive and flourishing trade has been built up, and premises comprising two floors of the dimensions each of 18x55 feet are occupied, and Dry and Fancy Goods, Carpetings, Feathers, Groceries, etc., are handled, and whether any or all of these commodities are wanted, this establishment will be found a most desirable place at which to procure the same, as the assortment is large, the quality excellent, the service prompt and the prices low. This is no doubt a strong indorsement, but it has not been made without careful study of, and examination into the subject, and we have no reason to suppose but what those who may favor Messrs. Howe & Ridlon with their patronage will have every reason to cordially subscribe to all that we have stated concerning their establishment and business methods. We know that the goods in stock are sufficiently varied to suit all tastes, and can assure our readers of polite treatment and strictly honorable dealings. Mr. E. W. Howe is a native of Sumner, Maine, and Mr. C. F. Ridlon of Albion, Maine, and both are highly respected in social as well as trade circles, Mr. Howe being a member of the Odd Fellows and Mr. Ridlon of the Masonic Order.

Noyes' Drug Store, Dealer in Drugs, Medicines, Toilet and Fancy Goods, Wall Paper and Window Shades, Physicians' Prescriptions carefully Compounded, Norway. One of the institutions of Norway is Noyes' Drug Store, and it would be well if all institutions, wherever found, were as worthy of liberal support as is the one referred to. It was established in 1861 by Mr. A. O. Noyes and his brother Lorenzo, the latter dying the same year and the business being continued by Mr. A. O. Noyes until his death, in 1878. Mr. Noyes is well-remembered in this vicinity although a full decade has elapsed since his decease, for he stood high in Masonic circles, was a member of the Portland Commandery and was also connected with the Knights Templars and Knights of Pythias. He was born in this town and was one of the original stockholders of the Norway National Bank, of which institution he was also a director. During the six years preceding his death he occupied the position of Town Treasurer, and was agent for the Canadian Express Co., for a long period, the agency being still continued in his name. Since his death, the Drug Store has been carried on by his widow, who was born in Fryeburg, Maine, her maiden name being Anna Chase. Mrs. Noyes has shown exceptional executive ability in the discharge of her present duties, and no higher meed of praise can be given her, than that she has fully maintained the high standard of excellence which her husband established. Employment is given to three competent assistants and the several departments of the business are in a most flourishing condition. One floor and a basement, measuring 32x60 feet, are occupied, and a heavy stock of Drugs and Medicines, Chemicals, Toilet and Fancy Goods is constantly carried. Wall Paper and Window Shades are also offered in great variety at low prices, some beautiful and novel designs being shown. Physicians' Prescriptions are prepared from selected materials, and no trouble is spared to secure absolute accuracy and avoid unreasonable charges.

THE FAMILY MEDICINE.

A SPEEDY CURE FOR

Colds, Croup, Sore Throat, Diptheria, Cuts, Burns, Sprains, Bruises, Neuralgia, Etc.

Mailed to any address on receipt of 30c. Your money refunded if it fails to benefit you when used strictly as directed on inside wrapper, so you take no risk in trying it. Sold by all dealers.

Browns' Instant Relief For Pain, Prepared by the Norway Medicine Co., Norway. Among the many thriving business enterprises carried on in this town, that conducted by the Norway Medicine Company deserves special mention, for despite the difficulty of successfully introducing a new proprietary remedy into a well-filled market, the demand for that prepared by the concern mentioned has already reached enormous proportions, although operations were only begun in August, 1887. This state of affairs is chiefly due to two things—first, the unusual merit of the article itself, and second, the intelligence and liberality shown in placing it before the public. Brown's Instant Relief for Pain is most happily named, for it does indeed afford instant relief, when used in accordance with the directions, and so thoroughly convinced are its proprietors of its infallibility, that they authorize dealers to refund the purchase money to those deriving no benefit from its use, provided the instructions given on the inside wrapper are conscientiously followed. As a Family Medicine we believe it to have no equal, for not only is it capable of curing most of the more common ailments in a very short time, if taken in season, but it has a decided advantage over the large majority of so-called "Pain-killers" insomuch as it is pleasant to the taste and hence will be readily taken by all children, even the most delicate. Every physician will agree that such maladies as Croup and Diptheria yield readily to prompt treatment but soon become dangerous if neglected. For this reason, if no other, every family should be supplied with Brown's Instant Relief, for it is a sure cure for the diseases mentioned and its timely use will save untold trouble and pa

It is also a specific for Coughs, Colds, Sore Throat, Chilblains, Sprains and Bruises, and its action on Fresh Cuts, Scalds and Burns, is inexpressibly soothing and healing. Rheumatism, Neuralgia and Palpitation soon give way to its beneficient influence, and its effect on the troubles peculiar to the gentler sex is simply magical, as many ladies have reason to know. Sufferers from that most exasperating and wearing of all common pains—Toothache, should waste no time in procuring a bottle of Brown's Instant Relief, for it is far superior to the various "Toothache Drops," which generally burn the inside of the mouth until eating is almost impossible, and its soothing effect is much more immediate and permanent. Dyspepsia, being a chronic complaint and the result of a morbid condition of the stomach, cannot be cured in a day by any means whatever; but by the persistent use of Brown's Instant Relief and some attention to diet, it can eventually be conquered, and during the progress of the treatment its annoying effects can be greatly mitigated. This remedy is of peculiar value to Farmers from the fact of its being equally good for man or beast. It has saved the life of many a valuable animal, and in this connection we would call attention to the experience of Mr. C. E. Rines, owner of the Norway bakery. His horse had the "Pink Eye" so badly as to refuse all food and be hardly capable of motion. One dose of Brown's Instant Relief enabled him to eat, and two more doses completely cured him. Is it surprising that Mr. Rines heartily recommends it as the most wonderful medicine he ever used? Mr. A. F. Andrews, from the nature of his business, should be well-posted concerning the value of medicines intended for stable use. Read what he says in relation to Brown's Instant Relief:—

NORWAY, ME., Nov. 30, '87.

Last night one of our valuable horses was taken with a severe chill and broke out in a cold sweat. We gave him Brown's Instant Relief according to directions and he immediately began to improve. We have used it many times for our horses and always with the same satisfactory results. We consider it to be a most valuable medicine.

A. F. ANDREWS.

One such letter from a practical man is worth pages of argument in establishing the value of a remedy, and many equally flattering testimonials could be given did space permit. Room must be made at least for the following communication from a widely-known gentleman who is accustomed to weigh his words well and to write precisely what he means:—

NORWAY. ME., Sept. 4, '87.

I have used Brown's Instant Relief and found it to be the best thing I have ever used for Cramp, Colic and Indigestion. I can cheerfully recommend it to all.

F. W. SANBORN,
Editor Oxford County Advertiser.

In closing, a few words may be said regarding the origin of this great remedy: Dr. G. W. Brown was called upon several years ago to treat a severe case of Gastric fever attended with paroxysms of pain. After exhausting the list of the usual remedies without result, the doctor prepared a combination of certain vegetable remedial agents, the external application of which immediately relieved the pain and stopped the vomiting. The fever abated and the patient soon recovered. Shortly after, a bad case of Colic was cured by internal use of the same remedy and, to make a long story short, after the doctor had used it in his practice for some three years, he found himself no longer able to properly supply the constantly increasing demand and so in order to give the public the full benefit of its use, the Norway Medicine Company was formed, with A. L. F. Pike as business manager. Since Brown's Instant Relief was placed in Norway Drug Stores in September, 1887, its sale has surpassed that of all other medicines combined, and that it is equally appreciated in a larger community, the following testimony from a representative Portland house will demonstrate:—

PORTLAND, ME., March 6, '88.

The sale of Brown's Instant Relief has much exceeded our expectations, and it has given universal satisfaction wherever introduced. We believe it is destined to have a large sale."
JOHN W. PERKINS & Co.

"The proof of the pudding is the eating," and it is obvious that no article could have won such phenomenal popularity in so short a time, if it did not accomplish all that is claimed for it.

Elm House Billiard Hall, Freeland Young, Proprietor, Norway. There are certain things that about every man who has not tried them, thinks he can do better than anybody else, and among these may be mentioned, driving a horse, keeping a hotel and managing a Billiard Hall. In point of fact, these things are, by no means, so easy to do as they seem to be, and in the last-named occupation, especially, it will be found by those who engage in it, that it is very hard to suit everybody, and that most of those who try to do so, generally end up by suiting nobody. However, the right man can achieve success in this the same as in any other business, and there can be no better proof of this assertion needed than that afforded by the popularity gained by the enterprise under the control of Mr. Freeland Young since it was started, in 1873. This gentleman occupies premises connected with the Elm Hotel, which are furnished with Billiard and Pool Tables. Mr. Young is a native of Paris, Maine, and has hosts of friends throughout this vicinity. He neglects no opportunity to improve the conveniences and facilities he has to offer his customers, and under his liberal management a very large trade has been built up. The tables, etc., are maintained in first-class condition, and all the requisits of a modern high-grade Billiard Hall are at hand. He was a member of Co. F., 23d Maine Regiment, and subsequently was a member of the 7th Maine Battery at the close of the war. For the past thirteen years he has been proprietor of the Elm House Billiard Hall. Mr. Young is a natural musician, has been an active member of musical organizations since 1866, and at the present time is the leader of Young's Orchestra and a member of the Norway Brass Band. Mr. Young gives lessons on several wind and stringed instruments, and is prominently connected with the Masonic Order.

LEADING BUSINESS MEN OF NORWAY.

C. N. Tubbs & Co., Dealers in Dry and Fancy Goods, Groceries, Flour, Salt, Crockery, Glass Ware, Paints, Oils and Varnishes; also Country produce, Norway. While calling attention to such an establishment as is carried on by Messrs. C. N. Tubbs & Co., it is hard to determine where to begin to mention the articles dealt in. Were these simply Dry Goods or Groceries or Glass Ware, it would be an easy matter to devote one's whole attention to the attractions offered, but where all these commodities are handled, together with many others of equal importance, there is no use in attempting to give a complete idea of the inducements extended in any one department. The best advice we can give, then, is "come and see for yourself." Messrs. C. N. Tubbs & Co. have a spacious store, measuring 85x28 feet, and although their stock is large, still there is chance enough for the public to call and examine what the firm have to offer in the way of standard goods at fair prices. Messrs. C. N. and James Tubbs began operations in 1874, and their trade has since steadily grown until it has reached its present large proportions. Mr. C. N. Tubbs is a native of this town and is connected with the Odd Fellows. The Dry and Fancy Goods carried in stock are well worthy the inspection of any lady, for some beautiful and novel effects are shown, and the assortment is certainly varied enough to suit all tastes and purses. Groceries of standard purity are supplied in quantities to suit, and especial attention is called to the Teas, Coffees and Spices handled, as the goods are warranted to be of uniformly superior quality. Crockery and Glass Ware are to be had at low prices, and a full supply of Paints, Oils and Varnishes are always on hand to choose from.

F. Q. Elliott, Dealer in Fine Ready-Made Clothing, Gent's Furnishings, Hats, Caps, etc., Opposite Elm House, Norway. There is really no excuse for any man presenting a shabby appearance nowadays, for not only can a neat and durable Suit of Clothes be purchased for a small sum of money, but all of the other articles going to make up a complete outfit are sold at extremely reasonable rates. It is necessary, of course, to use some discrimination in making such purchases, as all dealers are, by no means, equally low in their prices; but if a call be made on Mr. F. Q. Elliott at his store opposite the Elm House, Norway, the caller can feel sure that all he buys will be sold at prices as low as the lowest. Mr. Elliott's goods are perfectly reliable, and are, in fact, fully guaranteed to prove as represented, so that no fears need be entertained that anything bought of him will not prove satisfactory. The undertaking of which he is now the proprietor, was founded in 1888, this being the second time he has carried on business in Norway (having formerly carried on the same line of trade here for six years), and by his enterprise and liberal business methods, his trade is steadily increasing. Mr. Elliott is a native of Rumford, Maine, and a member of the Odd Fellows. He occupies premises in the Hathaway Block of the dimensions of 20x50 feet. Ready-Made Clothing, Hats, Caps and Gent's Furnishings in general, are handled very largely, and the latest fashionable novelties in these goods are early at hand and quoted at bottom prices. The services of courteous and well-informed assistants are employed, and customers are assured polite treatment and honorable dealings.

C. S. Tucker, Manufacturer and Dealer in Harnesses, Trunks and Valises, Carriage Robes and Mats, Whips, Curry-Combs and Brushes, Horse Blankets and Nets, Norway. Those who realize the importance of using Harnesses that are thoroughly well made in every respect, need no persuasion to induce them to buy goods of this kind at the establishment conducted by Cyrus S. Tucker, for if there is one thing more generally known than another in connection with this establishment, it is that every article sold there is sure to prove exactly as represented. For many years the name of Tucker has been identified with Norway's industrial interests, the grandfather of the present proprietor of the enterprise to which we have reference, having founded the undertaking in 1801. Mr. Cyrus Tucker was born in Norway and holds several positions of honor and responsibility in this town. He has been clerk of the Norway Village Corporation since 1867, and was Town Treasurer from 1880 to 1887. For more than ten years he has been connected with the Parish Committee of the First Universalist Church and he was the first Adjutant of Harry Rust Post, No. 54, G. A. R., he having served in the army throughout the Rebellion. He is Treasurer of all the Masonic bodies in town and is President of the Norway Savings Bank. Mr. Tucker not only deals in Harnesses, but also in Trunks, Valises, Carriage Robes and Mats, Whips, Curry-Combs and Brushes, Horse Blankets, Nets. and in short, all kinds of Horse Furnishings. Notwithstanding the uniform excellence of the articles handled by him, his prices are low as the lowest, for his facilities are unsurpassed, and the large business done makes a small margin of profit remunerative. Customers are given immediate and careful attention, and orders of all kinds are promptly and accurately filled.

Freeland Howe, Insurance Agent. Oxford County Insurance Agency; Established August, 1865, Norway. $275,000,000 is a good deal of money, so much, in fact, that no man alive can truly realize what an enormous sum it is. Yet vast as this amount of wealth is, it falls considerably short of the united assets of the Insurance Companies represented by Mr. Freeland Howe, at 102 Main Street. A single one of these corporations (the Mutual Life of New York) has $118,000,000 of assets, and there is not a company on his list but what may be as implicitly depended upon to pay its losses as the United States Government to redeem its bonds. During all of Mr. Howe's career in the Insurance Business (a career extending over a quarter of a century), he has proceeded on the same principle—that of affording his clients as absolute security as the world had to offer. He held the first Agency ever established by the famous Travelers' Insurance Company in this State, and has done much to bring the moral, "Insure in the Travelers'," home to the minds of those with whom he had to deal. Mr. Howe is a native of Sumner, Maine, and is a prominent member of the Free Masons. He is most certainly in a position to offer the most liberal inducements in the line of Fire, Life and Accident Insurance, and is, at all times, ready to give any information in his power to those who seek more light on the subject. We give a list of the companies represented by Mr. Howe, and repeat that no one can offer more favorable terms than he. Ætna, Hartford, Phœnix, Connecticut, Travelers' Life and Accident, of Hartford; New York Life Insurance Co., Niagara Insurance Co., Home Insurance Co., of New York; Insurance Co. of North America of Penn.; Union Mutual Life, of Portland; Mutual Life, of New York; Peoples' Insurance Company, of Manchester, N. H. Foreign Companies—Liverpool, London and Globe; City of London; Northern, of Aberdeen; Queen, of Liverpool.

G. M. Packard, Norway's Leading Millinery and Fancy Goods House, 113 Main Street, Norway. In singling out the business enterprises worthy of mention in a commercial history of this locality, no surer way can be found of arriving at a correct idea as to the comparative importance of any undertaking than that of consulting those who would naturally be called upon to support it. For example, who are more apt to give an intelligent judgment regarding the advantages offered by an establishment devoted to the sale of Millinery and Fancy Goods than the ladies on whom it depends for patronage? And if their verdict be accepted as a final one, then precedence must be given to the enterprise now conducted by G. M. Packard. This establishment was founded in 1885, by Mrs. W. Moore, who was succeeded in 1887 by the present proprietress. This lady has repeatedly given ample proof that she is sufficiently energetic and enterprising to afford her customers choice from the latest productions of the centers of fashion, both in the line of Millinery, Fancy Goods, Paper Patterns, and Ladies' Furnishing Goods She occupies an attractive store at No. 113 Main Street, where all visitors are courteously served by three efficient assistants. An inspection of the stock carried will disclose the fact that it is not only large but varied, also, while inquiry will show that the prices will bear the severest comparison with those of other houses in this line of trade. Miss Packard's taste is too well-known and appreciated to call for extended mention, and we will simply assure our readers that she is a mistress of the art of combining trimmings and colors, and is ever ready to give her patrons the benefit of her skill and experience.

Messrs. O'Connor & Owen, Manufacturers and Dealers in Marble and Granite Memorial Work, Monuments, Headstones, Tablets, Curbing, Buttresses, Steps, Building Work, etc., etc., done at Short Notice and at Reasonable Prices. Rough and Hammered Granite at Quarry, or delivered at depot. Designs furnished and estimates given. Shop Opposite Pine Grove Cemetery. P. O. Box 265, Norway. The monumental work produced in this country to-day, is far superior to that of a quarter of a century ago, for not only has the taste of the public been educated of late years, but the facilities for the production of first-class work have also been greatly improved. The residents of Norway and vicinity may well congratulate themselves on the opportunity they have to procure Monuments, Headstones, etc., of the very highest type, near at hand, for the Marble and Granite Memorial Work produced by Messrs. O'Connor & Owen at their shop, opposite the Pine Grove Cemetery, as admitted by competent judges to be fully equal to the best. Indeed this firm should be capable of meeting all honorable competition in this line of work, for they have had a varied and extensive experience in it, Mr. O'Connor having been employed by the United States Government for seven years, during which time he was engaged in Public Building work exclusively, on Post Office and Custom Houses in St. Louis and Cinnati, also in the War and Navy Department. He is a native of Portland, and begun business for himself in South Paris in 1885. Mr. E. S. Owen became associated with Mr. O'Connor in 1888. He has had twenty-four years experience at the business. Mr. Owen has recently returned from the Pacific coast where he has been engaged in business one and one-half years. He is a Maine man by birth and is well and favorably known in this section of the State. He is a member of the Odd Fellows, also of the order of Red Men. This firm employs two skilled assistants and is prepared to fill all orders at short notice. Their prices being placed as low as can be named on work of equal excellence. Designs will be furnished and estimates given on application, and communications addressed to P. O. Box 265, will receive early and careful attention. Building work is also carried on quite extensively and Buttresses, Steps, Curbing, etc., are made in any desired style. Rough and Hammered Granite may be bought here at the lowest market rates, either at the quarry or delivered at at the depot, as may be preferred.

LEADING BUSINESS MEN OF NORWAY.

Kenney & Swett, Dealers in Fine Boots, Shoes and Rubbers, Trunks and Valises. Hawkins Boot a Specialty. Norway. The importance of buying good-fitting Boots and Shoes can hardly be overestimated, for an ill-shaped article of foot-wear is not only uncouth in appearance but is most uncomfortable as well, and in not a few cases is positively dangerous to the general health. Especially is this the case where growing children are concerned, and parents cannot be too careful, when purchasing foot-wear, to see that it is neither too large nor too small and that the boot or shoe is properly shaped in every portion. The success which has attended the business venture of Messrs. Kenney & Swett, is largely due to their apreciation of the points we have mentioned and their intelligent efforts to handle only such goods as experience has shown to be both sightly and comfortable. Operations were begun in 1887, and the progress of the firm has been upward and onward ever since. Mr. J. A. Kenney is a native of Pownal, Maine, while Mr. E. N. Swett was born in South Paris. The former gentleman is a member of the Free Masons, Royal Arch Chapter, and is also connected with the Knights of Pythias. A store measuring 60x30 feet is occupied, and the stock carried comprises a full line of Fine Boots, Shoes and Rubbers, a specialty being made of the "Hawkin's Boot," and those who have tested that celebrated article of foot-wear need not be told that it is one of the most skillfully designed and honestly made boots in the market. Ladies, gentlemen, youths, boys and girls—all will find goods especially suited to their needs at this establishment, and the prices, like the goods, are just right in every particular.

S. B. & Z. S. Prince, Dry and Fancy Goods, Norway. The delight which the fair sex take in "shopping," has always been a a mystery to masculine comprehension, but still, if all stores were carried on as is that conducted by S. B. & Z. S. Prince, the problem would be comparatively easy to solve. At the establishment to which we have reference, every provision is made for the convenience of customers. The store is of the dimensions of 50x23 feet, and the heavy stock carried is always most attractively displayed. The assortment of Dry and Fancy Goods on hand is both varied and complete, and were we to attempt to even catalogue the many articles dealt in, our space would be exhausted before we had half completed the list. In a general way, however, we may give some idea of the attractions offered by stating that not only is there at all times a full selection of the many staple articles coming under the head of Dry and Fancy Goods, but that the latest fashionable novelties in these lines are also surely to be found at this popular store. Although a large business is done, no delay is experienced in waiting on customers, for the system in force is very effective, and the assistants are active as well as courteous. S. B. & Z. S. Prince have the reputation of selling at bottom prices, and we believe that no discriminating buyer can do business with them without cordially agreeing that this reputation is fully deserved. Strictly one price.

O. M. Cummings, Livery and Feed Stable; Passengers Conveyed to Adjoining Towns at Reasonable Rates; Stable on Danforth Street, Norway. The difference between an enterprising community and one that is of opposite tendencies, is chiefly observable in the manner in which opportunities are seen and taken advantage of in the former and neglected in the latter. We believe that Norway has never been seriously accused of lack of enterprise; but if it has, we fail to see on what the accusation was based. Certainly the Merchants, Manufacturers, etc., here are enterprising enough, and another instance of intelligent enterprise is that afforded by the Livery and Feed Stable maintained by Mr. O. M. Cummings. This gentleman is a native of Norway and a member of the Odd Fellows, being very well-known about town. His Stable is located on Danforth Street, and is thoroughly equipped with Single and Double Teams for general Livery purposes. He is also owner of the barge "Gypsy Queen," with a seating capacity for twenty persons, which he furnishes for excursion parties at the most reasonable rates. He is also contractor for carrying the U. S. mails between South Paris and Norway. Mr. Cummings became identified with his present enterprise in 1870, and has carried it on in a manner that has won for him the cordial approbation of the many people benefitted by it. The vehicles are kept in fine condition, and are easy-riding, while the Horses are strong and speedy, and very skillfully driven. Mr. Cummings is very reasonable in his charges, and furnishes a most enjoyable excursion for a small sum.

August Norway, Crown Laundry, Norway. When one comes to consider the immense number of pieces that have to be handled in a public Laundry, and the close resemblence that one piece has to another, it is difficult to see how mistakes are so successfully avoided as is the case with the great majority of such establishments. Of course each piece is marked, or is supposed to be, but even then it would seem as if things could not help getting mixed much more frequently than they really do. Eternal vigilence is the price of success in the Laundry Business, and a prominent example of what can be done by its exercise, is that afforded by the enterprise carried on by Mr. August Norway, and popularly known as the Crown Laundry. Business is done here under a very perfect system, and it is but the simple truth to say that annoying and delaying errors are few and far between. Mr. Norway, who is a native of Sweden, began operations in this country in 1888, and his success in building up a desirable patronage has been marked, although not more so than the earnestness of his efforts deserve. The guiding rule of the establishment is "satisfaction to all," as may be seen from the fact that the business is rapidly increasing. Three rooms are occupied, and every facility is at hand for the carrying on of operations to excellent advantage. Hand machine *only* being used. Employment is given to competent assistants, and work will be done at short notice and delivered promptly when promised.

Gilbert & Foss, Dealers in Groceries, Flour Meats and Provisions, Norway. Although there are doubtless many people who believe that no especial degree of ability is required to carry on a retail grocery store successfully, as a matter of fact it would be difficult to find a branch of trade which calls for more careful and skillful management. Of course there are some men in the business who let their stores run themselves, but the condition of their trade is not such as would encourage any good business man to adopt similar methods. A fine example of what may be done in the grocery line by industry and intelligence, is that afforded by the establishment carried on by Messrs. Gilbert & Foss, in this town. These gentlemen founded their present undertaking in 1886, and already the amount of their trade gives significant indications of what may be expected in the future. Mr. Lewis I. Gilbert is a native of Leeds, Maine, and Mr. Walter E. Foss of Wayne, in the same State. Both are members of the Ancient Order of United Workmen, and Mr. Gilbert is also connected with the Odd Fellows. Groceries, Flour, Meats and Provisions, are very extensively handled, and Confectionery, Tobacco and Cigars are also dealt in largely. It will thus be seen that the firm is prepared to supply housekeepers with everything needed in the food line, and the number of families dealing almost exclusively with this house shows how the inducements offered are appreciated. Prompt attention is given to all and the prices are as low as the goods are reliable.

W. C. Leavitt, Manufacturer and Dealer in Tin Ware and Plumbing Materials, Wholesale and Retail, Norway. It would be hard to find any article for domestic use of more value than Tin Ware, for there is not a housekeeper that would know how to get along if she were suddenly deprived of the many utensils made of this material. That there is a great difference in Tin Ware, everyone of any practical experience well knows, and there is nothing surer than that in the purchase of this, as of many other commodities, it is the most economical to get the best. For the best is the cheapest every time, and that some of the inferior Tin Ware on the market is positively dangerous to the health is a well-established fact. In calling attention to the Tin Ware manufactured and sold by Mr. W. C. Leavitt, we take pleasure in assuring our readers that it is thoroughly well made of selected stock. Indeed this is so generally understood hereabouts, that Mr. Leavitt does a very large business in this line alone, selling both at Wholesale and Retail and putting his prices as low as circumstances will permit. He was born in California and opened his present establishment in 1885. Plumbing materials are also manufactured and dealt in very extensively, and a fine and varied stock of kitchen furnishing goods is always kept on hand, all the useful novelties being included in it, and extra inducements being offered to all who want a good article at a low price.

C. C. Tebbetts, Hotel and Boarding House, Norway. The requirements of a good Hotel or of a first-class Boarding House, are comfortable accommodations and palatable food, and we are confident that it only needs a trial of the advantages offered by Mr. C. C. Tebbetts to demonstrate to anybody's satisfaction that this gentleman knows how to cater to the public. He is a native of Lovell, Maine, and is a member of the Odd Fellows, inaugurating his present enterprise in 1882. The premises made use of comprise three floors, some twenty-five rooms being available. There are many Hotels where more style can be found than at Mr. Tebbetts', but few men care a great deal for style, the average individual being much more fond of comfort. Well, comfort is to be had here if it is anywhere, and such of our readers as may wish a homelike place at which to stop during their stay in Norway, can do no better than to put up at Mr. Tebbetts'. The rooms are well-kept and conveniently furnished, and the table is supplied with an abundance of well-cooked food. Meals may be had at any reasonable hour, and the service will be found prompt as well as neat and attractive. Mr. Tebbetts desires to give no fair-minded person a chance to complain of his charges, and when his terms and accommodations are compared with those noticed elsewhere, they need not fear the result.

N. A. Trafton, Dealer in Cattle, Sheep and Lumber, Norway. Few men are better-known in this section of the state in connection with the purchase of Cattle and Sheep, for the market, than is Mr. N. A. Trafton, for this gentleman has given his attention to the branch of trade mentioned for a full score of years, having begun operations in Harrison in 1868. Mr. Trafton was born in Harrison and served on the board of selectmen in that town for several terms. He is connected with both the Free Masons and the Odd Fellows, and is as well-known socially as he is in a business way. Business was begun by him in Norway about five years ago, and he is now heavily interested in the Lumber trade as well as in the handling of Cattle and Sheep, furnishing the Pulp Company at Cumberland Mills with about 5,000 cords of wood per annum. Much of the live stock bought by him is shipped to Brighton, Mass., and his operations are a decided benefit to the community, as they are the means of putting a large amount of money in circulation just where it is needed—among farmers and stock growers. Mr. Trafton has not attained his present position without a good deal of hard and intelligent work, and it is gratifying to note the success of a man who has always done business on the principle that "honesty is the best policy," and whose word is known to be as good as his bond.

Partridge & Danforth, Millers; Dealers in Flour, Corn, Meal, Oats, Shorts, Graham, Choice Groceries, Dry Goods, Crockery, Hard Ware, Paints, Oils, etc. Store at Norway Lake, Mill at Norway. The Grist Mill carried on by Messrs. Partridge & Danforth in this town, enjoys a very large patronage, and the general store conducted by the same firm at Norway Lake, also stands deservedly high in the favor of the public. Messrs J. L. Partridge and F. A. Danforth are both natives of this town, and their business was inaugurated in 1884. They are both personally very generally known throughout this vicinity. Flour, Corn, Meal, Oats, Shorts and Graham are dealt in very extensively, for the firm's prices are always in accordance with the lowest market rates, and the goods they handle are of standard excellence. Large or small orders can be filled without delay, as the facilities at hand assure prompt and accurate delivery. At Norway Lake a fine stock of Choice Groceries, Dry Goods, Crockery, Hard Ware, Paints, Oils, etc., is always to be found, for the firm are constantly receiving new goods and aim to supply their customers with the latest novelties the market affords, as well as with all the staple articles usually found in a first-class general store. The groceries offered have been carefully selected for family use, and will prove perfectly satisfactory to the most fastidious. A good line of Domestic Dry Goods is carried.

C. L. Hathaway, Dealer in Lumber of all Kinds; also Dimension Lumber, Doors, Sash, Blinds and all Building Material; Office and Yard near Depot, Norway. Building operations have been much simplified of late years by the employment of machinery to do much of the work that was formerly done by hand, and the result is that a house can be constructed much more rapidly and cheaply now than ever before. One of the most important depots for Building Materials of all descriptions to be found in this State, is that conducted by Mr. C. L. Hathaway. This gentleman is a native of Norway, and became identified with his present business enterprise in 1877. He is very prominent in Masonic circles, having taken the 32d degree, and is also connected with the Odd Fellows, the Knights of Pythias and the Grand Army of the Republic. The premises utilized by him cover some three-quarters of an acre, and afford ample space for the storage of a very heavy and varied stock of Lumber of all kinds and Building Material in general. Doors, Sash and Blinds are supplied in any desired quantity at short notice, and orders for Dimension Lumber will be promptly and accurately filled, at the lowest market rates. In fact, Mr. Hathaway's facilities for the handling of the commodities in which he deals are so complete, and his relations with producers are so favorable that he is well-prepared to meet all competition and to supply perfectly reliable material as low as the same can be had anywhere.

J. C. Bennett & Co., Dealers in Meats, Provisions and Groceries, Norway, Me. The average American is a great meat-eater, and as the average American is at least the equal both mentally and physically of the average person of any nationality, it is hardly credible that the eating of meat can have the dire effects it is alleged to have, by the vegetarians. To be sure, meat to be healthful must come from sound animals and be neither too fresh nor too old, but it is easy to get meat of this kind if you visit the right place, and none better can be found than that carried on by Messrs. J. C. Bennett & Co., of Norway, Maine. This concern makes a specialty of the retailing of Meats, Groceries and Provisions of all kinds, and is prepared to furnish anything required in these lines of goods. Every care is taken to see that the public is supplied with strictly reliable articles, and as the prices are as low as they are in certain establishments where no such precautions are taken, it is not surprising that this store is a great favorite among discriminating buyers, and is patronized accordingly. Orders are filled promptly as well as carefully, and those who want the best food at low prices, should visit this establishment. The individual members of the firm are Messrs. J. C. and A. T. Bennett, both natives of Maine, and well known throughout this community, having been established in business here since 1871. Mr. A. T. Bennett is a member of the Odd Fellows, and both gentleman are highly respected in social as well as business circles.

HISTORICAL SKETCH.

—OF—

WINTHROP.

THE earliest name of the present town of Winthrop was "Pond Town." It was included in the "Plymouth Grant," or "Kennebec Purchase" of land in the District of Maine. Its original size was about five miles by eight. The first white known to have visited this spot was a hunter named Scott, who, about the middle of the eighteenth century, built a hut here and spent several years trapping and fishing in this vicinity. The first permanent settler was named Timothy Foster. He bought Scott's hut about 1764, but was troubled by creditors whom he seems to have sought to avoid by coming hither. They followed him up, sued him and succeeded for a time in imprisoning him, though as the law for imprisonment for debt was very severe at that time, it is probable that he was more unfortunate than guilty. Among the families which now began to come and build up the pioneer town, the most prominent were the Needhams, Wyrians, Halls, Waughs, Blunts, Howes, Floyds, Blys, Snows, Boyntons, Hopkins and Chandlers. These were all characterized by the energy and perseverance which mark the true pioneers, and under their sturdy efforts the foundations of the town began to be firmly set.

The immediate region was rather desolate in its character and appearance and was surrounded by large deserted tracts, consequently the early settlers had a very hard time and were compelled to exert every energy to maintain their position. But by burning large tracts of the timber land and thus forming new and rich soil, they succeeded in obtaining sufficient necessaries of life at home for a comfortable living. The town now began to grow rapidly, and by 1777 had become large enough to inaugurate measures for the establishment of a church, and with this view a lot was set apart for the minister. From this early period the town has always enjoyed the fame of being one of the most beautiful spots in the State. "Pond Town" was incorporated by the Legislature of Massachusetts in 1771, and at that time its name was changed to Winthrop, in honor of the first great governor of the Bay State. On the same day that it was incorporated, Hallowell, Vassalborough and Winslow also received that honor. The first town meeting in Winthrop was held May 6, 1771, at

Bishop's Inn. The first selectmen were: John Chandler, Timothy and Ichabod Howe, Robert Waugh and Jonathan Whiting, the latter also being town clerk and town treasurer. Although Winthrop was a very young town it contributed generously to the expenses of the Revolutionary War. In 1778 £30 were subscribed; in 1779, $260; in 1780, £3,000, and in 1781, 2,850 pounds of beef were forwarded to the army. The town also had a number of its citizens in the Continental Army. Great enthusiasm for the cause of the colonies was displayed throughout the war. In 1775, at the announcement of war, a military organization was formed, of which Ichabod Howard was chosen captain. Thirteen pounds were appropriated at this time for powder and lead. Nathaniel Fairbanks and eighteen others went to Cambridge and joined the Continental Army after the battle of Lexington.

In 1771, a temporary preacher had inaugurated the first religious services in the town, and in 1775 a church was organized, but was without a pastor for several years. The first settled pastor, Rev. David Jewett, came in 1788, but he left after a short settlement, and for many years great difficulty was experienced in obtaining a regular minister. The Methodists of the town first met together in 1794, and a church was first organized in 1825. The Baptists organized in 1792.

After the Revolution, progress was rapid up to the first decade of the present century. The town was greatly in favor, during the discussions which arose in 1785, of having York, Cumberland and Lincoln Counties set off from Massachusetts, as a separate State, and this feeling continued up to 1820, when Maine was finally set off. The town had grown sufficiently to be divided in 1791, the northern section being set off and incorporated as "Readfield." Among the early distinguished citizens of Winthrop were Capt. Ichabod Harvard, Jonathan Whiting, Justice of Peace and Representative in State Legislature in 1788, Col. Nathaniel Fairbanks and Lieut. Col. Simon Page.

The first inn in Winthrop was opened by Squire Bishop in 1767. Among other early store-keepers were Mr. John Cole, Maj. Elijah Wood, Capt. Barney Haskell, Mr. Joseph Tinkham, Mr. Samuel Holt. The first school in the town was taught by Mr. Benjamin Brainard, there being twelve scholars. This number increased every year until in 1822 the yearly appropriations for the maintenance of the schools was $650. The schools of Winthrop have long been marked by the most advanced methods and fine facilities, the greatest attention being given to this extremely important part of the town life. The culture of the town citizens has consequently been at the highest standard, so characteristic of the towns of New England. Among its prominent citizens have been and are many college graduates and professional men. The valuation of the town has steadily increased during this century. In 1820, it was $111,462.41; in 1830, $244,532; 1840, $459,380; 1854, $528,905. At the present time the valuation is about 1,000,000 and the population 2,200. In 1840, a survey of the town showed that it contained 16,800 acres of land, 8,342 acres of water, 318 acres of road; total, 25,540 square acres.

Winthrop has always been noted for its benevolent and philanthropic spirit, its devotion to every good work and interest in every new movement. In 1815, was established the "Winthrop Society for the Promotion of Good Morals." In 1816, a movement was inaugurated aiming at the crushing out of intemperance, which was one of the early influences which, united with others, succeeded after many years in establishing the Prohibitory Law of the State. In the year 1833, the anti-slavery spirit began to take definite form here and a society was formed to aid in the work for the abolition of slavery. From this time forward the spirit of freedom grew in force, strengthened by the various aggressions of the slave power during the century, and at the outbreak of the war in 1861, it broke forth in an enthusiastic support of the government. Men and money were devoted without stint throughout the war, and the most unflinching courage and patriotism displayed. Most of the soldiers who enlisted from Winthrop were enrolled in the 1st, 3rd, 9th, 11th, 13th, 14th, 21st, 24th, 28th and 29th Maine Volunteer Regiments.

LEADING BUSINESS MEN
OF
WINTHROP, ME.

Levi Jones & Co., Retail Dealers in Choice Groceries, Flour, Salt, Confectionery and Canned Goods, Tea, Coffee and Spices, Winthrop. Among the business enterprises of recent establishment deserving of more than passing mention, is that conducted by Messrs. Levi Jones & Co., on Main Street. This undertaking was begun in 1880, and has from the first been managed with marked liberality, and has consequently attained a popularity which many of its older competitors have failed to secure. Messrs. Levi Jones & Co., occupy three floors each measuring 30x60 feet, and waste none of the space under their control, for they carry an exceptionally varied, extensive and desirable stock of Choice Groceries, and strive to keep it so complete in every department that all orders can be filled without delay and with first-class goods. The line of Teas, Coffees and Spices carried is a very choice one, and we especially ask those who are judges of genuine excellence in these commodities to make a careful examination of what Messrs. Jones & Co., have to offer. Their prices are by no means higher than the average but, on the contrary, will be found to be as low as the lowest, quality considered. Flour, Salt, Confectionery, Canned Goods, and all the staple articles handled by this firm are offered at bottom rates, and those who give this house a trial order are sure to come again. Four capable and reliable assistants are constantly employed thus insuring courteous attention to all customers, and the prompt delivery of all orders, and an extensive wholesale and retail trade is transacted. The individual members of this firm are Mr. Levi Jones a native of Temple, Maine, and Mr. L. E. Jones of Winthrop, Maine. Both these gentlemen are thoroughly conversant with all the details of their business

Winthrop National Bank, Main Street, Winthrop. That a well equipped and well managed National Bank is capable of rendering most efficient aid in the development of a community is, of course an undisputed fact, and there can be no reasonable doubt but that Winthrop's prosperity is in no small measure due to the Bank that bears its name. The Winthrop National Bank was established in 1864, and its record during the almost quarter of a century that has passed since that time, is such as to thoroughly justify our local business men in putting every confidence in the institution and its management. Unquestionably it is often a difficult thing to choose between inclination and duty, and beyond a doubt the managing officers of the bank have repeatedly had to refuse assistance to local enterprises on account of their first duty being to the bank and those interested in it, but we believe that whenever such aid could be consistently rendered it was given promptly, cheerfully and gladly. The financial condition of the institution is very strong indeed, and the manner in which all the disturbances, panics, etc., of the last twenty years or so have been gone through with shows that the interests of the Bank have always been in competent and faithful hands. The capital is $100,000, and at no other time in its history was the Winthrop National Bank in a more satisfactory condition, or more easily able to continue the good work with which it has been identified in the past. The President, Mr. C. M. Bailey, and the Cashier, Mr. John M. Benjamin; and the Directors C. M. Bailey, Levi Jones, F. H. McIntire, Charles A. Wing and Henry Winslow, are known to all residents of this vicinity, and their names are enough to define the Bank's character and standing.

John Gower, Book Publications, Maine Street, Winthrop. As a representative of an important branch of business, the House of Mr. John Gower may be appropriately mentioned as one of the leading concerns in Winthrop, engaged in the business of Book Publications. The business was established in 1886, by Mr. Gower, and through his energy and ability displayed in its management, has secured a marked success. The premises occupied are located on Main Street, and comprise one entire floor. The trade of this concern extends throughout New England and the Middle States. Mr. Gower employs several clerks in his office; he has a branch office in Pennsylvania which is doing a good business. Some fifty men are employed as agents on the road to sell the books, the sale of which he controls. As these men are nearly all employed on a salary plan, and report daily the work they do, the care and responsibility involved is equal to that of two hundred men employed on commission. Mr. Gower is a native of Winthrop, but has spent most of his time for twenty years in the Subscription Book business in other States and in Canada. He is a prominent member of the Methodist Church and is active in Sunday-school and all other interests of religion. He is an earnest temperance worker and takes a deep interest in the politics of the day, being an active Republican. He combines a thoroughly practical knowledge of the business in which he is engaged, with liberality and business ability of a high order; being still a comparatively young man, there seems to be a prosperous and honorable future spreading out before him.

C. M. Bailey's Sons & Co., Manufacturers of and Dealers in Floor, Stair and Carriage Oil Cloths, Winthrop. Warerooms, 148 Duane Street, New York; 325 Arch Street, Philadelphia. As popular as Oil Cloth is as a floor-covering, etc., and as familiar as it is to us all in its finished state, there is probably not more than one person in a thousand (that is to say, in sections where no factory is located) who has the least idea of the processes gone through with in its manufacture. Yet the details of its making are interesting, and did not our space forbid, we would give our readers some description of the industry as carried on in the extensive works of Messrs. C. M. Bailey's Sons & Co., at Winthrop and Baileyville. This firm ranks with the great Oil Cloth Manufacturers of this country, its facilities for the turning out of the finished product being immense, and its goods being shipped to every portion of the Union. The enterprise was inaugurated in 1847, and during the forty odd years since intervening, the Bailey Oil Cloths have come to be generally accepted as the standard by dealers and the well-informed public everywhere. Extensive warerooms are maintained at No. 148 Duane Street, New York, and No. 325 Arch St., Philadelphia, and an immense and complete line of Floor, Stair and Carriage Oil Cloths, in all the latest patterns, is carried for the inspection of customers. As now constituted, the firm is made up of Messrs. C. I. Bailey, E. A. Bailey and J. E. Briggs, and under the energetic yet conservative management of these gentlemen, the industry is prospering greatly.

Employment is given to 200 hands, the monthly pay-roll amounting to some $10,000. The Winthrop plant covers an area of five acres of ground and includes a steam engine of 100 horse power, while that at Baileyville occupies two acres. Some thousand cords of wood are consumed annually, and about three hundred thousand gallons of linseed oil are also utilized. Great pains are taken to secure uniformity of manufacture, and those having a Bailey Oil Cloth may congratulate themselves on having the best in the market.

The Bazaar, Pinkham Block, Winthrop, E. O. Kelly, Proprietor.] Dry Goods, Yarns and Worsteds, Fancy Goods, Hosiery and Gloves. As a general rule it may be said that to attain success in the Dry Goods business, requires experience and ability. There may be certain circumstances or combinations of circumstances, that will make it possible for a man having neither of these advantages to build up a lucrative trade, but the chances are certainly all against it. Now Mr. E.O. Kelly of Pinkham Block, Winthrop, has experience, for his present enterprise was founded in 1882, and as for ability, let us briefly examine his business methods and judge for ourselves. A good index of anybody's business methods, is that afforded by the stock carried, and we think that no intelligent person can inspect the stock offered by Mr. Kelly without becoming convinced that this gentleman believes in putting the best goods obtainable before his customers, and quoting prices on the same as low as the lowest. The premises occupied are 20x45 feet in size and comprises one floor. The assortment of Dry and Fancy Goods carried at this establishment, which is popularly known as The Bazaar, is sufficiently complete to fill all available space, and includes a special variety of Dry Goods, Hosiery, Gloves, Yarns and Worsteds; also a fine line of the latest Fancy Goods. Mr. Kelly makes it a rule to misrepresent nothing in the slightest degree, and purchasers may depend upon getting what they pay for every time. Callers are given prompt and polite attention, and a thriving and growing retail business done. Mr. Kelly is a native of Winthrop and an active member of the Free Masons, well-known and highly respected in the community.

Winthrop House, J. W. Eaton, Prop., There is a Good Stable Connected with the House, Main Street, Winthrop. There are many attractions to draw strangers to the beautiful town of Winthrop, and not the least of these is the Winthrop House, which under its present management is without doubt one of the pleasantest hotels in the State. Here the guest feels at once at home, and although liberty is never allowed to degenerate into license, still there is a most agreeable absence of that painful stiffness and formality, so apparent in many houses which aspire to the front ranks. Mr. J. W. Eaton, the Proprietor, is a native of Massachusetts, and is a member of the Free Masons. He spares no pains to assure his patrons every possible accommodation and his liberal methods form a refreshing contrast to those in vogue in certain hotels, where the whole purpose of the management seems to be to supply the least possible amount of convenience for the greatest possible amount of money. The hotel the main part measures 40x60 feet, and ell 50x30 feet, contains 35 rooms, which are very comfortably furnished and which are kept in the most neat and attractive condition. Employment is given to five efficient assistants and the wants of guests are given immediate and courteous attention on all occasions. Mr. Eaton is careful to supply his table bountifully and with choice materials, as he recognizes the fact that though we may not live to eat, still eating has much to do with our bodily comfort. The cooking is first-class and the service prompt and cheerful. A thoroughly equipped Livery Stable is maintained in connection with the hotel, and managed by C. L. York, and teams will be furnished at all hours and at reasonable rates. There are some good roadsters in this stable and the carriages are stylish and easy-riding.

S. G. Davis, Manufacturer of Barrels, Coal Yard and Saw Mill, Corner Elm and Union Sts., Winthrop. If one-half of what we hear regarding the rough handling Barrels receive at the hands of Expressmen, "Baggage Smashers," etc., be true, there are no articles that should be more carefully and strongly made, and there are but few who have occasion to use barrels to any extent but what must feel that the greater part of these reports are founded on facts, at least. It is therefore only the truest economy to provide yourself with Barrels that are made to stand rough usage, and as appearances are often very deceitful in this, as in other things, the safest way to do is to visit some respectable manufacturer and procure those well-made, strong, and durable. Mr. S. G. Davis, (residence) corner Elm and Union Sts., Winthrop, Me., makes a specialty of the manufacture of Apple Barrels and we are convinced that it would be worth some little extra trouble to those who use these articles to make sure they get those Mr. Davis manufactures, for they are made of selected material and may be depended upon to give entire satisfaction. In addition to the manufacture of Barrels, Mr. Davis has in the same plant a Machine Shop and Shingle Mill, which are supplied with all necessary facilities for the conduct of the various departments of industry engaged in, and operated by a fifteen-horse power engine. He has recently secured the water-power formerly occupied by the Whitman Agricultural Works, and removed his Board Circular there, where he will manufacture long and short lumber. As soon as the buildings there are completed he will remove all his works from his Union St. establishment, leaving a very desirable opening for a shoe shop or any manufacturing requiring steam-power. Mr. Davis also runs a Coal and Wood Yard. He is a native of Mt. Vernon, Maine, but has resided in Winthrop thirty years and is well-known in various enterprises among them as the "Pioneer" Capt. of Lake Maranocook, owning two steamers, the Amarascoggin, licensed to carry two hundred passengers, and Annie, a staunch little propeller.

C. W. Dillingham, Coffins and Caskets, Main Street, Winthrop. Among the most enterprising and successful manufacturers of Winthrop, may be found Mr. C. W. Dillingham,

who carries on the manufacture of Coffins and Caskets. Business was inaugurated in 1877, by Mr. Dillingham, who has through his native ability and enterprise succeeded in building up his present prosperous manufacturing industry. The premises utilized by him are located on Main Street, and comprise two floors, each 28x33 feet in dimensions, and a large manufacturing business is done, employment being given to a sufficiently large force of workmen, and as the product of the house has met with great favor among those interested, the annual output is constantly increasing. All orders will receive prompt and painstaking attention and the goods are fully warranted to give the best satisfaction. Mr. Dillingham is a native of Turner, Me., and a member of the Odd Fellows. He is well-known throughout Winthrop, and is highly esteemed for his many excellent qualities.

Miss A. L. Emery, Dealer in Millinery and Fancy Goods. Particular attention given to Dress and Cloak-Making; Packard Block, Main Street, Winthrop. The past twenty years have seen some very pronounced changes take place in persons and in things, but in no department of trade has this interval of time been more prolific of change than in that concerned with the handling and production of Millinery and Fancy Goods. To say, therefore, that Miss A. L. Emery, located on Main Street, Winthrop, has carried on the business alluded to since 1883, is to say that she has proved herself competent to keep fully abreast of the times, notwithstanding the constant changes that are taking place in the public tastes. Miss Emery occupies a store 20x50 feet, and carries a well-selected assortment of goods in stock at all times. The thousand-and-one articles that are comprised under the head of Millinery and Fancy Goods, render the carrying of a complete stock of such commodities a practical impossibility, but we believe that the selection shown at this store is fully as large as the average, and is certainly made up of much fresher goods than is generally the case. The Dress and Cloak-Making Department is also very fully stocked, and not only are the latest fashions and fashionable novelties at hand, but the prices quoted are such as to make it well worth while to pay the establishment of Miss Emery an early visit. Three very capable assistants are employed, and all patrons of this establishment are assured entire satisfaction in both goods and work produced at this popular house. Miss Emery is also Agent for Lewando's French Dye House; sole Agent for Butterick's Patterns and Hall's Bazaar Forms for Draping Dresses.

HISTORICAL SKETCH

—— OF ——

RICHMOND.

OF the numerous and beautiful towns and cities along the banks of the great Kennebec, the progressive and delightful town of Richmond is worthy of special mention in many respects. Richmond was one of the earliest places settled in Maine, and in the Kennebec valley; as early as 1649, Christopher Lawson bought this whole region from the Indians for a mere song, and in 1651 he sold it again to Messrs. Clark & Lake who settled here about the same time Gardiner was being settled. During the French and Indian wars in the early part of the eighteenth century, Richmond was one of the most important points strategically on the whole frontier. Fort Richmond was built in 1719 and 1720, and up to the close of the wars it was the defensive center and place of refuge for this whole central section of the Kennebec valley. It was twice attacked by the Indians, once in 1722, and again in 1750, and successfully repelled them each time. After the cessation of the French and Indian wars it enjoyed comparative quiet and steady growth up to the time of the Revolution, when military matters again held full sway. After the Revolution, in which it joined with entire devotion and patriotism, it again continued to grow steadily up to the first decade of the present century, when for a time, and until the influence of the war of 1812 had been largely recovered from, a depression in the growth of the town intervened; but as the larger business in the river, especially through the introduction of the steamboat in the third and following decades of the century, developed its industries, Richmond again felt the spirit of growth and progressed rapidly for a time. At the time of the Civil War it had reached nearly its present extent, and it entered into that struggle with its old time enthusiasm and devotion. It spared neither men nor money, and all contributed to the advance of the national cause. Its soldiers enlisted mainly in the 11th, 14th, 15th, 24th, 28th and 29th regiments, and performed gallant service in the great campaigns throughout the war. The town has worthily commemorated the great memories of those who died in the war. Since the war the progress of the town, though interrupted by the various panics of the last two decades, has been in the main steady and increasing. The

Richmond Academy, a well-known institution was incorporated in 1861. In 1870, the population was 2,442 and the valuation $1,242,040; in 1880, the population was 2,658, and the valuation $1,221,354. At the present time the population has increased to about 3,000, and the town gives every promise of yet greater advances in the immediate future.

RICHMOND FROM THE KENNEBEC.

Richmond is so situated that it has a powerful supply of water privileges, both on the Kennebec and Mill Brook, and is enabled to offer great advantages to manufactories and mills. The Richmond Mineral Springs are also well known, and are much resorted to.

In its internal character and government Richmond is one of the most advanced of Maine towns. The local offices and all public matters are executed with great care and efficiency. Great attention has been paid to education, and its fine schools are widely known. It also has a fine public library of well-assorted books, containing about three thousand volumes. The sanitary and hygienic status of the town is of a high order. The climate is healthful and disease is at a minimum. All matters bearing on the public health receive the promptest and strictest attention. The religious interests of the town are also active and progressive in every good work. The churches represent all the leading denominations, and are well supported. All philanthropical works receive the generous and earnest co-operation of the people. The town is noted for its liberality and broad spirit. The business interests of the town are now progressing favorably. As the great advantages offered here become better known we can not doubt that the manufacturing and commercial interests will expand here and rapidly develop the rich resources of the town. To the careful foresight and strenuous exertions of its business, the town in the past has owed the largest part of its advance, and in the continuation of the same spirit of honor and enterprise is its greatest promise, and the assurance of indefinite and well-earned growth in prosperity and fame.

LEADING BUSINESS MEN

OF

RICHMOND.

Richmond Water Co., Richmond. The growing manufacturing interests of Richmond rendered some form of water service an absolute necessity, and the residents of this town are to be congratulated on the manner in which this necessity has been attended to, for the water system now in operation is a credit alike to those who constructed it, and to those who, by giving the project their support, rendered it an accomplished fact. The Richmond Water Company has identified with it two gentlemen, Messrs. Weston Lewis and Josiah S. Maxcy who have done much to earn the gratitude of every public spirited resident of Maine, for if he be a public benefactor who makes "two blades of grass grow where one grew before," what shall be said of he who, by furnishing an abundant and never-failing supply of water, promotes the health and comfort of thousands of people? The Richmond Water Works were built in 1886, and are sufficiently extensive to supply a population of from 8,000 to 10,000. Some six miles of mains are now utilized, and the water is raised to an earthen reservoir, situated on the Parks farm some two miles from the river, and two hundred feet above it, by means of machinery specially designed for the purpose by the Blake Manufacturing Company, of Boston, Mass. In estimating the power of the pump required, a liberal allowance was made for all contingencies, and as a consequence the means at hand are entirely adequate to maintain a constant and abundant supply of water under the most unfavorable circumstances. The pumping station is a delight to the eye of the admirer of neatness, for it is kept in "spick and span" condition, and those of æsthetic tastes will appreciate the tall brick chimney, it being the most handsomely designed of any on the Kennebec river. The reservoir has a capacity of one million gallons, and its height gives the water such a "head" that a hand-hose is converted into a most efficient fire engine. As to its quality, it is drawn through a system of scientifically constructed filters which effectually remove all saw-dust and other impurities, and as it originally comes from Moosehead Lake, its advantages as a drinking water are unequalled.

W. F. Morgan & Co., Shoe-manufacturers, Richmond. From the shoe-maker at his bench, to an establishment similar to that conducted by Messrs. W. F. Morgan & Co in this town, is a good deal of a step, and yet it is only of comparatively late date that machinery has superseded hand-labor in the production of shoes. The factory mentioned, is four stories in height and measures 50x150 feet, employment being given to three hundred hands. The pay-roll amounts to some $2,500 per week and a 150 horse-power steam-engine is required to furnish the motive power. These are pretty big figures, but this is a pretty big concern, and a little consideration of the methods of management employed in this establishment will go far to show just why the goods turned out here are in such active demand. There is no sentiment in business, and if a certain house's productions are preferred to those of other concerns, it is either because they are superior in quality or lower in price. To meet the sharp competition of the present day, it is necessary to exercise watchful care in every department and every detail of manufacture, and the system in operation at the factory of Messrs. W. F. Morgan & Co., is such as to assure this being done. The proprietors are residents of Lynn, Mass., and their interests in this town are well-attended to by Mr. Daniel P. Corcoran, who is a native of Stoneham, Mass. He exercises a close and unremitting supervision over the undertaking confined to his care, and is entitled to credit for the high position held by the Richmond factory.

LEADING BUSINESS MEN OF RICHMOND.

Chas. Flagg & Son, Furnishing Undertakers, Manufacturers of and dealers in Furniture. Ship, Office and Library Furniture made to order, Main Street, Richmond. The furniture business is immense in its proportions and the number of firms engaged in it, is increasing daily. Some of these firms are reliable and others are quite the reverse, so that careful discrimination should be used in the placing of orders, for ill-made and cheaply gotten-up furniture is dear at any price, and more of it is being put on the market every season. We take pleasure in calling attention to the Furniture manufactured and sold by Messrs. Chas. Flagg & Son, for this is carefully made from selected stock and is well worth the moderate price at which it is quoted. The house in question began operations in 1866, and is made up of Messrs. Chas. and J. C. Flagg. Their establishment is located on Main Street near the Rail Road and the premises occupied are very commodious, comprising three floors of the dimensions of 30x90 feet together with other buildings measuring 20x60 feet which are kept well stocked with well selected goods. Ship, Office and Library Furniture is made to order in the most skillful and durable manner at short notice, and at prices that will bear the severest comparison with those of other dealers handling articles of equal merit, a fine assortment of Finished Work is at hand to select from and anyone wanting anything in the Furniture line should not omit visiting this establishment. As Furnishing Undertakers and Funeral Directors the firm also holds a high reputation, and are prepared to supply Coffins and Caskets, Robes or any Funeral articles at short notice and at very reasonable rates, their rooms are open day and night. Residence of Chas. Flagg. Main Street, next door to rooms. Residence of J. Clark Flagg, Kimble Street.

Mrs. C. R. Wilson, Fancy Goods & Small Wares, Main Street, Richmond. What is conceded by good judges to be one of the most tasty and attractive establishments in Richmond, is that conducted by Mrs. C. R. Wilson, on Main Street, and as the goods therein handled, are such as are popular and extensively used, a flourishing and steadily increasing business is done. Mrs Wilson inaugurated the enterprise alluded to in 1881, and has more than justified the most sanguine expectations of herself, and friends, as the public have been quick to appreciate the many inducements offered, and have given evidence of the fact, by their liberal patronage. Fancy Goods, Small Wares and Hair Goods are exhibited in many styles, and those who are interested in the latest fashionable novelties should not fail to inspect the stock, as many of the newest productions in these lines are shown. The store is of the dimensions of 18x25 feet and employment is given to competent and polite assistants. Mrs. Wilson is a native of Bath, Me., and has attained a reputation for exceptional taste in the selection of the goods dealt in that is as high as it is deserved, and since her present establishment was opened she has filled all orders, in a manner that has given satisfaction to all concerned. Her prices will compare with any first-class establishment in Richmond.

W. G. Webber & Co., Dealers in Flour, Groceries and Provisions, Ship Stores and Country Produce, Richmond. Among the Richmond Grocery and Provision Stores that seem worthy of more than passing mention, reference should be made to that of which W. G. Webber & Co. are the proprietors, located on Main Street. This establishment had its inception in 1881, and has since become one of the best-known in the section wherein it is situated. The stock on hand is a most comprehensive one, for it includes Flour, Staple and Fancy Groceries and Provisions in great profusion. One floor and a basement is occupied, each covering an area of 25x75 feet, and employment is given to a sufficient force of assistants to insure all orders being promptly and conscientiously attended to. Messrs. Webber & Co. make it a rule to use their customers fairly, and that the latter appreciate this fact is proved by the universal confidence manifested in the goods coming from this store; not only the goods but also the prices will be found to be all right in every respect, and those who like to place their orders with a concern that will fill them faithfully, without constant watching, would do well to patronize the enterprise to which we have reference. Messrs. Webber & Co. do a large and increasing business, and are able to offer their goods at the lowest market rates, as during the past seven years they have established the most favorable relations with wholesalers and producers, and give their customers the full benefit of the same. Mr. Webber is a native of Richmond and well-known among our business men, having been engaged for twenty years in the photography business previous to his entering upon his present enterprise.

Jackson & Curtis, Grist Mill, off Main Street, Richmond. Considering the large use that is made of Flour, Feed, etc., in every community, it is not necessary to dwell upon the advantages attendant upon having a well-appointed Grist Mill operated in a city or town, and indeed, the people of Richmond need no further demonstration of the usefulness of the establishment conducted by Messrs. Jackson & Curtis, off Main Street, than that afforded by the advantages derived from the maintenance of this enterprise in their midst. The Mill is 40x50 feet in dimensions, and thirty horse-power is required to run the necessary machinery. It has been in operation since 1885, and deserves prominent mention among Richmond's industrial enterprises. Mr. Jackson is a native of Cape Cod, and Mr. Curtis was born in Perkins. Both these gentlemen are well known about town, and their liberal business methods have rendered them very popular. Flour is furnished in quantities to suit, at the lowest market rates, and the advantages derivable from the use of a fresh-ground article of this kind are known to every housekeeper. Prompt and careful attention is given to orders, and the best of Feed, etc., will be furnished at the very lowest market rates at all times. This firm also deal largely in Carriages of all kinds, Mowing Machines, Horse Rakes, and all kinds of Agricultural Implements; also Fertilizers in any quantity at lowest market rates.

A. W. Kimball, Photographer and Crayon Artist; also Kimball's Improved Crayon Portraits, the most Life-like Portraits that can be Produced; a careful examination will convince any one of this statement. Orders by mail promptly attended to; Main Street, Richmond. There are not a few people who think it necessary to visit the large cities in order to obtain a first-class portrait, and who would laugh at the idea of being able to get equally faithful and handsomely-finished likenesses at home; yet expert Photographers are not confined to the important cities by any means, and we have no hesitation in declaring without any reservation whatever, that Mr. A. W. Kimball is able to produce as good work at his studio on Main Street, as can be obtained in the State, nor do we ask anybody to take our word for it. Visit the studio, examine the finished work there on exhibition, compare it with that turned out at establishments of much greater pretensions, and see if you can find its superior. Mr. Kimball is a New Hampshire man by birth, and was, for several years, a resident of Boston, and has had a long and varied experience in the practice of his profession. He began operations here in 1880, and has steadily increased his patronage until now employment is given to two assistants, and a large number of orders are filled. Photographs of all kinds are produced at short notice, and at as low prices as can be named on work of this character. A specialty is made of Improved Crayon Portraits, and Mr. Kimball's claim that they are the most natural and life-like Portraits that can be found, is fully indorsed by those who have availed themselves of his skill in this direction. Orders by mail are given prompt attention, and no work is allowed to leave the studio that is not fully up to the high standard established by Mr. Kimball.

Clark & Milliken, Saw Mill, off Front Street, Richmond. One of the most thoroughly equipped establishments of the kind in this section of the State, is the Saw Mill carried on by Messrs. Clark & Milliken, off Front Street, and as machinery plays so important a part in the development of any community dependant upon manufacturing interests, it is gratifying to know that the mechanical equipment of this mill is equal to the best, thus putting its owners in a position to easily meet all competition, and maintain their present leading position in the trade. This firm began operations in 1885, and utilize a very extensive plant, which covers eight acres of ground, and includes a Planing Mill as well as a Saw Mill. Employment is afforded to eighty competent assistants, and 125 horse-power is required to run the necessary machinery. Mr. Clark is a native of Carratunk, Maine, and a Mason, and Mr. Milliken a native of West Gardiner, Maine, this latter gentleman being a member of the Masonic Order, also of the Odd Fellows. Both are well known in this community, and the enterprise under their control is so managed as to be a credit to the town as well as to its proprietors. Every facility is at hand for the prompt and accurate filling of orders, and no similar house in the State is in a position to offer more advantages to its customers.

William S. Hagar, Coal and Wood, Front Street, Richmond. There is every reason to believe that the practice of obtaining a winter's supply of Coal, during the season when the prices on this commodity rule low, will be more generally followed this year than ever before among those who have sufficient storage capacity under their control, for many of those who got caught in a corner during the labor trouble of last winter, resolved that in the future they would seek to protect themselves against another experience of the same kind. Well, whether you are going to buy Coal in large or in small quantities, it is policy to patronize a reputable firm, and we know of none more richly deserving confidence and support than that of William S. Hagar, doing business on Front Street. The premises are spacious and comprise an office 18x15 feet in dimensions, with yard-room covering an area of half an acre of ground, and the stock of Wood and Coal carried is correspondingly large, and the facilities for handling the same is satisfactory, employment being given to three capable and reliable assistants, and an extensive retail business is done. This enterprise was inaugurated in 1882, and the business methods pursued have been such as were bound to inspire confidence and build up an extensive trade and the success attained, although unusual in so short a time, is no more than was fairly won by hard work and enterprising methods. Mr. Hagar is known throughout this community as Postmaster and Justice of the Peace, and also as a member of the Free Masons.

Richmond Marble Yard, E. C. Boston, proprietor, Main Street, Richmond. Among the customs of days gone by, there are many that seem to people of the present time to be strange and undesirable, but of them all, there was not one more directly opposed to the prevailing beliefs and practices of to-day than that of placing representations of skulls, cross-bones etc., upon the memorials of the dead. Nowadays the emblems so placed are of a directly opposite character and tend to rob death of much of its terror, instead of adding to the same by ghastly reminders of our common mortality. Anchors to signify hope, Angels with up-pointing finger — such are the emblems called for by the existing state of feeling in the community, and when these are well-made and properly designed their effect is both consoling and commemorative. A house engaged in the production of all kinds of cemetery work, such as Monuments, Grave Stones Tablets etc., for many years and which has attained a high reputation for the artistic character of its productions, is that carried on by Mr. E. C. Boston on Main Street and popularly known as the Richmond Marble Yard. This enterprise was inaugurated by its present proprietor in 1878. The premises occupied by him comprise two floors each 20x50 feet in size and employment is given to three skilled workmen. It has often been remarked by good judges that there is never anything to offend the most refined taste in the works of this establishment as great pains are taken to select appropriate designs, and then to carry them out in a thoroughly first-class manner. Reasonable prices prevail and orders can be filled at short notice.

W. T. Hall, Insurance, Front Street, Richmond. To advise a man to insure his property nowadays, is a good deal like advising him not to drop a match into gun-powder or not to go out on the street without a hat—these being things that no person with an average amount of brains would think of doing. Arguments in favor of Insurance are no longer required. The ground has been thoroughly gone over time and time again, and the experience of years has shown the principle to be a correct one, and its practical application a duty devolving upon every man. Solvent and well-managed companies should be chosen, of course, but no great amount of trouble is necessary in order to accomplish this, for there are agents who represent several organizations and who are too well-known and highly esteemed in the community to make it possible that they would advise the placing of insurance in irresponsible corporations. For instance, there is Mr. W. T. Hall of this town. This gentleman is a native of Bowdoinham, and has been identified with Insurance matters for over a quarter of a century, having begun operations in 1861. His office is located on Front Street, and those who wish to obtain policies as good as gold, or get any information relating to Insurance, would best serve their own interests by consulting Mr. Hall at once. He is a member of the Free Masons and is the the Judge of Probate for this County. The Niagara and German-American Companies are both represented by him, and Insurance is written by him at the lowest rates.

I. F. Umberhine, Dealer in Hardware, Paints, Oils, Iron and Steel, Groceries, Salt, Lime, Cement, etc., Richmond. The stock carried in an establishment like that conducted by Mr. I. F. Umberhine on Main Street, Richmond, is so varied that even to enumerate the articles contained in it would more than fill our limited space, and yet these articles are as a rule so useful and even indispensable, that we hardly know which to call attention to and which to omit. Under the head of Hardware, Groceries, Paints, Oils, Iron and Steel, etc., are included scores of goods varying from a hammer to a pen-knife and embracing an immense variety of articles useful in every household. Mr. Umberhine is a native of Richmond and a member of the Odd Fellows, and is extremely well known among the business men of this city, having carried on his present business since 1885. The premises occupied consist of three floors, each 20x63 feet in dimensions, and afford considerable opportunity for the display of goods dealt in, and in addition to the goods already mentioned, Salt, Lime and Cement are quite largely dealt in. Those who may wish to purchase anything in the various lines of merchandise handled by Mr. Umberhine would do well to call and inspect his stock before purchasing elsewhere. All goods are sold at the lowest market rates and guaranteed to prove as represented. All callers will receive the polite and prompt attention which is the due of every customer and which has done much to gain for this establishment the abundant popularity it now enjoys.

A. C. Spaulding & Brother, dealers in Groceries and Paints, Oils, Main Street, Richmond. A firm that supply reliable Groceries at a fair price are, worthy of being liberally patronized, and even more decidedly is this the case when not only Groceries, but other equally useful commodities are furnished in a correspondingly acceptable manner. Messrs. A. C. Spaulding & Brother have done business here in Richmond ever since 1871, and the record they have made for fair dealing and active enterprise, is one of which they have abundant reason to be proud. Their establishment is located on Main Street, where two floors are utilized of the dimensions of 25x70 feet, and employment is given to three competent assistants. The firm is made up of Messrs. A. C. and M. E. Spaulding, both of whom were born in Carratunk; the latter being a member of the Odd Fellows and of the Knights of Pythias. A very large stock is carried, comprising choice Staple and Fancy Groceries, Corn, Flour, Feed etc., together with a full selection of Paints and Oils of standard quality. Every provision has been made for the accommodation of family trade, and the supplies furnished, will be found specially adapted to household use. Ready mixed Paints, which have become so popular of late years, are handled largely, one of the favorite brands being the "Atlas" which is made by Messrs. Geo. D. Wetherill & Co., of Philadelphia, and is guaranteed to give satisfaction when properly used. Messrs. A. C. Spaulding & Brother, do not confine themselves however to handling the productions of any one house, and their assortment of Painters' supplies is a large and desirable one.

Caldwell & Libby, Shoe Manufacturers, off Main Street, Richmond. If Maine continues to develop her Shoe-manufacturing industry at the same speed that it has been extended during the past decade, it is only a question of time when she will pass even Massachusetts in the race for supremacy. This is not the place to pass in review the many advantages which the State possesses in the way of manufacturing facilities, etc., and indeed the manner in which outside manufacturers have been improving these advantages of late, shows conclusively that they are already generally known and appreciated. One of the Shoe-manufacturing houses of comparatively recent establishment, is that of Messrs. Caldwell & Libby, located off Front Street. This enterprise was inaugurated in 1887, and occupies a two-story building measuring 45x100 feet. The latest improved machinery is utilized in this factory and the character and quantity of the product shows that the one hundred and fifty hands employed are skilled and experienced workmen. Mr. Caldwell is a native of the old Bay State, while Mr. Libby is a Maine man, having been born in Bethel. He is a member of the Odd Fellows, also the Grand Army, and gives close attention to the various details of the business. The goods produced at this factory meet with a ready sale, for they are uniform in quality and are supplied at the lowest market rates. This enterprise is evidently destined to develop largely and under present methods of management, this development cannot be long delayed.

LEADING BUSINESS MEN OF RICHMOND.

Warren S. Voter, Meats and Provisions, Front Street, Richmond. Many of our readers can no doubt sympathize with the individual who, when a friend sought to console him for the toughness of the meat he was chewing by reminding him that "exercise was healthy," replied that he preferred to take his meals and his exercise at different times. Even the most sweet-tempered person can be excused for exhibiting some anger or disgust when forced to wrestle with meat which is better fitted for shoe-leather than for food, especially when as is often the case, a high enough price has been paid to insure the procuring of the finest and choicest cut. But there are concerns engaged in the Meat and Provision trade which honestly strive to give full value for money in every case, and although mistakes may be made occasionally, they are always ready and willing to make proper amends for the same. It is owing to its adoption of this policy that the house of Warren S. Voter, doing business on Front Street, has attained so high a reputation and built up so large a business and we can sincerely commend this concern to all of our readers, who want a good article at a fair price. The business was started in 1887, by the present proprietor, who is a native of Phillips, Me., and a member of the Odd Fellows. One floor measuring 20x45 feet is occupied and a fine and complete stock of Meats, Provisions, etc., is carried. Capable assistants are employed and customers served with politeness and celerity. Mr. Voter enlisted in the Southern Rebellion in the 28th Me. Vols., and was actively engaged in the Siege of Port Hudson, Donalsonville and the Red River and others in the Southwest, and is Commander of John Merrill Post, G. A. R., of Richmond.

Harmon Smith, dealer in Dry Goods, Groceries, Flour, Richmond. Among the various popular and growing enterprises of Richmond, which bear mark of increasing prosperity, is the establishment of Mr. Harmon Smith located on Main Street. The proprietor established this business in 1854, and has since conducted its affairs with increasing facilities and signal success. The premises occupied for trade purposes, comprise a store 20x60 feet in dimensions, where a full and complete stock of Dry Goods, Groceries, Flour etc., are kept. The facilities possessed by the proprietor for obtaining a choice supply are unsurpassed by any contemporary concern. The greatest care is taken by Mr. Smith in selecting his choice and varied stock which is highly esteemed, by the citizens of Richmond for their excellence and low prices. Employment is given to two clerks, who are polite and prompt in their attention to the many customers, and every facility is at hand for the conduct of the large and prosperous retail trade. Mr. Smith is a native of Litchfield. He is a very able business man, and through his prompt and honorable methods the present large and successful business has been built up; which has won for him an eminently fine reputation throughout Richmond.

HISTORICAL SKETCH

—OF—

CANTON.

CANTON, the easternmost town of Oxford County, is one of the most beautiful and charming in all this attractive region. It is about six miles in length by nine broad, and is divided into two sections by the Androscoggin river, which runs through in a nearly easterly direction. This together with Whitney Pond and Brook furnishes six good water-powers. This power can be developed to a very great extent, and the business prospect it affords is very promising. Especially near Whitney Pond, the fine water privileges have already established a considerable business interest, forming the commercial center of the region. Here are large saw, lumber, stave and grist mills, manufactories of carriages, zinc wash-boards, moldings, furniture, tanneries and foundries. The town is surrounded by the hills, which form a protection to the smooth plain in which it sets. The scenery is very beautiful, the soil fertile and the agricultural interests are considerable. At Canton Point, there was formerly a headquarters of the Indians in this vicinity, who named it Rokomeko. This tribe was entirely exterminated by small-pox during the French and Indian wars. As usual through the river-valleys of the State, occasional reminiscenses of the former inhabitants are found in the shape of skeletons and implements of stone, for Rokomeko was the chief burying-place of the tribe. The town was first settled by the English in 1790, Wm. Livermore, Wm. French, Joseph Coolidge, and Alexander Sheppard, being the pioneers who first established themselves here. The place was included in the tract known as Phipps' Canada. It grew quite rapidly, and was incorporated as a part of Jay in 1795. It was set off from Jay and incorporated as Canton in 1821. It took an honorable and devoted part in the Mexican and Civil wars, the memories and traditions of the latter being most tenderly cherished. Most of its growth has been since the war of the Rebellion. Its population in 1870 was 984; valuation $395,993; population in 1880, 1,030; valuation, $367,693. Since the last census there has also been considerable advance and business expansion, and by 1890 it will have made large increase on the last census. Canton is twenty miles northeast of Paris, and sixty miles from Portland. It is situated at the terminus of the Rumford Falls & Buckfield Railroad. It is easily accessible and forms a most delightful summer residence, the surrounding country furnishing every rural attraction and recreation. The rates of accomodation are very low and the attractions are among the best. The town socially, educationally, and morally, is among the most advanced in the State, and is worthy of the pride which its citizens take in its condition. The business outlook is brightening every year as its unexcelled attractions become better known, and as this part of the State continues to develop, from the natural sequence of existing causes, Canton will go forward in the van; and guided by the same foresight and enterprise which has characterized its people in the past, will continue to maintain its enviable reputation.

LEADING BUSINESS MEN

OF

CANTON, ME.

Canton Steam Mill Company, (Gilbertville), Canton. The principal explanation of the marvelous quickness with which a large structure can be erected at the present day, is found in the practice of shaping the necessary timbers, etc., in large quantities by the aid of Steam power and ingenious machinery. To such perfection has this been brought, that it is said that the framing, etc., of a building of any desired size can be ordered from many of our large mills and shipped to any point where labor and material are dear, and there put together, with the certainty that as good a job will be made as if the shaping had been done on the spot. The Canton Steam Mill is probably as well equipped as any similar establishment in the country for the accurate and satisfactory filling of orders of this kind and the heavy business done, shows that the advantages it offers are fully appreciated by builders and others. The Canton Steam Mills were established in 1879, and the Company was composed of Messrs. C. H. and Z. E. Gilbert and Mr. O. A. McFadden, all being natives of Maine. Since January 1, 1888, it has been under the management of Mr. George B. Staples, who is a native of Carthage, Me. This mill has gained a reputation for thorough and accurate work that is unsurpassed, and it is no more than just to give it credit for the success attained. The energies of this enterprise are devoted to the manufacturing of Long and Short Lumber, and the premises utilized consist of two floors each covering an area of 116 by 50 feet, besides an engine house. This mill is supplied with the most improved methods of machinery which is operated by an engine of 175 horse power. The extensive business done requires the employment of 50 competent hands, and all work entrusted to this company will be executed in the most skillful and energetic manner possible.

J. W. Thompson, Editor and Publisher of The Maine Horse Breeders' Monthly; terms, $1.00 Per Annum. Circulation Larger than any Paper in Maine, outside of the Cities; write for Advertising Rates and Sample Copies; Canton. The wonderful improvement which has taken place in American horse-flesh within comparatively few years, is not the result of accident, by any means, but the legitimate outcome of hard, persistent and intelligent work, and the expenditure of large sums of money. American trotting stock is, as every ordinarily well-informed person knows, the best in the world, and the steady lowering of the mile record from year to year, proves that the limit of speed and bottom is not yet reached. That the results attained have been brought about by judicious breeding is also generally understood, and that those engaged in this work should be encouraged by the public, is as obvious as that the general average of horse-flesh is continually being raised by such operations. The horse breeders of this State are among the most advanced in the country, and that they form a numerous as well as an influential class, is proved by the circulation of the Maine Horse Breeders' Monthly—their representative paper —being larger than that of any other publication in the State, issued outside the cities. The paper in question was founded in 1879, by Mr. J. W. Thompson, a gentleman who is a recognized authority on all matters pertaining to horses and horse-breeding. He is a native of Turner, Maine, a member of the Free Masons, and is widely-known—aside from his journalistic capacity—as the author of that standard work, "Noted Maine Horses," which was published in 1874. In 1880, in response to an earnest and pressing demand, a second volume was issued, and the reception given to it has been cordial and flattering, the edition being already nearly exhausted. Mr. Thompson was, for several years, President of the Canton Driving Association, and was unanimously re-elected at the last annual meeting, and to him credit is largely due for the fine Driving Park, conceded to be one of the fastest and best tracks in the State. The Maine Horse Breeders' Monthly is indispensable to all engaged in that industry, and is both interesting and valuable to every lover of the delights of the road and track. It is published at $1.00 per annum, and for obvious reasons is one of the best advertising mediums in New England, especially for goods designed for the use of horsemen. Mr. Thompson acts as Editor and Publisher, and is ever on the alert to furnish the latest and most reliable information to his renders. Being thoroughly devoted to his work, he is constantly trying to improve his paper in every possible way, and it supplies a place which could be filled by no other publication of which we have knowledge.

C. H. Lucas, Manufacturer of the Little Giant Screw Driver, successor to Lucas & Bishop; also manufacturer of Watchmaker's Fine Tools of all kinds. A specialty is made of the manufacture of all kinds of Small Machinery, Patent Novelties, etc. Also Dealer in Plain, Galvanized and Enameled Steam, Gas and Water Pipe; all kinds of Valves Furnished. Canton. As might naturally be supposed, the Tools used by Watchmakers require especial skill in their making, and the plant necessary to an establishment devoted to their manufacture is both extensive and costly. Among the best equipped factories of the kind with which we are acquainted, a leading place is held by that carried on by Mr. C. H. Lucas, and the popularity of his productions among Watchmakers throughout New England, is convincing evidence of their unusual merit. Mr. Lucas not only makes Fine Watchmakers' Tools of all kinds, but is also extensively engaged in the manufacturing of Small Machinery of every description, Patent Novelties, etc., making a Specialty of this work and having every facility to carry it on to the best advantage. He is the manufacturer of the Little Giant Screw Driver, which was patented May 11, 1886, and has already become famous as one of those ingenious and efficient time saving devices for which American inventors are celebrated. Mr. Lucas does his own blacksmithing, maintaining a well-equipped shop for that purpose, and also carries on the Jewelry and Watch-Repairing Business, this branch being in charge of Mr. Jonas B. Look, than whom no more thoroughly competent person could be found, as he is a practical Watch and Clock Repairer of large experience, and does work that is guaranteed in every respect. Mr. Lucas is a native of Hartford, Maine, and is a prominent member of the Free Masons. He began operations in 1874, and with the exception of one year has always carried on business alone.

J. H. Hamlin, Dealer in Gent's Furnishings, Fancy Groceries, Farmers' Produce, Flour, etc., Canton. It is seldom that an enterprise of comparatively recent establishment shows such evident signs of prosperity as does that carried on by Mr. J. H. Hamlin in this town, and this success is all the more worthy of special mention from the fact that it has been brought about by strictly legitimate means, and not by the questionable methods too often followed at the present day. Mr. Hamlin was born in Waterford, Maine, and is a member of the Knights of Pythias. He is thoroughly acquainted with the various details of the business in which he is engaged, and as he gives them close personal attention, customers may safely depend upon a continuance of the prompt service and liberal methods which have already made his establishment so popular. The premises utilized are of the dimensions of 50x25 feet, and are well-stocked with a carefully selected assortment, comprising Fancy Groceries, Gentlemen's Furnishings, Farmers' Produce, Flour, etc. Mr. Hamlin only began operations in 1888, and his stock is consequently new and fresh in every department. He is constantly adding to it, and is evidently determined to give his customers the best goods obtainable, at prices that will bear the severest comparison with those named elsewhere.

A. S. Shaw & Co., Retail Dealers in Fine Boots and Shoes, Canton. A man who knows what the public wants in his line of business, and has the disposition and the ability to supply that want, is bound to make a success in whatever he undertakes, and those familiar with the methods followed by Messrs. A. S. Shaw & Co., since they began operations here in 1888, need not be told that this firm have shown precisely the ability indicated. The assortment of Fine Boots and Shoes to be found in their store is worthy of particular mention for a variety of reasons, not the least of which is that it is composed entirely of new, fresh goods, made by the most popular manufacturers. There is room enough to carry a large stock for the store occupied measures 50x20 feet, and as a matter of fact, both in extent and variety, the stock on hand is hard to equal. Boots and Shoes for all kinds of feet are handled. If you have children bring them here, for they can be fitted with Shoes that will both look well and wear well, and every one knows that a handsome and durable child's Shoe must be made carefully, from good stock. Yet the prices quoted on such goods are very low, as they are on all the styles dealt in by this enterprising firm. In Youth's, and Misses' Shoes there are also genuine inducements offered, and when we come to goods for adults, the best we can say is, go and see for yourself, for our space forbids even a hint at what may be expected in this line. A Specialty is made of Repairing, and the character of the work turned out is first class, the charges made being very reasonable

Nathan Reynolds, Dealer in Drugs, Medicines, Books and Stationery, Wall Paper, Paints, Oils, Varnishes, etc., Canton. One of the most popular establishments which we have met with in preparing this work, is that carried on by Mr. Nathan Reynolds. It was founded by its present proprietor in 1883, and the reputation since gained speaks well for the methods employed by its manager. Mr. Reynolds was born in this town and is a member of the Odd Fellows. He deals in Drugs, Medicines, etc., as well as in Books and Stationery, Wall Paper, Paints, Oils, Varnishes and kindred goods, and does a large business both wholesale and retail. It is Mr. Reynolds' endeavor to supply his customers with first class articles, strictly reliable in every respect, and he takes special pains in case of Drugs and Medicines as so much often depends upon the quality of such articles. Buying from the most reputable manufacturers and dealers, it is certainly no fault of his if his goods are not invariably up to the highest standard of merit. A fine selection of Books is to be found at his store, and fashionable and business Stationery in considerable variety, while the stock of Wall Paper comprises the latest and most popular designs and is offered at very low rates. Paints and Oils are handled extensively and the Varnishes on sale are from the best makers and may be depended upon to give full satisfaction if properly used. Customers are assured prompt and polite attention from Mr. Reynolds gives the business his careful, personal supervision. Mr. Reynolds has recently added to his stock a large assortment of Spectacles and Eye Glasses and can save his customers much trouble occasioned by buying of peddlers or parties away from home and furnish the goods at much lower prices.

S. Bicknell & Son, Manufacturers of Track Wagons; also General Jobbing, Canton. However much people may differ concerning the relative merits of certain articles manufactured in this country, and also in England, there are other productions in which there can be no question but what we lead the world, and prominent among these are Wheeled Vehicles of all kinds. Of course it would be idle to dispute that many English Carriages are imported into the United States annually; but this is no proof that they equal those produced here, for there are unfortunately some so-called Americans who would put up with the most cumbersome and inconvenient contrivances as long as they were "English, you know." There are Wagons made here in Canton which will compare favorably with the very best imported productions, and are sold at prices far below those quoted on such Vehicles. We have reference to the articles turned out by Messrs. S. Bicknell & Son, for, although the firm do not manufacture nearly so many Vehicles as some houses do, still what they *do* make may be relied upon absolutely. Selected stock and careful workmanship combine to produce the best results, and customers get the full value of their money, both in beauty and durability. Operations were commenced in 1886, and a thriving business has already been built up, not only in Wagon Making, but also in General Jobbing in Wood-Work, for which the firm have every facility. Both partners are natives of this town, and Mr. F. E. Bicknell is very prominent in Odd Fellowship. Two floors of the dimensions of 20x30 feet are occupied, and orders are filled at short notice and at moderate prices.

Childs & Staples, General Store, (Gilbertville) Canton. The amount of detail involved in the carrying on of any retail business is more or less large, but it is particularly noticeable in an establishment where a General Variety of Goods are handled. But the rewards of intelligent exertion in such a case are directly proportionate to the difficulty of the task, for some of these general stores are more largely patronized than any other establishments outside the cities. When $28,400 worth of goods are sold at retail from a single store in a little over eleven months, there must be good management somewhere, and the public must have learned that special advantages were to be gained by dealing with this house, and as this is the record held by Messrs. Childs & Staples, the obvious conclusion is that this is a good store to patronize. Now this conclusion is in perfect accord with the facts, for not only does the firm mentioned carry a stock that is complete in every department, but they quote prices on it that can hardly be equalled in this section, when goods of similar merit are concerned. Being very large buyers, they get exceptionally low rates from manufacturers and wholesalers, and as their business increases, their power to offer genuine inducements increases, also. The enterprise was started in 1885, by Messrs. Oscar Childs and George B. Staples. The former is a native of Canton and the latter was born in Carthage, both being connected with the Odd Fellows, while Mr. Childs is a member of the Free Masons, also. The premises in use comprise three floors, two of which measure 60x25 feet, while the other is 25x30 feet in size. A large storehouse is also utilized, its dimensions being 40x22 feet. A remarkably fine assortment of Clothing, Boots and Shoes, etc., is offered in connection with the many other goods handled, and any one dealing with this house has the satisfaction of knowing that every article is sure to prove as represented.

Geo. F. Towle, Dealer in the Celebrated Wilcox & White Parlor Organs, and Haines Bro.'s Pianos. Also Musical Instruments and Merchandise; Violin Strings a Specialty. Business Manager of Towle's Orchestra, Organized in 1859; Little Arcade. Canton. "Music hath charms to soothe the savage breast;" no doubt but it hath charms to accomplish a still more satisfactory result—make home what it should be, the pleasantest spot on earth. Anything that will promote good feeling in the domestic circle is to be encouraged, and certainly nothing is more valuable in this respect than music for a good, hearty family chorus is pleasant alike to singers and hearers. A Musical Instrument is, therefore, almost a necessity in every home, and for all around purposes the choice lies between a Piano and an Organ. Some will prefer the one and some the other, but one thing should be insisted upon—get a first-class Instrument, for such is not only the best but the cheapest in the end. A visit to the establishment of Mr. Geo. F. Towle will demonstrate the fact that a first-class Piano or Organ may be bought at a very low price, comparatively speaking, for this gentleman handles the celebrated Haines Bro.'s Pianos and the Wilcox & White Organs, the reputation of which is wide-spread and unsurpassed, and is prepared to quote bottom prices on both these popular instruments. He also deals in Musical Instruments in general, together with Musical Merchandise, making a Specialty of Violin Strings of the most desirable quality. Mr. Towle is a native of Gardiner, Maine, and began operations here in 1878. He is a member of the Free Masons and is very extensively known in musical circles in this State, being the Business Manager of Towle's Orchestra, which was organized by him in 1859, and has remained in existence continuously since that date. The Orchestra is very popular, and may always be depended upon to furnish thoroughly artistic music for all occasions.

M. B. Thomes, Druggist, Canton. To carry on a Retail Drug Store in the manner which is demanded by the present state of popular sentiment, is by no means so easy a task as many of our readers are probably disposed to believe, for we have noticed that the average man has but an imperfect conception of the true scope of a Pharmacist's duties. To discharge these in a proper manner, one must have a technical education as well as business ability and training, and there is hardly a branch of trade necessitating such close and arduous attention and confinement. Fortunately, however, we have many gentlemen in this State capable of carrying on an establishment of this kind in first-class style, and among them it is but just to notice Mr. M. B. Thomes, who is located in this town. Mr. Thomes was born in Denmark, Maine, and inaugurated his present enterprise in 1878. His record since that date amply justifies our estimation of him, and in this we are supported by the public he has served so faithfully. His store measures 45x20 feet, and contains a skillfully chosen stock of Drugs, Medicines and Chemicals, obtained from the most trustworthy sources, and renewed at frequent intervals. Physicians' Prescriptions are compounded with great care and accuracy, and the prices quoted in this department are as low as is compatible with the quality of the ingredients called for. Orders are filled at the shortest possible notice, and whether Medicines, Fancy and Toilet Articles, or anything kept in a First-Class Drug Store are required, we know of no better place at which to obtain them.

C. R. Houghton, Dealer in Cartridges, Powder, Shot and Caps, Fishing Tackle, Guns and Revolvers, Stoves, Tin and Hardware, Lead Pipe, Sheet Lead, Agricultural Implements, Hammocks, Phosphates, Cutlery, Granite, Agate and Wooden Ware, Pumps, Zinc, Fence Wire, Grindstones, Glass, Putty, Cordage, Etc., Iron, Steel and Blacksmiths Supplies, Barb and Plain Fence Wire, Wire Screen Cloth, Canton. It would be hard to find an establishment containing a more varied and more useful stock than that carried by Mr. C. R. Houghton, for this gentleman deals in Stoves, Tin and Hardware of every description besides a number of other articles which will be mentioned later. He was born in Woodstock, Maine, and is connected with the Free Masons, opening his present store in 1887. The premises utilized, comprise three floors of the dimensions of 30x36 feet each, as well as a commodious store house in which is kept a full assortment of Agricultural Implements, Poultry Netting, etc. He is a manufacturer of Tin Ware and offers special inducements to those wishing anything in this line. Stoves of all kinds are kept in stock or will be obtained at short notice and the prices quoted on them are in every instance in accordance with the lowest market rates. Lead Pipe and Sheet Lead are supplied in quantities to suit as are also Iron and Steel and Blacksmith's Supplies in general as well as Barbed and Plain Fence Wire and Wire Screen Cloth of standard quality. Cutlery, Granite, Agate and Wooden Ware are kept in great variety, together with Pumps, Zinc, Grindstones, Glass, Putty, Cordage, etc. Quite an extensive trade is done in Phosphate, and a carefully selected stock of Sporting Goods is at hand to choose from, comprising Fishing Tackle, Guns and Revolvers, Cartridges, Powder, Shot, Caps, Wads, etc. Prices are low in every department and prompt attention is given to customers.

HISTORICAL SKETCH
—OF—
FREEPORT, ME.

ONE of the most progressive and widely known towns of the Maine coast is Freeport, Cumberland County, situated at the head of a fine harbor opening into Casco Bay. In the earlier half of the century it was one of Maine's great shipping towns. Like Portland, Kennebunk, Bath, Boothbay, its harbor was frequented by in and out-going vessels, and on its docks there were always being made great monarchs of the deep; but like many other towns, its shipping fame has passed away. This interest, which developed continually after the Revolutionary War, reached its climax in the decade between 1850 and 1860. In one year ten great ships, from seven hundred to twelve hundred tonnage, were launched, and its commerce went upon all waters. In 1860 its population was two thousand seven hundred and ninety-two. But the disastrous effects of the war and succeeding years were fatal to its ship-building interests. There is yet hope that these will revive, and in these later years, when the prospect for American shipping has begun to brighten, signs of regeneration have appeared. The population of the town in 1870 was two thousand four hundred and fifty-seven; since then it has risen to about its former level. But the enterprising spirit of Freeport's citizens was not conquered by one rebuff. Since the war, increasing attention has been given to manufacturing, and this interest has now reached considerable importance. There are two good water powers in the town, situated respectively on the Harrasekett and Royal Rivers. The harbor is excellent also for commerce, connections being easy with Portland and Boston, and transportation cheap. The town is also on the line of the Maine Central R. R. Agriculture and the fisheries still receive considerable and profitable attention as well as manufacturing, though the tendency of things is clearly in the latter direction. Among the most important industries are those of fire-plates and shoes. There are four villages in Freeport, of which the most important one is Freeport Village, where the the business interests chiefly are situated. The town is only seventeen miles from Portland, and so enjoys those privileges only possible to a suburban town,— educational and social affairs on a high plane of culture. There are three churches in the town, and all religious and benevolent endeavors meet with hearty sympathy and co-operation. Situated on the sea, with its beautiful harbor opening out among the islands of Casco Bay, enjoying the united charms of the suburban villa, and most easily accessible, it is not surprising that Freeport is continually rising into higher estimation as a summer resort, and it can well bear all the criticism and admiration which can be bestowed by the increasing tide of summer visitors.

LEADING BUSINESS MEN

OF

FREEPORT, ME.

H. P. Dennison, Manufacturer of Boots, Shoes and Slippers, Pownal Street, Freeport. Freeport's manufacturing interests are not only very important now, but are rapidly becoming more so as the many advantages which a location here offers, become apparent to manufacturers. Prominent among Freeport's industries stands the manufacture of Shoes, and of the many houses engaged in that line here, none bear a higher reputation than does that of Mr. H. P. Dennison, located on Pownal St. This establishment was originally founded in 1879, by Messrs. Lemonte & Dennison, and in 1880 the firm-name was changed to Dennison & Lewis, and conducted under that style until 1883, when the present proprietor, Mr. H. P. Dennison, assumed full control of the business. His factory is located on Pownal Street, and comprises three floors, each 32x50 feet in dimensions. All the latest improved facilities and machinery are at hand, and the motive power is supplied by a five-horse-power engine. Employment is given to forty skilled and experienced hands. The energies of this establishment are devoted to the manufacture of Boots, Shoes and Slippers, of which he manufactures more than fifty styles. A specialty is made of Ladies' Kid Button Boots, and the large and increasing demand for these goods show how they are appreciated. Mr. Dennison is a native of Freeport, and has held the office of Selectman in that town and is a member of the Knights of Pythias. He has shown a vigor and liberality in the conduct of his business which has commanded and deserved success. The bulk of his business is through New England, although he ships a portion of his products to Chicago, Philadelphia and Milwaukee, Wisconsin. The superior quality of the product is rapidly extending the field and increasing the volume of trade.

E. B. Mallet, Jr., Dealer in Flour, Corn, Meal, Shorts, Oats and Barley, Opposite Depot, Freeport. There are probably but few citizens of Freeport who are not more or less familiar with the business enterprises of Mr. E. B. Mallet, jr. This gentleman established his Grist Mill in 1886, and his Saw Mill in 1887, the products of which are such as are indispensable to every community, and includes Flour, Corn, Meal, Shorts, Oats and Barley, and Grain of all kinds. The plant covers an area of one-quarter acre of ground; the Grist Mill comprises a three-story building. These mills are located opposite the depot and are operated by a sixty-horse-power engine. Employment is given to ten workmen, and an extensive wholesale business is transacted. In addition to the above-mentioned enterprises, Mr. Mallet owns an extensive Granite Quarry and Marble Works; all kinds of Granite and Marble Building, Cemetery Work and Steam Polishing; Designs and Estimates furnished on application. These enterprises cover an area of twenty acres of ground, and in which he employs about one hundred men. Also a Coal Yard about one-half acre in dimensions, containing sheds with a capacity for holding two thousand tons of Coal. His property in Freeport covers about three hundred acres of ground; in fact Mr. Mallet is *the* man of Freeport. In Pownal he ownes two hundred acres of property, running this for farming and stock purposes. Mr. Mallet is a native of Bath, Me., a member of the Knights of Pythias and the Free Masons (33d degree), and as might be expected in the case of one of his ability and experience, has a most comprehensive knowledge of his business in all its varied departments, and is consequently in a position to offer the most desirable and reliable merchandise at the lowest wholesale rates, which he guarantees to prove satisfactory in every particular.

LEADING BUSINESS MEN OF FREEPORT.

Gore & Davis, Dealers in Dry and Fancy Goods, Groceries, Boots and Shoes, Paints, Oils, etc., No. 8, Main Street, Freeport. Among the most enterprising, popular and firmly established of the business undertakings located in this section of the town, that conducted by Messrs. Gore & Davis merits special mention, and careful notice. The constant and intelligent efforts of the proprietors to extend special inducements to the public, have resulted in the building up of a trade, which as yet shows no signs of failing to keep up the constant ratio of increase which has so far distinguished it. This establishment was first started in 1831, by Messrs. Holbrook & Gore and with two or three changes up to 1875, when the firm name assumed its present style of Gore & Davis. Mr. Gore is a native of Roxbury, Mass., and Mr. Davis of Freeport, and both are so well-known to the residents of this place, that they require no further personal mention. The premises occupied, having the dimensions of 25x45 feet, and consisting of four floors, with four additional buildings used as storehouses, cover an area of one-fourth acre of ground. The services of four competent and polite assistants are constantly employed. Among the goods handled are Dry and Fancy Goods, Groceries, Boots, Shoes, Hardware, Fertilizers, Farming Tools, Paints, Oils, etc., and all these commodities are offered at the very lowest market rates. The line of Dry Goods carried includes the many staple articles coming under that head, while in the other lines a very choice assortment is at hand to select from. A full line of Groceries are also exhibited, and particular inducements are offered to purchasers of these productions. Mr. Davis is a member of the Knights of Pythias.

Miss A. Dillingham, dealer in Millinery and Fancy Goods, Stamping done to order, Depot Street, Freeport. An establishment which has great attractions for all ladies wishing to inspect or purchase fashionable and tasty goods is that carried on by Miss A. Dillingham on Depot Street; for at this store every effort is made to procure the most desirable novelties in the line of Millinery and Fancy Goods, as fast as they appear, and to offer them at the lowest possible rates. The premises occupied are of the dimensions of 20x30 feet and the extensive and varied stock on hand is displayed to excellent advantage. Miss Dillingham is a well-known resident of Freeport, and has a very wide circle of friends in this vicinity. Combining business ability and exceptional taste, her success in her chosen pursuits was only what was legitimately to be expected, and since the commencement of operations in 1880, a very select and heavy patronage has been attained. Miss Dillingham realizes that while there are some possessed of such abundant means that expense to them is a matter of but little consequence, there are others, who of course from the bulk of the community, who must consult economy in all their purchases, and it is to her intelligent and successful efforts, to furnish fashionable and durable articles, at prices within the reach of the people, that the chief part of the popularity of her establishment is due.

L. M. Bailey, Manufacturer of Ladies' and Misses' Boots and Shoes, All Hand Sewed, Bow Street, Freeport. An enterprise whose fame is by no means confined to the State in which it is located, is that conducted by Mr. L. M. Bailey, on Bow Street. Ladies' and Misses' Boots and Shoes, all hand sewed, are manufactured and sold at wholesale and are shipped to customers throughout the States. Business was inaugurated by Mr. Bailey in 1871, and during the years that have elapsed he has been very successful in building up a large and steadily increasing business. Mr. Bailey is a native of Freeport and a member of the Knights of Pythias. The premises occupied by him for business purposes are located on Bow Street, and consist of one floor 20x40 feet in dimensions, and employment is given to fifteen thoroughly capable assistants. The goods manufactured by this house are noted for their general desirability and good workmanship, and the large trade that is enjoyed is in a great measure the legitimate result of such a reputation. They are supplied at the very lowest market rates, and the prompt and capable filling of all orders is also a prominent feature of the proprietor's business methods. Mr. Bailey is thoroughly acquainted with the Boot and Shoe trade, and the discriminating care he shows in the selection of stock, and its treatment in his hands, is a guarantee that the high standard of merit set for his goods will be maintained.

W. A. Mitchell, General News Agent, and Livery Stable, off Main Street, Freeport. Numerous as Livery Stables are in this section, there are none too many of them and indeed in this, as in all other lines of industry there is always room at the top. The public find their chief difficulty not in choosing between the many good ones in operation, but in distinguishing the good from the bad; and as we confess to a weakness for that noble animal, the horse, and are besides, desirous to help along a deserving enterprise, we take great pleasure in calling the favorable attention of our readers to the establishment conducted by Mr. W. A. Mitchell, located at the corner of Main and School Streets. This stable is in more respects than one, a model of what such an undertaking should be, and that its many good points are not unappreciated is seen from the manner in which the advantages it has to offer have already been availed of. Business was begun by Mr. Mitchell in 1861, and the premises utilized for the Livery business consist of two stables and a carriage-house. One stable covers an area of 30x40 feet and the other 18x40 feet, and contains every facility for the comfort and rest of horses while intrusted to the care of this establishment, while the carriage-house is 40x44 feet in dimensions, and affords accommodations for a large number of carriages, etc. Experienced assistants are employed, and persons desiring horses and carriages of any description or for any purpose, are assured of being satisfactorily supplied at these stables. In connection with the Livery business Mr. Mitchell conducts a general News Agency and is prepared to supply all the popular publications of the day. He is a native of Freeport and has held the office of Town Clerk.

Harlow House and Restaurant, W. C. Harlow, proprietor, Freeport. Such of our readers as have had any extended experience in traveling, must have noticed the influence which the personality of the landlord of a hotel, has on the reception given to guests. Of course everybody knows that some hotels offer better sleeping accommodations, set better tables etc., than others, but we are not now referring to the difference to be noted in this respect, but to the way in which a guest is made to "feel at home," in one house, while in another he would feel strange and uncomfortable if he stayed there a month. Now, this depends entirely upon the proprietor. No one but a born hotel-keeper can make his guests his friends, and when it is said that the ability to keep a hotel must be born in a man, this is just what is meant. No better example of a home like hotel can be given than that afforded by the Harlow House, and the estimation in which this hotel is held by the traveling public, is well indicated by the answer of a well known commercial traveler, to our inquiry as to how he liked the accommodations, "The person who stops at the Harlow House once, will surely come again at the earliest opportunity" said he, and spoke as though he meant every word of it too. Mr. W. C. Harlow, the popular proprietor of the establishment in question, is a native of Augusta, and started his present enterprise in 1886. He has recently enlarged the house, improved it greatly throughout, and is now better prepared than ever before to furnish the best of accommodations at reasonable rates. The hotel is a two-story structure, 60x80 feet in dimensions, and the guests' rooms are light, pleasant and comfortable in every way. There are six assistants employed, and the service is both prompt and courteous at all times. Mr. Harlow sets an excellent table, providing an abundance of first-class food, which is well cooked and neatly served. There is a fine Livery Stable connected with the house, detailed mention of which is made in another column, and guests lack neither amusement nor facilities for pursuing their business operations. Mr. Harlow is a member of the Knights of Pythias and of the Grand Army, and has a very large circle of friends throughout this section.

George E. Legard, Harlow House Stable, Mechanic Street, Freeport. To say that the Harlow House Stable is fully worthy of its name, is to give it no light praise, for that popular Hotel has but few equals, and the same statement may truthfully be made concerning the Stable to which we have reference. Mr. George E. Legard, its proprietor, has carried it on since 1888, and has won golden opinions by reason of the accommodating spirit he displays, and the enterprise and liberality which characterize his methods of doing business. He is a native of Georgetown, Maine, and is connected with the Knights of Pythias. The premises measure about 60x70 feet, and comprise a Livery and Sale Stable, Carriage House, etc. They are well fitted up, and the vehicles and horses devoted to Livery purposes are far superior to what the public have been taught to expect in this connection. Teams may be had at any time at very short notice, and at prices that are bound to suit the most economically disposed. Mr. Legard makes a specialty of the sale of Canada Horses, and has a fine assortment of such animals on hand to select from. Those acquainted with his methods need not be told that no "jockeying" is practiced at his Stable, and to those who are not, we will simply say that every horse is warranted to the purchaser, and that Mr. Legard's guarantee is as good as gold, not only today but tomorrow, and as long as any reasonable man could wish. He has established a permanent business right here in Freeport; in other words, *he is here to stay*, and the advantages of buying horse flesh under these conditions must be obvious to all. Mr. Legard is in a position to quote the lowest market rates to his customers, and the most inexperienced purchaser need not fear getting "stuck," while the shrewdest buyer will find it worth his while to see what Mr. Legard has to offer. Carriages of all descriptions are dealt in as well as Horses, and the man who wants a stylish and satisfactory turn-out, and wishes to avoid having to pay fancy prices, will best serve his own interests by giving him a call.

J. C. Kendall, Insurance Agent, representing the following Companies:—Ætna, of Hartford, Conn.; Phœnix, of Hartford, Conn.; Home, of New York. Also Justice of the Peace; Pension Vouchers Executed; Office at Fred S. Soule's, Freeport. It is certain that as much caution and discrimination should be exercised in the placing of Insurance as in any other investment of equal importance; but how often is it the case that those whose business methods are commendable and successful in other departments, fail to appreciate the necessity for care in this special instance, and as a consequence, find the money they have paid out in premiums to be worse than wasted? Insurance that is not as sure as anything human can be, is—to speak plainly—simply a delusion and a snare, for it is much better to go without protection altogether than to rely upon that which will surely fail in the hour of need. The best way, undoubtedly, to place insurance, is to do so through an agency that will have an individual interest in the successful continuance of the same, for in that case, self-interest as well as business honor, combine to make the Insurance as satisfactory and as certain as possible. The Agency of which Mr. J. C. Kendall is the proprietor, whose office is located at Freeport, was established by him in 1882 and has already become well-known to the business men of this vicinity. Mr. Kendall is a native of Freeport and is very active in disseminating the blessings of reliable Insurance as widely as possible. He represents some of the most finely established and popular corporations in this country, prominent among which are the Ætna and Phœnix of Hartford, Conn., and the Home of New York, and can grant as favorable terms as any one in the writing of Policies. Mr. Kendall is also Justice of the Peace, and Executes Pension Vouchers in the most reliable and satisfactory manner. He is ready to give any desired information in regard to the various departments of his business, and his already attained success is rapidly increasing.

LEADING BUSINESS MEN OF FREEPORT. 317

M. V. B. Jordan, Manufacturer of Ladies' Fine Boots, Buskins and Slippers, Freeport. The manufacture of Ladies' Shoes has fittingly come to be recognized as one of the leading industries of New England, and some of the largest firms in this line have gained a national —and even international—reputation. Prominent among those engaged in the manufacture of these goods in Freeport, is Mr. Martin V. B. Jordan, who established his business in 1869, which now holds an honored place in this community; and since its establishment by great enterprise, integrity and fine order of workmanship, he has built up an extensive patronage which is alike honorable to the city and the efforts of its proprietor. The premises utilized by Mr. Jordan are located about two miles and a half out on the Southwest bend of the Durham and Freeport road, and comprise two floors, each 30x20 feet in dimensions, and fifteen hands are given constant employment. The class of goods manufactured by Mr. Jordan are highly celebrated for their beauty and durability, being carefully made in every detail, from the best materials. All orders by mail or otherwise receive the most careful and prompt attention, and the house has the universal reputation of being always thoroughly equal to all its claims in the entire satisfaction which it guarantees customers in the filling of their orders. Mr. Martin V. B. Jordan is a native of Freeport, and ranks among the truly representative manufacturers. He is an active member of the Free Masons and widely honored as a prominent citizen. Mr. Jordan manufactured the first case of shoes ever made in Freeport.

Fred S. Soule, Fashionable Tailor; Fine Woolens, etc., Main Street, Freeport. To dress well should be the aim of every man who has his own way to make in the world, for appearances count for a great deal in the battle of life, and money judiciously expended upon Clothing is never thrown away. When we say judiciously we mean used to the best advantage, and it cannot be too strongly impressed on the minds of those who seek to accomplish the best results, that the purchase of cheap and ill-fitting garments is never advisable, as whatever difference there may be between such goods and well-made Clothing in the first cost, is much more than made up in increased wear and superior appearance. Custom-made garments may be obtained at reasonable rates if the right kind of a house be patronized, and we may state right here, that there is none offering superior inducements in this line to Mr. Fred S. Soule, located on Main Street, Freeport. The establishment conducted by this gentleman covers an area of 40x65 feet, and employment is afforded to sixteen assistants. Any one in want of good, reliable, honestly-made and skillfully-fitted Clothing, should give Mr. Soule a call, as he can suit them if any one can, as both his goods and his prices are such as to win the highest approval of the public. Mr. Soule is thoroughly acquainted with his business in all its branches. He is a native of Freeport and a member of the Free Masons. St. Albans Commandry, No. 8, also of the Odd Fellows and Knights of Pythias.

J. F. Chickering, Dealer in Choice Family Groceries, Dry and Fancy Goods, Crockery and Glassware, Main Street, Freeport. Enterprising and intelligent business methods are pretty sure to make their influence felt without a great deal of delay, and therefore the large trade that has already been built up by Mr. J. F. Chickering, is only what might have been expected although this gentleman only began operations in 1887. His establishment is located on Main Street, and is as fine an example of a modern first-class business house, as can easily be found. The varied stock carried has many good points to recommend it and is constantly maintained at a high standard of excellence. To begin with, it is fresh and new of course, and then again it is most carefully selected, and will be found to contain a full assortment of Choice Family Groceries, Meats and Provisions, Crockery and Glass Ware, Boots and Shoes, all of the best quality obtainable. The prices are very moderate in every department, and customers are served with a promptness and politeness that are as acceptable as they are unusual. Mr. Chickering is a Massachusetts man by birth and a prominent Odd Fellow. He is evidently thoroughly acquainted with his business and his great success is the legitimate result of hard and intelligent work.

Cushing Hotel, Mrs. S. E. Cushing, proprietor, Depot Street, Freeport. Every experienced traveler will subscribe to the statement, that although it is comparatively easy to find so called "first-class hotels," it is a matter of the greatest difficulty to discover a house which combines the comforts of a home and the conveniences of a hotel, which is of the most unquestioned respectability, which does not have an atmosphere of Puritanical rigidity surrounding it. It is therefore with no small degree of pleasure that we call attention to that enterprise known as the Cushing Hotel, located on Depot Street in this town, for it is the unanimous verdict, so far as we have been able to learn, of those who have tested its resources and hospitality, that it has few equals and no superiors in this vicinity in all that goes to make up a desirable haven of rest for weary travelers. It was established in 1875 by Mrs. S. E. Cushing and is now under her able management. The building comprises two floors of the dimensions of 25x40 feet divided up into rooms of good size and most excellent arrangement. Employment is afforded to competent and polite assistants and nothing will be found wanting either in the fitting up and care of the rooms or the conduct of the *cuisine*, for an excellent table is set and the food is served promptly and courteously. The proprietress Mrs. Cushing is one of those ladies who seem to be born for such a position and those who have experienced her attention have nothing but praise to utter. The terms of this house are very moderate and the accommodations are strictly first-class.

O. W. Smith, Wholesale and Retail Dealer in all kinds of American and Imported Watches. Jewelry of all kinds, at the Lowest Living Profit. Fine Watch Repairing a Specialty. Orders by Mail Promptly Attended to; Freeport. No better illustration of the perfection which has been attained in the manufacture of Watches and Jewelry can be found than by an inspection of the stock of Mr. O. W. Smith, who has been actively engaged in business for thirty years, and founded his present establishment in 1886, which has, ever since its inception, been recognized among the leading ones in the Jewelry business of Freeport. The premises occupied by Mr. Smith consist of a finely appointed store, located on Main Street. There may be found a complete and extensive stock of elegant Watches and Jewelry of all kinds, including American and Imported Watches, of which a choice variety is constantly carried; also a good line of Holiday Goods throughout the holiday season. The extensive Wholesale and Retail trade requires the assistance of reliable clerks, and the entire business is most ably managed under the direct supervision of the proprietor, who is thoroughly and practically competent in all its branches. Fine Watch Repairing is made a specialty, and all orders are promptly attended to. The goods and work of this establishment are offered and executed at the lowest living profit. Mr. Smith is a native of Maine and a highly respected citizen of Freeport. He is a member of the Free Masons and Odd Fellows, and well-known in social as well as trade circles, and enjoys the esteem and confidence of the trade throughout New England and adjoining sections.

H. E. Davis & Co., Shoe Manufacturer, Mechanic Street, Freeport. The enormous consumption of Boots and Shoes in this country gives employment to thousands, for in spite of the valuable aid rendered by the ingenious machinery of the present day, by which one man can do the work of a score; the services of a vast army of skilled employes are still essential. One of the prominent establishments devoted to the Shoe Manufacturing industry of Freeport is that conducted by Messrs. H. E. Davis & Co., located on Mechanic Street. This enterprise has been in operation about two years, it having been founded in 1886, by Messrs. H. E. and J. F. Davis both natives of Freeport, and the business has since that date been conducted under the firm name of H. E. Davis & Co. The business premises utilized consist of three floors each 35x30 feet in dimensions and is supplied with all the requisite and approved machinery for the proper conduct of the Manufacturing business, which is operated by a fifteen-horse power engine. The services of twenty capable and reliable workmen are employed, and all orders of whatever magnitude, are given prompt and careful attention. The goods manufactured by H. E. Davis & Co., have acquired a prominent and desirable reputation in the market and can be relied upon for uniformity of material used, and workmanship. This firm have been in business for ten years in Freeport and are well known.

HISTORICAL SKETCH

—OF—

BUCKFIELD.

BUCKFIELD is in the southeast of Oxford County, on the Buckfield & Rumford Falls R. R. It is divided by the Nerinscot or Twenty-Mile river and also has other water supply which gives it a very large resource in this direction. Falls Brook Abbott, Washburn, Half-Moon, Shag, Tantrabagus, Wind, Bungamuck, Swan, Great and Little Labrador Ponds are some of the most important water reservoirs. There are also many hills in the town, the most prominent of which are Streaked Mountain, South Hills and Owl's Head Hill. Resting among these various elevations, the town is both sheltered and beautified. The soil, especially along the river, is fertile and agriculture advantageous. There are also in these hills several veins of magnetic iron and yellow ochre which have been mined a little and promise good results if developed. The town is the center of business for this part of the country, and its commercial interests are constantly progressing. The water supply has been a great advantage from the start. There are ten good powers on the Nerinscot river, and the outlets to the various ponds. This power is practically undeveloped and will admit of great

HISTORICAL SKETCH OF BUCKFIELD.

expansion. The present industrial interests are mainly in lumber, staves, wooden tools, grains, brushes, leather harnesses, shoes, tanneries, plaster, carding, shingles, powder kegs and powder. A slight outlay would make the water supply inexhaustible and abundantly capable of supplying a great manufacturing interest. The river is easily utilized for the purpose, other advantages are abundant, and transportation by railroad to all markets easy. There is a great granite ridge near the river, which will also be of great financial profit to some enterprising business man. The history of Buckfield is replete with interest. The first settler in the town was Benj. Spaulding, who came in 1776. He was followed in 1777 by Abijah Buck and Thomas Allen with their families. In 1785 the town was surveyed and the settlers paid two shillings an acre for it to the State of Massachusetts. The place was named after Abijah Buck and his mother, who were after that sturdy stock which has left the imprint of its life and name in various parts of the State. In 1793 the town was incorporated as Buckfield. In 1807 it sent its first representative to the Legislature in the person of Enoch Hall. A great fire across this part of the State in 1816, levelled the forest and incalculably damaged the towns. It was long before Buckfield recovered from the effects. The first preacher here was Rev. Nathan Chase, who had been a chaplain in the Revolution and exercised a strong and noble influence here for many years. The first church of which he was pastor, was organized by the Baptist denomination in 1821. Seba Smith, the well-known journalist and author was born here as was also Hon. Virgil D. Parson, member of Congress, and Hon. John D. Long, Ex-Gov. of Massachusetts, and member of Congress. The town took an active and devoted interest in the Civil War, and was represented at the front by some of Maine's most gallant soldiers. The sad, as well as the honored and joyful memorials of that great conflict have been affectionately treasured.

The town has made considerable advance in many lines since the war. In 1870 the population was 1,494, and the valuation $534,673. In 1880 the population was 1,579, and the valuation $397,598. Much business development has also been gained during the present decade. Altogether with its rich resources and the progressiveness of its people, the town's business outlook is most promising and it bids fair to become one of the chief centers of the inland trade of the State. The educational interests of the town have always been carefully considered and executed; the schools have a high and wide reputation. The town is also well advanced in social and religious culture, the churches and every charitable work are generously supported. The great natural beauty of the region is also attracting more tourists and summer visitors here every season.

RESIDENCE OF EX-GOV. JOHN D. LONG.

LEADING BUSINESS MEN

OF

BUCKFIELD, ME.

George D. Bisbee, Attorney At Law, Buckfield. The gentleman whose card we print above, is without doubt one of the best-known residents of this section of the State, for he has carried on operations for nearly a quarter of a century and is closely identified with the advancement of the best interests of Buckfield and vicinity. Mr. Bisbee was born in Hartford, Maine, and has held a number of public offices of importance and responsibility. He represented Buckfield in the State Legislature in 1873 and was elected to the Senate in 1881. For six years he filled the position of County Attorney and for four years served as United States Marshal for the District of Maine. Mr. Bisbee held a commission as Lieutenant during the Rebellion, and was connected with the Northern forces for three years, one-half which time he was confined in rebel prisons. He is a member of the Free Masons and has many warm personal friends both inside and outside of that order. It is not our purpose to speak in detail concerning Mr. Bisbee's capabilities as a lawyer, for his position in that profession is too clearly defined to need demonstation in these pages. That he is always heartily devoted to his clients' interests, our readers well know, and his painstaking care in the matter of apparently small and unimportant details shows how thoroughly he studies the cases confided to his direction. His offices are conveniently situated, and those in need of sound legal advice cannot do better in our opinion than to lay their case before Mr. Bisbee and be guided by his experienced counsel.

Homer N. Chase & Co., Nurserymen, the "Chase Nurseries, Geneva, N. Y.," Buckfield. The great enterprise carried on by the proprietors of the Chase Nurseries, whose headquarters are at Geneva, New York, and who maintain branch establishments in Philadelphia, Boston and Buckfield, is worthy of much more extended mention than the limits of our space enable us to give it, for the Chase Nurseries have a national reputation, and the undertaking is unique in one respect, being conducted by five brothers, who succeed their father, the late Hon. Thomas Chase, who founded the business over a quarter of a century ago. Some idea of the magnitude which this enterprise has attained, may be gained from the fact that the packing shed, cellars and grounds in Geneva, New York, cover an area of over three acres, and that over one hundred acres of Nursery Stock are under cultivation. The Geneva establishment is under the direct management of Messrs. R. G. and W. D. Chase, while Mr. H. A. Chase is in charge at Philadelphia, Mr. Geo. H. Chase at Boston, and Mr. Homer N. Chase here in Buckfield, this gentleman having begun operations here in 1883. He is a native of this town, and is connected with both the Free Masons and the Odd Fellows. The unsurpassed reputation held by the productions of the Chase Nurseries is the legitimate outcome of the constant employment of honorable, intelligent and liberal methods, for it has always been, and is today, the policy of the management, first to produce the best possible articles, second to bring their merits before the notice of those who would be liable to be interested, and third to sell at as low figures as circumstances will permit. To attain these ends, they have spared neither trouble nor expense in providing the most improved facilities, have advertised extensively in newspapers and elsewhere, and now have 250 agents on the road, introducing their goods to property owners. A standing offer is made to reliable men of salaried positions in connection with this department of the business, and the representative of Homer N. Chase & Co. is everywhere received for what he is,—an agent of an honorable firm, deserving of every consideration. The sale of Nursery Stock presents abundant opportunities for fraud and as our agricultural readers well know, these opportunities are eagerly availed of by many unscrupulous parties. Cheap stock is worthless stock, every time, and money spent on it is simply thrown away. The Chase Nurseries are among the best-equipped in the world, and are capable of turning out strictly reliable goods at a minimum cost. No misrepresentation is practiced or allowed by the proprietors, and we have no hesitation in saying that those who, knowing of the advantages to which we have referred, still persist in dealing with irresponsible parties in the delusive hope of saving a few dollars, richly deserve the disappointment and serious financial loss they will inevitably experience.

LEADING BUSINESS MEN OF BUCKFIELD.

C. Withington & Sons, Manufacturers of Brushes. Brushes for Cotton and Woolen Mills a Specialty, Buckfield. The almost numberless uses to which Brushes are put at the present day are hardly guessed at by the ordinary individual, for besides the more common employment of them for purposes familiar to all (such as cleaning clothes, boots, teeth, hands, etc.,) there are many manufacturing processes which could scarcely be carried on without their aid. Thousands of Brushes are used in Cotton and Woolen Mills, and it is largely owing to the perfection to which they have brought the articles adapted to such service that the firm of C. Withington & Sons may ascribe the present magnitude of their business. Although making a specialty of Brushes for Cotton and Woolen Mills, the firm by no means confine themselves to the manufacture of these goods but make Brushes of all descriptions, except those intended for Painting and Whitewashing. This enterprise is of long standing, having been started in 1855 by Messrs. Charles Withington and James H. Keyon. Twenty years later the present style was adopted, and although Mr. Charles Withington died in 1886 no change has been made in the firm name the partners now being Mr. F. P. Withington, Mr. C. C. Withington and Mr. O. H. Hersey. The first-named gentleman is a member of the Masons, and the second is connected with the Odd Fellows while Mr. Hersey belongs to both orders and is a member of the Oxford County Bar, occupying the position of County Attorney. The firm carry on a factory measuring 60x30 feet and comprising three floors, the necessary machinery being run by water-power and employment being given to twelve assistants. The product finds a ready market, chiefly in this State, for the Brushes turned out are of standard quality and are supplied at the lowest market rates.

F. A. Warren & Son, Dealers in Harnesses, Carriages, etc., Buckfield. The advantages of having a Harness properly fitted to the animal on which it is to be used, would seem to be plain enough to be apparent to every one, and yet there are many horses today seriously handicapped in their work by being improperly fitted out in this respect. Good Harnesses are not hard to find if sought for in the right place, and it is no secret in this community that the goods handled by Messrs. F. A. Warren & Son are not only equal to the best, but are sold at prices within the reach of all. Both members of the firm are natives of this town, and the junior partner (Mr. A. F. Warren), holds the office of Deputy Sheriff. Not only Harnesses, but Horse Furnishings of all descriptions are handled by this house, and any one wanting an article that is sure to prove as represented, at the lowest market rates, can do no better than to place their order right here. A large business is also done in Carriages and Sleighs, for the firm enjoy the most favorable relations with the manufacturers, and are consequently in a position to offer unusual advantages to their patrons. The Vehicles handled by them are durable as well as handsome and stylish, and are supplied with all the latest improvements known in the Carriage Makers' art.

R. S. Dorman, Dealer in Coffins, Caskets and Robes, Buckfield. Mr. R. S. Dorman has been one of Buckfield's prominent business men for over a quarter of a century, for he began operations here in 1862 and has always held a place in the front ranks. For a number of years Mr. Dorman confined himself to the manufacture of carriages, etc., but in 1881 he added Undertaking to his business and with characteristic energy, set to work to supply himself with the most improved and extensive facilities for the carrying on of the responsible duties connected with that useful field of labor. As a consequence, he is now prepared to furnish anything in the Undertaking line at short notice, for his stock of Caskets, Robes, etc., is both large and varied and bears evidence of careful and intelligent selection. Mr. Dorman makes a specialty of Embalming and announces his readiness to give immediate attention to orders by mail or telegraph. As to his competency, that may be judged from an examination of the following list of references, all the parties named being residents of this town and doubtless known to many of our readers: Dr. J. C. Caldwell, Dr. J. F. DeCoster, Mr. and Mrs. Charles Forster, Mr. James Roberts, Mrs. Silas Mitchell, Mr. and Mrs. H. N. Chase. Mr. Dorman strives to make his charges satisfactory in every case and is certainly in a position to supply Undertaking Goods at as low figures as can be named on articles of equal merit. He is a native of Mercer, Maine, a member of the Free Masons, and has a very wide circle of friends, not only in Buckfield but throughout this vicinity.

F. L. Irish & Company, Brush Block Mnfrs., Buckfield. The size of the business done in Brushes in this country, is appreciated by very few outside of those immediately interested, for the average man looks upon a Brush as a thing of no special consequence, and never realizes its usefulness until he is where such an article is not to be found. The rapidly growing demand for Brushes has caused the establishment of many expensively equipped factories, and, as in all other manufactures conducted on a large scale, the industry is divided up into many parts. For instance, the undertaking carried on by F. L. & I. M. Irish & Co., is devoted exclusively to the production of Brush Blocks, and the accuracy and rapidity with which this important portion (the foundation) of the complete Brush is turned out, must truly be seen to be appreciated. Two floors of the dimensions of 70x50 feet are occupied, and ample water-power is at hand to drive the ingenious machinery in use. There are four competent assistants employed and the facilities at hand render it easy for the firm to fill orders at very short notice, at prices that will bear the closest comparison with those quoted elsewhere. The advantages of dealing with F. L. & I. M. Irish & Co., are generally understood, and the products meet with a ready sale, being shipped practically to Boston and Pawtucket, R. I. Both members of the firm were born in Buckfield, and both belong to the Odd Fellows. They thoroughly understand their business in every detail, and give it the benefit of personal supervision, thus assuring the continued excellence of the product.

LEADING BUSINESS MEN OF BUCKFIELD

C. B. Atwood & Sons, General Store, Buckfield. The secret of successfully carrying on a retail store is after all no secret at all, for every observing person knows that honorable business methods and judicious enterprise are sure to win the favor and patronage of the public. A large and varied stock, well-selected and properly displayed, is sure to attract attention, and if the prices placed upon the articles composing it are reasonable, the goods are bound to sell as a matter of course. Therefore no further explanation is required in connection with the large business done by Messrs. C. B. Atwood & Sons. This firm has the right kind of articles, they are offered at the right kind of prices and customers are sure of the right kind of treatment, so that the business is of necessity prosperous. It was established in 1885, the partners being Messrs. C. B., E. F. and F. H. Atwood. Every member of the firm is a native of Buckfield and Mr. C. B. Atwood is connected with the Masons. Mr. F. H. Atwood being a member of the Odd Fellows. The premises in use comprise two floors measuring 80x30 feet and the stock on hand includes everything generally found in a first-class general store. No misrepresentation is practiced here and the firm strive to supply reliable goods at prices as low as the lowest.

Oxford County Dairying Association, A. F. Tilton, Manager, Buckfield. There have been many changes in the methods of butter making since the days of the old-fashioned upright churn with its up-and-down "plunger" motion, and these changes have affected not only the process of changing the cream into butter (which is, after all, but a small part of the business,) but the methods of obtaining and handling the cream, and the shipping of the finished product to the market. The "Oxford County Dairying Association" may be cited as an example of a concern using the most approved modern devices in the butter-making line, for this Association has only been in operation since 1887, and has spared neither trouble nor expense in fitting up its establishment. That the facilities at hand are quite extensive is proved by the fact that during a portion of the summer the daily product of the works amounted to 800 pounds, and that the plan under which operations are carried on is well-considered, needs no further guarantee than that afforded by the uniform excellence of the output. The cream is gathered by the Cooley process, and the direction of the enterprise is under the supervision of Mr. A. F. Tilton the efficient manager. This gentleman is a native of Livermore and is indefatigable in his efforts to advance the best interests of the undertaking under his control. President, Henry D. Irish. Directors, Henry D. Irish, Frank L. Warren, Hiram A. Conant, Elmer B. Austin, Homer N. Chase, Frank W. Bonney, William R. Carey. Clerk, Alfred Cole. Treasurer, Charles H. Prince.

J. A. Rawson, Apothecary, Buckfield. The Retailing of Drugs and Medicines is not a business to be entered into lightly, for it is by no means every man who is fitted by temperament, to say nothing of education, for such a task. Constant, unrelaxing and intelligent vigilance is the price of success in the true sense of the word, and the progressive Pharmacist must keep himself abreast of the latest scientific thought if he would conduct a really first-class establishment. It was in 1875 that Mr. J. A. Rawson began business in this town, and the confidence which has long been placed in his skill and his methods by those most conversant with both, is the most flattering possible proof of what his record has been in his responsible position. He is a native of Paris, Maine, and is connected with the Odd Fellows, besides holding a high degree in the Masonic Order. Mr. Rawson carries one of the most complete assortments of Pure Drugs, Medicines and Chemicals to be found in this section of the State, and is therefore exceptionally well-prepared to compound Physicians' Prescriptions without delay, in a perfectly satisfactory manner, especially as the apparatus at his command is of the most approved description. No chances are taken in this department, everything being done by precise rule, and the prices are put at the lowest possible figures for first-class service. Fancy Goods and Toilet Articles are handled to some extent, and the stock of these articles includes some of the latest novelties in the market.

C. M. & H. A. Irish, Brush Blocks, Easels, Lumber, etc., Buckfield. That Maine has a great future before it as a manufacturing State, no thoughtful and observing person can doubt. The natural wealth of the section—the mighty forests, and the broad rivers, forming easy highways for commerce—all contribute towards rendering this result possible, and if the development of the State continues at its present rate it will not be long before Maine products will be found in every market. The production of Long and Short Lumber has been one of the leading industries in the past, and among the most reliable firms engaged in it must be mentioned that of C. M. & H. A. Irish. This house has been before the public for 15 years, operations having been started in 1873. Both partners are natives of Hartford, Maine, and both are connected with the Odd Fellows. Premises measuring 75x22 feet are utilized, supplied with all the necessary machinery which is run by water-power. Besides dealing extensively in Long and Short Lumber, the firm manufacture Brush Blocks and school-room Easels, a force of four assistants being employed. Orders are invariably given immediate and careful attention and every care is taken to ensure that the goods supplied shall be fully up to the high standard long since placed on the productions of this establishment.

HISTORICAL SKETCH
— OF —
BRUNSWICK.

BRUNSWICK is an ideal town in New England, alike charming for its natural beauty and its quiet air of refinement. A subtle aroma of culture seems to pervade its streets and buildings and give peculiar dignity to its people. Whether it was peculiarly fitted for a college town, or has been transformed into harmony with the scholarly, academic spirit, it would not be easy to decide; but no one can escape the power of its beauty and charm. The history of Brunswick has been carefully studied and compiled by able men, so that its historical archives are unusually full. Its colonial history extends back to the very earliest activities of the English in this part of the new world. Thomas Purchase, an energetic pioneer and trader with the Indians had established himself here as early as 1628. His fame spread throughout the growing band of Englishmen along the Atlantic coast of New England, and in 1632 he was joined by George Way. These two obtained a patent from the Plymouth Company in England for a large piece of territory at the mouth of the Androscoggin River. It was about four miles square, and contained the great salmon fisheries, which were widely celebrated for their rich supplies of salmon, especially among the Indians. As early as 1639, the Indians already gave signs of an intention to do the English colonies no good, and in that year, for the sake of protection, Thomas Purchase placed his little colony under jurisdiction and control of Massachusetts. It continued to grow slowly but steadily up to the time of the outbreak of the King Philips War, in 1675. In that year the wrath of the Indians was poured out upon the little settlement, but though they devasted and burned the whole town, all the inhabitants succeeded in escaping. From this time for about a quarter of a century, the place lay desolate; but at the beginning of the eighteenth century, old families began to come back and the place so rapidly recovered its former size that it was incorporated as a township by the General Court of Massachusetts in 1717. Its territory comprised six square miles, and it was named Brunswick, in honor of the recently founded royal family of England. The first selectmen were Capt. M. Gyles, Thomas Wharton, James Storratt, John Cochran and John Heath, the latter also being the first town clerk.

In 1722, the township which had grown to number about forty families, had to be abandoned again, on account of the Indian wars. After a few years, however, it regained its former size and began again to grow, receiving a renewed charter as a town in 1738. In 1752 the town contained twenty dwelling-houses, four mills and one meeting-house. On account of the river, the salmon fishing, which was very extensive here, was the earliest and most important industry. The soil was also unusually fertile, and game furnished large quantities of fur. It is said that at this time one man caught thirty-nine barrels of salmon in three weeks. The town officers elected in 1639 were Samuel Hinkley, Town Clerk; Capt. B. Larrabee, Samuel Hinkley, John Getchell, James Dunning and David Dunning.

The Indians of this region belonged to the Anasagunticook tribe, and were of a bold, fiery nature, large in numbers and powerful in organization. Having their headquarters at Brunswick Falls, they gave the early inhabitants of this region a great deal of annoyance and trouble. Brunswick furnished about thirty men to the expedition against Louisburg in 1745, and other volunteers during the French and Indian wars. In 1760 among the leading families here, were the Pennell, Gross, Harding, Stone, Weston, Curtis and Melcher. In 1775 the town united with the rest of the colony in the agressive measures taken against the tyranny of England. It furnished a full quota of men and monies to the Revolutionary struggles, and spared no effort to help in establishing the liberty and government of the United States. Among other gallant officers from Brunswick were Col. Samuel Thompson, Col. Nathaniel Purinton, Major Nathaniel Larrabee and Capt. John Merrill. After the Revolutionary war the town continued to grow with increasing rapidity, and about 1800 the first stage line was opened between here and Portland. The population in 1740 was 160; in 1765, 506; in 1776, 867; in 1790, 1,387, and is now about two thousand. A considerable shipping interest was established here during the early years of this century, which was effectually killed by the Embargo Acts of 1807 and 1809, which caused immense indignation here as in other parts of New England. In the war of 1812 Brunswick furnished three hundred men, who nobly sustained the honor of the country and their native town. Though the war was locally disadvantageous, home issues were laid aside and the common cause supported with earnest devotion. After the war was over, the upward progress of the town was again resumed, and in 1820 the population had become 2,931, and the valuation $403,793.

In the war of the Rebellion, Brunswick took an honorable and distinguished part. The culture of the citizens and the added enthusiasm of the college, war made all the movements of the town thorough and generous. Several prominent field officers went from Brunswick, and over 700 private soldiers were enlisted here, a large proportion considering the number of inhabitants. In 1861, $7,000 were raised here for the support of the soldiers and government; in 1862, $15,700 were raised; in 1863, $42,800; 1864, $33,500; 1865, $33,200; making total of $132,200, during the war, which only represents a part of their generous contributions. The ladies of the town contributed great assistance in many ways, and throughout the war Maine had no more energetic and responsive town or city than Brunswick. Most of the soldiers who went from Brunswick enlisted in the 3d, 5th, 7th, 12th, 13th, 17th, 19th, 25th, or 30th, but the town was represented in almost every regiment that left the State. The memory of those who fell in the great conflict has ever been tenderly cherished, and no means spared to perpetuate the memorials of their glorious and patriotic devotion.

HISTORICAL SKETCH OF BRUNSWICK.

Bowdoin College, which has been so long and intimately connected with Brunswick, is deserving of more than passing notice, being the oldest and most famous educational institution of its kind in the State. The first movement for the college was started in 1788, by the Senator in Massachusetts Legislature from Cumberland Co., Hon. Josiah Thatcher, and the charter for the institution was granted by the Legislature in 1794. Brunswick was chosen as the cite because it made the most generous offers of land and support. It was named Bowdoin College in honor of the Hon. James Bowdoin, a graduate of Harvard, in 1745, delegate to the first Congress in 1776, and Governor of Massachusetts. One of the earliest and chief patrons of the college was the Hon. James Bowdoin, son of the former, a graduate of Harvard in 1771, who contributed money and land valued at $6,000. The original trustees were Rev. Thos. Brown, Falmouth; Samuel Deane, D.D., Portland; John Frothingham, Esq., Portland; Rev. Daniel Little, Wells; Rev. Thomas Lancaster, Scarboro; David Mitchell, Esq., North Yarmouth; Rev. Tristram Gilman, North Yarmouth; Rev. Alden Bradford, Wiscasset; Thomas Rice, Esq., Pownalboro; William Martin, North Yarmouth. The original purpose, as stated in charter, was "to found a seminary to promote virtue and piety, and a knowledge of the languages, and of the use of the liberal arts and sciences." Five townships of lands, each six miles square, were granted to the college by the Legislature. The college did not formally open until 1802, the Rev. Joseph McKeen of Beverly, Mass., having been chosen the first President in the preceding year. Massachusetts Hall, completed in 1802, was the first college building. In the first year there were eight students. Among the most prominent of the early professors were John Abbott, first professor of languages, and Parker Cleaveland, first professor of mathematics and sciences. In 1805 the Peucinian Society was founded. In 1807 there were forty-four students and 1,500 volumes in the library. In the same year President McKeen died and the Rev. Jesse Appleton of Dartmouth was chosen his successor. In 1808 the Athenæum Society was established. In 1811 the Hon. James Bowdoin died, leaving to the college another legacy of 2,000 books, many valuable maps, paintings, etc., valued at $15,000, and made the college his residuary legatee. In 1819, on the death of President Appleton, the Rev. William Allen, former President of Dartmouth, succeeded him. President Allen was followed in 1839 by the Rev. Leonard Woods of the Bangor Theological Seminary, who served the longest term of any President of the college, continuing in office until 1865, and was one of Bowdoin's ablest leaders and most distinguished. Among Bowdoin's other famous graduates were Henry W. Longfellow and Nathaniel Hawthorne, both of class of '25, and two of the most brilliant lights in American literature. Bowdoin has, indeed, been always distinguished for its strong literary tone and atmosphere, and is not surpassed at the present time in this respect by any college in New England. In 1855 King's Chapel was completed, and two years later the beautiful Memorial Hall, in honor of the Bowdoin men who fell during the war. The Rev. Samuel Harris was President from 1865 to 1871; he was succeeded by Gen. Joseph H. Chamberlain in 1871, and the latter by the Rev. William D. Hyde, D.D., the present incumbent. The total number of graduates up to 1876 was 1,887. The medical school, which is now in a flourishing condition, was established by the Maine

326   HISTORICAL SKETCH OF BRUNSWICK.

Three Brunswick Views

Legislature in 1820. Since 1820 this department has graduated 1,174 pupils. At the present time there are eighty-five students in the medical department and 137 in the academic department, making a total of 222. The college is now in a prosperous condition, and admirably maintaining the laurels of former years. The campus is spacious and beautiful, with wide lawns, long, shaded walks and beautiful buildings; among the chief of these are King's Chapel, Sargent's Gymnasium, Memorial Hall, Massachusetts Hall, Winthrop, Maine and Appleton Halls, the Medical School and Laboratory. The library now contains, together with those of the Athenæum and Peninian Societies, over 35,000 volumes, and there are large art collections and valuable scientific collections and apparatus. The faculty now numbers twenty-four, thirteen of whom are in the academical faculty, and the ability and scholarship of the teachers with the accumulated resources of many years, render Bowdoin's facilities for imparting higher instruction on a par with the best standard in the country.

The town of Brunswick is remarkable for the beauty of its environment, no less than the culture of its citizens. It seems to breathe the quiet air of refinement, and its broad streets, with arching elms, cool river drives and hilly outlooks, render its natural beauties of a high order. It is becoming more famed every year as a quiet and ideally restful summer resort. Although it has kept advancing, it has never cared to change its town government, which has worked with the greatest satisfaction. The population of Brunswick has increased as follows:—1740, 160; 1765, 506; 1776, 867, valuation, £19,000; 1790 1,378; 1810, 2,682—$325,280; 1820, 2,931—$403,793; 1830, 3,547—$815,178; 1840, 4,259; 1850, 4,975—$1,107,822; 1860, 4,723 —$1,421,091; 1870, 4,727; 1880, 5,384—$1,979,877.

It is probable that few people have a correct knowledge of Brunswick as a manufacturing center. That it affords regular employment to some sixteen hundred operatives in its various industries, is a matter of surprise to many who have been accustomed to look upon this good old town as a seat of learning and the abode of retired sea captains; and that there should be still better opportunities for a large increase of these manufacturing enterprises, where, on its lines of railroad, buildings can be erected affording the cheapest shipment obtainable.

The Board of Trade, with over one hundred members of the leading business men of the place, are seeking to bring some of the natural advantages offered by Brunswick to the attention of manufacturers, and any party of standing may be assured of a cordial welcome should he visit the place with a view to investigating the claims put forth.

At the present time the population is about six thousand, and the valuation $3,-496,128. All the town's interests are in a prosperous and progressive condition, and it seems that she has entered upon a period of unparalleled advances. The slowly accumulated forces of generations of enterprise and forethought are now being reaped in increasing abundance, and it cannot be other than a great satisfaction to all who have known this beautiful and delightful town to learn that its days of prosperity are lengthening into the deserved rewards of steady and upward growth.

LEADING BUSINESS MEN

OF

BRUNSWICK, ME.

Brunswick Savings Institution, Main Street, corner of Bank, Brunswick. Just about thirty years have elapsed since the Brunswick Savings Institution began operations, and it would be a most interesting and valuable study to trace out all the good it has wrought, all the wise resolutions it has prompted, and all the suffering it has obviated since the date of its incorporation—1858. But this is impossible. No one can tell what this worthy enterprise has accomplished, no one can tell what it may accomplish, but one thing is evident and sure—its influence is for good, first, last and all the time. Many a family is in comfortable circumstances by reason of the facilities for saving afforded by this Bank, and some idea of the extent to which the accommodations it offers are availed of, may be gained from the fact that it holds deposits aggregating some $368,000. The rate of interest allowed is in all cases as high as circumstances will permit, but those in charge of the Institution realize that the first requisite is safety, and never run extra risks for the sake of an extra per centage. They are all experienced and successful business men, and being able to conduct their own affairs successfully, may safely be intrusted with those of other people. The President, Mr. Henry Carvill and the Treasurer, Mr. Thomas H. Riley and Mr. John P. Winchell, Assistant Treasurer, are known to the great majority of the people in this vicinity, by reputation at least, while the Board of Trustees is constituted of other prominent citizens, such as Messrs. Weston Thompson, N. T. Palmer, Alonzo Day, Isaac Plummer, together with the President. Taken all in all, this Bank may be justly regarded as a worthy representative of the Savings Institutions of New England, and this is no small honor, for New England leads all other sections of the Union in the character and importance of its Savings Banks. New York, to be sure, holds the distinction of containing the largest bank in the country—the Bowery Savings Bank of New York City, which has about $44,000,000 in deposits and a surplus of $11,000,000, but outside of New York State, New England can challenge comparison. The aggregate capital of the various Savings Banks in the United States is $1,375,000,000—$125,000,000 of which is in Surplus, and $1,250,000,000 is due 3,457,352 depositors—figures which show the grand importance of these Institutions, but which are far too great to be appreciated by human comprehension. Industry and frugality will work wonders. Few men are so poor but what they could be poorer, and the number of those who actually *cannot* save money is very small indeed. "Spend less than you earn" is advice that only needs to be followed to ensure comfort and happiness, and every intelligent person should heed the lesson it conveys.

F. H. Purinton, Machinist and Gas Fitter, Main Street, Brunswick. Since the gentleman above named began operations, he has executed many commissions of no small importance, although he has been established in business for himself only since 1873. In the carrying out of these orders he has proved that no one in Brunswick is in a position to offer more decided advantages in the line of Machinist, Steam and Gas Fitting, and has conclusively shown that he possesses both the ability and the will to combine the greatest efficiency with the greatest economy, and to bear the interests of his customers in mind, without making any pretence of neglecting his own. Mr. F. H. Purinton is a native of Topsham and a member of the Free Masons, and is thoroughly experienced in this line of business and is known as a well-informed and energetic business man. The business premises utilized are located on Main Street and comprise one floor, 20x60 feet in dimensions. All orders left at this place will receive prompt attention. Estimates will be furnished for all kinds of Machinist Work, Steam Heating, and for the supplying of Manufacturers' workshops and private residences with Gas and Steam Heating. He is the patentee of a Steam Heater for heating dwelling houses, which is one of the very best heaters in use, and has given perfect satisfaction wherever they have been used. We need hardly mention the advantages of placing orders of this kind with a person who makes a specialty of them, and is fully responsible and prepared to contract to carry out such, at the lowest market rates. Employment is given to eight skilled workmen, and all order either for new work or repairing will be filled at short notice and in a superior manner.

C. W. Allen, Druggist and Apothecary, Lemont Block, cor. of Main and Pleasant Sts., Brunswick. One of the oldest established business enterprises to be found in Brunswick, is that conducted by Mr. C. W. Allen, Druggist and Apothecary, located in Lemont Block at the corner of Main and Pleasant Streets, for the undertaking in question was founded twenty-five years ago, having had its inception in the year 1863, under the present style of C. W. Allen, and it is but fair to say that, so far as the reputation of the enterprise is concerned the record made has been such as to confirm and strengthen the high degree of confidence placed in the undertaking by the community at large at its inception, and this confidence is fully deserved. A very large stock of Drugs, Medicines and Chemicals is carried at all times, complete in every department, and selected expressly with a view to the requirements of family trade. The premises occupied are 20x70 feet in size, and include one floor, being equipped with all the facilities and appliances, etc., to be found in a first-class city Drug Store. Mr. Allen is a native of Turner, Maine, and gives especial attention to the Compounding of Prescriptions, and no means are neglected to assure absolute accuracy in the filling of such orders, while the prices are put at the lowest figures consistent with the use of standard ingredients.

A. A. Davis, Dealer in Clocks and Jewelry; also Elgin, Hampden and Waltham Watches, etc., Brackett's Block, Brunswick, T. W. Davis, Manager. One of the most infallible signs of the culture and taste of an individual is that afforded by the character of the jewelry worn, and so decidedly is this the case, that a shrewd and experienced observer can generally tell at a glance the position held in society by those coming within the scope of his observation. But no matter how correct and refined the taste of a person may be in this respect, it will be of but little avail unless it is known where it can be fully gratified; and it is to supply this information that we have undertaken this article. The establishment of Davis, the Jeweler, located on Main street, in Brackett's Block, is one which well repays a visit as therein will be found a stock of Watches, Clocks and Jewelry, embracing many of the latest and most beautiful designs. The line of Watches handled include Elgin, Hampden and Waltham makes, all of which are offered at the lowest market rates. Mr. Davis was born in Brunswick and is extremely well known throughout this locality. His store covers an area of 20x30 feet and he has the assistance of Mr. T. W. Davis as Manager. Those desiring to purchase anything in the line of Watches, Clocks or Jewelry cannot afford to pass this establishment by, and should they call they will receive prompt and courteous attention. Special attention given to repairing in all its branches.

Pejepscott National Bank, Main, opposite Mason Street, Brunswick. That the Pejepscott National Bank deserves particular mention in a work treating of Brunswick's commercial history and present position, must be obvious to any one at all acquainted with that institution's career; for from the beginning this Bank has been a Brunswick enterprise, carried on by Brunswick men, and conducted with a jealous regard for Brunswick's interests. It was incorporated in 1865, and during the almost quarter of a century that has since elapsed, it has made a record for enterprise tempered with a just conservatism that is as gratifying as it is exceptional. The Bank has prospered as Brunswick has prospered, and has borne its share of what adversity the community has experienced since its incorporation, and by thus identifying itself with every-day affairs has won the confidence of the public to a marked degree. The list of the officers and directors controlling its affairs is in itself enough to vouch for the character of the institution, for the names found therein are known all through this section, and their owners are representative men in whom the community puts the utmost trust. Mr. H. C. Martin is the President, and Mr. L. H. Stover the Cashier; the Board of Directors being constituted of Messrs. H. C. Martin, W. S. Skolfield, J. L. Skolfield, Samuel Skolfield, John Bishop, P. C. Merriman and L. H. Stone. Certainly the Bank's affairs may be looked upon as quite secure in such hands as these, and there is every reason to hope and expect that the brilliant record of the past, will be equalled and even surpassed by that made in the future.

B. R. Jordan & Co., Dealers in Groceries, Paints, Oils and Glass, Main Street, Brunswick. As the health and strength of a people depend so largely on the food they eat, and as Groceries form so large a portion of the food eaten, it is of the highest importance to the welfare of a community that the Grocery trade should be in the hands of men of repute and integrity, and therefore when we find a house engaged in it that gives every evidence of being managed in a straightforward and liberal way, we take special pleasure in commending it to the public. Such a house is that maintained by B. R. Jordan & Co., on Main Street. This establishment was founded in 1865 under the firm name of Jordan & Snow, and so conducted until 1876, when its style was changed to the present one of B. R. Jordan & Co. These gentlemen have established a record for fair dealing and thorough business knowledge of which they may well be proud. One floor and a basement each 20x60 feet is occupied and a very extensive and varied stock is constantly carried comprising full lines of all descriptions of Groceries, selected expressly for family trade. Also Paints, Oils and Glass are extensively dealt in, and many inducements are offered to the public, as only the most reliable and popular goods are handled and sold at positively the lowest market rates and few if any establishments in this vicinity, can make a better showing, as the goods handled are fresh and first-class in every respect and warranted satisfactory. Mr. B. R. Jordan has held the office of Town Treasurer and Town Clerk, also Judge of Municipal Court.

S. T. & E. M. Brown, Manufacturers of Long and Short Lumber, Main Street, Brunswick. In a book of this character it is unavoidable that a great deal of prominence should be given to the Lumber business, for this industry plays so important a part in Maine's commercial interests, that no work treating of them would be complete did it not make extensive reference to this branch of trade. Among the best-known concerns handling Lumber in Brunswick or vicinity, must be placed that of Messrs. S. T. & E. M. Brown, which does business on Main Street. Both the gentlemen referred to are natives of Brunswick, and they have been identified with their present enterprise since 1886, their father, Truworthy Brown having carried on the business in the same mill sixteen years. Long and Short Lumber is very extensively handled, the entire plant utilized, covering an acre of ground, and comprising improved machinery of various kinds, being the inventors of a "Heavy Timber Planing Machine" run by water-power. Messrs. S. T. & E. M. Brown enjoy excellent facilities for obtaining timber at low rates, and having a thorough understanding of their business and a determination to give their customers a fair share of whatever advantages may be gained, they are enabled to supply anything in their line at rates as low as the lowest. Employment is given to twenty-five experienced assistants in the busy season, down to ten in the slackest time of the year. Orders are filled promptly, accurately and intelligently.

E. W. Johnson, M. D., Druggist and Apothecary, Main Street, Brunswick. There is no better known Druggist and Apothecary in Brunswick than Dr. E. W. Johnson, located on Main street, and he is especially well-known in this section of the State. Dr. Johnson is a native of Durham. He has been in practice and in the Drug business for twenty-five years, and as may be supposed in the case of one having his extensive experience, is thoroughly acquainted with every detail of his business. The old adage "Familiarity breeds contempt" is undoubtedly applicable to some cases, but it does not apply here, for Dr. Johnson realizes more and more with every year, the responsibilities of his position, and may be depended upon to neglect no means to serve the best interests of his customers. Prompt and decisive in the filling of orders, he is still very careful to avoid the least chance of error, and hence many prefer to have all their prescriptions compounded at this establishment, saying that they feel entirely secure when this course is pursued. There can be no higher compliment paid any Druggist and we are pleased to be able to say that it is well-deserved and will doubtless continue to be merited. Dr. Johnson carries a full stock of Drugs, etc., and also of Toilet Articles and similar goods. Employment is given to competent and well informed assistants, and callers may depend on receiving prompt and courteous attention. "Remedium," a perfect remedy for Chapped Hands, Face and Lips, Sunburn, Tan, and all Roughness of Skin. Apply to affected parts after washing and at bed-time. E. W. Johnson, M. D., Proprietor, Brunswick.

S. J. Boardman, Dealer in Dry and Fancy Goods, Cloaks, Shawls, etc. Geo. L. Thompson, Manager, Main Street, Brunswick. The ladies are noted for being "bargain hunters" especially so far as Dry and Fancy Goods are concerned, and as the establishment whose card we print above is known as the headquarters for bargains in those lines, it is but natural that it should be very liberally patronized by the fair sex. The enterprise in question, has been in operation a little over ten years, having been started in 1877. It is owned by Mrs. S. J. Boardman and is under the management of Mr. Geo. L. Thompson, who is admirably suited to the position he holds. Mrs. Boardman is a native of New Bedford, Mass., and Mr. Thompson was born in the same State, his birth-place being Newburyport. Two floors are occupied of the dimensions of 23x32 feet, and a very extensive stock is carried, comprising Dry and Fancy Goods, as well as a beautiful selection of Cloaks, Shawls, etc. As we have noted before, this is a famous store for bargains, and it is probably on account of this that one is always sure to find the stock made up entirely of fresh and seasonable goods, as prices are put at such figures that the public have to buy and thus "keep things moving." Employment is given to five careful and attentive assistants, and not the least popular feature of the management is the uniform politeness extended to every customer. Goods are cheerfully shown and any desired information given if possible. Mr. Thompson gives very close personal attention to the workings of this enterprise and is always on the alert to remedy defects and provide new features. He is deservedly popular and always has the welfare of his customers under consideration.

F. D. Snow, Bakery, Pleasant Street, Brunswick. There are a great many people who know of "Snow's Bakery" for this enterprise was inaugurated in 1884, and has been steadily and energetically carried on ever since. Mr. F. D. Snow, its proprietor, was born in Brunswick, and his place of business is located on Pleasant Street. The premises occupied, comprise two floors each of the dimensions of 22x60 feet, and include a spacious sales-room and a well fitted up bake-shop supplied with every modern convenience. Bread, Cake and Pastry of all kinds may be had here, and so popular are Mr. Snow's productions with the public, that the employment of five competent assistants is required to meet with the brisk and increasing demand of the large wholesale and retail trade transacted, and three teams are run by Mr. Snow to accommodate his patrons. The goods coming from this Bakery are made by skilled hands to be sure, but they would never have reached the point in the favor of the people that they now hold, were it not for the fact they are made of selected material and every detail of their manufacture carefully attended to. Mr. Snow may well take pride in the reputation his establishment holds, for it has been honestly earned and will be as honestly maintained in the future. The lowest market rates are quoted, and every patron assured polite attention. Weddings, parties and receptions supplied at reasonable rates and of as good quality as can be had in the best city bakeries.

LEADING BUSINESS MEN OF BRUNSWICK.

Tontine Hotel, W. B. Spear, Proprietor. Clerks, R. O. B. Dunning and G. W. Parker, Brunswick. It has been said that the true way to be prosperous and happy, is not so much to know how to earn money as to know how to spend it, and it must be confessed that this theory has much sound sense to recommend it. We all know people who are able to make a dollar go as far as twice that sum will in common hands, and a good part of this desirable result is due to knowing where to buy what you want. Clothing, books, luxuries—all of them may be bought to much better advantage at some places than at others and in the purchase of food and lodging, or in other words in the procuring of Hotel Accommodations, the rule holds equally good. A man may be supremely uncomfortable in a house charging from $3.00 to $6.00 per day, or he may be contented and well fed in one whose terms are not half so high. The Tontine Hotel is a fine example of first-class accommodations at second-class prices, and under its present management is unquestionably as desirable a House to stop at as can be found in this State. This is not our opinion alone, it is shared by hundreds who have experienced the hospitality of this popular Hotel and its wisdom is confirmed by the everyday experience of those making use of its facilities. A Hotel has been carried on here for about sixty years, but the present management assumed control in 1887. Mr. W. B. Spear is the Proprietor, while Mr. R. O. B. Dunning is the genial and accommodating Manager, and Mr. G. W. Parker the popular Clerk. There are fifty-five guest-rooms on the premises, which measure 40x70 feet and are three stories in height. Employment is offered to twelve assistants, and the rooms are kept in fine condition, while the table service is all that could be desired. The best that the market affords is furnished to guests, and the cooking is as a rule, excellent. A Livery Stable is connected with the Tontine House and teams may be had at all hours at low rates.

Spear & Whitmore, Dealers in Coal. Offices on Main and Cedar Streets, Brunswick. The inhabitants of this country are most fortunate in having abundant natural resources to draw from and in no particular are they more blessed in this direction than in the inexhaustible supplies of Coal which the United States contain. It would be difficult to over estimate the importance of an abundant fuel supply, for manufacturing, is out of the question; our comfort at home depends in a great measure upon it. One of the most popular firms in Brunswick engaged in handling Coal is that of Messrs. Spear & Whitmore, whose offices are located on Main and Cedar Streets. They inaugurated their enterprise in 1886, and have already established a large retail trade extending throughout Brunswick and adjoining towns. The facilities for handling and storing the immense stock carried are large and complete. Five competent assistants are employed, and premises are utilized, (in addition to the offices, already mentioned,) comprising a yard covering an acre of ground with buildings capable of holding three thousand tons of Coal. All orders, whether large or small, will receive prompt and careful attention, and those sent by mail will be acted upon with equal celerity to those given in person. Messrs. Spear and Whitmore are both natives of Maine and have many friends here. Mr. W. B. Spear is connected with the Free Masons and Mr. J. A. Whitmore with the Masons and Odd Fellows.

William M. Pennell, Dealer in Investment Securities and General Insurance Agent, Corner of Post-Office Square and Main Street, Brunswick. On the corner of Post-Office Square and Main Street is to be found one of the most sightly and pleasant offices on the street. Here all parties looking for safe and desirable Investments will find Mr. Pennell ready to supply their wants. He makes it a point to recommend only such Securities as will bear the closest investigation, and is building up a first-class business. He is also the representative of some of the leading Insurance Companies doing business. He has represented the Ætna Life of Hartford, as special agent over four years and has on his books the names of many of the leading citizens of this and other places in the State. The Employer's Liability Company is the Accident Company which Mr. Pennell represents in this department of his business. Fire Insurance is written in such companies as the Liverpool and London and Globe of England, the Connecticut of Hartford, the Orient of the same city, and other sound and well-known companies. He will be found ready to courteously give any information concerning the above lines of his business. Mr. Pennell is a native of Brunswick. He is Secretary of the Board of Trade and also of the Brunswick Loan and Building Association.

F. W. Barron, Groceries and Provisions, Main Street, Brunswick. The establishment conducted by Mr. F. W. Barron on Main Street, should certainly be familiar to the public in connection with the sale of Groceries and Provisions, for it has been occupied for this purpose, for the past fourteen years, having been established by its present proprietor in 1874. As long as it has been devoted to this trade, we feel that it is perfectly safe to assert that it was never so popular as it is at the present day for Mr. Barron has proceeded from the first with a determination to make his establishment second to none in Brunswick, so far as the offering of genuine inducements to the public is concerned and no better evidence of his success could be asked for than is supplied by his constantly increasing trade. Two floors are occupied each 20x50 feet in dimensions, and a remarkably complete stock of Choice Family Groceries are carried, also Provisions are very extensively handled, and always to be had here. Mr. Barron makes a specialty of "Fine Teas and Coffees." Particular attention is requested to the fresh and varied assortment of Food Supplies displayed, as they include only the best productions of the markets, all inferior and second-rate goods being entirely excluded. Orders are promptly and carefully delivered and moderate prices are quoted in every department.

F. H. Wilson, Pharmacist, Main Street, Brunswick. There is no need of enlarging upon the usefulness of a well-appointed and well-managed drug store in a community, for this usefulness is too plainly apparent to admit of its being disputed, and it is now generally conceded that the physician who heals a patient, must, in some cases, share whatever credit may attach to so doing, not only with the nurse but also with the apothecary who furnished the fresh and unadulterated drugs by which nature was aided in the battle against disease. It is unfortunate that some Drug Stores should be conducted by men totally unfitted for such a task, but still this is probably unavoidable, and on the whole the residents of Brunswick have reasons to congratulate themselves on the high standing to which the majority of pharmaceutical establishments located in this town are fairly entitled. It is but natural that the Pharmacy conducted by Mr. F. H. Wilson which was established in 1875 and located on Main Street, should be preferred by many people to any other in the vicinity, as it is generally understood that its proprietor is one of the most eminent of our Dispensing Chemists, and no patron of its prescription department can fail to observe the scrupulous nicety with which the most ordinary prescription is compounded. For this and for other reasons the prescription business of this establishment is a very large one, and as a consequence the consumption of the various Drugs and other agents employed in its carrying on, is very extensive thus necessitating their constant renewal and assuring their freshness. The premises occupied are spacious and attractively fitted up, fine "texture" ceiling work is one of the adornments of this model store. The assortment of fine Toilet Articles and other Fancy Goods is large and varied. Two thoroughly competent assistants are constantly employed and we need not add that prompt and courteous attention is extended to every caller. Mr. Wilson is a native of Topsham and a highly respected citizen of Brunswick, and a member of the Free Masons, Odd Fellows and Knights of Pythias. Mr. Wilson puts up and has a fine sale for his "Cough Annihilator." This medicine has been before the people several years and is said to be one of the very best remedies in the market.

E. D. Morin, Dealer in Groceries and Provisions, Main Street, Brunswick. It would probably be impossible to find an establishment more universally known in this vicinity than that conducted by Mr. E. D. Morin on Main Street, and the more thorough an investigation is made around town the more one is convinced in the idea that this enterprise ranks second to no other of a similar nature in Brunswick and vicinity. It was inaugurated in 1880 by its present proprietor, and the business has not reached its present development and magnitude on account of good luck, but simply because the furnishing of uniformly superior articles at uniformly low prices, is sure to result in the attainment of a large trade. The premises occupied comprise one floor and basement each covering an area of 20x40 feet and an additional storehouse for the accommodation of the large stock handled. The merchandise dealt in includes both Groceries and Provisions. No pains are spared to maintain the high reputation which the establishment has long since been accorded and both as regards quality and price, the articles handled will be found to give perfect satisfaction. Two assistants are employed and customers are served with a precision and celerity which are both novel and gratifying. The proprietor of this prosperous enterprise is a native of Canada, and is not only universally known throughout this locality but also generally esteemed.

Byron Stevens, Wholesale and Retail Bookseller and Stationer, Main Street, Brunswick. It is very certain that no account of the prominent business men of Brunswick would be complete were not mention made of Mr. Byron Stevens. The enterprise now conducted by Mr. Stevens was originally inaugurated in 1822 by Mr. G. Griffin, and popularly known as the College Book Store, and has been under the management of its present proprietor since 1884. The establishment is located on Main street, and may well be called the "Mecca" of those literarily inclined throughout Brunswick. The reasons for this are many, and prominent among them is the fact that any book published may be obtained through Mr. Stevens at publishers' rates, while he carries a full selection of the latest popular works as well as all the leading publications. One of the finest stocks of Fashionable and Commercial Stationery to be found in Brunswick, is also carried by Mr. Stevens, and the latest novelties in the line of Art Materials are always obtainable here at the earliest possible moment. Mr. Stevens is a native of Portland, Maine, but has resided in Brunswick ten years. The premises utilized are located on the corner of Main and Pleasant Streets, opposite the Tontine Hotel, and comprise two floors and a basement each covering an area of 20x60 feet, and an extensive retail trade is transacted, requiring the services of competent and well-informed assistants. It is a store that Brunswick people are very proud of, and well they may be, for few stores even in the cities display so attractive a stock the year around, as is to be found here. Their specialties are Wedding and other gifts, Fine Pictures, Artistic Wares and Fashionable Stationery.

J. F. Chaney, Dealer in Coal and Wood. Main Office, H. V. Stackpole's Shoe Store, Odd Fellows Block. Scale Office, at Wood Yard, near the Gas House, Brunswick. Recent developments in connection with the Coal trade have convinced many a worried house-holder that it would be a most desirable thing to have a private coal mine in his back-yard, and thus secure an unfailing supply at a fixed price, for the mining operations would not then be entirely stopped by "strikes" at uncertain intervals, and even should this occur, the matter could be settled without the employment of any "Board of Arbitration" or such ineffective and costly device. But as Coal in its natural state is unfortunately confined to certain regions far from here, the next best thing to do is to enter into relations with a house that makes a specialty of its handling, and that can be depended upon to supply its customers at the lowest market rates as long as there is any supply to draw from. Such a house is that carried on by Mr. J. F. Chaney, on Main street, Brunswick, and should any of our readers question the truth of this statement, we will simply refer them to the record made by this house during its four years of existence. The premises utilized comprise, in addition to the office on Main street, spacious yard-room with a capacity for the storage of 3,000 tons of Coal. This enterprise was started by Mr. Chaney in 1884. He is a Maine man by birth, and is well-known in the Coal trade of this vicinity and an extensive retail business is done, requiring the services of three assistants. All orders by mail or otherwise will receive prompt and careful attention and the best grade of Coal will be furnished in quantities to suit, at the lowest market rates. Mr. Chaney, also in connection with Coal keeps the largest Wood-Yard in town, with machinery for manufacturing all kinds of Wood, and sheds for seasoning it under cover. This enterprise started by him two years ago, has proven a great convenience to the community as well as a success to himself, so that now he has to keep a large number of men and teams at work during the winter months, cutting, hauling, fitting and delivering Wood to supply a large trade.

A. O. Reed, Photographer. Best facilities for Fine Work. Landscape Viewing Promptly Attended to. Main Street, Brunswick. The delicacy and dexterity required in the taking and finishing of photographs are by no means appreciated by the majority of people, although many, who think that anybody can take a good photograph if the necessary apparatus is at hand, must wonder why it is that one professional photographer does work which excites the admiration of all who see it, by its accuracy and beauty, while there are a dozen others apparently unable to even approach it in excellence. The truth is, photography is an art and not a a mere mechanical process. As the most gifted artist in colors must have a proper equipment of paints, brushes, etc., if he is to produce the best results, so the most experienced and artistic Photographer must have a first-class apparatus to allow his skill to display itself to advantage, but in neither case can anything worthy of the name of art be accomplished unless he who uses the materials furnished has the art-faculty within him. In the work produced by Mr. A. O. Reed of Brunswick, may be seen the happy effect of a combination of Artistic treatment and skillful handling of a subject, and as this gentleman does the largest business in Photography in this vicinity it is evident that his merits are appreciated. He is a native of Brunswick and founded his present undertaking in 1877. Two rooms are occupied of the dimensions of 20x60 feet each, which are supplied with the best facilities for fine work, and employment is given to two skilled assistants. A specialty is made of Landscape Viewing, and all orders are promptly attended to, and satisfaction guaranteed. Mr. Reed's reputation is too high to allow him to let any imperfect work leave his Studio and we may add that no one is a more severe critic of the results of his labor than he is himself. His prices are very low for the services rendered and all callers are treated with the utmost courtesy.

G. C. Stetson, Dealer in Dry and Fancy Goods, Cloaks, etc., Main Street, Brunswick. It is not a matter for wonderment that the house whose card we print above should be considered as a representative of its class in this vicinity for it is controlled by a man who has had an extended and varied experience in the business he conducts and who spares neither pains nor expense to fully maintain the leading position which he has for some time held. The enterprise in question was inaugurated in 1880 under the firm name of Stetson & Marsh and came under the sole control of the senior partner in 1886. Mr. George C. Stetson is a native of Brunswick and a member of Knights of Pythias, and is very widely known in this vicinity where he is highly esteemed. The premises occupied include two floors and a basement of the dimensions of 20x60 feet and the stock carried is not only heavy but complete foreign and domestic Dry Goods of every description as well as a fine line of Cloaks, etc. Employment is given to six assistants and customers are served with a promptness and courtesy as gratifying, as it is rare. The ladies of Brunswick have long since learned that when they wish to inspect the latest fashionable novelties this establishment is the place at which to find them and also that both Staple and Fancy Goods are offered at prices which will bear the strictest comparison with those asked elsewhere. The stock includes all grades and comprises some of the most beautiful designs and fabrics obtainable in the markets.

C. H. Colby, Contractor and Builder, and Manufacturer of Long and Short Lumber, Pump Tubing and Aqueduct Logs, Sash and Blinds, Doors and Ships' Cabin Work. Dimensions Sawed to Order. Moldings of all kinds. Ships' Wooden Tanks and Cisterns, Main Street, Brunswick. The enterprise carried on by Mr. C. H. Colby, has long ranked with the leaders in its special line, and indeed it is doubtful if there is another house in this vicinity of a similar character that is so well-known and so highly regarded. This undertaking was founded in 1845 by V. G. & E. Colby, afterward by S. & E. Colby and to C. H. Colby in 1878, who is a native of Webster. Mr. Colby is a Contractor and Builder as well as a manufacturer of Long and Short Lumber, and the scale on which he carries on business is indicated by the fact that the plant utilized covers an area of three acres of ground, employment being given to forty assistants. A large amount of valuable and efficient machinery is in operation, ample water-power being at hand, and among the specialties manufactured may be mentioned: Pump Tubing and Aqueduct Logs, Sash and Blinds, Doors and Ships' Cabin Work, Moldings of all kinds, Ships' Wooden Tanks and Cisterns, etc. Dimensions are sawed to order at short notice, and the character of the work turned out is of the highest order of excellence. Mr. Colby gives close attention to the more important details of his business, and takes pains to see that the high standard so long held by his productions is fully maintained. As may be supposed, he is in a position to quote bottom prices in the various departments of his business, for his facilities are unsurpassed, and long experience has reduced the expense of production to the lowest possible figure.

B. L. Dennison, Bookseller, Stationer, and dealer in Fancy Goods, Blank Books, Room Papers, Wrapping Paper, Paper Bags, Toys, etc. Five and Ten Cent Bargain Counter. Boston Daily Papers. also Circulating Library, Pictures and Picture Frames. Frames made to order at short notice. No. 1 O'Brien's Block, Main Street, Brunswick. Whether our readers be of a literary turn of mind or interested in learning the latest and most approved styles in the line of Fancy Goods and Paper Hangings they cannot fail to find that a visit to the establishment now conducted by Mr. B. L. Dennison on Main Street, No. 1 O'Brien's Block, both profitable and agreeable, for this gentleman carries an assortment of all the articles mentioned, so varied and complete that it must be seen to be appreciated; and what is even more to the purpose he is prepared to quote the very lowest market rates on anything he offers for sale. This house was inaugurated in 1808 by Mr. B. G. Dennison, and continued under his management until 1887, when the present proprietor Mr. B. L. Dennison assumed full control of the business. Both these gentlemen are natives of Brunswick and Mr. B. G. Dennison held the office of Post-Master from 1861 to 1866. The premises utilized are located on Main Street and comprise one floor and basement each 22x100 feet in dimensions. Employment is given to six thoroughly capable assistants thus insuring every caller prompt and courteous attention. The supply of Books carried is made up of the works of the standard authors as well as of those who are most popular at the present day. The Wall Paper in stock is new and original in design, and there is a sufficient variety of it on hand to allow both the tastes and the purses of customers to be fully suited. Fancy Goods of every description are largely dealt in as well as Stationery, Blank Books, Wrapping Paper, Paper Bags, Toys, etc., also Five and Ten Cent Goods, Boston Daily Papers, Pictures and Picture Frames, and Frames made to order at short notice. A large Circulating Library is also conducted at this establishment, and bottom prices are put upon every article.

Alexander & Hubbard, Livery, Sale and Boarding Stable, Next Door North of the Tontine Hotel, Main Street, Brunswick. The Livery Stable now carried on by Messrs. Alexander & Hubbard, on Main Street, next door North of Tontine Hotel, is, in some respect, a representative enterprise, for it has been under the management of the senior partner since 1866 (Mr. Hubbard have been admitted to the firm in 1882), and has an unblemished record for furnishing the best of accommodations. The proprietors are both natives of Maine, and it is safe to say that few men are better known, not only in Brunswick but also in adjoining communities. The premises occupied comprise a carriage-house, stable and office, and every facility is at hand for the proper accommodation of the extensive patronage received. No better Stable can be found in this vicinity at which to hire a turn-out for a spin on the road, for the Horses and Vehicles here furnished are good enough for anybody to use, and the terms in force are reasonable in the extreme. One of the most gratifying features connected with the management of this enterprise, is the way in which the Horses, Carriages, etc., are looked after, everything here being maintained in the most neat and trim condition. An important branch of the business is the Boarding of Horses, these animals being given excellent care and abundance of suitable food. Messrs. Alexander & Hubbard do quite an extensive Sale business, and if any of our readers are looking for a good Driving Horse, they will find it well worth while to see what these gentlemen have to offer. They also do General Trucking and Jobbing, and the Tontine Hotel work. Their prices are reasonable in the extreme, and guarantee perfect satisfaction in all branches of their business. Mr. Alexander is a member of the Free Masons and Mr. Hubbard of the Odd Fellows and the Grand Army, having enlisted in Co. D., 8th Maine Regiment as Musician; was at Beaufort, Hilton Island, Fort P., Cold Harbor, Fair Oaks, etc.; was stationed at Gen. Grant's headquarters in the General's band. Messrs. Alexander & Hubbard also have in readiness for the accommodation of large or small parties, Double Carriages and Sleighs; drivers furnished when required.

J. S. Towne, Pharmacist, Main Street, Brunswick. The establishment conducted by Mr. J. S. Towne, has peculiar claim to a prominent position in this review of the representative houses of Brunswick for this is one of the best appointed Pharmacies in this town, having been founded here in 1886 by the present proprietor who is a native of Buckfield, Maine, a member of the Free Masons and certainly ranks among the most highly esteemed business men in this vicinity. The store occupied covers an area of 18x45 feet and is located on Main Street and contains one of the most extensive assortments of Drugs, Medicines and Chemicals to be found in any retail Pharmacy in Brunswick. A sufficient number of assistants are employed to assure all necessary facility in the filling of orders. The compounding of Physicians' Prescriptions is the most important department of the business, and every means that science and practical experience can suggest is provided to make this service prompt and reliable. No risks are taken, conservative methods are invariably used, and so far as human foresight is capable of rendering accidents impossible, those doing business with this house are positively guaranteed against error. The charges are as low as the use of standard and tested ingredients will permit, and we are happy to say that the advantages offered are appreciated and a large business done. Mr. Towne is the inventor and proprietor of "Rose Balm" which stands without an equal as an invaluable and agreeable specific for Chapped Hands, Face, Lips and all Roughness of the Skin. Gentlemen will find it a fragrant and soothing application to the face after shaving as it allays all irritation and keeps the face smooth and free from soreness which is often caused by the razor. Don't confound "Rose Balm" with the many unsightly and disagreeable mixtures which are put up for the above complaints. "Rose Balm" is a scientific compound, the result of careful study and experiment to make it an elegant preparation in appearance without detriment to its curative properties, and it contains nothing that will injure the most delicate complexion.

Jordan Snow, Merchant Tailor and Dealer in Gent's Furnishing Goods, Main Street, Brunswick. No doubt many of our readers, especially those residing in Brunswick, have already heard favorable reports of the Merchant Tailoring establishment conducted by Mr. Jordan Snow, on Main Street; for those who do business with a house that is able to give perfect satisfaction both as regards its goods and its prices are very apt to communicate their experience to their friends so that they may take advantage of the same. Mr. Snow is a native of Brunswick and a member of the Knights of Pythias, and has been associated with his present enterprise since 1866. He is prepared to do Fine Tailoring of every description, but caters especially to the best class of trade, paying particular attention to the cutting and fitting of both old and young men's garments, and producing Fashionable Clothing for their wear that in every detail will bear the severest comparison with that turned out at much more pretentious establishments. One floor is occupied, 22x60 feet in dimensions, and an extensive and varied assortment of Gent's Furnishings are carried; also a complete line of Foreign and Domestic Fabrics are exhibited which will well repay careful inspection. Those who desire to dress with pleasing individuality will do well to remember that Mr. Snow makes a specialty of supplying Suitings, etc., that are uncommon in design without being unpleasantly conspicuous, and a sufficient variety in patterns is shown to allow all peculiarities of size and form, to be provided for. Although making a specialty of high-class Garments, Mr. Snow is by no means high in his prices and those who have been accustomed to the exhorbitant rates charged at some fashionable tailoring houses, will be most agreeably surprised on learning the prices quoted by Mr. Snow. The establishment is supplied with every facility for the doing of Fine Custom Work. Ten skilled assistants are employed, and only experienced hands intrusted with the various details of making, etc., and under these circumstances, Mr. Snow feels that he can confidently guarantee satisfaction, and warrant Perfect-Fitting, and Durable Garments.

F. C. Webb & Co., General Store, Main Street, Brunswick. "A worthy enterprise well conducted" seems to be the popular verdict on the business carried on by F. C. Webb & Co., in this town and after a somewhat exhaustive examination into its merits and advantages we are obliged to fully endorse this opinion. It is comparatively seldom that an instance is found where such cordial relations exist between a firm and its patrons as we can testify are observable in the present case, and when such a state of feeling is discovered, it requires no very deep knowledge of human nature to afford an explanation of it. Fair dealing on the one side and liberal patronage on the other, are all that is essential to the building up of a trade of mammoth proportions, and the establishment of a perfect confidence and appreciation. Mr. F. C. Webb is a native of Brunswick—a Director of the First National Bank and Vice President of the Board of Trade. For several years he was with the firm of J. T. Adams & Co., as bookkeeper, and upon the retirement of Mr. Adams eight years ago, took charge of the store. Extensive repairs were made on the interior of the building a year ago, and they now have the largest amount of floor room of any store in town. They now carry a large stock of General Goods suitable for their large and increasing trade. To accommodate thei. patrons they have the assistance of six experienced salesmen. Customers may rely upon prompt and polite treatment. In regard to prices, their reputation for being the lowest of any in town is not to be denied.

William R. Field, Fine Cigars and Tobacco, Main Street, Brunswick. The establishment carried on by Mr. W. R. Field on Main Street, is a resort of great and increasing popularity, not only for those who enjoy a good cigar, but also for those who find amusement and relaxation in a friendly game of Billiards and Pool, for Mr. Field has two Billiard tables and one Pool table on the premises and sees that they are kept in first-class condition so that a game on them is always enjoyable. A very large stock of Confectionery, Fruits, Cigars, and Tobacco is carried, and it is hard to say which department of this assortment is the most elaborate, for beginning at Cigars we find that all grades and kinds of both Foreign and Domestic Goods are offered, while the prices are put away down to the lowest notch. In Tobacco, we find all the popular brands of both Plug and Fine-Cut suitable for either chewing or smoking. In Pipes, there is certainly a sufficient variety to suit all tastes and purses. The premises occupied and located on Main Street, comprise two floors and a basement each 22x30 feet in dimensions. Mr. Field is a native of Brunswick and a member of the Free Masons. He does a very large business and deserves to for his prices are low and his goods of standard quality.

L. D. Snow, Dealer in Groceries, Provisions, Lime, Paints, Oils, Glass, etc., Main Street, Brunswick. One of Brunswick's representative establishments is that carried on by Mr. L. D. Snow, corner of Main and Center Streets. This enterprise is very extensively known, and the manner in which it is patronized by the very best class of trade, is most significent of its character and of the uniform superiority of the goods handled. Business was begun in 1876, and has since been continued with ever increasing success. Mr. Snow is a native of Brunswick, and is thoroughly acquainted with the Grocery trade giving close personal attention to its many details, and sparing no pains to constantly improve the efficiency of his service to the public. The premises utilized are 25x72 feet in size and include two floors. A very extensive and skillfully selected stock is always carried. It comprises Staple and Fancy Groceries of all descriptions, and a fine assortment of Provisions in almost endless variety. Also Paints, Oils, Glass, Lime and Cement. These goods are quoted at way-down prices, and are positively guaranteed to prove as represented in every instance. Employment is given to two efficient and courteous assistants, and every caller will receive prompt attention and satisfactory service.

E. A. Graves, Harness Manufacturer. Dealer in Sleigh and Carriage Robes, Horse Blankets, Whips, etc., Swift Block, Main Street, Brunswick. We talk of getting "a horse and carriage" as though no more was necessary in order to enjoy a ride, but nevertheless there is another item to be mentioned and a very important one it is too—the harness. Your horse may be a second edition of "Maud S," your carriage may be the latest production of the finest maker in the country, but unless you have a harness and a good one too, your chances for having an enjoyable drive are very small indeed. It is not everybody that advertises to be a harness-maker that understands his business by any means, but there are some first-class workmen here in Brunswick, and one of the best of them is Mr. E. A. Graves, carrying on operations on Main Street. This gentleman employs competent and skilled assistants and is enabled to fill every order without delay. He will make Harness to order in first-class style and at bottom prices, and carries in stock a fine assortment of Sleigh and Carriage Robes, Horse Blankets, Whips, etc., Horse Furnishings in general. Carriage Trimming and Repairing of every description, is done in the most skillful and durable manner. Fine Order Work is made a specialty of and satisfaction is confidently guaranteed to every customer. We therefore cordially recommend Mr. Graves and his popular establishment to all in this vicinity in need of anything in his line of business. Mr. Graves is a native of Brunswick and is extensively and favorably known throughout this section.

Miss E. A. Chase, Dealer in Millinery and Fancy Goods, Main Street, Brunswick. Enterprise and sagacity in the selection of goods and good taste, liberality, and accommodations in the arrangement and sale of them, are enough to insure success for any business undertaking, and perhaps some of those loud-mouthed philosophers who are so fond of disclaiming as to the unfitness of women for mercantile pursuits, would do well to stop talking long enough to investigate for themselves such cases of eminent success in this line as we have become conversant with in the preparation of this book. One of the most pronounced of them is the one to which we propose to allude in this article, and of itself it is enough to demonstrate that no monopoly of the qualities which bring about prosperity in business, is held by man. Miss E. A. Chase opened the establishment she has since conducted with profit to herself and to the community, in 1860, so that a sufficient time has since elapsed to enable an intelligent judgment to be formed as to the results attained. She is engaged in the Retailing of Millinery and Fancy Goods, etc., and has built up a patronage which could never have reached its present proportions had not genuine and continuous inducements been offered to the public. Four capable assistants are constantly employed and a store is occupied of the dimensions of 20x30 feet, and such arrangements are in force as to permit of every customer receiving prompt and careful attention. Miss Chase quotes very low prices on the articles handled, and depends more upon the extensive sales than upon large profits for the reward of her exertions.

A. W. Townsend, Bookseller and Stationer, Main Street, Brunswick. In a book intended for the people, as this is, all information as to how homes may be made beautiful at small expense, cannot fail to be of interest, and hence we need offer no apology for calling attention to the fine display of Wall Paper made by Mr. A. W. Townsend at his well-known establishment on Main Street, for there is nothing capable of so thoroughly changing the appearance of a room, or of an entire house, for that matter, as the substitution of New and Fashionable Paper-Hanging for those that are neither the one nor the other. Mr. Townsend offers a very skillfully-selected assortment to choose from, and whether a preference be had for large or small figures, bright or dark colors, he carries a sufficient variety to suit any caller. His prices are as low as the lowest, and no one interested should neglect visiting his establishment. Books, Stationery, etc., together with a full line of the latest novelties in the way of Fancy Goods, etc., are extensively handled, and the premises occupied measuring 28x70 feet and comprising one floor and basement, are none too spacious to accommodate the heavy stock carried. In this establishment the central offices for the telephone and New England Despatch Express are located. Mr. Townsend is a native of Brunswick and a member of the Odd Fellows and Knights of Pythias, and inaugurated his present enterprise in 1880. He has shown both liberality and foresight in the management of his business, and fully deserves the success he has won.

Mrs. M. A. Smith, Dealer in Millinery and Fancy Goods, also Hair Goods, Main Street, Brunswick. It is safe to assume, that when a business enterprise has been conducted steadily for twenty years it must be well managed, and must be concerned in the supplying of such goods as the public demands. Therefore when we say that the undertaking carried on by Mrs. M. A. Smith was founded in 1868, it is hardly necessary to add that it stands high in the favor of the people. No person can visit the store, inspect the attractions offered, and note the courteous attention paid to customers without being convinced that the establishment fully deserves its popularity, and when the prices quoted are learned, this conviction will be strengthened and confirmed. The premises utilized are of the dimensions of 20x40 feet and employment is afforded to four assistants. Millinery and Fancy Goods and Hair Goods of all descriptions are carried in stock, and no surer way of learning what are the latest novelties in these goods can be found than to examine the assortment here presented. Mrs. Smith is a native of Massachusetts and considering her long experience, it is hardly necessary to state, understands her business thoroughly in every detail. She gives close personal attention to the supervision of the various departments conducted by her, and is ever seeking to improve the efficacy of the service. Order work is done at short notice and in a neat and tasteful manner, and all goods are offered at the lowest market rates. Courtesy is extended to all and satisfaction is confidently guaranteed.

Bowdoin Paper Manufacturing Co., Main Street, Topsham (over the bridge). It is curious to remark the almost absolute ignorance that exists regarding the manner in which some of the most commonly used substances are produced, and in this connection nothing affords a better illustration of what we mean than the hazy and sometimes absurd ideas that are held concerning the manufacture of Paper. Perhaps ninety-nine men out of one hundred, if asked how Paper is made would say that rags, paper, etc., are put in a machine and ground up and then made into nice, new paper again; but if asked to give further particulars they would have to confess their ignorance. Paper is used for an immense variety of purposes nowadays, and its usefulness is being extended rapidly, and an immense amount of capital is employed in its manufacture, and some of the Paper-making machines in use are wonderful examples of mechanical ingenuity and skill. A well-known Paper Mill here in Topsham is that carried on by the Bowdoin Paper Manufacturing Company, located on Main Street, just over the bridge. This was inaugurated and the old mill built in 1868, the new mill being erected in 1883. Employment is given to one hundred and twenty-five hands, the pay-roll for which is $1,000 per week. The plant occupied covers an area of three acres of ground. The extensive system of machinery in use is run by water-power, and the product of the mill, which amounts to sixteen tons per day, is in active demand. The Bowdoin Paper Manufacturing Company is made up of Mr. W. H. Parson as President and Mr. M. C. Parson, Treasurer. both these gentlemen being natives of New York, and Mr. F. C. Whitehouse of Topsham, as Secretary. These gentlemen give close attention to their business interests, and the result is continued and steadily increasing prosperity.

Edward Beaumont, Dealer in Flour, Meal, Feed, Cotton Seed Meal. Wheat, Wheat Screenings, Ground Oyster Shells, Poultry Bone, Meat Scraps for Poultry, Topsham. It is an old and a well-proved rule, that it is always best to buy of the manufacturer under ordinary circumstances. This rule holds good in the purchase of Flour, Feed, etc., as well as in other things, and that many people think as we do on this subject, is proved by the large business done by Mr. Edward Beaumont who carries on a Grist Mill, as well as a large Wholesale and Retail Business, on Main Street, over the Bridge. This undertaking had its inception in 1858, the founder being Mr. W. B. Purinton, the present Proprietor, Mr. Edward Beaumont, being his successor. This gentleman has been connected with the business as Manager and Proprietor since 1860. He is extensively known in this vicinity and ranks with the representative manufacturers and merchants of Topsham. The George T. Smith Middlings Purifier Co., of Jackson, Michigan, the foremost and largest makers of improved Mill Machinery in the United States and will soon be in operation, making Refined Corn Meal, Granulated Corn Meal and Rye Meal on the Roller process. The Mill-Stone will not be discarded as it is an admitted fact that it cannot be superseded for Feed for Dairy Farming, and customers can have their choice of Roller or Stone Ground Meal and Feed. The premises occupied consist of four floors each 40x45 feet in dimensions, and are very completely fitted up with the most improved machinery and a complete Roller plant is now ordered from the makers, which is run by water-power. The commodities produced are supplied in quantities to suit, both a Wholesale and Retail Business being done, and all the goods handled will be the best money can purchase, as he does not buy inferior grades of any kind. Among the most important of these, may be mentioned Flour, Meal, Cotton Seed Meal, Wheat, Wheat Screenings, Ground Oyster Shells, Poultry Bone and Meat Scraps for Poultry. A specialty is also made of Pure Wheat Meal and warranted to be equal to any made; also refined Corn Meal, warranted superior to granulated and all other Corn Meal for domestic purposes, and the quality of all the articles, bought of this house, may be strictly depended upon to prove just as represented.

W. O. Peterson, Grocer, Main Street, Brunswick. The gentleman whose card we print above, has not carried on his present enterprise for a great length of time, as he only became identified with it in 1886, but nevertheless the record so far made under his management, has no reason to fear comparison with that of any other similar period in other establishments of this kind in this section, and that this is no slight praise, may well be thought when it is learned how large the number of such establishments are in Brunswick. Mr. W. O. Peterson is a native of this town and a member of the Odd Fellows. He has many friends, having added to his former large list since beginning to serve the public in his present capacity. The premises occupied include a store on Main Street of the dimensions of 25x60 feet, with an additional storehouse, and employment is given to one experienced and competent assistant, Mr. Robert Stanwood, who has been in the business many years. Groceries and General Stores are very extensively handled and as the stock is chosen especially with a view to the wants of family trade, it is worthy the inspection of every housekeeper. Groceries, both staple and fancy, are supplied at the lowest market rates, as well as everything usually included in General Stores and a full guarantee is given that every article shall prove as represented. Every department is equally liberally managed and a choice assortment of goods are offered in great profusion.

Miss A. Hacker, Dealer in Millinery and Fancy Goods, Main Street, Brunswick. Some of the would be "funny men" with which the newspaper press is infested at the present day, are fond of calling attention to certain things which they allege a "Woman can't do," but they apparently take no heed of the innumerable things a woman *can* do, among which may be prominently mentioned in this connection "mind her own business." As for things she can't do, it has baffled much wiser men than the jesters mentioned to discern just what are the limits of woman's powers when she sets her mind on the attainment of a certain object. It is not surprising of course that the best appointed Millinery Establishments should be conducted by the gentle sex for a "man milliner" is apt to be more of a curiosity than he is an artist and in these days artistic talent is essential to the highest success in the industry alluded to. The establishment of which Miss A. Hacker is the Proprietress, located on Main Street is one of the best and most favorably known in this vicinity and the heavy and increasing patronage it receives is fully deserved, as a large and fashionable assortment of Millinery and Fancy Goods are always to be found in the store, which is of the dimensions of 18x35 feet. Miss Hacker is a native of Brunswick and has carried on this undertaking since 1874. She has exceptional taste in the selection and arrangement of articles of Millinery and places her prices at such reasonable figures as to have built up a large patronage. Miss Hacker succeeded Mrs. J. M. Hacker (her mother) who carried on the Millinery and Fancy Goods business in Brunswick 39 years, having begun in 1842, she being the oldest Milliner in that town.

HISTORICAL SKETCH.

— OF —

BATH. ME.

NEW ENGLAND had many a romance in its younger years, which amid the mystic glamour of a primeval period would easily have developed into legend or myth or even epic song. But in no department of her life, perhaps, has there been more of romance and poetry than in the strugglings and voyagings of her sturdy sons upon the sea, of the old sea port towns of the New England coast; and few attained higher prestige or were more broadly typical of the restless, enterprising spirit which accomplished so many victories on the seas of the world, than Bath, Maine, and though the ardor of that spirit has been cooled, or turned into other directions by numerous reverses, there still lingers in the old city many memorials of the sea-faring days of the past. The old town sprung indeed from one of the most prominent shipping towns of New England, being settled in 1718 by Thomas Elkins from Salem, Mass., who came here with several other stout-hearted pioneers and founded the settlement in that year. During all the following years of that troubled century the village grew steadily, though slowly, and though the Indians gave considerable and serious annoyance, it does not seem, as many others round about were, to have ever been abandoned. The men who had come here had the purest and strongest blood in their veins of that race who had dared defy a king and plant a settlement in an unknown wilderness, and they were not going to be thwarted in their plans by any number of "blood-thirsty Red-men or wiley Frenchmen." But for many years the struggle for existence, not to say progress, looked doubtful, and in 1750, at the turning point of the century, there were only about two dozen houses here, and the Indians were still menacing them with destruction in fire and blood. But the following years witnessed a gradual adjusting of the disturbing influences, and the little town began to grow

HISTORICAL SKETCH OF BATH.

with more rapidity. In 1753 it was estimated that there were forty families settled here, and these formed the nucleus for a settlement which in a few decades had become one of the most important on the Northern part of the coast of New England. In 1760 the settlement had advanced to the dignity of erecting a meeting-house and seven years later the first settled minister, the Rev. Francis Winter was called, and

CENTER STREET IN 1889.

began a long and faithful work here. For a time in the middle part of the century, Bath might have been taken as an example of the famous Malthusian law of the geometrical progression of population, for in 1764 it had increased to over 400 and continued to do so up to the time of the Revolution.

The shipping interests of Bath are well worthy of careful study. As they developed the town saw some of its palmiest days, and the presence of its ships on all the waters of the world gave it an extended fame which has not died out at the present day, though the character of its industry has partially changed. It is a curious and noteworthy fact that the first vessel known to have been built in this country, was built at this spot. In 1607-8, the Popham Colony came here to build a vessel which, when completed, was called the "Virginia" after the Virgin Queen, and so far as known was the first constructed on the soil of the United States. The abundance of good timber and the excellent facilities for launching suggested to these early residents of the region the natural fitness which in after years developed so largely.

The aggregate number of ships built from 1781 to 1880 is 3,022, of tonnage 1,078,159, and the total valuation is $54,375,809. The shipping reached its apogee in the decade just before the last war and how disastrously that struggle affected it. Since that time, however, it has shown signs of rejuvenated life and has grown with comparative steadiness up to the present writing.

In the War of the Rebellion, Bath maintained its traditional laurels with increasing honor. It had received a city charter in 1847, and in 1854, upon the formation of the County of Sagadahoc, had been made the county seat. By virtue of its great shipping interests chiefly, it had become at the beginning of the War one or the largest and most influential cities of Maine, and nobly sustained its position from the start. It contributed liberally both of men and money and from it went forth

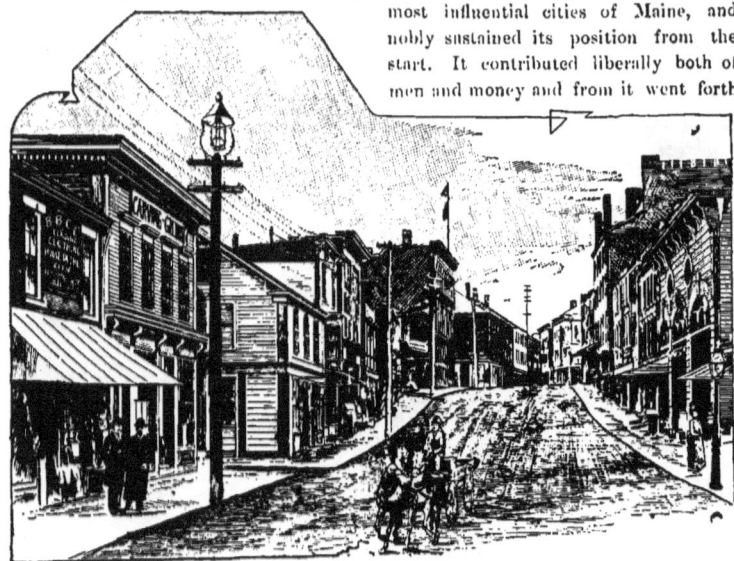

FRONT STREET IN 1889.

some of the most talented and able officers in the State Regiments. Its volunteers were chiefly enlisted in the 3d, 5th, 7th, 9th, 12th, 13th, 17th, 19th, 25th and 30th Maine Regiments, though it was represented in almost every one from the State. But the "pet Regiment" at Bath was the 19th, which was organized here, almost entirely composed of Bath men, and commanded by one of Bath's most prominent and honored citizens, Col. F. D. Sewall. This regiment served with distinguished honors at Fredericksburg, Gettysburg, the Wilderness Campaign and around Richmond in 1864 and '65. The honor list of Bath was very large and she was called also to mourn the loss of many of her noblest sons whose memory she has always tenderly cherished and fittingly perpetuated. Though a sufferer in her business interests from the great conflict, she never bated a jot of full patriotism and service and has since turned much of her enterprising spirit into other channels from those in which it ran before the War.

The city of Bath socially is one of the most famed in the State. The people are celebrated for their geniality and hospitality. The winter social seasons, unlike many parts of the Garden State which flourish only in summer, has a metropolitan atmosphere of social enlivenment and activity. The young people of the city have the wide-spread fame of being the leaders in the social world of Maine, and the season here has innumerable features of enjoyment and improvement which only those who have passed one here can at all appreciate or expect. Besides its own numerous shipping, Bath is connected with Boston and Portland by steamer and the Maine Central Railroad.

LEADING BUSINESS MEN

OF

BATH, ME.

Samuel Anderson, Druggist, Front Street, Bath. The well-known moral, "Familiarity breeds Contempt," has an apt illustration in the light manner in which the public at large regard the services rendered by those carrying on the numerous Pharmacies now in operation. The honorable and conscientious dispensing Chemist holds a position which is at once precarious and arduous. He is called upon to fill prescriptions of every imaginable kind, scrawled so illegibly at times that a grocer could not fill an order for goods so poorly written, held responsible for any ill effects that may follow the administration of the medicine, and accused of extortion if he charges one third as much for filling the prescription as the physician asked for writing it. Are these statements overdrawn? Think a moment and then answer. Under such circumstances a Chemist who has faithfully and acceptably served the public for more than thirty years, deserves special mention, and we take genuine pleasure in noting the fact that Mr. Samuel Anderson has such a record, for he has been associated with his present enterprise since 1856, operations having been begun in 1847, under the name of Samuel Anderson, senior. Mr. Anderson is a native of this city; no resident business man is more generally known or more highly esteemed in all quarters. The premises occupied are located on Front Street, and include one floor and a basement, measuring 20x60 feet. The assortment of Drugs, Medicines, Chemicals, etc., is very complete and skillfully chosen, and prescriptions can be filled at short notice with absolute correctness. No precautions are neglected, and the prices in every case are made as low as the use of first-class materials will permit. Mr. Anderson carries, also, a full line of Trusses, probably the largest stock in the State, including all the latest improvements. Every desirable style and all the modern appliances obtained as soon as introduced in the market. Fits are warranted in all cases, at prices lower than in Boston or New York. His stock also includes Supporters, Elastic Stockings, Shoulder Braces, etc.

The H. W. Howard Printing Company, Bath. From the time of Gutenberg to the present day, printing has made wonderful strides, and even during the past decade improvements have been brought about that add decidedly to the beauty and the practical value of "the art preservative." The day of the amateur has gone by, and although amateur printing accomplished a great deal of good by bringing home to every business man the fact that printer's ink could be used in his occupation to advantage, it has also educated the public to detect the difference between good and bad work in the typographical line. It is the neatly printed Circular, the symmetrical Bill-Head, the tasteful and concise Business Card that gives evidence that the concern whose name they bear is fully up to the times, and with very few exceptions a slovenly Card or Bill-Head means a slovenly way of doing business. Therefore it is worth while to take a little pains to have your Printing done in the best manner. This Company being centrally located, with the best material to be had, and employing none but competent workmen, with its electric motors and fine machinery, is able to turn out the best grades of work. Their Brunswick Office, newly fitted up some two years since, and under the able management of G. M. Wheeler, is acknowledged second to none in the State. Located in the new public building this Company is prepared to fill orders at short notice, and its prices are such as will bear comparison with those quoted any where else on work of similar quality. Every effort is made to strictly keep all promises in regard to time of delivery, etc., and estimates on any desired line of work will be cheerfully furnished on application. For extent, quality, variety and general excellence they are unsurpassed. A number of hands find constant employment in attending to the wants of the firm's patrons, the trade extending all over this section of the State. The characteristics which regulate the policy of this reliable house are such as to entitle it to universal consideration. All orders are promptly filled.

William B. Olys, Ship Broker and Commission Merchant; Fire and Marine Insurance Effected; Ice, Hay, Bricks and Wood Bought and Sold on Commission, Front Street, Bath. That the Commission Merchant fills an important place in the community, is well-known to all who are acquainted with the facilities of exchange afforded in our cities, and as Mr. William B. Olys is prominent among those engaged in this line of effort in Bath and vicinity, it is but right that we should notice his establishment in our columns. Mr. Olys has an office on Front Street, and has carried on operations here since 1885. He buys and sells Ice, Hay, Bricks and Wood, on Commission, and those having such commodities to dispose of, might do well to avail themselves of his services, as his facilities are of the best, and returns are made with promptness and accuracy. Mr. Olys is a native of Bath. He holds a commission as Justice of the Peace, and gives prompt and careful attention to business coming before him in that capacity. A large Insurance business is also done, as Mr. Olys acts for a number of companies of undisputed solidity, and places Insurance on both Fire and Marine risks, also Life and Accident. Among the corporations represented are the following:—American of Boston, Phœnix of Brooklyn, Merchants' of Newark, New Hampshire of Manchester, Peoples' of New Hampshire, New England Mutual Life Insurance Company, Employers' Liability Accident Assurance Company and Marine Limited of London, England, etc. Insurance will be effected in any of these celebrated companies on the most favorable terms, and conscientious effort will be made to discharge all commissions with fidelity and dispatch, thus adding to the already high reputation which this Agency now bears. Mr. Olys also makes a specialty of Ship Brokerage Business, his facilities being unsurpassed for procuring Ice, Lumber and other charters for small and large vessels. Mr. Olys furnishes estimates for building new vessels, and old vessels are bought and sold by him.

Walter S. Russell, Dealer in Choice Meats, Staple and Fancy Groceries, 188 Front Street, Bath. If everybody in this vicinity has not learned, as yet, that there is a market carried on at No. 188 Front Street, it is certainly not because the enterprise is a new one, for the market in question has been in operation about sixty years. The present proprietor is not the founder, however, for he only assumed control in 1882, but already has largely increased the business done, and is the acknowledged leader in his line of business in the city. His business was formerly conducted by his father, Mr. Chas. Russell, for fifty-three years. Mr. Walter S. Russell, the gentleman to whom we have reference, is a native of Bath, and widely known as a prominent and conservative business man. The premises utilized by him are of the dimensions of 70x55 feet, and are fully taken up by a large and skillfully selected stock of Choice Groceries, Meats, Fruits, Vegetables and Country Produce. Employment is given to two efficient and polite assistants, and callers may depend upon receiving courteous attention and honorable treatment. Mr. Russell makes a specialty of the furnishing of Choice Cuts, and is prepared to cater to the wants of the most fastidious. He does not confine himself to this class of trade, however, but spares no efforts to make his store attractive to all. The advantages of trading with him will be at once apparent.

J. A. Winslow & Son, Dealer in Stoves, Ranges, Furnaces, etc., Broad Street, Bath. When it is remembered during how many months in the year artificial heat is required in our Maine climate, it will be seen that the question of heating facilities is a most important one. It is important in two ways; first, as regards health, and second as regards expense. The air we breathe has much to do, of course, with our bodily health, and on the Stoves, or Furnaces used is much of the quality of the air dependent. One can be poisoned as surely with impure air—air impregnated with coal gas, or air that has been breathed several times—as with any other noxious agent, and too much care can not be used, not only in the selection but also in the management of stoves, etc. When we come to the financial side of the question, we see that some Stoves supply more heat than others without consuming more coal; this proves that they are constructed on more scientific principles, and the combustion being more perfect, the economical Stove must be the healthful one as well. No house in this section of the State is better known in connection with the sale of Stoves and Furnaces than that of Messrs. J. A. Winslow & Son, for this enterprise has been before the public for about a quarter of a century, and its standing is beyond cavil or dispute. The firm alluded to acts as agent for the Smith Anthony Company, the Magee Furnace and Messrs. Wood & Bishop, and offers an unsurpassed selection of the very highest type of Stoves and Furnaces for the inspection of customers. Three floors are occupied, four assistants employed, and any desired advice or assistance will be cheerfully given. The store is located on Broad Street and is very convenient of access. Messrs. J. A. Winslow & Son are in a position to offer unsurpassed inducements, and they warrant their goods to give satisfaction.

Mrs. E. A. W. Rouse, Dealer in Millinery and Fancy Goods, Center Street, Bath. An establishment which well deserves mention among the foremost in this city, is that conducted by Mrs. E. A. W. Rouse on Center Street, and indeed it would be difficult to pick out a more truly representative enterprise than that to which we have reference. It has been carried on since 1853, and one is always sure to find the latest fashionable novelties here, for Mrs. Rouse deals in Millinery and Fancy Goods, and takes special pains to see that her customers have the most approved styles to select from. The premises utilized are of the dimensions of 80x50 feet, and are conveniently located and excellently adapted for the purposes to which they are put. The stock of Millinery Goods is always very complete, and includes both Trimmed and Untrimmed Hats and Bonnets in all the latest shapes. Ribbons, Velvets, Feathers and other Trimming Materials are dealt in largely, and prompt and polite attention is given to every customer. Mrs. Rouse makes a specialty of

Millinery Work to order and has an unsurpassed reputation for thoroughness and good taste in this important department. Employment is given to five efficient assistants, and when necessity requires, work can be pushed through at surprisingly short notice. Prices are very moderate, and this fact taken in connection with the uniform excellence of the work, accounts for the magnitude of the business done.

George A. Tuttle, Dealer in Fancy Dry Goods, Hosiery, Gloves, Corsets, Ribbons, Trimmings, etc., Bath. We wish to make this book as interesting and as useful to the ladies as to the "lords of creation," and no surer way of doing so can be found than to have it contain reference to such establishments as that conducted by Mr. George A. Tuttle, on Center Street. This gentleman sells Fancy Dry Goods, and it is the simple truth that no dealer in the city has more real inducements to offer to his patrons. To begin with, his stock is extensive and varied, also comprising Hosiery, Gloves, Corsets, Ribbons, Trimmings, etc., as well as Jewelry, Toilet Articles, Infants' Wear of all kinds, Fine Knitting Yarns and Patterns, while a complete assortment of Choice Hair Goods is offered, which is worthy the careful inspection of those interested in artistic work of this kind. Mr. Tuttle was born in Tewksbury and began operations here in 1877. He has built up a thriving trade, and one of the most significant features of his business is the fact that his customers generally return again and again, being well satisfied with the treatment they receive. Care is taken to make only such representations as are warranted by the facts, and the prices are put at the lowest figure that circumstances will allow. Mr. Tuttle acts as Agent for Lewando's French Dye House, and sends goods to that establishment every Friday. The work done by Lewando needs no description here, for it is accepted as the standard wherever known. No exhorbitant rates are charged, and entire satisfaction is guaranteed. Zephyr, Worsted and Fine Knitting Yarns, Embroidery Materials of all kinds for Fancy Work, the largest line of Designs for Stamping East of Boston.

First National Bank, Front Street, Bath. The banking facilities of so important a commercial center as Bath, must naturally be somewhat extensive and the city has thus far been veryfortunate, both as regards the liberal manner in which these facilities have been provided and the able style in which they have been directed so as to do the most good. There is a more intimate connection between the mercantile and financial enterprises of a community than many people are ready to admit, and it is a fact that the most prosperous business centers are those in which the mutual relations of banker, manufacturer and merchant are most completely developed. The First National Bank of this city has accomplished a great deal of good since its incorporation in 1863 and is doubtless destined to wield a yet more important influence in the future. The secret of this success is—devotion to home interests. Not that the Bank has closed its eyes to all outside chances, and has not been able to see any good outside of Bath, but because after carefully surveying the field, home enterprises were invariably given the preference when such a course was possible. Owned and controlled by Bath men, the First National Bank has done its duty to the community, without jeopardizing the rights and property of stockholders. The President of the Institution is Mr. G. C. Moses, and the Cashier is Mr. W. D. Mussenden, both these gentlemen being natives of this city. The Board of Directors is composed of men well known to the majority of our readers as the following list will prove: G. C. Moses, H. W. Swanton, H. E. Palmer, A. Palmer, C. V. Miner, J. D. Robinson, M. G. Shaw, John R. Kelley and F. O. Moses. The Bank has a capital of $200,000 and a surplus of $50,000 and the last sworn statement made of its financial condition, proves it to be as thoroughly solvent an Institution as the most conservative stockholder could desire. This is the First National Bank incorporated in the State of Maine and was the sixty-first on the list in the United States.

James B. Drake, Ship and Insurance Broker, Granite block, Front Street, Bath. The gentleman whose card is printed above, ranks with the most widely-known business men of this section, for he has carried on operations for nearly a quarter of a century, and the nature of his business is such as to bring him in contact with all classes of people. Any defence of, or plea for insurance, must now be regarded as entirely unnecessary, for the experience of years has resulted in insurance becoming so universal, that the insurance expense account of a merchant, is looked upon as being as legitimate and necessary as his rent or tax bill. Mr. Drake represents a number of the strongest Insurance Companies in the world, and is prepared to furnish either Fire or Marine Insurance on the most favorable terms. The annexed list will give an idea of his resources, and after reading it, one cannot be surprised to learn that this is one of the most important agencies in the State. Royal Insurance Company; London & Lancashire; Liverpool and London and Globe; Phœnix of London; Ins. Co., of North America, Providence; Washington Fire and Marine, Hanover, Niagara, Northern, Queen, Continental, Westchester etc. Mr. Drake's office is centrally located in Granite Block, Front Street, and all desired information pertaining to Insurance matters will be cheerfully given on application. Policies can be issued at once and the instructions of customers will be carefully noted and faithfully followed. Another branch of Mr. Drake's business is the buying and selling of vessels, an extensive trade being carried on in this line. He is a large owner in vessels, managing ten or more himself, also a large stockholder and director in the Kennebec and Boston Steamboat Co. Associated as he is with prominent business men his circle of social and business friends is large.

Davis Hatch, Jr., Dealer in Boots, Shoes and Rubbers, Trunks, Bags, Valises, Sleigh Robes, Ladies' Furs, etc., 76 Front Street, Bath. Among the best-known business enterprises conducted in this city, mention must, of necessity, be made of that carried on by Mr. Davis Hatch, jr., at No. 76 Front Street. It is not at all surprising that this establishment *is* well-known, for Mr. Davis Hatch, senior, founded it over three-quarters of a century ago, and his son, Mr. Davis Hatch, jr., succeeded his father thirty years ago, and has spared no honorable means to keep it before the public. Boots, Shoes and Rubbers are among the more important articles in stock, and Trunks, Bags and Valises are also largely dealt in; Sleigh Robes, Ladies' Furs, etc., being extensively handled at the proper seasons. Mr. Hatch is a Bath man by birth, and is a member of the Free Masons. He employs two efficient and polite assistants, but gives close personal attention to the direction of affairs and is ever on the alert to add to the inducements offered customers. One floor and a basement of the dimensions of 20x65 feet are utilized, and the stock is plenty large enough to take up all the available space. The most prominent characteristic of goods bought at this store is their reliability. Mr. Hatch has always done business on the principle of giving his patrons all that they pay for, and taking pains to represent everything just as it is. He prefers to make no sale at all rather than to make one under false representations, and as a consequence, those who are familiar with his methods need no further guarantee than his simple word. His prices are as low as can be fixed on articles of similar quality, and those who wish to buy strictly reliable goods at the lowest market rates, will find it very difficult indeed to get more satisfactory results elsewhere. Davis Hatch, Jr., was the first man in the United States to manufacture and put up for sale Liquid Dressing for Ladies' Boots.

George W. Harrison, Dining Room, Front Street, Bath. It might seem at first thought, easy enough to manage a Restaurant, but there is no man who has had much occasion to patronize these places, but what will say that the really good ones are in a small minority. Why, is not for us to state. We may have our own theories on the subject, but our readers want facts rather than theories, and are naturally more interested in learning of one good Dining Room, than in hearing the reasons why a half dozen are not good. Therefore we will hasten to call to their attention the establishment conducted by Mr. George W. Harrison on Front Street, for this gentleman is one of the few who know how things should be done and spares neither time nor money in attaining satisfactory results. Mr. Harrison was born in Bath, and opened his present place of business in 1887. The premises measure 20x60 feet, and are nicely fitted up with all necessary facilities. But after all, the main point to be considered in an establishment of this kind is the food, and here Mr. Harrison comes out strong, for he supplies his customers with the best that the market affords, and takes measures to see that it is properly cooked and promptly and courteously served. Employment is given to two competent assistants and the comfort and convenience of patrons are looked out for on every hand. The prices here are very moderate, and a trial of the accommodations provided, will result in another call.

R. C. Harris, Dealer in Provisions, Groceries, Fruits and Vegetables, 106 Center Street, Bath. The gentleman whose card we print above has been engaged in his present line of business for just about twenty-one years, for it was in 1867 that he first opened his doors to the public. Of the comparative standing of his enterprise we need say but little; everybody who knows Bath at all intimately, knows of Mr. Harris' store, and there is not a Grocery and Provision House in town that is worthy of more unreserved commendation or that occupies a higher place in the esteem of the public. Mr. Harris was born in Brunswick and is a member of the Grand Army, having served as a Signal Officer in the Department of the Gulf during the Rebellion. The premises occupied by him are located at No. 106 Center Street, and measure 25x46 feet, being three stories in heighth. Employment is given to two experienced and well-informed assistants, and customers are at all times assured courteous attention and polite and fair treatment. Mr. Harris gives particular pains to supplying family trade, and the advantages he offers to those dealing with him are sufficiently pronounced to fully account for the heavy business done in this line. Provisions of all seasonable kinds are always in stock, and Staple and Fancy Groceries are also on hand in immense variety. Foreign and Domestic Fruits are very extensively dealt in, and Vegetables are sold in large quantities.

James H. Scott, Manufacturer of and Dealer in Harnesses of every Description; also Trunks, Bags, Valises, etc., Front Street, Bath. A thoroughly well-made Harness is not so often seen nowadays as it should be, for many manufacturers strive to produce a "cheap" article, rather than one that combines honest material and honest workmanship. Such harnesses are "cheap" only in name, for they have but little durability and are apt to give out at any time. To obtain a trustworthy Harness, one must patronize a trustworthy maker, such a one for instance as Mr. James H. Scott, whose place of business is located on Front Street. Operations were begun in 1876, under the firm name of R. Scott & Co., and in 1880 the present Proprietor assumed sole control. He is a native of this city and is a member of the Knights of Pythias. Premises measuring 20x50 feet are occupied and a fine stock of Horse Furnishings is carried, as well as a full assortment of Trunks, Valises, Bags and similar goods. Order work is done promptly, carefully and satisfactorily, and at prices that are reasonable and fair. Repairing is attended to at short notice and will be neatly and strongly done by skilled hands. Mr. Scott's Harness has the name of standing a deal of hard usage without giving out, and is therefore deservedly popular. He quotes low prices, considering the quality of the goods, and those who spend a dollar at his store, may depend upon receiving a full equivalent.

LEADING BUSINESS MEN OF BATH.

H. A. Bates, Dentist, Center and Front Streets, Bath. One of the favorite maxims of Americans is, "time is money," and it would be well for most of us if we realized that time is even more than money under certain circumstances. Promptness is especially desirable when taking action regarding the teeth, and if people would make it a rule to visit a competent Dentist at the first indications of decay or other trouble, there would be much suffering avoided, and the demand for false teeth would sensibly diminish. We are aware that about everybody has a sort of horror of being operated on by a Dentist, no matter how skillful and gentle he may be; but it should be remembered that there is no reason why the least pain should be experienced, provided you take time by the forelock, and do not delay until the keenly sensitive nerve has been exposed. It is an excellent idea to have the teeth examined at regular intervals whether they give any trouble or not; for by this means they are sure of being kept in first-class condition, and any incipient decay can be immediately arrested. This course is being pursued by a greater number of people yearly, and is particularly advisable in families containing young children. The chief precaution to be observed is the choosing of a thoroughly competent practitioner, and such of our readers as reside in Bath or vicinity, will have little trouble in selecting such a man, for there are a number of skilled Dentists in the city, and one of the most deservedly popular of them is Mr. H. A. Bates, whose rooms are at the cor. of Center and Front Streets. This gentleman is a native of Oakland and is connected with the Odd Fellows and Ancient Order of United Workmen. He began operations here in 1870, and his record during the past eighteen years affords the most satisfactory proof of his ability. Dr. Bates was the first Dentist to introduce in New England the Dental Electric Vibrator for Painless Extraction of Teeth. Four rooms are utilized, measuring 20x35 feet, and the latest improved facilities are at hand, enabling work to be done quickly and thoroughly, and at the lowest possible rates.

J. A. Hamm, Proprietor Commercial House Center Street, Bath. One of those unpretending but excellently managed Hotels, which every experienced traveler likes to stop at, is the Commercial House, located on Center St., and kept by Mr. J. A. Hamm. Guests are made to feel at home here at once, and great care is taken to give no reasonable cause for complaint to any patron. The Hotel contains twenty-two guest rooms, and is three stories in height, the apartments being spacious, airy, well-lighted and comfortably furnished. It is the aim of the management to supply the table with an abundance of well-cooked food, and also to arrange the bill of fare so as to allow of all tastes being satisfied. That this purpose is fully carried out will be disputed by none who have made practical trial of the accommodations here furnished, and as this system has been so successful in the past, there is no fear but what it will be continued in the future. The Commercial House is very conveniently situated and is one of the easiest Hotels to reach in town. Traveling-men are shown particular consideration and we feel that we speak the sentiments of many of them when we say it is worth while to "rush things" if necessary, in order to put up a day or two at this popular hostelry. The terms are very moderate, and one feels when paying a bill here as though he were getting the full worth of his money, cent for cent. The services are prompt and special instructions are carefully followed. A fine equipped Livery connected.

J. C. Piper, Manufacturer of Picture Frames and Dealer in Works of Art, Bragg's Block, Center Street, Bath. Philosophers tell us that everything that is useful is also beautiful, and from this point of view, even, a ton of coal may be said to have a beauty of its own; but the most of us are unable to appreciate the beauty of common articles of trade, and are obliged to visit such an establishment as that conducted by Mr. J. C. Piper, in Bragg's Block, Center Street, before we can find articles that are as beautiful as they are desirable in other respects. The gentleman to which we have reference began operations in 1854, and is, without doubt, one of the best-known Manufacturers of Picture Frames, etc., in the city. He is a native of East Newfield, York County, Me., and has a large circle of friends in this vicinity. We need not tell our readers that a Frame exerts a very powerful influence on the effect of a picture, for this is well-known; but it may be advisable to state that as Mr. Piper has made a special study of this subject, he is thoroughly competent to choose such a Frame as will be best adapted to the Picture it is designed to inclose. Orders for Frames are filled at short notice, and prices are as low as the lowest. Works of Art, Artists' Materials, etc., are also largely dealt in, and all callers are assured prompt attention, goods being cheerfully shown and all desired information given. The premises occupied measure 20x45 feet, and contain a beautiful selection of Paintings, Chromos, Etchings, Photographs, Engravings, etc. The Stock is displayed to excellent advantage, and Art-lovers would do well to give it an early examination.

N. & W. C. Covel, Carriage Trimmers, Harness Makers & Dealers in Whips, Curry-Combs, Brushes, Blankets, Trunks, Valises, etc., Washington Street, Bath. There are a great many excellent Carriages and Harnesses made in Maine annually; but there are also many poor ones turned out, and it is necessary to use some discrimination if imposition is to be avoided. There is no need of arguing as to the advantages of a good Harness or Carriage. There are really but two kinds made—one that is valuable and one that is worthless—and we will simply say that an unreliable Harness or Carriage is not only dangerous but useless, and should be cast aside as soon as its weakness is discovered. It is easy to purchase strong and well-made goods of this kind, and a visit to the establishment of which N. & W. C. Covel are the proprietors, located at 772 and 774 Washington Street, will result in the inspection of as trustworthy work as is done in this country. Messrs. Covel are as moderate in their prices as they are thorough in their work, and economy is best served by paying a fair sum and getting something that will last. They have carried on their present enterprise for many years, having started it early in the sixties, and are as well-known in Bath as though they were natives of that town, although they were born in Boston. Carriage trimming is also extensively carried on, and Repairing is done at short notice in a workmanlike manner, employment being given to three competent assistants and low rates are quoted. Carriages as well as Harnesses, also Whips, Curry Combs, Brushes, Blankets, etc., are dealt in largely, and not only staple goods but also novelties are to be found in stock.

Lincoln National Bank, Front Street, Bath. The National Banks of this State will, as a whole, compare favorably with those of any other portion of the Union, and are to be commended especially, for the liberality and good-judgement they show in encouraging local commercial enterprises. There are some exceptions of course, and there have been instances where Bank officials apparently preferred to aid out-of town houses rather than those nearer at hand, even when the security in both cases was eqally good, but this is fortunately of rare occurrence. We say fortunately, for it is undeniable that a Bank can exert a most effective influence in sustaining and building up the commerce of a community, and that too without ever endangering its own interests. Such of our readers as have watched the course of the Lincoln National Bank of this city since its incorporation in 1865, it being at that time the oldest Bank in Bath, need not be told that its management has ever been solicitous of local interests, for no observer could have failed to notice that the good of the community and that of the institution have been considered as identical. Other things being equal, the preference has always been given to home undertakings when financial aid was asked for, and under these circumstances, it is not surprising that Bath merchants and manufacturers should think highly of this Bank and those having it in charge. The President, Mr. Charles Davenport, and the Cashier, Mr. W. R. Shaw, are both personally well-known throughout the city, and it would be impossible to name two gentlemen in whom our resident business men would have more confidence. The Bank has a capital of $200,000 and a surplus of $40,000 its present financial standing fully justifies the choice of its officers and Directors. Directors: Charles Davenport, L. W. Houghton, Charles E. Patten, John S. Elliot, Charles W. Morse.

D. C. Gould & Co., Dealers in Groceries, Provisions, Flour, Coffee and Tea. Flour, Tea, Coffee and Spices a Specialty; Columbian Block, 182 Front Street, Bath. It is by no means the easy, simple thing it may seem to some, to carry on a Retail Grocery Store to the best advantage, and should any of our readers be disposed to question the accuracy of this statement, they may find proof of its truth in the many failures that occur in the line of business mentioned. But it is not of failures, but of success that we propose to treat, and a signal success is without doubt the establishment conducted by Messrs. D. C. Gould & Co., on Front Street. The enterprise in question was inaugurated in 1875, and has not reached its present popularity without constant and intelligent effort. Both D. C. and W. C. Gould were born in Jefferson, Maine, and have had extensive experience in the Grocery business. They make it a point to carry as large, if not the largest first-class and complete stock of Ship, Family and Fancy Groceries at Wholesale and Retail of any store in Bath, and are thus able to fill orders without delay. The quality of the goods supplied by them are bound to be satisfactory, for they purchase only of well-known and reputable houses and handle standard articles. The premises occupied measure 30x100 feet also storage building 30x80 feet including cellar, and employment is given to three competent assistants. The Messrs. Gould's prices will always bear the severest comparison with those of other dealers, for they are careful and experienced buyers and are satisfied with a living profit. They also handle all kinds of Choice Fruits in their season. The Flour sold by them comes direct from the Mills. A specialty is made of Chase & Sanborn's, of Boston, Fine Teas and Coffees. The Messrs. Gould keep two nice teams very busy all the time. All goods strictly as represented or money refunded.

H. S. Lord, Sail Maker. Awnings, Tents, Flags, Rail Nettings, Steam Pipe Coverings, Hammocks, etc., made to order. Yacht Sails a Specialty, Star of the East Wharf, Bath. Sailmaking is a branch of industry that requires especially close attention to detail, and there are few trades nowadays that are so independent of machinery and therefore so much affected by the individual skill of the workmen. A really good sail maker must have special fitness for the business as well as wide experience, and it is only when these are combined that strictly first-class work can be turned out. Mr. H. S. Lord of this city has the reputation of being one of the best sail makers in Maine, and indeed it only needs careful and intelligent inspection of the work leaving his establishment to show that this reputation is well-deserved. He is a native of West Brookville, and at the age of ten years commenced to learn the trade of sailmaking with S.T. Mugridge of Rockland, Me., and carries on business on Star of the East Wharf, having begun operations in 1885. Mr. Lord makes a specialty of Yacht Sails and certainly there is no branch of his business in which skill is more needed. The most beautiful yacht owes a great part of her good looks to her canvas and the speediest and finest model would have but little chance in a race if handicapped by ill-fitting sails. Therefore it is important to have not only hull, but also Sails and Rigging designed and made by perfectly competent parties, and it is the general opinion of yachtsmen hereabouts that Mr. Lord has no superior in his special line. Two floors are occupied, measuring 20x100 feet and employment is given to from 7 to 10 efficient and careful assistants. Mr. Lord makes Awnings, Tents, Flags, Rail Nettings, Steam Pipe Coverings, Hammocks, etc., as well as Sails, and not only fills orders promptly, but also places his rates at the lowest possible figures.

LEADING BUSINESS MEN OF BATH. 347

W. W. Mason, General Trucking, Broad Street, Bath. No matter how complete the railway and steamboat facilities of a business center may be, the best results cannot be attained unless ample teaming facilities are also provided. In fact, it may be said that the more perfect the former service is, the more perfect the latter should be also, and the business men and citizens of Bath in general have reason to congratulate themselves on the efficiency of that furnished by Mr. W. W. Mason, since he began operations in 1854. This gentleman is a native of Bath and has a large circle of friends in this vicinity. His office is conveniently located on Broad Street, and orders left there will receive the most prompt and careful attention. Although a very large business is done, it is easily handled, for Mr. Mason's facilities are very extensive, ten assistants being employed. The horses and vehicles utilized are kept in first-class condition, and the system in operation is so perfect as to render mistakes and annoying delays very rare indeed. Merchants dealing in goods apt to be injured by rough handling, find it especially to their advantage to make use of the facilities provided by Mr. Mason, for his drivers and helpers are careful and experienced and take special pains with packages marked fragile or otherwise distinguished from ordinary freight. Not only Trucking, but Jobbing of all kinds is attended to in a superior manner, and as both light and heavy teams are available. All varieties of articles can be quickly and economically transported for Mr. Mason's charges are as low as his service is satisfactory. Mr. Mason is also agent for the Eastern Steamboat Co.

J. L. Douglas, Dealer in Men's and Boys' Clothing, Hats, Caps and Gent's Furnishing Goods, etc., under Sagadahock House, Front Street, Bath. Strangers in Bath (or indeed in any other city) are frequently at a loss to know just where to purchase certain articles of which they stand in need, for while they of course desire to deal with a trustworthy house, still they do not feel like paying an extra profit for a name. Clothing and Gentlemen's Furnishing Goods are among the commodities in most common request and those stopping in Bath and wanting anything in this line, can possibly do no better than to visit the establishment carried on by Mr. J. L. Douglas, on Front Street, under the Sagadahoc House. This gentleman has had an extended experience in connection with the handling of Clothing, etc., for he has been identified with his present enterprise ever since 1862, it having been started in 1849 by Mr. John Ballou. Mr. Douglas is a native of Durham and is a member of the Free Masons. Of course he is well-known in Bath and vicinity, and his store is a favorite resort for the most careful buyers, as Mr. Douglas shows an exceptionally "clean" stock, no out of date articles being included. The store measures 20x45 feet, and a fine assortment of Men's and Boys' Clothing, Hats and Caps, Gentlemen's Furnishing Goods, etc., is always open to the inspection of those interested. Goods are cheerfully shown and as Mr. Douglas employs an experienced and efficient assistant, he is able to serve customers without delay.

Swanton, Jameson & Co., Dealers in Hardware and Ship Chandlery, Broad and Front Streets, Bath. One of the most extensive establishments of its kind in this portion of the State, is that carried on by Messrs. Swanton, Jameson & Co., at the corner of Broad and Front Streets. The premises occupied measure 40x70 feet and comprise three floors, all this space being required to accommodate the extremely heavy stock carried, which includes Hardware and Ship Chandlery, and is very complete in every department. The enterprise conducted by this firm was inaugurated in 1832, by Messrs. Hyde & Swanton, the present style being adopted in 1871. Messrs. J. B. Swanton, J. C. Jameson and H. W. Swanton constitute the firm, all of these gentlemen being natives of Bath. Both a Wholesale and Retail business is done, vessels being supplied at short notice, and the quality of every article sold being strictly guaranteed to prove as represented. No detailed description of the stock is possible in these pages, for the simple reason that lack of space forbids, the assortment on hand being so great that even a catalogue of it would have to contain a great many words. But it may be briefly described as being in keeping with the leading position which the concern enjoys, a position which is the legitimate result of earnest, intelligent and long-continued work. Customers are given prompt and painstaking attention, for employment is afforded to five efficient assistants and a great amount of business can thus be quickly disposed of. Low prices are quoted in each department, for no concern enjoys more favorable relations with producers.

John M. Clark, Undertaker, Casket warerooms Nos. 7 and 9 Broad Street, Bath. There is no question but that the establishment carried on by Mr. John M. Clark is one of the foremost of its kind in this State, and indeed it would be strange if such were not the case, for Mr. Clark began business a quarter of a century ago, and has since spared no pains to serve the public to the best of his ability. The premises made use of by him are situated at Nos. 28, 30, 32 and 34 Broad Street, and comprise two stores measuring 40x65 feet, six floors being occupied altogether. A very large stock of Caskets and Coffins is here carried, for Mr. Clark does an extensive business in the Undertaking line, and his facilities for filling orders without delay, are of the most effective character. He is prepared to supply everything needed on funeral occasions, and it is hardly necessary to say that he is in a position to supply anything in his line at prices as low as the lowest. His stock of funeral goods contains articles of all grades, and all orders are given equal care and executed with desirable promptness. Mr. Clark is a native of Limerick, Maine and is personally one of the most widely known of our resident merchants. His liberal methods have won for him many friends and his establishment may justly be pointed out as a truly representative one in every sense of the word. It deserves a prominent place in our columns and we take pleasure in giving it such a position.

Marine National Bank, Front Street, Bath. The condition of the banking institutions of a community, affords an accurate reflex of the state of trade in that section, for it is not possible to imagine a bank being flourishing and prosperous, when the industries and mercantile enterprises carried on in its vicinity are the reverse. For this reason, one acquainted with Bath and its present prospects, would naturally expect to learn that its banks were financially sound and extensive in resources, and that this is in accordance with the facts we need hardly say. One of the best-known institutions of this kind in the city, or for that matter in the State as well, is the Marine National Bank, and so intimately has this been connected with the business history of this community since 1864 (the year the institution was founded), that no work treating of that subject cou'd be looked upon as complete, did it not contain as extended mention of the Marine National Bank as circumstances would permit. It is not however our purpose to speak in detail of the beneficent influence this institution has extended over the many local enterprises it has fostered. Our resident merchants know well the record of the bank in this respect, and could all the individual instances of timely aid rendered be brought to light, this record would be almost indefinitely extended. Suffice it to say that its managers have ever had the best interests of Bath at heart, and have acted with ability and zeal to advance those interests by all honorable means. The President of the bank, Mr. S. D. Bailey, is a native of Bath and has most acceptably filled the mayor's chair, while the cashier, Mr. H. A. Duncan, is also a native of this city. The institution has a capital of $100,000 and is under the control of the following representative gentlemen as directors: S. D. Bailey, E. C. Hyde, P. M. Whitmore, H. W. Field, J. M. Hayes.

Charles W. Dunning, Livery Stable, Front Street, Bath. When inquiring about a Livery Stable, one of the first questions asked is "Are the horses good?" this being followed by "Are the carriages of modern style and easy riding?" Both these questions can unhesitatingly be answered in the affirmative, so far as the establishment carried on by Mr. Charles W. Dunning is concerned, for there is not a similar enterprise in this vicinity conducted on more liberal principles. Mr. Dunning has been identified with his present undertaking since 1860, and is one of the best-known stable-keepers in the State. He was born in this city, and is connected with both the Free Masons and the Odd Fellows. Premises of the dimensions of 50x80 feet are utilized, located on Front Street, and employment is given to two efficient assistants. Mr. Dunning's horses are carefully selected for the especial service required of them, and will be found docile, willing and quite speedy. He does not pretend to supply his patrons with race-horses, but he does seek to furnish strong and trustworthy animals that can give a good account of themselves on the road, and that are easy drivers. Nothing is so destructive to the pleasure of driving as to have to continually urge your horse along, and patrons of Mr. Dunning's stable speak in the highest terms of the manner in which his horses get over the road without any forcing. His prices are low, and orders are promptly filled.

William Ledyard, Men's Youths', Boys' & Children's Fine Clothing, and Men's Furnishings, 48 and 50 Centre Street, Bath. Many of our readers can remember no doubt, when those who had any considerable amount of clothing to buy, could best serve their own interests by visiting Portland, or even Boston, as the prices quoted in those cities were more than enough lower than home prices, to make up for the expense of travel, etc. But this ceased to be the case some time ago, and it is but the simple truth that the retail purchaser of clothing can now get as much for his money right here in Bath as he can in any part of New England. Of course he must use common sense in placing his orders, for there are unscrupulous dealers here as there are in all cities, and there are others who, with the best of intentions, have neither the capital nor the business ability to compete successfully with better-equipped houses; but it is not difficult to judge as to the comparitive merits of our local retail Clothing concerns, and many residents of Bath and vicinity have decided unequivocally in favor of that conducted by Mr. William Ledyard, at Nos. 48 and 50 Centre Street, opposite City Hall. The proprietor of this popular establishment is a native of Bath, and is connected with the Free Masons. He has carried on his present enterprise since 1888, and has already established an extensive and rapidly increasing trade two floors are occupied, each forty-two feet square, and an immense stock of Men's, Youth's, Boy's, and Children's Clothing, and Men's Furnishings is constantly carried. The nature of these goods and the general policy of the house are so well indicated by the guarantee issued by Mr. Ledyard, that we can do no better than to give it in full, as follows : — 1st, That the prices of our goods shall be as low as the same quality of material and manufacture can be bought in New England; 2d, One price to everyone for same quality of goods, on same day of purchase; 3d, All goods to be exactly as represented; 4th, That the full amount of purchase money will be refunded in all cases where goods are unsatisfactory and are returned unworn and uninjured. This "covers the whole ground," and we can only add that in spite of the large business done, prompt service is assured to all, as employment is given to three efficient and polite assistants. Mr. J. C. Ledyard, father of Mr. Wm. Ledyard, can need no introduction to our Bath readers, as he has long been prominent in the community, being very extensively engaged in handling Real Estate, and having long been considered an authority in such matters. He is agent for the Cambridge Iron Roofing, which is guaranteed Fire and Water Proof, and has been thoroughly indorsed by underwriters in general. This Roofing will be furnished in quantities to suit, or will be applied at a moderate charge, satisfaction being guaranteed in either case, providing the explicit directions given are properly carried into effect. Mr. Ledyard's office is in his son's store, Nos. 48 and 50 Centre Street, and he will be happy to give full information on application.

Bath Savings Bank, Front St., Bath. While no doubt it is true that the opportunities for amassing a competency are not so numerous or so plain to see nowadays as they were half a century ago, still, it is within the power of the large majority of people to secure themselves against want if they go to work about it in the right way. Too many of us seek to win a fortune by one brilliant stroke, disdaining the building up of one little by little, but having a hazy idea that some day we shall have riches within our grasp and only need to reach out and pluck them. We set our minds on having a balance of ten, twenty, thirty or forty thousand dollars to our credit before we die, but never seem to realize that everything must have a beginning, and that the largest sum of money is made up of a number of single dollars. Few of us are financiers: not all of us have business instincts, but every man in health has within him the capacity for earning money, and the capacity to earn involves the capacity to save. To save, then, is within the reach of practically all, and so important is the formation of the habit of saving, that every working man should save something under all circumstances, if it be but a quarter of a dollar a week. Save all you honorably can and deposit it in a secure and well-managed Bank; then should trouble come you have some resource and feel that you have done your duty as a man, at least. Our Maine Savings Banks are, as a rule, worthy of the highest praise, and one of the most deserving of them is that which has been carried on in this city since 1852 under the name of the Bath Savings Bank. It has rendered efficient aid to thousands in the past, and has still the capacity for a continuance of its noble work in the future, for it is managed with a rare combination of prudence and enterprise, and is thus enabled to give a good rate of interest without indulging in hazardous speculation. The names of its officers and trustees are those of well-known and representative citizens, and no stronger guarantee of the institution's good faith and worthiness could be asked than that afforded by the fact that the following gentlemen are responsible for its direction:—President, Chas. Davenport; Treasurer, J. H. Humphreys. Trustees, L. W. Houghton, J. H. Kimball, H. W. Swanton, E. B. Drummond, M. S. Briory.

Troy Laundry, Front St., Opp. Railroad Depot, Bath. Troy, New York, is famous as the home of the improved method of doing Laundry Work, now so popular throughout the country; but there are few establishments outside of the city mentioned that are so deserving of the title, "Troy Laundry," as that conducted by Mr. H. E. Hatch, on Front Street, opposite the railroad depot. Mr. Hatch is a native of Chester, Maine. He opened the establishment to which we have reference in 1888, and has already advanced it to a high position in the favor of the public. This success has been won by hard work and earnest determination, and is fully deserved, as all work has been received on the understanding that should it fail to give satisfaction, no charge would be made. Employment is given to five assistants, and orders can be filled at short notice, goods being sent for and delivered free of charge. Special attention is given to Family Washings, and those housekeepers who wish to be relieved of the worst drudgery they have to perform or supervise, would do well to give Mr. Hatch's establishment a trial. Orders by mail will receive prompt and painstaking attention, and every effort will be made to sustain the high reputation for efficiency now enjoyed.

G. J. Mitchell, Dealer in Corn, Meal, Oats, Shorts and Middlings, Commercial Street, Foot of Broad, Bath. But little thought is required to convince anybody that the business of those dealing in Corn, Meal, Oats, Shorts, etc., must of necessity be one of the most important branches of commerce in the country. These articles are not merely commodities, they are necessities, and being both for man and beast, their consumption cannot help being very great. Bath has many concerns dealing in these goods within her borders, but not one of them is more deserving of all the confidence and patronage it receives than that carried on by Mr. G. J. Mitchell, on Commercial Street, Foot of Broad. This gentleman founded the undertaking in question in 1865, and has long since built up a thriving business and established a name for filling orders with promptness and intelligence that speaks volumes for the attention he gives to the interests of his customers as well as of himself. The premises occupied comprise two floors, and are of the dimensions of 45x45 feet. Mr. Mitchell handles Corn, Meal, Oats, etc., both at Wholesale and Retail, and is prepared to furnish any or all of these commodities in any desired quantity without delay. His prices are always as low as the lowest, and his goods equal to the best.

J. Varney, Dealer in Lumber, Front Street, North Bath. Of course everybody knows that Maine is a great Lumber State, but still, no one can really gain a correct idea of the vastness of this interest until he has traveled from one end of this section to the other, and seen with his own eyes the variety and extent of the establishments more or less directly connected with it. Some of these establishments are old and others are of recent date; but all of them, generally speaking, are prosperous, and many of Maine's most prominent citizens are concerned in their management. The firm of J. Varney was formed in 1859, and the volume of business done shows a constant and most gratifying increase. This concern deals in Lumber, both at Wholesale and Retail, and utilizes yard room of the dimensions of 100x150 feet, located on Front Street, Bath, the mill being located at North Bath. The most favorable relations are enjoyed with producers and the lowest market rates are quoted to large and small buyers. A large and varied stock is generally to be found in this yard, and many extensive consumers place the bulk of their orders here on account of the promptness and accuracy with which they are filled. Employment is given to four assistants, and customers are assured early attention and uniformly fair treatment. Orders for dimensions solicited and promptly filled. Satisfaction guaranteed.

Sagadahoc National Bank, Front St, Bath. The Sagadahoc National Bank is a great favorite with our resident business men, and deservedly so, for since its incorporation its policy has ever been to encourage legitimate local enterprises as liberally as circumstances would permit. Having been founded in 1865, it has been in operation nearly a quarter of a century, and has been largely instrumental in developing Bath's commercial possibilities to their present extent. There are probably few who have never been immediately connected with the management of a National Bank, who realize the difficulty of administering the affairs of such an institution to the general satisfaction of the community and to the profit of the Bank itself. The course to be steered lies between rash speculation and undue conservatism; should the first extreme be approached, there is a cry of alarm from the business public and confidence is badly shaken; while if too much caution be exercised the management will find themselves characterized as "fossils," and patronage will be transferred to a more wide-awake institution. It is the easiest thing in the world to criticize Bank management; but the number of those who are really competent to improve upon existing financial methods, is extremely small. The Sagadahoc National Bank is carried on by gentlemen who may fairly be considered as representative citizens, and their special fitness for their present duties is best evidenced by the high esteem in which the enterprise is held among those most conversant with its operations. The President, Mr. Franklin Reed, is a native of this city, as is also the Cashier, Mr. Henry Eames. The Board of Directors is made up of Messrs. Franklin Reed, Alfred Lamonte, W. F. Moses, H. F. Morse and John G. Morse. The Bank has a capital of $100,000, and a surplus of $30,000, and is in most excellent financial condition, being thoroughly well perpared for the carrying on of a General Banking Business. Its career has been a most honorable one, and its future gives every indication of being worthy of its past history.

B. B. C. C., Dealers in Men's, Youths' and Children's Clothing, Hats, Caps and Furnishing Goods, Bertram L. Filene, Manager, Front Street, Opposite Elm, Bath. The mystic letters "B. B. C. C." have occasioned a good deal of natural curiosity since they were brought before the public in connection with the popular Clothing establishment located on Front Street, opposite Elm, and many have been the guesses made as to what they stand for. They might mean "Big Bath Clothing Concern," and still be entirely justified by the facts, for there is not a house in this city dealing in similar goods that offers more genuine inducements to its customers. The proprietor of the enterpise is Mr. William Filene, who resides in Lynn, the manager being Mr. B. L. Filene, a native of Lynn, Mass. The "B. B. C. C." occupies two floors and employs three assistants, who give prompt and courteous attention to every caller, and carry into effect the guiding principle of the establishment—uniform politeness and fair dealing to all. This is emphatically a "one price" store, and rich or poor, experienced or inexperienced, are charged the same rates and used the same way. Men's, Boys' and Youths' Clothing is kept in stock in great variety, and one may visit this store with the full assurance that a perfect fit is to be had there. The garments dealt in are of new and stylish cut and materials, and are thoroughly well-made, being durable as well as handsome. A complete outfit may be bought here, for Hats, Caps and Furnishing Goods are all handled largely, and quoted at bottom prices. No more popular store can be found in town than this, and it is gratifying to record a success so intelligently worked for and so honestly won.

M. M. Lemont, Boots and Shoes, Centre Street, Bath. It is not an easy thing to carry a sufficiently large and varied stock of Boots and Shoes to enable all tastes to be suited, but experience will do wonders, and during the three years that Mr. M. M. Lemont has carried on his present establishment on Centre Street, he has gained a very accurate idea of what is wanted by those to whom he caters. His store is 20x45 feet in dimensions, and employment is given to two efficient assistants, thus assuring prompt service to all. Boots and Shoes of all descriptions are handled by Mr. Lemont, and if he cannot fit and suit you, you must be a very exceptional person. Of course the quality of the stock on hand is governed in a great measure by the time of year, but one is always sure to find within it, thick boots and thin boots, shoes for hard service and shoes for dress purposes, together with full lines of slippers, rubbers, etc. One popular feature of Mr. Lemont's management, is his guarantee that each article sold shall prove just as represented, and inexperienced buyers can depend absolutely on this warrant being lived up to in every respect. Repairing is done at short notice, and prices in every department are very reasonable.

S. J. Watson, Brass Founder, Broad Street, Bath. The art of casting metals has been brought to great perfection of late years in this country, and results are now attained that would have been looked upon as impossible a quarter of a century ago. Casting in brass is one of the most advanced departments of this industry, for this composition is comparatively easy to handle, and everybody has some idea of the immense variety of articles that are wholly or partially composed of it. A Brass Foundry that will compare favorably, as regards the excellence of the work done, with any similar establishment in this section, is that carried on by Mr. S. J. Watson on Broad Street. This industry was founded in 1868, and during the score of years it has been in operation, it has gained a reputation that is as high as it is well-deservd. Mr. Watson, who is a native of Castine, has always given close personal attention to every detail of his business, and has neglected no means to improve the efficiency of the establishment, and the record it has for uniformly superior work and prompt filling of orders, shows the result of such business methods. Two floors are occupied, measuring 35x85 feet. The most improved facilities are provided, and parties wishing anything in Mr. Watson's line, would do well to take advantage of his excellent work and low prices.

People's Twenty-Five Cent Savings Bank, Galen C. Moses, President, F. W. Weeks, Treasurer, Bath. An institution for which we feel a hearty respect, and which we take especial pleasure in calling the favorable attention of our readers to, is that whose title heads this article, the People's Twenty five Cent Savings Bank. It is well named. Since its inception a score of years ago, it has been carried on in the interest of the people, has been so managed as to conclusively prove that the intention of those having it in charge, is to provide a place where the public may leave savings and feel perfectly confident that they are even more secure than if in the custody of the owners. Thus there is an additional incentive given to save, and working men and women are made to feel that prudence and economy really pay in more senses than one. It is not high interest that should be regarded so much as safety, in the making of an investment by those of limited means, and the majority of working people, even though they do not enjoy the advantages for obtaining correct information on financial matters that some others may, thoroughly understand that under all ordinary circumstances, a high rate of interest and reasonable security are incompatible. Do not put your money into enterprises which promise fabulous returns; such chances would not require advertising were they genuine, and speculation should be left to those who can afford it. Then again, you want your money where you can get it at short notice in case of emergency, and the People's Twenty-five Cent Savings Bank is just such a place, all unnecessary formalities being avoided and prompt and polite attention being assured to all. The institution is in charge of Mr. Galen C. Moses, President, Mr. F. W. Weeks, Treasurer, and Messrs. James D. Robinson, John R. Kelley, R. S. Hunt and G. S. Preble, Trustees. These gentlemen require no introduction to our readers for they are all well known, and their place in the community is marked and high. Deposits approximating $300,000 are held, and the surplus above actual liabilities amounts to some $35,000 the resources of the bank lying in mortgages, Public Funds and Bank Stock almost entirely.

J. G. Washburn, Dealer in Musical Instruments, Pictures and Frames, Stationery, etc., 36 Center Street, Bath. The very handsomest furnished house that could be produced, would be bare and incomplete without the presence of pictures, and as there is no home so beautiful but what such works of art will improve it, so there is none so mean and humble but what a well chosen engraving or photograph can brighten it up wonderfully. There is no need of spending a great deal of money, unless one is perfectly able to do so, and in fact it is really surprising how far a few dollars will go in the purchase of Pictures and Frames. It is, however of no small importance to know where to buy, for there are dealers and dealers, and while some are very moderate in their prices, others seem to believe in keeping works of art out of the reach of common people. This is by no means the principle on which Mr. J. G. Washburn does business, and if you want proof of this, just visit his store at No. 36 Center Street; you will find it well-stocked with Pictures and Frames of all kinds, and should you leave an order for a Frame, it will be filled at surprisingly short notice and at bottom rates. Mr. Washburn is a native of Massachusetts and a member of the Knights of the Golden Cross. He has carried on his present enterprise since 1886, and has already built up a flourishing trade. Artists' Materials of standard quality are dealt in in great variety, and Stationery is handled to some extent, while Pianos and Organs may be bought here to better advantage than at some much more pretentious establishments. Mr. Washburn carries a very large variety of Pianos and Organs, ranging in prices —Pianos, from $150 up, and Organs ranging from $50 up. These goods are sold for cash or on installments cheaper than the same quality in the Boston or New York markets. He also carries a large variety of Violins, Banjos, Guitars, etc.

Watson & Co., Dealers in Stoves, Furnaces, Ranges, Tin, Iron and Copper Ware, House Furnishing Goods, Galley and Cabin Outfits, Vessels' Stoves, Water Closets, Lead Pipe, Sheet Lead, &c., &c.; House and Ship Plumbers, 102, 104 Front, Head of Broad Street, Bath. The firm of Watson & Co., is a representative one in every sense of the word, and the magnitude of their business will compare favorably with that of any house in the State engaged in a similar line of trade. Operations were begun in 1853, by Messrs. S. J. & W. H. Watson, both of whom are natives of Castine, Me., and are well known personally throughout Bath and vicinity. The premises occupied are located at Nos. 102 and 104 Front Street, Head of Broad, and comprise three floors. each of which measures 40x65 feet. A very heavy and varied stock is carried, consisting of Stoves, Furnaces, Ranges, Tin, Iron and Copper Ware, together with House Furnishing Goods, Galley and Cabin Outfits, Vessels' Stoves, Water Closets, Lead Pipe, Sheet Lead, etc., the goods being obtained from the most reliable sources, and being guaranteed in every instance to prove just as represented. Employment is given to six efficient assistants, and House and Ship Plumbing of all descriptions will be done to to order at short notice, and at a moderate price. The paramount importance of having Plumbing Work done in an honest and scientific manner, is now too generally understood to render it necessary to dwell upon the subject, for so many dangerous and even deadly diseases have been traced to defective Plumbing, that carelessness in this respect is inexcusable. Messrs. Watson & Co. have every facility at their command to do House and Ship Plumbing as it should be done. They have that knowledge of ways and means which can only come from experience, and they employ only skilled and trustworthy workmen, the result being that their work has an enviable reputation for efficiency and durability. The lowest rates consistent with the attainment of the best results, are quoted on large and small orders, and the rule "the best is the cheapest," is proved by the experience of their customers. The latest improved Stoves, etc., may be bought of this firm at the lowest market rates, and any information concerning such goods will be cheerfully given on application.

LEADING BUSINESS MEN OF BATH.

C. W. Clifford, Jeweler, Bath. The most of us find it plenty hard enough to get a living under the most favorable circumstances, and hence cannot afford to hamper ourselves in any avoidable manner. This being the case, what further argument is necessary as to the importance of carrying a reliable watch? "Time is money," says the proverb, and no man is in a position to waste his own or his neighbor's time with impunity. Without a reliable timepiece in your pocket, you cannot be sure of filling any agreement as agreed upon, and therefore it is of the utmost importance that everyone should own a dependable watch. It is not necessary to pay an extravagant price for an article of this kind, for modern invention has reduced the cost of watches wonderfully, and while time is now more valuable than ever before, the machines for measuring it were never so excellent and cheap. A good place to buy a watch is at the establishment of Mr. C. W. Clifford, located on Front Street. This gentleman makes a specialty of Waltham and Elgin Watches, but can furnish an article of any reliable make. He has carried on business here since 1877, and has built up a good business by low prices and honorable dealing. Mr. Clifford was born in Bath, and is a member of Polar Star F. and A. M., Montgomery and St. Bernard R. A. C., also Dunlap Commandery, No. 5, K. T. He served the City Council as Common Councilman in 1888, was re-elected in 1889. His store measures 20x40 feet, and his stock includes Diamonds, Jewelry, Silver-Ware, Clocks, etc., as well as Watches. It is varied and skillfully selected, comprising fashionable novelties of the most popular description, which are quoted at very reasonable rates, as indeed are all the articles offered at this popular store.

James E. Haley, Lumber Yard. Dealer in Doors, Sashes, Blinds, Shingles, Clapboards, Laths, Moldings, Gutters, Ship Plugs and Wedges, Stair Posts, Rails, etc.; Contactor and Builder, Commercial Street, Bath. Among the best-known dealers in Lumber and Building Stock in Bath and vicinity, mention should be made of Mr. James E. Haley, who has carried on operations in this city (of which he is a native) since 1866. The premises utilized are located on Commercial Street, and include a Lumber Yard measuring 100 x 126 feet, and a building of the dimensions of 20x70 feet. Doors, Sashes, Blinds, Shingles, Clapboards, Laths, Moldings and Gutters, are very largely dealt in, together with Stair Posts, Rails, etc. Is also State Agent for the Patent Actinolite Cement Roofing, which is furnished and applied, and guaranteed fire and water proof. Mr. Haley is in a position to supply anything in this line at the very lowest market rates, and can fill the heaviest orders at short notice. Particular attention is given to Contracting and Building, and those contemplating the erection of a house of any kind, would do well to acquaint themselves with what advantages Mr. Haley is prepared to offer. He will furnish estimates on application, and, for many reasons which are too apparent to require detailed mention, is able to figure as closely as any builder in the State. Those dealing with him know that they are doing business with a responsible party, and this of itself is no small item to be considered.

M. S. Dunning, Manufacturer of Clothing, Bath. When a man visits a Clothing Store and buys a suit for $7.00, $10.00, $15.00 or $20.00, as the case may be, it is very rarely that he bothers his head about the system of manufacture which permits the selling of ready-made garments at from 25 to 50 per cent discount from custom prices. Yet this system is worthy of some thought, for it is the outgrowth of years of experience, and is as nearly perfect as human ingenuity can make it. One of its chief characteristics is the dividing up of operations into many specialties. One manufacturer makes coats, another pants and vests, and the help become so skilled in their special duties as to be able to carry them on with surprising accuracy and speed. Among the largest Clothing Manufacturers in this section, mention must be made of Mr. M. S. Dunning, for this gentleman employs nearly 200 hands, and turns out Coats by the thousands. He began operations in 1877, and his business shows a marked and gratifying increase annually. Notwithstanding the large scale on which operations are carried on, there is no confusion, for everything is reduced to a system and each employé is held responsible for the excellence of his or her work. Mr. Dunning is a native of Bath, and is very widely known among the trade. His productions are in active demand, for they are uniform in quality, and are always thoroughly and durably made. Mr. Dunning also keeps for sale or exchange, the best makes of Sewing Machines in the market, at prices that defy competition.

S. L. Farrar, Manufacturer of Stoves and Tin Ware, Ship Plumber and Pump Repairer. Stove Repairing and House Work of all kinds done with neatness and dispatch. Stove and Range Linings constantly in stock, Haley's block, Centre Street, Bath. The enterprise carried on by Mr. S. L. Farrar, in Haley's Block, Center Street, was started in 1879, and has since become one of the most prominent of its kind in the city. Mr. Farrar is a native of Searsmont, Maine, and is connected with both the Free Masons and the Odd Fellows. He handles Stoves and Tin Ware in general besides doing Ship Plumbing, Pump Repairing etc., and acts as sole agent for the celebrated "Elmwood" Range, which in the the opinion of many experienced housekeepers, combines more good points than any other stove in the market. Each of these ranges is sold under a strict guarantee that it will do all that is claimed for it, with proper handling, and the price will bear comparison with that at which any first-class range can be sold. Mr. Farrar gives especial attention to Stove Repairing and family work of all kinds, and can fill such orders at very short notice in a thorough and workmanlike manner. A full selection of Stove and Range Linings is constantly in stock, and Stove goods in general are offered at bottom prices. Employment is given to two competent assistants and callers will be treated courteously and waited upon promptly. Any desired information will be cheerfully given, and those thinking of buying a range, will best serve their own interests by investigating the merits of the "Elmwood."

LEADING BUSINESS MEN OF BATH. 353

A. F. Williams, Grocer, Center Street, Bath. There is probably not a more firmly established business enterprise in this city than that carried on by Mr. A. F. Williams on Center Street, for this undertaking was founded in 1869, and known by the name of L. Williams & Brother, corner of Vine and Washington Sts. The firm was dissolved in 1879, L. Williams continuing at the old stand. A. F. Williams bought out the store on Center Street occupied by E. H. Turner and went into business for himself, one door from his present location, where he continued for four years, his business in the meantime had so increased that a larger store was a necessity. The one he now occupies at 69 Center, was newly constructed, and, like its predecessor, is full of the best goods the market affords. Mr. Williams is a prominent member of the Odd Fellows and has a very large circle of friends throughout the city and its vicinity. He handles Groceries and Meats in great variety, and occupies premises measuring 20x60 feet. The stock on hand is complete in every department and is well worthy of inspection, for it has been selected with care, especially for first-class trade, and is offered at the same prices often quoted on inferior goods. Sugar and flour are two of the most staple commodities that can be named, and there is no household but what makes more or less extensive use of them. Mr. Williams supplies either in quantities to suit, and we ask particular attention to the Flour, Corn, Meal, and Grain of all kinds. Butter and Cheese are specialties of this house and of the very finest quality. The Finest Patent Roller Flour and the Common Grades are sold by the bag or barrel at absolutely bottom rates. Teas and Coffees are also dealt in largely, and the assortment of Canned Goods on hand is of choice quality, and is deserving of examination.

J. F. Hayden, Coal, Wholesale and Retail, yard, Commercial Street, north of Boston Steamboat landing. Office, opposite Sagadahock House, Bath. The old saying "an ounce of fact is worth a ton of theory" is as true as it is old, and cases come up daily to prove that this is correct. Some people say that Coal can be bought to as much advantage of one dealer as of another, when similar quantities are ordered; this perhaps may be theoretically true — practically, the reverse is the case. It does not require a very extended experience to convince any person that more genuine satisfaction is to be had from placing orders with some houses than with others, and when Coal is wanted, there is no establishment in Bath, that it is more profitable to patronize than that conducted by Mr. J. F. Hayden. This gentleman has an office opposite the Sagadahock House, and the yard is located on Commercial Street, north of the Boston Steamboat Landing. This yard covers about half an acre and contains storage capacity for 4000 tons of coal. Mr. Hayden is a native of Bath and has been identified with his present enterprise since 1879. He handles Coal very extensively, doing a wholesale and retail business, and employing five competent assistants, while the lowest market rates are always quoted by Mr. Hayden, the quality of the Coal furnished is strictly reliable, and as consumers appreciate good Coal,

good weight and good service, it is not to be wondered at that this, is one of the most largely patronized enterprises of this kind in this vicinity.

Spinney & Hayes, Manufacturers of and Wholesale and Retail Dealers in Confectionery, Nuts, Figs, etc. 152 Front Street, Bath. Messrs. Spinney & Hayes began operations in 1888, and the magnitude of their present business proves that the public are quick to appreciate genuine merit and enterprising methods; for the firm in question have striven from the first to handle only dependable goods, and to offer the best possible service to their patrons; and the degree of success attained is significantly indicated by the prosperity noticeable in connection with their establishment. The concern is made up of Messrs. E. E. Spinney and F. W. Hayes, both of whom were born in this city. They are manufacturers of and wholesale and retail dealers in Confectionery and Ice Cream, and also handle Nuts, Figs and Foreign and Domestic Fruits very extensively. The premises utilized are located at No. 152 Front Street, and comprise one large apartment measuring 40x22 feet, and a work-room of the dimensions of 15x25 feet. A very large and varied assortment of Confectionery is constantly on hand, and as the firm are manufacturers as well as dealers, it is obvious that they are in a position to know and to guarantee the quality of the goods composing the same. Pure, fresh Candy, free from injurious flavoring matter, will hurt no one, and we take pleasure in calling the attention of our readers to the Candies etc., offered by this firm, for we are confident that they are healthful, and we know they are delicious to the taste. The prices quoted are very low, and every caller is assured prompt and polite attention. Messrs. Spinney & Hayes have the best of facilities for large or small orders.

Highest Award For Our Exhibit.

ESTABLISHED 1843.

J. T. DONNELL & CO.,

—MANUFACTURERS OF—

CORDAGE,

From Manila, American, Russia and Sisal Hemp.

—DEALERS IN—

WIRE ROPE, OAKUM, &c.

Washington St., Bath.

J. T. Donnell,   C. R. Donnell,   J. G. Donnell.

23

S. Dillaway, Manufacturer of all kinds of Thin Clothing, and agent for the Remington, White, Household and New Home Sewing Machines, Houses to rent, Bath. In a general way, everybody realizes that the fifty millions of inhabitants contained in this country must be clothed somehow, but very few stop to think of the magnitude of the job. It is made all the larger by the variability of our climate, for a suit that would be entirely comfortable at one time of year, would be insufferably hot at another. But "many hands make light work" and that there are "many hands" engaged in the manufacture of clothing hereabouts, may be seen from the fact that a single maker, Mr. S. Dillaway, doing business on Centre Street, employs three hundred assistants. The gentleman mentioned, manufactures all descriptions of Thin Clothing and occupies premises of the dimensions of 20x65 feet, comprising two floors. He is well known to dealers throughout the State, and the product of his work rooms finds a ready and constant sale. Mr. Dillaway has been identified with his present line of business since 1857, and was born in Belfast. He acts as agent for the "Remington" the "White" Household and New Home Sewing Machines, and can quote bottom prices on any one of these popular articles, Mr. Dillaway is heavily interested in real-estate matters and is looked upon as a high authority concerning such. He has many desirable houses to rent, and no one contemplating an investment in local real estate should omit giving him a call.

George Snell, successor to Samuel D. Haley, Manufacturer and Dealer in House and Ship Furniture, Feathers, Mattresses, Looking-Glasses, &c., Warehouse at the old stand, Front Street, Bath. One of the landmarks of Bath, is the building occupied by Mr. George Snell as a furniture warehouse, for this structure was erected over half a century ago and has been identified with the Furniture business since 1837, operations having been begun at that time by Mr. Samuel D. Haley who was succeeded by the present proprietor in 1882. Mr. Snell was born in Boston, Mass., and is generally regarded as one of the most enterprising, as he is certainly one of the most popular, merchants in this city. The premises occupied, are of the dimensions of 25x60 feet and comprises three floors, a very heavy stock being carried consisting of House and Ship Furniture, Feathers, Mattresses, Looking Glasses and House Furnishing Goods in general. One reason of the high standing held by this establishment, is the perfect dependence that may be placed on the quality of the articles sold here. Mr. Snell takes his customers into his confidence and uses them as he would like to be used himself were the positions reversed. While prices here rule as low as anywhere, in no case is mere show attained by the sacrifice of genuine merit, and as a consequence Mr. Snell's goods have a well earned reputation for durability and general excellence. The assortment carried is sufficiently varied to make it easy to find articles suited for use under all circumstances, and polite assistants are at hand to lend all desired aid, in making a selection.

John L. Purington, Dealer in Dry Goods, and full assortment of Mme. Demorest's reliable Patterns, 3 Bank Block, near the Post Office, Front Street, Bath. One of the oldest established business enterprises carried on in this city, is that of which Mr. John L. Purington is the proprietor, located at No. 3 Bank Block, near the Post Office, Front Street. The undertaking in question is as well-known as it is well-established, for Mr. Purington does a large business, and there are very few ladies who think of "shopping" in Bath, without calling at this popular store. There they are sure to find as fine a line of Dry Goods as can be shown in this vicinity, and are also sure of being courteously received and promptly waited upon. The premises occupied, comprise one floor and a basement and measure 20x60 feet. The stock on hand consists of Dress Goods, Laces, Hamburgs, Gloves, Hosiery, Hoop Skirts, Corsets, Gossamer Capes, Table Linen, Mme. Demorest's Reliable Patterns, Cloth for men and Boys wear etc., and embraces all the most fashionable novelties, in addition to the staple goods always in demand. Mr. Purington was born in Bath, and is a member of the Free Masons. He begun operations in 1861, and has therefore been identified with his present business for considerably over a quarter of a century. As may be supposed, he has an exceptionally thorough knowledge of it in every department, and as he enjoys the most favorable relations with wholesalers, he is in a position to buy to the best advantage, and therefore to offer his patrons reliable goods at prices as low as can be named on articles of equal excellence.

J. H. Shepard, House, Ship, Sign, Fresco, and Ornamental Painting, Gilding, Glazing and Paper Hanging, 787 Washington Street, Bath. It is rather curious, how reluctant some people are to spend a dollar on Painting, for it would seem as if everybody must understand that there is some use to paint, aside from its value for ornamental purposes, "Beauty is only skin deep" it is true, but a surface beautified by paint, is made more durable as well as more pleasant to the eye, and hence a gain is made in two ways. There is one thing however that should be borne in mind, and that is, that the kind of stock used and the manner in which it is applied, have everything to do with the economy of the process. Cheap and poor stock is practically useless, and even good stock must be used properly to get satisfactory results. The moral is plain, have your painting done by a reputable man, who has a reputation for skill as well as for honesty. No one could be found, more exactly filling these requirements, than Mr. J. H. Shepard of this city, and since he founded his present business in 1874, he has repeatedly proved himself capable of undertaking anything in the house-painting and decorating line, and carrying it out to the entire satisfaction of all parties concerned. Mr. Shepard is a native of Bath, and his place of business is conveniently located at the corner of Center and Washington Streets. Employment is given to an average force of six assistants, and all orders are filled at short notice, and at the lowest rates consistent with the use of standard stock and the employment of skilled labor.

J. C. Higgins & Son, Photographers, Landscape Work and Interiors a Specialty, Front Street, Bath. The art of Photography has its divisions and sub-divisions, the same as any other industry or profession of equal importance, and in order to be sure of obtaining the best possible results, it is an excellent idea to learn what photographers make specialties of certain things, and to place orders accordingly. For instance, if anything in the line of Landscape or Interior Work is wanted, it would be foolish to go a photographer who seldom or never does anything in this department, when such a house as that of Messrs. J. C. Higgins & Son exists, for the firm in question make a specialty of Landscape Work and Interiors, and obtain effects which would otherwise be impossible. Mr. J. C. Higgins began operations over a quarter of a century ago, for it was in 1862 that he started his present enterprise. In 1887 his son became associated with him under the present firm-name, and the future of the business looks as promising as its past has been honorable. Mr. Higgins is a native of Boston, and is connected with the Free Masons, the Odd Fellows and the Knights of Pythias. It is hardly necessary to mention that he is extremely well-known throughout this vicinity, for during his long business career, it is but natural that he should have made many friends and almost innumerable acquaintances. The premises utilized are located on Front Street, and are of the dimensions of 18x75 feet. They are very completely equipped, and every facility is at hand for the prompt and artistic filling of orders. Employment is given to three assistants, and Portraits, Landscapes or Interiors will be furnished at short notice, finished in the highest style of the art, at prices that are sure to prove entirely satisfactory.

Read Nichols, Dealer in Lime, Cement, Hair, Sand, Calcine Plaster, Centers and Brackets, Fire and Common Brick, Pressed Hay, Cement and Akron Pipe for Drains, etc., Commercial Street, Bath. It is obvious that those houses dealing in Building Materials must occupy a very important place in the community, for building is constantly going on, and the demand for Lime, Cement, Bricks, etc., is correspondingly great. Prominent among those dealing in these and similar commodities, is Mr. Read Nichols, doing business on Commercial Street, in this city, and those wishing anything in the line of Cement, Hair, Sand, Calcine Plaster, Centers and Brackets, Fire and Common Brick, etc., should by all means give him a call, as he is prepared to quote bottom prices on *strictly reliable articles*. Pressed Hay, Drain Pipe, (Cement and Akron) are also handled very extensively, and mason work is done at very short notice in a thoroughly satisfactory manner. Mr. Nichols was born in Bowdoin, Me., and has been identified with the present enterprise since 1876. The premises utilized by him comprise a store of the dimensions of 20x70 feet, and yard room measuring 20x40 feet. A sufficient number of assistants are employed to enable all orders to be attended to without delay, and the stock on hand is so varied and complete as to render it easy to meet all demands at short notice. Only goods of standard quality are handled, and satisfaction is guaranteed to every customer.

Johnson Bros., (Successors to George Fisher), Ship Chandlery and Hardware of All Descriptions, Paints, Oils and Varnishes, Agents for the New Bedford Cordage Co., Front Street, Bath. An establishment doing a very large business and occupying a foremost position among similar houses in this section, is that carried on by Messrs. Johnson Brothers on Front Street. This enterprise had its inception in 1847, under the management of Messrs. Kendall, Richardson & Co., the present firm succeeding Mr. George Fisher in 1885. It is made up of Messrs. George W., Edward F., and Ernest A. Johnson, all of whom are natives of Bath, Edward F. being connected with both the Free Masons and the Odd Fellows. Both a wholesale and retail business is done, and the premises occupied comprise two floors and a basement, measuring 25x70 feet, and a storehouse 35x60 feet in size, containing two floors and a basement. Ship Chaudlery is very extensively dealt in, and Hardware of All Descriptions is also handled very largely. Messrs. Johnson Brothers act as Agents for the New Bedford Cordage Co., John A. Roebling's Sons' Co. Wire Rope, J. B. Carr & Co.'s Troy Chain Works, American Ship Windlass Co. of Providence, R. I., Taunton Copper Co., Woodbury Duck, etc., all of which are the leading houses in the Ship Chandlery business in New England; also Agents for the Buckeye Mowing Machine. A full line of Paints, Oils and Varnishes is offered to select from, and orders can be filled without delay, any desired quantity being furnished at bottom prices. The management of this enterprise is liberal and progressive, and customers will find that their interests are considered as identical with those of the firm. No false representations are made under any circumstances, and mistakes will be cheerfully rectified, if due to any fault of the concern or its employes.

T. L. Nichols, Dealer in Provisions, Groceries and Ship Stores, Corner of Washington and South Streets, Bath. It is not difficult to obtain a correct idea of the estimation in which the establishment carried on by Mr. T. L. Nichols, at the corner of Washington and South Streets, is held by its patrons and by the public in general, for few, if any enterprises of the kind, located in this city, are better known or more highly spoken of. Mr. Nichols is a native of Georgetown, Maine, and has been identified with the establishment referred to since 1860, so that there has certainly been ample opportunity for him to make the public familiar with his methods. One floor and a basement are occupied, their dimensions being 20x50 feet, and employment is given to two efficient assistants. The stock on hand bears evidence of skillful selection, and comprises Provisions, Groceries and Ship Stores in almost endless variety. Mr. Nichols is in a position to obtain his supplies on as advantageous terms as any dealer in town, and as he is satisfied with small profits, it follows that his prices will bear the severest comparison with those quoted by other houses. We need hardly say that no misrepresentation is allowed in this establishment, for no store could hold the reputation that this one does unless it were conducted on strictly honorable principles.

LEADING BUSINESS MEN OF BATH.

A. J. Snow, Merchant Tailor, Front Street, Bath. One of the best ways in which to save money, is to know how to spend it, and although this may seem a paradox, it is nevertheless undeniably true. The question of first cost is, to be sure, an important one, but it is no more so than several others which should be considered when making purchases, for durability, fit, suitableness, etc., all have a decided bearing on the question of whether clothing, for instance, be cheap or dear. A thoroughly-made custom garment will, with proper usage, look shapely and trim after six months of wear, while a ready-made article will generally be shabby and unpresentable by that time. The different materials used in the trimmings, the difference in the care with which the sewing, etc., is done—all these points go to make up the superiority of custom work, and the slight difference in price is fully compensated for, as those who have tried both kinds of clothing will generally agree. Mr. A. J. Snow of this city, is well-known among those who pay careful attention to dress, and his establishment on Front Street is a favorite resort with the most discriminating buyers. Premises of the dimensions of 20x60 feet are occupied, and every facility is at hand to do a strictly first-class merchant tailoring business. A full and skillfully selected assortment of Standard and Fashionable Fabrics is always kept on hand, and visitors will find both Foreign and Domestic Manufacturers of Fine Woolens fully represented. Employment is given to from eight to ten efficient assistants, and the individuality of each customer is carefully studied, a perfect fit being guaranteed. Mr. Snow is a native of Bath, and is master of his business in every detail. His prices are low, and no poor work is allowed to leave his establishment.

C. A. Hooker, Manufacturer and Dealer in Coffee, Cream Tartar and Spices, Salt, Corn, Meal, Feed, &c., Commercial Street, Bath. Grist mills are by no means so uncommon as to be special objects of interest to the public, but spice mills are not so frequently met with, and the community is so immediately and deeply concerned in the securing of a supply of Pure Spices, Coffee, etc., that an establishment which provides these commodities is worthy of special mention in our pages. Therefore we need not apologize to our readers for calling their attention to the enterprise carried on by C. A. Hooker on Commercial Street, for since this gentleman began operations in 1875, he has gained an enviable reputation on account of the uniform excellence of the goods in which he deals. He has a well-equipped Grist, Spice and Salt Mill, also the largest Roller Mill in the State for Grinding Corn into Meal, and does a large and increasing business, both wholesale and retail, employing two competent assistants. Coffee, Cream Tartar and Spices of All Kinds are supplied in quantities to suit, and Salt, Corn, Meal, Feed, etc., are also offered at the lowest market rates. As may be supposed from the facilities at his command, Mr. Hooker is able to fill orders without delay, and to meet all competition, both in quality and price. He is a native of Gardiner, and his success is in a great measure due to the close personal attention he gives to every detail of his business.

A. Hatch, Photographer, Front Street, Bath. It is a curious fact that many people who would never think of placing all artists on a level, seem to believe that all photographers can attain equally good results. Even were photography purely a mechanical process, (which is by no means the case), this assumption would be illogical, for everyone knows that mechanics following the same trade vary greatly in skill, and when it is borne in mind that a perfect photographic portrait is the result of artistic "retouching," lightning, etc., and that these processes must be varied to suit different individuals, it becomes plainly evident that really first-class photographers are artists as well. Compare such work as is done by Mr. A. Hatch, at his studio on Front Street, with that too often set before the public, and the difference is discernable at a glance. Mr. Hatch has carried on business here fully a score of years, having began operations in 1860, and his reputation is unsurpassed, having been built up by conscientious and skillful work. He is a native of Litchfield, and is connected with the Free Masons and the Knights Templars. Three rooms are utilized, measuring 20x60 feet, and all the facilities employed are first-class in kind, and modern in style, enabling Mr. Hatch to carry on photography, in its various branches, to the satisfaction of all concerned. Particular attention is given to the proper representation of ladies dresses, etc., and some very beautiful results have been obtained in this line. Children are also given especial care, and all work is done at very reasonable rates.

L. H. Andrews, Merchant Tailor, Centre Street, Opposite City Hall, Bath. Every man, and especially every young man, owes it to himself to dress neatly and in good taste, for appearances have to be consulted in every-day life, and dress certainly influences appearances to a marked degree. There are many people who have all their clothing made to order, and there doubtless would be many more, were it generally understood that this involves no such great expense as is imagined by the majority. A call at L. H. Andrews' on Centre Street, opposite the City Hall, will result in much being learned regarding this matter, for Mr. Andrews is one of our leading Merchant Tailors, and is well-prepared to give information concerning Clothing and its cost. Premises of the dimensions of 20x60 feet are made use of, and employment is afforded to four competent assistants. Mr. Andrews has carried on his present enterprise since 1876, and has built up a very satisfactory amount of trade. The strong points of the Clothing made at this establishment are the perfection of fit attained, and the durable nature of the garments turned out, while the prices are but a trifle in excess of those named on First-class Ready-made Clothing. Goods of all description are carried in stock, and both the man of fashion and the merchant of quiet taste, can here find fabrics expressly adapted to their use. Mr. Andrews is always fully up to the times as regards the adoption of the latest fashionable novelties, and his garments will not suffer by comparison with those produced at Portland, Boston, or other large cities. In fit, cut and style they are unexceptionable, while for workmanship they are equalled by few.

LEADING BUSINESS MEN OF BATH.

H. L. & W. E. Chase, Successors to H. L. Chase, Dealers in Provisions & Groceries, Teas, Coffees & Spices a specialty; also best grades of Flour, cor. Washington & Center Sts.; also Pork Packers, Wholesale and Retail Dealers in Pork, Lard, Hams, Ribs, Bologna, Ham and Pork Sausages, Head Cheeses, etc., 773, 775, 777 Washington St., Bath. The firm of H. L. & W. E. Chase is of comparatively recent origin, being formed in 1887, but the enterprise carried on by this concern was inaugurated over a quarter of a century ago, it being started by Mr. H. L. Chase in 1862. This gentleman is a member of the Free Masons and Mr. W. E. Chase is connected with the Knights of Pythias, both are natives of this city. Groceries and Provisions are dealt in very extensively and particular attention is paid to the handling of Teas, Coffees, Spices and Molasses, some of the choicest grades in the market being constantly carried in stock and the prices being placed extremely low for goods of such superior quality. The most desirable and popular brands of Flour are also to be had at this store in quantities to suit as well as Canned Goods of every description. The store is 40x60 feet in dimensions and employment is given to two efficient assistants besides a bookkeeper. A very important department of the business is that devoted to Pork Packing, this being carried on a large scale in a three story building measuring 40x40 feet. Here there are six assistants employed and both a Wholesale and Retail trade is conducted. Pork in all its many forms being supplied at the very lowest market rates. Lard, Hams, Ribs, Bologna, Ham and Pork, Sausages, Head Cheese, etc., are all offered at moderate prices and orders will be filled at short notice, satisfaction being guaranteed. They have recently enlarged their quarters and added a full stock of Grain and Feed. Buying in car lots, shipped direct from the West they are enabled to sell in large or small quantities at a low figure. In this as well as the other departments their trade is steadily increasing.

J. S. Jackson & Son, Block Manufacturers, Front Street, Bath. A well-known and old established house, and one of the oldest Block making establishments in the country is that of J. S. Jackson & Son on Front Street. No better recommendation can be asked for than the fact that this factory has stood the storms of competition successfully for one hundred years. This business was established by the father of the late William Ingalls. The latter succeeded to the business. On his death the present firm assumed control and are excelling all previous efforts, and are now to be excelled by no one in this country. The greatest stride which the Block industry has witnessed is that of making a Block with the wearing parts so arranged that a sufficient amount of lubricant is stored within the Block as to keep the parts well oiled as long as the Block lasts, and although the quickest steam hoisting has been done with this new patent, yet there seems to be no end to the amount of work which can be done with hardly any perceptible wear. This new invention has been very successfully put forth by this firm. They also make a specialty of Galvanizing, and this department is the most thoroughly equipped in this part of the country, for vessel work of almost any length and size.

W. Hawthorne, Merchant Tailor, Front Street, Bath. No man can afford to despise the influence of dress. There is, of course, such a thing as wasting money on clothing, but the mistake many men make is in going to the other extreme and dressing cheaply and shabbily, and the result can hardly be favorable. To dress well and fashionably need not cost a great deal of money. Exercise discrimination in choosing a tailor, and be guided in some degree by his advice. It is for his interest to use you well, and it is for your interest to use him well. He will do his best to keep a steady customer, and you will find that a tailor accustomed to your form can fit you more perfectly than a stranger. Mr. W. Hawthorne of Front Street, has many a steady patron, for he has been in business here since 1844, and has built up an extensive and desirable trade. Our readers will find it very difficult to learn of an establishment offering more solid advantages to its customers than this one, for Mr. Hawthorne is liberal in his methods and makes it a point to give a generous equivalent for all that he receives. A Large and Varied Stock of Fine Foreign and Domestic Suitings, etc., is constantly carried, so that selection is rendered an easy matter. Employment is given to from eight to ten competent assistants, and all that good workmanship and low prices can do to satisfy patrons, is done at this popular store.

LEADING BUSINESS MEN OF BATH.

Boothbay Harbor. Boothbay Harbor is situated on the coast of Maine between the mouths of the Kennebec and Damariscotta Rivers, distant about twelve miles from the city of Bath in a direct line, and about sixteen miles by the winding course of the lovely deep water channel, which is navigated daily by the steamers running between Bath and Boothbay. This is one of the best locations on the coast of Maine for summer residences and tourists. Each year brings renewed evidence of this fact, in the increasing tide of summer travel which seeks rest and recreation among its picturesque islands and shores. Some of the best lands about this harbor have been taken up by land companies and other associations, and are being rapidly improved by building of roads, clearing, grading and building of handsome cottages. Boothbay has a solid basis of prosperity in its safe, beautiful and capacious harbor, its picturesque surrounding hills and scenery, and its accessibility to railroad and steamboat communication at Bath without making a rough sea trip. This harbor is a paradise to lovers of yachting, rowing and fishing. Its deep-sheltered bays are free from strong tides and squally winds, and excellent fishing grounds are reached by less than an hour's sail. It is the constant resort of coasting and fishing vessels and passing yachts and steamers. The town of Boothbay Harbor presents an exceedingly neat, cleanly and prosperous appearance, has good stores and markets, excellent roads and fine drives about the surrounding hills, from which views of the coast are constantly obtained of unsurpassed beauty. The town will soon be supplied with pure spring water from a system of water-works to be immediately built. Travelers are well provided for at two good public houses, and a fine summer hotel has been planned by the Boothbay Land Co., and will no doubt soon be erected. One of the great attractions of a trip to Boothbay is a sail on the lovely and picturesque route of the neat, fast steamers of the Eastern Steamboat Co. Crossing the Kennebec and leaving it directly opposite Bath, the steamer passes the draw-bridge spanning the narrow passage between Woolwich on the left and the island of Arrowsic on the right, crosses Nequasset Bay and enters the narrow tortuous and rushing waters of Hellgate, which soon widen into the broad bay of Hockomock, crossing which a narrow, deep channel is entered which divides the islands of Westport on the left from Georgetown on the right. After a beautiful sail the steamer enters the narrow strait between Boothbay on the left and the island of Southport on the right. This passage opens directly upon Mouse Island, where the first landing in the harbor is made. To the left one and one-half miles is the beautiful and growing village of Boothbay. In front about a mile east is Spruce Point with its handsome evergreen woods and new club house and landing. Beyond lies Ocean Point, with its hotel and neat cottages. Seaward is seen Squirrel Island with its hundred well-kept cottages, chapel, hall, etc.

Geo. P. Davenport, Broker, Insurance, Bonds, Stocks, Shipping and Real Estate. Office over Telegraph Office, opposite Sagadahock House, Bath. One of the busiest offices to be found in this city, is that of Mr. George P. Davenport, son of Hon. Charles Davenport, President of the Bath Savings Institution, also President of the Lincoln National Bank, located on Front Street, Opposite the Sagadahoc House, for this gentleman does a very extensive Brokerage Business in Bonds, Stocks and Real Estate, and conducts one of the most popular Insurance Agencies in this section. He is a native of Bath, and is widely known here, having been identified with his present enterprise since 1878. Much of Mr. Davenport's popularity with the general public is due to the policy he pursues of cheerfully giving information relative to the varied interests which he represents. He recognizes the fact that many who wish to make investments have not time at their disposal to personally make investigation as to the desirability of the many securities on the market, and hence is always ready to lend the benefit of his experience and knowledge, or render any other aid that is in his power to give. Fire, Marine and Accident Insurance Policies are written in the most reliable and liberal companies, among those represented being the Lancashire Insurance Co., the Western Assurance Co., the Commercial Union Assurance Co., the Holyoke Mutual Insurance Co., the Traders' and Mechanics' Mutual Insurance Co., and the Accident Insurance Co. of North America, which have already paid out hundreds of dollars to Bath claimants alone. No more liberal terms can be made elsewhere than those offered by Mr. Davenport, and such of our readers as wish to obtain the most absolutely certain insurance at the lowest possible rates, will find it for their interest to place their orders here. But while Mr. Davenport has a large correspondence in connection with Insurance, Bonds, Stocks and Real Estate, the largest proportion of his business is in connection with *Shipping*. All classes of Shipping Property are Bought and Sold by Mr. Davenport. Being a large owner in Shipping, he is brought in contact with parties owning this kind of property, and knows the value of vessels. Parties having them for sale, and those wishing to buy, can obtain desirable information in connection with Shipping, as well as in regard to Bonds, Stocks, Real Estate and Insurance, by calling at the office of Geo. P. Davenport, Broker, Bath.

LEADING BUSINESS MEN OF BATH.

Hotel Phœnix, formerly Bath Hotel, 716 Washington Street, Bath. Terms $2.00 per day; Welch Bros., Proprietors. This Hotel is pleasantly situated on Washington Street, two minutes walk south from the depot. It commands a fine view of the Kennebec River and harbor. It has been thoroughly renovated and newly furnished; contains all the modern improvements, such as electric lights, electric bells, hot and cold water, bath-rooms, &c., &c. Since March, 1888, when the house was opened, it has been favored by a liberal patronage, and all speak in praise of the management and service. Although new to the business, the Messrs. Welch Bros. have succeeded in placing the Phœnix to the front as one of the best two-dollar houses in the country. Tourists and traveling men will find at the Phœnix all the comforts of home.

Charles F. Hayden, Watches, Jewelry, Nautical Instruments and Publications, 106 Front Street, Bath. Although the most of us think that we can select such commodities as clothing, groceries, boots, shoes, etc., or any articles in common use, with considerable confidence, when we buy Watches, Jewelry or Silverware, we depend almost entirely upon the honesty of the dealer. Of course all persons have their tastes in these articles, and know what suits them, so far as mere appearance is concerned, but, if we desire to be sure of our money's worth, and to know just what we are buying, it is obvious that ordinary prudence demands our purchasing anything in this line from thoroughly reputable dealers, and those who neglect this precaution have only themselves to blame if the result is not satisfactory. Without desiring to exalt one house at the expense of another, we must still call our readers attention to the advantages offered to patrons of the establishment of Mr. Charles F. Hayden, 106 Front Street, for the goods sold here are not only excellent in quality, but are low-priced, as a careful comparison will soon prove to anyone's satisfaction. Mr. Hayden, a native of this city, continues a business which has been both actively and honorably carried on by closely connected concerns for nearly forty years in the same store. The Watch and Jewelry business has also in connection with it a large one in Nautical Instruments, Charts and Publications, Mr. Hayden being agent of the U. S. Coast Survey, and also Hydrographic offices. His Jewelry and Silverware stock is both extensive and attractive, being almost entirely of the latest styles and novelties, and will pay an examination. Everything sold being warranted to be as represented at the time of sale.

C. T. Hooper & Sons, Dealers in Wall Paper, Curtains and Fixtures, Paints, Oils, etc., 154 Front Street, Bath. The enterprise carried on by Messrs. C. T. Hooper & Sons, in their elegantly fitted-up store, No. 154 Front Street, was inaugurated a quarter of a century ago, operations having been begun by Messrs. Howes & Hooper in 1864. In 1883 Mr. C. T. Hooper became sole proprietor, and in 1889 the existing firm was formed. It is constituted of Messrs. C. T., C. H. and F. E. Hooper, the senior partner being a native of Skowhegan, while both his sons were born in this city. Mr. C. T. Hooper served in the army during the Rebellion, first acting as Orderly Sergeant and subsequently holding a commission as Lieutenant in the Third Maine. He was a member of the Bath City Council for five years, and is very widely known throughout this city and vicinity. The firm do a very large business, as may easily be judged from the magnitude and the variety of the stock carried, and the prices quoted on the goods offered go far to explain the popularity of the establishment, the lowest rates are adhered to, and the goods are in every instance guaranteed to prove as represented. The premises utilized comprise three floors, the ground floor being 54x18 feet in dimensions, while the combined area of the two upper floors is about the same. The store has recently been elaborately fitted up, and is supplied with electric lights and other modern improvements, the stock being displayed to excellent advantage, and customers being given every opportunity to choose intelligently and satisfactorily. The assortment of Wall-Papers includes the latest artistic novelties, as well as a full line of Staple Patterns, the leading manufacturers being represented, and so great a variety of styles and shades offered that all tastes and all purses can be suited. Curtains and Fixtures, Paints, Oils, Varnishes, etc., are largely dealt in. Orders for Painting and Paper-Hanging will also be executed in first-class style. This is one of the most important departments of the business, and no concern in the State has better facilities or a higher reputation to maintain.

D. T. Percy & Son, Dry Goods and Carpetings, (Percy Block); Crockery and Paper-Hangings, (Union Block); Dry and Fancy Goods, (Granite Block), Bath. There are three mercantile establishments carried on in this city, each representative in its line and independent of the others, and yet all three are conducted by members of one family, under the common firm-name of D. T. Percy & Son. The original establishment is located in Percy Block, Front Street, and occupies three floors and a basement, of the dimensions of 20x90 feet. Dry Goods and Carpetings are the chief commodities handled here, and the stock on hand is certainly large and varied enough to allow of all tastes and all purses being suited. Mr. D. T. Percy was born in this city, and has had more than thirty-five years experience in his present line of business. He caters to all classes of trade, sells every description of Floor Covering, as well as Foreign and Domestic Dry Goods in general, and quotes bottom prices on dependable articles in every department, employing seven courteous assistants, who show callers prompt and painstaking attention. Paper-Hangings are as important as Carpets, where interior decoration is concerned, and in order to choose such intelligently, no better course can be taken than to visit the spacious store in Union Block, carried on by Messrs. D. T. and Frank H. Percy. This firm have been in business a little over ten years, and from the first have carried a full line of Paper-Hangings and Borders, which they offer at very reasonable prices. The stock comprises the latest artistic novelties, as well as more staple products, and must be seen to be appreciated. Silverplated Ware, Crockery, Glass, Lamps, Chandeliers, etc., are also largely dealt in, the premises utilized comprising three floors, measuring 20x90 feet, the space thus obtained being fully availed of. Three assistants are employed, and goods will be cheerfully shown and prices given. The third and last of the stores to which this article has reference is located in Granite Block, Front Street, and is devoted explessly to Dry and Fancy Goods, Messrs. D. T, and Augustus A. Percy being the proprietors. This enterprise has been under its present management since 1836, and is steadily developing, greater inducements being offered every year, and no pains being spared to continue to deserve the full confidence of the public. Two floors and a basement 20x90 feet in size are made use of, and employment is given to five assistants. Dry and Fancy Goods of all kinds are dealt in, and a specialty is made of offering the latest novelties as soon as they make their appearance in the market. It is generally conceded that no house in this section makes a better showing in this respect, and the prices quoted will also bear the most severe comparison with those named elsewhere.

Equitable MORTGAGE COMPANY.

STATEMENT.

Capital Subscribed,	$2,000,000.00
Capital Paid in (Cash),	1,000,000.00
Surplus and Undivided Profits,	115,444.82
Assets,	4,935,940.25

SIX PER CENT DEBENTURES
AND
GUARANTEED FARM MORTGAGES,

The interest coupons of these Debentures and Mortgages are payable semi-annually at any of our offices, and the coupons will be accepted by all banks as cash. Our mortgages are upon improved farms only. We loan no money on the unduly stimulated property of the towns and cities. We loan no money upon any farm until the property has been examined by a salaried employe of the company, and the borrower investigated. Our Debentures are secured by an equal amount of mortgages deposited with the American Loan and Trust Co. of New York, as trustee, and are further secured by the capital and assets of the Equitable Mortgage Co. Also,

MUNICIPAL BONDS.

OFFICES:

NEW YORK,	208 Broadway
BOSTON,	117 Devonshire Street
PHILADELPHIA,	Fourth and Chestnut Streets
LONDON, ENGLAND,	150 Leadhall Street

SEND FOR PAMPHLET.

THE PENN MUTUAL LIFE INSURANCE CO.,

OF PHILADELPHIA, PA.

is one of the oldest and most reliable Life Insurance Companies in the city. It has issued its forty-first annual report. This excellent institution is a purely mutual organization—all profits being divided among the insured. Its directors are chosen by and from among the policy-holders. The work of forty-one years is both admirable and grandly charitable. During this time it received $30,684,408 in premiums; in interest, profits on stocks, etc., $9,392,990; in accrued interest, $89,049; increase in value of stocks, etc., $416,176; and net deferred and unreported premiums, $330,277; making a grand total of $40,912,903. It has during this time paid in death claims $9,837,221; in matured endowments, $785,849; in surplus or dividends returned to policy-holders, $7,505,721; for surrendered and lapsed policies, $2,542,524; for re-insurance, $270,594; taxes, $611,579; commissions, agency expenses, rents, salaries, etc., $5,571,984. The balance on hand on the first day of the present year was $13,787,428. Of this sum the life rate endowment accumulations, and the general surplus on a four per cent. basis, including returns to members not yet due, was $2,210,151. During the year just completed the company received in premiums, $2,640,561, and for interest, rents, etc. $717,464, making a grand total income of $3,358,025. It paid in death claims, $823,324; in matured endowments, $75,237; for re-insurance, $4,269; for surrendered policies, $202,002, and in surplus returned to members, $519,552. This was truly a good year's work. It is a notable fact, that during the whole history of the company the interest profit on stocks, accrued interest, and increased value of the stocks owned by the company, more than paid the entire death claims. It is a fact worthy of mention, that during the existance of this office, the gains arising from the actual being less than the tabular mortality, have been in the neighborhood of two millions of dollars. During the last year the company issued 5,666 policies, insuring $14,630,744. The total amount of insurance in force at the end of the year was $68,372,882. The following facts are significant : The gain in new premiums during the year 1888 was $67,321 ; in renewal income, $222,249; in interest income, $55,407 : in gross income. $358,261 : in assets, $1,187,160; and in insurance in force, $7,354,077. The company recently modified its policy contracts so as to embrace more liberal features than the former contracts. The new polices were made incontestable after two years, and the limits of residence were enlarged. The Board, recognizing the justice of extending these provisions, adopted a resolution declaring that "on and after the first day of January, 1888, all members insured under policies then in force, issued by the company prior to January 1st, 1885, be and they are hereby declared entitled to all the provisions or advantages as to suicide, residence, travel and employment embraced in the new forms of policies issued by the company." We are sure that in economy of management; in careful selection of risks; in careful investment of funds; in liberality towards the policy-holders, and in returns of surplus, it is not a whit behind the largest and best of its peers. A call at the principal offices in this state, and a careful inspection of its books, reports and methods, will conserve the best interests of all our readers. Mr. A. M. Austin, general agent, 93 Exchange street, Portland, Me., is a native of Canton, Me., and ranks among our most influential and honorable business men and citizens.

A. M. AUSTIN, General Agent, 93 Exchange St., Portland.

www.ingramcontent.com/pod-product-compliance
Lightning Source LLC
Chambersburg PA
CBHW020232240426
43672CB00006B/502